THE BOISTEROUS SEA OF LIBERTY

THE BOISTEROUS SEA OF LIBERTY

A Documentary History of America from Discovery through the Civil War

David Brion Davis and Steven Mintz

New York • Oxford

Oxford University Press

1998

Oxford University Press

Oxford New York
Athens Auckland Bangkok Bogotá Buenos Aires Calcutta
Cape Town Chennai Dar es Salaam Delhi Florence Hong Kong Istanbul
Karachi Kuala Lumpur Madrid Melbourne Mexico City Mumbai
Nairobi Paris São Paulo Singapore Taipei Tokyo Toronto Warsaw

and associated companies in
Berlin Ibadan

Published by Oxford University Press, Inc.
198 Madison Avenue, New York, New York 10016

Library of Congress Cataloging-in-Publication Data
The boisterous sea of liberty : a documentary history of America from discovery through the Civil War / [edited by] David Brion Davis and Steven Mintz.
p. cm.
Includes index.
ISBN 0-19-511669-0 (alk. paper)
1. United States—History—Colonial period, ca. 1600–1775—Sources. 2. United States—History—Revolution, 1775–1783—Sources. 3. United States—History—1783–1865—Sources. 4. United States—Race relations—Sources. 5. United States—Social conditions—To 1865—Sources. I. Davis, David Brion. II. Mintz, Steven, 1953–
E187.B65 1998
973—dc21 98-7332

1 3 5 7 9 8 6 4 2

Printed in the United States of America
on acid-free paper

Contents

Acknowledgments

We should like to express our deepest gratitude to Richard Gilder and Lewis Lehrman, who not only made this book possible but also whose immense generosity and ongoing collecting project has already done much to increase the American public's knowledge and understanding of our complex past. We also wish to thank James G. Basker, president of the Gilder Education Group, and Seth T. Kaller, the main liaison of Mr. Gilder and Mr. Lehrman to various manuscript owners. Paul W. Romaine, the curator and executive director of the collection, and Sandra M. Trenholm, his archives and reference specialist, both provided us with innumerable photocopies and much invaluable information. Lesley S. Herrmann, executive director of the Gilder Lehrman Institute of American History, first suggested the creation of such an anthology, and has provided us with much encouragement and support. We are also grateful to S. Parker Gilbert, president of the Morgan Library Board of Trustees, Charles E. Pierce, Jr., director of the library, and such curators as Robert Parks, Christine Nelson, and Lori E. Gilbert, who have helped us and other researchers make use of the collection. David Brion Davis would like to thank Michael Kammen, John Stauffer, Bertram Wyatt-Brown, Adam J. Davis, Thomas LeBien, and Paul Romaine for valuable criticism and suggestions regarding the Introduction. Many of the documents, it should be stressed, are available on microfilm or on the Internet. Inquiries about Gilder Lehrman Collection holdings may be addressed to Ms. Leslie Fields, Assistant Curator, The Pierpont Morgan Library, 29 East 36th Street, New York, NY 10016.

For invaluable help translating, transcribing, and interpreting documents, Steven Mintz would like to thank Kenneth Lipartito, Catherine Patterson, and especially Susan Kellogg. He is also very grateful to Paul Romaine and Sandra Trenholm for their helpful advice, detailed comments, and indispensable help in selecting illustrations.

THE BOISTEROUS SEA OF LIBERTY

Introduction

by David Brion Davis

I. THE PURPOSE AND NATURE OF THIS ANTHOLOGY

Nothing can overcome apathy, boredom, or contempt for the past as quickly and effectively as primary sources. Eyewitness accounts of a battle or bitter legislative debate can have the power of a fax or e-mail just received, evaporating the gap between past and present. Such sources enable readers to identify with men and women long dead and to suddenly understand how decisions made in the past continue to haunt our lives. No less important, as we learn to listen to these voices we gain a growing sense of the complexity and *contingency* of past events. How different would America be today if the British had defeated the Americans in their struggle for independence, or if the United States had been drawn into England's war against Revolutionary and Napoleonic France, or if Jefferson had lost the election of 1800 to Aaron Burr, or if the South had moved before the Civil War toward gradual emancipation of slaves while enacting strict "black codes" to maintain a servile labor force and white supremacy, or if Britain and France had recognized and actively aided the southern Confederacy?

Primary sources can encourage readers to see history from opposing viewpoints and to understand the values and perspectives of history's losers. If we wish to comprehend the decisions, forces, and institutions that have shaped American society, it is essential to hear the arguments of Loyalists and British generals as well as American patriots, Jefferson and Madison as well as Hamilton and John Marshall, proslavery theorists as well as abolitionists. If we are to benefit from history we must even learn to see the world through the eyes of rogues and villains, including the worst perpetrators of evil, such as eighteenth-century slave traders and twentieth-century Nazis. How else, after all, can we understand the roots of human depravity or the convergence of events that make evil happen? Like it or not—and America's antihistorical culture has long attempted to conceal this fact—the past shapes and governs much of our present-day reality; and whatever liberation we can achieve from that unknown past depends in large part on accurate knowledge. To deny this truth is to chain ourselves even more rigidly to a past misunderstood and easily mythologized in terms of the children of light overcoming the children of darkness, or of demonic forces subverting a golden age.

This interpretive anthology of 366 documents moves from the European discovery of America to the end of the Civil War. The central theme is human power: power exemplified by racial slavery and the relations between Indians and whites, but also issues of power in transatlantic connections, in the formation and conduct of new governments, and in the interactions of class and domesticity. While our major focus shifts to the public domain, we also show how new challenges to public authority led to the beginnings of a reexamination of gender and the private sphere. This anthology is unique in the range, significance, and novelty of its selections and in its extensive introductions and commentary, which provide continuing linkage while also addressing five organizing themes and four pivotal issues that will be discussed below. Our goal in giving such explanatory context is not to impose a fashionable new "interpretation" on American history but rather to open the way to new questions and insights, to see our past in a new and far more contingent light.

In spelling out some of our basic assumptions about history I would like to update a statement I made some years ago: A sharp distinction must be drawn between, on the one hand, paternalizing the past for not knowing what we think we now know—what has been termed "generational chauvinism"—and, on the other, using all the tools and concepts at our disposal for understanding our own "paternity." No doubt in the future our own mixtures of insight and blindness will be interpreted from that then-present perspective from which one tries to understand the past. We will then be perceived in ways in which we cannot perceive ourselves. And only a proper respect for evidence will prevent reckless assaults on our muteness by omniscient and all-embracing explanation. I am prepared to believe that nothing in history is absolute or clear-cut; that truth is always framed in ambiguity; that good and evil, though by no means "relative," are always colored by human ambivalence; that all liberations are won at a cost; and that all choice involves negation. I also think that history is filled with moral ironies and that one can point to ironies but never prove them. Yet when all this is frankly acknowledged, there is something left that is primary and irreducible. Whatever one believes about historical progress—or the lack of it—we are the beneficiaries of past struggles, of the new and often temporary sensitivities of a collective conscience, and of brave men and women who thought that the time was right not only for appealing to unfulfilled promises of the past, but also for breaking the proprieties of the present—for saying, in new contexts and to new audiences, as John Adams, Thomas Jefferson, and many others said in 1776, and as Martin Luther King, Jr. said nearly two centuries later, "How long? Not long!"

The anthology is divided into eight units that are organized temporally as well as by topic. As far as possible, the organization reflects the concerns and presuppositions of the authors of the documents. While these authors are often well-known leaders, we have also included the personal letters of farmers, artisans, housewives, Indians, blacks, radicals, moderates, and conservatives.

Part One, "First Encounters," begins with a letter Columbus wrote on his first voyage and then moves quickly to some Spanish sources on the first interactions with the Indians and African slaves, which greatly complicated the original "meaning" of the New World. Part Two, "European Colonization North of Mexico," moves from Richard Hakluyt's arguments in the 1580s for promoting English colonization in the New World to King Philip's War in 1675 and to new definitions of English liberties that include Samuel Sewall's memorial of 1700 attacking African-American slavery.

The twenty documents in Part Three, "A Land of Contrasts," include a 1650 description of New Netherlands, "America's first multicultural society," statements by Oneida and Seneca Indians, materials on the founding of Georgia, the shocking condition of redemptioners (white immigrants who were sold to pay off the cost of their transport), the British slave trade, and Daniel Horsmanden's notes on an alleged Negro conspiracy in 1741 to burn down the city of New York. Part Four centers on the crucial Seven Years' War (or French and Indian War), which transformed the prospects of both Indians and American colonists, freeing the latter from dependence on British protection against the French. Indirectly, the war also gave a new impetus to antislavery thought.

In view of the supreme importance of the subject, we have selected forty-eight documents for Part Five, "The Age of Revolution, 1765–1783." Along with such well-known subjects as British taxation of the colonists, the Boston Massacre and Tea party, and the Articles of Confederation, we have given particular attention to methods of resistance, ideology and media, and the theme of slavery and enslavement—both the conviction of white colonists that Britain intended to enslave *them,* and the role in the war of free and enslaved African Americans. What accentuates the importance of the latter point is the fact, little known to the general public, that the War for Independence was largely fought and won in the South.

Part Six, "Creating a New Nation," begins with the Loyalists' exodus to Canada in 1783 and ends with Andrew Jackson's defeat of the Creek Indians, the Hartford Convention, and John Quincy Adams's report in 1815 that British naval commanders, in the War of 1812, "have carried away from the United States all the slaves they have taken." Intervening documents help to illuminate Shays' Rebellion, the Northwest Ordinance, the Constitutional Convention, the impact of the Haitian and French Revolutions, the birth of political parties, the perilous nature of American foreign policy at a time of global conflict, and issues of slavery and race in Jeffersonian America.

Part Seven, "Antebellum America," constitutes the heart of the anthology. Its 130 selections are subdivided into sixteen sections that give some sense of the content of the documents: A. Shifts in Sensibility, Family, Gender Roles, and the Rise of Humanitarianism; B. Origins of the American Reform Tradition; C. 1818 and 1819: Watershed Years in American History; D. The Missouri Crisis; E. Slavery and Sectionalism; F. The Rise of the Second Party System; G. Ideology and Power in Jackson's America; H. Antebellum Reform: The Shift to Immediatism; I. Abolition and Slavery; J. From Antislavery to Women's Rights; K. Manifest Destiny; L. Mounting Sectional Antagonisms; M. The Mexican War; N. America at Mid-Century; O. The Gathering Storm; P. The Secession Crisis.

The final forty-seven documents, in Part Eight, "Civil War," capture some of the powerful emotions of hope, grief, despair, hatred, and prayer that punctuated America's greatest crisis and formative experience. The voices of little-known or unidentified soldiers and citizens mix with those of General Beauregard, Colonel Custer, Samuel P. Chase, Edwin M. Stanton, Robert E. Lee, and Abraham Lincoln. The volume ends with a glimpse of the future, "Toward Reconstruction."

II. FIVE ORGANIZING THEMES

I would like to ask readers to keep in mind five themes or organizing concepts I have long found useful in my own work as a historian and teacher of history. These five categories should help give added meaning to many of the primary sources and especially to connections between or among the sources.

The first and most central theme pertains to the spectrum between human power and authority, on the one hand (whether held by a sovereign individual, a group, or public opinion), and powerlessness, shame, dehumanization, and enslavement, on the other. For example, most American colonists in 1776, and most southerners in 1861, believed that they were compelled to resist being "enslaved" by an expansive, aggressive, and illegitimate authority. The complexities and ironies of exercising power and influence will be the major organizing theme of this anthology.

Power, as we all know, can be exerted by many means. Armies and police often use physical force and the threat of death to curb certain behavior or impose the policies of a government or would-be government. Governments enact laws controlling behavior and employ various administrative tools to achieve their ends. Economic power can take such forms as strikes; boycotts; firing or laying off employees; lowering wages; or the control of markets, interest rates, and currency. Power, despite the word's association with physical force, can be largely psychological, as in advertising or public appeals to guilt, honor, or patriotism. Much of human history can be read as a series of conflicts over the legitimation of power as different leaders, tribes, factions, classes, ethnicities, and nations have struggled for esteem, respect, honor, freedom, and material well-being.

"[I]f every Man had his will," John Peter Zenger wrote in 1733, "all Men would exercise Dominion, and no Man would suffer it." An American jury acquitted Zenger, a German immigrant and publisher of a New York newspaper, of seditious libel in a pivotal trial that helped establish both freedom of the press and freedom to criticize all governing authority. As Zenger's attorney told the jury, "Every Man who prefers Freedom to a Life of Slavery will bless and honour You, as Men who have...given us a Right,—the Liberty—both of exposing and opposing arbitrary Power...by speaking and writing Truth." The United States is unique in attempting to create a political system committed to *individual* dignity and freedom of choice. "At the heart of liberty [as protected by the Fourteenth Amendment]," the U.S. Supreme Court has said, "is the right to define one's own concept of existence, of meaning, of the universe, and of the mystery of human life."[1]

Unfortunately, while political and economic power are indispensable for true liberty as well as for social order and economic growth, the exercise of power has generally been linked with the domination and subordination of certain populations. And for thousands of years, the institution of slavery has stood as the most extreme example of and metaphor for domination and submission. Although slave labor was never a part of the original European plans for New World settlement, Indian and especially African slaves became the essential driving force in the New World economies from the mid-sixteenth to the mid-nineteenth centuries. Paradoxically, therefore, when the Anglo-

1. Planned Parenthood v. Casey, 505 U.S. at 851 (1992)

American colonists began to angrily resist British encroachments of power in the 1760s and 1770s, they were surrounded by African-American slaves, their own living examples of the dishonor and dehumanization of total powerlessness.

The second theme involves the spectrum between evil and good, sin and virtue, and the widespread human anticipation of providential rewards and punishments on earth. For Thomas Jefferson, in sharp contrast to John Adams, the moral distinctions between good and evil were seldom clouded by ambiguity. Like many idealists, Jefferson saw history essentially as a story of the children of light struggling against the children of darkness in an unending crusade for human liberty and enlightenment. But Jefferson could also express the fear that, because God was just, Jefferson's own children of light would eventually be convulsed in a cataclysm of racial retribution if they failed to abolish slavery and somehow remove the black population to a safe refuge.

As some of the early selections show, the Indians of the Caribbean and North America were perceived both as noble savages (but "timid beyond cure," as Columbus put it) and as the incarnation of evil. This was partly because they represented human life *removed* from the complex structures, boundaries, and coercions of European civilization. For Christians who believed in humanity's innate propensity for evil, the Indians' alleged cannibalism and delight in torture confirmed the conviction that only repressive and authoritarian societies, like those in Europe, could mitigate the sinful impulses of "natural man." Even some Christian missionaries, however, concluded that the Indians in regions such as Canada exhibited a simplicity of life and a purity of mind that stood in sharp contrast to the greed and corruption of the Old World.

In English eyes, the Spaniards who massacred and looted the Aztecs and Incas epitomized evil, yet the Spaniards' spectacular conquests and acquisition of wealth evoked English envy and emulation, though on a level of self-professed virtue and mission. Conceptions of evil often help to define goodness. Thus as the institution of slavery came to be seen by a small minority as the epitome of sin, the abolitionist cause took on the mantle of selfless virtue. If a noble movement promised to ennoble its participants, many abolitionists soon became more preoccupied with internal wars over doctrinal purity than with finding common ground for an effective assault on southern slavery. Still, American abolitionism gained much strength from the religious conviction that fighting slavery was God's work and that the nation's emancipation from its central sin was as certain as Christ's Second Coming. One question touched on by various documents from the seventeenth century to Lincoln's second inaugural address concerns the influence of the Old Testament in conditioning Americans to expect collective rewards, such as the opening of the great West, and collective punishments, such as the Civil War.

Collective rewards and punishments tie in closely with our third theme: the ways in which time and historical change are perceived. During the long decades of the Cold War between the United States and the Soviet Union, most peoples came to think of the world as permanently divided between the democratic and the Communist superpowers. Any important changes could move only at a glacially slow pace. As historians looked backward in time, it became increasingly difficult to comprehend sudden revolutionary transformations. But then beginning in 1989, the Soviet empire started to collapse, and even the best-informed specialists in international relations looked on with dismay as maps, alliances, and the most basic assumptions about the future suddenly became obsolete. The unexpected ending of the Cold War and the evaporation of communism in the Soviet Union and Eastern Europe should help us better understand such sudden transformations as the American Revolution and the Civil War.

Actually, much of American history has been based on the secular belief in the possibility of continuous, gradual human improvement in accordance with the natural laws of cause and effect—the underlying assumption being that morality, justice, and happiness (as specified, famously, in the Declaration of Independence) are capable of the same cumulative advances as modern science and technology.

It's useful to contrast this belief in gradual progress, which I will refer to as "gradualism," with the sense of a "revolutionary moment," a decisive time of qualitative change, of being abruptly catapulted into a wholly new frame of time. Gradualism refers to steady chronological, clocklike change, but change so slow and incremental that it is often imperceptible. For some religious thinkers, especially, revolutionary moments were never inevitable or predictable, and were largely based on visions of a new messianic age. Yet as various documents will show, Americans tended to view the War of Independence and the Civil War in precisely this light, as eschatological leaps that overcame a "demonic power." An even more dramatic example, to which virtually all Americans were forced to react, was the French Revolution, which attempted to abolish all enslavement to the past, with the Jacobins' wholly new calendar and Reign of Terror.

Tension between gradualism and revolutionary moments often took the form of mundane debates over the consequences of religious revivals, the means of punishing criminals, and the timing of local reforms, such as the laws of northern states that emancipated the children of slaves when they reached an age, sometime in their twenties, when their labor had presumably paid for the cost of their maintenance. Far more central, however, were the ways in which conflicting conceptions of time and social change came to dominate the national debate over slavery and racial difference after the northern states had defined themselves as "free soil." In the early 1830s a new generation of abolitionists took up the cry "Immediate emancipation!" This slogan, which had different connotations and consequences in England, was much misunderstood in America; yet immediatism directly challenged complacency as well as the prevailing conviction, quietly affirmed by George Washington in 1786, that only the state legislatures could abolish slavery and only "by slow, sure & imperceptible degrees." What could not be allowed to be perceptible, or *perceived,* was any change in white supremacy or racial intermixture. The immediatists, one should note, were immediately denounced as "amalgamationists"—as "nigger-lovers" who would surrender their white daughters to the lusts of African-American men.

This nuclear racist obsession leads to our fourth theme or organizing concept, human differences as exemplified and symbolized by "race." Responsible scientists have long discredited any biological or genetic definition of racial groups. Humans have always been sensitive to the physical and mental differences that distinguish the people they encounter—height, strength, bulk, physiognomy, friendliness, sexiness, special skills, and so on. But we now know from studies of DNA that there is far greater genetic variation *within* various African groups that there is *between* an African group and a random collection of people from Europe or Asia. In other words, such outer physical traits as skin color, hair texture, and physiognomy do not correlate with major genetic variation. But for many centuries at least, humans have tended to define their differences, including cultural differences, in terms of racial stereotypes. In part this may be due to the way in which dominant and recessive genetic physical traits are inherited.

The arbitrary and cultural character of race has often been illustrated by contrasting the North American "Negro," defined to include anyone with a "drop" of "African blood," with the complex gradations of racial intermixture found in Latin America. Why is someone who has six or seven white European great-grandparents classified as "black"? We no longer speak of an Alpine race, a Mediterranean race, or a Hebrew race. But by what means did the Irish, Jews, and Arabs, at one time regarded as barbarous and even subhuman, become "white"? If race differentiates and divides groups of people, how important has it also been as a means of unification?

Of course, racial categories are no less *real* even when deprived of biological substance. Like serfdom, social castes, and royal or noble "blood," concepts of race influence perception, including self-perception, and can above all represent a shared historical experience, such as that of the Native Americans and African Americans in the United States. Our documents trace the meaning of these shared racial experiences from Columbus's view in 1493 that the Caribbean Indians "are of a very keen intelligence" to the interrogation for witchcraft, in 1691, of Tituba, an Indian slave brought from Barbados to Salem, Massachusetts; from the panic in New York City in 1741 *"that the Negroes were rising,"* to the actual insurrection of Nat Turner in 1831 and the complex debates over the enlistment of slaves or former slaves in the Union and Confederate armies.

The fifth and final theme concerns the development and fate of transcendent ideals, particularly liberty, equality, and democracy (and their antitheses). From Columbus on, the New World stimulated and nourished European visions of liberation and perfection, which at first seemed quite compatible with hereditary hierarchy and even with slavery (in 1516 Thomas More prescribed slavery as a punishment in his famous book describing an imaginary ideal society, *Utopia*). Our early documents give much attention to the developing republican ideals of liberty, independence, equality, and virtue, which were to play a crucial role in the American Revolution and the framing of state and federal governments. While American leaders drew on the republican ideals of ancient Greece and Rome, they were also indebted to a tradition of radical republican thought that arose in the Renaissance and especially in the English civil wars and Commonwealth of the mid-seventeenth century.

This republican ideology was passionately opposed to the corruptions of entrenched privilege and hereditary power—to a society like those in Europe in which the poverty-stricken masses were obliged to show humiliating obeisance to a haughty elite. In this respect it is worth noting that the Quakers, who originated in the turmoil of mid-seventeenth-century England and who later became pioneers in the British and American antislavery movements, refused to kneel, bow, uncover their heads, or prostrate themselves before supposedly "superior" human beings.

Is it liberty or equality that stands as the antithesis of slavery? How much is equality a matter of feeling and behavior—that is, a matter of *treating* people as equals even when there are immense differences in wealth, power, and status? One of our early documents, dated 1705, shows the rage expressed by the governor of Massachusetts, Joseph Dudley, when two cart drivers refused to make way for his carriage and then failed to exhibit what Dudley considered the proper kind of deference: "Winchester [a cart driver] answered boldly...I am as good flesh & blood as you. I will not give way." A century later the kind of deference Dudley expected was much rarer, and some politicians were beginning to present themselves as "men of the people."

American champions of republicanism, such as Thomas Jefferson, were deeply troubled by the growing inequalities of pre-Revolutionary colonial society, which they associated with the self-serving patronage of the royal governors and their courts. Republicans envisioned independent commonwealths populated by virtuous yeoman farmers whose ownership of freehold property would ensure their lack of dependence on a wealthy elite. This republican emphasis on liberty, independence, and virtue—an unselfish devotion to the public good—was eventually forced to make room for Benjamin Franklin's and Abraham Lincoln's craving for *opportunity,* for a fluid society in which, ideally, no man is permanently required to work for other men.

There are obvious tensions and contradictions between the ideal of equality and the kind of opportunity that enables some men and women to far surpass all others. Yet the brilliant and much-quoted French traveler and observer Alexis de Tocqueville found in 1831 that "equality of condition" was the single most striking fact about American democratic society. Similarly, Abraham Lincoln said that the "equality of men" was the central idea behind public opinion and the American government. In his original wording of the Declaration of Independence, Jefferson wrote that "all men are created equal & independent." It was from this equal creation that "they derived rights inherent & inalienable, among which are the preservation of life, & liberty, & the pursuit of happiness." According to the philosopher Morton White, these words can be translated into a "because" clause: Because all men have been created equal in the sense of sharing a common nature and belonging to the same species, "they should also be treated as equal in the sense that no one of them should depend on the will of any other man."[2] This linkage of equality and independence challenges traditional boundaries of race, class, and gender.

Certainly this is the Declaration's message that inspired reformers of all kinds, including early feminists, labor leaders, and black and white abolitionists. In one of our documents the abolitionist Gerrit Smith draws a distinction between the British abolitionists, who merely claimed that "a *man* ought not to be a *slave,*" and the American abolitionists, who contended that abolition "is demanded by the principle that 'all men are created equal' and that no man is to be excluded from the rights of manhood." For all of these American agitators, the Declaration was above all the sacred fount of democracy (a word not used in a positive sense by Jefferson, Madison, and John Adams in the Revolutionary era).

Yet John Adams was not alone in insisting that hierarchies, like other inequalities,

2. Morton White, *The Philosophy of the American Revolution* (New York: Oxford University Press, 1978), pp. 62–78, 160–84.

were inevitable and thus in need of recognition and control. Even Jefferson talked of a "natural aristocracy" based on merit alone, and proposed an educational system and selective examination, in that "twenty of the best geniuses will be raked from the rubbish annually" to form an educated elite. Some historians have argued that the egalitarian rhetoric of Jacksonian democracy simply cloaked the emergence of different kinds of elites. The early extension of suffrage in America to virtually all white males, at a time when England, for example, limited voting to men of considerable property, distracted attention from the denial of suffrage to women and from the fact that the gap between rich and poor in America was rapidly widening; moreover, as John C. Calhoun candidly admitted, the illusion of white equality rested in good part on the belief in black inferiority.

On the other hand, the rhetoric of democracy and the spread of democratic manners greatly reduced the arrogant disdain and fawning obeisance that unequals had traditionally expressed toward each other. Virtually every European traveler to America commented on the informal and relaxed way in which ordinary white citizens talked to men of higher rank. As Duke François de La Rochefoucault-Liancourt put it: "The rich man shakes hands with the worker and talks with him, not as elsewhere in order to honour him, but as one who may need his help one day—and further, without calculation, by habit, by education."

Meanwhile, with the documents written by Samuel Sewall in 1700 and John Woolman in 1757, we see the earliest development of antislavery ideals that were based on the Golden Rule and on a belief that it is wrong morally and politically to treat humans either as infallible demigods endowed with unlimited power, or as contemptible objects, mere instruments of another's will. These antislavery ideals acquire new meanings in the later selections by William Lloyd Garrison, Gerrit Smith, John Brown, and even Abraham Lincoln, who said in the 1850s, "As I would not be a *slave,* so I would not be a *master.* This expresses my idea of democracy. Whatever differs from this, to the extent of the difference, is no democracy."

The five themes we have just examined interact in countless ways. Thus the second theme, regarding good and evil, depends in large measure on the way power is used, as in the violent crimes of an individual or the arbitrary, unconstitutional acts of a government. Similarly, a revolutionary moment—let us say the sudden and unexpected emancipation of slaves in French colony of St. Domingue (later Haiti)—depended on the *loss* of power by French planters and administrators. The theme of race helps to explain why various nations governed by whites responded so differently to the black Haitian as opposed to the later Latin American wars for independence. The theme of transcendent ideals ties in closely with more basic notions of good and evil. Equality of respect or esteem, for example, would seem to be related to a sense of empathetic fairness, as in the Hebrew and Christian versions of the Golden Rule found in the Old and New Testaments: "Love your neighbor as yourself"; "You and the stranger shall be alike before the Lord"; "The stranger who resides with you shall be to you as one of your citizens; you shall love him as yourself, for you were strangers in the land of Egypt"; "Therefore all things whatsoever ye would that men should do to you, do ye even so unto them: for this is the law and the prophets."[3]

3. Lev. 19:18; Num. 15:15; Lev. 19:34; Matt. 7:12.

III. FOUR PIVOTAL ISSUES IN EARLY AMERICAN HISTORY

The five conceptual themes also cut across a large number of substantive issues that the documents address. I shall here limit the discussion to four major historical issues, beginning with the seemingly irreversible development of the African slave trade and New World slavery.

This subject clearly presents us with the most extreme example of unlimited power and dehumanization—linked, ironically, with the seemingly liberating "consumer revolution" in northern Europe as slave-grown sugar and tobacco provided the first luxury products for a mass market. Racial slavery also provided, after a considerable lapse of time, a model or paradigm of social evil. As Abraham Lincoln put it in a profound and yet typically simple way, "If slavery is not wrong, nothing is wrong."[4] And as I have already suggested, the bitter and tumultuous debates over slavery revolved, in large part, over the question of time. In both Britain and the United States, abolitionism became a serious force only when reformers began demanding the "immediate" emancipation of all slaves. While this slogan appeared absurdly unrealistic, the American Civil War, with its wholly unexpected emancipation of more than four million African-American slaves, seemed to millions of both blacks and whites to be a true revolutionary moment, the sudden purgation of what James Madison had much earlier called the fruit of America's "original sin."

For that very reason, the Thirteenth, Fourteenth, and Fifteenth Amendments to the Constitution gave new force and substance to the older republican ideals of liberty, equal protection of the laws, and equality of opportunity. Yet emancipation did little to dissolve the deeply rooted racial prejudice that had evolved along with the institution of slavery. Another century would elapse before white Americans would begin serious implementation of ideals embodied in the Fourteenth Amendment and the Declaration of Independence.

Like slavery, the second issue—America's relation to Europe and the Old World—connects many primary-source selections from Columbus to the end of the Civil War. Europe's domination and influence over America were most explicit, of course, during the long colonial era, when the periodic wars between England and France had a decisive effect on the colonists' own sense of identity and their relations with Native Americans. After the War of 1812 (and the fall of Napoleon), the immense power of the British navy silently protected the United States. The spell of isolation was then broken by the attempted secession of the southern states. In 1861 the fate of the United States lay more in European hands than at any time since 1815 or perhaps even 1781. Britain's decision to resist French pressure to intervene did not guarantee a Union victory in the Civil War. But a formal recognition of the Confederacy would almost certainly have led to Confederate independence and thus a divided America.

The third issue, closely related to the second, is American exceptionalism, or the degree to which America had escaped the dismal laws, cycles, conditions, and coercions

4. Letter to Albert G. Hodges, April 4, 1864, in *The Collected Works of Abraham Lincoln,* Vol. VII, ed. Roy P. Basler, (New Brunswick, N.J.: Rutgers University Press, 1953), p. 281.

of Old World history. In the initial era of discovery, conquest, and piracy, Europeans often saw the New World as exceptional in the negative sense of being wholly out of control, subject to no laws, order, or civil restraints. As the saying went, there was no peace "beyond the line," an invisible longitudinal barrier in the Atlantic that marked the limits of European treaties.

By Thomas Jefferson's time, however, many Americans (and even some Europeans) had concluded that America was synonymous with a new beginning for mankind. It was the antipode of European constraints and corruption. The reverse side of our Great Seal, emblazoned on every dollar bill, proclaims "Novus Ordo Seclorum" (a new cycle of the ages). Jefferson's own vision included an expanding "empire for liberty," which by 1804, with the annexation of Louisiana, also meant an empire for slavery. Jefferson fervently believed that westward expansion into territories claimed by France and Spain would preempt the danger of any European interference or intervention. He also advocated the "living generation's" self-liberation from the laws, limits, and debts of the past. Yet John Adams, Jefferson's lifelong but "dialectical" friend, was appalled by the naïveté of this Garden of Eden faith. For Adams, human nature would always be the same on both sides of the Atlantic: The universal human obsession with status, power, ambition, recognition, and honor, to say nothing of human greed and lust, would always need the checks and balances of law and government. But as Adams understood all too acutely, his form of secular puritanism was doomed in the ages of Jefferson and Jackson.

As in Europe, nationalism often brought together Americans of different religious faiths, social classes, and ethnicities. The fourth and final issue centers on a sense of *"Americanness,"* which was strongly felt even by the increasingly persecuted free African Americans who resisted the popular white crusade to "colonize" American free blacks in Liberia or some other distant refuge. What was it, we must ask the documents, that Americans increasingly shared? Even in the colonial period, as the selections make clear, Americans could be of Dutch, French, German, Swedish, Irish, Jewish, African, or Native American ethnicity (while many American Jews consider Judaism a religion, Jews were seen as members of a "nation"). This diversity would increase over time, especially with the massive Irish and German immigration of the 1840s and 1850s. Yet there was something distinctively American in the very affirmation of a freedom to be *different.*

Even the southern secessionists thought of themselves as being the truly authentic Americans, the true heirs of the American Revolution, as distinct from the wayward Northerners who had been corrupted by European fashions and values and who had betrayed their noble Revolutionary heritage. As Robert Edgar Bonner has recently written, drawing on sermons, tracts, and diaries of southern soldiers, southern secession meant that "it was not only the future of 'the South' but of the entire American experience that hung in the balance."[5]

5. Bonner, "Americans Apart: Nationality in the Slaveholding South," Ph.D. diss., Yale University (December 1997), Chap. 5, p. 294.

IV. THOUGHTS AND REFLECTIONS ON SOME OF THE DOCUMENTS

A. THE REVOLUTIONARY PERIOD

With these themes and issues in mind, I would like to suggest some ways of reading selected documents and thus provide a preview of the richness and diversity of this interpretive anthology.

John Jay, who turned thirty in 1775, was one of the leaders of the American Revolution and a member and then president of the Continental Congress. Contrast Jay's speech to the State Constitutional Convention of New York, delivered on December 23, 1776, with the later petition of Peter Kiteridge, a black Revolutionary War veteran, to the selectmen of Medfield, Massachusetts.

Jay, a New Yorker who still owned slaves, says we are "determined to die free rather than live slaves and entail bondage on our children." He also interprets American military defeats as divine punishment for our sins, "like the Jews of old." If Americans could not be persuaded to fight for their liberty, he declares, then they *deserve* to be slaves! Jay later joined the New York Manumission Society and supported the gradual abolition of slavery. Kiteridge had been a slave for "the best part of my life," but in 1775, "in the twentyfifth [sic] of my age I entered into the service of the U.S. as a private soldier wherein I continued five years and...contracted a complaint from which I have suffered in a greater or less degree ever since." Now, after years as a day laborer and at age fifty-eight, with an unusable arm and incurable diseases, he seeks assistance, "as a stranger accidentally fallen within your borders," in supporting his wife and four children. Jay had the will and the power to free his own slaves. Kiteridge, an illiterate Revolutionary War veteran who signed an "X" where his benefactor, an amanuensis, wrote "His mark," found that freedom for a black could lead to pleas for assistance from a white community.

I am most impressed by the number of eminent Americans, including such figures as James Otis, Mercy Otis Warren, and John Adams, who sought to explain the American cause to the sympathetic mind of Catharine Macaulay, an Englishwoman and the author of the multivolume *History of England from the Accession of James I to that of the Brunswick Line.* Catharine Macaulay, who after the war spent ten days visiting George Washington, personified the tradition of English dissent stemming from Oliver Cromwell's seventeenth-century Commonwealth. Her correspondence with American leaders dramatizes the importance of radical Anglo-American ties and English sympathy for the oppressed colonists. Yet readers may also ask, even after reading the gripping eyewitness accounts of the Boston Massacre and the Battle of Concord, why more Americans didn't respond to the remarkable amnesty proclamations of the British generals Thomas Gage and Sir Henry Clinton. Other documents do convey the Americans' outrage over being invaded by mercenary foreign troops—"Barbarians of Germany"—and there is a surprising emphasis on pillage and the rape of wives and daughters as a foreign army continues to capture more and more American territory.

The constant and significant refrain that free white colonists were in literal danger of being *"enslaved,"* or in the striking biblical phraseology, of being forced to become "hewers of wood and drawers of water," dramatized the danger that *any* government could become tyrannical. And the American rebels faced the immediate need to form new governments while resisting the armed force of their former British "parent." In November 1775 John Adams sent Richard Henry Lee a remarkable "Sketch" of a three-branch government that foreshadowed the basic principles of later state and federal constitutions:

> A Legislative, an Executive and a judicial Power, comprehend the whole of what is meant and understood by Government. It is by ballancing [sic] [each] of these Powers against the other two, that the Effort in human Nature toward Tyranny can alone be checked and restrained and any degree of Freedom preserved in the Constitution.

It was Adams who took the lead in 1775 and 1776 in calling for each colony to adopt a new independent constitution, a step that marked the de facto secession from the British Empire.

The Revolution, which challenged the legitimacy of kings and all hereditary ranks, even provoked new questions about gender. Lucy Knox, the eloquent wife of the patriot General Henry Knox, was willing to make allowances for the long lapses in her husband's correspondence. She knew that Henry was in the midst of battles, and she did her best to boost his morale. Yet Lucy expresses the very explicit hope that when the war is over, Henry will not consider himself "commander in chief of your own house, but be convinced that there is such a thing as equal command."

Various documents underscore the *contingency* of the War of Independence, which like most wars could easily have had an altogether different outcome. Far too often American history is taught as if everything were inevitable, as if the nation's development, driven by some deep underlying forces, proceeded in accordance with a preordained plan. But in 1781, six years after the beginning of armed resistance, George Mason could survey the British occupation of the South and conclude, "Our affairs have been for some time growing from bad to worse." Writing from North Carolina, the British commander Charles Cornwallis could speak of adopting "effectual measures for suppressing the remains of Rebellion in this Province." We sense the deep despair of real American people, people who wonder, for example, about the motives and commitment of America's French ally. Was it possible, as one writer suggests, that the French government wanted to prolong the war to transform the independent states into a weakened French satellite that would provide a gateway for restoring French power in North America? The documents also enable us to reexperience the perceptions of American Loyalists as they lost their houses and possessions and fled to Canada.

The ideals popularized by the Revolution could have paradoxical effects. In a letter of 1786, George Washington vows never "to possess another slave by purchase." Two years earlier James Pemberton, a leading American Quaker and abolitionist, attempts to coordinate antislavery strategy with his British Quaker counterpart James Phillips. But after describing the American Quakers' attempts to send antislavery petitions to Congress and the New Jersey legislature, Pemberton moves on to the controversial issue of admitting free blacks to membership with the Society of Friends. Such membership, Pemberton explains, might imply "the privilege of intermarriage and I believe there are few who would freely consent to introduce such a union in their families which mixture some think would reverse the order of Divine Providence who in his wisdom inscrutable to us has been pleased to form distinction of Colour." This prejudice, we must remember, was being expressed by people who represented the most radical and enlightened stance regarding slavery and race.

Consider another example of an American radical compromising Revolutionary ideals: Thomas Jefferson's policy regarding Native Americans in 1780, when he was governor of Virginia. The British had opposed rapid settlement of the western frontier since they were mainly interested in the fur trade and in maintaining friendly relations with Indian allies. Most of the Indians, accordingly, sided with the British during the Revolution. On April 19, 1780, nearly four years after writing the Declaration of Independence, Jefferson expressed "much concern" over "the many murders committed by the Indians...in the neighborhood of Pittsburg[h]." "We have been too diverted by interests of Humanity," he continued, "from enforcing good behavior by severe punishment. Savages are to be curbed by fear only." The only ultimate solution, Jefferson made clear, would be the removal of tribes like the Shawnees "beyond the Mississippi or the [Great] Lakes."

The very success of the War of Independence presented American leaders with formidable problems of "reality": How were the independent American people to govern themselves and avoid disunion, disintegration, and anarchy? Writing to General Henry Knox on the subject of Shays' Rebellion in 1786, George Washington echoes many of the fears and themes of the earlier Tories: "There are combustibles in every State, which a spark might set fire to." One can understand Washington's fear that given such violent defiance of law in Massachusetts (Shays' Rebellion), Britain, still an enemy, would do everything possible to incite Indian attacks and "to foment the spirit of turbulence within the bowels of the United States, with a view of distracting our governments, and promoting divisions." Only "[v]igilance in watching, and vigour in acting," Washington felt, could prevent the new nation from losing everything that had been won in the Revolution.

B. EARLY NATIONAL CRISES, 1787–1815

One may blandly observe that these years witnessed very rapid economic, demographic, and even urban growth as the borders of the United States expanded to include Kentucky, Tennessee, Ohio, and Louisiana (Indiana, Mississippi, Illinois, and Alabama would quickly follow by 1819). But it can also be argued that these twenty-eight years were the most critical period in American history, as hazardous and fraught with peril as the Civil War itself. The Constitution had hardly been drafted and ratified and the new federal government put to test when the French Revolution erupted and then ignited European and global wars that quickly spread to the Caribbean, the nerve center of the Atlantic slave system.

While many readers of American history and biography are familiar with president Washington's Neutrality Proclamation, the struggle between Jeffersonian Francophiles and Hamiltonian Anglophiles, the XYZ Affair, and America's "undeclared war" with France (which President Adams courageously ended before it brought on disaster), little has been done to widen this narrative to include the Haitian Revolution; France's emancipation of colonial slaves; America's military aid to the black leader Toussaint-Louverture, in what would soon be Haiti; the British recruitment of many regiments of black troops who fought the French and Spaniards and even engaged in the Battle of New Orleans; the massive 1811 slave insurrection in Louisiana; or the overall impact of the European wars on southern slaves and Indian tribes.

It is no exaggeration to say that the vicissitudes of the French Revolutionary and Napoleonic wars determined whether the United States would control the Mississippi River, gain a claim to Florida and the vast Louisiana Territory stretching westward to the Rocky Mountains, avoid a cataclysmic slave insurrection, expand cotton plantations westward from Georgia to Louisiana, successfully "remove" the large Indian tribes who lived east of the Mississippi, and enjoy economic growth stimulated either by foreign trade or early industrialization in the Northeast.

Our documents go far in bringing the awesome uncertainties of this era to life. I am thinking, for example, of the detailed material on the conflicts at the Constitutional Convention and the arguments over the Constitution's ratification. Mercy Otis Warren, a respected historian of the Revolution, conveys the sense of uncertainty in a letter of September 1789 to Catharine Macaulay. This letter was written at a time when women, according to the dominant male-centered ideology, were supposed to be wholly uninterested in politics: "It is time we have a government established & Washington at its head. But we are too poor for Monarchy, too wise for despotism, too dissipated[,] selfish & extravagant for Republicanism." After condemning the leaders' desire for "exorbitant salarics" and "ostentatious pomp," Warren took note of the French Revolution, which had just begun: "would it not be surprising if that nation should [show] a greater advantage from the spirit of liberty diffused through the continent than the American's may be able to boast after all their struggle and sacrifice to become a free people."

The issue of America's security and future expansion is highlighted by a previously unpublished letter Thomas Jefferson wrote as secretary of state on August 12, 1790. At that moment Britain and Spain were on the brink of war, and Jefferson, addressing the U.S. commissioner to England, Gouverneur Morris, was deeply concerned about a possible British conquest of Florida and other adjacent regions held by Spain. Jefferson was confident that American settlers would eventually infiltrate Florida and take over other frontier areas from the feeble Spaniards. But at a time when the British refused to evacuate soldiers from the American Northwest posts, as stipulated by the 1783 treaty of peace, nothing seemed more alarming than the prospect of more British troops to the South and the West.

A novel way to read the documents concerning the famous struggle over the national debt and Alexander Hamilton's program for a strong economy that would balance agriculture with manufacturing is to see Hamilton's economic vision as a political economy in which there would be no place for slavery. That was not Hamilton's explicit purpose, and slavery was not part of the increasingly angry debates between Federalists and Republicans. Yet before the 1790s, no one offered a serious alternative to the central linkage between the North American economy and the Atlantic slave system—America's dependence, in particular, on Caribbean markets. Hamilton's program pointed the way toward the kind of self-sufficient industrial economy that eventually emerged in the free-soil North and that became more and more intolerant of the demands of the slaveholding south.

Ironically, Hamilton was born and reared in the slave colonies of the Leeward Islands. But after some philanthropic merchants sent him to New York City for a college education, he became increasingly dedicated to reorienting the economy away from its dependence on slave labor and trade with the Caribbean. In contrast to Jefferson, his bitter rival who refused to join the Virginia antislavery society, Hamilton became a leader in the New York Manumission Society, one of the first antislavery groups in world. It must be added that Hamilton also favored the employment of women and children in factories (but at Monticello Jefferson closely supervised the young slaves who worked at his own small nailmaking factory). Above all, Hamilton's vision of urban banks, investment, and manufacturing threatened Jefferson's ideal of a simple agrarian republic.

As one of our previously unpublished documents shows, however, Hamilton played a role in choosing Jefferson (as a least of possible evils) as president of the United States. John Adams, the incumbent president, would have won the election in 1800 if Southerners had not been able to count three-fifths of their slaves in calculating electoral votes. Even so, because of a constitutional oversight, Jefferson received the same number of electoral votes as the Republican vice-presidential candidate, Aaron Burr. This anomaly, which was corrected in 1804 by the Twelfth Amendment, threw the contest into the Federalist-controlled House of Representatives.

At this point Hamilton wrote an urgent letter to Harrison Gray Otis, urging the Federalists in the House to vote for Jefferson: "Mr. Jefferson, though too revolutionary in his notions, is yet a lover of liberty and will be desirous of something like orderly Government—Mr. Burr loves nothing but himself—Thinks of nothing but his own aggrandizement—and will be content with nothing short of permanent power in his own hands.... In a choice of Evils, let them take the least—Jefferson is in my view less dangerous than Burr."

After thirty-five deadlock ballots, James Bayard, a Federalist congressman from Delaware, made a deal with Jefferson and then changed his vote, ensuring Jefferson's victory.[6] It seems highly probably that Hamilton's continuing influence contributed to the deadlock and thus to Jefferson's ultimate triumph. In 1804 Burr killed Hamilton in a celebrated duel. We include a later letter of Burr's regarding his trial for treason, which had nothing directly to do with his killing Hamilton.

I can only briefly touch on the many paradoxes of slavery in Jeffersonian America, beginning with the all-important Haitian Revolution, which converted St. Dominigue, the richest colony in the Caribbean, into a black republic governed by former slaves. Again, the documents question any sense of inevitability. In a remarkable letter of August 1802, eleven years after the first great slave uprising in St. Domingue and following the arrival of a large French army sent by Napoleon, the French general

6. I am indebted for this information to Bruce Ackerman, who shows in his forthcoming book for *The Roots of Presidentialism: The Marshall Court Confronts the Jeffersonian Revolution* that before Bayard's defection, which Jefferson later rewarded, some Federalists were maneuvering to make John Marshall president. In 1804, before the duel, Hamilton also helped to block Burr's election as governor of New York.

Charles Victor Emmanuel LeClerc reassures General Rochambeau, his successor, that "[t]his insurrection is in its last crisis. By the first month of the revolutionary calendar, with a month of campaigning, all will be over." Exhorting Rochambeau to "[s]how no mercy," LeClerc adds that "[o]ne must be unflinching and inspire great terror; it is the only thing that will suppress the blacks." At this point Toussant-Louverture had already been captured and shipped off to die in a French prison; Jacques Dessalines and other black leaders had temporarily gone over to the side of the French. Yet by January 1, 1804, the French had been expelled and Dessalines, as emperor, proclaimed the independence of the black Haitian republic.

It was this French defeat in 1803 that led Napoleon to sell the vast Louisiana Territory to the United States. The autocratic government that the Jefferson administration imposed on the people of Louisiana evoked an interesting memorial to Congress in 1804 from "Planters, Merchants and other inhabitants of Louisiana":

> Without any agency in the events which have annexed our country to the United States, we yet consider them as fortunate, and thought our liberties secured even before we knew the terms of the cession.... [But the law] does not "incorporate us in the Union"...vested us with none of the "Rights," gives us no advances and deprives us of all the "immunities" of American citizens.... A Governor is to be placed over us, whom we have not chosen, whom we do not even know, who may be ignorant of our language, uninformed of our institutions, and who may have no connections with our Country or interest in its welfare.

The principal concerns of these petitioners, it turns out, were the restrictions placed on the importation of slaves and an absolute prohibition on the slave trade from Africa. In 1803, in response to the presumed markets that the Louisiana Purchase would open up, South Carolina had opened its ports to a massive slave trade from Africa. The South Carolinians knew that Congress, pressured by the economic, moral, and racist interests of the Upper South, would probably ban such African slave imports altogether in 1808, when first permitted to do so by the U.S. Constitution.

C. ANTEBELLUM AMERICA, 1815–60

The victories and defeats of the Napoleonic wars, including the War of 1812, profoundly shaped the following decades of American history. After 1815, there was little risk of French or even British intervention westward from the Atlantic or northward from the Caribbean. Spain, occupied by Napoleon and devastated by the Peninsular War (1808–14), faced a series of independence movements throughout its New World empire. By the mid-1820s, coinciding with revolutionary movements within Spain itself, all the Spanish colonies except Cuba and Puerto Rico had achieved independence. Spain's vulnerability made it easy in 1818 for Andrew Jackson to invade Spanish Florida (which had become a refuge for fugitive slaves and a base for Seminole Indian raids) and for Secretary of State John Quincy Adams to negotiate a treaty with Spain in 1819 ceding Florida and expanding U.S. claims to the Pacific.[7]

7. West Florida, or the "Florida panhandle," had been annexed in 1810.

The decline or disappearance of European power also opened the way for the removal of eastern and especially large southeastern Indian tribes west of the Mississippi. Even earlier, thanks in part to the invention of the cotton gin and the explosive growth of the textile industry in Britain and New England, southern merchants and planters began marching hundreds of thousands of black slaves into the Old Southwest, which soon became the heart of the Cotton kingdom. Westward settlement expanded so fast that by 1819 Arkansas was being organized as a territory and Missouri, also west of the Mississippi and part of the Louisiana Purchase, was applying for admission to the Union as a slave state.

Meanwhile, the War of 1812 had stimulated manufacturing in New England and the Northeast, where, partly as a result of the religious revivals of the Second Great Awakening, the middle classes experienced a deep shift in moral sensibility. Women stood at the forefront of this characterological transformation. Often left behind as increasing numbers of men gravitated to the West, women became more active as schoolteachers, factory workers, and members of various kinds of benevolent, religious, and reform associations. As many of the documents indicate, eighteenth-century ideals of order, wit, and restraint slowly gave way to a romantic insistence on feelings, love, affection, and piety. Examples can be seen in the romantic conception of marriage, romantic fiction and poetry, and the new interest in nurturing and even indulging children.

No less important was the focus of the religious revivals on human moral *ability.* Contradicting the traditions of Calvinism, quietism, and their secular counterparts, which emphasized the limitations of human life, a new generation of clergymen preached that all humans CAN say "yes!" Men and women had the power to accept divine grace and even to change the world. Thus in addition to the secular Revolutionary heritage, with its lesson that the oppressions of the past can be thrown off and a new nation founded, there emerged an even more powerful religious message of *possibility*. The disciples of John Wesley, the English father of Methodism, like the secular disciples of Thomas Paine, fervently believed that we have it in our power to transform the world. But in the North, far more than in the South, economic and scientific advances undercut traditions of fatalism and hostility to change.

Of all the reform movements that sprang to life in the antebellum era, "temperance," which soon meant abstinence from *all* alcoholic drinks, attracted the most followers. There is considerable evidence that alcoholism had become by the early nineteenth century a serious national problem. The per capita consumption of alcohol was much higher than it is today, and relatively few women drank. The temperance reformers could be quite explicit:

> There is death in it. It contains Ardent Spirits, and it will destroy you. One Glass will not destroy me! you say. So said the man whom you saw drunk, on the floor, wallowing in his vomit. So said the man whom you saw beating his wife. So said the wretch whom you saw on the gallows, for committing murder, while intoxicated. And so you still say as you become like them.

The temperance movement was like a tree trunk with branches leading into abolitionism, feminism, pacifism, and other causes. Despite the paradoxical meaning of the word "temperance," reformers led the way in attacking "moderation" as a form of hypocrisy and immoral compromise. As one New Hampshire speaker puts it in a speech on July 4, 1829: "But they are all alike, the drunkard and the drinker....Temperate, moderate drinkers; temperate, moderate slavedealers; temperate, moderate gamblers; temperance, moderate sinners, all alike. It is the drinking which is wrong." The model, clearly, was the ancient concept of original sin. As various Protestant denominations abandoned this doctrine or at least adopted a more optimistic view of inherent human goodness, activists searched for secular embodiments of sin as a way of comprehending and struggling to correct an evil world.

The commitment to reform an evil world clashed in interesting ways with the idealization of the Revolutionary fathers and exhortations to remain faithful to their heritage. While reformers pointed out, for example, that the British tax on tea was a minor evil compared to African-American slavery, they still felt the need to quote Jefferson and pay tribute to the Founders. This deference to a sacred past often pitted American nationalism against the sectional rivalry of North and South. The theme of filial duty, far from declining as the Revolutionary generation passed away, took on added power with the approach of the Civil War. Each section claimed to be the legitimate and faithful Revolutionary heir.

An early act of this drama can be seen in President James Monroe's Fourth of July address in 1817 to the Massachusetts Society of the Cincinnati, an organization of Revolutionary War officers. Monroe himself was a Revolutionary War veteran from Virginia who still wore his hair in a powdered wig, often along with eighteenth-century attire; his nationalism had been attested to by his role in negotiating the Louisiana Purchase and his service as U.S. minister to both France and England (and by his later winning a second presidential term by an electoral college vote of 231 to 1!). In 1817 many New Englanders felt guilty over the "treasonous" moves toward secession some New England extremists had taken in opposition to the War of 1812 (the Hartford Convention). It was in this context that Monroe assured his listeners, "[Y]ou do but justice to yourselves in claiming the confidence of your country, that you can never desert the standard of freedom." "May your children," he then told the aging audience, "never forget the sacred duties devolved on them, to preserve the inheritance so gallantly acquired by their fathers."

In 1820–21 the debates over admitting Missouri as a new slave state provoked disturbing threats of disunion and civil war. The two-party system, which reemerged in American politics in the early 1830s and united Northerners and Southerners by instilling allegiance to the Democratic or Whig Parties, can be understood as a way of promoting nationalism, mitigating sectionalism, and suppressing public discussion of the explosive issue of slavery.

President Andrew Jackson was a slaveholding planter who hated abolitionists and knew that his election depended on southern votes. Yet no document better expresses the nationalist view of the Union than Jackson's proclamation of December 10, 1832, condemning South Carolina's attempt to "nullify" the tariff laws passed in 1828 and 1832. According to Jackson, "the power to annul a law of the United States, assumed by one State, {is} INCOMPATIBLE WITH THE EXISTENCE OF THE UNION, CONTRADICTED EXPRESSLY BY THE LETTER OF THE CONSTITUTION, UNAUTHORIZED BY ITS SPIRIT, INCONSISTENT WITH EVERY PRINCIPLE ON WHICH IT WAS FOUNDED, AND DESTRUCTIVE OF THE GREAT OBJECT FOR WHICH IT WAS FORMED." In surprisingly strong language defining his own duty as president—and anticipating the stand later taken by Abraham Lincoln—Jackson told the citizens of South Carolina that their leaders "know that a forcible opposition could alone prevent the execution of the laws, and they know that such opposition must be repelled. Their object is disunion: but be not deceived by names: disunion, by armed force, is TREASON."

Jackson's main political rival, Henry Clay, was also a southern slaveholder and even more of a nationalist (favoring federal aid to transportation and other "internal improvements"). In an important private letter of 1831, the year of Nat Turner's slave insurrection and of the first printing of William Lloyd Garrison's abolitionist newspaper *The Liberator,* Clay openly declares that "Slavery is undoubtedly a manifest violation of the rights of man. It can only be justified in America, if at all, by necessity." Clay even expresses regret that his native state of Kentucky had failed to adopt a law like Pennsylvania's, providing for gradual emancipation. Yet coming to the crucial point, Clay clearly affirms what historians have come to call "the federal consensus," which was shared by the overwhelming majority of antebellum Americans: "Congress has no power...to establish any system of emancipation, gradual or immediate, in behalf of the present or any future generation. The several states alone, according to our existing institutions, are competent to make provision on that subject." This was exactly the position later taken by Abraham Lincoln, an ardent admirer of Clay. When in 1862 Lincoln concluded that "necessity" required the emancipation of Confederate slaves, he did not look to Congress for the needed authority, but to the war powers of the chief executive, as commander in chief.

The literate and privileged slave Nat Turner was not willing to wait that long. Beginning on August 22, 1831, Turner led a group of sixty to eighty slaves on a rampage through Southampton County, Virginia, killing more than fifty whites, mostly women and children. Local newspapers were most struck by "the horrible ferocity of these monsters.... Nothing is spared; neither age nor sex is respected—the helplessness of women and children pleads in vain for mercy."

A highly revealing "Authentic and Impartial Narrative" by Samuel Warner refers to past southern fears that whites would someday "witness scenes similar to those which but a few years since, nearly depopulated the once flourishing island of St. Domingo {St. Domingue} of its white inhabitants." Nat Turner, according to Warner, assumed the character of a preacher and told his fellow slaves about "the happy effects which had attended the united efforts of their brethren in St. Domingo, and elsewhere, and encouraged them with the assurance that a similar effort on their part, could not fail to produce a similar effect, and not only restore them to liberty but would produce them wealth and ease!" Warner, who asserted that "all men are born equal" and that slavery was a form of tyranny, cast much blame on the original slave traders "who first brought them from their native plains—who robbed them of their domestic joys...and doomed them in this 'Land of Liberty' to a state of cruel bondage!"

Garrison, who had just begun his abolitionist paper a few months before the uprising, interpreted Turner's killings as the "fulfillment" of his own predictions, "[t]he first step of the earthquake, which is ultimately to shake down the fabric of oppression." According to Garrison, "IMMEDIATE EMANCIPATION" could alone save the United States from a racial "war of extermination" and from "the vengeance of Heaven."

In a fascinating earlier letter, Garrison compares his own incarceration in a Baltimore jail to the much worse sufferings of the poor slave: "My food is better and more abundant, I get a pound of bread and a pound of meat, with a plentiful supply of pure water, *per diem.* I can lie down or rise up, sit or walk, sing or declaim, read or write.... Moreover, I am daily cheered with the presence and conversation of friends;—I am constantly supplied with fresh periodicals from every section of the country." In contrast, the field hand, poorly fed and whipped, "must toil early and late *for the benefit of another*....For the most trifling or innocent offence, he is felled into the earth, or scourged on his back till it streams with blood." Yet after taking up the abolitionist cause, Garrison has been dismayed to find "the minds of the people strangely indifferent to the subject of slavery. Their prejudices were invincible—stronger, if possible, than those of slaveholders."

It is interesting to note that the major nineteenth-century slave revolts in the British West Indies were quite disciplined, resulting in the loss of extremely few white lives. While these insurrections were brutally suppressed, the slaves did not alienate English public opinion. Turner's lack of any apparent plan or strategy besides revenge and mass killing made it easy for southern defenders of slavery, led by Thomas R. Dew, to dismiss Turner as a madman, "a fanatical Negro preacher...whose confessions proved without a doubt mental aberration." Dew exerted enormous influence by calling for calm and reason in the aftermath of mass hysteria and panic, which had led the Virginia legislature, "composed of an unusual number of young and inexperienced members," to an imprudent public debate on slavery and emancipation. After 1832 there would be no further legislative debates; the South would become much more closed to antislavery speech and writing; and for the thirty-three remaining years of racial slavery there would be no further slave uprisings.

We have included some especially rich documents on the winning of Texan independence from Mexico and the stormy debates, including the long filibuster of former president and now elderly congressman John Quincy Adams, regarding the annexation of slaveholding Texas to the United States. On May 22, 1836, E.G. Fisk reports to his sister that General Sam Houston has just arrived in New Orleans, confirming the news "of the capture of Santa Anna & entire destruction of the Mexicans." A major uprising of Indians in Alabama and Georgia had cut off mail from New York for nearly a week. While a referendum held soon after the Battle of San Jacinto showed that Texans favored annexation by a vote of 3,277 to 93, John Quincy Adams and many other northern leaders were adamant against adding more slave states and thus increasing southern dominance, or what was becoming known as "the Slave Power." As one northern clergyman put it in 1845, after Congress narrowly approved a resolution admitting Texas, "The annexation of Texas is a great offense against humanity & a monstrous transgression of the law of God. It is a violation of the constitution of the U. States."

Abolitionists, moderate antislavery whites, and especially free blacks became increasingly disillusioned and depressed by the events that followed Texan annexation—especially the Mexican War, the growing truculence of the South, and the Fugitive Slave Law of 1850. The latter imperiled every free black in the North, since the law denied alleged fugitives the right to a jury trial or the right to testify in their own defense, required all citizens to assist in the capture of alleged fugitives, and decreed that the judges or so-called commissioners were to be paid twice as much when they decided that an accused black was a slave than when they determined that the black was a free person. At least these southern proslavery victories stimulated a much broader antislavery movement throughout the North.

Robert C. Nell, a black Bostonian, led his black community in an eloquent denunciation of the Fugitive Slave Law. Appealing to the Massachusetts Bill of Rights and "[t]he example of the Revolutionary Fathers in resisting British oppression," Nell condemns the system of American slavery as "the vilest that ever saw the sun" and resolves that "any Commissioner who would deliver up a fugitive slave to a Southern highwayman, under this infamous and unconstitutional law, would have delivered up Jesus Christ to his persecutors for one-third the price that Judas Iscariot did."

Similarly, at a meeting of protest in Syracuse, New York, Gerrit Smith and the famous escaped slave and black abolitionist Frederick Douglass pledge themselves to resist the Fugitive Slave Law "actively, as well as passively, and by all such means, as shall...promise the most effectual resistance." But while Smith and Douglass condemn the "corrupt politics" and "corrupt churches" that made the enactment and execution of such a law possible, they also feel the need to quote Jefferson, "the immortal writer of the Declaration of Independence," as saying, "If we do not liberate the enslaved by that generous energy of our own minds, they must, they will, be liberated by the awful process" that had driven the Haitian Revolution. And according to Smith and Douglass, Jefferson's words are "rapidly approaching their fulfillment."

As we hurtle on toward some kind of showdown over the seemingly unsolvable problem of slavery, other documents enable us to pause briefly and survey America at midcentury. Clearly slavery did not preoccupy the minds of most white Americans, and the Compromise of 1850 (which included the Fugitive Slave Law) gave the illusion at least of a permanent settlement. This was, we need to remember, the beginning of an era of railroads and iron mills, of revolutionary advances in science and technology; a time of massive immigration and hysterical nativism; it was the world of John Stuart Mill, Herbert Spencer, Karl Marx, and Charles Darwin. And in the Rocky Mountain West, where the Mormons had finally found a refuge from savage persecution and had been amazingly successful in founding their own Zion, their leader, Brigham Young, could write in 1854: "In our Mountain home we feel not the withering sources of influence of political or even fashionable despotism. We breathe fresh air, drink from the cool mountain stream, and feel strong in the free exercise of outdoor life."

After moving through the later politics of crisis—"Bleeding Kansas," the Dred Scott decision, the Lincoln-Douglas debates, and John Brown's raid at Harpers Ferry and attempt to arouse the slaves of the South—I strongly urge readers to look carefully at the text of South Carolina's secession convention of December 20, 1860, "Declaration of the Immediate Causes which Induce and Justify the Secession of South Carolina from the Federal Union." This document sums up a lot. It also provides insight into the mentality that led to the Civil War.

After reviewing the way that sovereign, independent states had supposedly agreed on the Constitution of the United States, the South Carolinians set forth the principle "that the failure of one of the contracting parties to perform a material part of the agreement, entirely releases the obligation of the other." For many years, the secessionists then charge, fourteen northern states have deliberately refused to honor their constitutional obligations, specifically the Fourth Article of the Constitution regarding the return of the fugitive slaves. Indeed, northern states have enacted so-called personal liberty laws "which either nullify the Acts of Congress, or render useless any attempt to execute them."

The fugitive slave issue has become absolutely central, we begin to see, because it proves that Northerners no longer respect and honor the Southerners' property rights in African-American slaves, as recognized and sanctioned by the Constitution:

> They have denounced as sinful the institution of Slavery; they have permitted the open establishment among them of societies, whose avowed object is to disturb the peace.... They have encouraged and assisted thousands of our slaves to leave their homes; and those who remain, have been incited by emissaries, books and pictures to servile insurrection.
>
> For twenty-five years this agitation has been steadily increasing, until it has now secured to its aid the power of the Common Government. Observing the forms of the Constitution, a sectional party has found within that article establishing the Executive Department, the means of subverting the Constitution itself.

The latter point refers to the election of Abraham Lincoln, a man "whose opinions and purposes are hostile to slavery," a man whose party "has announced, that the South shall be excluded from the common Territory...and that a war must be waged against slavery until it shall cease throughout the United States." This open hostility to the rights and interests of the South, in the eyes of the secessionists, clearly required South Carolina to resume "her separate and equal place among nations."

Twenty-five days later, on January 14, 1861, a correspondent for the *New York Herald* reports that in Galveston, Texas, "the great majority are for secession without compromise on any terms." Lincoln's election proved to Texans that "hostility to African slavery" not only pervaded "the churches, the Sunday schools, the moral propagandist societies," but that the northern people as a whole had become "indoctrinated with hatred to an institution which they know theoretically only." The reporter then astutely concludes that honor was the key, that this moral condemnation

> of an institution which, in a community of mixed races, is considered to be the most wise, and consequently the most productive of high moral results, touches the honor of

> every Southern man and woman, and leads to that blind resentment which discards all considerations of material interest. The coming administration of Lincoln is looked upon as the embodiment of this moral slur upon southern society and hence it is believed that submission to it will be an admission of inferiority in the face of the whole world.

D. CIVIL WAR

Following a few documents on futile attempts at compromise, in the preceding section, we begin to get a vivid view of what now is at stake. Writing on July 22, 1861, a day after the First Battle of Bull Run, an Indiana soldier describes a night alarm and near panic:

> one of the Sentinels got frightened, & fired his gun, & then the alarm raged all around the camp until some guns were fired, all the men was called out, & placed in line of battle...all in the most perfect silence for three long hours. When we were told the alarm was failed, & ordered to our quarters, It was amusing to see the boys...coming out half dressed, some without their guns, others their shoes and hats.

The amusement soon fades as we begin to read of bodies literally torn to pieces, heads gone, bodies cut in two, yet soldiers exultant with victory.

The Lincoln administration faced two critical issues that strongly weighed against any direct moves to undermine slavery in the South. First, Union armies would have to move through the slaveholding border states, Maryland (which controlled access to the city of Washington), Delaware, Kentucky, and Missouri. Without the support of these four states, which resisted Lincoln's proposals for even compensated, very gradual emancipation, the war probably could not be won. Second, contrary to the widespread southern myth of a united antislavery North, the Democratic Party remained strong, and many Democrats were virulent racists who supported slavery and even opposed the war. To win the broadest possible support for the war effort, the Republican Congress reassured the public in July 1861 that the war was not being waged to interfere with or overthrow slavery. For a short time, some Union officers even returned fugitive slaves to their southern owners.

As the documents show, however, the Union armies could not evade or remain neutral with respect to slavery. From the outset, enormous crowds of black slaves fled behind the supposedly protective Union lines. Many of them contributed to the Union war effort by reporting the movements of Confederate forces or showing how to navigate southern harbors and inland waterways, a factor that encouraged the least racist northern soldier to support the Emancipation Proclamation. In 1863 the Western Sanitary Commission reported to President Lincoln that as many as fifty thousand blacks,

> chiefly women and children...[were now living] within our lines...for whom no adequate provision has been made.... they are very poorly clad—many of them half naked—and almost destitute of beds and bedding—thousands of them sleeping on the bare ground.... No language can describe the suffering, destitution and neglect which prevail in some of their "camps." The sick and dying are left uncared for...and the dead unburied.

In some respects it was the massive flight of slaves that undermined the institution of slavery and exerted pressure on Lincoln to formally transform the Union army into an army of liberation. Yet the selected documents reveal many of the complexities that led to and surrounded Lincoln's Emancipation Proclamation and the decision to enlist nearly two hundred thousand blacks in the Union army.

The war brought rapid changes in race relations that left many white Southerners in a state of shock and alarm. In 1864, for example, Tobias Gibson exclaims in a letter to his daughter that "White children are to...mix in the same cabin with the Negro with the same Yankee Marm for the teacher!" Gibson fears that this northern "tendency to fanaticism" will lead to "miscegenation," a new word that, as Edwin H. McCaleb later explains, means the mixture of races—something "odious, destructive & contrary to the laws of God & Man." This was a view shared not only by Northerners but even by many ardent foes of slavery.

Civil War military battles often detract attention from the absolutely crucial election of 1864. "The Two Roads to Peace," with excerpts from the Democratic platform and the Republican platform, is one of the most remarkable and revealing documents in the entire anthology. The Democrats, who deny that the war has anything to do with slavery (their candidate for president, General George B. McClellan, opposed the Emancipation Proclamation), condemn the Lincoln administration for "four years of failure to restore the Union by experiment of war, during which, under the pretense of military necessity or war power higher than the Constitution, the Constitution itself has been disregarded in every part." The Democrats then demanded that "IMMEDIATE EFFORTS BE MADE FOR A CESSATION OF HOSTILITIES, with a view to the ultimate Convention of all the States, or other peaceable means, to the end that at the earliest practicable moment peace may be restored on the basis of the Federal Union of the States."

In sharp contrast, the Republican platform speaks of "rebels and traitors" and demands the unconditional surrender of "the rebellion now raging against [the government's] authority." No less significant, the Republicans resolve "That as slavery was the cause, and now constitutes the strength of this rebellion, and as it must be always and everywhere hostile to the principles of republican government, justice and the national safety demand its utter and complete extirpation from the soil of the Republic." Upholding Lincoln's Emancipation Proclamation and approving the "employment as Union soldiers of men heretofore held in slavery," the platform also favors a constitutional amendment that shall "terminate and forever prohibit the existence of Slavery within the limits of the jurisdiction of the United States."

The immense disparity between these two documents underscores the fact that in the midst of war McClellan's Democrats and Lincoln's Republicans were not like the political parties that have characterized most of U.S. history. The Democratic platform contained no words against slavery, no words of censure for the southern "rebels." In effect the Democrats would have settled for a truce that included an agreement to maintain slavery—and the vast majority of slaves were still under firm southern control. Moreover, during the summer of 1864 Lincoln was privately convinced that he would lose the election. It was the great and unexpected Union victory at Atlanta, in September, that turned the tide.

The hatred of Lincoln reached such a peak that some Republicans called for his being court-martialed, and antiwar Democrats rejoiced at his assassination. The war stimulated such anger and desire for revenge that it is remarkable, especially in view of Lincoln's martyrdom, that the northern victory was not followed by a massive extermination of Confederate leaders and northern sympathizers. In contemporary China, for example, the Taiping Rebellion led to the massacre of many millions.

But the South did suffer appalling devastation in addition to the loss of about one quarter of its white male population of military age. In 1834, when Parliament emancipated British colonial slaves, the slaveholders suffered little financial loss since they were compensated with £20 million, to say nothing of four more years of "free" labor from the so-called apprentices, who were to receive no wages. In contrast, Southerners lost about $2.5 billion in human property, a staggering figure for the mid-nineteenth century. One can reasonably ask why the Confederates accepted total defeat and did not carry on guerrilla warfare against the northern army of occupation.[8]

Edwin H. McCaleb's letter of June 1, 1865, the last document in our anthology, may provide a hint concerning the lack of further resistance when he speaks of "the national quiet and law abiding disposition of our people" as a force preventing "lawlessness and outrage." Though McCaleb was a Confederate veteran of the war that had just ended, he can assure T. P. Chandler, his northern correspondent, that "[a]ll good citizens deeply deplore the assassination of Pres. Lincoln....Mr. L—was a great man and more than that was a good man and the country could ill afford to lose his services at this important crisis."

McCaleb's letter is important because it gives expression to an often neglected but widespread national consensus on the issues of slavery and race. McCaleb was a southern moderate who at age seventeen, when the war commenced and he was about to leave college for the army, made a speech "against secession and advocating the sovereignty of the Federal Government." Deeply resentful of any form of Reconstruction, McCaleb argues that since the South was willing to accept its defeat, Americans should forgive and forget and proceed as if the war had been a tragic mistake. And in a sense, that is exactly what happened after the end of Radical Reconstruction in 1877.

Any attempt to understand that momentous failure must come to terms with McCaleb's revealing and highly typical views of slavery and race:

> By this sudden system of Emancipation, this spasmodic transformation of the ignorant Negro from a peaceful laborer who has been accustomed to have all needs...provided... both in sickness & health to a self reliant citizen will paralyze the productive resources of

8. The historian George Fredrickson has recently explored this question, comparing the Confederates with the Boers in South Africa, and has concluded that southern guerrillas might well have won many concessions if not total independence. Fredrickson, "Why the Confederacy Did Not Fight a Guerrilla War After the Fall of Richmond: A Comparative View," 35th Annual Robert Fortenbaugh Memorial Lecture (Gettysburg College, 1996). Aside from the professionalism and sense of honor of Robert E. Lee and other generals, one must remember that the Ku Klux Klan and other paramilitary organizations *did* use guerrillalike violence in opposing any steps toward racial equality.

> the South.... If we could have a system of gradual emancipation & colonization our people would universally rejoice & be glad to get rid of slavery which has ever been a cancer upon the body politic of our social organization....We would gladly substitute white for slave labor but we can never regard the Negro our equal either intellectually or socially. ...If such a detestable dogma [miscegenation] becomes a law we shall soon have a race of mulattoes as fickle & foolish as the Mongrel population of Mexico never content with their present condition but always desiring a change of government & rulers.

Such deep-rooted racial prejudices were pervasive in the North as well as the South. The McCalebs of America never explained why, given the repugnance most whites felt for blacks, miscegenation would become common enough to transform Americans into a "mongrel" race. Nor did they ask, as abolitionists usually did, whether the supposedly innate and undesirable traits they found in "the Negro" were the products of slavery itself, including the prohibition of literacy, the separate sale of family members, and the masters' continuous efforts to destroy self-respect.

While Radical Reconstruction brought immense political, social, and educational gains for the freedpeople, it was not long before men with views like Edwin McCaleb's were in power. Despite their growing dislike for slavery, American whites had not been prepared for a revolutionary moment, a truly "immediate" emancipation; and as the history of Reconstruction soon proved, the northern public had little genuine interest in the welfare of former slaves.

Still, it is important to stress that slavery was not declining in economic importance in the years before the Civil War. It was a healthy, expanding, and immensely profitable institution that might have persisted, had there been no war, well into the twentieth century. Thus the Emancipation Proclamation and the Thirteenth, Fourteenth, and Fifteenth Amendments were highly contingent events and landmarks of impressive political and legal progress. For all its evils, the sharecropping system was considerably better than slave gang labor. And by 1880, after years of black suffrage and officeholding, some 20 percent of southern blacks owned their own land. One can always stress the positive or negative dimensions of the same historical facts. But there can be little doubt that Radical Reconstruction, with its constitutional amendments, civil rights acts, and precedents of free blacks as elected office holders and representatives, laid a foundation for the civil rights breakthroughs of the 1960s and 1970s.

PART ONE

First Encounters

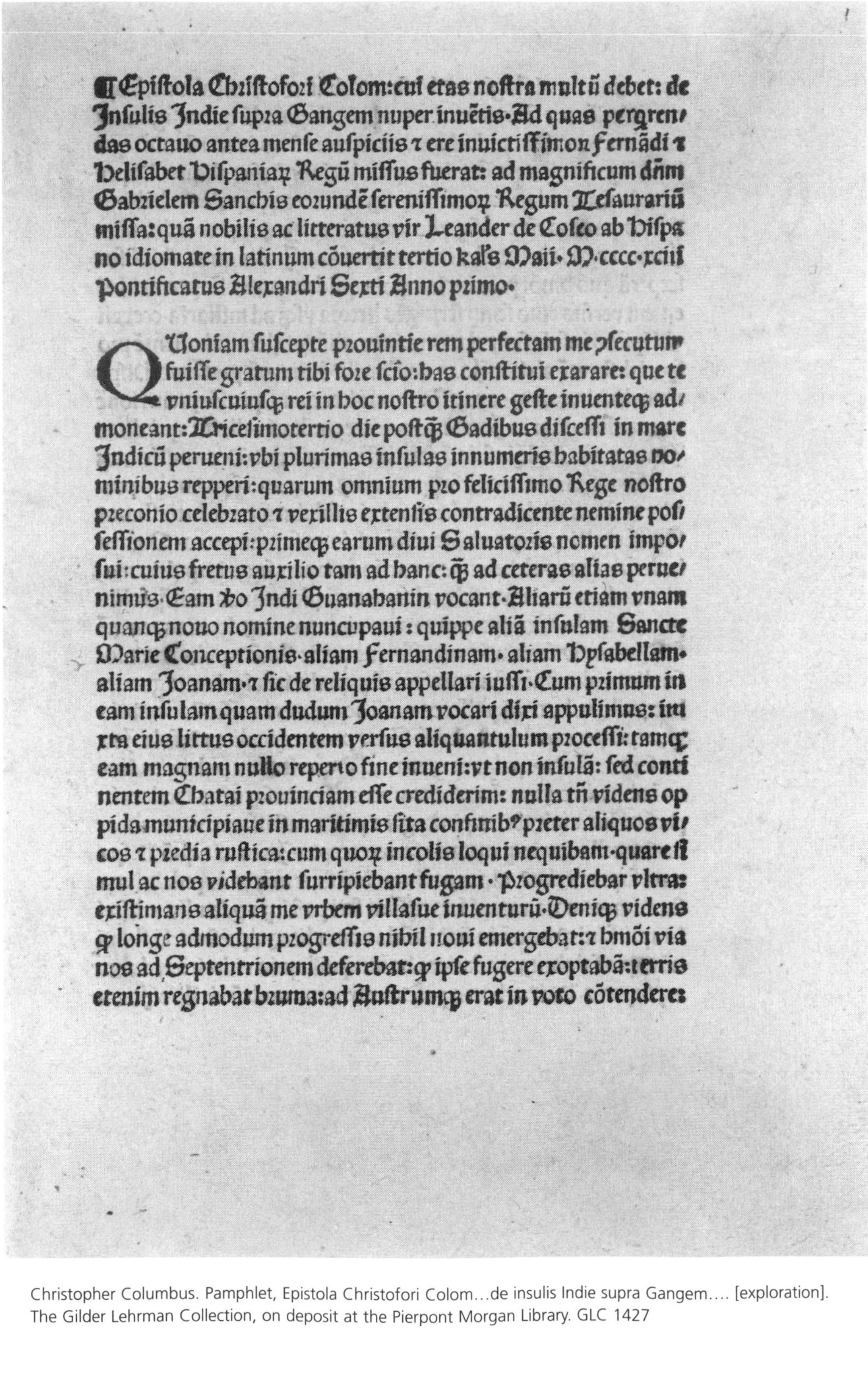

¶ Epistola Christofori Colom: cui etas nostra multũ debet: de
Insulis Indie supra Gangem nuper inuẽtis. Ad quas perquiren/
das octauo antea mense auspiciis ⁊ ere inuictissimorũ Fernãdi ⁊
Helisabet Hispaniarũ Regũ missus fuerat: ad magnificum dñm
Gabrielem Sanchis eorundẽ serenissimorũ Regum Tesaurariũ
missa: quã nobilis ac litteratus vir Leander de Cosco ab Hispa
no idiomate in latinum cõuertit tertio kal's Maii. M.cccc.xciii
Pontificatus Alexandri Sexti Anno primo.

Quoniam suscepte prouintie rem perfectam me ꝯsecutum
fuisse gratum tibi fore scio: has constitui exarare: que te
vniuscuiusqꝫ rei in hoc nostro itinere geste inuenteqꝫ ad/
moneant: Tricesimotertio die postq̃ Gadibus discessi in mare
Indicũ perueni: vbi plurimas insulas innumeris habitatas ho/
minibus repperi: quarum omnium pro felicissimo Rege nostro
preconio celebrato ⁊ vexillis extensis contradicente nemine pos/
sessionem accepi: primeqꝫ earum diui Saluatoris nomen impo/
sui: cuius fretus auxilio tam ad hanc: q̃ ad ceteras alias perue/
nimus. Eam ꝟo Indi Guanahanin vocant. Aliarũ etiam vnam
quanqꝫ nouo nomine nuncupaui: quippe aliã insulam Sancte
Marie Conceptionis. aliam Fernandinam. aliam Hysabellam.
aliam Joanam. ⁊ sic de reliquis appellari iussi. Cum primum in
eam insulam quam dudum Joanam vocari dixi appulimus: iu
xta eius littus occidentem versus aliquantulum processi: tamqꝫ
eam magnam nullo reperto fine inueni: vt non insulã: sed conti
nentem Chatai prouinciam esse crediderim: nulla tñ videns op
pida municipiaue in maritimis sita confinib⁹ preter aliquos vi/
cos ⁊ predia rustica: cum quorũ incolis loqui nequibam. quare si
mul ac nos videbant surripiebant fugam. Progrediebar vltra:
existimans aliquã me vrbem villasue inuenturũ. Deniqꝫ videns
ꝙ longe admodum progressis nihil noui emergebat: ⁊ hmõi via
nos ad Septentrionem deferebat: ꝙ ipse fugere exoptabã: terris
etenim regnabat bruma: ad Austrumqꝫ erat in voto cõtendere:

Christopher Columbus. Pamphlet, Epistola Christofori Colom…de insulis Indie supra Gangem…. [exploration]. The Gilder Lehrman Collection, on deposit at the Pierpont Morgan Library. GLC 1427

The four-hundredth anniversary of Christopher Columbus's "discovery" of the New World was commemorated with the massive "World's Columbian Exposition" in Chicago in 1893. The exposition celebrated Columbus as a man of mythic stature, an explorer and discoverer who carried Christian civilization across the Atlantic Ocean and initiated the modern age.

The five-hundredth anniversary of Columbus's first voyage of discovery was treated quite differently. Many peoples of indigenous and/or African descent identified Columbus with imperialism, colonialism, and conquest. The National Council of Churches adopted a resolution calling October 12 a day of mourning for millions of indigenous people who died as a result of European colonization.

More than five hundred years after the first Spaniards arrived in the Caribbean, historians and the general public still debate Columbus's legacy. Should he be remembered as a great discoverer who brought European culture to a previously unknown world? Or should he be condemned as a man responsible for an "American Holocaust," a man who brought devastating European and Asian diseases to unprotected native peoples, who disrupted the American ecosystem, and who initiated the Atlantic slave trade? What is Columbus's legacy—discovery and progress, or slavery, disease, and racial antagonism?

To confront such questions, one must first recognize that the encounter that began in 1492 among the peoples of the Eastern and Western Hemispheres was one of the truly epochal events in world history. This cultural collision not only produced an extraordinary transformation of the natural environment and human cultures in the New World, it also initiated far-reaching changes in the Old World.

New foods reshaped the diets of people in both hemispheres. Tomatoes, chocolate, potatoes, corn, green beans, peanuts, vanilla, pineapple, and turkey transformed the European diet, while Europeans introduced sugar, cattle, pigs, cloves, ginger, cardamom, and almonds to the Americas. Global patterns of trade were overturned, as crops grown in the New World—including tobacco, rice, and vastly expanded production of sugar—fed growing consumer markets in Europe.

Even the natural environment was transformed. Europeans cleared vast tracts of forested land and inadvertently introduced Old World weeds. The introduction of cattle, goats, horses, sheep, and swine also transformed the ecology as grazing animals ate up many native plants and disrupted indigenous systems of agriculture. The horse, extinct in the New World for ten thousand years, transformed the daily existence of many indigenous peoples. The introduction of the horse encouraged many farming peoples to become hunters and herders. Hunters mounted on horses were also much more adept at killing game.

Death and disease—these, too, were consequences of contact. Diseases against which Indian peoples had no natural immunities caused the greatest mass deaths in human history. Within a century of contact, smallpox, measles, mumps, and whooping cough had reduced indigenous populations by 50 to 90 percent. From Peru to Canada, disease reduced the resistance that Native Americans were able to offer to European intruders.

With the Indian population decimated by disease, Europeans gradually introduced a new labor force into the New World: enslaved Africans. Between 1502 and 1870, when the Atlantic slave trade was finally suppressed, from 10 million to 15 million Africans were shipped to the Americas.

Columbus's first voyage of discovery also had another important result: It contributed to the development of the modern concept of progress. To many Europeans, the New World seemed to be a place of innocence, freedom, and eternal youth. The perception of the New World as an environment free from the corruptions and injustices of European life would provide a vantage point for criticizing all social evils. So while the collision of three worlds resulted in death and enslavement in unprecedented numbers, it also encouraged visions of a more perfect future.

THE MEANING OF AMERICA

1 / *"They have no iron or steel or weapons, nor are they capable of using them"*

At the time of the first discoveries, Europeans tended to view the New World from one of two contrasting perspectives. Many saw America as an earthly paradise, a land of riches and abundance, where the native peoples led lives of simplicity and freedom similar to those enjoyed by Adam and Eve in the biblical Garden of Eden.

Other Europeans described America in a much more negative light: as a dangerous and forbidding wilderness, a place of cannibalism and human misery, where the population lacked Christian religion and the trappings of civilization. This latter view of America as a place of savagery, cannibalism, and death would grow more pronounced as the Indian population declined precipitously in numbers as a result of harsh labor and the ravages of disease and as the slave trade began transporting millions of Africans to the New World.

But it was the positive view of America as a land of liberty, liberation, and material wealth that remained dominant. America served as a screen on which Europeans projected their deepest fantasies of a land where people could escape inherited privilege, corruption, and tradition. The discovery of America seemed to mark a new beginning for humanity, a place where all Old World laws, customs, and doctrines were removed, and where scarcity gave way to abundance.

In a letter reporting his discoveries to King Ferdinand and Queen Isabella of Spain, Christopher Columbus (1451–1506) paints a portrait of the indigenous Taino Indians as living lives of freedom and innocence near the Garden of Eden.

CHRISTOPHER COLUMBUS, *letter to the sovereigns on his first voyage, February 15–March 4 1493, GLB 216*

...The people of this island [Hispaniola] and of all the other islands which I have found and seen, or have not seen, all go naked, men and women, as their mothers bore them, except that some women cover one place with the leaf of a plant or with a net of cotton which they make for that purpose. They have no iron or steel or weapons, nor are they capable of using them, although they are well-built people of handsome stature, because they are wondrously timid. They have no other arms than the arms of canes, [cut] when they are in seed time, to the end of which they fix a sharp little stick; and they dare not make use of these, for oftentimes it has happened that I have sent ashore two or three men to some town to have speech, and people without number have come out to them, as soon as they saw them coming, they fled; even a father would not stay for his son; and this was not because wrong had been done to anyone; on the contrary, at every point where I have been and have been able to have speech, I have given them of all that I had, such as cloth and many other things, without receiving anything for it; but they are like that, timid beyond cure. It is true that after they have been reassured and have lost this fear, they are so artless and so free with all they possess, that no one would believe it without having seen it. Of anything they have, if you ask them for it, they never say no; rather they invite the person to share it, and show as much love as if they were giving their hearts; and whether the thing be of value or of small price, at once they are content with whatever little thing of whatever kind may be given to them. I forbade that they should be given things so worthless as pieces of broken crockery and broken glass, and lace points, although when they were able to get them, they thought they had the best jewel in the world.... And they know neither sect nor idolatry, with the exception that all believe that the source of all power and goodness is in the sky, and in this belief they everywhere received me, after they had overcome their fear. And this does not result from their being ignorant (for they are of a very keen intelligence and men who navigate all those seas, so that it is wondrous the good account they give of everything), but because they have never seen people clothed or ships like ours.

UTILIZING THE NATIVE LABOR FORCE

2 / "With fifty men they can all be subjugated and made to do what is required of them"

Christopher Columbus's voyages of discovery were part of a much broader pattern of European commercial and financial expansion during the fifteenth century. In the span of fewer than four decades, European countries revolutionized sea travel. Led by tiny Portugal, fifteenth-century European mariners adapted from the Arabs a small, sturdy ship known as a caravel, capable of sailing against the wind. They also refined such navigational aids as the astrolabe and quadrants, allowing sailors to accurately chart their latitude, while mapmakers and geographers greatly improved the quality of maps. In just a decade, from 1488 to 1498, European sailors mastered the winds and currents of the South Atlantic, making it possible for the first time to sail from western Europe to West Africa and into the Indian Ocean.

With financial support from German and Italian bankers and merchants, Portugal was able to exploit these discoveries and create a system of long-distance trade and commerce based on sugar and slavery. As early as 1420, the Portuguese began to settle islands off the West African coast. In Madeira, the Azores, the Canary Islands, and other islands, the Portuguese introduced sugar cane. Beginning in 1443, Portugal established a string of trading posts along the West African coast, which soon became major sources of slave labor for the Iberian Peninsula and especially for the Atlantic island sugar plantations.

Christopher Columbus was very familiar with this network of Atlantic trade. Born in Genoa in 1451, the son of an Italian wool weaver, Columbus was pushed by his father into trade. In 1476 he settled in a Genoese trading community in Portugal. There he met his wife, whose father was the Portuguese governor of an island off Africa's Atlantic coast. For ten years Columbus lived in Madeira and made voyages to the Azores, the Canary Islands, and West Africa. Forty-one years old at the time he made his first voyage of discovery to the New World, Columbus was obsessed with the idea of finding a new route to the Far East, which would provide him with enough wealth to pay for the liberation of the Holy Land from Islamic rule. Personally familiar with slavery and sugar production when he arrived in the Caribbean, he quickly saw the opportunity to extract riches from this new land.

As the following extracts from his journal reveal, within days of his arrival in the New World Columbus regarded the Indian population as a potential labor source. As he and other Europeans would soon discover, the Indians, especially the Caribs, were not as timid or as easily dominated as Columbus originally thought.

Christopher Columbus, journal, October 14, 1492, December 16, 1492

Sunday, 14th of October

...these people are very simple as regards the use of arms, as your Highnesses will see from the seven that I caused to be taken, to bring home and learn our language and return; unless your Highnesses should order them all to be brought to Castile, or to be kept as captives on the same island; for with fifty men they can all be subjugated and made to do what is required of them....

Sunday, 16th of December

...your Highnesses may believe that this island [Hispaniola], and all the others, are as much yours as Castile. Here there is only wanting a settlement and the order to the people to do what is required. For I, with the force I have under me, which is not large, could march over all these islands without opposition. I have seen only three sailors land, without wishing to do harm, and a multitude of Indians fled before them. They have no arms, and are without warlike instincts; they all go naked, and are so timid that a thousand would not stand before three of our men. So that they are good to be ordered about, to work and sow, and do all that may be necessary, and to build towns, and they should be taught to go about clothed and to adopt our customs.

"Journal of the First Voyage of Christopher Columbus, 1492–93," in E.G. Bourne, *The Northmen, Columbus and Cabot, 985–1503. Edited by Edward Gaylord Bourne. New York: C. Scribner's Sons, 1906, pp. 114, 145–146, 182.*

Engravings of "Landing of Columbus" [From collection: Portraits of historical figures: engravings, lithographs, photographs &c., 1790–1980 ca.]. The Gilder Lehrman Collection, on deposit at the Pierpont Morgan Library. GLB 0486

NEW WORLD FANTASIES

3 / *"All slavery, and drudgery...is done by bondsmen"*

The European voyages of discovery of the late fifteenth century played a critical role in the development of modern conceptions of progress. From the ancient Greeks onward, Western culture tended to emphasize certain unchanging and universal ideas about human society. But the discovery of the New World threw many supposedly universal ideals into doubt. The Indians, who seemingly lived free from all the traditional constraints of civilized life—such as private property or family bonds—offered a vehicle for criticizing the corruptions, abuses, and restrictions of European society.

In 1516 the English humanist Sir Thomas More (1478–1535) published *Utopia,* his description of an ideal society where crime, injustice, and poverty did not exist. Writing just twenty-four years after Columbus's first voyage to the Caribbean, More located his perfect society in the Western Hemisphere. More's book, written in the form of a dialogue, contrasts the simplicity of life in Utopia with contemporary Europe's class divisions. In Utopia, property is held in common, gold is scorned, and all inhabitants eat the same food and wear the same clothes. And yet several features of More's Utopia strike a jarring note. For one thing, his book justifies taking land from the indigenous people because, in European eyes, they did not cultivate it. And further, the prosperity and well-being of More's ideal society ultimately rest on slave labor.

Sir Thomas More, *Utopia*, London, 1516

...When I consider within myself and weigh in my mind the wise and godly ordinances of the Utopians, among whom with very few laws all things be so well and wealthily ordered, that virtue is had in price and estimation, and yet, all things being there common, every man hath abundance of everything.

...No household or farm in the country hath fewer than forty persons, men and women, besides two bondmen, which be all under the rule and order of the good man, and the good wife of the house, being both very sage and discreet persons....For they dividing the day and the night into twenty-four hours, appoint and assign only six of those hours to work....

In this hall all vile service, all slavery, and drudgery, with all laboursome toil and business, is done by bondsmen....

The Utopia of Sir Thomas More. Translated by Ralph Robinson with an introduction and notes by H.B. Cotterill. London: Macmillan & Co. Ltd., 1908, Second Book, pp. 67, 75, 79–80, 83–84.

LABOR NEEDS

4 / "This is the best land in the world for Negroes"

Christopher Columbus believed that Indians would serve as a slave labor force for Europeans, especially on the sugar cane plantations off the western coast of North Africa. Convinced that the Taino Indians of the Caribbean would make ideal slaves, he transported five hundred to Spain in 1495. Some two hundred died during the overseas voyage. Thus Columbus initiated the African slave trade, which originally moved from the New World to the Old, rather than the reverse.

By the beginning of the sixteenth century, Spain's experiments in enslaving Indians were failing. To meet the mounting demand for labor in mining and agriculture, the Spanish began to exploit a new labor force: slaves from western Africa.

Slavery was a familiar institution to many sixteenth-century Europeans. Although slavery had gradually died out in northwestern Europe, it continued to flourish around the Mediterranean Sea. Ongoing warfare between Christianity and Islam produced thousands of slave laborers, who were put to work in heavy agriculture in Italy, southern France, eastern Spain, Sicily, and eastern Europe near the Black Sea. Most slaves in this area were "white"—Arabs, or natives of Russia or eastern Europe. But by the mid-fifteenth century, the expansion of the Ottoman Empire cut off the supply of white slaves. It was during the mid-fifteenth century that Portugal established trading relations along the West African coast, and discovered that it was able to purchase huge numbers of black slaves at low cost.

Several factors made African slaves the cheapest and most expedient labor source. The prevailing ocean currents made it relatively easy to transport Africans to the Caribbean. Further, because Africans came from developed agricultural societies, they were already familiar with highly organized tropical agriculture. The first African slaves were brought to the New World as early as 1502, where they mined precious metals and raise sugar, coffee, and tobacco—the first goods sold to a mass consumer market.

The African slave trade would be an indispensable part of European settlement and development of the New World. By the mid-eighteenth century, slaves could be found everywhere in the Americas from French Canada to Chile. Indeed, the number of Africans forcibly imported into the New World actually exceeded the number of whites who would come to the Americas before the 1830s. Between 1492 and 1820 approximately ten million to fifteen million Africans were forcibly brought to the New World, while only about two million Europeans had immigrated. In this excerpt Alonso de Zuazo (1466–1527), the Spanish judge of Hispaniola, argues that slavery is essential for Caribbean development.

Alonso de Zuazo to Cardinal Ximenes, regent of Spain, January 22, 1518

Indeed, there is urgent need for Negro slaves, as I have written to inform His Highness, and in as much as Your Lordship will see that part of my letter to His Highness, I shall not repeat it here, except to say that it is urgent to have them brought. Ships sail from these islands for Seville to purchase essential goods such as cloth of various colors as well as other merchandise, which is used as ransom of Cape Verde whither the goods are carried with the permission of the King of Portugal. By virtue of the said ransom, let ships go there and bring away as many male and female Negroes as possible, newly imported and between the ages of fifteen to eighteen or twenty years. They will be made to adopt our customs in this island and they will be settled in villages and married to their women folk. The burden of work of the Indians will be eased and unlimited amounts of gold will be mined. This is the best land in the world for Negroes, women and old men, and it is very rarely that one of these people die.

J. A. Saco, *Historia de la Esclavitud de las Raza Africana,* Tomo I, pp. 143-44

THE BLACK LEGEND

5 / *"Under the guise of developing the country, the Christians (as they call themselves)...engaged in plunder and slaughter"*

Late in the eighteenth century, around the time of the three-hundredth anniversary of Columbus's voyage of discovery, the Abbé Raynal (1713–96), a French philosopher, offered a prize for the best answer to this question: "Has the discovery of America been beneficial or harmful to the human race?"

Eight responses to the question survive. Of these, four argued that Columbus's voyage had harmed human happiness. The European discovery of the New World had a devastating impact on the Indian peoples of the Americas. Oppressive labor, disruption of the Indian food supply, deliberate campaigns of extermination, and especially disease decimated the Indian population. Isolated from such diseases as smallpox, influenza, and measles, the indigenous population proved to be extraordinarily susceptible. Within a century of contact, the Indian population in the Caribbean and Mexico had shrunk by more than 90 percent.

During the sixteenth century, when the House of Habsburg presided over an empire that included Spain, Austria, Italy, Holland, and much of the New World, Spain's

Copia de la bula del decreto y concessi on q̄ hizo el papa Alexandro sexto al Rey y a la Reyna nuestros señores de las Indias conforme al capitu. Per venerabilem. §. rationibus/qui filij sint legitimi/y al cap. … on. xxiij. q. iiij.

In nomine dñi. Amen. Nouerint vniuersi hoc presens publicum trāsumptū inspecturi qd nos Jacobus cōchillos dei ⁊ apostolice sedis grã epūs Cathaniensis: habuim⁹, vidim⁹, ⁊ diligēter inspexim⁹ infrascriptas litteras felicis recordationis Alexādri pape sexti eius vera bulla plūbea cū cordulis sericeis, croceiq̄ coloris more Romane curie impēdentis bullatas sanas siquidē ⁊ integras ac oīmoda suspitione carentes huiusmodi sub tenore. ALEXANDER epūs seruus seruorū dei carissimo in xp̄o filio Ferdinādo Regi ⁊ carissime in xp̄o filie Elisabeth Regine Castelle Legiōis, Aragonū, Sicilie ⁊ Granate illustrib⁹ salutē ⁊ apostolicā benedictionē. Inter cetera diuine maiestati beneplacita opera ⁊ cordis nr̄i desiderabilia illud ꝑfecto potissimū existit vt fides catholica ⁊ xp̄iana religio nr̄is presertim tēporib⁹ exaltetur ac vbilibet amplietur ⁊ dilatetur animarū q̄z salus ꝓcuretur ac barbare natiōes deprimātur ⁊ ad fidē ipsam reducantur. Unde cū ad hāc sacrā Petri sedē diuina fauente clemencia (meritis licet imparibus) euocati fuerim⁹ cognoscentes vos tanq̄ veros catholicos Reges ⁊ principes q̄les semp fuisse nouimus ⁊ a vobis preclare gesta toti pene iā orbi notissima demostrāt: nedū id exoptare sed omni conatu, studio ⁊ diligencia: nullis laboribus, nullis impēsis, nullisq̄z pcēdo periculis etiā ꝓpriū sanguinē effundēdo efficere ac omnē animū vestrū omnesq̄z conat⁹ ad hoc iamdudū dedicasse quē admodū recuperatio regni Granate a tirānide Saracenorū hodiernis tēporib⁹ per vos cū tanta diuini nominis gloria facta testatur. Digne ducimur nō immerito ⁊ debem⁹ illa vobis etiā sponte ⁊ fauorabiliter cōcedere per que huiusmodi sanctū ⁊ laudabile ac immortali deo acceptū propositū in dies feruentiori animo ad ipsius dei honorem ⁊ imperij xp̄iani propagationē prosequi valeatis. Sane accepimus qd vos qui dudū animū proposueratis aliquas insulas ⁊ terras firmas remotas ⁊ incognitas ac per alios hactenus nō reptas querere ⁊ inuēire vt illarū incolas ⁊ habitatores ad colēdū redēptorē nr̄m ⁊ fidē catholicā ꝓfitendū reduceretis: hacten⁹ in expugnatiōe ⁊ recupatiōe ipsi⁹ regni Granate plurimū occupati huiusmodi sāctū ⁊ laudabile ꝓpositū vr̄um ad optatū finē pducere nequiuistis sed tandē sicut dño placuit regno predicto recuperato, volētes desideriū adimplere vestrū dilectū filiū Christophorū colon virū vtiq̄z dignū ⁊ plurimū cōmendandū ac tanto negocio aptū cū nauigijs ⁊ hominibus ad similia instructis nō sine maximis laborib⁹ ⁊ periculis ac expēsis destinastis vt terras firmas ⁊ insulas remotas ⁊ incognitas huiusmodi per mare vbi hactenus nauigatū nō fuerat diligēter inquireret. Qui tandē (diuino auxilio facta extrema diligentia in mari oceano nauigantes certas insulas remotissimas ⁊ etiā terras firmas que per alios hactenus reperte non fuerant) inuenerunt in quib⁹ q̄ plurime gentes pacifice viuentes ⁊ vt asseritur nudi incedentes nec carnibus vescentes inhabitant, ⁊ vt prefati Nuncij vestri possunt opinari gētes ipse in Insulis ⁊ terris predictis habitantes credunt vnū deum creatorē in celis esse ac ad fidem catholicā amplexandū ⁊ bonis moribus imbuendū satis apti videntur spesq̄z habetur quod si erudirētur nomē saluatoris dñi nr̄i Jesu xp̄i in terris ⁊ insulis predictis facile induceretur. Ac prefatus Christophorus in vna ex principalibus Insulis predictis iam vnā turrim satis munitam in qua certos christianos qui secum iuerāt in custodiā ⁊ vt alias insulas ac terras firmas remotas ⁊ incognitas inquirerent posuit: construi ⁊ edificare fecit. In quibus quidē insulis ⁊ terris iam repertis aurū aromata ⁊ alie q̄ plurime res ꝓtiose diuersi generis ⁊ diuerse q̄litatis reperiuntur. Unde oībus diligenter ⁊ ꝓsertim fidei catholice exaltatione ⁊ dilatatione (prout decet catholicos Reges ⁊ principes) cōsideratis: more progenitorū vestrorū clare memorie regū: terras firmas ⁊ insulas p̄dictas illarum q̄z incolas ⁊ habitatores vobis diuina fauente clemētia subijcere ⁊ ad fidem catholicā reducere proposuistis. Nos igitur huiusmodi vestrum sanctum ⁊ laudabile propositū plurimū in dño cōmendantes ac cupientes vt illud ad debitū finē perducatur ⁊ ipsum nomē saluatoris nostri in partibus illis inducatur: Hortamur vos q̄ plurimū in dño ⁊ per sacri lauacri susceptionē qua mādatis apostolicis obligati estis ⁊ Uiscera misericordie dñi nr̄i Jesu xp̄i attēte requirimus vt cū expeditionē huiusmodi omnino prosequi ⁊ assumere pronamente orthodoxe fidei zelo intendatis populos in huiusmodi insulis ⁊ terris degentes ad christianā religionē suscipiendū inducere velitis ⁊ debeatis nec pericula nec labores vllo vnq̄ tēpore vos deterreāt firma spe fiduciaq̄z cōceptis qd deus omnipotēs conatus vr̄os feliciter prosequetur. Et vt tāti negocij prouinciā apostolice gratie largitate donati liberius ⁊ audatius assumatis Motu proprio nō ad vestrā vel alterius pro vobis super hoc nobis oblate petitionis instātiā sed de nostra mera liberalitate ⁊ ex certa scientia ac de apostolice potestatis plenitudine omnes insulas ⁊ terras firmas inuentas ⁊ inueniendas detectas ⁊ detegendas versus occidētē ⁊ meridiē fabricādo ⁊ cōstruendo vnā lineā a polo artico scilicet septētrione ad polū antarcticū scilicet meridiē siue terre firme ⁊ insule inuente ⁊ inueniende sint: versus indiā aut versus aliā quācumq̄z ptem que linea distet a q̄libet insularū que vulgariter nūcupantur de los Azores ⁊ Cabo verde centum leucis versus occidentē ⁊ meridiem. Itaq̄z omnes insule ⁊ terre firme reperte ⁊ reperiende detecte ⁊ detegende a prefata linea versus occidentē ⁊ meridiē per alium regē aut principē christianū nō fuerint actualiter possesse vsq̄z ad diē natiuitatis dñi nr̄i Jesu xp̄i ꝓxime preteritū a quo incipit Annus presens millesi. q̄dringē. nonagesi. tertius q̄ndo fuerūt per Nūcios ⁊ Capitaneos vestros inuente alique predictarū insularū. Auctoritate omnipotētis dei nobis in beato Petro concessa ac vicariatus Jesu xp̄i qua fungimur in terris cū omnibus illarū dominijs ciuitatibus castris locis ⁊ villis iuribusq̄z ⁊ iurisditionibus ac ptinentijs vniuersis vobis heredibusq̄z ⁊ successoribus vestris Castelle ⁊ Legionis regib⁹ in perpetuum tenore presentiū donamus concedimus ⁊ assignamus vosq̄z ⁊ heredes ac successores prefatos illarū dominos cū plena libera ⁊ oīmoda potestate auctoritate ⁊ iurisditione facimus constituimus ⁊ deputamus. Decernentes nihilominus per huiusmodi donationē concessionem ⁊ assignationē nr̄am nulli xp̄iano principi qui actualiter prefatas insulas ⁊ terras firmas possederit vsq̄z ad predictum diē Natiuitatis dñi nr̄i Jesu xp̄i iusquesitū sublatū intelligi posse aut auferri debere. Et insuper mandamus vobis in virtute sācte obedientie (vt sicut etiā pollicemini ⁊ nō dubitamus pro vestra maxima deuotione ⁊ regia magnanimitate vos esse facturos) ad terras firmas ⁊ insulas predictas viros ꝓbos ⁊ deū timētes doctos peritos ⁊ expertos ad instruendū incolas ⁊ habitatores prefactos in fide catholica ⁊ bonis moribus imbuendum destinare debeatis, omnē debitā diligētiam in premissis adhibentes. Ac quibuscūq̄z personis cuiuscūq̄z dignitatis etiam imperialis ⁊ regalis status gradus ordinis vel cōditionis sub excōmunicationis late sētentie pena quam eo ipso si cōtra fecerint incurrant districtius inhibemus ne ad insulas ⁊ terras firmas inuentas ⁊ inuemēdas detectas ⁊ detegendas versus occidentem ⁊ meridiē fabricando ⁊ construendo lineam a polo arctico ad polū antarcticū siue terre firme ⁊ insule inuente ⁊ inueniēde sint: versus indiam aut versus aliam quācūq̄z partem: que linea distet a qualibet insularum que vulgariter nūcupātur de los Azores ⁊ Cabo verde centum leucis versus occidentem ⁊ meridiem vt prefertur pro mercibus habendis vel quauis alia de causa accedere presumāt absq̄z vestra ac heredum ⁊ successorū vestrorum predictorum licentia speciali. Nō obstantibus cōstitutionibus ⁊ ordinationibus apostolicis ceterisq̄z contrarijs quibuscūq̄z: in illo a quo imperia ⁊ dominationes ac bona cuncta procedunt confidentes: quod dirigente dño actus vr̄os si huiusmodi sanctū ⁊ laudabile propositū prosequamini breui tempore cū felicitate ⁊ gloria totius populi xp̄iani vestri labores ⁊ conatus exitum felicissimū consequentur. Uerum quia difficile foret presentes litteras ad singula queq̄z loca in quibus expediens fuerit deferri: volumus ac motu ⁊ scientia similibus decernimus: quod illarum trāsumptis manu publici Notarij inde rogati subscriptis ⁊ sigillo alicuius psone in ecclesiastica dignitate cōstitute seu curie ecclesiastice munitis ea prorsus fides in iudicio ⁊ extra ac alias vbilibet adhibeatur que presentibus adhiberetur si essent exhibite vel ostense. Nulli ergo omnino hominum liceat hanc paginā nr̄e cōmendationis, hortationis, requisitionis, donationis, cōcessionis, assignationis, constitutionis, deputationis, decreti, mandati, inhibitionis ⁊ voluntatis, infringere vel ei ausu temerario cōtraire, Si quis autem hoc attentare presumpserit indignationē oīpotentis dei ac beatorū Petri ⁊ Pauli apostolorū eius se nouerit incursurum. Datis Rome apud sanctum Petrum Anno incarnationis dñice millesimo quadringentesimo nonagesimo tertio quarto nonas maij pontificatus nr̄i anno primo.

Pope Alexander VI. Broadside, Demarcation bull, granting Spain possession (in Latin and Spanish), [1550 ca.].
The Gilder Lehrman Collection, on deposit at the Pierpont Morgan Library. GLC 4093

enemies created an enduring set of ideas known as the "Black Legend." Propagandists from England, France, Germany, Italy, and the Netherlands vilified the Spanish as a corrupt and cruel people who subjugated and exploited the New World Indians, stole their gold and silver, infected them with disease, and killed them in numbers without precedent. In 1580, William I, prince of Orange (1533–84), who led Dutch Protestants in rebellion against Spanish rule, declared that Spain "committed such horrible excesses that all the barbarities, cruelties and tyrannies ever perpetrated before are only games in comparison to what happened to the poor Indians."

Ironically, the Black Legend drew upon criticisms first voiced by the Spanish themselves. During the sixteenth century, observers such as Bartolomé de las Casas (1474–1566), the bishop of Chiapas, condemned maltreatment of the Indians. As a way to protect Indians from utter destruction, las Casas proposed an alternative labor force: slaves from Africa. Given the drastic decline of the Indian population and the reluctance of Europeans to perform heavy agricultural labor, African slaves would raise the staple crops that provided the basis for New World prosperity: sugar, coffee, rice, and indigo.

Las Casas would come to regret his role in encouraging the slave trade. Although he rejected the idea that slavery itself was a crime or sin, he did begin to see African slavery as a source of evil. Unfortunately, las Casas's apology was not published for more than three hundred years.

Bartolomé de las Casas, *A Short Account of the Destruction of the Indies*, 1542

New Spain [Mexico] was discovered in 1517. The explorers treated the inhabitants offensively and murdered some Indians. Under the guise of developing the country, the Christians (as they call themselves) in 1518 engaged in plunder and slaughter. From 1518 until the present day, and it now 1542, the iniquity, injustice, violence, and tyranny that the Spanish have committed against the Indians has escalated as the perpetrators lost all fear of God and the King and all self-respect as well....

During the 12 years [from 1518 to 1530], the Spanish killed more than four million men, women, and children with swords and lances, and by burning people alive.... This does not count those who have died, and continue to die every day, from the slavery and oppression that the Spanish impose....

Among other massacres perpetrated by the Spanish was one that took place in Cholula, a city with thirty thousand inhabitants. Dignitaries and priests from the city and the surrounding countryside greeted the Spanish with great solemnity and respect, and escorted them into the city and lodged them in the homes of the local nobility. The Spanish decided to stage a massacre—or a "chastisement" as they call it—in order to terrorize the population.

It has been Spain's practice in every land they have discovered to stage a massacre in order to make the meek and innocent tremble with fear.

To accomplish this, the Spanish summoned the local dignitaries. As soon as they arrived to hold talks with the Spanish commander, they were taken captive and had no opportunity to warn others. Then the Spanish demanded five or six thousand Indians to carry their loads.... Once these poor wretches assembled in the courtyard, guards blocked the gates while Spanish soldiers slaughtered the Indians with swords and lances. Not one escaped....

That same day, according to an eye-witness, the Spanish managed to capture Montezuma by trickery. They put him in fetters and placed a guard of eighty soldiers over him....

The pretext under which the Spanish invaded these areas, massacred their harmless inhabitants, and depopulated the country was to make the Indians subjects of the King of Spain. Otherwise, they threatened to kill the Indians or burn them alive. And those who did not promptly submit to such an unjust demand, and refused to obey cruel and beastly men, were called rebels who were in revolt against His Majesty the King.

Bartolomé de las Casas, *Brevisima relaction de la destruccion de las Indias* (Seuilla: Truggillo [1552]).

A CRITIQUE OF THE SLAVE TRADE

6 / "A thousand acts of robbery and violence are committed in the course of bartering and carrying off Negroes"

Las Casas was not alone in recognizing the evils of slavery. In this selection, another Spanish cleric, Fray Tomas de Mercado (d. 1575?), argues that the slave trade was the product of deception, robbery, and violence.

The European colonization of the New World brought three disparate geographical areas together: the Americas, western Europe, and western Africa. Some of the consequences of this intercultural contact are well known, such as the introduction of horses, pigs, and cattle into the New World, and the transfer of potatoes, beans, and tomatoes to Europe. But other consequences of the Columbian exchange are less noted. As a result of the Atlantic slave trade, such New World food crops as cassava, sweet potatoes, squash, and peanuts were carried to Africa, sharply stimulating African population growth and therefore increasing the population in ways that helped make the slave trade possible.

Fray Tomas de Mercado, *Suma de Tratos y Contratos*, Seville, 1587

It is public opinion and knowledge that no end of deception is practiced and a thousand acts of robbery and violence are committed in the course of bartering and carrying off Negroes from their country and bringing them to the Indies and to Spain.... Since the Portuguese and Spaniards pay so much for a Negro, they go out to hunt one another without the pretext of a war, as if they were deer; even the very Ethiopians, who are different, being induced to do so by the profit derived. They make war on one another, their gain being the capture of their own people, and they go after one another in the forests where they usually hunt.... In this way, and contrary to all justice, a very great number of prisoners are taken. And no one is horrified that these people are ill-treating and selling one another, because they are considered uncivilized and savage. In addition to the pretext, of parents selling their children as a last resort, there is the bestial practice of selling them without any necessity to do so, and very often through anger or passion, for some displeasure or disrespect they have shown them.... The wretched children are taken to the market place for sale, and as the traffic in Negroes is so great, there are Portuguese, or even Negroes themselves, ready everywhere to buy them. There are also among them traders in this bestial and brutal business, who set boundaries in the interior for the natives and carry them off for sale at a higher price on the coasts or in the islands. I have seen many acquired in this way. Apart from these acts of injustice and robberies committed among themselves, there are thousands of other forms of deception practiced in those parts by the Spaniards to trick and carry off the Negroes finally as newly imported slaves, which they are in fact, to the ports, with a few bonnets, gewgaws, beads and bits of paper under which they give them. They put them aboard the ships under false pretenses, hoist anchor, set sail, and make off towards the high seas with their booty.... I know a man who recently sailed to one of those Islands and, with less than four thousand ducats for ransom, carried off four hundred Negroes without license or registration.... They embark four and five hundred of them in a boat which, sometimes, is not a cargo boat. The very stench is enough to kill most of them, and, indeed, very many die. The wonder is that twenty percent of them are not lost.

J.A. Saco, *Historia de la Esclavitud de la Raza Africana,* Tomo II, pp. 80–82.

PART TWO

European Colonization North of Mexico

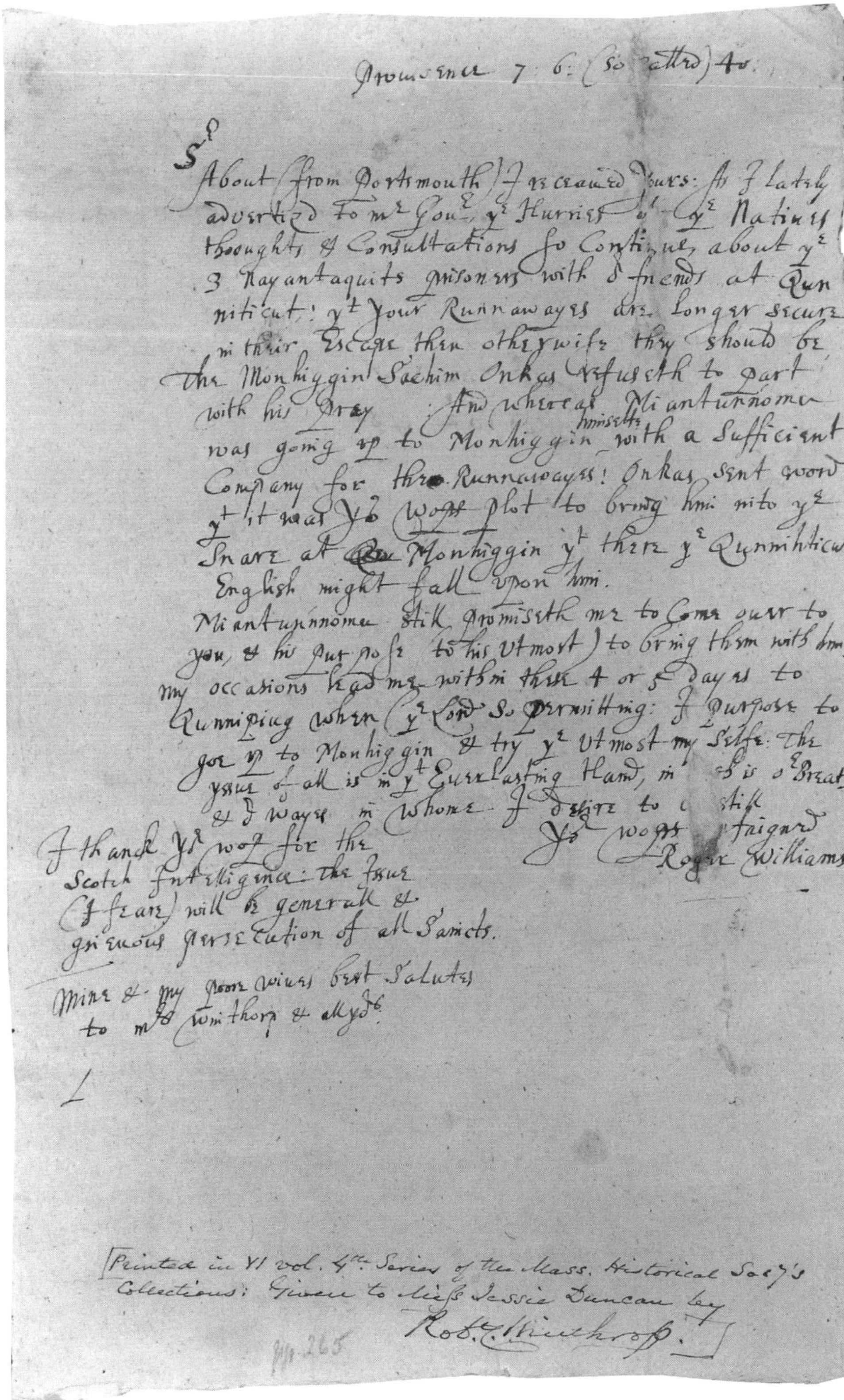

Providence 7. 6. (so called) 40.

Sir

About (from Portsmouth) I received yours: As I lately advertized to mr Gover, ye Hurries of ye Natives thoughts & Consultations so continue, about ye 3 Nayantaquits prisoners with o friends at Qunniticut: yt your Runnawayes are longer secure in their Escape then otherwise they should be: the Monhiggin Sachim Onkas refuseth to part with his Prey: And whereas Miantunnome himselfe was going up to Monhiggin with a sufficient Company for three Runnawayes: Onkas sent word yt it was yo worst plot to bring him into ye Snare at Monhiggin yt there ye Qunnihticut English might fall upon him.

Miantunnome still promiseth me to come over to you, & his purpose (to his utmost) to bring them with him.

My occasions lead me within these 4 or 5 dayes to Qunnipiug: when (ye Lord so permitting) I purpose to goe up to Monhiggin & try ye utmost my selfe: the yssue of all is in yt Everlasting Hand, in whom is o breath & o wayes in whome I desire to … still

Yor worsps unfeigned

Roger Williams

I thanck yr wor for the Scotch Intelligence: the yssue (I feare) will be generall & grievous persecution of all Saincts.

Mine & my poore wives best salutes to mrs Winthrop & all yrs.

[Printed in VI vol. 4th Series of the Mass. Historical Socy's Collections: Given to Miss Jessie Duncan by Robt. C. Winthrop.]

pp. 265

Roger Williams. Autograph letter signed, to John Winthrop, 1640/06/07 [?]. The Gilder Lehrman Collection, on deposit at the Pierpont Morgan Library. GLC 1590

Prior to the seventeenth century, all European attempts to plant permanent colonies north of Mexico—with the exception of a Spanish fortress at St. Augustine in Florida and a small Spanish settlement in New Mexico—failed. Unprepared for the harsh and demanding environment, facing staunch resistance from the indigenous population, and lacking adequate financing and supplies, sixteenth-century French and English efforts to establish permanent North American settlements in Newfoundland, Nova Scotia, the St. Lawrence Valley, Florida, and Roanoke Island off the coast of North Carolina were short-lived failures.

During the early seventeenth century, however, national and religious rivalries and the growth of a merchant class eager to invest in overseas expansion and commerce encouraged renewed efforts at colonization. England established its first enduring settlement in Jamestown in 1607; France in Québec in 1608; the Dutch in what would become Albany in 1614; and the Swedes a fur-trading colony in the lower Delaware Valley in 1638. As early as 1625 nearly ten thousand Europeans had immigrated to the North American coast. But only about eighteen hundred were actually living on the continent in that year, due mainly to the staggeringly high number of deaths from disease during the initial stages of settlement.

Seventeenth-century European settlement took sharply contrasting forms. Perhaps the most obvious difference was demographic. The English immigration was far larger and more gender-balanced than that of the Dutch, the French, or the Spanish. The explanation for the rapid growth of England's North American colonies lies in the existence of a large "surplus" population. Early seventeenth-century England contained a large number of immigrant farmhands as well as unemployed and underemployed workers. Most English immigrants to North America were recruited from the lower working population—farm workers, urban laborers, and artisans—who were suffering from economic distress, including sharply falling wages (which declined by half between 1550 and 1650) and a series of failed harvests. Outside of New England, most English immigrants—perhaps as many as 70 percent or more—were indentured servants, who agreed to serve a term of service in exchange for transportation across the Atlantic.

Religious persecution was a particularly powerful force motivating English colonization. England allowed religious dissidents to immigrate to the New World. Some thirty thousand English Puritans immigrated to New England, while Maryland became a refuge for Roman Catholics, and Pennsylvania, southern New Jersey, and Rhode Island, havens for Quakers. The refugees from religious persecution included Baptists, Congregationalists, Presbyterians, and a small number of Catholics, to say nothing of religious minorities from continental Europe, including Huguenots and members of the Dutch and German Reformed churches.

Europe's North American settlements differed markedly in their economies. While the Dutch, French, and Swedish settlements relied mainly on trade in fish and furs, English settlement took a variety of forms. In New England, the economy was organized largely around small, family farms and urban communities engaged in fishing, handicrafts, and Atlantic commerce, with most of the population living in small, compact towns. In the Chesapeake colonies of Maryland and Virginia, the economy was structured largely around larger and much more isolated farms and plantations raising tobacco, with an average of only about two dozen families living in a twenty-five-square-mile area. In the Carolinas and the British West Indies, economic life was organized around larger but less isolated plantations growing rice, indigo, coffee, cotton, and sugar.

By the beginning of the eighteenth century, the population in Britain's North American colonies was growing at an unprecedented rate. At a time when Europe's population was increasing by just 1 percent a year, New England's growth rate was 2.6 or 2.7 percent annually. By the early eighteenth century, the population was also growing extremely rapidly in the middle Atlantic and southern colonies, largely as a result of a low death rate and a sex ratio that was more balanced than in Europe itself.

By 1700 Britain's North American colonies offered an unprecedented degree of social equality and political liberty for white men. The colonies differed from England itself in the proportion of white men who owned property and were able to vote, as well as in the population's ethnic and religious diversity. Yet by the beginning of the eighteenth century it was also clear that colonial expansion involved the displacement of the indigenous population and that the colonial economy depended heavily on various forms of unfree labor, of which the most rapidly growing form consisted of black and sometimes Indian slaves, who could be found in every one of Britain's North American colonies.

JUSTIFICATIONS FOR ENGLISH INVOLVEMENT IN THE NEW WORLD

1 / "The Kings of Spain...have rooted out above fifteen millions of reasonable creatures"

Foreign propagandists seized on the writings of las Casas and Mercado and turned them to their own purposes. In one version of the Black Legend, an English writer explained that the Indians "were simple and plaine men, and lived without great labour." The Spaniards in the lust for gold, however, "forced the people...to stande all the daie in the hotte sunne gathering golde in the sande of the rivers. By this means a great nombre of them...died, and a great number of them (seeing themselves brought from so quiet a life to such miserie and slaverie) of desperaction killed them selves. And many wolde not mary, bicause they wolde not have their children slaves to the Spaniards." An English reprint of the writings of las Casas bore this sensational title: "Popery Truly Display'd in its Bloody Colours: Or, a Faithful Narrative of the Horrid and Unexampled Massacres, Butcheries, and all manners of Cruelties that Hell and Malice could invent, committed by the Popish Spanish."

Religious differences and national interests contributed to the Black Legend.

Dutch Protestants were rebelling against Spanish rule, while the French, Germans, and Italians were bitter over defeats at Spain's hands. England, which had become a Protestant country during the Reformation, not only aided the Dutch struggle for independence, it also encouraged English mariners such as Francis Drake (1540–96) and John Hawkins (1532–95) to raid Spanish ships and towns in the Americas. In response, King Philip II of Spain (1527–98) assembled an armada that tried unsuccessfully to invade England in 1588 and make it a Catholic country again.

The Black Legend provided powerful ideological sanction for English involvement in the New World. By seizing treasure from Spanish ships, staging raids on Spanish ports and cities in the Americas, and enlisting runaway slaves known as Cimarons to prey on the Spanish, Protestant England would strike a blow against Spain's aggressive Catholicism and rescue the Indians from Spanish slavery. But it is a pointed historical irony that the very English seamen, such as Drake and Hawkins, who promised to rescue the Indians from Spanish bondage, also bought and enslaved Africans along the West African coast and transported them to Spanish America, where they sold them to Spanish colonists.

Richard Hakluyt (1552–1616), a London lawyer, was one of the most influential promoters of English colonization in North America. In this selection, he justifies English predations against Spanish shipping and ports in the New World. He also argues that the Pope's decision in 1494 to divide the New World between Spain and Portugal was in error.

In 1494 papal ambassadors had persuaded Spain and Portugal to accept the Treaty of Tordesillas, which established a "line of demarcation" about eleven hundred miles west of the Azores. Spain received the right to all undiscovered territory west of the line, and Portugal was given all lands east of this boundary, which by the early sixteenth century included Brazil.

Richard Hakluyt, "A particular discourse concerning the great necessity and manifold commodities that are like to grow to this Realm of England by the Western discoveries lately attempted," 1584

If you touch him [King Phillip II of Spain] in the [West] Indies, you touch the apple of his eye; for take away his treasure...[and] his old bands of soldiers will soon be dissolved, his purpose defeated, his power and strength diminished, his pride abated, and his tyranny utterly suppressed....

To confute the general claim and unlawful title of the insatiable Spaniards to...America...we...[must] answer the...most injurious and unreasonable donation granted by Pope Alexander the Sixth...to the great prejudice of all other Christian princes but especially to the damage of the Kings of England....

No Pope had any lawful authority to give any such donation...our Savior Christ confessed openly to Pilate that his kingdom was not of this world....

The inducements that moved His holiness to grant those unequal donations unto Spain were, first, (as he saith) his singular desire and care to have the Christian Religion and Catholic faith exalted, and to be enlarged, and spread abroad throughout the world...and that the salvation of souls should be procured of everyone, and that the barbarous nations should be subdued....

The Kings of Spain have sent such hellhounds and wolves thither as have not converted but almost quite subverted them, and have rooted out above fifteen millions of reasonable creatures, as Bartholomew de Casas...doth write....

Richard Hakluyt, "A Discourse on Western Planting," *Documentary History of the State of Maine*, Maine Historical Society Collections, 2nd Ser., (Cambridge, Mass., 1877), vol. II, pp. 36–41.

A RATIONALE FOR NEW WORLD COLONIZATION

2 / "All...our...trades in all Europe...may...[count] for little... [compared with] America"

During the early and mid-sixteenth century, the English tended to conceive of North America as a base for piracy and harassment of the Spanish. But by the end of the century, the English began to think more seriously about North America as a place to colonize: as a bulwark against Catholic Spain, a market for English goods, a source of raw materials and commodities such as furs, and a market for finished products. America would also provide a place to send the English poor and ensure that they would contribute to the nation's wealth.

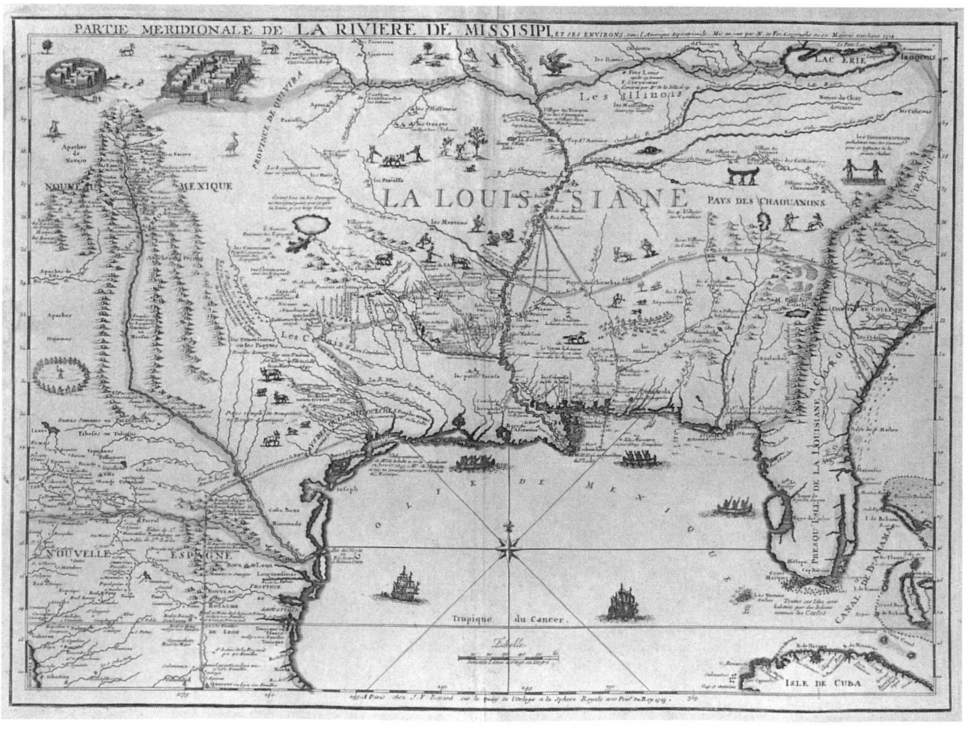

Nicolas De Fer. Map, Partie meridionale de la riviere de Missisipi [sic] et ses environs..., 1718. The Gilder Lehrman Collection, on deposit at the Pierpont Morgan Library. GLC 4254

During the late sixteenth and early seventeenth centuries, the English poor increased rapidly in number. As a result of the enclosure of traditional common lands (which were increasingly used to raise sheep), many common people were forced to become wage laborers or else to support themselves hand-to-mouth or simply as beggars.

Here Richard Hayluyt recounts the advantages of New World colonization. Later Hakluyt invested his own money in the company that colonized Virginia.

RICHARD HAKLUYT, "A PARTICULAR DISCOURSE CONCERNING THE GREAT NECESSITY AND MANIFOLD COMMODITIES THAT ARE LIKE TO GROW TO THIS REALM OF ENGLAND BY THE WESTERN DISCOVERIES LATELY ATTEMPTED," 1584

...All the commodities of all our old decayed and dangerous trades in all Europe, Africa, and Asia...may in short space [count] for little or nothing [compared with]...that part of America which lieth between 30 and 60 degrees of northerly latitude, if by our slackness we suffer not the French or others to prevent us....

For all the statutes that hitherto can be devised, and the sharp execution of the same in punishing idle and lazy persons, for want of sufficient occasion of honest employments, cannot deliver our commonwealth from multitudes of loiterers and idle vagabonds. Truth it is that through our long peace and seldom sickness (two singular blessings of Almighty God) we are grown more populous than ever heretofore; so that now there are...so many, that they can hardly live one by another, nay rather they are ready to eat up one another; yea many thousands of idle persons are within this realm, which having no way to be set on work, be either mutinous and seek alteration in the state, or at least very burdensome to the commonwealth and often fall to pilfering and thieving and other lewdness, whereby all the prisons of the land are daily pestered and stuffed full of them, where either they pitifully pine away or else at length are miserably hanged, even 20 at a clap out of some jail. Whereas if this voyage [to the New World] were put in execution, these petty thieves might be condemned for certain years in the western parts, especially in Newfoundland, in sawing and felling of timber and masts of ships...; in burning of the firs and pine trees to make pitch, tar, rosin, and soap ashes; in beating and working of hemp for cordage; and, in the more southern parts, in setting them to work in mines of gold, silver, copper, lead, and iron; in dragging for pearls and coral; in planting of sugar canes, as the Portingales [Portuguese] have done in Madeira; in maintenance and increasing of silk worms for silk, and in dressing the same; in gathering of cotton whereof there is plenty; in tilling of the soil there for grain; in dressing of vines whereof there is great abundance for wine; olives, whereof the soil is capable, for oil; trees for oranges, lemons, almonds, figs, and other fruits, all which are found to grow there already;... in building of forts, towns, churches; in powdering and barrelling of fish, fowls, and flesh, which will be notable provision for sea and land; in drying, sorting, and packing of features, where of may be had there marvelous great quantity....

In sum, this enterprise will minister matter for all sorts and states of men to work upon; namely, all several kinds of artificers, husbandmen, seamen, merchants, soldiers, captains, physicians, lawyers, divines, cosmographers, hydrographers, astronomers, historiographers; yea, old folks, lame persons, women, and young children, by many means...shall be kept from idleness, and be made able by their own honest and easy labour to find themselves without surcharging others.

Richard Hakluyt, "A Discourse on Western Planting," *Documentary History of the State of Maine*, Maine Historical Society Collections, 2nd Ser., (Cambridge, Mass., 1877), vol. II, pp. 36–41.

ENGLAND'S FIRST ENDURING NORTH AMERICAN SETTLEMENT

3 / *"Being ready with clubs to beat out his brains, Pocahontas... got his head in her arms"*

After unsuccessful attempts to establish settlements in Newfoundland and at Roanoke, the famous "Lost Colony," off the coast of present-day North Carolina, England established its first permanent North American settlement, Jamestown, in 1607. Located in swampy marshlands along Virginia's James River, Jamestown's residents suffered horrendous mortality rates during its first years. Immigrants had just a 50–50 chance of surviving five years.

The Jamestown expedition was financed by the Virginia Company of London, which believed that precious metals were to be found in the area. From the outset, however, Jamestown suffered from disease and conflict with Indians. Approximately thirty thousand Algonquian Indians lived in the region, divided into about forty tribes. About thirty tribes belonged to a confederacy led by Powhatan.

Food was an initial source of conflict. More interested in finding gold and silver than in farming, Jamestown's residents (many of whom were either aristocrats or their servants) were unable or unwilling to work. When the English began to seize Indian food stocks, Powhatan cut off supplies, forcing the colonists to subsist on frogs, snakes, and even decaying corpses.

Captain John Smith (1580?–1631) was twenty-six years old when the first expedition landed. A farmer's son, Smith had already led an adventurous life before arriving in Virginia. He had fought with the Dutch army against the Spanish and in eastern Europe against the Ottoman Turks, when he was taken captive and enslaved. He later escaped to Russia before returning to England.

Smith, serving as president of the Jamestown colony from 1608 to 1609, required the colonists to work and traded with the Indians for food. In 1609, after being wounded in a gunpowder accident, Smith returned to England. After his departure, conflict between the English and the Powhatan confederacy intensified, especially after the colonists began to clear land in order to plant tobacco.

In this excerpt, Smith describes the famous incident in which Powhatan's 12-year-old daughter, Pocahontas (1595?–1617), saved him from execution. Although some have questioned whether this incident took place (since Smith failed to mention it in his *Historie*'s first edition), it may well have been a "staged event," an elaborate adoption ceremony by which Powhatan symbolically made Smith his vassal or servant. Through similar ceremonies, the Powhatan people incorporated outsiders into their society.

Pocahontas reappears in the colonial records in 1613, when she was lured aboard an English ship and held captive. Negotiations for her release failed, and in 1614, she married John Rolfe, the colonist who introduced tobacco to Virginia. Whether this marriage represented an attempt to forge an alliance between the English and the Powhatan remains uncertain.

JOHN SMITH, *Generall Historie of Virginia*

[1608] At last they brought him [John Smith] to...Powhatan, their emperor. Here more than 200 of those grim courtiers stood wondering at him [Smith], as he had been a monster; till Powhatan and his train had put themselves in their braveries. Before a fire upon a seat like a bedstead, he sat covered with a great robe made of racoon skins, and all the tails hanging by....

Having feasted him after their best barbarous manner they could, a long consultation was held, but the conclusion was: two great stones were brought before Powhatan; then as many as could laid hands on him [Smith], dragged him to them, and thereon laid his head, and being ready with their clubs to beat out his brains, Pocahontas, the king's dearest daughter, when no entreaty could prevail, got his head in her arms, and laid her own upon his to save him from death. Whereat the emperor was contented he should live to make him hatchets, and her bells, beads, and copper....

[1609] As for corn provisions and contributions from the savages, we had nothing but mortal wounds, with clubs and arrows. As for our hogs, hens, goats, sheep, horses, or what lived, our commanders, officers, and savages daily consumed them; some small proportions sometimes we tasted, till all was devoured. Then swords, arms, pieces, or anything we traded with the savages, whose cruel fingers were so oft imbued in our blood, that what by their cruelty, our governor's indiscretion, and the loss of our ships, of 500 within six months after Captain Smith's departure there remained not past 60 men, women, and children—most miserable and poor creatures. And those were preserved for the most part by roots, herbs, acorns, walnuts, berries, now and then a little fish. They that had starch in these extremities made no small use of it; yea, even the very skins of our horses.

Nay, so great was our famine that a savage we slew and buried, the poorer sort took him up again and ate him; and so did diverse one another boiled and stewed with roots and herbs. And one among the rest did kill his wife, powdered [salted] her, and had eaten of her before it was known; for which he was executed, as he well deserved. Now whether she was better roasted, boiled, or carbonated [broiled], I know not; but of such a dish as powdered wife I never heard.

This was that time, which still to this day, we call the starving time. It were too vile to say, and scarce to be believed, what we endured; but the occasion was our own for want of providence, industry, and government, and not the barrenness and defect of the country, as is generally supposed.

Edward Arber, ed., *Works 1608–1631,* (Westminster: Archibald Constable, 1895,) pp. 391–401, 497–516.

LIFE IN EARLY VIRGINIA

4 / *"My brother and my wife are dead"*

Early Virginia was a death trap. Of the first three thousand immigrants, all but six hundred were dead within a few years of arrival. Virginia was a society in which life was short, diseases ran rampant, and parentless children and multiple marriages were the norms.

In sharp contrast to New England, which was settled mainly by families, most of the settlers of Virginia and neighboring Maryland were single men bound in servitude. Before the colonies turned decisively to slavery in the late seventeenth century, planters relied on white indentured servants from England, Ireland, and Scotland. They wanted men, not women. During the early and midseventeenth century, as many as four men arrived for every woman.

Why did large numbers of people come to such an unhealthful region? To raise tobacco, which had been introduced into England in the late sixteenth century. Like a number of other consumer products introduced during the early modern era—such as tea, coffee, and chocolate—tobacco was related to the development of new work patterns and new forms of sociability. Tobacco appeared to relieve boredom and stress and to enhance people's ability to concentrate over prolonged periods of time. Tobacco production required a large labor force, which initially consisted primarily of white indentured servants, who received transportation to Virginia in exchange for a four- to seven-year term of service.

In one of the earliest surviving letters from colonial Virginia, Sebastian Brandt (fl. 1600–1625?), an early settler, casually describes the extent of mortality in the colony. He also shows that the search for precious metals persisted even after the colonists had begun to raise tobacco.

SEBASTIAN BRANDT, JANUARY 13, 1622, GLC 708

Well beloved good friend Henry Hovener

My comendations remembered, I heartily wish your welfare for God be thanked I am now in good health, but my brother and my wife are dead about a year past. And touching the business that I came hither is nothing yet performed, by reason of my sickness and weakness I was not able to travel up and down the hills and dales of these countries but do now intend every day to walk up and downe the hills for good Mineralls here is both golde silver and copper to be had and therefore I will doe my endeavour by the grace of God to effect what I am able to perform....It may please the aforesaid Company to send me...two little runletts of wine and vinegar some spice and sugar to comfort us here in our sickness....And whatsoever this all costeth I will not only w[i]th my most humble service but also w[i]th some good Tobacco, Beaver, and Otterskins and other commodities here to be had recompence the Company for the same.

RACE WAR IN VIRGINIA

5 / *"They basely and barbarously murdered, not sparing either age or sex"*

Since tobacco production rapidly exhausted the soil of nutrients, the English began to acquire new lands along the James River, encroaching on Indian hunting grounds. In

1622, Powhatan's successor, Opechancanough, tried to wipe out the English in a surprise attack. Two Indian converts to Christianity warned the English; still, 347 settlers, or about a third of the English colonists, died in the attack. Warfare persisted for ten years, followed by an uneasy peace. In 1644 Opechcanough launched a last, desperate attack. After about two years of warfare, in which some 500 colonists were killed, Opechcanough was captured and shot and the survivors of Powhatan's confederacy, now reduced to just 2,000, agreed to submit to English rule.

Edward Waterhouse, a prominent Virginia official, offers a firsthand account of Opechcanough's attack and suggests how the attack removed all restraints on the Virginians' quest for revenge.

Edward Waterhouse, 1622

And such was the conceit of firm peace and amity as that there was seldom or never a sword worn and a piece seldomer, except for a deer or fowl.... The houses generally sat open to the savages, who were always friendly entertained at the tables of the English, and commonly lodged in their bed-chambers...to open a fair gate for their conversion to Christianity....

Yea, such was the treacherous dissimulation of that people who then had contrived our destruction, that even two days before the massacre some of our men were guided through the woods by them in safety....Yea, they borrowed our own boats to convey themselves across the river (on the banks of both sides whereof all our plantations were) to consult of the devilish murder that ensued, and of our utter extirpation, which God of his mercy (by the means of some of themselves converted to Christianity) prevented....

On the Friday morning (the fatal day) the 22nd of March, as also in the evening, as in other days before, they came unarmed into our houses, without bows or arrows, or other weapons, with deer, turkeys, fish, furs, and other provisions to sell and truck with us for glass, beads, and other trifles; yea, in some places, sat down at breakfast with our people at their tables, whom immediately with their own tools and weapons either laid down, or standing in their houses, they basely and barbarously murdered, not sparing either age or sex, man, women or child; so sudden in their cruel execution that few or none discerned the weapon or blow that brought them to destruction....

And by this means that fatal Friday morning, there fell under the bloody and barbarous hands of that perfidious and inhumane people, contrary to the laws of God and man, and nature and nations, 347 men, women, and children, most by their own weapons. And not being content with taking away life alone, they fell after again upon the dead, making, as well as they could, a fresh murder, defacing, dragging, and mangling the dead carcasses into many pieces, and carrying away some parts in derision....

Our hands, which before were tied with gentleness and fair usage, are now set at liberty by the treacherous violence of the savages...so that we, who hitherto have had possession of no more ground than their waste and our purchase at a valuable consideration to their contentment gained, may now by right of war, and law of nations, invade the country, and destroy them who sought to destroy us; whereby we shall enjoy their cultivated places.... Now their cleared grounds in all their villages (which are situate in the fruitfulest places of the land) shall be inhabited by us, whereas heretofore the grubbing of woods was the greatest labor.

Susan Kingsbury, ed., *The Records of the Virginia Company of London,* (Washington: Government Printing Office, 1906–1985,) pp. 550–51, 556–57

INDENTURED SERVITUDE

6 / *"[Virginia] is reported to be an unhealthy place, a nest of Rogues... [and] dissolute...persons"*

Raising tobacco required a large labor force. At first it was not clear that this labor force would consist of enslaved Africans. Virginians experimented with a variety of labor sources, including Indian slaves, penal slaves, and white indentured servants. Convinced that England was overpopulated with vagabonds and paupers, the colonists imported surplus Englishmen to raise tobacco and to produce dyestuffs, potash, furs, and other goods that England had imported from other countries. Typically, young men or women in their late teens or twenties would sign a contract of indenture. In exchange for transportation to the New World, a servant would work for several years (usually four to seven) without wages.

The status of indentured servants in early Virginia and Maryland was not wholly dissimilar from slavery. Servants could be bought, sold, or leased. They could also be physically beaten for disobedience or running away. Unlike slaves, however, they were freed after their term of service expired, their children did not inherit their status, and they received a small cash payment of "freedom dues."

The English writer Daniel Defoe (1661?–1731) set part of his novel *Moll Flanders* (1683) in early Virginia. Defoe described the people who settled in Virginia in distinctly unflattering terms: There were convicts, who had "been found guilty of felonies...punishable by death," and there were those "brought over by masters of ships to be sold as servants. Such as we call them, my dear, but they are more properly called slaves."

George Alsop, an indentured servant in Maryland, echoed these sentiments in 1666. Servants "by hundreds of thousands" spent their lives "here and in Virginia, and elsewhere in planting that vile tobacco, which all vanishes into smoke, and is for the most part miserably abused." And, he went on, this "insatiable avarice must be fed and sustained by the bloody sweat of these poor slaves."

In this extract, John Hammond (d. 1707) describes servitude in Virginia during the tobacco boom years.

JOHN HAMMOND, *Leah and Rachel, or, The Two Fruitful Sisters Virginia and Mary-land,* 1656

It is the glory of every Nation to enlarge themselves, to encourage their own foreign attempts, and to be able to have their own, within their territories, as many several commodities as they can attain to, that so others may rather be beholding to them, than they to others....

But alas, we Englishmen...do not only fail in this, but vilify, scandalize and cry down such parts of the unknown world, as have been found out, settled and made flourishing, by the charge, hazard, and diligence of their own brethren, as if because removed from us, we either account them people of another world or enemies.

This is too truly made good in the odious and cruel slanders cast on those two famous Countries of Virginia and Mary-land, whereby those Countries, not only are many times at a standstill, but are in danger to moulder away, and come in time to nothing....

The Country [Virginia] is reported to be an unhealthy place, a nest of Rogues, whores, dissolute and rooking persons; a place of intolerable labour, bad usage and hard Diet, &c.

To Answer these several calumnies, I shall first shew what it was? Next, what it is?

At the first settling and many years after, it deserved most of those aspersions (nor were they aspersions but truths).... Then were Jails emptied, youth seduced, infamous women drilled in, the provisions all brought out of England, and that embezzled by the Trustees (for they durst neither hunt fowl, nor Fish, for fear of the Indian, which they stood in awe of) their labour was almost perpetual, their allowance of victual small, few or no cattle, no use of horses nor oxen to draw or carry, (which labours men supplied themselves) all of which caused a mortality; no civil courts of justice but under a martial law, no redress of grievances, complaints were repaid with stripes...in a word all and the worst that tyranny could inflict....

And having briefly laid down the former state of Virginia, in its Infancy, and filth, and the occasion of its scandalous aspersions: I come to my main subject, its present condition of Happiness (if anything can be called happy in this transitory life)....

The usual allowance for servants is (besides their charge of passage defrayed) at their expiration, a year's provision of corn, double apparel, tools necessary, and land according to the custom of the Country, which is an old delusion, for there is no land customarily due to the servant, but to the Master, and therefore that servant is unwise that will not dash out that custom in his covenant and make that due of land absolutely his own, which although at the present, not of so great consequences; yet in few years will be of much worth....

When ye go aboard, expect the Ship somewhat troubled and in a hurlyburly, until ye clear the lands end; and that the Ship is rummaged, and things put to rights, which many times discourages the Passengers, and makes them wish the Voyage unattempted: but this is but for a short season, and washes off when at Sea, where the time is pleasantly passed away, though not with such choice plenty as the shore affords.

But when ye arrive and are settled, ye will find a strange alteration, an abused Country giving the lie to your own approbations to those that have calumniated it....

The labour servants are put to, is not so hard nor of such continuance as Husbandmen, nor Handicraftmen are kept at in England, I said little or nothing is done in winter time, none ever work before sun rising nor after sun set, in the summer they rest, sleep or exercise themselves give hours in the heat of the day, Saturdays afternoon is always their own, the old Holidays are observed and the Sabbath spent in good exercises.

The women are not (as is reported) put into the ground to work, but occupy such domestic employments and housewifery as in England, that is dressing victuals, right up the house, milking, employed about dairies, washing, sewing, &c. and both men and women have times of recreations, as much or more than in any part of the world besides, yet some wenches that are nastily, beastly and not fit to be so employed are put into the ground, for reason tells us, they must not at charge be transported then maintained for nothing, but those that prove so awkward are rather burthensome than servants desirable or useful....

Those Servants that will be industrious may in their time of service gain a competent estate before their Freedoms, which is usually done by many, and they gain esteem and assistance that appear so industrious: There is no Master almost but will allow his Servant a parcel of clear ground to cut some Tobacco in for himself, which he may husband at those many idle times he hath allowed him and not prejudice, but rejoice his Master to see it, which in time of Shipping he may lay out for commodities, and in Summer sell them again with advantage and get a Pig or two, which any body almost will give him, and his Master suffer him to keep them with his own, which will be no charge to his Master, and with one years increase of them may purchase a Cow Calf or two, and by that time he is for himself; he may have Cattle, Hogs and Tobacco of his own, and come to live gallantly; but this must be gained (as I have said) by Industry and affability, not by sloth nor churlish behavior.

And whereas it is rumoured that Servants have no lodging other then on boards, or by the Fire side, it is contrary to reason to believe it: First, as we are Christians; next as people living under a law, which compels as well the Master as the Servant to perform his duty; nor can true labour be either expected or exacted without sufficient clothing, diet, and lodging; all which their Indentures (which must inviolably be observed) and the Justice of the Country requires.

But if any go thither, not in a condition of a Servant, but pay his or her passage, which is some six pounds: Let them not doubt but it is money well laid out...although they carry little else to take a Bed along with them, and then few Houses but will give them entertainment, either out of courtesy, or on reasonable terms; and I think it better for any that goes over free, and but in a mean condition, to hire himself for reasonable wages of Tobacco and Provision, the first year, provided he happen in an honest house, and where the Mistress is noted for a good Housewife, of which there are very many (notwithstanding the cry to the contrary) for by that means he will live free of disbursement, have something to help him the next year, and be carefully looked to in his sickness (if he chance to fall sick) and let him so covenant that exceptions may be made, that he work not much in the hot weather, a course we always take with our new hands (as they call them) the first year they come in.

If they are women that go after this manner, that is paying their own passages; I advise them to sojourn in a house of honest repute, for by their good carriage, they may advance themselves in marriage, by their ill, overthrow their fortunes; and although loose persons seldom live long unmarried if free; yet they match with as dissolute as themselves, and never live handsomely or are ever respected....

Be sure to have your contract in writing and under hand and seal, for if ye go over upon promise made to do this or that, or to be free, it signifies nothing.

John Hammond, *Leah and Rachel, or, The Two Fruitful Sisters Virginia and Mary-land* (London, Printed by Mabb, 1656).

THE SHIFT TO SLAVERY

7 / *"All children...shall be held bond or free only according to the condition of the mother"*

Black slavery took root in the American colonies slowly. Historians now know that small numbers of Africans lived in Virginia before 1619, the year a Dutch ship sold some 20 blacks (probably from the West Indies) to the colonists. But it was not until the 1680s that black slavery became the dominant labor system on plantations there. As late as 1640 there were probably only 150 blacks in Virginia, and 300 in 1650. But by 1680 the number had risen to 3,000 and by 1704, to 10,000.

Until the mid-1660s the number of white indentured servants was sufficient to meet the labor needs of Virginia and Maryland. Then, in the mid-1660s, the supply of white servants fell sharply. Many factors contributed to the growing shortage of servants. The English birth rate had begun to fall and with fewer workers competing for jobs, wages in England rose. The great fire that burned much of London in 1666 created a great need for labor to rebuild the city. Meanwhile, Virginia and Maryland became less attractive as land grew scarcer. Many preferred to immigrate to Pennsylvania or the Carolinas, where opportunities seemed greater.

To replenish its labor force, planters in the Chesapeake region increasingly turned to enslaved Africans. In 1680 just 7 percent of the population of Virginia and Maryland consisted of slaves; twenty years later, the figure was 22 percent. Most of these slaves did not come directly from Africa, but from Barbados and other Caribbean colonies or from the Dutch colony of New Netherlands, which the English had conquered in 1664 and renamed New York.

The status of blacks in seventeenth-century Virginia was extremely complex. Some were permanently unfree; others, such as indentured servants, were allowed to own property and marry and were freed after a term of service. Some were even allowed to testify against whites in court and purchase white servants. In at least one county, black slaves who could prove that they had been baptized sued successfully for their freedom. There was even a surprising degree of tolerance of sexual intermixture and marriages across racial lines.

As early as the late 1630s, however, English colonists began to distinguish between the status of white servants and black slaves. In 1639 Maryland became the first colony to specifically state that baptism as a Christian did not make a slave a free person.

During the 1660s and 1670s Maryland and Virginia adopted laws specifically designed to denigrate blacks. These laws banned interracial marriages and sexual relations and deprived blacks of property. Other laws prohibited blacks from bearing arms or traveling without written permission. In 1669 Virginia became the first colony to declare that it was not a crime to kill an unruly slave in the ordinary course of punishment. In that same year Virginia also prohibited masters from freeing slaves unless the freedmen were deported from the colony. Virginia also voted to banish any white man or woman who married a black, mulatto, or Indian.

The imposition of a more rigid system of racial slavery was accompanied by improved status for white servants. Unlike slaves, white servants and free workers could not be stripped naked and whipped. As the historian Edmund S. Morgan has suggested, a hardening of racial lines contributed to a growth in a commitment to democracy, liberty, and equality among white men.

Virginia slave laws

December 1662

Whereas some doubts have arisen whether children got by any Englishman upon a Negro woman should be slave or free, *be it therefore enacted and declared by this present Grand Assembly*, that all children born in this country shall be held bond or free only according to the condition of the mother; and that if any Christian shall commit fornication with a Negro man or woman, he or she so offending shall pay double the fines imposed by the former act.

September 1667

Whereas some doubts have risen whether children that are slaves by birth, and by the charity and piety of their owners made partakers of the blessed sacrament of baptism, should by virtue of their baptism be made free, *it is enacted and declared by this Grand Assembly, and the authority thereof*, that the conferring of baptism does not alter the condition of the person as to his bondage or freedom; that diverse masters, freed from this doubt may more carefully endeavor the propagation of Christianity by permitting children, though slaves, or those of greater growth if capable, to be admitted to that sacrament.

September 1668

Whereas it has been questioned whether servants running away may be punished with corporal punishment by their master or magistrate, since the act already made gives the master satisfaction by prolonging their time by service, *it is declared and enacted by this Assembly* that moderate corporal punishment inflicted by master or magistrate upon a runaway servant shall not deprivate the master of the satisfaction allowed by the law, the one being as necessary to reclaim them from persisting in that idle course as the other is just to repair the damages sustained by the master.

October 1669

Whereas the only law in force for the punishment of refractory servants resisting their master, mistress, or overseer cannot be inflicted upon Negroes, nor the obstinacy of many of them be suppressed by other than violent means, *be it enacted and declared by this Grand Assembly* if any slave resists his master (or other by his master's order correcting him) and by the extremity of the correction should chance to die, that his death shall not be accounted a felony, but the master (or that other person appointed by the master to punish him) be acquitted from molestation, since it cannot be presumed that premeditated malice (which alone makes murder a felony) should induce any man to destroy his own estate.

William Waller Hening, *Statutes at Large; Being a Collection of all the Laws of Virginia* (Richmond, Va.: Samuel Pleasants, 1809–23), Vol. II, pp. 170, 260, 266, 270

REGIONAL CONTRASTS

8 / "We walked in the woods amongst wild beasts... at least 20 miles,...expecting to die"

In 1680 Thomas Culpepper (1635–89), the royal governor of Virginia, traveled to Boston. On his way, he suffered a near-shipwreck and then had to walk through the Massachusetts wilds. Later, unhappy in Virginia, he left his post to live with his mistress in London. Due to his absenteeism he was removed from the governorship.

Culpepper's letter suggests significant demographic and economic contrasts between the Chesapeake region and New England. Because of its cold winters and low population density, seventeenth-century New England was perhaps the most healthful region in the world. After an initial period of high mortality, life expectancy quickly rose to levels comparable to our own. Men and women, on average, lived about sixty-five to seventy years, fifteen to twenty years longer than in England. One result was that seventeenth-century New England was the first society in history in which grandparents were common.

Descended largely from families who arrived during the 1630s, New England was a relatively stable society settled in compact towns and villages. It never developed any staple crop for export of any consequence, and about 90 to 95 percent of the population was engaged in subsistence farming.

The farther south one looks, however, the higher the death rate and the more unbalanced the sex ratio. In New England, men outnumbered women about three to two in the first generation. But in New Netherlands there were two men for every woman, and the ratio was six to one in the Chesapeake. Whereas New England's population became self-sustaining as early as the 1630s, New Jersey and Pennsylvania did not achieve this until the 1660s to the 1680s, and Virginia until after 1700. Compared to New England, Virginia was a much more mobile and unruly society.

In his letter, Culpepper alludes to Bacon's Rebellion in 1676, when friction among backcountry farmers, landless former indentured servants, and coastal planters in Virginia exploded in violence. Convinced that Virginia's colonial government had failed adequately to protect them against Indians, backcountry rebels, led by Nathaniel Bacon, a wealthy landowner, burned the capital at Jamestown, plundered their enemy's plantations, and offered freedom to any indentured servants who joined them. In the midst of the revolt, Bacon died of dysentery. Without his leadership, the uprising collapsed, but fear of servant unrest encouraged planters to replace white indentured servants with black slaves, set apart by a distinctive skin color. In 1660 there were fewer than a thousand slaves in Virginia and Maryland. But during the 1680s, their number tripled, rising from about forty-five hundred to twelve thousand.

Thomas Culpepper, September 20, 1680, to his sister, GLC 4298

I suppose it will not be unacceptable to you to hear from me and therefore I write this not[e] only to let you know that I am here. But that both my self and all with me are perfectly well, and that on the 10th Day of August that I left Virginia, every individual person that came over with me in the Oxford (soldiers as well as servants) were so too, except only Mr Jones, who had been very sick of the seasoning (though occassion'd first by drinking) but was on the mending hand also.... I was received here with all the militia viz. (twelve companies) in arms and have been highly treated beyond my expectation or desert. I am lodged to my wish, and find no difference between this place, and old England but only want of Company. I have not been sick one day since I saw you (w[hi]ch was more than I could say last summer.) Nor since taken any kind of physick, but for prevention of acute diseases have been twice let Blood and now and then fasted at nights. The last time of my bleeding was here the 10th Instant w[hi]ch I shall remember a good while for going out some time after though I was very well let blood, yet my arm being ill fixed, the orifice burst out bleeding afresh, w[hi]ch I did not so soon perceive but that I lost at Least 7 or 8 ounces of Blood, before I could have help to remedy it, but I verily believe it will prove to be the better for me. Besides this small accident, I have had nothing memorable during my whole voyage but the great danger I escaped on the 22th August (being Sunday) about 2 in the morning in coming hither that our ship run aground in unknown shoals with a great gust of wind, and lay beating two or three houres in a night as dark as a pit five miles from any land and every minute or rather knock, expecting our last doom, and that she would bulge and break in pieces but we being but on the tail of the land, and deep water to the leeward of us, the strength of the wind made us bear it over, and when we absolutely despaired of any help but our long boat, w[hi]ch could hardly have lived with six persons in that rough sea, when we were four and twenty, we found our selves afloat again miraculously I think verily. The owner of the ship was Mr Jarvis (that married our Cousin Nat Bacon the rebels Widow)...and conclude my direction under God Almighty was our preservat[i]on. I was resolved to stay no longer aboard but made my self be set on shore next morning (though on an unknown shore and not without some danger of drowning also) with J Polyn and The Cook, each of us with a gun, w[hi]ch proved to be 130 or 140 miles from hence. [T]hat day we walked in the woods amongst wild beasts, and more savage Indians at least 20 miles, when expecting to die in the woods or worse, we met an Englishman, who brought us to his cottage, and the next morning showed us the way to Sandwich (a small English Village in this country) where we were furnished with horses and a guide that with much adieu, through uncouth places, brought us hither at last, but our ship (in w[hi]ch was all my plate, goods, and furniture to a considerable value) did not arrive here till 10 dayes after us.

THE PILGRIMS ARRIVE IN PLYMOUTH

9 / "In 2 or 3 months time, half of their company died"

In sixteenth-century England, a religious movement known as Puritanism arose that wanted to purge the Church of England of all vestiges of Roman Catholicism. The Puritans objected to elaborate church hierarchies and to church ceremonies and practices that lacked biblical sanction and elevated priests above their congregation.

Late in the sixteenth century, some Puritans, known as separatists, became convinced that the Church of England was so corrupt that they withdrew from it and set up their own congregations. In 1609 a group of separatists (later known as Pilgrims) fled from England to Holland, eager to escape the corrupting wickedness around them. In his classic *History of Plimouth Plantation*, William Bradford (1588–1657), the Pilgrim leader, explains why the Pilgrims decided to leave the Netherlands in 1619 and establish a new community in the New World—as it turned out, in Massachusetts. In this selection he also describes how at Plymouth the Pilgrims were assisted by an Indian named Squanto.

Squanto's story illustrates the way in which the entire Atlantic world became integrated in wholly new ways during the seventeenth century and the impact this transformation had upon real-life individuals and communities. A Patuxet Indian born in about 1585, Squanto had grown up in a village of two thousand near where the Pilgrims settled in 1620. In 1614 Captain John Smith had passed through the region, and one of his lieutenants kidnapped Squanto and some twenty other Patuxets, planning to sell the Indians in the slave market of Málaga, Spain. After escaping to England, where he learned to speak English, Squanto returned to New England in 1619, only to discover that his village had been wiped out by a chicken pox epidemic—one of many epidemics that killed about 90 percent of New England's coastal Indian people between 1616 and 1618. Squanto then joined the Wampanoag tribe.

After the Pilgrims arrived, Squanto served as an interpreter between the Wampanoag leader, Massasoit, and the colonists and taught the English settlers how to plant Indian corn. He also tried to use his position to challenge Massasoit's leadership, informing neighboring tribes that the Pilgrims would infect them with disease and make war on them unless they gave him gifts. Squanto's scheme to use his connections with the Pilgrims to wrest power from Massaoit failed. In 1622, two years after the English settlers arrived, Squanto fell ill and died of an unknown disease.

WILLIAM BRADFORD, *History of Plimouth Plantation*, 1620–47

After they had lived in this city [Leyden in the Netherlands] about some 11 or 12 years...and sundry of them taken away by death; and many others began to be well stricken in years...those prudent governors, with sundry of the sagest members began both deeply to apprehend their present dangers, and wisely to foresee the future and think of timely remedy. In the agitation of their thoughts, and much discourse of things hereabout, at length they began to incline to this conclusion, of removal to some other place. Not out of any newfangledness, or other suchlike giddy humour by which men are oftentimes transported to their great hurt and danger, but for sundry weighty and solid reasons, some of the chief of which I will here briefly touch.

...Of all sorrows most heavily to be borne, was that many of the children...[as a result of] the great licentiousness of youth in that country, and the manifold temptations of the place, were drawn away by evil examples into extravagant and dangerous courses, getting the reins off their necks and departing from their parents. Some became soldiers, others took upon them far voyages by sea, and other some worse courses, tending to dissoluteness, and the danger of their souls, to the great grief of their parents and dishonor of God. So that they saw their posterity would be in danger to degenerate and be corrupted.

Lastly, (and which was not least) a great hope and inward zeal they had of laying some good foundation (or at least to make some way thereunto) for propagating and advancing the gospel of the Kingdom of Christ in those remote parts of the world....

Being thus passed the vast ocean and a sea of troubles before in their preparation... they had now [in Massachusetts] no friends to welcome them, nor inns to entertain or refresh their weather beaten bodies, no houses or much less towns to repair to, to seek for succor.... And for the season it was winter, and they that know the winters of that country know them to be sharp and violent and subject to cruel and fierce storms, dangerous to travel to known places, much more to search an unknown coast. Besides, what could they see but a hideous and desolate wilderness, full of wild beasts and wild men, and what multitudes there might be of them they knew not.... If they looked behind them, there was the mighty ocean which they had passed, and was now as a main bar and gulf to separate them from all the civil parts of the world....What could now sustain them but the spirit of God and his grace?...

But that which was most sad and lamentable was that, in 2 or 3 months time, half of their company died, especially in January and February, being the depth of winter and wanting houses and other comforts, being infected with the scurvy and other diseases which this long voyage and their inaccommodate condition had brought upon them. So, as there died sometimes 2 or 3 a day in the aforesaid time that, of 100 and odd persons, scarce 50 remained. And of these, in time of most distress, there was but 6 or 7 sound persons, who, to their great commendations be it spoken, spared no pains, night nor day, but with abundance of toil and hazard of their own health, fetched them wood, made them fires, dressed them meat, made their beds, washed their loathesome clothes, clothed and unclothed them; in a word, did all the homely and necessary offices for them which dainty and queasy stomachs cannot endure to hear named....

All this while the Indians came skulking about them and would sometimes show themselves aloof of, but when any approached near them, they would run away. And once they stole away their tools where they had been at work and were gone to dinner. But about the 16 of March a certain Indian came boldly amongst them and spoke to them in broken English, which they could well understand, but marveled at it. At length, they understood, by discourse with him, that he was not of these parts, but belonged to the eastern parts, where some English ships came to fish, with whom he was acquainted and could name sundry of them by their names, amongst whom he had got his language.... His name was Samasett. He told them also of another Indian whose name was Squanto, a native of this place who had been in England and could speak better English than himself. Being, after some time of entertainment and gifts, dismissed, a while after he came again, and 5 more with him, and they brought again all the tools that were stolen away before, and made way for the coming of their great sachem, called Massachoit, who, about 4 or 5 days after, came with the chief of his friends and other attendance, with the aforesaid Squanto. With whom, after friendly entertainment and some gifts given him, they made peace with him (which hath now continued this 24 years)....

After these things he returned to his place called Sowams, some 40 miles from this place, but Squanto continued with them and was their interpreter and was a special instrument sent of God for their good beyond their expectation. He directed them how to set their corn, where to take fish, and to procure other commodities, and was also their pilot to bring them to unknown places for their profit, and never left them till he died....

William Bradford, History of Plimouth Plantation (Boston: Wright & Potter, 1901), pp. 29–30, 32–35, 93–97, 109–12, 114–16

REASONS FOR PURITAN IMMIGRATION

10 / *"Most children...are perverted, corrupted, & utterly overthrown by the multitude of evil examples"*

No group has played a more pivotal role in shaping American values than the New England Puritans. The seventeenth-century Puritans contributed to our country's sense of mission, its work ethic, and its moral sensibility. Today, eight million Americans can trace their ancestry to the fifteen to twenty thousand Puritans who immigrated to New England between 1629 and 1640.

Few people, however, have been as frequently subjected to caricature and ridicule. The journalist H.L. Mencken defined Puritanism as "the haunting fear that someone, somewhere, might be happy." And particularly during the 1920s, the Puritans came to symbolize every cultural characteristic that "modern" Americans despised. The Puritans were often dismissed as drably clothed religious zealots who were hostile to the arts and were eager to impose their rigid "Puritanical" morality on the world around them.

This stereotypical view is almost wholly incorrect. Contrary to much popular thinking, the Puritans were not sexual prudes. Although they strongly condemned sexual relations outside of marriage—levying fines or even whipping those who fornicated, committed adultery or sodomy, or bore children outside of wedlock—they attached a high value to the marital tie. Nor did Puritans abstain from alcohol; even though they objected to drunkenness, they did not believe alcohol was sinful in itself. They were not opposed to artistic beauty; although they were suspicious of the theater and the visual arts, the Puritans valued poetry. Indeed, John Milton (1603–74), one of England's greatest poets, was a Puritan. Even the association of the Puritans with drab colors is wrong. They especially liked the colors red and blue.

Although the Puritans wanted to reform the world to conform to God's law, they did not set up a church-run state. Even though they believed that the primary purpose of government was to punish breaches of God's laws, few people were as committed as the Puritans to the separation of church and state. Not only did they reject the idea of establishing a system of church courts, they also forbade ministers from holding public office.

Perhaps most strikingly, the Puritans in Massachusetts held annual elections and extended the right to vote and hold office to all "freemen." Although this term was originally restricted to church members, it meant that a much larger proportion of the adult male population could vote in Massachusetts than in England itself—roughly 55 percent, compared to about 33 percent in England.

John Winthrop (1606–76) was a well-off landowner who served as governor of the

Massachusetts Bay Colony for much of its early history. Unlike the Pilgrims, Winthrop and the other Puritans who traveled to Massachusetts were not separatists. Rather than trying to flee the corruptions of a wicked world, they hoped to establish in New England a pure church that would offer a model for the churches in England. In this selection, Winthrop offers religious and economic arguments in support of moving to New England.

John Winthrop, 1629

Reasons for Puritan migration

1. It will be a service to the Church of great consequence to carry the Gospel into those parts of the world...& to raise a Bulwark against the kingdom of AnteChrist w[hi]ch the Jesuits labour to reare up in those parts.

2. All other churches of Europe are brought to desolation, & o[u]r sins, for w[hi]ch the Lord begins already to frown upon us & to cut us short, do threaten evil times to be coming upon us, & who knows, but that God hath provided this place to be a refuge for many whom he means to save out of the general calamity, & seeing the Church hath no place left to fly into but the wilderness, what better work can there be, then to go & provide tabernacles & food for her against she comes thither:

3. This Land grows weary of her Inhabitants, so as man, who is the most precious of all creatures, is here more vile & base then the earth we tread upon, & of less price among us than an horse or a sheep: masters are forced by authority to entertain servants, parents to maintain there own children, all towns complain of the burthen of their poore, though we have taken up many unnecessary yea unlawful trades to maintain them, & we use the authority of the Law to hinder the increase of o[u]r people....

4. The whole earth is the Lords garden & he hath given it to the Sons of men w[i]th a gen[era]l Commission: Gen: 1:28: increase & multiply, & replenish the earth & subdue it,...why then should we stand striving here for places of habitation...& in the meane time suffer a whole Continent as fruitful & convenient for the use of man to lie waste w[i]thout any improvement?

5. All arts & Trades are carried in that deceitful & unrighteous course, as it is almost impossible for a good & upright man to maintain his charge & live comfortably in any of them.

6. The fountaine of Learning & Religion are so corrupted as...most children (even the best wittes & of fairest hopes) are perverted, corrupted, & utterly overthrown by the multitude of evil examples....

R.C. Winthrop, *Life and Letters of John Winthrop* (Boston: Ticknor and Fick's, 1864), Vol. I, pp. 309-311

THE IDEA OF THE COVENANT

11 / "Some must be rich, some poor, some high and eminent in power... others mean and in subjection"

A central element in Puritan social and theological life was the notion of the covenant. All social relationships—between God and man, ministers and congregations, magistrates and members of their community, and men and their families—were envisioned in terms of a covenant or contract that rested on consent and mutual responsibilities.

Seventeenth-century New England churches were formed by a voluntary agreement among the members, who elected their own ministers. Similarly, the governments in Plymouth Colony (before it merged with Massachusetts) and in New Haven Colony (before it merged with Connecticut) were based on covenants. In each seventeenth-century New England colony, government itself rested on consent. Governors and legislative assemblies were elected, usually annually, by the freemen of the colony. In contrast, England appointed Virginia's governor, while in Maryland, the governor was appointed by the Calvert family, which owned the colony. Even marriage itself was regarded as a covenant. Connecticut granted nearly a thousand divorces between 1670 and 1799.

In this famous essay written aboard the *Arabella* during his passage to New England in 1630, John Winthrop (1606–76) proclaims that the Puritans had made a covenant with God to establish a truly Christian community, in which the wealthy were to show charity and avoid exploiting their neighbors while the poor were to work diligently. If they abided by this covenant, God would make them an example for the world—a "city upon a hill." But if they broke the covenant, the entire community would feel God's wrath.

In his stress on the importance of a stable community and reciprocal obligations between rich and poor, Winthrop implicitly criticized the disruptive social and economic changes that were rapidly transforming English society. As a result of the enclosure of traditional common lands, many rural laborers were thrown off the land, producing a vast floating population. As many as half of all village residents left their community each decade. In his call for tightly knit communities and families, Winthrop was striving to re-create a social ideal that was breaking down in England itself.

John Winthrop, "A Modell of Christian Charity," 1630

God Almighty in His most holy and wise providence hath so disposed of the Condition of mankind, as in all times some must be rich, some poor, some high and eminent in power and dignity; others mean and in subjection.

The Reason Hereof:...so that the rich and mighty might not eat up the poor, nor the poor and despised rise up against their superiors and shake off their yoke; second, in the regenerate in exercising His graces in them, as in the great ones their love, mercy, gentleness, temperance, &c.; in the poor and inferior sort, their faith, patience, obedience, &c....

When God gives us a special commission He wants it strictly observed in every article....

Thus stands the case between God and us. We are entered into covenant with Him for this work.... But if we neglect to observe these articles, which are the ends we have propounded, and—dissembling with our God—we shall embrace and prosecute our carnal intentions, seeking great things for ourselves and our posterity, the Lord will surely break out in wrath against us and be revenged on such a perjured people, and He will make us know the price of the breach of such a covenant.

Now the only way to avoid this shipwreck and to provide for our posterity is to follow the counsel of Micah: to do justly, to love mercy, to walk humbly with God. For this end, we must be knit together in this work as one man; we must hold each other in brotherly affection; we must be willing to rid ourself of our excesses to supply others' necessities; we must uphold a familiar commerce together in all meekness, gentleness, patience, and liberality. We must delight in each other, make others' conditions our own and rejoice together, mourn together, labor and suffer together, always having before our eyes our commission and common work, our community as members of the same body.

So shall we keep the unity of the spirit in the bond of peace....We shall find that the God of Israel is among us, and ten of us shall be able to resist a thousand of our enemies. The Lord will make our name a praise and glory, so that men shall say of succeeding plantations: "The Lord make it like that of New England." For we must consider that we shall be like a City upon a Hill; the eyes of all people are on us.

Massachusetts Historical Society Collections (Boston, 1838), pp. [31]–48.

SERVITUDE IN NEW ENGLAND

12 / "[Ill] reports is given of my Wyfe for beatinge the maid"

In his famous *Two Treatises on Government* (1690), the English philosopher John Locke (1632–1704) declared that in the beginning "all the world was America." By this he meant that freedom was people's natural condition and that even after they formed a social compact and subjected themselves to government, they retained certain fundamental rights. Ironically, despite his philosophy of inalienable rights, Locke was the last major philosopher to justify slavery.

Locke, like many Europeans before and after, associated the New World with freedom and equality. In colonial New England, however, many young people served a term of service prior to marriage. While frequently idealized as a family-like relationship in which a master and a mistress functioned as parents and teachers, service could also involve exploitation and resistance.

In the following selection, John Winter of Richmond Island, Maine, defends his wife against charges that she had cruelly beaten Priscilla, their servant. This selection not only informs us about the kinds of work that servants performed and the conditions under which they labored, but also suggests how a shortage of labor in New England made it difficult to regulate servants' lives.

John Winter, 1639

You write me of some yll reports is given of my Wyfe for beatinge the maid; yf a faire waye will not do yt, beatinge must, sometimes, uppon such Idlle girrells as she is. Yf you think yt fitte for my wyfe to do all the worke & the maide sitt still, she must forbeare her hands to strike, for then the worke wll ly undonn. She hath bin now 2 years 1/2 in the house, & I do not thinke she hath risen 20 times before my Wyfe hath bin up to Call her, and many tymes light the fire before she Comes out of her bed. She hath twize [runaway]...in the woodes, which we have bin faine to send all our Company to seeke. We Cann hardly keep her within doores after we a gonn to beed, except we Carry the key of the doore to beed with us. She never Could melke Cow nor goat since she Came hither.... She Cannot be trusted to serve a few piggs, but my wyfe most Commonly must be with her.

James Pinney Baxter, ed., *Trelawny Papers* (Portland, Me.: Hoyt, Fogg, and Donham, 1884)

MOUNTING CONFLICT WITH NATIVE AMERICANS

13 / *"For the number of our people...be in all about 4000 souls"*

In a letter written in Boston four years after its founding, John Winthrop (1606–76) explains the difficulties of establishing a self-sustaining, self-governing settlement and describes the colonists' mounting conflict with the Indians.

Compared to the Southeast, it was much more difficult for native peoples of New England to resist the encroaching English colonists. For one thing, the Northeast was much less densely populated. Epidemic diseases introduced by European fishermen and fur traders reduced the population of New England's coastal Indians about 90 percent by the early 1620s. Further, this area was fragmented politically into autonomous vil-

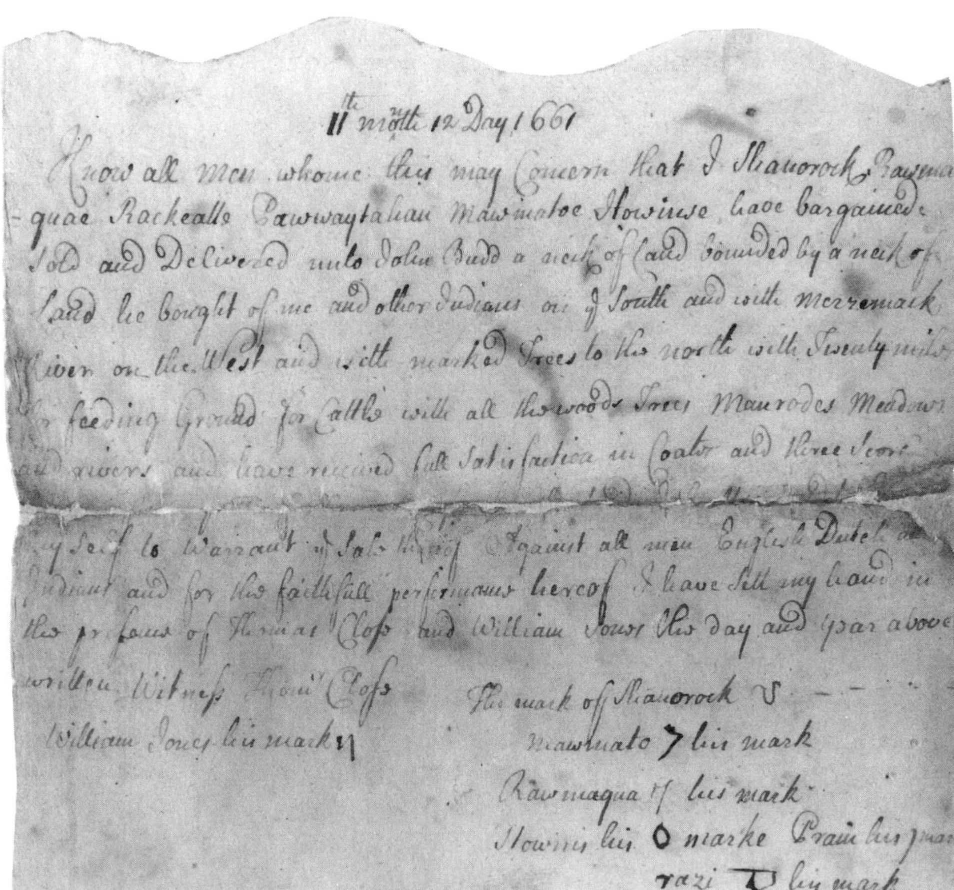
11th month 12 Day 1661

Know all men whome this may Concern that I Maurorock Rawmaquae Rackealls Pawwaytahan Mawmatoe Howinse have bargained sold and Delivered unto John Budd a neck of land bounded by a neck of land he bought of me and other Indians on the South and with Merremack River on the West and with marked Trees to the north with Twenty miles for feeding Ground for Cattle with all the woods Trees Maurodes Meadows and rivers and have received full Satisfaction in Coats and three Score [illegible] my Self to Warrant the Sale thereof Against all men English Dutch and Indians and for the faithfull performance hereof I have Sett my hand in the presence of Thomas Close and William Jones this day and year above written

Witness Thomas Close
William Jones his mark

The mark of Maurorock
Mawmato his mark
Rawmaqua his mark
Howinse his O marke Prain his mark
razi his mark

Manuscript document signed, Sale of land on Long Island Sound to English Quaker John Budd by Indian tribe, 1661/11/12. The Gilder Lehrman Collection, on deposit at the Pierpont Morgan Library. GLC 5305

lages with a long history of bitter tribal rivalries. Such factors allowed the Puritans to expand rapidly across New England.

Some groups, notably the Massachusetts, whose number had fallen from about 20,000 to just 750 in 1631, allied with the Puritans and agreed to convert to Christianity in exchange for military protection. But the migration of Puritan colonists into western Massachusetts and Connecticut during the 1630s provoked bitter warfare, especially with the Pequots, the area's most powerful people. In 1636, English settlers accused a Pequot of attacking ships and murdering several sailors; in revenge, they burned a Pequot settlement on what is now Block Island, Rhode Island. Pequot raids left about 30 colonists dead. A combined force of Puritans and Narragansett and Mohegan Indians retaliated by surrounding and setting fire to the main Pequot village on the Mystic River.

In his *History of Plimouth Plantation*, William Bradford described the destruction by fire of the Pequots' major village, in which at least 300 Indians were burned to death: "Those that escaped from the fire were slain with the sword; some hewed to pieces, others run threw with their rapiers [swords].... It was a fearful sight to see them thus frying in the fier, and the streams of blood quenching the same." The survivors were enslaved and shipped to the Caribbean. Altogether about 800 of 3,500 Pequots were killed during the Pequot War. In his epic novel *Moby Dick*, Herman Melville names his doomed whaling ship *The Pequod*, a clear reference to earlier events in New England.

John Winthrop, May 22, 1634, to Sir Nathaniel Rich, GLC 1105

That you are pleased among your many and weighty employments to spend so much serious thoughts and good wishes upon us, and the work of the Lord in our hands, I must needs acknowledge it among others the special favours of God towards us, and an undoubted testimony of your sincere Love towards us: which makes me the more careful to satisfy your desire, of being truly informed of our estate....You may please therefore to understand that first, for the number of our people, we never took any survey of them, nor do we intend it, except enforced through urgent occasion (David's example sticks somewhat with us) [some Protestants interpreted the Bible as forbidding a census] but I esteem them to be in all about 4000 souls and upward: in good health (for the most part) and well provided of all necessaries: so as (through the Lords special providence) there hath not died about 2 or 3 grown persons, and about so many Children all in the last year, it being very rare to hear of any sick of agues or other diseases, nor have I known of any quartan Ague amonge us since I came into the Country. For our subsistence here, the means hitherto hath been the yearly access of newcomers, who have supplied all our wants, for Cattle, and the fruits of our la[b]ours, as board, pale, smiths work etc: If this should fail, then we have other meanes which may supply us, as fish, viz: Cod, bass and herring, for which no place in the world exceeds us, if we can compass salt at a reasonable rate: our grounds likewise are apt for hemp and flax and rapeseeds, and all sorts of roots, pumpkins and other fruits, which for taste and wholesomeness far exceed those in England: our grapes also (wherewith the Country abounds) afford a good hard wine. Our ploughs go on with good success, we are like to have 20 at work next year: our lands are aptest for Rye and oats. Our winters are sharp and longe, I may reckon 4

> months for storing of cattle, but we find no difference whither they be housed or go abroad: our summers are somewhat more fervent in heat than in England. Our civil Government is mixt: the freemen choose the magistrates every year...and at 4 courts in the year 3 out of each town (there being 8 in all) do assist the magistrates in making laws, imposing taxes, and disposing of lands: our Juries are chosen by the freemen of everye town. Our Churches are governed by Pastors, Teachers, ruling Elders and Deacons, yet the power lies in the whole Congregation and not in the Presbytery [not in a larger council of churches] further than for order and precedence. For the natives, they are near all dead of the smallpox, so the Lord hath cleared our title to what we possess.

NATIVE AMERICANS AS ACTIVE AGENTS

14 / "The Monhiggin [Mohican]...refuseth to part with his prey"

Although most of New England's settlers were Puritans, these people did not agree about religious doctrine. Some, such as the Pilgrims of Plymouth, believed that the Church of England should be renounced, while others, such as Massachusetts Bay's leaders, felt that the English church could be reformed. Other issues that divided Puritans involved who could be admitted to church membership, who could be baptized, and who could takc communion.

Disagreements over religious beliefs led to the formation of a number of new colonies. In 1636 Thomas Hooker (1586–1647), a Cambridge, Massachusetts, minister, established the first English settlement in Connecticut. Convinced that government should rest on free consent, he extended voting rights beyond church members. Two years later, another Massachusetts group founded New Haven colony in order to combat moral laxness by setting strict standards for church membership and basing its laws on the Old Testament. This colony was incorporated by Connecticut in 1662.

In 1635 Massachusetts Bay colony banished Roger Williams (1604–83), a Salem minister, for claiming that the civil government had no right to force people to worship in a particular way. Williams had even rejected the ideal that civil authorities could compel observance of the Sabbath. Equally troubling, he argued that Massachusetts's royal charter did not justify taking Indian land. Instead, Williams argued, the colonists had to negotiate fair treaties and pay for the land.

Instead of returning to England, Williams headed toward Narragansett Bay, where he founded Providence, which later became the capital of Rhode Island. From 1654 to 1657 Williams was president of Rhode Island colony.

In Rhode Island, Williams found allies among certain Indian tribes. Like other colonial leaders, he would play off different tribes against one another (not unlike the way tribes would play off the French and English). The Sachem (chief) of the Mohican Indians, Uncas, allied himself with English settlers in Massachusetts but sometimes fought other tribes allied to the English, such as the Narragansetts. In this letter Williams writes to Winthrop about Uncas holding three Narragansetts ("Nayantaquits") and five "friends," apparently captured in battle or raiding. Miantonomi of the Narragansetts, an ally of the English and friend of Williams, was sent to get the prisoners.

Prior to this letter, Miantonomi had received permission from the English to fight Uncas. In 1643 Governor Winthrop would allow Uncas to execute Miantonomi, whom he had defeated in battle. Uncas managed to defeat neighboring tribes in war and thus helped to more firmly establish English hegemony in New England.

The nineteenth-century American novelist James Fenimore Cooper (1789–1851) would give the name Uncas to the title character in his classic tale of Indian-white friendship and conflict, *The Last of the Mohicans*, which he set a century later in time, amid the French and Indian War.

Roger Williams, July 6, 1640, to Governor John Winthrop of Massachusetts, GLC 1590

As I lately advertized to Mr. Gov[erno]r...Consultations so Continue, about the 3 Nayantaquits {Narragansetts} prisoners with 5 friends at Qunniticut....

The Monhiggin {Mohican} Sachim {leader} Onkas refuseth to part with his prey. And whereas, Miantunnomu {Miantonomi, a Narragansett ally of the English and friend of Williams} was going up to Monhiggin himselfe with a Sufficient Company for three Runnawayes, Onkas {Uncas} sent word th[a]t it was yr Wo[rshi]ps plot to bring him into [th]e Snare at Monhiggin that there [th]e Quinnitcut English might fall upon him.

Miantunnomu still promiseth me to Come over to you, & his purpose (to his utmost) to bring them with him: my occasions lead me within these 4 or 5 dayes to Qunnipiug when (the Lord so permitting): I purpose {propose} to goe up to Monhiggin & try the utmost my Selfe: The yssue {issue} of all is in th[a]t Everlasting Hand, in which is o[u]r Breath & o[u]r Wayes.

PURITAN ECONOMICS

15 / *"Some false principles are these"*

The New England Puritans, like many Americans before the nineteenth century, rejected the idea that prices should fluctuate freely according to the laws of supply and demand. Instead, they believed that there was a just wage for every trade and a just price for every good. Charging more than this just amount constituted "oppression," and authorities sought by law to prevent prices or wages from rising above a customary level.

Yet within a few decades of settlement, the Puritan blueprint of an organic, close-knit community, a stable, self-sufficient economy, and a carefully calibrated social hierarchy began to fray as New England became increasingly integrated into the Atlantic economy. To try to maintain traditional social distinctions, Massachusetts Bay colony in 1651 adopted a sumptuary law, which spelled out which persons could wear certain articles of clothing and jewelry.

But as early as the second half of the seventeenth century, a growing number of New Englanders were engaged in an intricate system of Atlantic commerce, selling fish, furs, and timber not only in England but also throughout Catholic Europe, investing in shipbuilding and transporting tobacco, wine, sugar, and slaves. Particularly important was trade with the West Indies and the Atlantic islands off of northwestern Africa. Such trade was highly competitive and risky, but over time it gradually created distinct classes of merchants, tradesmen, and commercially-oriented farmers.

In this document, John Winthrop refers to an episode in 1639 when Robert Keayne (1595–1656), a Boston merchant, was tried, convicted, and fined one hundred pounds sterling for selling imported goods for higher prices than those set by the Massachusetts General Court. In his will, Keayne protested a censure he received from his own church. "If they should have cast me out of the church 20 times for this," he wrote, "I should have chosen it rather than to have confessed myself guilty."

John Winthrop, 1640

After the court had censured him [Puritan merchant Robert Keaynes], the church of Boston called him also in question, where (as before he had done in court) he did, with tears, acknowledge and bewail his covetous and corrupt heart, yet making some excuse for many of the particulars, which were charged upon him, as partly by pretence of ignorance of the true price of some wares, and chiefly by being misled by some false principles, as, 1. That, if a man lost in one commodity, he might help himself in the price of another. That if, through want of skill or other occasion, his commodity cost him more than the price of the market in England, he might then sell it for more than the price of the market in New England &c. These things gave occasion to Mr. [John] Cotton [a leading Puritan minister], in his publick exercise the next lecture day, to lay open the errour of such false principles, and to give some rules of direction in the case.

Some false principles are these:

1. That a man might sell as dear as he can, and buy as cheap as he can.

2. If a man lose by casualty of sea, &c. in some of his commodities, he may raise the price of the rest.

3. That he may sell as he bought, though he paid too dear, &c. and though the commodity be fallen, &c.

4. That, as a man may take the advantage of his own skill or ability, so he may of another's ignorance or necessity.

John Winthrop, *The History of New England from 1630 to 1649* (Boston, Little, Brown, 1853), Vol. I, pp. 313–17

KING PHILIP'S WAR

16 / *"Various are the reports...of the causes of the present Indian warre"*

For nearly half a century following the Pequot War, New England was free of major Indian wars. During this period, the region's indigenous people declined rapidly in numbers and suffered severe losses of land and cultural independence. During the first three quarters of the seventeenth century, New England's indigenous population fell from 140,000 to 10,000, while the English population grew to 50,000. Meanwhile, the New England Puritans launched a concerted campaign to convert the Indians to Protestantism. John Eliot, New England's leading missionary, convinced about 2,000 to live in "praying towns," where they were expected to adopt white customs. New England Indians were also forced to accept the legal authority of colonial courts.

Faced with death, disease, and cultural disintegration, many of New England's native peoples decided to strike back. In 1675 the chief of the Pokanokets, Metacomet (whom the English called King Philip), forged a military alliance including about two thirds of the region's Indians. In 1675 he led an attack on Swansea, Massachusetts. Over the next year, both sides raided villages and killed hundreds of victims. Twelve of ninety New England towns were destroyed.

The last major Indian war in New England, King Philip's War was the most destructive conflict, relative to the size of the population, in American history. Five percent of New England's white population was killed—a higher proportion than Germany, Britain, or the United States lost during World War II. Indian casualties were far higher; perhaps 40 percent of New England's Indian population was killed or fled the region. When the war was over, the power of New England's Indians was broken. The region's remaining Indians would live in small, scattered communities, serving as the colonists' servants, slaves, or tenants.

In 1675, England dispatched Edward Randolph (1632–1703) to determine the conflict's causes and assess the damage. As Randolph notes, the government of Puritan Massachusetts viewed the Indian attacks as punishment for their own sins. This idea of divine punishment derives from the Old Testament, which continually interprets attacks on the ancient Israelites as punishment for sin. This provided a model for the Puritans and their descendants down to Abraham Lincoln's Second Inaugural Address, which pictured the Civil War as God's punishment on the American people for the sin of slaveholding.

Edward Randolph, 1675

Various are the reports and conjectures of the causes of the present Indian warre. Some impute it to an imprudent zeal in the magistrates of Boston to christianize those heathen before they were civilized and enjoining them the strict observation of their laws, which, to a people so rude and licentious, hath proved even intolerable, and that the more, for that while the magistrates, for their profit, put the laws severely in execution against the Indians, the people, on the other side, for lucre and gain, entice and provoke the Indians to the breach thereof, especially to drunkenness, to which those people are so generally addicted that they will strip themselves to their skin to have their fill of rum and brandy....

Some believe there have been vagrant and jesuitical priests, who have made it their business, for some years past, to go from Sachem to Sachem, to exasperate the Indians against the English and to bring them into a confederacy, and that they were promised supplies from France and other parts to extirpate the English nation out of the continent of America. Others impute the cause to some injuries offered to the Sachem Philip; for he being possessed of a tract of land called Mount Hope...some English had a mind to dispossess him thereof, who never wanting one pretence or other to attain their end, complained of injuries done by Philip and his Indians to their stock and cattle, whereupon

Philip was often summoned before the magistrate, sometimes imprisoned, and never released but upon parting with a considerable part of his land.

But the government of the Massachusetts...do declare these are the great evils for which God hath given the heathen commission to rise against them.... For men wearing long hair and perewigs made of womens hair; for women...cutting, curling and laying out the hair.... For profaneness in the people not frequenting their meetings....

With many such reasons...the English have contributed much to their misfortunes, for they first taught the Indians the use of arms, and admitted them to be present at all their musters and trainings, and shewed them how to handle, mend and fix their muskets, and have been furnished with all sorts of arms by permission of the government....

The loss to the English in the several colonies, in their habitations and stock, is reckoned to amount to 150,000 l. [pounds sterling] there having been about 1200 houses burned, 8000 head of cattle, great and small, killed, and many thousand bushels of wheat, pease and other grain burned...and upward of 3000 Indians men women and children destroyed.

Albert B. Hart, ed., *American History Told by Contemporaries* (New York: Macmillan 1897), Vol. 1, pp. 458–60

STRUGGLES FOR POWER

17 / "Take, kill, & destroy [th]e enemy without limitation of place or time"

Two parallel struggles for power took place in eastern North America during the late seventeenth and early and mid-eighteenth centuries. One was an imperial struggle between France and England. Four times between 1689 and 1763, France, England, and their Indian allies engaged in struggles for dominance. The other was a power struggle among Indian groups, pitting the Iroquois and various Algonquian-speaking peoples against one another.

These two struggles were closely interconnected. Both France and England were dependent on Indian peoples for furs and military support. The English outnumbered the French by about twenty to one during this period, and therefore the survival of French Canada depended on the support of Algonquian-speaking nations. For Native Americans, alliances with England and France were sources of wealth, providing presents, supplies, ammunition, and captives whom the Indians either adopted or sold. Such alliances also kept white settlers from encroaching on Indian lands.

During times of peace, however, Indians found it much more difficult to play England and France off against each other. It was during the period of peace in Europe that followed the Treaty of Utrecht in 1713 that England and France destroyed the Natchez, the Fox, and the Yamasee Nations.

In this letter, Thomas Danforth (1622–99), who had served as deputy governor of Massachusetts Bay colony and president of Maine, refers to King William's War (1689–97), the first French and Indian War. Like Queen Anne's War (1702–13) and King George's War (1744–48), two later French and Indian wars, this conflict grew out of a struggle in Europe. After Indians allied to the English raided French settlements near

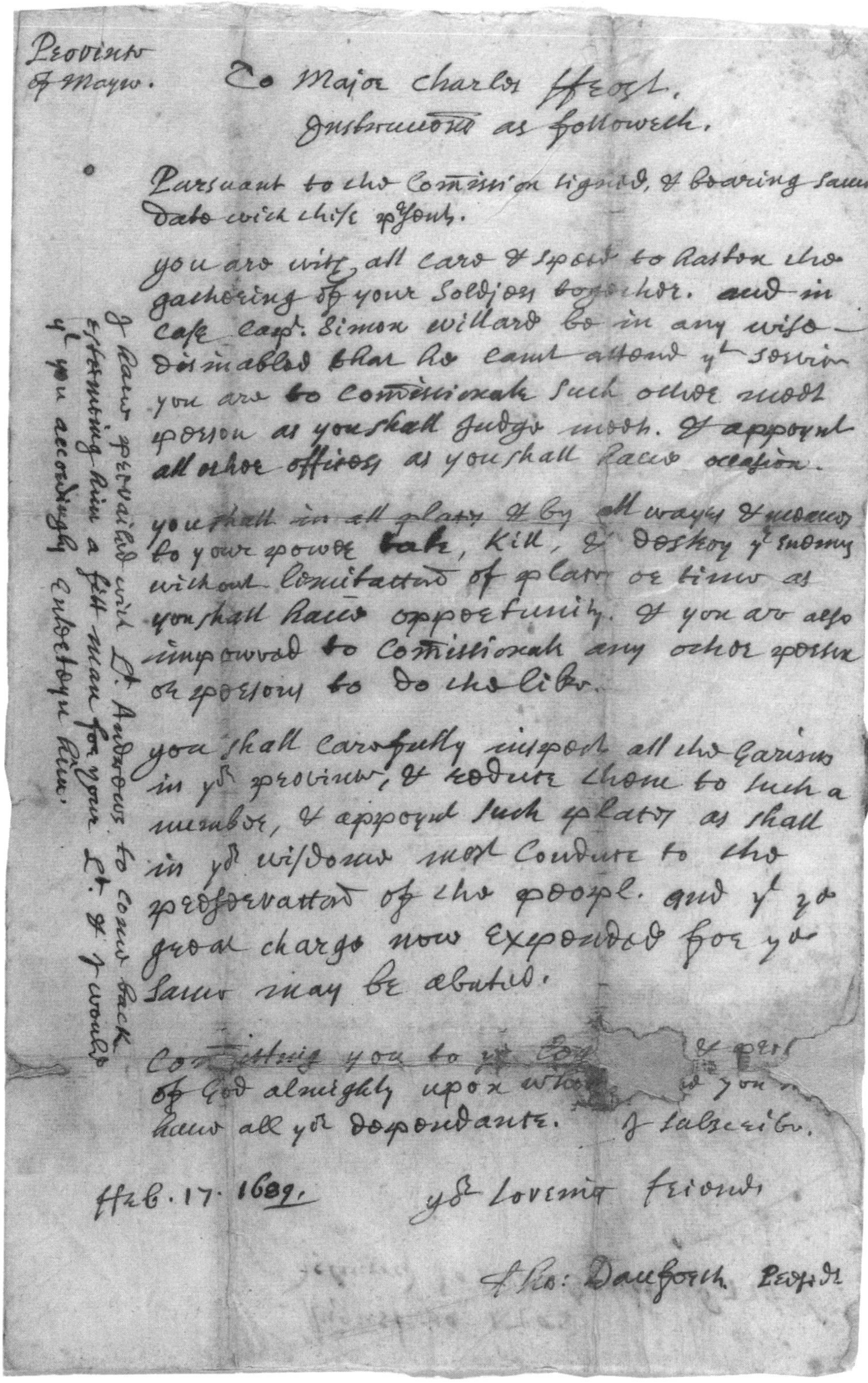
Province of Mayne.

To Major Charles ffrost.
Instructions as followeth.

Pursuant to the Commission signed, & bearing same date with this p[re]sents.

you are with all care & speed to hasten the gathering of your Soldiers together. and in case Capt. Simon Willard be in any wise disinabled that he cannot attend ye service you are to Commissionate such other meet person as you shall judge meet. & appoint all other officers as you shall have occasion.

you shall in all places & by all wayes & meanes to your power take, kill, & destroy ye enemy without limitation of place or time as you shall have opportunity. & you are also impowred to Commissionate any other person or persons to do the like.

you shall carefully inspect all the Garisons in yor province, & reduce them to such a number, & appoint such places as shall in yor wisdome most conduce to the preservation of the people. and yt ye great charge now expended for ye same may be abated.

Committing you to ye [illegible] & [illegible] of God almighty upon who[m] [illegible] you may have all yor dependance. I subscribe.

Feb. 17. 1689. yor Loveing friend

Tho: Danforth Presidt

I have prevailed with Lt. Andrews to come back esteeming him a fitt man for your Lt. & I would yt you accordingly entertayne him.

Thomas Danforth. Autograph letter signed, to Charles Frost, 1689/02/17. The Gilder Lehrman Collection, on deposit at the Pierpont Morgan Library. GLC 5580

Montreal, the French and their Indian allies retaliated by staging raids on New York and New England. Two English assaults on the province of Québec ended in failure, and a stalemate ensued. The war was finally ended in 1697 by the Treaty of Ryswick, which returned to England and France all territory each side had lost during the war.

THOMAS DANFORTH, FEBRUARY 17, 1689, GLC 5580

You are [to take] all care & go to Boston [to] gather of your soldiers together....You shall in all glory & by all ways & means to your power take, kill, & destroy [th]e enemy without limitation of place or time as you shall have opportunity, & you are also empowered to commission any other person...to do the like.

You shall carefully inspect all the garrisons in your purview, & reduce them to such a number, & appoint such [officers] as shall do most to the preservation of the people....

AN INDIAN SLAVE WOMAN CONFESSES TO WITCHCRAFT

18 / *"Tituba an Indian woman [was] brought before us... upon Suspicion of witchcraft"*

In 1691 a group of girls in Salem, Massachusetts, accused an Indian slave named Tituba of witchcraft. Tituba's confession ignited a witchcraft scare that left 19 men and women hanged, one man pressed to death, and more than 150 other people in prison awaiting trial.

For two decades New England had been in the grip of severe social stresses. A 1675 conflict with the Indians known as King Philip's War had resulted in more deaths relative to the size of the population than any other war in American history. A decade later, in 1685, King James II's government revoked the Massachusetts charter. A new governor, Sir Edmund Andros, sought to unite New England, New York, and New Jersey into a single Dominion of New England. He also tried to abolish elected colonial assemblies, restrict town meetings, and impose direct control over militia appointments, and permitted the first public celebration of Christmas in Massachusetts. After William III replaced James II as king of England in 1689, Andros's government was overthrown, but Massachusetts was required to eliminate religious qualifications for voting and to extend religious toleration to sects such as the Quakers. The late seventeenth century also marked a sudden increase in the number of black slaves in New England.

The 1637 Pequot War produced New England's first known slaves. While many Indian men were transported into slavery in the West Indies, many Indian women and children were used as household slaves in New England. The 1641 Massachusetts Body of Liberties recognized perpetual and hereditary servitude (although in 1643, a Massachusetts court sent back to Africa some slaves who had been kidnapped by New England sailors and brought to America). Tituba was one of the growing number of slaves imported from the West Indies.

Probably an Arawak born in northeastern South America, Tituba had been enslaved in Barbados before being brought to Massachusetts in 1680. Her master, Samuel Parris, had been a credit agent for sugar planters in Barbados before becoming a minister in Salem, Massachusetts. In late 1691 two girls in Parris's household and two girls from nearby households began to exhibit strange physical symptoms, including convulsions and choking. To counteract these symptoms, Tituba made a "witchcake" out of rye meal and urine. This attempt at counter-magic led to Tituba's arrest for witchcraft. She and two other women—Sarah Good and Sarah Osborne—were accused of bewitching the girls. Tituba confessed, but the other two women protested their innocence. Good was executed; Osborne died in prison.

As Elaine G. Breslaw has shown, Tituba's confession that she had consorted with Satan and attended a witches' coven fueled fears of a diabolical plot to infiltrate and destroy Salem's godly community. In her testimony, Tituba drew upon Indian and African, as well as English, notions of the occult.

Tituba later recanted her confession, saying that she had given false testimony to save her life. She claimed "that her Master did beat her and otherways abuse her, to make her confess and accuse...her Sister-Witches."

Salem Village, March 1st 1691

Tituba an Indian woman brought before us by Const[able] Joseph Herrick of Salem upon Suspicion of witchcraft by her committed according to [th]e complaint of Jos[eph] Hutcheson and Thomas Putnam &c of Salem Village as appears per warrant granted Salem 29 Febr[uar]y 1691/2. Tituba upon examination and after some denial acknowledged the matter of fact according to her examination given in more fully will appear, and who also charged Sarah Good and Sara Osburne with the same....

(H) Tituba what evil spirit have you familiarity with.

(T) None.

(H) Why do you hurt these children.

(T) I do not hurt them.

(H) Who is it then.

(T) The devil for ought I know.

(H) Did you never see the devil.

(T) The devil came to me and bid me serve him.

(H) Who have you seen.

(T) Four women sometimes hurt the children.

(H) Who were they.

(T) Goode Osburn and Sarah Good and I do not know who the others were. Sarah Good and Osburne would have me hurt the children but I would not. She further saith there was a tall man of Boston that she did see.

(H) When did you see them.

(T) Last night at Boston.

(H) what did they say to you.

(T) They said hurt the children

(H) And did you hurt them

(T) No there is 4 women and one man they hurt the children and they lay upon me and they tell me if I will not hurt the children they will hurt me.

(H) But did you not hurt them

(T) Yes but I will hurt them no more.

(H) Are you not sorry you did hurt them.

(T) Yes.

(H) And why then doe you hurt them.

(T) They say hurt children or wee will doe worse to you.

(H) What have you seen.

[T] A man came to me and say serve me.

(H) What service.

(T) Hurt the children and last night there was an appearance that said kill the children and if I would not go on hurting the children they would do worse to me.

(H) What is this appearance you see.

(T) Sometimes it is like a hog and sometimes like a great dog, this appearance she saith she did see 4 times.

(H) What did it say to you?

(T) ...The black dog said serve me but I said I am afraid he said if I did not he would doe worse to me.

(H) What did you say to it.

(T) I will serve you no longer. Then he said he would hurt me and then he looked like a man and threatens to hurt me, she said that this man had a yellow bird that kept with him and he told me he had more pretty things that he would give me if I would serve him.

(H) What were these pretty things.

(T) He did not show me them.

(H) What also have you seen

(T) Two rats, a red rat and a black rat.

(H) What did they say to you.

(T) They said serve me.

(H) When did you see them.

(T) Last night and they said serve me, but I said I would not

(H) What service.

(T) She said hurt the children.

(H) Did you not pinch Elizabeth Hubbard this morning

(T) The man brought her to me and made me pinch her

(H) Why did you goe to Thomas Putnams last night and hurt his child.

(T) They pull and hall me and make me goe

(H) And what would have you doe.

[T] Kill her with a knife.

Fuller and others said at this time when the child saw these persons and was tormented by them that she did complain of a knife, that they would have her cut her head off with a knife.

(H) How did you go?

(T) We ride upon stickes and are there presently.

(H) Doe you goe through the trees or over them.

(T) We see nothing but are there presently.

[H] Why did you not tell your master.

[T] I was afraid they said they would cut of[f] my head if I told.

[H] Would you not have hurt others if you co[u]ld.

[T] They said they would hurt others but they could not

[H] What attendants hath Sarah Good.

[T] A yellow bird and shee would have given me one.

[H] What meate did she give it?

[T] It did suck her between her fingers.

[H] Did not you hurt Mr Currins child?

[T] Goode good and goode Osburn told that they did hurt Mr Currens child and would have had me hurt him too, but I did not.

[H] What hath Sarah Osburn?

[T] Yellow dog, she had a thing with a head like a woman with 2 legges, and wings. Abigail Williams that lives with her Uncle Parris said that she did see the same creature, and it turned into the shape of Goode Osburn.

[H] What else have you seen with Osburn?

[T] Another thing, hairy it goes upright like a man it hath only 2 legges.

[H] Did you not see Sarah Good upon Elizabeth Hubbard, last Saturday?

[T] I did see her set a wolfe upon her to afflict her, the persons with this maid did say that she did complain of a wolfe.

(T) She further saith that shee saw a cat with good at another time.

[H] What cloathes doth the man go in?

[T] He goes in black clothes a tall man with white hair I thinke.

[H] How doth the woman go?

[T] In a white hood and a black hood with a top knot.

[H] Doe you see who it is that torments these children now.

[T] Yes it is Goode Good, shee hurts them in her own shape

[H] And who is it that hurts them now.

[T] I am blind now. I cannot see.

William E. Woodward, comp., *Records of Salem Witchcraft* (Roxbury, Mass., Priv. print for W.E. Woodward 1864), Vol. I, pp. 11–48.

19 / *"The devil is now making one attempt more upon us"*

Most people in the early modern world believed in the existence of witches who gained supernatural power by signing a pact with Satan. The Salem witch trials were not unique events. In continental Europe, where witch-hunts were much more common than in America, thousands of people were executed—often isolated and impoverished older women, who were regarded as a drain on community resources. As late as 1787, outside of Independence Hall, where the framers were drafting the U.S. Constitution, a Philadelphia mob killed an accused witch.

In the half century before the Salem trials, more than eighty people were put on trial for witchcraft in Massachusetts and Connecticut alone. During the seventeenth century, some thirty-two people were executed for witchcraft in the American colonies.

What was unique about the Salem witch trials was the number of people who were accused and convicted. In previous witch trials, judges had imposed high standards of proof, which resulted in a majority of the accused being acquitted. But when England revoked Massachusetts's charter in 1685, it threw the judicial system into disarray. The special court set up in Salem allowed the use of "spectral evidence": testimony from victims of a vision that they had of the person who was tormenting them. Further, the court permitted the use of psychological pressure and even torture to obtain confessions and ruled that anyone who confessed, identified fellow witches, and repented would go free.

The Salem witch scare had complex social roots. It drew upon preexisting rivalries and disputes within the rapidly growing Massachusetts port town: between urban and rural residents; between wealthier commercially-oriented merchants and subsistence-oriented farmers; and between Congregationalists and other religious denominations: Anglicans, Baptists, and Quakers. The witch trials offer a window into the anxieties and social tensions that accompanied New England's increasing integration into the Atlantic economy.

For the educated Puritan elite, there was double irony in the fact that the witch scare erupted in Salem. The word "salem" means peace, and the town's founders had hoped that Salem would be a village of peace. Further, they had drawn "salem" from Jerusalem, hoping that this new village would serve as a foundation for a new Jerusalem.

In this selection, written a year after the Salem episode, Cotton Mather (1663–1728), one of New England's leading Puritan theologians, defends the trials, depicting New England as a battleground where the forces of God and the forces of Satan will clash. But guilt over this grisly episode gradually ate into the New England conscience, and in 1697 Massachusetts held a public fast to mourn the blood that had been unjustly shed.

A descendant of one of the witchcraft judges, the novelist Nathaniel Hawthorne (1804–64), dwelled in his writings on hidden guilt—sexual, moral, and psychological. In an early tale, he wrote: "In the depths of every heart, there is a tomb and dungeon, though the lights, the music, the revelry above us may lead us to forget their existence, and the...prisoners whom they hide." One might speculate that his preoccupation with the complexities of human motivation and his lack of faith in progress and human perfectability stemmed in part from his awareness of his ancestor's involvement in the witchcraft affair.

COTTON MATHER, *The Wonders of the Invisible World*, 1693, GLC 264

The New Englanders are a people of God settled in those, which were once the devil's territories. And it may easily be supposed that the devil was exceedingly disturbed when he perceived such a people here accomplishing the promise of old made unto our Blessed Jesu—that He should have the utmost parts of the earth for His possession....

The devil is now making one attempt more upon us; an attempt more difficult, more surprising, more snarled with unintelligible circumstances than any that we have hitherto encountered; an attempt so critical, that if we get well through, we shall soon enjoy halcyon days, with all the vultures of hell trodden under our feet. He has wanted his incarnate legions to persecute us, as the people of God have in the other hemisphere been persecuted; he has, therefore, drawn his more spiritual ones to make an attack upon us. We have been advised by some credible Christians yet alive that a malefactor, accused of witchcraft as well as murder, and executed in this place more than forty years ago, did then give notice of a horrible *plot* against the country by *witchcraft*, and a foundation of *witchcraft* then laid, which if it were not seasonably discovered would probably blow up and pull down all the churches in the country.

And we have now with horror seen the discovery of such a *witchcraft*! An army of devils is horribly broke in upon the place which is the center, and after a sort, the first-born of our English settlements. And the houses of the good people there are filled with the doleful shrieks of their children and servants, tormented by invisible hands, with tortures altogether preternatural. After the mischiefs there endeavored, and since in part conquered, the terrible plague of evil angels has made its progress into some other places, where other persons have been in like manner diabolically handled.

These our poor afflicted neighbors, quickly, after they become infected and infested with these demons, arrive to a capacity of discerning those which they conceive the shapes of their troublers; and notwithstanding the great and just suspicion that the demons might impose the shapes of innocent persons in their spectral exhibitions upon the sufferers (which may prove no small part of the witch plot in the issue), yet many of the persons thus represented, being examined, several of them have been convicted of a very damnable witchcraft. Yea, more than twenty-one have confessed that they have signed unto a book, which the devil showed them, and negated in his hellish design of bewitching and ruining our land....

Now, by these confessions it is agreed that the devil has made a dreadful knot of witches in the country, and by the help of witches has dreadfully increased that knot; that these witches have driven a trade of commissioning their confederate spirits to do all sorts of mischiefs to the neighbors; whereupon there have ensued such mischievous consequences upon the bodies and estates of the neighborhood as could not otherwise be accounted for; yea that at prodigious witch meetings the wretches have proceeded so far as to concert and consult the methods of rooting out the Christian religion from this country, and setting up instead of it perhaps a more gross diabolism than ever the world saw before. And yet it will be a thing little short of miracle if, in so spread a business as this, the devil should not get in some of his juggles to confound the discovery of the rest.

THE SIN OF SLAVEHOLDING

20 / "Liberty is in real value next to life"

On January 14, 1697, Samuel Sewall (1652–1730), a leading merchant and one of the Salem judges, publicly repented his role in the witch trials. Three years later he published one of the first antislavery tracts in American history.

In colonial America there was no sharp division between a slave South and a free-labor North. New England was involved in the Atlantic slave trade from the mid-1600s to the 1780s. In the years preceding the American Revolution, slavery could be found in all the American colonies. By the mid-eighteenth century, slaves made up almost 8 percent of the population in Pennsylvania, 40 percent in Virginia, and 70 percent in South Carolina. During the second quarter of the eighteenth century, a fifth of Boston's families owned slaves; and in New York City in 1746, slaves performed about a third of the city's manual labor.

In the North, slaves were used in both agricultural and nonagricultural employment, especially in highly productive farming and stock-raising for the West Indian market in southern Rhode Island, Long Island, and New Jersey. Slaves not only served as household servants for an urban elite—cooking, doing laundry, and cleaning stables—they also worked in rural industry, in saltworks, iron works, and tanneries. In general, slaves were not segregated into distinct racial ghettos; instead, they lived in back rooms, lofts, attics, and alley shacks. Many slaves fraternized with lower-class whites. But in the mid-eighteenth century, racial separation increased as a growing proportion of the white working class began to express bitter resentment over competition from slave labor. The African-American response in the North to increased racial antagonism and discrimination was apparent in a growing consciousness and awareness of Africa and the establishment of separate African churches and benevolent societies.

In this extract, Sewall critically examines the rationalizations that were used to justify slavery. His tract's title refers to the Old Testament story in which Joseph's brothers sold him into slavery.

Samuel Sewall, *The Selling of Joseph: A Memorial*, 1700

Forasmuch as liberty is in real value next to life, none ought to part with it themselves, or deprivate others of it, but upon most mature consideration.

The numerousness of slaves at this day in the province, and the uneasiness of them under their slavery, has put many upon thinking whether the foundation of it be firmly and well laid, so as to sustain the vast weight that is built upon it. It is most certain that all men, as they are the sons of Adam, are coheirs, and have equal right unto liberty, and all other outward comforts of life....

Originally and naturally, there is no such thing as slavery. Joseph was rightfully no more a slave to his brethren than they were to him; and they had no more authority to sell him than they had to slay him....

And all things considered, it would conduce more to the welfare of the province to have white servants for a term of years than to have slaves for life. Few can endure to hear of a Negro's being made free, and indeed they can seldom use their freedom well; yet their continual aspiring after their forbidden liberty renders them unwilling servants. And there is such a disparity in their conditions, color, and hair that they can never embody with us and grow up into orderly families, to the peopling of the land, but still remain in our body politic as a kind of extravasat[ed] blood.... Moreover, it is too well known what temptations masters are under to connive at the fornication of their slaves, lest they should be obliged to find them wives, or pay their fines....

It is likewise most lamentable to think, how in taking Negroes out of Africa and selling of them here, that which God has joined together men do boldly rent asunder—

men from their wives, parents from their children. How horrible is the uncleanness, mortality, if not murder, that the ships are guilty of that bring great crowds of these miserable men and women. Methinks, when we are bemoaning the barbarous usage of our friends and kinfolk in Africa, it might not be unseasonable to inquire whether we are not culpable in forcing the Africans to become slaves among ourselves. And it may be a question whether all the benefit received by Negro slaves will balance the account of cash laid out upon them, and for the redemption of our own enslaved friends out of Africa, besides all the persons and estates that have perished there.

Objection 1. These blackamoors are of the posterity of Ham, and therefore under the curse of slavery (Gen. 9:25–27).

Answer.... If this ever was a commission, how do we know but that it is long since out of date?... But it is possible that by cursory reading this text may have been mistaken....

Objection 2. The Negroes are brought out of a pagan country into places where the Gospel is preached.

Answer. Evil must not be done that good may come of it....

Objection 3. The Africans have wars one with another. Our ships bring lawful captives taken in those wars.

Answer.... If they be between town and town, provincial or national, every war is upon one side unjust. An unlawful war can't make lawful captives. And by receiving, we are in danger to promote and partake in their barbarous cruelties.

Samuel Sewall, *The Selling of Joseph: A Memorial* (Boston: Printed by Bartholomew Green and John Allen, 1700).

ENGLISH LIBERTIES

21 / "The Constitution of our English Government [is] the best in the World"

In 1556 John Ponet (1516–56), an English writer, pointedly warned Mary, queen of Scots, that she ruled over "a bodie of free men and not of bondemen" and that she could not "give or sell them as slaves and bondemen." The idea that the English, unlike their counterparts on the European continent, had more rights, greater security of property, and a higher standard of living than those who wore "wooden shoes" was already a common viewpoint in the sixteenth century. But the concept of "English liberties" took on added resonances as a result of the English Civil War of the mid-seventeenth century.

During the seventeenth century, members of Parliament drew upon the Magna Carta—a charter signed by King John in 1215 that granted many rights to the English aristocracy—to rally support in their struggle against the autocratic rule of the Stuart kings. Members of Parliament viewed the charter as a constitutional check on royal power. They cited it as a legal support for their argument that there could be no laws or taxation without the consent of Parliament. And members of Parliament used the charter to demand guarantees of trial by jury and safeguards against unfair imprisonment.

In 1628 the English Parliament presented to King Charles I the Petition of Right, which declared unconstitutional certain actions of the king, such as levying taxes without the consent of Parliament, billeting soldiers in private homes, imposing martial law, and imprisoning citizens illegally. A repudiation of the divine right of kings, the Petition of Right asserted the supremacy of law over the personal wishes of the King. Charles I failed to obey the Petition of Right, and his autocratic rule led to his execution in 1649.

In 1689, seven years after the publication of a volume on English liberties by Henry Care (1646–88), Parliament presented King William III and Queen Mary with a declaration that became known as the Bill of Rights. The 1689 English Bill of Rights listed certain rights that were "true, ancient, and indubitable rights and liberties of the people" of England. It limited the powers of the king in such matters as taxation and keeping a standing army. In the colonies, as in England itself, Americans would celebrate English liberties as their birthright.

HENRY CARE, *English Liberties, Or, The Free-Born Subject's Inheritance*, BOSTON, [THE VOLUME WAS ORIGINALLY PUBLISHED IN 1685, BUT THE GILDER LEHRMAN COLLECTION COPY, THE FIRST EDITION PUBLISHED IN THE COLONIES, WAS PRINTED IN 1721]

The Constitution of our English Government (the best in the World) is no Arbitrary Tyranny like the Turkish Grand Seignior's, or the French Kings, whose Wills (or rather Lusts) dispose of the Lives and Fortunes of their unhappy Subjects; Nor an Oligarchy where the great men (like Fish in the Ocean) prey upon, and live by devouring the lesser at their pleasure. Nor yet a Democracy or popular State, much less an Anarchy, where all confusedly are hail fellows well met, but a most excellently mixt or qualified Monarchy, where the King is vested with large Prerogatives sufficient to support Majesty; and restrained only from power of doing himself and his people harm, which would be contrary to the very end of all Government, and is properly rather weakness than power.... The Commonality too, so Guarded in their Persons and Properties by the fence of Law, and renders them Freemen, not Slaves.

In France and other Nations the mere Will of the Prince is Law, his Word takes off any...Head, imposes Taxes, or seizes any man's Estate, when, how, and as often as he wishes, and if one is Accused or but so much as suspected of any Crime, he may either presently Execute him, or Banish or Imprison him at pleasure.... Nay if there be no Witnesses, yet he may be put to the Rack, the Tortures whereof make many an Innocent Person confess himself guilty....

But in England, the Law is both the Measure and the Bond of every Subject's Duty and Allegiance, each man having a fixed Fundamental Right born with him as to the Freedom of his Person and Property in his Estate, which he cannot be deprived of, but either by his consent, or some Crime for which the Law has Imposed such a Penalty as Forfeiture.

PART THREE

A Land of Contrasts

Jan Jansson. Map, Recens Edita totious Novi Belgii [New Netherlands—New York], 1730. The Gilder Lehrman Collection, on deposit at the Pierpont Morgan Library. GLC 3583

Even in the colonial era, the distinguishing characteristic of American society was the diversity of its population. By European standards, America was extraordinarily diverse ethnically, religiously, and regionally. The first federal census, conducted in 1790, found that a fifth of the entire population was African American. Among whites, three-fifths were English in ancestry and another fifth was Scottish or Irish. The remainder was of Dutch, French, German, Swedish, or some other background.

This astonishing diversity was in large part a product of the way that colonial America was originally settled. During the early seventeenth century, the most dynamic countries in Europe scrambled to establish overseas colonies and trading posts. The Dutch set up outposts in Brazil, Curaçao, New Netherlands, the Pennsylvania region, and West Africa; the English in the Bahamas, Barbados, Jamaica, and Nova Scotia, as well as along the mainland Atlantic coast; the French in the Caribbean, Canada, Guadeloupe, St. Domingue, Louisiana, and Martinique. The first phase of colonization was highly decentralized. The earliest settlements were established not under the direction of government, but by commercial companies, religious organizations, and individual entrepreneurs.

By the mid-seventeenth century, however, it became apparent that the colonies could be an important source of national wealth for the parent nation. Mercantilist thinkers saw colonies as a source of revenue and raw materials, a market for manufactured goods, and a way to strengthen a nation's economic self-sufficiency. The English government adopted a more systematic approach to colonization: It moved aggressively to annex Jamaica, New Netherlands, and New Sweden, and it began to grant territory to a specific person or persons called proprietors.

Although major goals of the new colonial system were to expand trade and assert greater control over the colonies, many of the proprietors projected utopian fantasies onto the lands they were granted. George Calvert, Lord Baltimore, established the first proprietary colony. He envisioned Maryland as a haven for Roman Catholics and as a place where he could re-create a feudal order. A group of eight nobles who received a gift of land in the Carolinas envisioned a hierarchical manorial society with a proprietary governor and a hereditary nobility. William Penn sought a refuge for himself and other Quakers. A group of proprietors led by James Oglethorpe envisioned Georgia as a haven for debtors and a buffer against Spanish Florida.

In practice it proved impossible to confine colonial development to a predetermined design. To attract settlers, it proved necessary to guarantee religious freedom, offer generous land grants, and have self-government through a representative assembly. But it was not merely schemes to set up feudal manors or to maintain proprietary rule that failed. The proprietors of Georgia banned the importation of hard liquor and outlawed slavery (not out of a moral concern about slavery, but because of anxiety that slavery would promote economic inequality and discourage industrious habits among white settlers). Yet within a few years, mounting opposition from Georgians and migration out of the colony led the trustees to revoke the restrictions on liquor and slaves.

MERCANTILIST IDEAS

1 / *"Although this Realm be already exceedingly rich... yet might it be much increased"*

In 1776 a Scottish professor named Adam Smith (1723–90) published the most influential book on economics ever written. Titled *The Wealth of Nations*, this book directed a withering attack against earlier notions of how nations attain wealth and power. An advocate of free trade and laissez-faire, trusting in the "Invisible Hand" of unregulated market forces, Smith called this older viewpoint "mercantilism." Under mercantilism, every nation sought to sell more than it bought. To maximize the state's welfare, government tried to regulate and protect industry and commerce. Colonies existed to enhance national self-sufficiency, provide essential raw materials, and serve as a market for finished products.

In this selection, Thomas Mun (1571–1641), a seventeenth-century English economist, offers a succinct summary of the mercantilist ideas Smith later repudiated and explains how overseas colonies can contribute to the nation's wealth.

THOMAS MUN, 1664

1. First, although this Realm be already exceedingly rich by nature, yet might it be much increased by laying the waste grounds (which are infinite) into such employments as should no way hinder the present revenues of other manured [cultivated] lands, but hereby to supply our selves and prevent the importations of Hemp, Flax, Cordage, Tobacco, and divers other things which now we fetch from strangers to our great impoverishing.

2. We may likewise diminish our importations, if we would soberly refrain from excessive consumption of forraign wares in our diet and rayment,...which vices at this present are more notorious amongst us than in former ages. Yet might they easily be amended by enforcing the observation of such good laws as are strictly practiced in other Countries against the said excesses; where likewise by commanding their own manufactures to be used, they prevent the coming in of others....

4. The value of our exportations likewise may be much advanced when we perform it ourselves in our own Ships, for then we get only not the price of our wares as they are worth here, but also the Merchants gains, the charges of insurance, and freight to carry them beyond the seas....

Thomas Mun, *England's Treasure by Forraign Trade,* (New York: Macmillan, 1903 ed.), pp. 9-12

NEW NETHERLANDS: AMERICA'S FIRST MULTICULTURAL SOCIETY

2 / *"There are, also, various other Negroes in this country"*

In 1648, after an eighty-year struggle, the Dutch Republic won its independence from Spanish rule. The seventeenth century was the Netherlands' golden age, during which

Engraving detail: Pilgrims departing for America [From collection: Portraits of historical figures: engravings, lithographs, photographs &c., 1790–1980 ca.] The Gilder Lehrman Collection, on deposit at the Pierpont Morgan Library. GLB 0486

the Dutch produced some of the world's greatest painters, such as Rembrandt; great philosophers, such as Spinoza; and great mathematicians and astronomers, such as Christian Huygens. During the golden age, the Netherlands also developed a colonial empire with bases stretching from Indonesia, Sri Lanka, and Brazil to Aruba, the Antilles, and the southern tip of Africa. It was also the only Western country permitted to trade with Japan. A major sea power, the Dutch in 1650 owned sixteen thousand of the twenty thousand ships engaged in European commerce.

In an effort to find a sea route around the Americas to Asia, the Dutch East India Company sent Henry Hudson and a crew of twenty to search for a westward passage. On his third voyage, in 1611, Hudson sailed into the harbor of present-day New York City and journeyed up the river named after him as far as Albany, thereby establishing Dutch claims to the region. In 1621 the Dutch West India Company (which had been founded to trade in West Africa and the Americas) began to colonize New Netherlands, which encompassed parts of present-day New York, Delaware, New Jersey, and Connecticut.

From the outset, New Netherlands was a multiethnic and multireligious society. Only about half the population was Dutch; the remainder included French, Germans, and Scandinavians, as well as a small number of Jews from Brazil. The Dutch considered New Netherlands a minor part of their colonial empire, valuable primarily as a source of furs. But many merchants were attracted by the colony's promise of freedom of worship, local self-government, and free land that would remain tax-exempt for ten years.

Even before an English fleet captured New Amsterdam in 1664, many of the colony's residents had been alienated by corruption, trade monopolies, arbitrary taxation, and ongoing conflict with neighboring Indian nations. In this selection Adriaen Van Der Donck (1620–55) and others lay out the residents' grievances.

Adriaen Van Der Donck et al.; *The Representation of New Netherland*, 1650

As we shall speak of the reasons and causes which have brought New Netherlands into the ruinous condition in which it is now found to be, we deem it necessary to state the very first difficulties and for this purpose, regard it as we see and find it in our daily experience. As far as our understanding goes, to describe it in one word (and none other better presents itself), it is *bad government*, with its attendants and consequences, that is the true and only *foundation stone* of the decay and ruin of New Netherlands....

Trade, without which, when it is legitimate, no country is prosperous, is by their acts so decayed that the like is nowhere else. It is more suited for slaves than freemen, in consequences of the restrictions upon it and the annoyances which accompany the exercise of the right of inspection....

In the meantime, the Christians are treated almost like Indians in the purchase of the necessaries with which they cannot dispense. This causes great complaint, distress, and poverty; as, for example, the merchants sell those goods which are liable to little depreciation at 100 percent and more profit, when there is no particular demand or scarcity of them....

There are, also, various other Negroes in this country, some of whom have been made free for their long service, but their children have remained slaves, though it is contrary to the laws of every people that anyone born of a Christian mother should be a slave and be compelled to remain in servitude.

Collections of the New-York Historical Society, 2nd series, (New York: Macmillan, 1849) Vol. II, pp. 288-321.

NEW NETHERLANDS BECOMES NEW YORK

3 / *"All people shall continue free"*

Between 1652 and 1674 the Dutch fought three naval wars with England. The English had hoped to wrest control of shipping and trading from the Dutch but failed. As a result of these conflicts, the Dutch won what is now Suriname from England, while the English received New Netherlands from the Dutch. In 1664, the English sent a fleet to seize New Netherlands, which surrendered without a fight. The English renamed the colony New York, after James, the Duke of York, who had received a charter to the territory from his brother King Charles II. The Dutch briefly recaptured New Netherlands in 1673, but the colony was returned to the English the next year.

Under Dutch rule, New Netherlands had suffered from ethnic tension, political instability, and protracted Indian warfare, which retarded immigration. Similar problems persisted under English administration. One source of tension was the Duke of York's refusal to permit a representative assembly, which was not established until 1683.

Another source of tension was the "patroon" system, which the Dutch West India Company set up in 1629 to promote settlement. Patroons were given huge estates, which they rented to tenant farmers. Patroons had the power to control such aspects of settlers' lives as their right to move, establish businesses, and marry. The duke of York allowed Dutch landowners to retain these estates, and gave equally large tracts of land to his supporters. By 1703 five families held approximately 1.75 million acres of New York. By 1750 these families had become among colonial America's wealthiest landed elite. Although these landowners lost their feudal privileges as a result of the Revolution, they still owned about 1.8 million acres of land in the early nineteenth century. Between 1839 and 1846, tenant farmers on these properties staged "Anti-Rent Wars," demanding title to lands that they felt rightfully belonged to them. In 1846, New York granted the tenants their farms.

True copy of articles whereupon...the New Netherlands were surrendered, JANUARY 1674, GLC 377

We consent that the States General, or the West India Company shall freely enjoy all Farms & Houses (except such as are in the forts) and that within six months they shall have free liberty to transport all such arms and ammunition as do belong to them, or else they shall be paid for them.

2. All publick Houses shall continue for the uses, which now they are for.

3. All people shall continue free Denizens and enjoy their Lands, Houses, Goods, Ships wherever they are within this Country, and dispose of them as they please.

4. If any Inhabitants have a mind to remove himself he shall have a year and six weeks from this day to remove himself, wife, children, serv[an]ts, goods...

5. If any officer of State or public Minister of State have a mind to go for England they shall be transported freight free in His Ma[jesty']s frigates when the frigate shall return thither.

6. It is consented to that any people may freely come from the Netherlands and plant in this Country....

7. All Ships from the Netherlands or any other places, and goods therein, shall be received here and sent hence after the manner which formerly they were before our coming hither for six months....

8. The Dutch here shall enjoy their Liberty of their Consciences in Divine worship and Church Discipline.

9. No Dutchman here or Dutch ship here shall upon any occasion be forced to serve in war against any Nation whatsoever.

10. That...Manhattan shall not have any Soldiers quartered among them without being...payd for them, by their officers....

11. The Dutch here shall enjoy their own Customs concerning their Inheritances....

INDIAN AFFAIRS

Along the eastern coast, England, France, the Netherlands, and Spain all competed over trade with the Indians. In the Northeast, the English, French, and Dutch struggled to control the immensely valuable fur trade. In the Southeast, it was not only furs that attracted the English, the Spanish, and later the French, but also deerskin (used to make clothes, gloves, and book bindings) and Indian slaves. During the early eighteenth century, Indian slaves (many of whom had been converted to Catholicism at Spanish missions before capture) made up a third of the slaves in South Carolina.

Competition over furs, skins, and slaves had many destructive effects on Native Americans. It made Indians increasingly dependent on European manufactured goods and firearms. The trade also killed off animals that provided a major part of the hunting and gathering economy. And traders spread disease and alcohol. The fur trade also conflicted with traditional Indian religious beliefs, which charged hunters with never killing more animals than they needed for subsistence.

Above all, competition over trade encouraged intertribal warfare and therefore undermined Native Americans' ability to resist white expansion. Competition for hunting grounds drove many people out of their traditional homelands. In what is now New York, the Iroquois—a federation of tribes that included the Cayuga, Mohawk, Oneida, Onondaga, Seneca, and later the Tuscarora—pushed many Algonquian-speaking Indians eastward toward the Atlantic coast, where they came into conflict with New Englanders, or northward and westward.

During the late seventeenth and eighteenth centuries, Native Americans frequently became embroiled in European wars to control North America. Four times between 1689 and 1763, France, England, and their Indian allies waged wars over land between the Allegheny Mountains and the Mississippi River, fishing grounds off Nova Scotia and Newfoundland, and control of the fur trade. Nevertheless, it would be a mistake to view Native American–European relations during this period as entirely one-sided. The Iroquois were able to use their European connections to achieve hegemony over the northern frontier.

One of the most complete sets of records of negotiations among Native Americans and the English was compiled by Robert Livingston (1654–1728), founder of one of New York's most prominent families. These records provide a graphic record of the interactions between the English and neighboring Native Americans, especially in New York, and indicate that power in these negotiations was not only on one side.

4 / *"Yours having entered our houses, taken away and destroyed our goods and People"*

Few subjects are more clouded by myths and misconceptions than the history of Native Americans. Quite unconsciously, many contemporary Americans have picked up a complex set of myths about Indians. Many assume that pre-Columbian North America was sparsely populated virgin land; in fact, it probably had 7 million to 12 million inhabitants. Often, when Americans think of early Indians, they imagine hunters on horseback. In fact, many Native Americans were farmers, and horses had been extinct in the New World for ten thousand years before Europeans arrived.

The most dangerous misconception is the easiest to slip into. It is to think of the Indians as a people somehow fated for extinction, the passive victims of an acquisitive, land-hungry white population. Far from being passive, Native Americans were active agents who responded to threats to their land and culture through physical resistance, cultural adaptation, and establishment of strategic alliances.

Especially during the early colonial period, as the following selection reveals, the English felt forced to deal with Native Americans as nations. Through formal diplomacy, the English felt a continuing need to make pacts and treaties with Indian peoples. Among the ways the Dutch, the English, and eastern Indians would seal agreements were through ceremonies involving peace pipes, peace medals, wampum, and burying a hatchet. Later, the United States would take these symbols to the Trans-Mississippi West, where they did not carry their original meaning.

Propositions of Colonel William Kendall authorized by the Governour, Council, and Burgesses of Virginia at a Grand Assembly held in James City to the Oneydes [Oneidas] in the Court house of Albany this 30th day of October 1679, Livingston Indian Papers, GLC 3107

I am come from Virginia being as all these countries under our great King Charles, to speak to you, upon occasion of some of yours having entered our houses, taken away and destroyed our goods and People, and brought some of our women and Children Captives in your Castles contrary to your faith and promises, and is also a breach of your Peace made with Colonel Coursey without any Provocation or Injury in the Least done by us, or disturbing you in your hunting trade, or Passing until you were found taking our Corn, out of our fields and Plundering and burning our houses.

Though your Actions already done, are Sufficient Reasons to Induce us to a Violent war against you which might Engage all our Confederated English neighbours, subjects to our great king Charles, yet upon the Information the governor here hath given us, that you have quietly and Peaceably, delivered to him, the Prisoners you had taken from us, Who are also Returned in Safety to our Country, and your excusing [th]e Same, We are therefore willing and have and do forgive all ye Damages you have done our People (though very great) Provided you nor any Living amongst you or coming from you, for the future do not offend or molest our People or Indians Living amongst us, *Which if it shall appear that you do not truly Perform, then we Expect full Satisfaction for all the Injuries that you have already done us to the utmost farthing.*

And one of your Squaws being taken alive in our Country, and now Returned here, being freed, I Return her to you.

And whereas you have still a Christian Girl of our Parts with you, doe expect, that you likeways free & Return ye Same.

We have a Law in our Country, that all Indians coming near a Christian any where, must Stand Still, and lay down there Arms, as a token of their being friends, otherwise are Looked upon and taken or destroyed as Enemies, and having many of our People in the woods abroad every way, *we doe acquaint you (therewith) that if your People shall go to war towards our Parts against any Indians not in friendship with us that you forbear to come near our Plantations.*

5 / "The English...shot some of our People dead"

The history of Native Americans is commonly viewed as tragedy. Indian history, from this point of view, is the story of declining population, lost homelands, and cultural dislocation. There is, however a much more positive side to this history. This is a story of cultural persistence and survival in the face of extraordinary challenges, dislocations, and population loss. Despite the destructive effects of disease, Native Americans maintained a remarkable capacity for resistance and independent action.

The Oneydes Answer upon the Propositions of Colonel William Kendall, agent for ye Country of Virginia in the Court house of Albany this 31 of October 1679, Livingston Indian Papers, GLC 3107

...It is Represented to us yesterday the damage that we have done in Virginia, in destroying your goods and People, & in taking of your women and children Captives &c. we Confess to have done so But there is a Covenant made 2 Year ago with Colonel Coursey in the Presence of his honor the governor that we might freely come towards your Plantations, when we went out a fighting to our Indian Enemies to Refresh our selves if we were hungry, & we came there, & got nothing, then we took Indian Corn and Tobacco, whereupon the English coming out shot some of our People dead, and afterwards wee defended ourselves out of which these disasters are Proceeded, You say that it is our faults, and we think that the firing upon us is the Occasion....

Yesterday it was told us, that which is already Past is forgiven, for which we do thank you, Yea we thank you heartily, and Confess that the Pole or Stake of unity hath been fallen, but now Reared up again; Let all that which is Past not only be forgotten but be Buried in a Pit of oblivion, yea I say in a Bottomless Pitt where a Strong Currunt of a River Runs through, that which is now thrown in it, may never appear more....

We have understood Yesterday, that if wee come nigh any Christians in your Country, that we must Stand Still, and lay down our armes. Tis good, we accept of it. But let it not be of so bad a Consequences as Colonel Coursey saying was, for he said Likeways, that we might come there as friends, when we went out fighting against our Indian Enemies, But our going thither did bring these disasters. Let us have Victuals when we go fighting against our foresaid Enemys....

6 / "The Governor of Canada is Intended to Destroy us"

In rejecting the exaggerated and distorted view that casts Native Americans in the role of passive victims, it is also important to recognize the realities that limited Indians' freedom of action. Even in the late seventeenth century, Indian peoples such as the Five Nations who lived in what is now New York felt intense pressure to forge alliances with Europeans in order to obtain arms, manufactured goods, and protection from enemy peoples, especially the French and their Huron allies. The need for European allies would remain a crucial theme in Native American history from the late sixteenth century until the War of 1812, which removed the native peoples' last reliable outside source of support.

Propositions made by four Sinnekes [Senecas] To the Commander & Justices of Peace in the Court house of Albany ye 29 June 1685, Livingston Indian Papers, GLC 3107

1. There is news Brought us in our Country by 4 Indians...& they tell us that the Governor of Canada is Intended to Destroy us....

2.The government of Canada's design is kept very Secret, & as it were Smothered in a Pot that is covered, but nevertheless tis broke out as far as our Country & wee are acquainted with it....We Desire that you would be Pleased to order that our Young Soldiers do not go out a fighting; but Stay at home to Defend their Country; if it should happen that the French should Come & fall upon our Country, for wee are Informed that he Design to be there about 3 months hence....

Answer to the aforesaid Propositions, 29 June 1685

We have heard your Propositions and Perceive that you are fearful of the French, which you ought not to be, nor give any Credit to Such Stories, for you having Submitted your Selves under this government and obeying the governor. Last year in not making a Peace with the French without his Consent...you need not doubt but the governor will take all fitting care to Preserve you and your Country. In the mean Time you must Tell your young men from the governor, That they are not to goe out a fighting against their Indian Enemies but stay at home till the time of the Beaver hunting approaches, which will be in the fall, and then you are to Pursue & follow your hunting as formerly, & Bring your Beaver hither where you will find you are Civilly Treated, and have all Sorts of goods very cheap.

THE SCHENECTADY MASSACRE

7 / *"As to the causes of this...war...jealousy arising from the trading of our people...seems to be the principal one"*

Robert Livingston (1654–1728) offers a vivid account of an attack by the French and their Indian allies on the Dutch and English settlement at Schenectady in New York on February 8 and 9, 1690. The attack came in retaliation for a series of devastating Iroquois raids on Canada, which had essentially stopped the French fur trade for two years. The raid was an attempt to punish the English for supplying arms and ammunition to the Iroquois and to bolster the morale of the French Canadians and western tribes with an easy victory, since the Iroquois were impossible to defeat.

Approximately sixty people were killed in the raid on Schenectady (including ten women and twelve children) and between eighty and ninety were taken prisoner. The Schenectady raid was part of a three-pronged French attack on isolated northern and western settlements. The two other prongs of the attack were at Salmon Falls, New Hampshire, where thirty were killed and fifty-four prisoners were tortured to death, and

Fort Loyal (today, Portland, Maine), where the inhabitants were killed or taken prisoner. Overall, the raids convey a strong impression of cruelty by the French and their allies and carelessness and greediness of the English and the Dutch.

ROBERT LIVINGSTON, FEBRUARY 9, 1689–90, LIVINGSTON PAPERS, GLC 3107

This sad story should not pass from our memory but remain engraved on it and we should grieve over our sins rather than bewail our loss, for it is clearly shown that when the measure of our iniquities is full, we are cut down and almost exterminated, of which the present smoking ruins of houses and barns bear ample witness before the eyes of our few remaining people. As to the causes of this bloody war, which they pretend originated with us, jealousy arising from the trading of our people...seems to be the principal one, for the Indians, that is to say, the Five Nations, were very friendly disposed toward us. The French begrudged us this and therefore made every effort to make them hostile to us.... The French...invited several Indians to come into the[ir]...fort to be entertained...but they met with a different reception, for as soon as they entered the fort they were bound securely and carried off to Cubeck [Québec], to the number of 60.... Having at once assembled an army, [the French]...marched against the Indians...with the intention of destroying them, but this failed. The Indians were so embittered by this that like madmen they fell upon the French farmers, murdering and burning to revenge this breach of faith, so that many suffered great loss and damage. Showing themselves greatly perturbed about this and holding us responsible for it...they [the French] found and cruelly murdered the Dutch, saying: "The Dutch are urging you to fight against us, therefore we shall excuse you."...

The bloodthirsty people [the French and their Indian allies], then, to accomplish their evil purpose, according to their own statement made the journey from Canada to this place in 11 days.... They divided themselves into three troops and after they had everything well spied out and found that the gates were open and that nowhere there was any sentinel on duty and that on account of the heavy snow which had fallen the day before no one had been in the woods by whom they could have been detected, the full wrath of God was poured out over us. Having posted three or four men before every house, they attacked simultaneously at the signal of a gun. They first set fire to the house of Adam Vroman, who when he offered resistance was shot through the hand. After several shots had been fired, his wife, hoping to find an opportunity to get away, opened the back door, whereupon she was immediately shot dead and devoured by the flames.... His eldest daughter...had her mother's child on her arm.... Asked...whether the child was heavy...she said yes, whereupon [one of the invaders]...took the child from her and taking it by the legs dashed its head against the sill of the house, so that the brains scattered over the bystanders....

The women and children fled mostly into the woods, almost naked and there many froze to death.... Oh, we poor, miserable people, how we were scattered during that dreadful night, the husband being separated from his wife and the children from both, one hiding for 2 or 3 days in the woods and in swampy and marshy land, where God in His mercy nevertheless did not forget them....

The rest, then, who escaped the bloody sword, were condemned to be prisoners, but here again God's guiding hand clearly appears, for many sorrowful women and children and some old men, seeing this dreadful journey ahead of them, which meant practically death, doubtless offered up their prayers to God, who from the depths of their woe granted them delivery.... Considering that the old men and children and also the women would be a hindrance to them in their flight, they [the French and their allies] discharged them from their place of confinement to the great joy of all....

In all as many as 60 people have been murdered by these fiends and 40 houses and 22 barns, all filled with cattle, have been almost completely destroyed.

8 / *"The French of Canada have killed [and] Imprisoned...your People"*

Although the popular retrospective view emphasizes whites or Europeans fighting to dispossess Indians of their land, in the crucial colonial years, when European colonists could have suffered devastating defeat, various Indian nations were allied with France or England or Spain. One of the key goals of England's "forest diplomacy" was to forge alliances with Indian peoples against the French.

The struggle between Britain and France was motivated not only by the prospects of economic profit but also by religion, national honor, and dreams of empire. A major battleground in this contest took place in upstate New York, where the English formed an alliance with the Iroquois to disrupt French trade in the interior.

PROPOSITIONS MADE BY THE HONORABLE COLONEL RICHD. INGOLDESBY LIEUTENANT GOVERNOR. & COMMANDER IN CHIEF OF HER MAJESTY'S PROVINCES OF NEW YORK, THE JERSEYS & TERRITORIES DEPENDING THEREON IN AMERICA TO YE MAQUASE, ONEYDES, ONNONDAGES, & CAYOUGES IN ALBANY THIS 14 DAY OF JULY 1709, LIVINGSTON INDIAN PAPERS, GLC 3107

Brethren

I have sent for you upon an Extraordinary occasion, to assist in an Expedition for ye Reducing Canada, which you have So much Long'd for, That neighbourhood you know hath been of a long time Very Troublesome to you, & many of her Majesty's good Subjects In these Parts.

We will not now Enumerate the many Perfidious and base actions they [the French] have been guilty off. We have whole Volumes full of Complaints which you have made to us of their Treacherous dealings. The French of Canada have killed, Imprisoned, Carried away, and Transported your People, burnt your Castles, and used all means which lay in their Power to Impoverish you, and bring you to a low and miserable Condition.

They have not only Seduced your People, and Enticed them away from your Country, but Encouraged even your own Brethren to make war upon you, on purpose to weaken you.

They have Set the Far Indians upon you and furnished them with arms and Ammunition in order to Destroy you. The Pains they have taken to accomplish your Ruin hath been Indefatigable.

> They encroached upon your rights and Liberties by building Forts upon your Land against your wills, Possessing the Principall Passes and hunting Places, whereby all your hunting (your only Support) was rendered not only Precarious, but dangerous.
>
> Their treacherously murdering of Montour, one of your Brethren, before your Faces, in your own Country this Summer is an Evident mark of their Insolence and how they Intend to use you. Most of these and other things having been truly Represented to the Great queen of Great Britain [Queen Anne] (who is victorious over the French King in Europe). She hath taken them into her Royal Consideration and has been Graciously Pleased (notwithstanding the vast Expence her Majesty is daily at in Carrying on this necessary just war against France in Europe) to Send over at a great charge a Considerable Fleet, with men, Ammunition, Provision, and Artillery and other things necessary for ye Effectuall Reducing of Canada, to Redeem you from that Bondage and Slavery the French designed to bring you under. I must therefore Earnestly exhort you to be cheerful and resolute in joining with all your Strength with her Majesty's Forces....
>
> This will be the only and Effectual means to Procure a firm and durable Peace and quiet Possession of our Settlements for us, and for you and your Posterity for ever....

PERSECUTION OF THE QUAKERS

9 / "We are...necessitated to lay before the Governor an oppression that we lye under"

The social upheaval ignited by the seventeenth-century English Civil War spawned many radical millennarian religious groups, including the Diggers, who rejected private property; and the Ranters, who claimed to worship God through drinking, smoking, and fornicating. Only one of the radical religious group that emerged during the tumultuous years of the 1640s and 1650s has survived until now: the Society of Friends (the Quakers).

Today the Quakers are often associated with austerity and self-discipline, but in the sect's early days, members behaved in very rebellious ways. Some marched into churches, where they denounced ministers as dumb dogs and hirelings. They also refused to doff their hats before magistrates or to swear oaths. They opposed war and gave women the right to speak at public meetings, holding that both sexes were equal in their ability to expound God's teachings.

The Quakers rejected the orthodox Calvinist belief in predestination. Instead, the Quakers insisted that salvation was available to all. It came, however, not through an institutional church, but from within, by following the "inner light" of God's spirit. It was because Friends seemed to shake when they felt religious enthusiasm that they became known as Quakers.

In England as well as in a number of American colonies the Quakers faced violent persecution. Some fifteen thousand Quakers were jailed in England between 1660 and 1685. In 1660 Edward Burrough cataloged the maltreatment of Quakers in New England: Sixty-four Quakers had been imprisoned; two Quakers lashed 139 times, leaving one "beat like into a jelly"; another branded with the letter H, for heretic, after being whipped with 39 stripes; and three Quakers had been executed.

Even in New York, which tolerated a wide variety of religious persuasions, the Quakers faced hostility. After arriving in Long Island in 1657, some Quakers were fined, jailed, and banished by the Dutch, who (like Puritan New Englanders) were outraged by Quaker women proselytizing. In this selection, New York's Quakers inform the province's royal governor about ways in which they are mistreated.

Over time, the Quakers found successful ways to channel their moral idealism and religious enthusiasm. The sect established weekly and monthly meetings that imposed structure and discipline on members, and beginning in the mid-eighteenth century, directed their energies against a wide variety of social evils, including slavery. By the early nineteenth century, Quakers were engaged in moral reform movements in numbers wildly disproportionate to the sect's size. As many as a third of all early nineteenth-century feminists and antislavery activists were Quakers.

Petition of New York Quakers to the Governor, November 11, 1702, GLC 2509.01

The Humble Address of the People called Quakers in the Province of New York

...We are now forced to approach humbly the Governor with our complaint in a matter of the highest moment relating to our privileges as freeborn subjects being lately denied the undoubted right of choosing our own representation at an election in Queens county on the island of Nassau...because we could not (for conscience sake) swear we were freeholders although it was well known to the sheriff & judge too....

We are also necessitated to lay before the Governor an oppression that we lye under being imposed upon by some of our neighbors....Yet they have presumed to take away our substance by...disposing of [our goods]...at their own will & pleasure, because we could not think it our duty to contribute with them to build their Noncomformist Preacher a dwelling house, & we do humbly conceive they have no legal...[ground] to impose any such tax upon us.

THE QUAKER IDEAL OF RELIGIOUS TOLERANCE

10 / *"Persons have been flung into Jails"*

The Quakers had remarkable success in attracting a number of socially prominent individuals to their cause. Among these, none was more important than William Penn (1644–1718). The son of an English naval officer and a friend of James II, Penn became a Quaker at age twenty-two. He was imprisoned several times for writing and preaching about Quakerism, including an eight-month confinement in the Tower of London.

In 1680 Penn asked Charles II of England to repay an eighty-thousand-dollar debt owed to Penn's father with wilderness land in America. The next year, he was granted a charter. Penn viewed his new colony as a "Holy Experiment" that would provide colonists religious liberty and cheap land. He made a treaty of friendship with Indians shortly after he arrived in Pennsylvania in 1682, paying them for most of the land that King Charles had given him.

Compared to many other colonies, Pennsylvania, from the outset, was a remarkable success. It experienced no major Indian wars. Strong West Indian demand for grain generated prosperity and made Philadelphia a major port. Nevertheless, the colony did not live up to Penn's dream of a "peaceable kingdom." In 1685 he pleaded with the colonial legislature: "For the love of God, me, and the poor country, be not so governmentish; so noisy and open in your disaffection."

In this essay, written seven years before founding Pennsylvania, Penn offers arguments in favor of religious tolerance.

William Penn, "England's present interests discovered..." London, 1675, GLC 1672

Certain it is, that there are few Kingdoms in the World more Divided within themselves [by religion than England]....

Your Endeavours for a [religious] Uniformity have been many; Your Acts not a few to Enforce it, but their Consequence, whether you intended it or not, through the Barbarous Practices of those that have had their Execution, hath been the Spoiling of several Thousands of the free inhabitants of this Kingdom of their Unforfeited Rights. Persons have been flung into Jails, Gates and Trunks broke open, Goods destroyed, till a stool hath not been left to sit down on, Flocks of Cattle driven, whole Barns full of Corn seized, Parents left with out Children, Children without their Parents, both without subsistence....

Finding then by Sad Experience, and a long Tract of Time, That the very Remedies applied to cure Dissension increase it; and that the more Vigorously a Uniformity is coercively prosecuted, the Wider Breaches grown, the more Inflamed Persons are, and fixt in their Resolutions to stand by their Principles; which, besides all other Inconveniences to those that give them Trouble, their very Sufferings beget that Compassion in the Multitude...and makes a Preparation for not a few Proselytes....

The Question. What is most Fit, Easie and Safe at this Juncture of Affairs to be done, for Composing, at least Quieting Differences; for Allaying the Heat of Contrary Interests, and making them Subservient to the Interest of the Government, and Consistent with the Prosperity of the Kingdom?

The Answer.

I. An Inviolable and Impartial Maintenance of English Rights.

II. Our Superiours governing themselves upon a Balance, as near as may be, towards the several Religious Interests.

III. A sincere Promotion of General and Practical Religion....

I shall not at this time make it my Business to manifest the Inconsistency that there is between the Christian Religion, and a forced Uniformity; not only because it hath been so often and excellently done by Men of Wit, Learning and Conscience, and that I have elsewhere largely deliver'd my Sense about it; but because Every free and impartial Temper hath of a long time observ'd, that such Barbarous Attempts were so far from being indulged, that they were most severely prohibited by Christ himself....

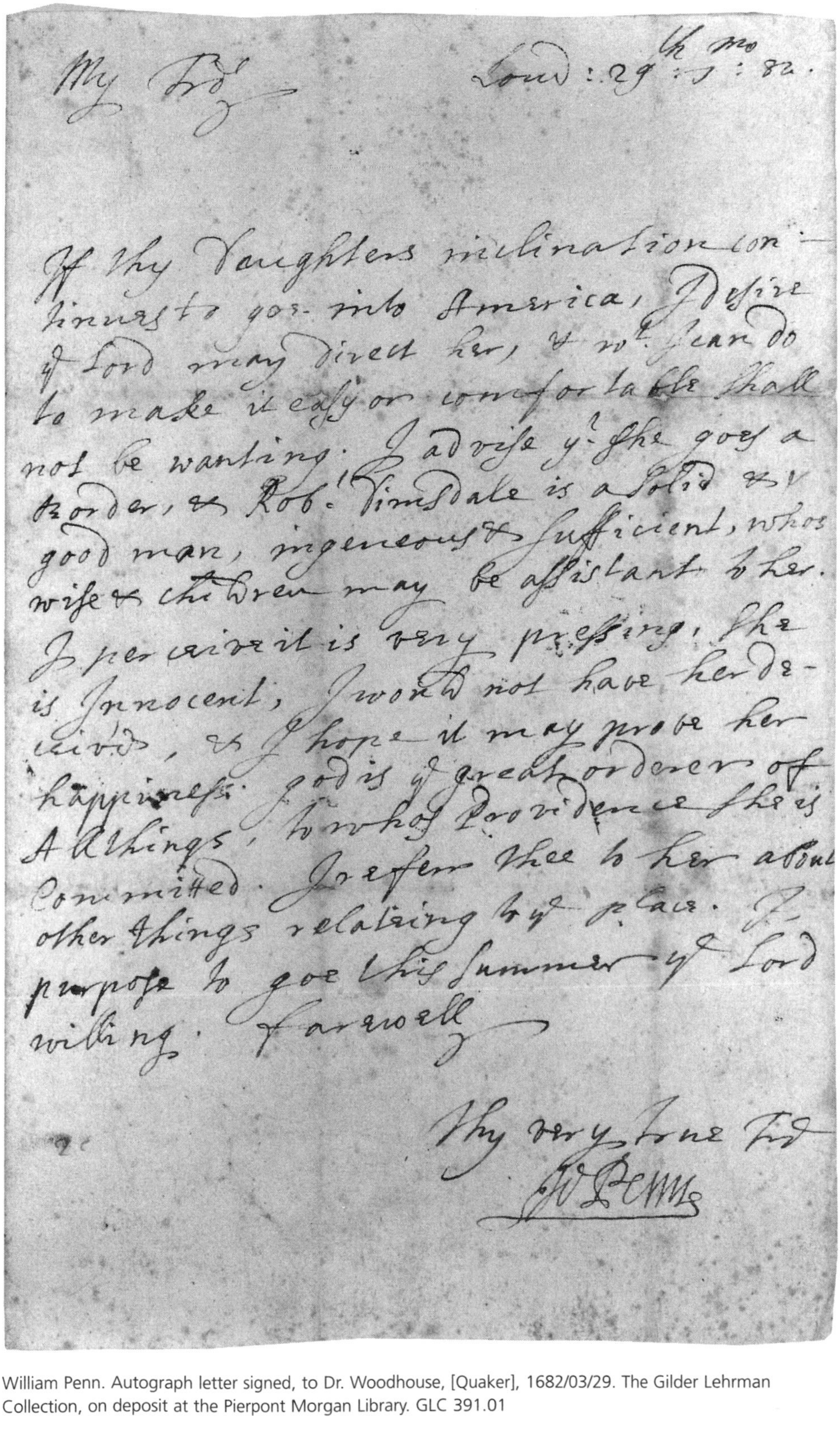

My Frd

Lond: 29th: 1mo: 82.

If thy Daughters inclination continues to goe into America, I desire
ye Lord may direct her, & wt I can do
to make it easy or comfortable shall
not be wanting. I advise yt she goes a
border, & Robt Timsdale is a solid & v
good man, ingeneous & sufficient, whos
wife & children may be assistant to her.
I perceive it is very pressing, she
is Innocent, I would not have her deceived, & I hope it may prove her
happiness. God is ye great orderer of
All things, to whos Providence she is
Committed. I refer thee to her about
other things relating to ye place. I
purpose to goe this Summer ye Lord
willing. Farewell

Thy very true Frd
W Penn

William Penn. Autograph letter signed, to Dr. Woodhouse, [Quaker], 1682/03/29. The Gilder Lehrman Collection, on deposit at the Pierpont Morgan Library. GLC 391.01

Instead of Peace, Love and good Neighborhood, behold Animosity and contest! One Neighbour watcheth another...; this divides them, their Families and Acquaintance....

Nor is this Severity only Injurious to the Affairs of England, but the whole Protestant World: For besides that it calls the Sincerity of their Proceedings against the Papists into Question, it furnisheth them with this sort of unanswerable Interrogatory: "The Protestants exclaim against us for Persecutor, and are they now the very men themselves?..."

But there are...objections that some make against what I have urged, not unfit to be consider'd. The first is this: If the Liberty desired be granted, what know we but Dissenters may employ their Meetings to insinuate against the Government, inflame the People into a Dislike of their Superiours, and thereby prepare them for Mischief.... Answer....What Dissenter can be so destitute of Reason and Love to common Safety, as to expose himself and Family; by plotting against a Government that is kind to him, and gives him the Liberty he desire....

SOUTH CAROLINA

11 / *"Reflecting S[i]r on the weakness of this our Colony"*

South Carolina's proprietors envisioned establishing a feudal society in their land grant. They kept huge landed estates for themselves, and, with the assistance of the English philosopher John Locke, drew up a plan, known as the Fundamental Constitutions of Carolina, which would have given them the power of feudal lords. The scheme called for a three-tiered hereditary nobility—consisting of "proprietors," "landgraves," and "caciques"—who would own 40 percent of the colony's land and serve as a Council of Lords and recommend all laws to a parliament elected by small landowners. But like other feudal visions, this one failed. South Carolina's settlers rejected virtually all of this plan, and immigrants refused to move to the region until it was replaced by a more democratic system of government.

Emigrants from Barbados played a decisive role in South Carolina's early settlement in 1679 and 1680, and brought black slaves with them. Within a decade, they had found a staple crop—rice—that they could raise with slave labor. The grain itself had probably come from West Africa, and African slaves were already familiar with rice cultivation. The result was to transform South Carolina into the mainland society that bore the closest resemblance to the Caribbean. As early as 1708, slaves actually outnumbered whites, and by 1730 there were twice as many slaves as whites in the colony. About a third of South Carolina's slaves during the early eighteenth century were Indians.

The rapid growth in the slave population raised the specter of slave revolt. In 1739 the Stono Rebellion, the largest slave uprising in colonial America, took place about twenty miles from Charleston. Led by a slave named Jemmy, the rebels burned seven plantations and killed approximately twenty whites as they headed for refuge in Spanish Florida. Within a day, however, the Stono rebels were captured and killed by the white militia.

South Carolina was also the scene of some of the most bitter Indian-white warfare. In 1711, after incidents in which whites had encroached on their land and kidnapped Indians as slaves, the Tuscaroras destroyed New Bern. Over the next two years the colonial militia, assisted by the Yamassees, killed or enslaved a fifth of the Tuscaroras. Many survivors subsequently migrated to New York, where they became the Sixth Nation of the Iroquois Confederacy. Then, in 1715, the Yamassees, finding themselves increasingly in debt to white traders and merchants, allied themselves with the Creeks and attempted to destroy the colony. With help from the Cherokees, the colonial militia successfully repelled the offensive, largely ending Indian resistance to white expansion in the Carolinas.

Writing just twenty years after the establishment of the first permanent English settlement in South Carolina, James Moore recounts a journey he had taken eight years earlier, during which he had uncovered several kinds of ores and minerals. Indians he encountered informed him that the Spanish had been operating mines in the area; and that the indigenous people had killed the Spaniards in order to avoid being enslaved by them. Moore expresses concern about making a discovery of silver public, for it might "incite & encourage the French in America." He asks Edward Randolph, the royal surveyor, to bring this information to the attention of the royal government.

JAMES MOORE, MARCH 1, 1698–99, TO EDWARD RANDOLPH, GLC 5758.02

As well out of curiosity to see what sort of Country we might have in land as to find out and make a new & farther discovery of Indian Trade, I made a Journey in the year 1690 over the Apalathean [Appalachian] Mountains in which Journey I took up seven sorts of ores or mineral stones, all differing either in weight, color, smell or some other qualities.

By my friend col[one]l Maurice Mathews I sent these to be try'd [tested] to England, he had them try'd and sent me a word two of the seven sorts were very good and one Indifferent. By the Help of my Journal I can go to every Individual place I took up any of the seven sorts of ores. In the same Journey I was informed that the Spaniards had been actually at work upon mines within Twenty miles of me I enquired of the Natives of the truth of that matter and the reason why they desisted. They told me it was true and described to me their great Bellows & furnaces, and that they killed the Spaniards...when...the Spaniards grew Numerous [fearing that] they [the Spanish] should make slaves of them to worke in those mines as they had Millions of other Indians as they said they had been informed....

Reflecting S[i]r on the weakness of this our Colony & considering that the report of a silver mine among us would incite & encourage the French in America, if not in Europe, to Invade us, I thought it convenient during the War between the Crowns of England & France not to make any discovery of them. Now S[i]r By the Peace the Emperor hath made with the Turks and the recovery of the King of Spain (if those reports are true) the Peace between England and France seems to be well confirmed and Lasting. I think this poor little colony of ours may not only be out of Danger of an Invasion, but be peopled and enriched by the working of these mines....

GEORGIA

12 /"The Trustees intend to relieve such unfortunate persons as cannot subsist here [in England]"

Prior to the American Revolution, only one colony, Georgia, temporarily sought to prohibit slavery, because the founders did not want a workforce that would compete with the debtors they planned to transport from England. Settlers, however, illegally imported slaves into the colony, forcing the proprietors to abandon the idea of a slave-free colony.

In this selection, James Oglethorpe (1696–1785), Georgia's founder, describes the idealistic objectives behind this venture.

JAMES OGLETHORPE, 1733

The Trustees intend to relieve such unfortunate persons as cannot subsist here [in England], and establish them in an orderly manner, so as to form a well-regulated town. As far as their fund goes, they will defray the charge of their passage to Georgia; giving them necessaries, cattle, land, and subsistence till such time as they can build their houses and clear some of their land....

By such a colony many families who would otherwise starve will be provided for, and made masters of houses and lands. The people in Great Britain, to whom these necessitous families were a burden, will be relieved. Numbers of manufacturers will be here employed for supplying them with clothes, working tools, and other necessities. And by giving refuge to the distressed Salzburgers [Austrians], and other persecuted Protestants, the power of Britain, as a reward for its hospitality, will be increased by the addition of so many religious and industrious subjects.

The colony of Georgia lying about the same latitude with part of China, Persia, Palestine, and the Madeiras, it is highly probable that when hereafter it shall be well peopled and rightly cultivated, England may be supplied from thence with raw silk, wine, oil, dyes, drugs, and many other materials for manufactures which she is obliged to purchase from southern countries. As towns are established and grow populous along the rivers Savannah and Altamaha, they will make such a barrier as will render the southern frontier of the British colonies on the continent of America safe from Indian and other enemies.

Peter Force, comp., *Tracts* (Washington: Printed by P. Force, 1836), Vol. I, pp. 2, 5, 6

ENGLISH LIBERTIES AND DEFERENCE

13 / "I am as good flesh & blood as you"

The social history of eighteenth-century America presents a fundamental paradox. In certain respects, colonial society was becoming more like English society. The power of royal governors was increasing, social distinctions were hardening, lawyers were paying closer attention to English law, and a more distinct social and political elite was gradually emerging, as a result of the expansion of Atlantic commerce, the growth of the tobacco and rice economies, and especially the sale of land. To be sure, compared to the English aristocracy, the wealthiest merchants, planters, and landholders were much more limited in wealth and less stable in membership. Nevertheless, there was a growth of regional elites who intermarried, aped English manners, and dominated the highest levels of colonial government.

Yet the eighteenth century also witnessed growing claims of "English liberties" against all forms of tyranny and subservience. A 1705 legal case pitting Governor Joseph Dudley (1647–1720) of Massachusetts against two cart drivers, whom the governor charged with insubordination, offers a vivid example of the mounting challenges to social deference. This case became a landmark in limiting the authority of public officials.

Governor Joseph Dudley and Thomas Trowbridge, January 23, 1705, to Massachusetts Superior Court Justices, GLC 461.01

Account of Governor Joseph Dudley

The Governour informs the Queens Officers of her majesty's Superior Court that on Friday the seventh of December last past he took his journey from Roxbury towards New Hampshire and the Province of Maine for her majesty's immediate service there.... [He] had not proceeded above a mile from home before he met two carts in the Road Loaded with wood, of which the Carters were as he is since informed Winchester and Trowbridge.

The Charet [coach] wherein the Governour was had three sitters and their Servants... drawn by four horses, one very unruly, & was attended only at that instant by Mr. William Dudley, the Governour's son.

When the Governour saw the two carts approaching he directed his son to bid them to give him the way having a Difficult drift with four horses & a tender Charet [coach] so heavily loaden not fit to break the way, Who accordingly did Ride up & told them the Gov[erno]r was there, & they must give way. Immediately upon it the second Carter came up to ye first...& one of them says aloud he would not go out of the way for the Governour whereupon the Gov[erno]r came out of the Charet and told Winchester he must give way to the Charet. Winchester answered boldly...I am as good flesh & blood as you. I will not give way. You may go out of the way, & came towards the Governour. Whereupon the Governour drew his sword to secure himself & command the Road & went forward; yet without either saying or intending to hurt the carters or once pointing or passing at them but justly supposing they would obey & give him the way; and again commanded them to give way. Winchester answered that he was a Christian & would not give way & as the Governour came toward him he advanced & at len[g]th laid hold on the Gov[erno]r & broke the sword in his hands. Very soon after came a Justice of the Peace, & sent the Carters to prison...the Gov[erno]r demanded their names which they would not say...nor did they once in the Gov[erno]r[']s hearing or sight pull of[f] their hatts...or any word to excuse the matter but absolutely stood...on each side of the fore-horse laboured & put forward to drive upon and over the Governour. And this is averred upon the honour of the Governor.

Account of Thomas Trowbridge:

I passed through the town of Roxbury in the lane between the house of Ebenezer Davis and the widow Pierpont in which lane are two plain cart paths which meet in one at the de[s]cent of the hill. I being...on the west side of the land I seeing the Governor[']s coach where the paths meet in one...drove leisurely so that the coach might take that path on the east side...which was the best...when I came near the paths met I made a stop thinking they would pass by me in the other.... And the Governor[']s son...biding that it was easier for the coach to take the other path than for me to turn out of that; then did he strike my horse and...drew his sword and told me he would stab one of my horses. I stept betwixt him and my horses and told him he should not if I could help it. He...made several passes at me with his sword which I fended of[f] with my stick. Then came up John Winchester of Muddyriver alias Brookline...who gives the following account.

...I left my cart and came up and laid down my whip by Trowbridge and his Team. I asked Mr. William Dudley why he was so rash. He replied this dog won't turn out of the way for the Governour. Then I passed to the Governour with my hat under my arm hoping to moderate the matter, saying may it pleas[e] your Excellency, it is very easy for you to take into this path.... He answered...you rogue or rascal, I will have that way. I then told his excellency, if he would but have patience a minute or two I would clear that way for him. I turning about and seeing Trowbridge his horses twisting about ran to stop them....The Governour followed me with his drawn sword and said run the dogs through and with his naked sword stabbed me in the back. I facing about, he struck me on the head...giving me there a bloody wound. I then expecting to be killed dead on the spot to prevent his Excellency from such a bloody act in the heat of his passion. I caught hold of his sword and it broke but yet...in his furious rage he struck me divers blows with the hilt and piece of the sword remaining.... I called to the standers by to take notice that what I did in defense of my life.... The Governour said you lie you dog you lie you Devil.... Then said I, such words don't become a Christian. His Excellency replied, a Christian you dog, a Christian you Devil.... I was a Christian before your were born.

I Thomas Trowbridge further declare that...the Governour struck me divers blows then taking Winchester's driving stick and with the great end there of struck me several blows as he had done to Winchester afore. Winchester told his Excellency he had been a true subject to him and served him and had honoured him.... His Excellency said...you shall go to Jail you dogs; then twas asked what should become of our teams. His Excellency said, let them sink into the bottom of the earth.

QUEEN ANNE'S WAR

14 / "They are animated...to such barbarity by the French"

Queen Anne's War (1702–13) was the second of four great wars for empire fought between France, England, and their Indian allies. This struggle broke out when the French raided English settlements on the New England frontier. Fighting then spread to the southern frontier, where English colonists in the Carolinas attacked Spanish territory in Florida. An English invasion of Québec in 1710 failed, but in the Treaty of Utrecht ending the conflict, France ceded Newfoundland, Nova Scotia, and the French territory around Hudson Bay to England, and abandoned its claim to sovereignty over the Iroquois. Following the war, conflict persisted in the South, where English settlers destroyed the Yamassee Indians, who had been French allies, while the French brutally put down resistance by the Natchez Indians and their Chickasaw allies. This letter to the English queen examines the conflict's costs to New England.

The on-going challenge from the French and the Indians significantly shaped colonial society. It impeded westward settlement; led colonists to locate many early towns on sites chosen for military, not economic, reasons; and encouraged New Englanders to maintain compact communities. Further, it led colonists to adopt Indian methods of guerrilla warfare.

The French and Indian threat also carried profound consequences for American identity, generating a sense of a collective "us" transcending ethnic and regional lines. Conflict with French "papists" and "godless" Indians not only made colonists sensitive to the danger of tolerating "enemies within," it also reinforced a sense of themselves as a "Chosen People" with a special mission to defend civilization against Satan's forces. Finally, the costs of warfare severely strained relations between the colonies and England. Ultimately, war debts and defense costs would set into motion the train of events that culminated in the American Revolution.

THOMAS OLIVER, OCTOBER 20, 1708, TO QUEEN ANNE, GLC 4891

May it please yr Majesty.

It's nothing short of Twenty years, That your Majesty's good Subjects of this Province have been wasting under the Calamities of a Distressing and Expensive War, taking the Commencement Hereof from the Rebellion and Eruption of the Eastern Indians in the year 1688...save only the intervention of three or four years cessation....Yet in those years we were put to a very considerable charge in keeping constant guards and espyals over them, to prevent surprizals by their perfidy and treacherys.

And very soon upon the new declaration of war with France they broke out again in open rebellion and hostility, committing diverse barbarous murders, just after a repeated and fresh recognition of their duty and allegiance to your majesty.

We have been sharers in common with other our fellow subjects to a great degree in losses, both of men and estate, at home and at sea, both in the former & the present war, our trade is greatly diminished, and we are very much exhausted; our yearly expences for our necessary defence, and to prevent the incursions of the enemy is vastly great....

But we have no prospect of the end of these Troubles, & of being eased of our heavy and insupportable charge and burthen, whilst we can act only defensively, and have to do with the Enemy's Revels within our very bowels, who like beasts of prey seek their living by rapine and spoils, and are such monsters that their barbarities and cruelties are horrendous to human nature. And they are animated & encouraged to such barbarity by the French setting the heads of your Majesty's subjects, at a price upon bringing in the scalps, and they kill many in cold blood.... They have the advantage of retiring for shelter to the obscure recesses of a vast wilderness full of woods, lakes, rivers, ponds, swamps, rocks, and mountains, whereto they make an easy and quick passage, by of their...canoes of great swiftness and light of carriage; the matter whereof they are made being to be found almost everywhere and their skill and dexterity for the making and using of them is very extraordinary, which renders our tiresome marches after them ineffectual.

These rebels have no fixt settlements, but are ambulatory, & make frequent removes, having no other Houses, but tents or huts made of barque or kinds of trees, mats, etc. which they soon provide in all places where they come, so that it is impracticable to pursue or follow them with any body of regular troops. They are supported and encouraged by the French, who make them yearly presents gratis, of clothing, arms, and ammunition besides the supplies they afford them for the beaver and furs...and constantly keep their priests & emissaries among them, to steady them in their interests and bigotries which they have instilled into them. The French also oft times join them in their marches on our frontiers.

We humbly conceive with submission that the most probable method of doing execution upon them & reducing them is by men of their own color, way, & manner of living.

And if your Majesty shall be graciously pleased to command the service of the Mohawks and other Nations of the Western Indians that are in friendship and Covenant with your Majesty's several Governments, against these Eastern Indian rebels, for which they express themselves to stand ready and to whom they are a terror, they would with the blessing of God in short time extirpate or reclaim them and prevent the incursions made upon us from Canada or the east.

IMMIGRATION AND ETHNIC DIVERSITY

15 / *"During the voyage there is...terrible misery"*

During the eighteenth century, the colonial population grew at an astounding rate, doubling every twenty-five years. A significant part of this growth was the result of natural increase. At a time when the average English family had just three or four children survive to adulthood, the figure in the colonies was about seven. But the increase in population also reflected rapid immigration.

Immigration had a variety of sources. During the eighteenth century between 500,000 and 600,000 slaves were forcibly imported into the North American colonies. Another source of newcomers was the Scotch-Irish, descendants of sixteenth-century Scottish Presbyterians who had settled in northern Ireland. Fleeing rising rents imposed by absentee English landlords as well as a tax system that required them to pay tithes to support the Anglican Church, about 100,000 people from Ireland came to the American colonies between 1720 and 1755.

During this same period, some 65,000 Protestants left an area in Germany's Rhine River valley known as the Rhenish Palatine for the American colonies, fleeing religious persecution and crop failures. By 1775 the Pennsylvania Dutch (actually "Deutsch," for Germans) made up a third of the colony's population.

South of New England, half of all immigrants arrived in various forms of unfreedom: as indentured servants, apprentices, tenants, convicts, or slaves. George Washington's namesake—a member of the Virginia House of Burgesses named George Erskine, who served as Washington's mother's legal guardian—had been kidnapped as a boy in Wales and sold as a servant in Virginia. Thomas Paine (1737–1809) arrived in Philadelphia in 1774 on a vessel carrying 122 indentured servants.

About a third of eighteenth-century Germans came as "redemptioners," who sold themselves or their children for a term of years in return for transportation to the American colonies. By 1750, when Gottlieb Mittelberger, a schoolteacher from the duchy of Wurttemberg, left his wife and children to travel to America, recruitment and transportation of German settlers was controlled by Dutch shippers, who charged the emigrants by the day. Upon arrival in Philadelphia, the emigrants were kept on shipboard until someone agreed to pay the costs of their transportation. To obtain payment, many redemptioners agreed to serve a three or more years term of service and bound out their children until age twenty-one.

Gottlieb Mittelberger, *Journey to Pennsylvania in the Year 1750*

During the voyage there is on board these ships terrible misery, stench, fumes, horror, vomiting, many kinds of sea-sickness, fever, dysentery, headache, heat, constipation, boils, scurvy, cancer, mouth-rot, and the like, all of which come from old and sharply salted food and meat, also from very bad and foul water, so that many die miserably.

Add to this, want of provisions, hunger, thirst, frost, heat, dampness, anxiety, want, afflictions, and lamentations, together with other trouble, as for example, the lice abound so frightfully, especially on sick people, that they can be scraped off the body. The misery reaches the climax when a gale rages for two or three nights and days, so that every one believes the ship will go to the bottom with all human beings on board. In such a visitation the people cry and pray most piteously....

At length, when, after a long and tedious voyage, the ships come in sight of land, so that the promontories can be seen, which the people were so eager and anxious to see, all creep from below on deck to see the land from afar, and they weep for joy, and pray and sing, thanking and praising God....

But alas! When the ships have landed at Philadelphia after their long voyage, no one is permitted to leave them, except those who pay for their passage or can give good security. The others, who cannot pay, must remain on board the ships till they are purchased, and are released from the ships by their purchasers. The sick always fare the worst, for the healthy are naturally preferred and purchased first. And so the sick and wretched must often remain on board in front of the city for two or three weeks, and frequently die; whereas many a one, if he could pay his debt and were permitted to leave the ship immediately, might recover and remain alive....

The sale of human beings in the market on board the ship is carried on thus: every day Englishmen, Dutchmen, and High-German people come from the city of Philadelphia and other places, in part from a great distance, say 20, 30, or 40 hours away, and go on board the newly arrived ship that has brought and offers for sale passengers from Europe, and select among the healthy persons such as they deem suitable for their business, and bargain with them how long they will serve for their passage-money, which most of them are still in debt for. When they come to an agreement, it happens that adult persons bind themselves in writing to serve 3, 4, 5, or 6 years for the amount due by them, according to their age and strength. But very young people, from 10 to 15 years, must serve till they are 21 years old.

Many parents must sell and trade away their children like so many head of cattle; for if their children take the debt upon themselves, the parents can leave the ship free and unrestrained. But as the parents often do not know where and to what people their children are going, it often happens that such parents and children, after leaving the ship, do not see each other again for many years, perhaps no more in all their lives.

When people arrive who...have children under 5 years, the parents cannot free themselves by them; for such children must be given to somebody without compensation to be brought up, and they must serve for their bringing up till they are 21 years old. Children from 5 to 10 years, who pay half price for their passage, viz. 30 florins, must likewise serve for it till they are 21 years of age. They cannot, therefore, redeem their parents by taking the debt of the latter upon themselves. But children above 10 years can take part of their parents' debt upon themselves.

A woman must stand for her husband if he arrives sick, and in like manner a man for his sick wife, and take the debt upon herself or himself, and thus serve 5 to 6 years, not alone for his or her own debt, but also for that of the sick husband or wife. But if both are sick, such persons are sent from the ship to the sick-house, but not until it appears probable that they will find no purchasers. As soon as they are well again they must serve for their passage, or pay if they have means.

It often happens that whole families—husband, wife, and children—are separated by being sold to different purchasers, especially when they have not paid any part of their passage-money.

When a husband or wife has died at sea when the ship has made more than half of her trip, the survivor must pay or serve not only for himself or herself, but also for the deceased....

If some one in this country runs away from his master, who has treated him harshly, he cannot get far. Good provision has been made for such cases, so that a runaway is soon recovered. He who detains or returns a deserter receives a good reward.

Gottlieb Mittelberger, *Journey to Pennsylvania in the Year 1750* (Philadelphia: J.J. McVey, 1898), pp.20-29.

INDENTURED SERVITUDE

16 / "An apprentice or servant...for...ye Term of fifteen years & five Months"

Colonial Americans were extremely familiar with various forms of unfree labor. Many youths served a term of years apart from their families as servants or apprentices. At the age of twelve, Benjamin Franklin (1706–90) was indentured to his much older brother for a nine-year term, and was only supposed to receive wages the last year.

The prevalence of various forms of voluntary and involuntary servitude gave a highly charged meaning to words such as "liberty," "freedom," and "tyranny." Franklin would later write in his autobiography that his brother's harsh treatment "might be a means of impressing me with that aversion to arbitrary power that has stuck to me through my whole life." It seems likely that their familiarity with servitude contributed to the colonists' suspicions of power and their fear that America would be subjected to slavery as a result of arbitrary British rule and autocratic trade and tax policies.

INDENTURE APPRENTICING JAVIN TOBY, JANUARY 9, 1747, GLC 3002.01

This Indenture Witnessesth that Hannah Toby Indian Woman of So[uth] Kingstown of...ye Colony of Rhode Island...hath put her son Javin Toby, Molatto of her own free will & accord an apprentice or servant of John Steadman of South Kingstown yeoman & to Purthany his Wife...after the manner of an apprentice from of Day of ye date hereof for and during ye Term of fifteen years & five Months which Will be compleat on ye Seventh day of June 1763. During all which Term of apprentice or service his master & mistress faithfully shall serve their secrets keep their Lawful Commands of labor & every Where he shall do no damage to his s[ai]d Master & Mistress nor see it done by others. Without giving notice thereof to his s[ai]d Master & Mistress he shall not waste his Master & Mistresses goods nor lend them unlawfully to any. He shall not use any unlawful games nor contract matrimony nor commit Fornication. During s[ai]d Term he shall not absent himself either by day or by night Without Leave nor Haunt Taverns ale Houses...but in all things behave as a faithful servant ought to do during the s[ai]d term and his s[ai]d Master & Mistress...by their Parts are to find and provide sufficient apparel meat Drink Washing & Lodging Suitable for Such an apprentice. During s[ai]d Term at ye Expiration thereof to Dismiss Him With one new Suit of apparel fitting for his body besides his usual wearing Clothes.

SUSPICION OF ARBITRARY POWER

17 / *"If every Man had his Will, all Men would exercise Dominion"*

A pivotal jury decision in New York in 1735 helped establish the principle of freedom of the press. Opponents of New York's royal governor, William Cosby, had set up John Peter Zenger (1697–1746), a German immigrant, as publisher of the *New York Weekly Journal* in 1733. The next year, after New York's governor dismissed one of his leading opponents, Chief Justice Lewis Morris, from office, the *Weekly Journal* severely criticized Cosby. Because the articles attacking Cosby were published anonymously, the governor had Zenger indicted and tried for seditious libel. English law defined any criticism of a public official—true or false—as libel. But Zenger's attorney, Andrew Hamilton (1676–1741) of Philadelphia, persuaded the jury that Zenger had printed the truth and that the truth is not libelous.

In stirring words, Hamilton told the jury that "the Question before the Court...is not the Cause of a poor Printer, nor of *New-York* alone....No! It may in its Consequence, affect every Freeman that lives under a British Government on the Main of *America*....It

Numb. XIX.

THE
New-York Weekly JOURNAL.

Containing the freſheſt Advices, Foreign, and Domeſtick.

MUNDAY March 11th, 1733.

Mr. Zenger,

Pray incert the following Sentiments of CATO, *and you'll oblige Yours*, &c.

CONſidering what ſort of a Creature Man is, it is ſcarce poſſible to put him under too many reſtraints, when he is poſſeſſed of great Power: He may poſſibly uſe it well; but they act moſt prudently, who ſuppoſing that he would uſe it ill, incloſe him within certain Bounds, and make it terrible to him to exceed them.

It is nothing ſtrange, that Men, who think themſelves unaccountable, ſhould act unaccountably, and that all Men would be unaccountable if they could; even thoſe who have done nothing to diſpleaſe, do not know but ſometime or other they may; and no Man cares to be at the intire Mercy of another. Hence it is, that if every Man had his Will, all Men would exerciſe Dominion, and no Man would ſuffer it. It is therefore, owing more to the Neceſſities of Men, than to their Inclinations, that they have put themſelves under the Reſtraint of Laws, and appointed certain Perſons, called Magiſtrates, to execute them; otherwiſe they would never be executed, ſcarce any Man having ſuch a Degree of Virtue as willingly to execute the Laws upon himſelf; but on the contrary, moſt Men thinking them a Grievance, when they come to medle with themſelves and their Property.

Hence grew the Neceſſity of Government, which was the mutual Contract of a Number of Men, agreeing upon certain Terms of Union and Society, and putting themſelves under Penalties, if they violated theſe terms, which were called Laws, and put into the Hands of one or more Men to execute. And thus men quitted Part of their natural Liberty to acquire civil Security. But frequently the Remedy prov'd worſe than the Diſeaſe; and humane Society had often no enemies ſo great as their own Magiſtrates; who, wherever they were truſted with too much Power, always abuſed it, and grew miſchievous to thoſe who made them what they were. Rome, while ſhe was free, (that is, while ſhe keept her Magiſtrates within due bounds,) could defend herſelf againſt all the world, and conquer it; but being enſlaved (that is her Magiſtrates having broke their Bounds) ſhe could not defend her ſelf againſt her own ſingle Tyrants; nor could they defend her againſt her foreign Foes and Invaders: For by their Madneſs and Cruelties they had deſtroyed her Virtue and Spirit, and exhauſted her Strength. This ſhews that thoſe Magiſtrates, that are at abſolute differance with a Nation, either cannot ſubſiſt long, or will not ſuffer the Nation to ſubſiſt long; and that mighty Traitors, rather than fall them ſelves, will pull down their Country.

The common People generally think that great Men have great Minds, and ſcorn baſe Actions; which Judgment is ſo falſe, that the baſeſt and worſt of all Actions have been done by great Men; perhaps they have not picked private Pockets, but they have done worſe, they have often diſturbed, deceived and pillaged the World: And he who is capable of the higheſt Miſchiefs, is capable of the Meaneſt. He who plunders a Country of a Million of Money, would in ſuitable Circumſtances ſteal a Silver Spoon; and a Conqueror, who ſteals and pillages a

Kingdom,

John P. Zenger. Newspaper, *The New York Weekly Journal,* Numb. XIX, 1733/03/11. The Gilder Lehrman Collection, on deposit at the Pierpont Morgan Library. GLB 0326

is the Cause of Liberty....Every Man who prefers Freedom to a Life of Slavery will bless and honour You, as Men who have...given us a Right...both of exposing and opposing arbitrary Power (in these Parts of the World, at least) by speaking and writing Truth."

An excerpt from Zenger's *Weekly Journal* gives vivid expression to the popular suspicion of arbitrary power.

JOHN P. ZENGER, *New York Weekly Journal*, NO. XIX, MARCH 11, 1733, GLB 326

Mr. Zenger,

Pray insert the following sentiments of Cato, and you'll oblige Yours, &c.

Considering what sort of a Creature Man is, it is scarce possible to put him under too many restraints, when he is possessed of great Power: He may possibly use it well; but they act most prudently, who supposing that he would use it ill enclose him within certain Bounds and make it terrible to him to exceed them.

It is nothing strange, that Men, who think themselves unaccountable, should act unaccountably, and that all Men would be unaccountable if they could...; and no Man cares to be at the entire Mercy of another. Hence it is that if every Man had his Will, all Men would exercise Dominion, and no Man would suffer it. It is therefore owing more to the Necessities of Men, than to their Inclinations, that they have put themselves under the Restraint of Laws, and appointed certain persons, called Magistrates, to execute them; otherwise they would never be executed, scarce any Man having such a Degree of Virtue as unwillingly to execute the Laws upon himself....

Hence grew the Necessity of Government, which was the mutual Contract of a Number of Men, agreeing upon certain Terms of Union and Society, and putting themselves under Penalties if they violated these terms, which were called Laws, and put into the Hands of one or more Men to execute. And thus men quitted Part of their natural Liberty to acquire civil Security. But frequently the Remedy prov'd worse than the Disease; and humane Society had often no enemies so great as their own Magistrates; who, wherever they were trusted with too much Power, always abused it, and grew mischievous to those who made them what they were. Rome, while she was free, (that is, while she kept her Magistrates within due bounds) could defend herself against all the world, and conquer it; but being enslaved (that is her Magistrates having broke their Bounds) she could not defend her self against her own single Tyrants; nor could they defend her against her foreign Foes and Invaders: For by their Madness and Cruelties they had destroyed her Virtue and Spirit, and exhausted her Strength....

The common People generally think that great Men have great Minds, and scorn base Actions; which Judgment is so false, that the basest and worst of all Actions have been done by great Men; perhaps they have not picked private Pockets, but they have done worse, they have often disturbed, deceived and pillaged the World: And he who is capable of the highest Mischiefs, is capable of the Meanest. He who plunders a Country of Millions of Money, would in suitable Circumstances steal a Silver Spoon; and a Conqueror, who steals and pillages a Kingdom, would in an humbler Fortune rifle a Portmanteau or rob an Orchard.

Political Jealousy, therefore, in the people is a necessary and laudable Passion. But in a Chief Magistrate, a Jealousy of his People is not so justifiable, their Ambition being only to preserve themselves; whereas it is natural for Power to be striving to enlarge itself, and to be encroaching upon those that have none.... Now because Liberty chastises and shortens Power, therefore Power would extinguish Liberty; and consequently Liberty has too much cause to be exceeding jealous and always upon her Defence. Power has many Advantages over her; it has generally numerous Guards, many Creatures, and much Treasure; besides it has more Craft and Experience, and less Honesty and Innocence: And whereas Power can, and for the most Part does subsist where Liberty is not, Liberty cannot subsist without Power; so that she has, as it were, the Enemy always at her Gates.

To Conclude: Power without Control appertains to God alone; and no Man ought to be trusted with what no Man is equal to. In Truth, there are so many passions and Inconsistencies, and so much Selfishness, belonging to humane Nature, that we can scarce be too much upon our Guard against each other. The only Security we have that men will be Honest, is to make it their Interest to be Honest; and the best Defence we can have against their being Knaves, is to make it terrible to them to be Knaves. As there are many Men, wicked in some Stations, who would be innocent in others; the best way is to make Wickedness unsafe in any Station.

THE GREAT AWAKENING

18 / *"A great...concern about...Things of Religion...became Universal"*

The Great Awakening, the most important event in American religion during the eighteenth century, was a series of emotional religious revivals that spread across the American colonies in the late 1730s and 1740s. The mid-eighteenth century witnessed a wave of evangelism without precedent in America, England, Scotland, and Germany. In England this wave would culminate in the Methodist revivals led by John Wesley (1703–91), while in Germany the revivals would give rise to a movement known as Pietism. In colonial America, in contrast to England and Germany, the revivals tended to cross class lines and to take place in urban as well as rural areas.

In New England, in particular, the Great Awakening represented a reaction against the growing formality and the dampening of religious fervor in the Congregational churches. Elsewhere in the colonies, no single church was able to satisfy the population's spiritual and emotional needs.

The periodical *The Christian History* reported the revivals in England, Scotland, and America as they took place. It published Jonathan Edwards's account of the revivals he led in Northampton, Massachusetts, that helped ignite the Great Awakening. Edwards (1703–58), one of this country's most brilliant theologians, sought in his theological writings to reconcile Calvinist teachings and Enlightenment thought. In Northampton, Edwards deliberately directed his sermons at the young, and by 1734 the whole town was engaged in a religious revival. But by 1750 he had been ousted from his church and spent most of his remaining years evangelizing among New England's Indians.

The Great Awakening carried profound consequences for the future. It was the first experience shared by large numbers of people throughout all the American colonies, and therefore contributed to the growth of a common American identity. It also produced a deepened consciousness of sin within the existing social order and aroused a faith that Americans stood within reach of Christ's Second Coming. Even though the Great Awakening contributed to a splintering of American Protestantism, as supporters of the revivalists known as New Lights and their opponents, known as Old Lights, established separate congregations, it also sent a powerful spiritual message: that God works directly through the people, rather than through churches or other public institutions.

The Christian History, July 11, 1743, GLB 423

In the Night after the Lord's Day, October 29, 1727, there was a general and amazing Earthquake throughout New England & the neighbouring Provinces; which with several repeated Shocks afterwards in divers Parts of the Land, was a Means of awakening many to serious Thoughts of God and Eternity, and of reviving Religion among us....

But a more remarkable Revival of Religion in this Country follows in a Time of great Security; when there was no terrible Dispensation of Providence to awaken the minds of Men, in the Years 1734, 35, and 36. An Account of this is given in a printed Treatise entitled, A faithful Narrative of the surprising Work of God in the Conversion of many hundred Souls in Northampton...in the Province of the Massachusetts,...written by the Rev. Mr. Jonathan Edwards Minister of Northampton, Nov. 6. 1736....

Just after my Grandfather's [Solomon Stoddard (1634–1729)] Death, it seemed to be a time of extraordinary Dullness in Religion: Licentiousness for some Years greatly prevailed among the Youth of the Town; they were many of them very much addicted to Night-walking, and frequenting the Tavern, and lewd Practices, wherein some, by their Example, exceedingly corrupted others. It was their Manner very frequently to get together, in Conventions of both Sexes, for Mirth and Jollity, which they called Frolicks; and they would often spend the greater part of the Night in them, without regard to any Order in the Families they belonged to: and indeed Family-Government did too much fail in the Town. It was become very customary with many of our young People, to be Indecent in their Carriage at Meeting, which doubtless, would not have prevailed to such a Degree, had it not been that my Grandfather through his great Age (tho' he retained his Powers surprisingly to the last) was not able to Observe them. There had also long prevailed in the Town, a Spirit of Contention between two Parties, into which they had for many Years been divided, by which, was maintained a Jealousy one of the other, and they were prepared to oppose one another in all public Affairs.

But in two or three Years after Mr. Stoddard's Death, there began to be a sensible Amendment of these Evils; the young People...by degrees left off their Frolicking, and grew observably more Decent in their Attendance on the public Worship, and there were more that manifested a Religious Concern than there used to be.

At the latter end of the Year 1733, there appeared a very unusual flexibleness, and yielding to Advice, in our young People. It had been too long their manner to make the Evening after the Sabbath, and after our public Lecture, to be especially the Times of their

Mirth, and Company keeping. But a Sermon was now preached on the Sabbath before the Lecture, to shew the Evil Tendency of the Practice, and to persuade them to reform it; and it was urged on Heads of Families, that it should be a thing agreed upon among them to govern their Families, and keep their Children at home, at these times.... But Parents found little, or no occasion for the exercise of Government in the Case; the young People declared themselves convinced by what they had heard from the Pulpit, and were willing of themselves to comply with the Counsel that had been given: and it was immediately, and, I suppose, almost universally complied with; and there was a thorough Reformation of these Disorders thenceforward, which has continued ever since....

Presently upon this, a great and earnest Concern about the great Things of Religion, and the eternal World, became universal in all Parts of the Town, and among Persons of all Ages.... All other Talk but about spiritual and eternal Things, was soon thrown by.... The Minds of People were wonderfully taken off from the World; it was treated amongst us as a Thing of very little Consequence....The Temptation now seemed to lie on that Hand, to neglect worldly Affairs too much, and to spend too much Time in the immediate Exercise of Religion....

There was scarcely a single Person in the Town, either old or young, that was left unconcerned about the great Things of the eternal World. Those that were wont to be the vainest, and loosest, and those that had been most disposed to think, and speak lightly of vital and experimental Religion, were now generally subject to great Awakenings.

FEAR OF SLAVE REVOLTS

19 / *"The Negroes were rising"*

In 1741 New York City executed thirty-four people for conspiring to burn down the city. Thirteen African-American men were burned at the stake and another seventeen black men, two white men, and two white women were hanged. An additional seventy blacks and seven whites were banished from the city.

In 1741 New York's economy was depressed, and, as a result of a punishing winter, the population suffered severe food shortages. The British Empire was at war with France and Spain, and there were reports that the Spanish were threatening to invade New York or organize acts of arson. There was also troubling news about the Stono slave uprising in South Carolina. With one-fifth of Manhattan's population consisting of black slaves, it was apparently easy to believe that they, perhaps assisted by Irish Catholic immigrants, were conspiring to set the city ablaze. It seems unlikely that there was an organized plan to set fire to the city and murder its inhabitants, as the authorities alleged. There is, however, evidence of incidents of arson, and it appears that some slaves talked about retaliating against their enslavers and winning their freedom.

While slavemasters described their slave populations as faithful, docile, and contented, slaveowners always feared slave revolt. Probably the first slave revolt in the New World erupted in Hispaniola in 1522. During the early eighteenth century there were slave uprisings on Long Island in 1708 and in New York City in 1712. Slaves in South

Carolina staged several insurrections, culminating in the Stono Rebellion of 1739, when they seized firearms, killed whites, and burned houses. In 1740 a slave conspiracy was uncovered in Charleston. During the late eighteenth century slave revolts took place in Guadeloupe, Grenada, Jamaica, Suriname, St. Domingue (Haiti), Venezuela, and the Windward Islands. Many fugitive slaves, known as maroons, fled to remote regions such as Spanish Florida or Virginia's Great Dismal Swamp.

The main result of slave insurrections, throughout the Americas, was the mass execution of blacks. In 1712, when a group of enslaved Africans in New York set fire to a building and ambushed and murdered about nine whites who arrived to put out the fire, fourteen slaves were hanged, three were burned at the stake, one was starved to death, and another was broken on the wheel.

The following account was originally published in 1744 by Daniel Horsmanden (1694–1778), who presided over the trial and later served on New York's Supreme Court.

DANIEL HORSMANDEN, *A Journal of the Proceedings in the Detection of the Conspiracy formed by Some White People, in Conjunction with Negro and other Slaves, for burning the city of New-York in America, and Murdering the Inhabitants*, 1744, GLC 4205

Wednesday, March 18 [1741]

About one o'clock this day a fire broke out of the roof of his majesty's house at Fort George, within this city, near the chapel; when the alarm of fire was first given, it was observed from the town, that the middle of the roof was in a great smoke, but not a spark of fire appeared on the outside for a considerable time.... Upon the chapel bell's ringing, great numbers of people, gentlemen and others, came to the assistance of the lieutenant governor and his family; and...most of the household goods, etc. were removed and saved.... But the fire got hold of the roof...and an alarm being given that there was gun powder in the fort, whether through fear and an apprehension that there was, or whether the hint was given by some of the conspirators themselves, with artful design to intimidate the people, and frighten them from giving further assistance, we cannot say; though the lieutenant governor declared to every body that there was none there.... Such was the violence of the wind, and the flames spread so fast, that in about an hour and a quarter's time the house was burnt down to the ground....

Monday, April 6 [1741]

About ten o'clock in the morning, there was an alarm of a fire at the house of serjeant Burns, opposite fort Garden....

Towards noon a fire broke out in the roof of Mrs. Hilton's house...on the East side of captain Sarly's house.... Upon view, it was plain that the fire must have been purposely laid.... There was a cry among the people, *the Spanish Negroes; the Spanish Negroes; take up the Spanish Negroes*. The occasion of this was the two fires...happening so closely together.... and it being known that Sarly had purchased a Spanish Negro, some time before brought into his port, among several others.... and that they afterwards pretending to have been free men in their country, began to grumble at their hard usage, of being sold as slaves. This probably gave rise to the suspicion, that this Negro, out of revenge, had been the instrument of these two fires; and he behaving insolently upon some people's asking him questions concerning them.... It was told to a magistrate who was near, and he ordered him to jail, and also gave direction to constables to commit all the rest of that cargo [of Africans], in order for their safe custody and examination....

While the justices were proceeding to examination, about four o'clock there was another alarm of fire....

While the people were extinguishing the fire at this storehouse, and had almost mastered it, there was another cry of fire, which diverted the people attending the storehouse to the new alarm...but a man who had been on the top of the house assisting in extinguishing the fire, saw a Negro leap out at the end window of one of them...which occasioned him to cry out...*that the Negroes were rising*....

Supreme Court, Wednesday, April 22 [1741]

Deposition, No. 1-Mary Burton [a servant], being sworn, deposeth,

1. "That Prince [Mr. Auboyneau's slave] and Caesar [Mr. Varack's slave] brought the things which they had robbed...to her master, John Hughson's house...about two or three o'clock on a Sunday morning [March 1, 1740].

2. That Caesar, Prince and Mr. Philipse's Negro man (Cuffee) used to meet frequently at her master's house, and that she had heard them (the Negroes) talk frequently of burning the fort; and that they would go down to the Fly [the city's east end] and burn the whole town; and that her master and mistress said, they would aid and assist them as much as they could.

3. "That in their common conversation they used to say, that when all this was done, Caesar should be governor, and Hughson, her master, should be king.

4. "That Cuffee used to say, that a great many people had too much, and others too little; that his old master had a great deal of money, but that, in a short time, he should have less, and that he (Cuffee) should have more....

7. "That she had known at times, seven or eight guns in her master's house, and some swords, and that she had seen twenty or thirty Negroes at one time in her master's house...."

This evidence of a conspiracy, not only to burn the city, but also destroy and murder the people, was most astonishing to the grand jury, and that any white people should become so abandoned as to confederate with slaves in such an execrable and detestable purpose, could not but be very amazing to every one that heard it....

[A Justice administers the sentence to Quack and Cuffee]

You both now stand convicted of one of the most horrid and detestable pieces of villainy, that ever satan instilled into the heart of human creatures to put in practice; ye, and the rest of your colour, though you are called slaves in this country; yet are you all far from the condition of other slaves in other countries; nay, your lot is superior to that of thousands of white people. You are furnished with all the necessaries of life, meat, drink, and clothing, without care, in a much better manner than you could provide for yourselves, were you at liberty; as the miserable condition of many free people here of your complexion might abundantly convince you. What then could prompt you to undertake so vile, so wicked, so monstrous, so execrable and hellish a scheme, as to murder and destroy your own masters and benefactors? nay, to destroy root and branch, all the white people of this place, and to lay the whole town in ashes.

I know not which is more astonishing, the extreme folly, or wickedness, of so base and shocking a conspiracy.... What could it be expected to end in, in the account of any rational and considerate person among you, but your own destruction?

AMERICA AS A LAND OF OPPORTUNITY

20 / "Why increase the Sons of Africa...where we have so fair an Opportunity...of increasing the lovely White and Red?

Perhaps the most important essay written by an American during the eighteenth century, Franklin's "Observations Concerning the Increase of Mankind" was one of the first serious studies of demography. In the early nineteenth century it would serve as an inspiration for Thomas Malthus (1766–1834), who based his grim law of population (that population would inevitably outstrip the food supply) on Franklin's calculations. But Franklin's argument was, in fact, quite different from Malthus's bleak prophesy. Franklin, like other Americans as late as Lincoln, held to a belief that no man in America needed to long remain a laborer for others. Despite the doubling of the population every twenty years or so, America remained a land of opportunity, where wages remained high and even slaves were expensive.

What is perhaps most striking about Franklin's essay today is his sophisticated use of "social science" data to convince the British ministry to alter its colonial policies. Particularly jarring, however, is Franklin's plea that America be maintained as an entirely Anglo-Saxon society.

Benjamin Franklin, "Observations Concerning the Increase of Mankind, Peopling of Countries, &c.," 1755

Europe is generally full settled with Husbandmen, Manufacturers, &c. and therefore cannot now much increase in People: America is chiefly occupied by Indians, who subsist mostly by Hunting. But as the Hunter, of all Men, requires the greatest Quantity of Land from whence to draw his Subsistence, (the Husbandman subsisting on much less, the Gardener on still less, and the Manufacturer requiring the least of all), The Europeans found America as fully settled as it well could bee by Hunters; yet these having large Tracks, were easily prevail'd on to part with Portions of Territory to the new Comers, who did not much interfere with the Natives in Hunting, and furnish'd them with many Things they wanted.

Land being thus plenty in America, and so cheap as that a labouring Man, that understands Husbandry, can in a short Time save Money enough to purchase a Piece of new Land sufficient for a Plantation, whereon he may subsist a Family; such are not afraid to marry; for if they even look far enough forward to consider how their Children when grown up are to be provided for, they see that more Land is to be had at Rates equally easy, all Circumstances considered.

Hence Marriages in America are more general, and more generally early, than in Europe. And if it is reckoned there, that there is but one Marriage per Annum among 100 Persons, perhaps we may here reckon two; and if in Europe they have but 4 Births to a Marriage (many of their Marriages being late) we may here reckon 8, of which if one half grow up, and our Marriages are made, reckoning one with another at 20 Years of Age, our People must at least be doubled every 20 Years.

But notwithstanding this Increase, so vast is the Territory of North-America, that it will require many Ages to settle it fully; and till it is fully settled, Labour will never be cheap here, where no Man continues long a Labourer for others, but gets a Plantation of his own, no Man continues long a Journeyman to a Trade but goes among those new Settlers, and set up for himself, &c. Hence Labour is no cheaper now, in Pennsylvania, than it was 30 Years ago, tho' so many Thousand labouring People have been imported.

The Danger therefore of these Colonies interfering with their Mother Country in Trades that depend on Labour, Manufactures, &c. is too remote to require the Attention of Great-Britain.

But in Proportion to the Increase of the Colonies, a vast Demand is growing for British Manufacturers, a glorious Market wholly in the Power of Britain, in which Foreigners cannot interfere, which will increase in a short Time even beyond her Power of supplying, tho' her whole Trade should be to her Colonies: Therefore Britain should not too much restrain Manufactures in her Colonies. A wise and good Mother will not do it. To distress, is to weaken, and weakening the Children, weakens the whole Family....

'Tis an ill-grounded Opinion that by the Labour of Slaves, America may possibly vie in Cheapness of Manufactures with Britain. The Labour of Slaves can never be so cheap here as the Labour of working Men is in Britain. Any one may compute it. Interest of Money in the Colonies from 6 to 10 per Cent. Slaves one with another cost L30 Sterling per Head. Reckon then the Interest of the first Purchase of a Slave, the Insurance or Risque on his life, his Clothing and Diet, Expences in his Sickness and Loss of Time, Loss by his Neglect of Business (Neglect is natural to the Man who is not to be benefitted by his own Care or Diligence), Expense of a Driver to keep him at Work, and his Pilfering from Time to Time, almost every Slave being *by Nature* a Thief, and compare the whole Amount with the Wages of a Manufacturer of Iron or Wool in England, you will see that Labour is much cheaper there than it can ever be by Negroes here. Why then will Americans purchase Slaves? Because Slaves may be kept as long as a Man pleases, or has Occasion for their Labour; while hired Men are continually leaving their Master (often in the midst of his Business) and setting up for themselves.

....There are suppos'd to be now upwards of One Million English Souls in North-America, (tho' 'tis thought scarce 80,000 have been brought over Sea) and yet perhaps there is not one the fewer in Britain, but rather more, on Account of the Employment the Colonies afford to Manufacturers at Home. This Million doubling, suppose but once in 25 Years, will in another Century be more than the People of England, and the greatest Number of Englishmen will be on this Side the Water. What an Accession of Power to the British Empire by Sea as well as Land! What Increase of Trade and Navigation! What Number of Ships and Seamen! We have been here but little more than 100 Years, and yet the Force of our Privateers in the late War, united, was greater, both in Men and Guns, than that of the whole British Navy in Queen Elizabeth's Time....

And since Detachments of English from Britain sent to America, will have their Places at Home so soon supply'd and increase so largely here; why should the Palatine Boors [Germans] be suffered to swarm into our Settlements, and by herding together establish their Language and Manners to the Exclusion of ours? Why should Pennsylvania, founded by the English, become a Colony of *Aliens*, who will shortly be so numerous as to Germanize us instead of our Anglifying them, and will never adopt our Language or Customs, any more than they can acquire our Complexion.

Which leads me to add one Remark: That the Number of purely white People in the World is proportionably very small. All Africa is black or tawny. Asia chiefly tawny. America (exclusive of the new Comers) wholly so. And in Europe, the Spaniards, Italians, French, Russians and Swedes, are generally of what we call a swarthy Complexion; as are the Germans also, the Saxons only excepted, who with the English, make the principal Body of White People on the Face of the Earth. I could wish their Numbers were increased. And while we are, as I may call it, *Scouring* our Planet, by clearing America of Woods, and so making this Side of our Globe reflect a brighter Light to the Eyes of Inhabitants in mars or Venus, why should we in the Sight of Superior Beings, darken its People? why increase the Sons of Africa, by Planting them in America, where we have so fair an Opportunity, by excluding all Blacks and Tawneys, of increasing the lovely White and Red? But perhaps I am partial to the complexion of my Country, for such Kind of Partiality is natural to Mankind.

Benjamin Franklin, "Observations Concerning the Increasing of Mankind, Peopling of Countries, &c." (Boston: Printed by S. Kneeland, 1755).

PART FOUR

The Seven Years' War

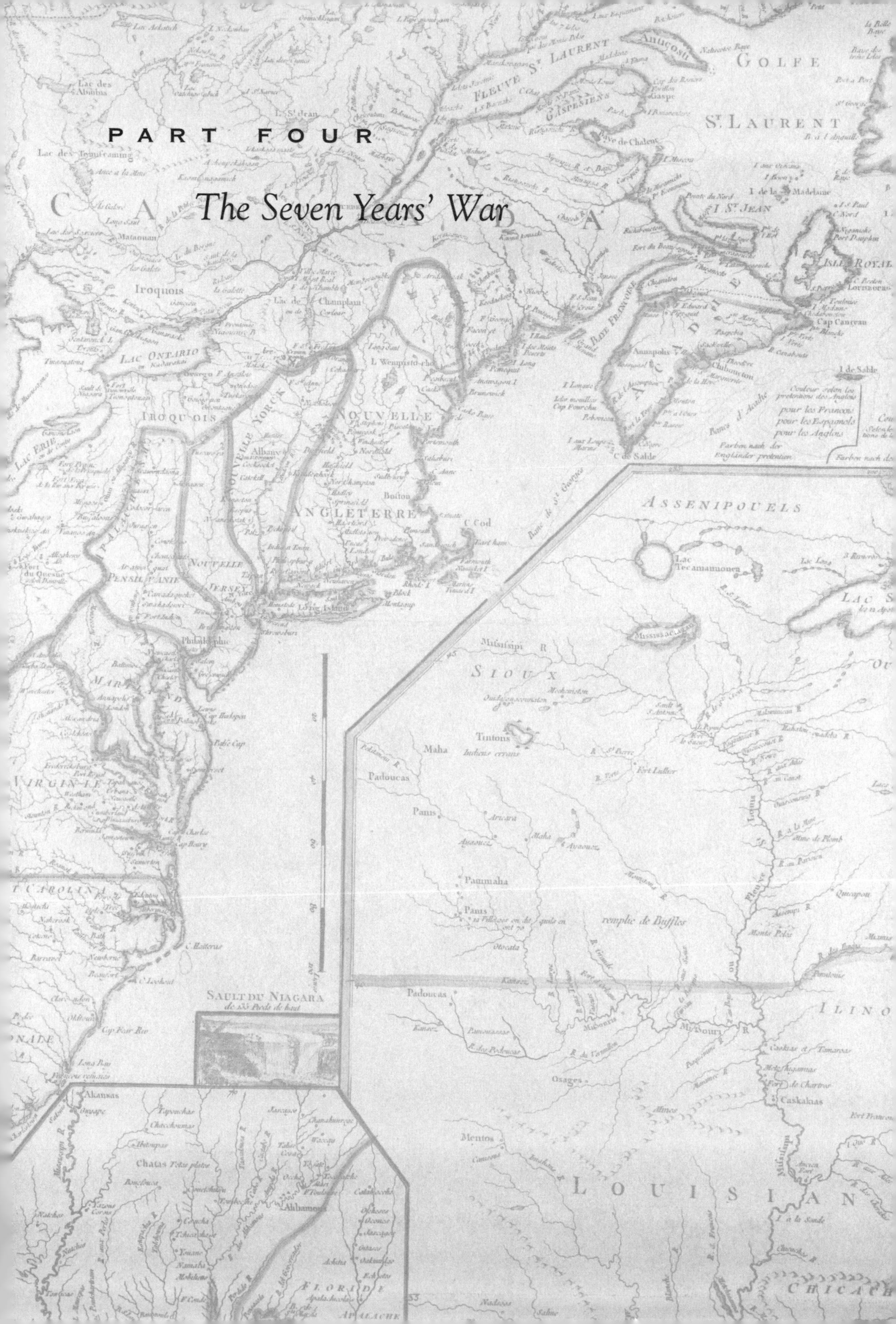

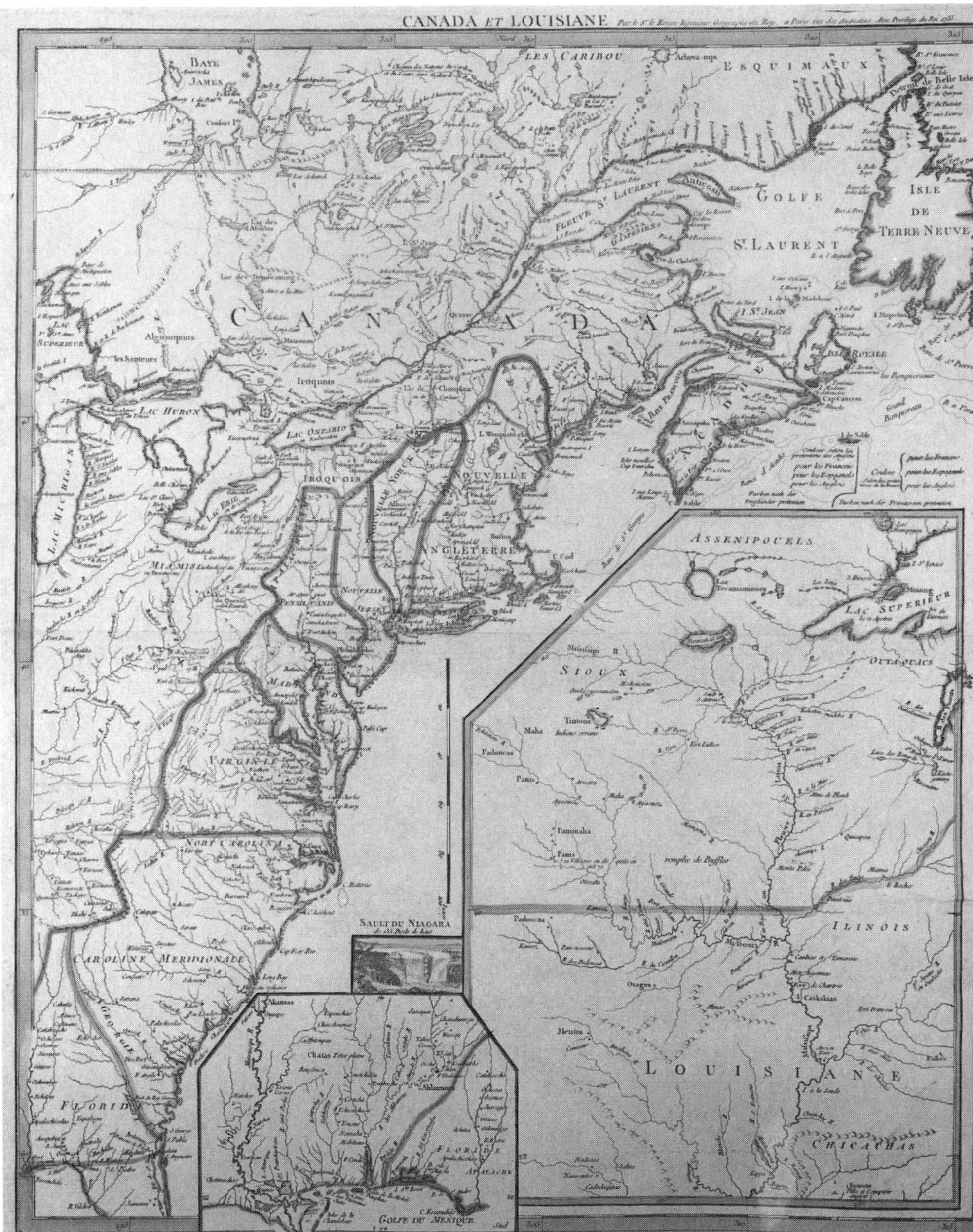

George L. Le Rouge. Map, Canada et Louisiane [double page engraving with handcoloring], 1755. The Gilder Lehrman Collection, on deposit at the Pierpont Morgan Library. GLC 5714

Half a century of conflict between Britain and France over North America culminated in the French and Indian War. When the war began, there were more than about 2 million British colonists in America and about 65,000 French in Canada.

Unlike the three previous Anglo-French wars, which were outgrowths of European conflicts, this one began with colonial initiatives. Fur traders from Pennsylvania and Virginia were eager to trade with Indians in the Ohio River valley. Leading Virginia planters, who were interested in developing the region, had formed the Ohio Company, and with support of London merchants, had received a royal grant of 200,000 acres in the Ohio River valley in 1749.

The French, determined to secure the territory against encroaching British and American traders and land speculators, built a chain of forts along Pennsylvania's Allegheny River. The British ministry ordered colonial governors to repel the French advance, "by force" if necessary.

In 1753, Virginia's governor, Robert Dinwiddie, an investor in the Ohio Company, sent George Washington, a twenty-one-year-old major in the Virginia militia, to Pennsylvania to demand a French withdrawal from the forts. The French refused. In the spring of 1754, Washington returned to Pennsylvania with about 160 men. The French defeated Washington at Fort Necessity, the first battle of the French and Indian War.

Meanwhile, representatives of seven colonies met in Albany, New York, with representatives of the Iroquois Confederacy. The goal of the Albany Congress was to solidify friendship with the Iroquois in light of the approaching war with France and to discuss the possibility of an intercolonial union. At the conference Benjamin Franklin presented a "plan of union" that would establish a Grand Council that would be able to levy taxes, raise troops, and regulate trade with the Indians. The delegates at the congress approved the plan, but the colonies refused to ratify it, since it threatened their power of taxation.

Following the surrender of Fort Necessity, Britain ordered sixty-year-old Major General Edward Braddock and a combined force of 3,000 redcoats and colonial militia to attack the French stronghold of Fort Duquesne at the site of present-day Pittsburgh. French and Indian forces ambushed the expedition eight miles from the fort, killing Braddock and leaving two-thirds of his soldiers dead or wounded.

In 1756 William Pitt became the king's new chief minister. Viewing America as the place "where England and Europe are to be fought for," Pitt let Prussia bear the brunt of the Seven Years' War in Europe, while concentrating British military resources in America. He united the previously divided colonies by guaranteeing payment for military services and supplies. He also installed younger and more capable officers.

Pitt's strategy worked. In 1758 the British, with colonial forces assisting, seized

Louisbourg, a French fortress guarding the mouth of the St. Lawrence River. In 1759 British forces sailed up the river, laid siege to the city of Québec for three months, and defeated French forces in September. The next year, Montreal also surrendered to the British, ending the fighting in America.

The war came to an official end in 1763, with the signing of the Treaty of Paris. The treaty gave Britain all French land in Canada except for two tiny fishing islands south of Newfoundland. To the south, the treaty gave Britain all of France's holdings east of the Mississippi River, which now became the boundary between the British colonies and Louisiana, which Spain received from France before ceding Florida to Britain. In effect, triumphant Britain chose to keep Canada rather than the conquered Caribbean slave colonies Guadeloupe and Martinique, which were returned to France.

BRITISH NORTH AMERICA IN 1755

1 / *"Canada must be subdued"*

Immediately before the American Revolution, there were not just thirteen British colonies in the New World; there were thirty, stretching from Guiana on the South American coast to Hudson Bay. Many people in Britain regarded the Caribbean as the most valuable portion of Britain's New World empire. Through the seventeenth century, the revenue produced in the West Indies was vastly greater than that produced by the mainland colonies. A single island, Barbados, had more people in 1676 than all of New England. By the mid-eighteenth century, however, the value of the mainland colonies both as a source of raw materials and as a market for British goods was becoming increasingly apparent.

A Maryland newspaper, excerpting a report from an English magazine, offers a perspective on why the French and Indian War had begun and why the American colonies were worth protecting.

The Maryland Gazette, MAY 22, 1755, NO. 524, GLB 321

A General View of the Conduct of the French in America, of our Settlements there.

But what engrosses the Attention at present is their Invasion of Virginia, in a profound Peace; and well it may, since that our Colonies on that Continent are of the utmost Importance....

Nova Scotia is a Country which has laid long neglected, but is capable of being made very considerable. Great Part of its Soil is very good, and wants only People to cultivate it, and produce every Kind of Corn which grows in England. The Country abounds in many Sorts of Timber, as Oak, Beech, Birch, Walnut, Fir &c. so that they can build what Number of Ships they please; but the principal Thing that will make this Colony very considerable is the Cod Fishery.... So that by this Trade you plant a Colony, increase your Number of Seamen, put off your Manufactures, and enrich yourselves.

The next Colony is New Hampshire and Main[e]: This is also known for its fishery: But is most famous for the excellent Masts and Yards that it furnishes to the Royal Navy of England, which you could not get in such Abundance, nor on such Conditions, in any Country of the World; for they do not take a Guinea from you: But for all their Fish, Masts, Etc., you pay them in Goods.

The Province of Massachusetts...comes next, of which Boston is the Capital. It...has a large Sea Coast, and many very good Harbours.... Their soil is indifferent, producing Rye, Oats, Barley, Indian Corn, but no Wheat; They have excellent Pasture Land, and of course good Provisions. A principal Article of their Trade is Cod Fish, which they send to Spain, Portugal, Italy, &c. and the Whale Fishery is more considerable here than in any of the other Colonies....

From the Populousness of this country, it may easily be judged what Quantities of Manufactures are required there, all of which are paid for in Fish...in building us Ships, in Oil, Pitch, Tar, and in Gold and Silver....

The Colony gave Peace to Europe; for it is well remembered what a Figure the Allies made in Flanders the late War; France carried every Thing before her, and nothing could check her Designs, till the Governor and Council of Boston resolved the Reduction of Cape Breton [northern Nova Scotia], laid an Embargo, beat up for Volunteers, enlisted 4000 Men, bought Arms, Provisions, hired Transports, and sailed in 40 days after the resolution first taken. They took the Place, which greatly alarmed the French King, who was then in Flanders. A Congress was held about two Years after at Aix la Chapelle; What had we to offer France in Lieu of all her Conquests? Why, nothing but Cape Breton; and for her Cape Breton she gave up all Flanders [because of the return of Louisbourg Fortress].

We come next to Rhode-Island, which is about the Size of the Isle of Wight.... The principal Articles of their Trade are Horses, Lumber, and Cheese.... They bring a great deal of Silver, every Dollar of which finds its Way to London to pay for our Manufactures; they also build very fine Ships, with which they do good Service in Time of War.

Travelling Westward we next come to Connecticut.... The Soil of this Country is better than that of Boston, and is productive of every Kind of European Corn, they have a great Plenty of black Cattle, [wheat], Sheep, Hogs, and Horses; and abound in every Necessary of Life....The consumption of our Manufactures in this Country is very great, and the Product of all the Provisions, Horses, and Lumber, that they export to other countries, comes to London for Goods.

The next Colony is New York.... They have for many Years carried on a considerable Trade to London and other Ports of this Kingdom, as well as to Spain, Portugal, all Italy, Africa, and all the West India Islands, and take several Hundred Pounds per Annum of our Manufactures; for which we are paid in Gold and Silver...and many Thousands per Annum in Beaver, and other Furs, Ships, and several other Articles.

We go on to New-Jersey, most of which is a very level Country, and its Produce the same as that of New-York, and in great abundance.... They have but very little foreign Trade; New York is the principal Market for their Provisions; and supplies them with English Goods. This Colony was unfortunately granted to a certain Number of Proprietors; who often had Disputes about the Divisions of the Lands; so that Titles were precarious, which discouraged People from settling it; but within these 25 Years past, it is become very prosperous, and very populous.

Pennsylvania['s]...Product is the same in every particular as that of New-York, and full as abundant.... There have gone only from the Port of Rotterdam, from 4 to 8,000 Palatines to Pennsylvania per Annum...besides many English, Scots, and Irish....

The next Colony is Maryland, of which Lord Baltimore is Proprietor: But whatever the cause, it is thinly inhabited. It is a very fruitful Country, and produces very good Wheat, and other European Corn, and a great deal of Indian Corn. The Inhabitants have Abundance of black Cattle and Hogs; but their principal Article is Tobacco, of which they send a great deal to England.... Unhappily for this Colony, the Felons of England are thought good enough to be incorporated with its Inhabitants. However the People take all our Manufactures that they have Occasion for, which they pay in Tobacco, Deer-Skins, and Fur.

Virginia is the most ancient of all the Colonies.... The Soil is extremely good, producing all Sorts of European and Indian Corn, in great Abundance, but is most famous for Tobacco.... The People live in great Plenty, but are not quite so Numerous as in some other colonies, because they employ Negroes in the raising of their Tobacco....

North Carolina...is very hot in Summer, and not very cold in Winter...and has been very indifferently managed. It is a very fruitful Country. Its Produce is Indian Corn, Rice, Pulse, Tobacco, Pitch, Tar, Deer-Skins, Fur, Wax, and Tallow. It contains many Sorts of Timber, the Principal is Pine of several Kinds. As the Inhabitants have but little Winter, they abound in Cattle and Hogs; of the latter the Woods are full; They fatten themselves on Chestnuts &c. so that they are no Expense to the Farmer. The greatest disadvantage is, that they have a dangerous Sand Bar all along their Coast, and but one good Harbour for Ships of Burden, which is Cape Fear, their principal Town....

South Carolina...is very hot and has but very little winter. Its Produce is the same with that of North Carolina; but its principal Produce is Rice, with which it supplies almost all Europe; and if the Article of Indigo, which they have lately fallen on, will succeed, this will soon become one of the richest Colonies we have; and we shall save the vast sums which we pay France annually for that Article....

The last Colony is Georgia...and is extremely hot, a poor light Soil, and but thinly inhabited; it was settled as our Frontier next to the Spaniards; and we had great Hopes of making there great Quantities of Silk. Some has been made, and more might...and if they bring the Affair to Perfection, it will be a prodigious Advantage to England.

Such is the British Empire in North America; which from Nova-Scotia to Georgia is a Tract of 1600 Miles Sea-Coast; a Country productive of all the necessaries and Conveniences of Life; and which already contains a greater Number of People than either the Kingdom of Naples and Sicily, Sardinia, Portugal, Spain, Denmark, Sweden, or Prussia, or the Republic of Holland. In short, there are but three Powers in Europe, which surpass them in Number, the German Empire, France, and perhaps England. America is become the Fountain of our Riches, for with America our greatest trade is carried on....

This is the Country, which the French have many Years envied us, and which they have been long meditating to make themselves Masters of: They are at length come to a Resolution to attack us, in profound Peace, in one of the best of those Colonies, Virginia; and in that part of it which lies on the River Ohio, to which Country they never pretended before. Every one knows that the English were the first and only Europeans who settled Virginia.... The French however if they find their Way to the Coast of Virginia, will easily over-run the provinces, because each Province considers itself as independent of the Rest, and the Invaders from Canada all act under one Governor; to unite 13 Provinces which fill an Extent of 1600 Miles is not easy.... Canada must be subdued.

A SOLDIER'S DIARY

2 / "Cutlasses and hatchets playing on every quarter with much effusion of blood"

A soldier's diary provides a vivid firsthand account of fighting in northern New York during the early stages of the Seven Years' War, when the British and colonial forces suffered a series of punishing defeats at the hands of the French and their Indian allies.

ROBERT MOSES, 1755, GLC 4944

...We were informed that a number of Indians killed two men in a very barbarous manner. Destroyed eight cattle carried away the value of three. A scout consisting of thirty men pursued them on Friday July 25th [1755] but could not discover them....

...we received intelligence that a number of Indians supposed to consist of one hundred killed two men about two miles from the Fort [Bellowe's Fort], took the man's heart and cut it in two and laid it on his neck, and butchers the other most barbarously, sought a house near the Fort, wounded one man that he died about an hour after our arrival....

Saturday 7th [of September]: in the afternoon one of the Mohawks that came in informed Colonel Blanchard that he discovered a vast number of French & Indians about 4 miles from the camp & tract [tracked] thirty about a mile from the Camp. The Colonel ordered a scout of one hundred and 20 men to go and know the certainty of it, who returned and made no discovery excepting few tracks which they supposed was made by some of their own men which were a hunting.

Monday the 8th: day of September 1755—a scout went out from Lake George commonly called by the Indians Lake Sacremaw, under the command of Colonel William being in number hundred they receiving intelligence that an Army of French & Indians were on the borders and that their intention chiefly was to beset Fort Lyman. The Colonel with five men was making the best of his way down to reli[e]ve them in case any such emergency should happen but he had marched not exceeding 4 miles from the Lake when he entered where the Enemy ambushed themselves on each side of the path in the form of a half moon. The Colonel had no sooner come up, with his men conveniently in the midst of them but he was fired on every quarter very briskly. The Colonel's men behaved themselves cowardly for some minutes but [were] overpowered by such a vast company their number suppose to consist of 2500 men compelling Colonel with his 600 to fight & retreat until they came to the Fort at the Lake. The Enemy pursued them very boldly with their firelocks shouldered and their Bay[o]nets fixed to them marched in towards ye Front of our Army and thought to rush into the camp. They in the camps took them to be New Hampshire forces never fired a gun until the Enemy came so near them that they could discover a Frenchman from an Englishman upon which discovery the whole camp was alarmed & withstood them on the front fixed their cannons and played on them for an hour with the loss of many men to the French. They immediately begin to charge on the right & left...but at both places they met with strong resistance. The Indians on the Left Wing were so ambitious that they would feign enter into ye Artillery ground. Two cannon were mounted on that quarter on[e] of which being fired on them swept away sixteen which put the rest in such a terror that they drawed off as quick as possible.

The Regiments which were camped at Fort Lymon...14 miles [away] heard the cannons roaring...immediately dispatched to the Lake the New Hampshire Regiment together with part of New York Regiment which number met ye enemy after they drawed off from ye Lake with a new salutation of firelocks.

Cutlasses and hatchets playing on every quarter with much effusion of blood but our New Hampshire forces being fresh & courageous and the Enemy tired and much discouraged with the Defeat they met with, retreated and made their escape toward a Creek. The next day they were pursued. A vast quantity of plunder was taken up which they dropped in the creek. The day after ye battle three Frenchmen were taken up by the Guard of Fort Lymon who upon examination declared that their Army was entirely broke....

FASTING AND REPENTANCE

3 / "The English Colonies...are fallen under the Chastising hand of Heaven"

In 1756 the French and their Indian allies won a series of military victories in what is now upstate New York and southern Ontario. Following the British and colonial defeats in the early stages of the conflict, Governor Stephen Hopkins (1707–85) of Rhode Island issued a proclamation calling for a day of fasting and repentance. Because the United States has not been the scene of bloody battles, invasions, and wartime atrocities for well over 130 years (except, of course, for the Native American population), it is easy to forget the ravages and perils of the first 258 years of our history.

Stephen Hopkins, governor of Rhode Island, proclamation of a day of fasting and rest, May 12, 1756, GLC 1412.11

All who acknowledge God's moral Government of the World, believe that the Sins of Mankind draw down his Judgments upon them. And as the English Colonies on the Continent are fallen under the Chastising hand of Heaven who has permitted the barbarous and cruel Savages of the Wilderness to spoil and destroy their Borders to murder their young Men and to carry their Sons and Daughters into the most Calamitous

Captivity and are threatened with Wars Still more General and Judgments which portend their utter Extirpation Under such Circumstances Reason Suggests and Revelation Demonstrates that our whole Safety depend on deeply humbling ourselves before God Sincerely repenting of our Sins and religiously resolving to reform our Lives and Actions for the Time to come.

Such Considerations have moved the General assembly of the said Colony to direct Me to proclaim Thursday the Twentieth Day of this Instant May to be observed as a Day of Fasting and Prayer throughout the Colony and that no Servile Labor be done on that Day but that all Societies of Christians within the Same Assemble themselves together at their Several usual Places of public Worship and there humbly address the Throne of Grace for the Preservation of George the Second our present King of his Royal Family and of the British Constitution and for the Peace and Safety of all his Colonies. And principally that we may break off from our Sins by hearty Repentance and may avert the Judgments of God and obtain his Favor by true Amendment of Life.

THE CAPTURE OF QUÉBEC

4 / "We...clambered up one of the steepest precipices that can be conceived"

The climactic battle of the conflict took place on September 12–13, 1759. After laying siege to the city of Québec for three months, five thousand British regulars sailed past the city and secretly scaled the cliffs leading to the Plains of Abraham, west of the city, under cover of darkness. The French moved quickly to repel the surprise attack, but within fifteen minutes, the battle was decided. Captain John Knox offers a firsthand account of the decisive battle that brought an end to French rule over Canada.

Captain John Knox, *An Historical Journal of the Campaigns in North America, 1757–60*

Before daybreak this morning we made a descent upon the north shore, about half a quarter of a mile to the eastward of Sillery, and the light troops were fortunately, by the rapidity of the current, carried lower down, between us and Cape Diamond; we had, in this debarkation, thirty flat-bottomed boats, containing about sixteen hundred men. This was a great surprise on the enemy, who, from the natural strength of the place, did not suspect, and consequently not prepared against, so bold an attempt. The chain of sentries, which they had posted along the summit of the heights, galled us a little, and picked off several men, and some officers, before our light infantry got up to dislodge them.

This grand enterprise was conducted and executed with great good order and discretion; as fast as we landed, the boats put off for re-enforcements....We lost no time here, but clambered up one of the steepest precipices that can be conceived, being almost a perpendicular, and of an incredible height. As soon as we gain the summit all was quiet, and not a shot was heard.... The general then detached the light troops to our left to rout the enemy from their battery, and to disable their guns, except they could be rendered serviceable to the party who were to remain there; and this service was soon performed. We then faced to the right, and marched toward the town by files, till we came to the Plains of Abraham: an even piece of ground which Mr. [British General James] Wolfe had made choice of, while we stood forming upon the hill. Weather showery; about six o'clock [a.m.] the enemy first made their appearance upon the heights, between us and the town; whereupon we halted, and wheeled to the right, thereby forming the line of battle.

About eight o'clock we had two pieces of short brass six-pounders playing on the enemy, which threw them into some confusion, and obliged them to alter their disposition, and Montcalm [the French commander] formed them into three large columns; about nine the two armies moved a little nearer each other....

About ten o'clock the enemy began to advance briskly in three columns, with loud shouts and recovered arms, two of them inclining to the left of our army, and the third towards our right, firing obliquely at the two extremities of our line, from the distance of one hundred and thirty, until they came within forty, yards; which our troops withstood with the greatest intrepidity and firmness, still reserving their fire, and paying the strictest obedience to their officers. This uncommon steadiness, together with the havoc which the grapeshot from our fieldpieces made among them, threw them into some disorder, and was most critically maintained by a well-timed, regular, and heavy discharge of our small arms, such as they could no longer oppose. Hereupon they gave way, and fled with precipitation, so that, by the time the cloud of smoke was vanished, our men were again loaded, and, profiting by the advantage we had over them, pursued them almost to the gates of the town and the bridge over the little river, redoubling our fire with great eagerness, making many officers and men prisoners.

An Historical Journal of the Campaigns in North America for the Years 1757, 1758, 1759, and 1760, Vol. I, ed. Arthur G. Doughty (Toronto: Champlain Society, 1914–16), Vol. II, pp. 94–101.

THE SEVEN YEARS' WAR AND THE GROWTH OF ANTISLAVERY SENTIMENT

5 / *"Though we made slaves of the Negroes...I believed that liberty was the natural right of all men equally"*

During the eighteenth century Great Britain dominated the Atlantic slave trade. Exports of Africans, during the 1700s, exceeded 6 million, three times the number shipped between 1450 and 1700. Of these, 2.9 million were shipped by Englishmen or Anglo-Americans.

During the eighteenth century, the slave trade become one of Britain's largest and most profitable industries. By mid-century a third of the British merchant fleet was engaged in transporting 50,000 Africans a year to the New World. But it was not just slave traders or planters who benefited from the slave trade. American shipowners, farmers, and fisherman also profited from slavery. Slavery played a central role in the growth of commercial capitalism in the colonies. The slave plantations of the West Indies became the largest market for American fish, oats, corn, flour, lumber, peas, beans, hogs, and horses. And New Englanders distilled molasses produced by slaves in the French and Dutch West Indies into rum.

Although slavery did not create a major share of the capital that financed the industrial revolution (profits from the slave trade and New World plantations added up to about 5 percent of Britain's national income in the mid-eighteenth century), slaves did produce the major consumer goods that were the basis of world trade during the seventeenth, eighteenth, and nineteenth centuries. These slave-grown products stimulated a consumer revolution, enticing the masses of Britain and then Western Europe to work harder and more continuously to enjoy the pleasures of sugar, tobacco, rum, coffee, and eventually cotton clothing. It was New World slave labor that ushered in the consumer culture we know today. In addition, the slave trade provided stimulus to shipbuilding, banking, and insurance; and Africa became a major market for iron, textiles, firearms, and rum.

Among the people deeply implicated in the Atlantic slave system were the Quakers. Some Quakers in the West Indies owned slave plantations, while Quaker merchants in London, Philadelphia, and Newport, Rhode Island, were engaged in the Atlantic slave trade. The Seven Years' War, however, produced a spiritual crisis within the Society of Friends and inspired the Quakers to become the first religious group to actively discourage its members from owning or trading in slaves.

In the following selections from his journal, written during the Seven Years' War, the Quaker John Woolman (1720–72) describes his growing recognition that slavery was sinful and that it threatened America's destiny. His deep misgivings over enslaving Africans sprang entirely from religious sources—especially from the biblical precept that "God is no respecter of persons." Yet to his horror, Woolman discovered that even Quakers used the Bible to justify racial slavery.

John Woolman, journal, 1757

Soon after I entered this province [Maryland] a deep and painful exercise came upon me...as the people in this and the Southern Provinces live much on the labor of slaves, many of whom are used hardly....

As it is common for Friends on such a visit to have entertainment free of cost, a difficulty arose in my mind with respect to saving my money by kindness received from what appeared to me to be the gain of oppression. Receiving a gift, considered as a gift, brings the receiver under obligations to the benefactor, and has a natural tendency to draw the obliged into a party with the giver.....

Many were the afflictions which attended me, and in great abasement, with many tears, my cries were to the Almighty for his gracious and fatherly assistance.... Being thus helped to sink down into resignation, I felt a deliverance from that tempest in which I had been sorely exercised....The way in which I did it was thus: when I expected soon to leave a Friend's house where I had entertainment...I spoke to one of the heads of the family privately, and desired them to accept of those pieces of silver, and give them to such of their Negroes as they believed would make the best use of them; and at other times I gave them to the Negroes myself, as the way looked clearest to me....

[May 9.] We pursued our journey.... On the way we had the company of a colonel of the militia, who appeared to be a thoughtful man. I took occasion to remark on the difference in general betwixt a people used to labor moderately for their living, training up their children in frugality and business, and those who live on the labor of slaves; the former, in my view, being the most happy life. He concurred in the remark, and mentioned the trouble arising from the untoward, slothful disposition of the Negroes, adding that one of our laborers would do as much in a day as two of their slaves. I replied, that free men, whose minds were properly on their business, found a satisfaction in improving, cultivating, and providing for their families; but Negroes, laboring to support others who claim them as their property, and expecting nothing but slavery during life, had not the like inducement to be industrious.

After some further conversation I said, that men who have power too often misapplied it; that though we made slaves of the Negroes, and the Turks made slaves of the Christian, I believed that liberty was the natural right of all men equally. This he did not deny, but said the life of the Negroes were so wretched in their own country that many of them lived better here than there. I replied, "There is great odds in regard to us on what principle we act"; and so the conversation on that subject ended. I may here add that another person, some time afterwards, mentioned the wretchedness of the Negroes, occasioned by their intestine wars, as an argument in favor of our fetching them away for slaves. To which I replied, if compassion for the Africans, on account of their domestic troubles, was the real motive of our purchasing them, that spirit of tenderness being attended to, would incite us to use them kindly, that, as strangers brought out of affliction, their lives might be happy among us. And as they are human creatures, whose souls are as precious as ours, and who may receive the same help and comfort from the Holy Scriptures as we do, we could not omit suitable endeavors to instruct them therein; but that while we manifest by our conduct that our views in purchasing them are to advance ourselves, and while our buying captives taken in war animates those parties to push on the war, and increase desolation amongst them, to say they live unhappily in Africa is far from being an argument in our favor....

Soon after, a Friend in company began to talk in support of the slave-trade, and said the Negroes were understood to be the offspring of Cain, their blackness being the mark which God set upon him after he murdered Abel his brother; that it was the design of Providence they should be slaves, as a condition proper to the race of so wicked a man as Cain was. Then another spake in support of what had been said. To all which I replied in substance as follows: that Noah and his family were all who survived the flood, according to Scripture; and as Noah was of Seth's race, the family of Cain was wholly destroyed. One of them said that after the flood Ham went to the land of Nod and took a wife; that Nod was a land far distant, inhabited by Cain's race, and that the flood did not reach it; and as Ham was sentenced to be a servant of servants to his brethren, these two families, being thus joined, were undoubtedly fit only for slaves. I replied, the flood was a judgment upon the world for their abominations, and it was granted that Cain's stock was the most wicked, and therefore unreasonable to suppose that they were spared.... I further reminded them how the prophets repeatedly declare "that the son shall not suffer for the iniquity of the father, but every one be answerable for his own sins." I was troubled to perceive the darkness of their imaginations, and in some pressure of spirit said, "The love of ease and gain are the motives in general of keeping slaves, and men are wont to take hold of weak arguments to support a cause which is unreasonable."...

Many of the white people in those provinces take little or no care of Negro marriages; and when Negroes marry after their own way, some make so little account of those marriages that with views of outward interest they often part men from their wives by selling them far asunder, which is common when estates are sold.... Many whose labor is heavy being followed at their business in the field by a man with a whip, hired for that purpose, have...little else allowed but one peck of Indian corn and some salt, for one week, with a few potatoes; the potatoes they commonly raise by their labor on the first day of the week. The correction ensuing on their disobedience to overseers, or slothfulness in business, is often very severe, and sometimes desperate.

Men and women have many times scarcely clothes sufficient to hide their nakedness, and boys and girls ten and twelve years old are often quite naked amongst their master's children. Some of our Society, and some of the society called Newlights, use some endeavors to instruct those they have in reading; but in common this is not only neglected but disapproved. These are the people by whose labor the other inhabitants are in a great measure supported, and many of them in the luxuries of life. These are the people who have made no agreement to serve us, and who have not forfeited their liberty that we know of. These are the souls for whom Christ died, and for our conduct toward them we must answer before Him who is no respecter of persons. They who know the only true God, and Jesus Christ whom he hath sent, and are thus acquainted with the merciful, benevolent, gospel spirit, will therein perceive that the indignation of God is kindled against oppression and cruelty, and in beholding the great distress of so numerous a people will find cause for mourning.

The Journal and Essays of John Woolman, ed. Amelia Mott Gummere (New York: Macmillan, 1892), pp. 188–95.

THE FATE OF NATIVE AMERICANS

6 / "I most heartily congratulate you on the surrender of Canada"

No longer able to play the French off against the British, Native Americans found it increasingly difficult to slow the advance of white settlers into the western parts of New York, Pennsylvania, North and South Carolina, and Virginia. To stop encroachments on their lands in the Southeast, the Cherokees attacked frontier settlements in the Carolinas and Virginia in 1760. Defeated the next year by British regulars and colonial militia, the Cherokees had to allow the English to build forts on their territory.

Indians in western New York and Ohio also faced encroachment onto their lands. With the French threat removed, the British reduced the price paid for furs, allowed settlers to take Indian land without payments, and built forts in violation of treaties with local tribes. In the spring of 1763 an Ottawa chief named Pontiac led an alliance of Delaware, Seneca, Shawnee, and other western Indians in rebellion. Pontiac's alliance attacked forts in Indiana, Michigan, Pennsylvania, and Wisconsin that Britain had taken over from the French, destroying all but three. Pontiac's forces then moved eastward, attacking settlements in western Pennsylvania, Maryland, and Virginia, killing more than two thousand colonists. Without assistance from the French, however, Pontiac's rebellion petered out by the year's end.

The following letter, which describes the encroachment of colonists onto Indian homelands, provides context for Pontiac's uprising.

Richard Peters to Sir William Johnson, Superintendent of Indian Affairs, February 12, 1761, GLC 766

The Connecticut People are making their grand push both in England for a new Grant from the King, and in this Province for a forcible entry and detainer of the Indian Land, on no other Pretence than that their Charter extends to the South Seas, and so like mad men they will cross New York and New Jersey, and come and kindle an Indian war in the Bowels of this poor Province....

The Governor has wrote you at large on this wicked revival of the Connecticut Claims, and I wish either you or General Amherst could fall on some means to have it

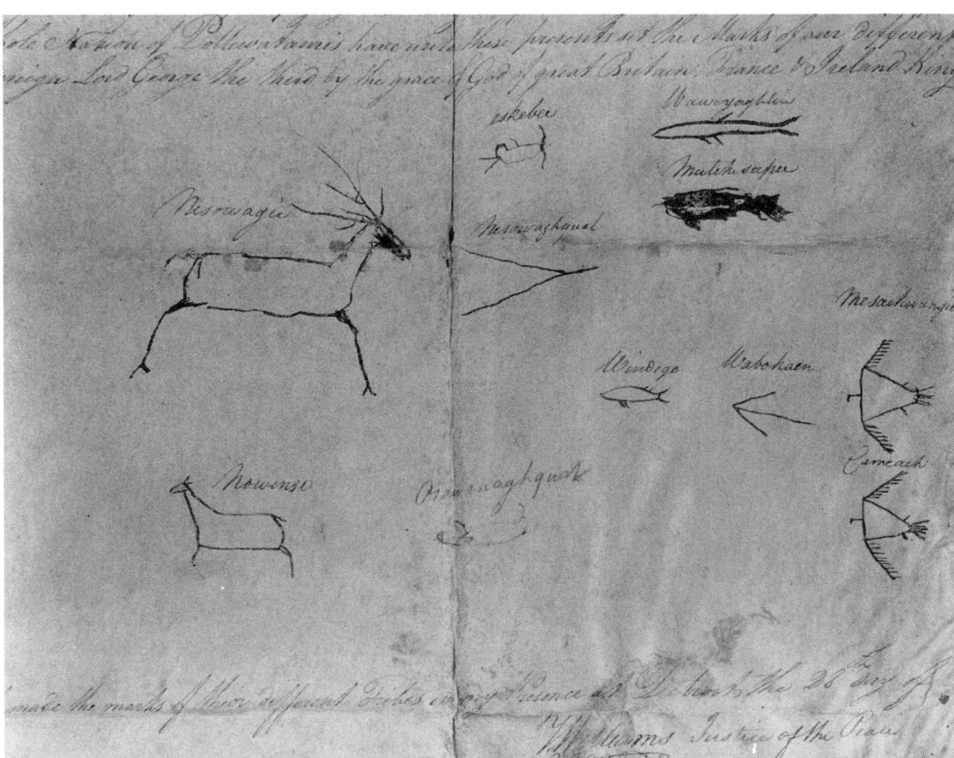

Pottwatomi Indian Nation. Document signed, Land grant to Maj. Arent Schuyler De Peyster (Detroit area), 1780/07/20. The Gilder Lehrman Collection, on deposit at the Pierpont Morgan Library. GLC 1450.808

laid aside, for it will breed a civil war among our Back Inhabitants, who are sucking in, all over the frontiers, the Connecticut Poison and Spirit & will actually in my Opinion, go into open Rebellion in the opening of the Spring.

I could heartily wish that the Delaware Complaints were heard and adjusted....

I most heartily congratulate you on the surrender of Canada and on the most favourable Situation of all our Affairs....

PART FIVE

The Age of Revolution, 1765–1825

Paul Revere. Print, The Bloody Massacre perpetrated in King-Street… [engraving of Boston Massacre], 1770.
The Gilder Lehrman Collection, on deposit at the Pierpont Morgan Library. GLC 1868

On the morning of August 14, 1765, to protest the Stamp Act— a law obligating Americans to purchase special stamped paper for newspapers and many legal forms—a Boston crowd hanged an effigy of the city's stamp collector, Andrew Oliver, from a tree. When Oliver failed to resign his position immediately, the mob demolished the stamp collector's warehouse at the city dock. The crowd then beheaded the effigy's head and "stamped" it to pieces. After giving Oliver time to flee, they ransacked his house, shattering the windows and smashing the furniture. Three days later, a second house wrecking occurred in Newport, Rhode Island, after the local stamp distributor failed to resign.

The protests and disorder that broke out in the American colonies in 1765 marked the beginning not only of the American struggle for independence, but also more than half a century of popular protest, revolution, and war across the Western world. From the Ural Mountains in Russia to the Alleghenies and the Andes in the Americas, rioting, revolutions, and popular struggles against undemocratic rule took place in areas as diverse as France (in 1789), Geneva in Switzerland, Ireland, and Mexico.

Revolution took on an entirely new meaning in 1791, when civil war erupted in St. Domingue (Haiti) and slaves in the French colony's northern province rose in revolt. In 1770 a French philosophe, the Abbé Raynal, had called for a "black Spartacus" to overthrow slavery. Spartacus was a Thracian slave and gladiator who led a great slave revolt against the Romans in southern Italy in 73–71 B.C.E. Under the leadership of a new Spartacus, Toussaint Louverture, Haiti's slaves defeated the armies of France, Spain, and Britain, and, in 1801, adopted a constitution prohibiting slavery forever. Haiti became independent in 1804 after expelling a second French expeditionary force, sent by Napoleon.

The age of revolution culminated with the Latin American wars of independence. In 1790 five European countries—Britain, France, the Netherlands, Portugal, and Spain—controlled all of Latin America. But in 1821, Mexico won its independence from Spain, and two years later Costa Rica, El Salvador, Guatemala, Honduras, and Nicaragua broke away from Mexico. In South America during the 1820s, Argentina, Bolivia, Chile, Colombia, Ecuador, Peru, and Venezuela won their freedom from Spanish rule.

So, the American Revolution was not an isolated event. Despite many significant differences, the popular protests and upheavals of the age of revolution reflected certain common ideals and aspirations that had been unleashed by the American and French Revolutions. Unifying all of these revolutions was a shared political language invoking such potent terms as "constitutional rights," "the sovereignty of the people," and "the consent of the governed."

The Roots of Revolution

Few in Britain or its colonies could have imagined in 1763 that a war for independence would erupt within a dozen years. The American colonists had a long history of squabbling with one another, and, before 1765, relations among the colonists were much more quarrelsome than their relations with Great Britain.

Rapid population growth within the colonies was a source of many intercolonial disputes, including conflicts over colonial boundaries. New York clashed with Connecticut and Massachusetts; Pennsylvania with Connecticut and Virginia; and New York and New Hampshire over claims to present-day Vermont.

Westerners and Easterners within individual colonies also fought over issues of representation, taxation, Indian policy, and the slow establishment of governmental institutions in frontier areas. In 1764 the Paxton Boys, a group of Scotch-Irish frontier settlers from western Pennsylvania, marched on Philadelphia, and withdrew only after they were promised a greater representation in the Quaker-dominated provincial assembly and greater protection against Indians. In the late 1760s in backcountry South Carolina, where local government was largely nonexistent, frontier settlers organized themselves into vigilante groups known as Regulators to maintain order. Only extension of a new court system into the backcountry kept the Regulators from attacking Charleston. In North Carolina in the early 1770s, the eastern militia had to suppress conflict in the backcountry, where settlers complained about underrepresentation in the colonial assembly, high taxes, exorbitant legal fees, and manipulation of debt laws by lawyers, merchants, and officials backed by eastern planters.

These regional conflicts often coincided with ethnic lines. Many backwoods residents were Scotch-Irish or German in descent, and they deeply resented the Anglo-American establishment of the more settled parts of the colonies. Conflict also surged periodically in areas where wealthy proprietors owned substantial amounts of land. In eastern New Jersey during the 1740s, and New York's Hudson River valley in 1757 and 1766, tenant farmers refused to pay rents and staged insurrections against landlords.

Yet for all their squabbles, the colonists did share certain characteristics in common, which became increasingly apparent during the years leading up to the Revolution. These included the absence of a titled, hereditary aristocracy; a widespread distribution of land; an unprecedented degree of ethnic and religious diversity; and broad eligibility to vote—50 to 75 percent of adult white males, compared to only about 20 percent in England. In contrast to the way Britons conceived of Parliament, the colonists thought of the members of the colonial assemblies as representatives of the people, accountable to their constituents and obligated to follow public instructions.

Certain shared economic grievances also gave a degree of common identity to the colonists, such as dependence on British and Scottish financial agents. The sharing of Protestant religious revivals as well as anti-Catholicism, too, proved to be important elements in an emerging American identity.

During the 1760s and 1770s all of these conditions, trends, and experiences contributed to a distinctive sense of American identity. Many colonists began to conceive of America as a truly "republican" society. By a republican society they meant something more than a government based on popular elections. Such a society emphasized personal independence, public virtue, and above all a suspicion of concentrated power as essential ingredients of a free society. Increasingly, Americans contrasted their society with Britain, with its landed aristocracy, political corruption, patronage, and bloated governmental bureaucracy. For decades, various European writers had idealized Americans as an industrious, egalitarian people, content with the simple joys of life. In the years preceding the Revolution, many Americans began to self-consciously reflect on this distinctive republican identity.

The Ideology of Independence

In the Declaration of Independence, Thomas Jefferson traced the causes of the Revolution to "a history of repeated injuries and usurpations, all having in direct object the establishment of an absolute Tyranny over these States." But the Revolution was not simply the result of a series of British abuses of power; it was also a product of the way the colonists *perceived* and *interpreted* those events.

At the beginning of the imperial crisis, American leaders were not outspoken in their opposition to Britain. They defended the British constitution and assumed that their grievances would be resolved. Gradually, however, they became convinced that wicked and designing ministers were conspiring to deprive them of their liberties. By 1776 they believed that the king himself was part of this conspiracy.

The colonists viewed the events of the 1760s and 1770s through an ideological prism that had been shaped by English thinkers who had tried to deny the throne to Charles II's Catholic brother James between 1679 and 1681. This tradition held that liberty was always fragile and vulnerable, that power was always aggressive and corrupting, and that political liberty required constant vigilance. These ideas had been kept in circulation during the eighteenth century by radical Whig politicians in Britain, including Thomas Gordon and John Trenchard. The colonists avidly read their warnings about the dangers posed by a standing army, the government corruption caused by government officials lusting after power, and the evils caused by public debt. When Parliament began to tax Americans, regulate their trade, station troops in their midst, and deny colonists the right to expand westward, many Americans perceived these efforts as part of a design to deprive them of their property and reduce them to slavery.

The Consequences of the Seven Years' War

During the Seven Years' War, Britain debated whether at the end of the conflict it should claim French Canada or the rich sugar island of Guadeloupe in the Caribbean. Some in Britain believed that the sugar colony offered a greater source of wealth, while others believed that Canada would serve as an expanding market for British manufactured goods. Some worried that without the French presence in Canada, the mainland colonists might begin to seek independence from the British Empire. Fatefully, Britain chose Canada in the Peace of Paris of 1763.

The Seven Years' War gave Britain undisputed control of North America east of the Mississippi River. But the war also produced a host of problems and costs that could not be ignored. The most immediate problem was the British debt, which had jumped from £75 million to £137 million during the Seven Years' War. To raise revenue, Parliament had imposed a new tax on cider produced in England, but this tax provoked uprisings in apple-growing counties. The British government was determined that the colonists should assume a greater financial burden. At the time, taxes in the colonies were about 1 shilling per person a year, compared to 26 shillings a year in Britain.

Related to the debt problem was the issue of colonial smuggling. During the Seven Years' War, American merchants illegally traded with French and Spanish ports in the Caribbean. As a result of flagrant evasions of British navigation acts, the customs system in the colonies cost Britain much more than it raised in revenue. Customs officials' salaries cost the treasury about £8,000 a year, more than four times what the officials collected.

Britain was also worried about the financial burden of Indian warfare on the colonial frontier, if the colonists migrated too rapidly onto Indian hunting grounds. In the spring of 1763 Pontiac and an alliance of western tribes had launched attacks on white settlements from New York to Virginia. And while the warfare was ultimately suppressed in the autumn, it revealed the potential costs of unrestrained white settlement.

These problems led to a series of new British policies during the 1760s. To protect the western Indian and fur trades and prevent costly Indian wars, Britain issued the Proclamation of 1763, which restricted colonial settlement west of the Appalachian Mountains. To cut down on smuggling, George Grenville, the chancellor of the Exchequer, stationed British naval vessels in American waters to seize colonial merchant ships suspected of illegal trading activities. And to raise tax revenue and defray the cost of maintaining troops in the British colonies, the British Parliament passed a series of measures. It adopted the Sugar Act of 1764, which cut the duty on molasses in half to encourage colonists to *pay* the duty rather than evade it by smuggling; the Quartering Act of 1765, which passed responsibility for housing British troops onto the colonists; and the Stamp Act of 1765, which required payment of a tax on legal documents and newspapers. The Stamp Act was the first direct tax (as opposed to a customs duty) levied on the colonists.

THE PROCLAMATION OF 1763

1 / "The several Nations...of Indians...should not be molested"

In 1773 Benjamin Franklin (1706–90) published a brief history of the British government's actions during the preceding decade. Its title: *Rules by Which a Great Empire May Be Reduced to a Small One*. Beginning in 1763, successive British ministries made a series of political missteps that gradually stirred the colonists to assert American liberties against British oppression.

Before 1763 the colonists largely accepted Parliament's right to take actions on their behalf—and even the primacy of England's economic interests over their own. Prior to the Seven Years' War, however, almost all parliamentary actions had been designed to regulate trade, and while the colonies sometimes regarded these acts as unfair or inexpedient, they did not regard them as especially oppressive or burdensome.

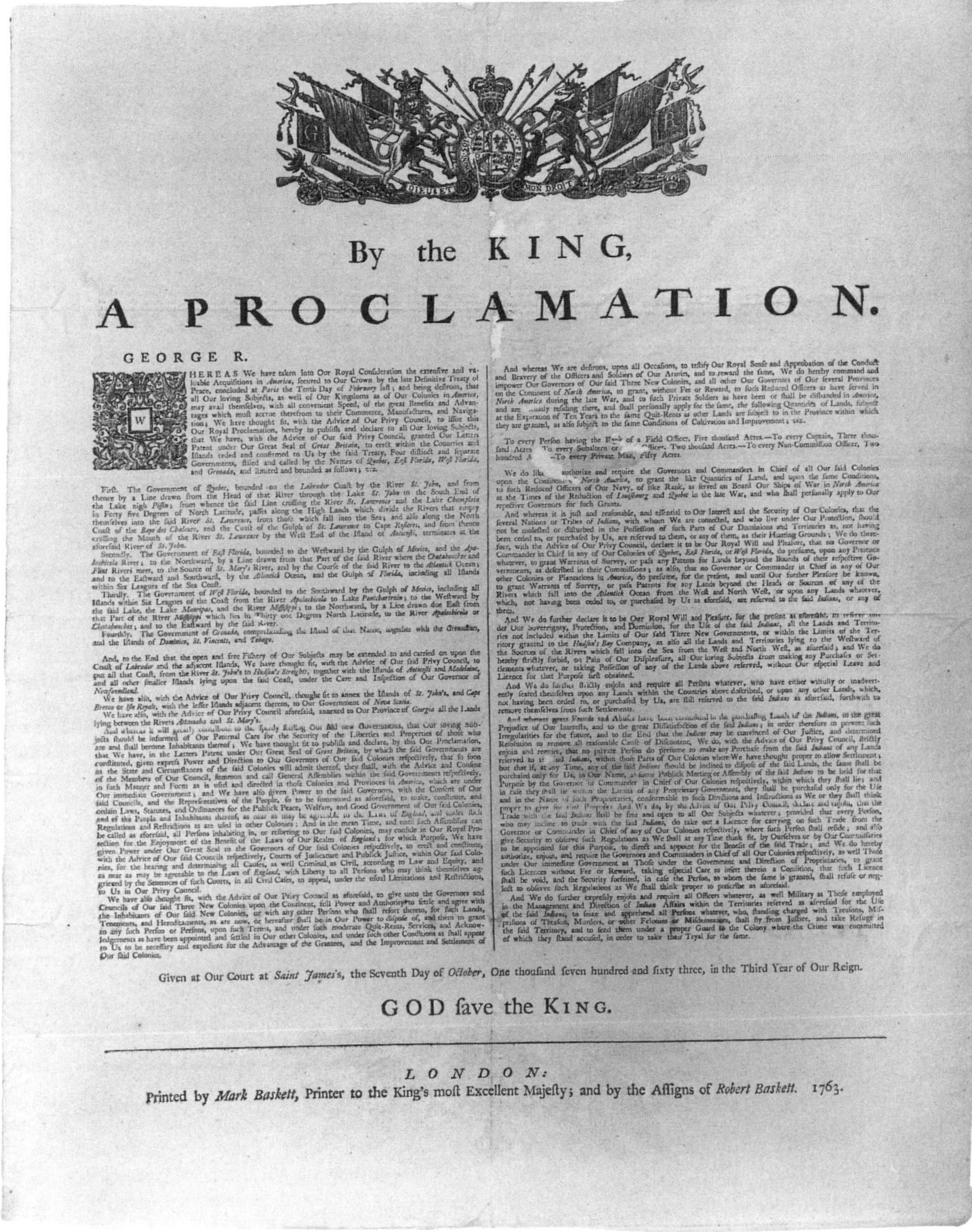

DIEU ET MON DROIT

By the KING,

A PROCLAMATION.

GEORGE R.

WHEREAS We have taken into Our Royal Consideration the extensive and valuable Acquisitions in *America*, secured to Our Crown by the late Definitive Treaty of Peace, concluded at *Paris* the Tenth Day of *February* last; and being desirous, that all Our loving Subjects, as well of Our Kingdoms as of Our Colonies in *America*, may avail themselves, with all convenient Speed, of the great Benefits and Advantages which must accrue therefrom to their Commerce, Manufactures, and Navigation; We have thought fit, with the Advice of Our Privy Council, to issue this Our Royal Proclamation, hereby to publish and declare to all Our loving Subjects, that We have, with the Advice of Our said Privy Council, granted Our Letters Patent under Our Great Seal of *Great Britain*, to erect within the Countries and Islands ceded and confirmed to Us by the said Treaty, Four distinct and separate Governments, stiled and called by the Names of *Quebec*, *East Florida*, *West Florida*, and *Grenada*, and limited and bounded as follows; viz.

First. The Government of *Quebec*, bounded on the *Labrador* Coast by the River *St. John*, and from thence by a Line drawn from the Head of that River through the Lake *St. John* to the South End of the Lake nigh *Pissin*; from whence the said Line crossing the River *St. Lawrence* and the Lake *Champlain* in Forty five Degrees of North Latitude, passes along the High Lands which divide the Rivers that empty themselves into the said River *St. Lawrence*, from those which fall into the Sea; and also along the North Coast of the *Baye des Chaleurs*, and the Coast of the Gulph of *St. Lawrence* to Cape *Rosieres*, and from thence crossing the Mouth of the River *St. Lawrence* by the West End of the Island of *Anticosti*, terminates at the aforesaid River of *St. John*.

Secondly. The Government of *East Florida*, bounded to the Westward by the Gulph of *Mexico*, and the *Apalachicola* River; to the Northward, by a Line drawn from that Part of the said River where the *Chatahouchee* and *Flint* Rivers meet, to the Source of *St. Mary's* River, and by the Course of the said River to the *Atlantick* Ocean; and to the Eastward and Southward, by the *Atlantick* Ocean, and the Gulph of *Florida*, including all Islands within Six Leagues of the Sea Coast.

Thirdly. The Government of *West Florida*, bounded to the Southward by the Gulph of *Mexico*, including all Islands within Six Leagues of the Coast from the River *Apalachicola* to Lake *Pontchartrain*; to the Westward by the said Lake, the Lake *Maurepas*, and the River *Mississippi*; to the Northward, by a Line drawn due East from that Part of the River *Mississippi* which lies in Thirty one Degrees North Latitude, to the River *Apalachicola* or *Chatahouchee*; and to the Eastward by the said River.

Fourthly. The Government of *Grenada*, comprehending the Island of that Name, together with the *Grenadines*, and the Islands of *Dominico*, *St. Vincents*, and *Tobago*.

And, to the End that the open and free Fishery of Our Subjects may be extended to and carried on upon the Coast of *Labrador* and the adjacent Islands, We have thought fit, with the Advice of Our said Privy Council, to put all that Coast, from the River *St. John's* to *Hudson's Streights*, together with the Islands of *Anticosti* and *Madelaine*, and all other smaller Islands lying upon the said Coast, under the Care and Inspection of Our Governor of *Newfoundland*.

We have also, with the Advice of Our Privy Council, thought fit to annex the Islands of *St. John's*, and *Cape Breton* or *Isle Royale*, with the lesser Islands adjacent thereto, to Our Government of *Nova Scotia*.

We have also, with the Advice of Our Privy Council aforesaid, annexed to Our Province of *Georgia* all the Lands lying between the Rivers *Attamaha* and *St. Mary's*.

And whereas it will greatly contribute to the speedy settling Our said new Governments, that Our loving Subjects should be informed of Our Paternal Care for the Security of the Liberties and Properties of those who are and shall become Inhabitants thereof; We have thought fit to publish and declare, by this Our Proclamation, that We have, in the Letters Patent under Our Great Seal of *Great Britain*, by which the said Governments are constituted, given express Power and Direction to Our Governors of Our said Colonies respectively, that so soon as the State and Circumstances of the said Colonies will admit thereof, they shall, with the Advice and Consent of the Members of Our Council, summon and call General Assemblies within the said Governments respectively, in such Manner and Form as is used and directed in those Colonies and Provinces in *America*, which are under Our immediate Government; and We have also given Power to the said Governors, with the Consent of Our said Councils, and the Representatives of the People, so to be summoned as aforesaid, to make, constitute, and ordain Laws, Statutes, and Ordinances for the Publick Peace, Welfare, and Good Government of Our said Colonies, and of the People and Inhabitants thereof, as near as may be agreeable to the Laws of *England*, and under such Regulations and Restrictions as are used in other Colonies: And in the mean Time, and until such Assemblies can be called as aforesaid, all Persons inhabiting in, or resorting to Our said Colonies, may confide in Our Royal Protection for the Enjoyment of the Benefit of the Laws of Our Realm of *England*; for which Purpose, We have given Power under Our Great Seal to the Governors of Our said Colonies respectively, to erect and constitute, with the Advice of Our said Councils respectively, Courts of Judicature and Publick Justice, within Our said Colonies, for the hearing and determining all Causes, as well Criminal as Civil, according to Law and Equity, and as near as may be agreeable to the Laws of *England*, with Liberty to all Persons who may think themselves aggrieved by the Sentences of such Courts, in all Civil Cases, to appeal, under the usual Limitations and Restrictions, to Us in Our Privy Council.

We have also thought fit, with the Advice of Our Privy Council as aforesaid, to give unto the Governors and Councils of Our said Three New Colonies upon the Continent, full Power and Authority to settle and agree with the Inhabitants of Our said New Colonies, or with any other Persons who shall resort thereto, for such Lands, Tenements, and Hereditaments, as are now, or hereafter shall be in Our Power to dispose of, and them to grant to any such Person or Persons, upon such Terms, and under such moderate Quit-Rents, Services, and Acknowledgements as have been appointed and settled in Our other Colonies, and under such other Conditions as shall appear to Us to be necessary and expedient for the Advantage of the Grantees, and the Improvement and Settlement of Our said Colonies.

And whereas We are desirous, upon all Occasions, to testify Our Royal Sense and Approbation of the Conduct and Bravery of the Officers and Soldiers of Our Armies, and to reward the same, We do hereby command and impower Our Governors of Our said Three New Colonies, and all other Our Governors of Our several Provinces on the Continent of *North America*, to grant, without Fee or Reward, to such Reduced Officers as have served in *North America* during the late War, and to such Private Soldiers as have been or shall be disbanded in *America*, and are [illegible]ually residing there, and shall personally apply for the same, the following Quantities of Lands, subject at the Expiration of Ten Years to the same Quit-Rents as other Lands are subject to in the Province within which they are granted, as also subject to the same Conditions of Cultivation and Improvement; viz.

To every Person having the Ra[illegible] of a Field Officer, Five thousand Acres.—To every Captain, Three thousand Acres.—To every Subaltern or [illegible]fficer, Two thousand Acres.—To every Non-Commission Officer, Two hundred A[illegible]—To every Private Man, Fifty Acres.

We do lik[illegible] authorize and require the Governors and Commanders in Chief of all Our said Colonies upon the Continen[illegible] *North America*, to grant the like Quantities of Land, and upon the same Conditions, to such Reduced Officers of Our Navy, of like Rank, as served on Board Our Ships of War in *North America* at the Times of the Reduction of *Louisbourg* and *Quebec* in the late War, and who shall personally apply to Our respective Governors for such Grants.

And whereas it is just and reasonable, and essential to Our Interest and the Security of Our Colonies, that the several Nations or Tribes of *Indians*, with whom We are connected, and who live under Our Protection, should not be molested or disturbed in the Possession of such Parts of Our Dominions and Territories as, not having been ceded to, or purchased by Us, are reserved to them, or any of them, as their Hunting Grounds; We do therefore, with the Advice of Our Privy Council, declare it to be Our Royal Will and Pleasure, that no Governor or Commander in Chief in any of Our Colonies of *Quebec*, *East Florida*, or *West Florida*, do presume, upon any Pretence whatever, to grant Warrants of Survey, or pass any Patents for Lands beyond the Bounds of their respective Governments, as described in their Commissions; as also, that no Governor or Commander in Chief in any of Our other Colonies or Plantations in *America*, do presume, for the present, and until Our further Pleasure be known, to grant Warrants of Survey, or pass Patents for any Lands beyond the Heads or Sources of any of the Rivers which fall into the *Atlantick* Ocean from the West and North West, or upon any Lands whatever, which, not having been ceded to, or purchased by Us as aforesaid, are reserved to the said *Indians*, or any of them.

And We do further declare it to be Our Royal Will and Pleasure, for the present as aforesaid, to reserve under Our Sovereignty, Protection, and Dominion, for the Use of the said *Indians*, all the Lands and Territories not included within the Limits of Our said Three New Governments, or within the Limits of the Territory granted to the *Hudson's Bay* Company, as also all the Lands and Territories lying to the Westward of the Sources of the Rivers which fall into the Sea from the West and North West, as aforesaid; and We do hereby strictly forbid, on Pain of Our Displeasure, all Our loving Subjects from making any Purchases or Settlements whatever, or taking Possession of any of the Lands above reserved, without Our especial Leave and Licence for that Purpose first obtained.

And We do further strictly enjoin and require all Persons whatever, who have either wilfully or inadvertently seated themselves upon any Lands within the Countries above described, or upon any other Lands, which, not having been ceded to, or purchased by Us, are still reserved to the said *Indians* as aforesaid, forthwith to remove themselves from such Settlements.

And whereas great Frauds and Abuses have been committed in the purchasing Lands of the *Indians*, to the great Prejudice of Our Interests, and to the great Dissatisfaction of the said *Indians*; in order therefore to prevent such Irregularities for the future, and to the End that the *Indians* may be convinced of Our Justice, and determined Resolution to remove all reasonable Cause of Discontent, We do, with the Advice of Our Privy Council, strictly enjoin and require, that no private Person do presume to make any Purchase from the said *Indians* of any Lands reserved to t[illegible] said *Indians*, within those Parts of Our Colonies where We have thought proper to allow Settlement; but that if, at any Time, any of the said *Indians* should be inclined to dispose of the said Lands, the same shall be purchased only for Us, in Our Name, at some Publick Meeting or Assembly of the said *Indians* to be held for that Purpose by the Governor or Commander in Chief of Our Colonies respectively, within which they shall lie; and in case they shall lie within the Limits of any Proprietary Government, they shall be purchased only for the Use and in the Name of such Proprietaries, conformable to such Directions and Instructions as We or they shall think proper to give for that Purpose: And We do, by the Advice of Our Privy Council, declare and enjoin, that the Trade with the said *Indians* shall be free and open to all Our Subjects whatever; provided that every Person, who may incline to trade with the said *Indians*, do take out a Licence for carrying on such Trade from the Governor or Commander in Chief of any of Our Colonies respectively, where such Person shall reside; and also give Security to observe such Regulations as We shall at any Time think fit, by Ourselves or by Our Commissaries to be appointed for this Purpose, to direct and appoint for the Benefit of the said Trade; and We do hereby authorize, enjoin, and require the Governors and Commanders in Chief of all Our Colonies respectively, as well Those under Our immediate Government as Those under the Government and Direction of Proprietaries, to grant such Licences without Fee or Reward, taking especial Care to insert therein a Condition, that such Licence shall be void, and the Security forfeited, in case the Person, to whom the same is granted, shall refuse or neglect to observe such Regulations as We shall think proper to prescribe as aforesaid.

And We do further expresly enjoin and require all Officers whatever, as well Military as Those employed in the Management and Direction of *Indian* Affairs within the Territories reserved as aforesaid for the Use of the said *Indians*, to seize and apprehend all Persons whatever, who, standing charged with Treasons, Misprisions of Treason, Murders, or other Felonies or Misdemeanors, shall fly from Justice, and take Refuge in the said Territory, and to send them under a proper Guard to the Colony where the Crime was committed of which they stand accused, in order to take their Tryal for the same.

Given at Our Court at *Saint James's*, the Seventh Day of *October*, One thousand seven hundred and sixty three, in the Third Year of Our Reign.

GOD save the KING.

LONDON:
Printed by *Mark Baskett*, Printer to the King's most Excellent Majesty; and by the Assigns of *Robert Baskett*. 1763.

King George III. Broadside, proclamation [establishing British rule over Quebec, etc. recognizing Indians], 1763.
The Gilder Lehrman Collection, on deposit at the Pierpont Morgan Library. GLC 5214

After 1763, however, Parliament's actions appeared to clash with the colonists' interests. At the end of the Seven Years' War, France surrendered Canada and much of the Ohio and Mississippi valleys—two thirds of eastern North America—to British rule. Many colonists regarded these new lands as a godsend. But the Proclamation of 1763 reserved lands west of the Appalachian Mountains for Indians and forbade white settlement there.

Equally disturbing, new British politics restricted Indian trade to traders licensed by the British government. For the first time, power over westward expansion was placed in the hands of British officials, outside the colonists' control. By preventing the colonial population from moving inland, the British ministry hoped to avoid costly Indian wars, protect the western fur trade, and keep western land speculation under the control of the crown. To enforce the proclamation, the British cabinet decided to station up to ten thousand troops along the frontier, at a cost of £250,000 annually. The colonists, who wanted to expand westward without the interference of British troops, deeply resented the proclamation. They feared that if they were walled in along the eastern coast, the results would be overpopulation, the growth of crowded cities, and social stratification along rigid class lines.

GEORGE III, PROCLAMATION OF 1763, OCTOBER 7, 1763, GLC 5214

WHEREAS WE have taken into Our Royal Consideration the extensive and valuable Acquisitions in America, secured to Our Crown by the late Definitive Treaty of Peace, concluded at Paris...and being desirous that all Our loving Subjects...may avail themselves with all convenient Speed, of the great Benefits and Advantages which must accrue therefrom to their Commerce, Manufactures, and Navigation, We have thought fit...to issue this Our Royal Proclamation....

And whereas it is just and reasonable and essential to Our Interest and the Security of Our Colonies, that the several Nations or Tribes of Indians with whom We are connected, and who live under Our Protection should not be molested or disturbed...no Governor...in any of Our other Colonies or Plantations in America, do presume for the present...to grant Warrants of Survey, or pass Patents for any Lands beyond the Heads or Sources of any of the Rivers which fall into the Atlantic Ocean....

And whereas great Frauds and abuses have been committed in the purchasing Lands of the Indians, to the great Prejudice of Our Interests, and to the great Dissatisfaction of the said Indians; in order to prevent such Irregularities for the future, and to the End that the Indians may be convinced of Our Justice and determined Resolution to remove all reasonable cause of Discontent, We do...enjoy and require that no private Person do presume to make any Purchase from the said Indians of any Lands reserved to the said Indians....

THE STAMP ACT CRISIS

2 / *"There is a violent spirit of opposition raised on the continent"*

Eleven years before the Declaration of Independence, a crisis took place that defined the issue that would help provoke the American Revolution: taxation without representation.

To raise new revenue, Parliament in 1764 passed the Sugar Act, which imposed new charges on foreign wines, coffee, textiles, and indigo imported into the colonies and enlarged the customs service, requiring shippers to fill out documents detailing each ship's cargo and destination. The British navy was ordered to patrol the American coast to search for smugglers, who, if caught, were to be tried in a special court without a jury. That same year, the Currency Act banned the colonists from issuing paper money. Since the colonies had trouble getting gold or silver coins, the prohibition on paper money forced many colonists to resort to barter.

Also in 1764, the British ministry announced plans to institute a stamp tax, to go into effect on November 1, 1765, to make the colonists pay part of the cost of stationing British troops in America. This act required the colonists to pay a tax, represented by a stamp, on newspapers, playing cards, diplomas, and legal documents. Violations of the Stamp Act would be tried in vice-admiralty courts, which had traditionally been used only in cases involving maritime law. Thus the Stamp Act also appeared to threaten the right to trial by jury.

Reactions to the Stamp Act included riots and boycotts of British goods. Crowds calling themselves Sons of Liberty prevented stamped papers from being unloaded from British ships. Daughters of Liberty, organizations formed by colonial women, promoted the manufacture of homespun cloth, as a substitute for imported British cloth, and circulated protest petitions.

In October 1765, delegates from nine colonies met in New York City and prepared a statement protesting the Stamp Act. The Stamp Act Congress, which was the first united action by the colonies against unpopular British policies, acknowledged that Parliament had a right to regulate colonial trade. It denied, however, that Parliament had the power to tax the colonies, since the colonies were unrepresented in Parliament. The power of taxation resided only with the colonists themselves and their representatives.

Under pressure from London merchants, Parliament abolished the Stamp Act in 1766. But at the same time it passed the Declaratory Act, which stated that the king and Parliament had full legislative authority over the colonies in all matters.

In December 1765, John Adams (1735–1826), who would later become the second president of the United States, wrote that this had "been the most remarkable year of my life." The Stamp Act, "that enormous engine...for battering down all the rights and liberties of America," had raised a spirit of resistance throughout mainland British North America. "In every colony, from Georgia to New Hampshire inclusively," he observed, "the stamp distributors and inspectors have been compelled by the unconquerable rage of the people to renounce their offices. Such and so universal has been the resentment of the people, that every man who has dared to speak in the favor of the stamps, or to soften the detestation in which they are held, how great soever his abilities and virtues had been esteemed before, whatever his fortune, connections, and influence had been, has been seen to sink into universal contempt and ignominy."

Adams was particularly struck by the political consequences of the Stamp Act. "The people, even to the lowest ranks, have become more attentive to their liberties, more inquisitive about them, and more determined to defend them, than they were ever before known.... Our presses have groaned, our pulpits have thundered, our legislatures have resolved; our towns have voted; the crown officers have everywhere trembled, and all their little tools and creatures been afraid to speak and ashamed to be seen...."

The following document offers a first-person account of the escalating conflict over the Stamp Act from a pro-British perspective.

ARCHIBALD HINSCHELWOOD, AUGUST 19, 1765, TO JOSHUA MAUGER, GLC 3902

I had the pleasure to receive your letter...and am greatly obliged to you for your kind remembrance of me, and the pains you have taken to get me appointed for the disposal of the stamps in this province [Nova Scotia]....

There is a violent spirit of opposition raised on the continent against the execution of the Stamp Act, the mob in Boston have carried it very high against the Secre[tar]y [Andrew Oliver]...for his acceptance of an office in consequence of that Act. They have even proceeded to sow violence, and burnt him in effigy. They threaten to pull down & burn the stamp office row building; and that they will hold every man as infamous that shall presume to carry the Stamp Act into execution, so it is thought Mr. Oliver will resign.

I don't find any such turbulent spirit to prevail among us, if it should, the means are in our Hands to prevent any tumults or Insults; what the consequences may be in the colonies who have no military force to keep the rabble in order, I cannot pretend.

3 / *"There is not gold and silver enough in the colonies to pay the stamp duty for one year"*

His is one of the most remarkable success stories in American history. The eighteenth child of a Boston candlemaker and soapmaker, Benjamin Franklin (1706–90) was apprenticed to his brother, a printer, but ran away. As a publisher in Philadelphia, he was so successful that he was able to retire at age forty-two and devote the rest of his life to science and politics.

While serving in England as a representative of the colonies of Pennsylvania, Massachusetts, New Jersey, and Georgia, Franklin promoted the idea of American liberties and testified against the Stamp Act. He had been out of touch with sentiment in the colonies, and in his testimony before Parliament, Franklin suggested that the colonists objected only to direct taxes, not to duties placed on imported goods. His testimony helped to secure the repeal of the Stamp Act and greatly enhanced his reputation in both England and America.

BENJAMIN FRANKLIN, "THE EXAMINATION OF DOCTOR BENJAMIN FRANKLIN BEFORE AN AUGUST ASSEMBLY, RELATING TO THE REPEAL OF THE STAMP ACT," 1766, GLC 1719

Q. What is your name, and place of abode?

A. Franklin, of Philadelphia.

Q. Do the Americans pay any considerable taxes among themselves?

A. Certainly many, and very heavy taxes.

Q. What are the present taxes in Pennsylvania, laid by the laws of the colonies?

A. There are taxes on all estates, real and personal; a poll tax; a tax on all offices, professions, trades, and businesses, according to their profits; an excise on all wine, rum, and other spirit; and a duty of ten pounds per head on all Negroes imported, with some other duties.

Q. For what purposes are those taxes laid?

A. For the support of the civil and military establishment of the country, and to discharge the heavy debt contracted in the last war [the Seven Years' War]....

Q. Are not all the people very able to pay those taxes?

A. No. The frontier counties, all along the continent, having been frequently ravaged by the enemy and greatly impoverished, are able to pay very little tax....

Q. Are not the colonies, from their circumstances, very able to pay the stamp duty?

A. In my opinion there is not gold and silver enough in the colonies to pay the stamp duty for one year.

Q. Don't you know that the money arising from the stamps was all to be laid out in America?

A. I know it is appropriated by the act to the American service; but it will be spent in the conquered colonies, where the soldiers are, not in the colonies that pay it....

Q. Do you think it right that America should be protected by this country and pay no part of the expense?

A. That is not the case. The colonies raised, clothed, and paid, during the last war, near 25,000 men, and spent many millions.

Q. Were you not reimbursed by Parliament?

A. We were only reimbursed what, in your opinion, we had advanced beyond our proportion, or beyond what might reasonably be expected from us; and it was a very small part of what we spent. Pennsylvania, in particular, disbursed about 500,000 pounds, and the reimbursements, in the whole, did not exceed 60,000 pounds....

Q. Do not you think the people of America would submit to pay the stamp duty, if it was moderated?

A. No, never, unless compelled by force of arms....

Q. What was the temper of America towards Great Britain before the year 1763?

A. The best in the world. They submitted willingly to the government of the Crown, and paid, in all their courts, obedience to acts of Parliament....

Q. What is your opinion of a future tax, imposed on the same principle with that of the Stamp Act? How would Americans receive it?

A. Just as they do this. They would not pay it.

Q. Have not you heard of the resolutions of this House, and of the House of Lords, asserting the right of Parliament relating to America, including a power to tax the people there?

A. Yes, I have heard of such resolutions.

Q. What will be the opinion of the Americans on those resolutions?

A. They will think them unconstitutional and unjust.

Q. Was it an opinion in America before 1763 that the Parliament had no right to lay taxes and duties there?

A. I have never heard any objection to the right of laying duties to regulate commerce; but a right to lay internal taxes was never supposed to be in Parliament, as we are not represented there....

Q. Did the Americans ever dispute the controlling power of Parliament to regulate the commerce?

A. No.

Q. Can anything less than a military force carry the Stamp Act into execution?

A. I do not see how a military force can be applied for that purpose.

Q. Why may it not?

A. Suppose a military force sent into America; they will find nobody in arms; what are they then to do? They cannot force a man to take stamps who chooses to do without them. They will not find a rebellion; they may indeed make one.

Q. If the act is not repealed, what do you think will be the consequences?

A. A total loss of the respect and affection the people of America bear to this country, and of all the commerce that depends on that respect and affection.

Q. How can the commerce be affected?

A. You will find that, if the act is not repealed, they will take very little of your manufactures in a short time.

Q. Is it in their power to do without them?

A. I think they may very well do without them.

Q. Is it their interest not to take them?

A. The goods they take from Britain are either necessaries, mere conveniences, or superfluities. The first, as cloth, etc., with a little industry they can make at home; the second they can do without till they are able to provide them among themselves; and the last, which are much the greatest part, they can strike off immediately. They are mere articles of fashion, purchased and consumed because the fashion in a respected country; but will now be detested and rejected. The people have already struck off, by general agreement, the use of all goods fashionable in mournings, and many thousand pounds worth are sent back as unsaleable....

Q. If the Stamp Act should be repealed, would it induce the assemblies of America to acknowledge the right of Parliament to tax them, and would they erase their resolutions [against the Stamp Act]?

A. No, never.

Q. Is there no means of obliging them to erase those resolutions?

A. None that I know of; they will never do it, unless compelled by force of arms.

Q. Is there a power on earth that can force them to erase them?

A. No power, how great soever, can force men to change their opinions....

Q. What used to be the pride of the Americans?

A. To indulge in the fashions and manufactures of Great Britain.

Q. What is now their pride?

A. To wear their old clothes over again, till they can make new ones.

THE TOWNSHEND ACTS

4 / *"Taxes...are imposed upon the People, without their consent"*

Based in part on Benjamin Franklin's arguments before Parliament, Charles Townshend (1725–67), the British chancellor of the Exchequer, believed that the colonists would find a duty on imported goods more acceptable than the Stamp Act, which taxed them more directly. In 1767 Parliament passed the Townshend Acts, which placed duties on such imported items as glass, tea, lead, paint, and paper. Colonists not only objected to the new duties, but also to the way they were to be spent—and to the new bureaucracy that was to collect them. The new revenues were to be used to pay the expenses of governors and judges. Because colonial assemblies were traditionally responsible for paying colonial officials, the Townshend Acts appeared to be an attack on their legislative authority.

The Townshend Acts also set up a board of customs commissioners, which was supposed to be a more efficient way of organizing the customs system. But many merchants saw it as an attempt to introduce a new bureaucracy and official corruption into the colonies.

Merchants from Boston adopted a nonimportation agreement in 1768, vowing not to import certain articles rather than pay the duties. By 1769, after merchants in other cities had joined the boycott, imports of British goods had fallen by 40 percent. Women played an active role in the protests against the Townshend Acts. Daughters of Liberty led campaigns against consumption of British tea and clothing.

Meanwhile, to cut costs, the ministry closed many western forts and redeployed British forces in coastal cities. Under the Quartering Act of 1765, the colonists would be responsible for housing and providing for the troops. When New York refused to provide supplies for the soldiers, Townshend responded by threatening to nullify all laws passed by the New York assembly until the Quartering Act was obeyed. The other colonies rallied to New York's support by threatening to resist all taxes imposed by the Crown.

In the face of this united opposition, Townshend modified the Quartering Act. Instead of requiring colonists to open their homes to soldiers, he allowed them to house them in barracks, unoccupied buildings, and barns. But even this weakened act stirred resistance.

Many colonists also objected to the unscrupulous actions of British customs officials, some of whom began to enrich themselves by accusing shipowners and merchants of smuggling and then confiscating ships and cargoes. In June 1768, a crowd attacked local customs collectors who had seized a sloop owned by John Hancock (1737–93), one of the colonies' richest merchants. The commissioners fled to an island in Boston for safety, and pleaded for military protection. The British government sent two regiments of troops to Boston in September 1768.

In this letter, John Hancock and four other Boston selectmen protest the Townshend Acts and the impending arrival of British troops.

John Hancock and four other Boston selectmen, September 14, 1768, to the Selectmen of Medway, Massachusetts, GLC 3110

You are already too well acquainted with the melancholy and very alarming Circumstances to which this Province, as well as America in general, is now reduced. Taxes equally detrimental to the commercial interests of the Parent country and the colonies are imposed upon the People, without their consent; Taxes designed for the Support of the Civil Government in the Colonies, in a Manner clearly unconstitutional, and contrary to that, in which 'till of late, Government has been supported, by the free Gift of the People in the American Assemblies or Parliaments; as also for the Maintenance of a large Standing Army; not for the Defence of the newly acquired Territories, but for the old Colonies, and in a Time of Peace. The decent, humble and truly loyal Applications and Petitions from the Representatives of this Province for the Redress of these heavy and very threatening Grievances, have hitherto been ineffectual, being assured from authentick Intelligence that they have not yet reach'd the Royal Ear: The only Effect of transmitting these Applications...has been a Mandate from one of his Majesty's Secretaries of State to the Governor of this Province, to Dissolve the General Assembly, merely because the late House of Representatives refused to Rescind a Resolution of a former House, which imply'd nothing more than a Right in the American Subjects to unite in humble and dutiful Petitions to their gracious Sovereign, when they found themselves aggrieved: This is a Right naturally inherent in every Man, and expressly recognized by the glorious Revolution as the Birthright of an Englishman....

The Concern and Perplexity in which these Things have thrown the People, have been greatly aggravated by a late Declaration of his Excellency Governor [Francis] Bernard, that one or more Regiments may soon be expected in this Province.

The Design of these Troops is in every one's Apprehension nothing short of Enforcing by military Power the Execution of Acts of Parliament in the forming of which the Colonies have not, and cannot have any constitutional Influence. This is one of the greatest Distresses to which a free People can be reduced....

5 / *"The governors of too many of ye colonies are not only unprincipled, but...rapacious"*

In this selection, James Otis (1725–83), one of the early leaders in the colonists' struggle for independence, informs Catharine Macaulay (1731–91), an English liberal sympathetic to the colonies' cause, about the situation in America. A year before he wrote this letter, Otis had rejected in outspoken terms the British demand that the Massachusetts assembly withdraw its demand that colonists repudiate the Townshend Acts. "We are asked to rescind?" he asked rhetorically. "Let Great Britain rescind her measures, or the colonies are lost to her forever."

The colonists considered Macaulay, an eminent English historian with many valuable political connections, one of the most important figures in Britain with whom they could present their grievances. Steeped in the seventeenth-century English traditions of revolution, Lady Catharine played a critical role in reviving knowledge of seventeenth-century English radicalism. Many colonists likened their situation to that of seventeenth-century radicals who had sought to protect English liberties against the usurpations of the Stuart kings. Lady Catharine later toured an independent United States in 1787.

JAMES OTIS, JULY 27, 1769, TO CATHARINE MACAULAY, GLC 1796

You have condescended to intimate your pleasure that I should transmit you an account of American affairs. Were I equal to the business it would require an album. At present I can only say No. America is really distressed as you justly perceive. The governors of too many of ye colonies are not only unprincipled, but...rapacious.... The revenue officers in general are to the last degree oppressive. The commerce of the Country is...dying—[a mutual friend] told of captures & prizes taken from truly loyal subjects here inasmuch as the same [practice] as is sent out against traitors, rebels, and others the worst of his enemies. Indeed, all the least endearing appellations are liberally bestowed on the colonists for no apparent fault...[except] petitioning ye King, & living as...peaceably as possible....

6 / *"The army...is now publicly declared to be for the purpose of enforcing obedience to the authority of Parliament"*

Born in Ulster, Charles Thomson (1729–1824) came to Philadelphia as a young schoolmaster. During the 1765 Stamp Act crisis, Thomson became a significant figure in local politics, orchestrating resistance to the measure in Philadelphia. Over the next decade, Thomson continued to be a central figure in the organization of Philadelphia opposition to British trade policies. With the coming of the Revolution, Thomson became secretary of the Continental Congress, a post he retained until the creation of the federal government in 1789. Ignored by the Washington administration, he spent the last thirty-five years of his life out of public office.

Here Thomson, writing as a member of the Philadelphia Merchants' Committee, which strongly supported the nonimportation efforts, argues that British actions—the imposition of illegal taxes, the bloated customs bureaucracy, the stationing of an army among the people—all were part of a plot to deprive Americans of their liberties.

CHARLES THOMSON, NOVEMBER 26, 1769, TO BENJAMIN FRANKLIN, GLC 1018

First the parliament claims a right to levy taxes upon the Americans without their consent;...they declare that they have a power to make laws to bind them in all cases whatever: By another act they suspend the legislative authority of an American Assembly for daring to dispute their commands.... The army, which was left in America after the late war under the pretence of securing and defending it, is now publicly declared to be for the purpose of enforcing obedience to the authority of Parliament. The remonstrances and Petitions of the Assemblies in favour of their rights, and against these claims of Parliament, are treated as sedition and the attempts of the people to procure a redress of grievances are deemed rebellion and treason: and, in order to intimidate the colonies, an antique, obsolete law is revived and the crown addressed to send for persons accused of treasonable practices in America & try them in England. How much further they may proceed is uncertain; but from what they have already done the colonies see that their property is precarious & their liberty insecure. It is true the impositions already laid are not very grievous; but if the principle is established, and the authority, by which they are laid, admitted, there is no security for what remains. The very nature of freedom supposes that no tax can be levied on a people without their consent given personally or by their representatives.

...I have often viewed with infinite satisfaction the prodigious growth & power of the British Empire and have pleased myself with the hopes that in a century or two the British colonies would overspread this immense territory added to the crown of Britain [i.e. Canada], carrying with them the religion of Protestants, and the laws, customs, manners, & language of the country from whence they sprung;... But alas! the folly of a weak administration has darkened the prospect.

THE BOSTON MASSACRE

7 / *"A most horrid murder was committed...by 8 or 9 Soldiers"*

By the beginning of 1770 there were four thousand British soldiers in Boston, a seaport with only fifteen thousand inhabitants. On the evening of March 5, crowds of day laborers, apprentices, and merchant sailors began to pelt British soldiers with snowballs and rocks. A shot rang out, and then several soldiers fired their weapons; when it was over, five civilians lay dead or dying, including Crispus Attucks, a mulatto merchant sailor. A firsthand account of the Boston massacre, by the Deacon John Tudor (1709?–95), follows.

At a trial later that year, John Adams defended the soldiers in a belief that the men had a right to effective legal counsel. Convinced that America should not lose the moral advantage of showing that the soldiers could receive a fair trial, Adams also wanted to remind Bostonians of the "Dangers...which must arise from intemperate heats and irregular commotions." Adams obtained deathbed testimony from one of the five men who had been mortally wounded by the British soldiers, who swore that the crowd, not the troops, was to blame for the massacre. As a result of this testimony, all but two of the soldiers were acquitted and the worst punishment any of the soldiers received was a branding on the thumb.

DEACON JOHN TUDOR, 1770

March [1770]

On Monday Evening the 5th current, a few Minutes after 9 O'Clock a most horrid murder was committed in King Street before the Customhouse by 8 or 9 Soldiers under the Command of Capt[ain] Tho[ma]s Preston...

March 5th

This unhappy affair began by Some Boys & young fellows throwing Snow Balls at the sentry placed at the Customhouse Door. On which 8 or 9 Soldiers Came to his assistance. Soon after a Number of people collected, when the Capt commanded the Soldiers to fire, which they did and 3 Men were Kill'd on the Spot & several Mortally Wounded.

The Capt soon drew off his Soldiers up to the Main Guard, or the Consequences might have been terrible, for on the Guns firing the people were alarm'd & set the Bells a Ringing as if for Fire, which drew Multitudes to the place of action.

Lieut. Governor [Thomas] Hutchinson, who was commander in Chief, was sent for & Came to the Council Chamber, w[h]ere some of the Magistrates attended. The Governor desired the Multitude about 10 O'Clock to separate & go home peaceable & he would do all in his power that Justice should be done &c....

The people insisted that the Soldiers should be ordered to their Barracks 1st before they would separate, Which being done the people separated about 1 O'Clock....

The next forenoon the 8 Soldiers that fired on the inhabitants were also sent to Jail.

Tuesday A.M. the inhabitants met at Faneuil Hall & after some pertinent speeches, chose a Committee of 15 Gentlemen to wait on the Lieut. Governor in Council to request the immediate removal of the Troops.

The message was in these Words. That it is the unanimous opinion of this Meeting that the inhabitants & soldiery can no longer live together in safety; that nothing can Rationally be expected to restore the peace of the Town & prevent Blood & Carnage but the removal of the Troops: and that we most fervently pray his Honor that his power & influence may be exerted for their instant removal.

His Honor's Reply was. Gentleman I am extremely sorry for the unhappy difference & especially of the last Evening, & Signifying that it was not in his power to remove the Troops &c &c.

March 6

The Above Reply was not satisfactory to the Inhabitants, as but one Regiment should be removed to the Castle Barracks.

In the afternoon the Town Adjourned to Dr. Sewill's Meetinghouse [Old South Church] not large enough to hold the people, their being at least 3,000, some suppos'd near 4,000, when they chose a Committee to wait on the Lieut. Governor to let him & the Council Know that nothing less will satisfy the people than a total & immediate removal of the Troops out of the Town....

His Honor communicated this advice of the Council to Col Dalrymple & desir'd he would order the Troops down to Castle William. After the Col. had seen the Vote of the Council He gave his Word & honor to the Town's Committee that both the Regiments should be remov'd without delay....

March 8

Agreeable to a general request of the Inhabitants, were follow'd to the Grave in succession the 4 Bodies of Saml Gray, Saml Maverick, James Caldwell & Crispus Attucks, the unhappy Victims who fell in the Bloody Massacre.

On this sorrowful Occasion most of the shops & stores in Town were shut, all the Bells were order'd to toll a solemn peal in Boston, Charleston, Cambridge & Roxbery.

The several Hearses forming a junction in King Street, the Theatre of that inhuman Tragedy, proceeded from thence thro' the main street, lengthened by an immense Concourse of people, So numerous as to be obliged to follow in Ranks of 4 & 6 abreast and brought up by a long Train of Carriages.

The sorrow Visible in the Countenances, together with the peculiar solemnity,

Surpass description; it was suppos'd that the Spectators & those that follow'd the corps amounted to 15000, some supposed 20,000.

Note: Capt Preston was tried for his Life on the affare of the above October 24 1770. The Trial lasted 5 Days, but the Jury brought him in not Guilty.

William Tudor, ed,. *Deacon Tudor's Diary.* Boston: Press of W. Soooner, 1896.

8 / "What are all the Riches...of Life compared with...Liberty"

The revolutionary era greatly increased popular participation in politics. Political pamphlets proliferated, and newspapers were transformed from business organs into vehicles for political discussion. Not only did the number of subscribers multiply, but so, too, did the number of letters to the editor, as did circulation outside of cities. Popular demonstrations, many of which were initially and traditionally orchestrated from top down, grew more frequent and more independent of elite control. And the number of examples of people acting independently of government through conventions and voluntary committees also increased.

In this document, a colonist who identifies himself as "Brutus" defends the right of ordinary mechanics and artisans to take an active political role over the objections of gentlemen.

BRUTUS [ATTRIBUTED TO ALEXANDER MCDOUGALL], TO THE FREE AND LOYAL INHABITANTS OF THE CITY AND COLONY OF NEW-YORK, MAY 16, 1770, GLC 2552

Nothing can be more flagrantly wrong than the Assertion of some of our mercantile Dons [leading merchants], that the Mechanics have no Right to give their Sentiments about the Importation of British Commodities. For who, I would ask, is the Member of Community, that is absolutely independent of the rest? Or what particular Class among us, has an exclusive Right to decide a Question of general Concern? When the Non-Importation Agreement took Place, what End was it designed to answer? Not surely the private Emolument of Merchants, but the universal Weal [well-being] of the Continent. It was to redeem from Perdition, from total Perdition, the Stock of English Liberty, to which every Subject, whatever may be his Rank, is equally entitled. Amidst all the Disparity of Fortune and Honours, there is one right as common to all Englishmen as Death. It is that we are all equally free. Sufficient it is therefore to shew the matchless Absurdity of the exclusive Claim, of which a few interested Merchants have lately attempted, in a most assuming Manner, to avail themselves, in determining on the Question, whether the Non-Importation Agreement shall be rescinded, to observe, that it was not solemnly entered into for the Good of the Merchants alone, but for the Salvation of the Liberties of us all. Of this the trading Interest of this City were convinced, when, after forming themselves into a Society for executing that Agreement, they not only requested a similar Association of the Mechanics, but by frequent Meetings conspired with them in support of the important Compact.... Every Man saw, that between an Importation of Goods, which stern Virtue ought ever to despise as a Means to encourage Luxury, and the Sacrifice of our inestimable Rights as Englishmen, there was no Medium. This view of the Subject began and brought to Perfection, the important Resolution to repeal all the odious Duties, but that on Tea; and this remains unrepealed for no other Reason than that a tyrannical Ministry will not stoop to it unasked; and the East-India Company scorn to request it of that tyrannical Ministry. Has not our Mother Country, by solemn Act of Legislation, declared that she has a right to impose internal Taxes on us? And is not such an Imposition incompatible with our Liberty?... And shall we not, for our own Sakes, shew that we can live without them? What are all the Riches, the Luxuries, and even the Conveniences of Life compared with that Liberty where with God and Nature have set us free, with that inestimable Jewel which is the Basis of all other Enjoyments?...

9 / *"I trust we have Virtue & Resolution"*

The escalating conflict with Britain after 1763 forced the colonists to define their identity as well as the nature of sovereignty and authority through practical action and philosophic reflection. Republican ideology served as a way to articulate a sense of identity. Increasingly, the colonists envisioned themselves as a people emancipated from religious and political despotism, as a simple, cooperative people whose virtue and independence rested on land ownership.

A Philadelphia landlord and lawyer, John Dickinson (1732–1808), played a critical role in mobilizing popular opposition to the Townshend Acts. In a series of newspaper essays, he argued against all parliamentary taxes—both "direct" taxes and "indirect" taxes. Far from being duties to regulate trade, the Townshend Acts were taxes to raise revenue. Taxes disguised as trade duties, he wrote, were "a most dangerous innovation," with the potential for turning the colonists into "abject slaves." Significantly, like Brutus, Dickinson can assume that all white colonists, regardless of class or occupation, are "free," and are thus vulnerable to British "enslavement."

In this letter Dickinson associates the colonial cause with virtue and piety and implicitly identifies Britain with luxury and corruption. It is notable that so many colonists addressed their appeals to an English woman.

John Dickinson, October 31, 1770, to Catharine Macaulay, GLC 1790.01

A class of men in all states too fondly devoted to profitable tho inglorious Tranquility, have the same addiction to private interests here, that they have shewn in every other part of the world. But the freeholders of this Continent, the really respectable Body of the People, I think, are still firm to the Cause of Liberty. To engage them to act with more spirit of headiness in controlling the sliding patriotism of merchants, it will...wait...[until] the administration encouraged by a supposed Victory, shall with still more indolent audacity renew their attacks on our Freedom....

I trust we have Virtue & Resolution. Yet certain it is—that no mortal can engage in a more difficult Enterprise to rouse a People in vindication of their artfully invaded Rights—to unite them—& to maintain that union, in a persevering adherence to... measures for obtaining Redress.

Your generous Labors, Madam, in rendering Justice...will I doubt not, facilitate the Endeavors of future Patriots throughout the British Dominion in every age. Your attention to America in particular is very obliging....

10 / *"My Enemies were forced to content themselves with abusing me... in the Newspapers"*

As late as 1775, Benjamin Franklin (1706–90) was convinced that the issues dividing Britain and the colonies were "a Matter of Punctilio, which Two or three reasonable People might settle in half an Hour." But years earlier, his enemies were already trying to use their influence within the British government to get him dismissed from his position as postmaster, an effort he describes in the following letter, which was written while Franklin was in London. In fact, he was not dismissed from the post until 1774.

BENJAMIN FRANKLIN, DECEMBER 30, 1770, TO HIS SISTER JANE MECOM, GLC 5508.003

As to the Rumor you mention (which was, as Josiah tells me, that I had been deprived of my Place in the Post Office on Account of a letter I wrote to Philadelphia) it might have this Foundation, that some of the Ministry had been displeas'd at my Writing such Letters, and there were really some Thoughts among them of shewing that Displeasure in that manner. But I had some Friends too, who unrequested by me advised the contrary. And my Enemies were forced to content themselves with abusing me plentifully in the Newspapers, and endeavoring to provoke me to resign. In this they are not likely to succeed, I being deficient in that Christian Virtue of Resignation. If they would have my Office, they must take it—I have heard of some great Man, whose Rule it was with regard to Offices, *Never to ask for them, and never to refuse them:* To which I have always added in my own Practice, *Never to resign them.* As I told my Friends, I rose to that office thro' a long Course of Service in the inferior Degrees of it: Before my time, thro' bad Management, it never produced the Salary annexed to it; and when I received it, no Salary was to be allow'd if the office did not produce it.... I had been chiefly instrumental in bringing it [the Post Office] to its present flourishing State, and therefore thought I had some kind of Right to it. I had hitherto executed the Duties of it faithfully, and to the perfect Satisfaction of my Superiors, which I thought was all that should be expected of me on that Account. As to the Letters complained of, it was true I did write them, and they were written in Compliance with another Duty, that to my Country. A Duty quite Distinct from that of Postmaster. My Conduct in this respect was exactly similar with that I held on a similar Occasion but a few Years ago, when the then Ministry were ready to hug me for the Assistance I afforded them in repealing a former Revenue Act. My Sentiments were still the same, that no such Acts should be made here for America; or, if made should as soon as possible be repealed; and I thought it should not be expected of me, to change my Public Opinions every time his Majesty thought fit to change his Ministers.... My rule in which I have always found Satisfaction, is, Never to turn aside in Public Affairs thro' Views of private Interest; but to go strait forward in doing what appears to me right at the time, leaving the Consequences with Providence. What in my younger Day enabled me to more easily walk upright, was, that I had a Trade; and that I could live upon a little; and thence (never having had views of making a Fortune) I was free from Avarice, and contented with the plentiful Supplies my business afforded me. And now it is still more easy for me to preserve my Freedom and Integrity, when I consider, that I am almost at the End of my Journey [Franklin would live nearly twenty more productive years]....

THE REGULATORS

11 / *"Lawyers,* bad everywhere, *but in Carolina worse than bad"*

Even as tension between the colonies and Britain was rising, disputes among colonists continued. In western North Carolina, many farmers, known as Regulators, rose up against wealthy lawyers and merchants, who charged excessive fees for legal services and manipulated debt laws. The royal governor needed more than a thousand troops to defeat the Regulators at the Battle of Alamance on May 16, 1771. In this letter, Richard Henry Lee (1732–94), a signer of the Declaration of Independence and a leader of the patriot cause in Virginia, discusses the North Carolina Regulator movement and Gov. William Tryon's suppression of it by force.

RICHARD HENRY LEE, JUNE 19, 1771, TO WILLIAM LEE, GLC 3719

...you may know, that the Lawyers, *bad everywhere*, but in Carolina worse than bad, having long abused the people in the most infamous manners at length brought things to such a pass, that a bond of £500 was taken for a single fee in trifling causes, and this bond put in suit and recovered before the business was done for which the fee was paid. Grieved in this manner without being able to obtain redress, the people were at length driven by repeated injuries to do what otherwise they would never have thought of. The Governor himself in his speech to the Assembly acknowledges the grievances and recommends enquiry & redress, but instead of accompanying the redress with an Act of Amnesty...it was at length agreed by the Governor to allow a certain space of time for the Insurgents to consider about laying down their Arms, and that before the allowed time was elapsed, he fell upon the unsuspecting multitudes and made great slaughter with his Cannon....

SAMUEL ADAMS

12 / *"The Wretch who betrays his Country"*

As one of the chief organizers of protests against the imperial policies adopted by Britain after the Seven Years' War, Samuel Adams (1722–1803) was, in Thomas Jefferson's words, "truly the *man of the Revolution*." A founder of the Sons of Liberty, the Boston-born, Harvard-educated Adams was also a key instigator of protests against the Stamp Act and the Townshend Acts.

Samuel Adams's animosity to arbitrary royal authority had deep personal roots. To promote economic growth in Massachusetts, his father had helped establish a land bank, which lent paper money backed by real estate. In 1741 wealthy merchants led by Thomas Hutchinson (1711–80), fearful that the bills would be used to pay debts, called on the royal Massachusetts governor to declare the land bank illegal. When he did, Adams's father lost tremendous sums of money and never recovered financially.

In 1771 Thomas Hutchinson succeeded Francis Bernard (1712–79) as governor of

Massachusetts. Both Bernard and Hutchinson punished Boston for its resistance to the Townshend Acts by moving the colonial legislature to Cambridge.

SAMUEL ADAMS, JULY 16, 1772, TO COLONEL JAMES WARREN, GLC 1215

The Session is at length over. Since your Departure I have been, as I expected, almost plagued to Death with the Deputations of Whigs [opponents of royal oppression], & the Advantage the Tories [defenders of royal authority] constantly make of them. The Resolves have finally passed, & even as they now appear, I believe they chagrin him whom they call the Governor & his Adherents. We have since resolved on a Petition & Remonstrance to the King, a copy of which I will send you if you promise not to publish them....

The Governor [Thomas Hutchinson] at the close, sent down a message in the Bernardian tone [the arrogant tone of former Governor Francis Bernard] which I *intend* to look over. To speak truth plainly, when the Secretary made it I thought it a very indecent *thing*, in which there appeared a *studied* affront to the House; and it *seemed* to me that I myself had a particular share of it. Pray let me know your Sentiments.

As we have been adherents with each other, & I believe ever shall, you have shared with me in the Curses of a Circle of Tories at Cambridge on the Commencement Day; when Confusion to me & my Adherents was given as a Toast, after too many for the reputation of the Company had been already drunk. This will appear to you, the greater Honor done me....

Don't you think that Mr. [Governor Thomas] Hutchinson aims at irritating this Country in everlastingly introducing his Creatures into all the public Assemblies? Some of the young Gentlemen honored themselves in their performances & particularly Mr. Austin, a promising young Whig, whose Oration you would have [heard] with particular pleasure. "While the Wretch who betrays his Country for the Sake of Places Embodiments & Passions," but I [rely] no more upon my Memory, least I should unhappily detract from the true spirit & stile of it. May Heaven bless the Lad & preserve him from the Contagion of the World!

13 / *"A System of Tyranny gaining ground upon us every day"*

In this letter, John Adams (1735–1826) describes the escalating tensions in Massachusetts during the winter and early spring of 1773, and the mounting opposition to Governor Thomas Hutchinson. Two months after this letter was written, Samuel Adams read a private letter of Hutchinson's before a secret session of the Massachusetts legislature. This letter, which had been acquired by Benjamin Franklin, stressed the need to limit the colonists' rights. The Massachusetts House subsequently petitioned the king for Hutchinson's removal. On March 30, 1774, Hutchinson dismissed the legislature before it could initiate impeachment proceedings against him.

JOHN ADAMS, APRIL 19, 1773, TO CATHARINE MACAULAY, GLC 1785

My own absence from town, my ill State of Health and the melancholy Situation of our public affairs, a System of Tyranny gaining ground upon us every day and overbearing every Man, who will not bow his head to Baal, must be my excuse for the [lateness of this] post....

The Intelligence that Salaries were granted by the Crown to our Judges, already dependent for their Continuance in office, on the mere Will of a Governor and Council spread a general Alarm here. To lull the people, the Courtiers had resorted to a very odd Stratagem. They gave out that the Judges were already in, during good Behavior, and that this Grant of Salaries from the Crown would render them completely independent....

You will find however in these papers, a part of a controversy between the Governor and the House. This Controversy will amuse you. It ought never to have been begun by the Governor. For the consequence of it must be that the People of this Continent will be convinced, too clearly, and too soon that upon Principles of the British Constitution, the British Parliament have no Authority over us.

However, we must resign to Fate. This Man [Thomas Hutchinson] was born, to disturb this Continent and the British Empire, and if he is Suffered with his Family Connections to hold the places they now fill he will effectively answer the evils of his creation. A thorough Master in Theory and practice of the Political Principles of Machiavelli there is no Quantity of public Mischief, no Sacrifice of Truth, Honor Virtue or Country through which he will not cheerfully force his way to wealth and power....

THE BOSTON TEA PARTY

14 / "Nothing but equal Liberty...can secure the attachment of the Colonies to Britain"

The Townshend duties were a dismal failure. Only £21,000 in new duties were collected, while sales of British goods to the colonies fell by more than £700,000. In 1770 Parliament repealed all the Townshend duties except one, a duty on tea, to symbolize Parliament's right to tax the colonies. To avoid paying the duty, colonial merchants smuggled in tea illegally from the Netherlands.

The East India Tea Company, a huge British trading company with eighteen million pounds of unsold tea cramming its warehouses, was tottering on the edge of bankruptcy. To sell its tea for less than smuggled Dutch tea, the company asked for the right to ship tea directly from India to America, instead of stopping first in England. The East India Company also wanted to name its own local tea distributors.

Lord Frederick North (1732–92), who had become the king's chief minister in 1770, thought that the colonists would buy the cheaper British tea and thereby recognize Parliament's right to tax them. Many colonists, however, viewed the Tea Act as an insidious plot to get them to abandon their argument against taxation without representation.

In November 1773, three ships carrying tea for the East India Company docked at Boston Harbor. Opponents of the Tea Act, led by Samuel Adams, insisted that the ships return to their home port. Massachusetts governor Thomas Hutchinson, knowing that after a twenty-day waiting period the tea would be impounded for nonpayment of duties and sold at auction, refused to issue the permits required for the ships to leave the harbor. On December 16, patriots, disguised as Indians, threw 342 chests of tea, valued at £10,000, into the harbor.

Writing just five days before Bostonians dumped the cargoes of tea overboard, John Adams still assumed that the British ships would return to England.

JOHN ADAMS, DECEMBER 11, 1773, TO CATHARINE MACAULAY, GLC 1787

The last ministerial Maneuver has created a more open and determined Resistance than ever has been made before. The Tea Ships are all to return, whatever may be the Consequence. I suppose your wise Minister will put the Nation to some expense of a few Millions to quell this Spirit by another Fleet and Army. The Nation is so independent, so clear of Debt and so rich in Funds and Resources, as yet untried, that there is no doubt to be made, she can well afford it.

But let me tell those wise Ministers, I would not advise them to try many more such Experiments. A few more such Experiments will throw the most of the trade of the Colonies, into the Hands of the Dutch, or will erect an independent Empire in America—perhaps both.

Nothing but equal Liberty and kind Treatment can secure the attachment of the Colonies to Britain.

15 / *"There arrived from England 450 chests of tea"*

A Bostonian named John Andrews (1764–1845) offered the following account of the Tea Party. "A general muster was assembled, from this and all ye neighbouring towns, to the number of five or six thousand, at 10 o'clock Thursday morning in the Old South Meeting house, where they pass'd a *unanimous* vote that the *Tea* should go out of the *harbour* that afternoon.... They muster'd, I'm told, upon Fort Hill, to the number of about two hundred, and proceeded, two by two, to Griffin's wharf...and before *nine* o'clock in the evening, every chest from on board the three vessels was knock'd to pieces and flung over ye sides. They say the actors were *Indians* from *Narragansett*. Whether they were or not, to a transient observer they appear'd as *such*, being cloath'd in Blankets with the heads muffled, and copper color'd countenances, being each arm'd with a hatchet or axe, and pair of pistols, nor was their *dialect* different from what I conceive these geniuses to *speak*, as their jargon was unintelligible to all but themselves."

In a letter to his father, a Boston merchant name John Easson also mentions the Boston Tea Party. The letter is written from the commonsense perspective of a man in commerce worried about losses from rowdy Bostonians.

JOHN EASSON, DECEMBER 18, 1773, TO DAVID EASSON, GLC 191

...If you have any of your tea left, you must tak[e] good care of it for there will be Non[e] to be Gott[.] [H]ere about a fortnight ago there arrived from England 450 chests of tea[.] Last night the Sons of Liberty went and forced the Ships, brock all the Chests and Empt[i]ed all the tea into the Sea this I believe will be as bad as the Stamp Act.

16 / *"We consider each Colony on this Continent as parts of the same Body"*

Britain responded to the Boston Tea Party with outrage. Convinced that rebels in Boston had to be taught a lesson, Parliament passed several laws that the colonists called the "Intolerable Acts." One act closed Boston Harbor until Bostonians paid for the destroyed

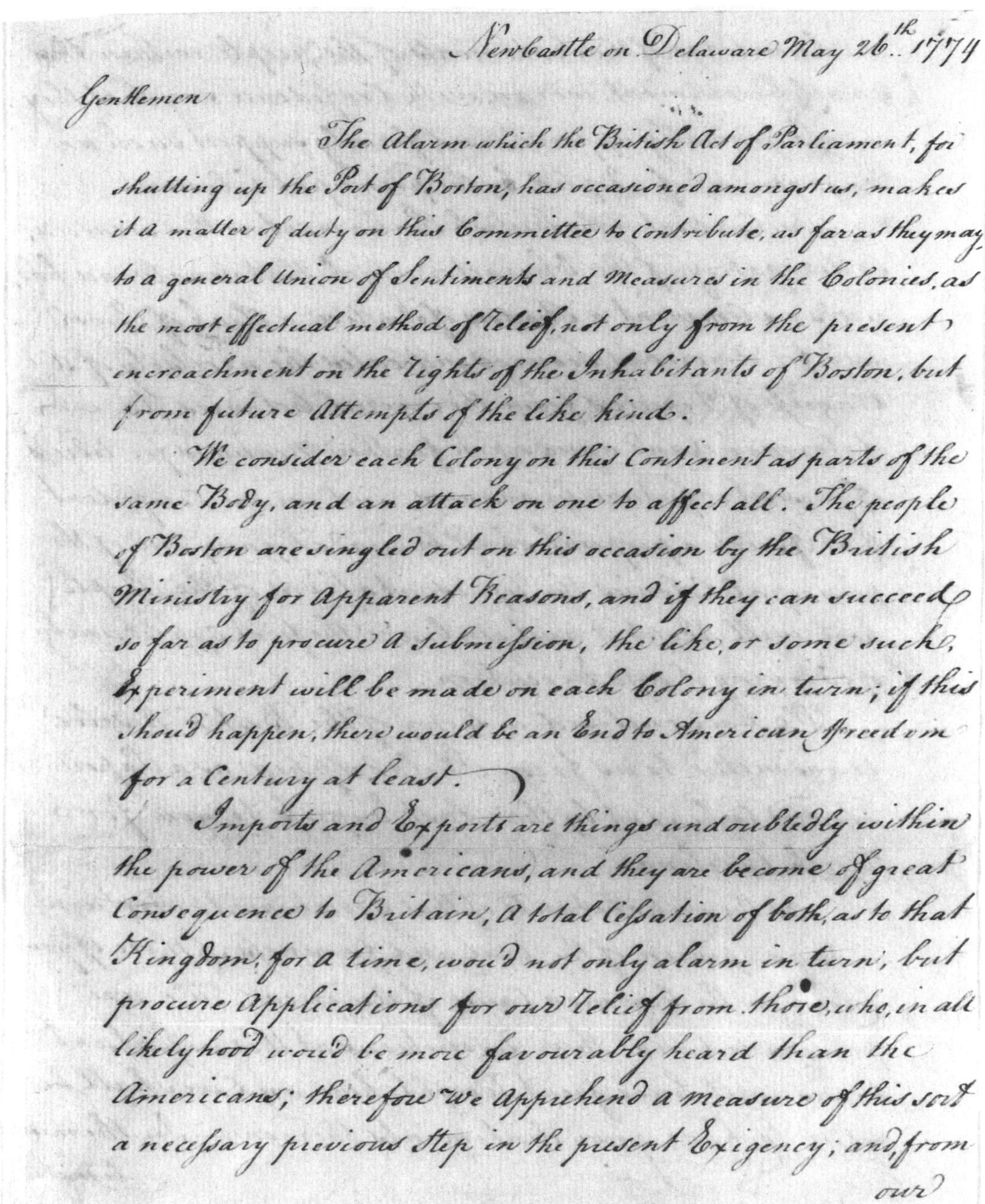
Newcastle on Delaware May 26th 1774

Gentlemen

The Alarm which the British Act of Parliament, for shutting up the Port of Boston, has occasioned amongst us, makes it a matter of duty on this Committee to contribute, as far as they may, to a general Union of Sentiments and Measures in the Colonies, as the most effectual method of relief, not only from the present encroachment on the rights of the Inhabitants of Boston, but from future Attempts of the like kind.

We consider each Colony on this Continent as parts of the same Body, and an attack on one to affect all. The people of Boston are singled out on this occasion by the British Ministry for Apparent Reasons, and if they can succeed so far as to procure a Submission, the like, or some such Experiment will be made on each Colony in turn; if this shoud happen, there would be an End to American freedom for a Century at least.

Imports and Exports are things undoubtedly within the power of the Americans, and they are become of great Consequence to Britain; a total Cessation of both, as to that Kingdom, for a time, woud not only alarm in turn, but procure Applications for our relief from those, who, in all likelyhood woud be more favourably heard than the Americans; therefore we apprehend a measure of this sort a necessary previous step in the present Exigency; and, from our

George Read. Autograph letter signed, to Va. Committee of Correspondence, 1774/05/26. The Gilder Lehrman Collection, on deposit at the Pierpont Morgan Library. GLC 3718

tea. Another measure gave the governor the right to move trials of those who injured customs collectors to another colony or to England. A third act allowed Britain to house troops in unoccupied private houses, as long as the army paid a fair rent. A fourth measure suspended Massachusetts's royal charter, expanded the powers of the royal governor, and declared that town meetings could be held only with the governor's permission. Thomas Hutchinson, the Massachusetts royal governor, asked for a leave of absence and went to England. The crown named Lieutenant General Thomas Gage, the commander in chief of British forces in North America, the new governor.

Colonial leaders viewed the "Intolerable Acts" as confirming the worst tendencies of imperial legislation over the past decade. These measures suggested that Britain could disband colonial legislatures, abolish local self-government, interfere with normal judicial procedures, and elevate military authority over civil authority.

At the same time, Parliament enacted the Québec Act, which fixed the southwestern boundary of the province at the Ohio River (extending Québec to the modern southern borders of Ohio, Indiana, and Illinois) and declared Roman Catholicism to be Québec's established religion. This measure further antagonized militantly anti-Catholic Protestants, who believed that the act transformed the West into a preserve for savages and Papists.

In the following letter, three leading Bostonians, serving on the town's Committee of Correspondence, warn other colonists about the dangers that British actions posed to their liberties, demand a cession of British imports and exports, and call for a convention of delegates from the colonies to organize resistance to the Intolerable Acts. This convention, which would later be called the First Continental Congress, assembled in Philadelphia on September 5, 1774, and included every colony except Georgia.

George Read, cosigned by Thomas McKean and Jonathan McKinley, May 26, 1774, GLC 3718

The Alarm which the British Act of Parliament, for shutting up the Port of Boston, had occasioned among us, makes it a matter of duty on this Committee to contribute as far as they may, to a general Union of Sentiments and Measures in the Colonies, as the most effectual method of relief, not only from the present encroachments on the Rights of the Inhabitants of Boston, but from future Attempts of the like kind.

We consider each Colony on this Continent as parts of the same Body, and an attack on one to affect all. The people of Boston are singled out on this occasion by the British Ministry for Apparent Reasons, and if they can succeed so far as to procure a submission. Experiment will be made on each Colony in turn, if this should happen, there would be an End to American Freedom for a Century at least.

Imports and Exports are things undoubtedly within the power of the Americans, and they are become of great Consequence to Britain, a total cessation of both, as to that Kingdom, for a time, would not only alarm in turn, but procure application for our relief...; therefore we apprehend a measure of this sort a necessary previous step in the present Exigency; and, from our knowledge of the Sentiments of the people within that small Government, we can with Confidence say that they would generally approve, and firmly support such an Engagement if adopted by the principal Colonies.

The Conduct of the British Parliament on this occasion, so derogatory of the character which that Senate once had, needs no Comment, a Shadow of Justice, a Cloak of Power used for America's Scourge indicates the necessity of a Congress of Deputies from the several Colonies to determine and agree upon further measures for Redress of present or future Grievances; and we are Confident that if such a proposal shall be made by any one of the principal Colonies the Representatives of the People here will adopt it and embrace the first opportunity of carrying it into Execution....

17 / *"They found upwards of fifty thousand men well armed, actually on their march to Boston"*

A signer of the Declaration of Independence from Delaware, Caesar Rodney (1728–84) served as a major general in the state militia and as president of Delaware during the Revolution. In this letter, Rodney describes the rumors and paranoia following a false report of a British attack on Boston. He supports the claim of the Friends of Liberty that the rumor may have been started by loyalists to measure the support for the patriots in the countryside.

CAESAR RODNEY, SEPTEMBER 17, 1774, TO AN UNKNOWN RECIPIENT, GLC 983

Some time ago, I do not doubt but you were all much alarmed on a Report that the Kings Ships were firing on the Town of Boston. When that news came to this City, the Bells were muffled, and kept Ringing all that day; However in a few days after, that news was contradicted here....When the Expresses went to Contradict this false Report they found upwards of fifty thousand men well armed, actually on their march to Boston for the Relief of the inhabitants; and that every farmer who had a cart or wagon (and not able to bear arms) were with them Loaded with Provisions, ammunition and Baggage & [tha]t all headed by Experienced officers who had served in the late American war. And that vast numbers now were prepared to March upon the news being Contradicted, they Returned peaceably to their several places of Abode, but not till they had sent some of their officers from the different parts to Boston to know the...Affairs there and to direct them. What principal officers of different part of the Country they should hereafter send in case they should stand in need of their assistance. It is supposed by some of the friends of Liberty at Boston that the alarm was set on foot by some of the friends to the ministerial plan in order to try whether there was that true valor in the people—if this was the case, I suppose you will think with me that by this time they can have no doubts remaining—Indeed I think it is proved by the General's own conduct, for, ever since that, he has been fortifying himself, which I imagine is now for his own security, than to attack the Inhabitants.

18 / *"Ruinous system of colony administration... calculated for enslaving these Colonies"*

At the start of the quarrel with Britain following the Seven Years' War, Americans had little sense of how much they had in common. But by 1774, when the first Continental Congress met, there was a growing sense of unanimity. Although the delegates did not call for independence, they did vote to cut off colonial trade with Britain unless

The Aſſociation,

Agreed upon by the GRAND AMERICAN CONTINENTAL CONGRESS.

WE his Majeſty's moſt loyal Subjects, the Delegates of the ſeveral Colonies of New Hampſhire, Maſſachuſetts Bay, Rhode-Iſland, Connecticut, New-York, New Jerſey, Pennſylvania, the Three Lower Counties of Newcaſtle, Kent, and Suſſex, on Delaware, Maryland, Virginia, North-Carolina, and South Carolina, deputed to repreſent them in a Continental Congreſs, held in the city of Philadelphia, on the fifth day of September, 1774, avowing our allegiance to his Majeſty, our affection and regard for our fellow ſubjects in Great-Britain and elſewhere, affected with the deepeſt anxiety, and moſt alarming apprehenſions at thoſe Grievances and diſtreſſes, with which his Majeſty's American ſubjects are oppreſſed, and having taken under our moſt ſerious deliberation, the ſtate of the whole continent, find, that the preſent unhappy ſituation of our affairs, is occaſioned by a ruinous ſyſtem of colony adminiſtration adopted by the Britiſh Miniſtry about the year 1763, evidently calculated for enſlaving theſe Colonies, and, with them, the Britiſh Empire. In proſecution of which ſyſtem, various Acts of Parliament have been paſſed for raiſing a Revenue in America, for depriving the American ſubjects, in many inſtances, of the conſtitutional trial by jury, expoſing their lives to danger, by directing a new and illegal trial beyond the ſeas, for crimes alledged to have been committed in America: And in proſecution of the ſame ſyſtem, ſeveral late, cruel and oppreſſive Acts have been paſſed reſpecting the town of Boſton and the Maſſachuſetts Bay, and alſo an Act for extending the province of Quebec, ſo as to border on the weſtern frontiers of theſe Colonies, eſtabliſhing an arbitrary government therein, and diſcouraging the ſettlement of Britiſh ſubjects in that wide extended country; thus by the influence of civil principles and ancient prejudices to diſpoſe the inhabitants to act with hoſtility againſt the free Proteſtant Colonies, whenever a wicked Miniſtry ſhall chuſe ſo to direct them.

To obtain redreſs of theſe grievances, which threaten deſtruction to the lives, liberty, and property of his Majeſty's ſubjects in North-America, we are of opinion, that a non importation non-conſumption, and non exportation agreement, faithfully adhered to, will prove the moſt ſpeedy, effectual, and peaceable meaſure: — And therefore we do, for ourſelves, and the inhabitants of the ſeveral Colonies, whom we repreſent, firmly agree and aſſociate under the ſacred ties of virtue, honor, and love of out country, as follows:

Firſt. That from and after the firſt day of December next, we will not import into Britiſh America, from Great Britain or Ireland, any goods, wares or merchandize whatſoever, or from any other place any ſuch goods, wares or merchandize, as ſhall have been exported from Great-Britain or Ireland; nor will we, after that day, import any Eaſt-India tea from any part of the world; nor any molaſſes, ſyrups, paneles, coffee, or piemento, from the Britiſh plantations, or from Dominica; nor wines from Madeira, or the Weſtern Iſlands; nor foreign indigo.

Second. That we will neither import, nor purchaſe any ſlave imported after the firſt day of December next, after which time, we will wholly diſcontinue the ſlave trade, and will neither be concerned in it ourſelves, nor will we hire our veſſels, nor ſell our commodities or manufactures to thoſe who are concerned in it.

Third. As a non conſumption agreement ſtrictly adhered to, will be an effectual ſecurity for the obſervation of the non-importation, we, as above, ſolemnly agree and aſſociate, that, from this day, we will not purchaſe or uſe any tea imported on account of the Eaſt-India company, or any on which a duty hath been or ſhall be paid; and from and after the firſt day of March next, we will not purchaſe or uſe any Eaſt-India tea whatever, nor will we, nor ſhall any perſon for or under us, purchaſe or uſe any of thoſe goods, wares or merchandize, we have agreed not to import, which we ſhall know, or have cauſe to ſuſpect, were imported after the firſt day of December, except ſuch as come under the rules and directions of the tenth article hereafter mentioned.

Fourth. The earneſt deſire we have, not to injure our fellow-ſubjects in Great Britain, Ireland, or the Weſt Indies, induces us to ſuſpend a non-exportation until the tenth day of September, 1775; at which time if the ſaid Acts and parts of Acts of the Britiſh parliament, herein after mentioned, are not repealed, we will not, directly or indirectly, export any merchandize or commodity whatſoever, to Great-Britain, Ireland or the Weſt-Indies, except Rice to Europe.

Fifth. Such as are merchants, and uſe the Britiſh and Iriſh trade will give orders as ſoon as poſſible, to their factors, agents and correſpondents, in Great Britain and Ireland, not to ſhip any goods to them on any pretence whatſoever, as they cannot be received in America; and if any merchant reſiding in Great-Britain or Ireland, ſhall directly or indirectly ſhip any goods, wares or merchandize, for America, in order to break the ſaid non importation agreement, or in any manner contravene the ſame, on ſuch unworthy conduct being well atteſted, it ought to be made public; and, on the ſame being ſo done, we will not from thenceforth have any commercial connection with ſuch merchant.

Sixth. That ſuch as are owners of veſſels will give poſitive orders to their captains, or maſters, not to receive on board their veſſels any goods prohibited by the ſaid non-importation agreement, on pain of immediate diſmiſſion from their ſervice.

Seventh. We will uſe our utmoſt endeavours to improve the breed of ſheep and increaſe their numbers to the greateſt extent, and to that end we will kill them as ſparingly as may be, eſpecially thoſe of the moſt profitable kind; nor will we export any to the Weſt Indies, or elſewhere; and thoſe of us who are or may become overſtocked with, or can conveniently ſpare any ſheep, will diſpoſe of them to our neighbours, eſpecially to the poorer ſort, on moderate terms.

Eighth. That we will in our ſeveral ſtations encourage frugality, œconomy, and induſtry; and promote agriculture, arts, and the manufactures of this country, eſpecially that of wool; and will diſcountenance and diſcourage, every ſpecies of extravagance and diſſipation, eſpecially all horſe-racing, and all kinds of gaming, cock-fighting, exhibitions of ſhews, plays, and other expenſive diverſions and entertainments. And on the death of any relation or friend, none of us or any of our families will go into any further mourning dreſs, than a black crape or ribbon on the arm or hat for Gentlemen, and a black ribbon and necklace for Ladies, and we will diſcontinue the giving of gloves and ſcarfs at funerals.

Ninth. That ſuch as are venders of goods or merchandize, will not take advantage of the ſcarcity of goods that may be occaſioned by this aſſociation, but will ſell the ſame at the rates we have been reſpectively accuſtomed to do, for twelve months laſt paſt. — And if any vender of goods or merchandize, ſhall ſell any ſuch goods on higher terms, or ſhall in any manner, or by any device whatſoever, violate or depart from this agreement, no perſon ought, nor will any of us deal with any ſuch perſon, or his or her factor or agent, at any time hereafter, for any commodity whatever.

Tenth. In caſe any merchant, trader, or other perſons ſhall import any goods or merchandize after the firſt day of December, and before the firſt day of February next, the ſame ought forthwith at the election of the owner, to be either re-ſhipped or delivered up to the committee of the county, or town wherein they ſhall be imported, to be ſtored at the riſque of the importer, until the non-importation agreement ſhall ceaſe, or be ſold under the direction of the committee aforeſaid; and in the laſt mentioned caſe, the owner or owners of ſuch goods, ſhall be reimburſed (out of the ſales) the firſt coſt and charges, the profit if any, to be applied towards relieving and employing ſuch poor inhabitants of the town of Boſton, as are immediate ſufferers by the Boſton Port-Bill; and a particular account of all goods ſo returned, ſtored or ſold, to be inſerted in the public papers; and if any goods or merchandizes ſhall be imported after the ſaid firſt day of February, the ſame ought forthwith to be ſent back again, without breaking any of the packages thereof.

Eleventh. That a committee be choſen in every county, city, and town, by thoſe who are qualified to vote for Repreſentatives in the Legiſlature, whoſe buſineſs it ſhall be attentively to obſerve the conduct of all perſons touching this aſſociation; and when it ſhall be made to appear to the ſatisfaction of a majority of any ſuch committee, that any perſon within the limits of their appointment has violated this aſſociation, that ſuch majority do forthwith cauſe the truth of the caſe to be publiſhed in the Gazette, to the end that all ſuch foes to the rights of Britiſh America may be publickly known, and univerſally contemned as the enemies of American liberty; and thenceforth we reſpectively will break off all dealings with him or her.

Twelfth. That the committee of correſpondence in the reſpective colonies do frequently inſpect the entries of their cuſtom-houſes, and inform each other from time to time of the true ſtate thereof, and of every other material circumſtance that may occur relative to this aſſociation.

Thirteenth. That all manufactures of this country be ſold at reaſonable prices, ſo that no undue advantage be taken of a future ſcarcity of goods.

Fourteenth. And we do further agree and reſolve, that we will have no trade, commerce, dealings or intercourſe whatſoever, with any colony or province, in North-America, which ſhall not accede to, or which ſhall hereafter violate this aſſociation, but will hold them as unworthy of the rights of freemen, and as inimical to the liberties of their country.

And we do ſolemnly bind ourſelves and our conſtituents, under the ties aforeſaid, to adhere to this aſſociation until ſuch parts of the ſeveral Acts of parliament paſſed ſince the cloſe of the laſt war, as impoſe or continue duties on Tea, Wine, Molaſſes, Syrups, Paneles, Coffee, Sugar, Piemento, Indigo, Foreign Paper, Glaſs, and Painters Colours, imported into America, and extend the Powers of the Admiralty courts beyond their ancient limits, deprive the American Subject of trial by jury, authorize the Judge's certificate to indemnify the proſecutor from damages, that he might otherwiſe be liable to from a trial by his peers, require oppreſſive ſecurity from a claimant of ſhips or goods ſeized, before he ſhall be allowed to defend his property, are repealed. — And until that part of the Act of the 12. G. 3. chap. 24, entitled, "An Act for the better ſecuring his Majeſty's dock yards, magazines, ſhips, ammunition, and ſtores," by which, any perſons charged with committing any of the offences therein deſcribed, in America, may be tried in any ſhire or county within the realm, is repealed — And until the four Acts paſſed in the laſt ſeſſion of parliament, *viz.* That for ſtopping the port and blocking up the harbour of Boſton — That for altering the charter and government of the Maſſachuſetts Bay — And that which is entitled "An Act for the better adminiſtration of juſtice, &c. — And that "For extending the limits of Quebec," &c. are repealed. And we recommend it to the provincial conventions, and to the committees in the reſpective Colonies, to eſtabliſh ſuch further regulations as they may think proper, for carrying into execution this Aſſociation.

The foregoing Aſſociation being determined upon by the CONGRESS, was ordered to be ſubſcribed by the ſeveral Members thereof; and thereupon we have hereunto ſet our reſpective names accordingly.

In Congreſs, Philadelphia, October 20, 1774.

Signed,

PEYTON RANDOLPH, Preſident.

NEW-HAMPSHIRE.
John Sullivan, Nathaniel Folſom.

MASSACHUSETTS-BAY.
Thomas Cuſhing, Samuel Adams,
John Adams, Robert-Treat Paine.

RHODE-ISLAND.
Stephen Hopkins, Samuel Ward.

CONNECTICUT.
Eliphalet Dyer, Roger Sherman,
Silas Deane,

NEW-YORK.
Iſaac Low, John Alſop,
John Jay, James Duane,
William Floyd, Henry Wiſener,
S. Boerum.

NEW JERSEY.
James Kinſey, William Livingſton,
Stephen Crane, Richard Smith.

PENNSYLVANIA.
Joſeph Galloway, John Dickinſon,
Charles Humphreys, Thomas Miſflin,
Edward Biddle.

NEW-CASTLE, &c.
Cæſar Rodney, Thomas M'Keane,
George Read.

MARYLAND.
Matthew Tilghman, Thomas Johnſon,
William Paca, Samuel Chaſe.

VIRGINIA.
Richard Henry Lee, George Waſhington,
P. Henry, jun. Richard Bland,
Benjamin Harriſon, Edmund Pendleton.

NORTH-CAROLINA.
William Hooper, Joſeph Hewes,
R. Caſwell.

SOUTH-CAROLINA.
Henry Middleton, Thomas Lynch,
Chriſtopher Gadſden, John Rutledge,
Edward Rutledge.

Boſton: Printed by *Edes & Gill*, in Queen-Street.

Broadside, The Association Agreed with the Grand American Congress... [non-importation], 1774/10/20.
The Gilder Lehrman Collection, on deposit at the Pierpont Morgan Library. GLC 4489

Parliament abolished the Intolerable Acts. The delegates also approved resolutions advising the colonies to begin training their citizens for war. Note that the spirit of self-sacrifice and ascetic anticonsumerism extended to a closing of the African and West Indian slave trade.

The Association, agreed upon by the Grand American Continental Congress, October 20, 1774, GLC 4489

We his Majesty's most loyal Subjects, the Delegates of the Several Colonies...deputed to represent them in a Continental Congress, held in the City of Philadelphia, on the fifth day of September, 1774, avowing our allegiance to his Majesty, our affection and regard for our fellow subjects in Great Britain and elsewhere, affected with the deepest anxiety, and most alarming apprehensions at those Grievances and distresses, with which his Majesty's American subjects are oppressed, and having taken under our most serious deliberation the state of the whole continent, find, that the present unhappy situation of our affairs, is occasioned by the ruinous system of colony administration adopted by the British Ministry about the year 1763, evidently calculated for enslaving these Colonies, and, with them, the British Empire. In prosecution of which system, various Acts of parliament have been passed for raising a Revenue in America, for depriving the American subjects, in many instances of the constitutional trial by jury, exposing their lives to danger, by directing a new and illegal trial beyond the seas, for crimes alleged to have been committed in America: And in prosecution of the same system several late, cruel and oppressive Acts have been passed respecting the town of Boston and the Massachusetts Bay, and also an Act for extending the province of Quebec, so as to border on the western frontiers of these Colonies, establishing an arbitrary government therein, and discouraging the settlement of British subjects in that wide extended country....

To obtain redress of these grievances, which threaten destruction to the lives, liberty and prosperity of his Majesty's subjects in North America, we are of opinion, that a non-importation, non-consumption, and non-exportation agreement, faithfully adhered to, will prove the most, speedy, effectual, and peaceable measure: And therefore we do, for ourselves, and the inhabitants of the several Colonies, whom we represent, firmly agree and associate under the sacred ties of virtue, honor, and love of our country, as follows:

First. That from and after the first day of December next, we will not import into British America, from Great Britain or Ireland, any goods, wares, or merchandize whatsoever, or from any other place such goods, wares or merchandize as shall have been exported from Great Britain or Ireland; nor will we, after that day, import any East India tea from any part of the world; nor any molasses, syrups...coffee, or pimento from the British plantations, or from Dominica, nor wines from Madeira, or the Western Islands, nor foreign indigo.

Second. That we will neither import nor purchase any slave imported after the first day of December next, after which time, we will wholly discontinue the slave-trade....

Eighth. That we will in our several situations encourage frugality, economy, and industry; and promote agriculture, arts, and the manufactures of this country, especially that of wool; and will discountenance and discourage every species of extravagance and dissipation, especially all horse-racing, and all kinds of gaming, cock-fighting, exhibitions of shows, plays, and other expensive diversions and entertainments. And on the death of any relation or friend, none of us or any of our families will go into any further mourning of dress, than a black crape or ribbon on the arm or hat for Gentlemen, and a black ribbon and necklace for Ladies, and we will discontinue the giving of gloves and scarfs at funerals.

Ninth. That such as are venders of goods or merchandize will not take advantage of the scarcity of goods that may be occasioned by this association, but will sell the same at the rates we have been respectively accustomed to, for twelve months last past. And if any vender of goods or merchandize shall sell any such goods on higher terms, or shall in any manner or by any device whatsoever, violate or depart from this agreement, no person ought, nor will any of us deal with any such person, or his or her factor or agent, at any time hereafter, for any commodity whatever....

And we do solemnly bind ourselves and our constituents...to adhere to this association until such parts of the several Acts of Parliament passed since the close of the last war, as Impose or continue duties on Tea, Wine, Molasses, Syrups...Coffee, Sugar Pimento, Indigo, Foreign Paper, Glass and Painters Colours, imported into America, and extend the Powers of the Admiralty courts beyond their ancient limits, deprive the American subject of trial by jury, authorize the Judge's certificate to indemnify the prosecutor from damages, that he might otherwise be liable to from a trial by his peers, require oppressive security from a claimant of ships or goods seized, before he shall be allowed to defend his property, are repealed. And until that [act]...by which, any persons charged with committing any of the offenses therein described, may be tried in any shire or county within the realm, is repealed. And until the four Acts passed in the last session of parliament, viz. That for stopping the port and blocking up the harbour of Boston—That for altering the charter and government of the Massachusetts Bay—And that which is entitled "An Act for the better administration of justice, &c.—And that "For extending the limits of Quebec," &c. are repealed....

19 / *"We...lay our grievances before the throne"*

Many members of the Continental Congress blamed the imperial crisis on the acts of malevolent ministers and implored King George to intercede with Parliament to find some means to preserve English liberties in America. In fact, the king was so invested in the imperial policies that he was unable to serve a mediating role in the conflict. It is interesting to contrast the language of this petition with that of the Declaration of Independence, drafted only twenty months later.

PETITION FROM THE GENERAL CONGRESS IN AMERICA TO THE KING, OCTOBER 26, 1774, GLC 1671

Most Gracious Sovereign,

We your majesty's faithful subjects...[beg] to lay our grievances before the throne.

A standing army has been kept in these colonies ever since the conclusion of the late war, without the consent of our assemblies; and this army, with a considerable naval armament, has been employed to enforce the collection of taxes;

The authority of the commander in chief, and, under him, of the brigadier general, has in time of peace been rendered supreme in all the civil governments in America.

The commander in chief of your majesty's forces in North-America has in time of peace been appointed governor of a colony.

The charges of usual officers have been greatly increased, and new, expensive, and oppressive officers have been multiplied.

The judges of the admiralty and vice-admiralty courts are empowered to receive their salaries and fees from the effects condemned by themselves. The officers of the customs are employed to break open and enter houses without the authority of any civil magistrate, founded on legal information.

The judges of courts of common law have been made entirely dependent on one part of the legislature for their salaries, as well as for the duration of their commissions....

Commerce has been burthened with many useless and oppressive restrictions....

In the last session of parliament, an act was passed for blocking up the harbour of Boston; another empowering the governor of Massachusetts-bay to send persons indicted for murder in that province to another colony, or even to Great-Britain, for trial, whereby such offenders may escape legal punishment; a third for altering the...constitution of government in the province; and a fourth extending the limits of Québec...whereby great numbers of British freemen are subjected to [French laws]...and establishing an absolute government, and Roman catholick religion, throughout those vast regions that border on the westerly and northerly boundaries of the free protestant English settlements; and a fifth, for the better providing suitable quarter for officers and soldiers in his majesty's service in North-America....

Had our Creator been pleased to give us existence in a land of slavery, the sense of our condition might have been mitigated by ignorance and habit: But thanks be to his adorable goodness, we were born in...freedom and ever enjoyed our right under the auspices of your royal ancestors, whose family was seated on the British throne to rescue and secure a pious and gallant nation from the popery and despotism of a superstitious and inexorable tyrant....

The apprehension of being degraded into a state of servitude, from the pre-eminent rank of English freemen, while our minds retain the strongest love of liberty, and clearly foresee the miseries preparing for us and our posterity, excites emotions in our breasts, which, though we cannot describe, we should not wish to conceal. Feeling as men, and thinking as subjects in the manner we do, silence would be disloyalty. By giving this faithful information, we do all in our power to promote the great objects of your royal cares, the tranquility of your government, and the welfare of your people....

20 / *"When a Nation...turns advocate for Slavery and Oppression, there is reason to suspect she has...ceased to be virtuous"*

Leaders of the patriot cause repeatedly argued that imperial policies would literally make the colonists slaves of the British. As the historian Bernard Bailyn has demonstrated, the colonists' talk of being enslaved was not hyperbole or lurid rhetoric; it expressed a genuine fear of being subjected to "the arbitrary will and pleasure of another."

Letter from the General Congress at Philadelphia, September 5, 1774, to the people of Great Britain, September 5, 1774, GLC 4774

Friends and Fellow Subjects,

When a Nation led to Greatness by the Hand of liberty, and possessed of all the Glory, the Heroism, Munificence, and Humanity can bestow, descends to the ungrateful Talk of bringing Chains to her Friends and Children, and, instead of Giving Support to Freedom, turns Advocate for Slavery and Oppression, there is reason to suspect she has either ceased to be virtuous, or been extremely negligent in the appointments of her rulers....

At the conclusion of the late war...under the influence of that man [Lord Grenville], a plan of enslaving your fellow subjects in America was concerted, and has ever since been pertinaciously carrying into execution....

Prior to this era, you were content with drawing from us the wealth produced by our commerce. You strained our trade in every way that could conduce to your emolument; you exercised unbounded sovereignty over the sea; you named the ports and nations to which alone our merchandise should be carried, and with whom alone we should trade, and though some of these restrictions were grievous, we nevertheless did not complain; we looked up to you as to our parent state, to which we were bound by the strongest ties, and were happy in being instrumental to your prosperity and your grandeur....

Before we had recovered from the distresses which ever attend war, an attempt was made to drain this country of all its money, by the oppressive Stamp Act. Paint, glass, and other commodities, which you would not permit us to purchase of other nations, were taxed; nay, although no wine is made in any country subject to the British state, you prohibited our procuring it of foreigners without paying a tax, imposed by your parliament, on all we import. These, and many other impositions, were laid upon us most unjustly and unconstitutionally, for the express purpose of raising a revenue. In order to silence complaint, it was indeed provided that this revenue would be expended in America, for its protection and defence. These exactions, however, can receive no justification from a pretended necessity of protecting and defending us. They were lavishly squandered on court favorites and ministerial dependents, generally avowed enemies to America....

To enforce this unconstitutional and unjust scheme of taxation, every fence that the wisdom of our British ancestors had carefully erected against arbitrary power has been violently thrown down in America, and the inestimable right of trial by jury taken away in cases that touch both life and property....

Nor are these the only capital grievances under which we labour. We might tell of dissolute, weak, and wicked governors having been set over us; of legislatures being suspended for asserting the rights of British subjects; of needy and ignorant dependents on great men advanced to the seats of justice, and to other places of trust and importance; of hard restrictions on commerce, and a great variety of lesser evils....

Now mark the progression of the ministerial plan for enslaving us. Well aware that such hardy attempts to take our property from us, to deprive us of that valuable right of trial by jury, to seize our persons and carry us for trial to Great Britain, to blockade our ports, to destroy our charters, and change our forms of government, would occasion and had already occasioned, great discontent in all the colonies, which might produce opposition to these measures, an act was passed to protect, indemnify, and screen from punishment, such as might be guilty even of murder, in endeavoring to carry their oppressive edicts into execution; and by another act, the dominion of Canada is to be expanded...and governed as that by being disunited from us, detached from our interest, by civil as well as religious prejudices, that by their numbers daily swelling with catholic emigrants from Europe, and by their devotion to administration, so friendly to their religion, they might become formidable to us, and on occasion, be fit instruments in the hands of power to reduce the ancient free Protestant colonies to the same state of slavery with themselves....

May not a ministry, with the same armies, enslave you?... Remember the taxes from America, the wealth, and we may add the men and particularly the Roman catholics, of this vast continent, will then be in the power of your enemies; nor will you have any reason to expect that, after making slaves of us, many among us should refuse to assist in reducing you to the same abject state.

AMERICAN RESISTANCE TO BRITAIN

21 / "It will produce Resistance, and Reprisal, and a Flame through all America"

In the following letter, in which he describes the grievances he feels threaten to reduce the colonists to political slavery, John Adams (1735–1826) revives memories of the Puritan struggle against the religious tyranny of the Stuart monarchs during the English Civil War, a subject dear to the heart of Catharine Macaulay, who was writing an eight-volume history of England from the time of James I.

JOHN ADAMS, DECEMBER 28, 1774, TO CATHARINE MACAULAY, GLC 1788

It is not easy to convey to you, Madam, an Adequate Idea of the State of this Province.—It is now at last, true that we have no Government,—legislative, executive, or judicial.—The People determined never to Submit to the Act for destroying their Charter, so dearly purchased, preserved and defended by the Toil Treasure and Blood of their Ancestors, are, every where devoting themselves to Arms....What the Ministry will do is uncertain.—All the British Fleet and Army cannot change Minds [or] Opinions.—They cannot make a Juror Serve, nor a Representative.—An attempt to cram a form of Government down the Throats of a People,—to impose a Constitution, upon a united and determin'd People by Force, is not within the Omnipotence of an English Parliament.... If they Send the Sword and Fire, to ravage this Country, they will find in New England, an hundred Thousand descendants of the Puritan in Charles and James's days, who have not yet lost entirely the Spirit of English men under the English Commonwealth.... If this should be attempted, it will produce Resistance, and Reprisal, and a Flame through all America, Such as Eye hath not yet Seen, nor Ear heard nor hath it entered into the Heart of the Minister or his Minions to conceive.

22 / "Kings are servants, not the proprietors of the people"

Two years before the Declaration of Independence, Thomas Jefferson (1743–1826), then thirty-one, distributed an essay to the delegates at the first Continental Congress in which he outlined grievances against the British government. At the time, this statement was considered too radical by most colonial leaders. In this document, Jefferson appeals not only to an English tradition of political liberty, but also to the idea of certain natural and inalienable rights—a concept he would develop two years later in the Declaration of Independence .

THOMAS JEFFERSON, "A SUMMARY VIEW OF THE RIGHTS OF BRITISH AMERICA," 1774, GLC 962

These are our grievances which we have thus laid before his majesty, with that freedom of language and sentiment which becomes a free people claiming their rights, as derived from the laws of nature, and not as the gift of their chief magistrate: Let those flatter who fear; it is not an American art. To give praise which is not due might be well venal, but would ill beseem those who are asserting the rights of human nature. They know, and will therefore say, that kings are servants, not the proprietors of the people. Open your breast, sire, to liberal and expanded thought.

23 / *"We consider ourselves as laying the foundation of a glorious future Empire"*

Ezra Stiles (1727–95), a future president of Yale College, was serving as pastor in Newport at the time he wrote this letter. He describes how Parliament's repressive laws have inflamed Americans, who fled Europe for freedom. He criticizes Britain for not sharing its triumph over France with its colonists. Convinced that the colonists are capable of governing themselves, he predicts future greatness for America.

EZRA STILES, APRIL 15, 1775, TO CATHARINE MACAULAY, GLC 1798

Not only Britain, but all Europe are Spectators of the Conflict, the Arduous Struggle for Liberty. We consider ourselves as laying the foundation of a glorious future Empire, and acting a part for the Contemplation of Ages. America is ambitious of conducting with that Prudence, Wisdom, Counsel, and true Greatness, which may com[m]end them to the Admiration of Posterity and the World.... The Resolutions of Parliament instead of intimidating only add Fuel to the Flame, invigorate & strengthen the Resolutions of the Americans. We have the united Wisdom of the Continent incessantly exercised in deliberating, projecting & resolving the public Measures adapted to the present momentous Exigency: and if deserted by our Brethren in Great Britain, and abandoned by the World, we confidently trust in Our GOD that he will deliver us.... America is ready for the last Appeal, which however shocking and tremendous, is by the Body of the Colonies judged less terrible than the Depredations of Tyranny & arbitrary Power....

Our Fathers fled hither for Religion and Liberty: if extirpated from hence, we have no new World to flee to. God has located us here, and by this Location has com[m]anded us here to make a Stand, and see the Salvation of the Lord. In repeated Days of Prayer and Fasting, we have asked Council of Heaven, and com[m]itted our Cause to God....We are embarked in a glorious and animating Cause, and proceed in it with undoubted Confidence of final Success...

The Maryland Congress has already proceeded to levy Taxes for an Armament. So.

Carolina Congress have shut up the Courts of Law. The System proceeds, and may perhaps terminate in an entirely new Colony-Police, by erecting the Congress into the Legislatures of free allied States. And on this Alliance and Confederacy may arise a stated [sic] Continental or Imperial Congress for deliberating Matters of universal Moment. I do not say that this Change would be happiest, wisest & best: but this I say, that the present Measures of Administration & Parl[iamen]t will precipitate & ensure such a Revolution, and if not desisted and departed from, all will very soon terminate in this. If there be no Relaxation speedily, a Continental Army will be raised, and under repeated supposed Defeats, will survive and perpetuate itself, till such or a similar system of Policy shall be eventually established.

THE BATTLES OF LEXINGTON AND CONCORD

24 / "Troops...marched to Lexington & there Killed a number of our American Soldiers"

In February 1775, Parliament declared Massachusetts to be in a state of rebellion. This declaration permitted soldiers to shoot suspected rebels on sight. In April, General Thomas Gage (1721–87) received secret orders to arrest the ringleaders of colonial unrest. Having already learned of the orders, colonial leaders fled Boston to avoid arrest.

Gage decided to seize and destroy arms the patriots had stored at Concord, twenty miles northwest of Boston. On the night of April 18, 1775, 700 British soldiers began to march toward Concord. When Joseph Warren (1741–75), a Boston patriot, discovered that British troops were on the march, he sent Paul Revere (1735–1818) and William Dawes (1745–99) to ride to Concord to warn the people about the approaching forces.

At dawn on April 19, the troops reached the town of Lexington, five miles east of Concord. About 70 volunteer soldiers called minutemen lined the Lexington Green to warn the redcoated British troops not to trespass on the property of freeborn English subjects. A shot rang out; the British troops fired. Eight minutemen were killed and another ten were wounded.

The British continued to Concord, where they searched for hidden arms. At North Bridge, a group of redcoats and minutemen clashed, leaving 3 redcoats and 2 minutemen dead. The British then retreated to Boston, while citizen-soldiers fired at the soldiers from behind trees and stone fences. British soldiers killed or wounded totaled 273; colonists losses were 95. The resistance displayed on April 19, 1775, indicated that the American Revolution would truly be a popular revolution.

The battles of Lexington and Concord occurred three weeks after Patrick Henry (1736–99) delivered his famous words, "Give me liberty or give me death." Although an earlier battle with the British had been fought in North Carolina, at Moore's Creek Bridge, Lexington and Concord became fixed in the public mind as the valiant start of American resistance.

Several first-person accounts of these battles survive. Phineas Fullam, a Committee of Safety postrider, reported seeing "some of the Men killed the whole number on both sides as near as can be estimated is 200 among whom are a Considerable Number of

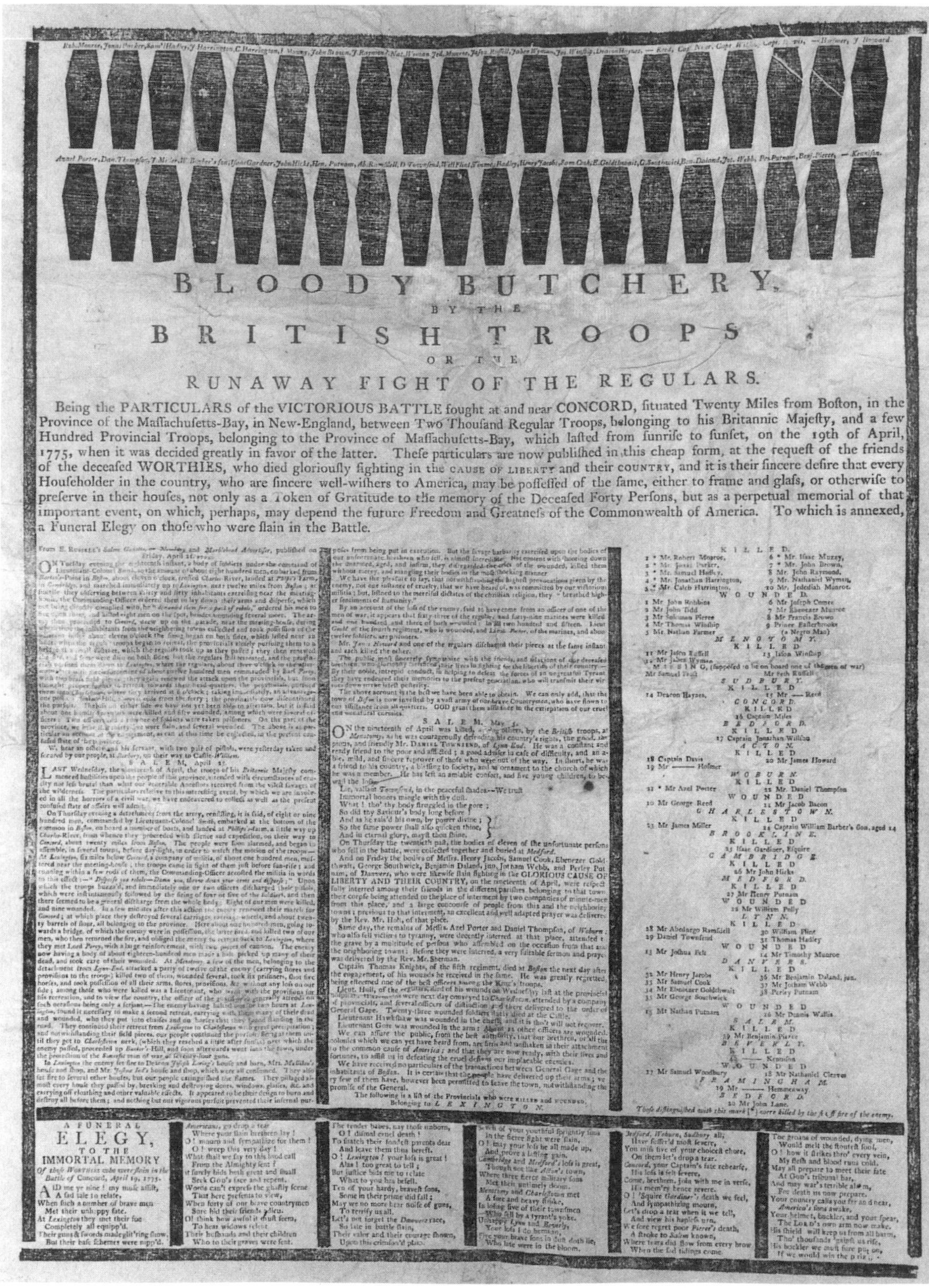

BLOODY BUTCHERY,

BY THE

BRITISH TROOPS:

OR THE

RUNAWAY FIGHT OF THE REGULARS.

Being the PARTICULARS of the VICTORIOUS BATTLE fought at and near CONCORD, situated Twenty Miles from Boston, in the Province of the Massachusetts-Bay, in New-England, between Two Thousand Regular Troops, belonging to his Britannic Majesty, and a few Hundred Provincial Troops, belonging to the Province of Massachusetts-Bay, which lasted from sunrise to sunset, on the 19th of April, 1775, when it was decided greatly in favor of the latter. These particulars are now published in this cheap form, at the request of the friends of the deceased WORTHIES, who died gloriously fighting in the CAUSE OF LIBERTY and their COUNTRY, and it is their sincere desire that every Householder in the country, who are sincere well-wishers to America, may be possessed of the same, either to frame and glass, or otherwise to preserve in their houses, not only as a Token of Gratitude to the memory of the Deceased Forty Persons, but as a perpetual memorial of that important event, on which, perhaps, may depend the future Freedom and Greatness of the Commonwealth of America. To which is annexed, a Funeral Elegy on those who were slain in the Battle.

A FUNERAL ELEGY, TO THE IMMORTAL MEMORY Of those WORTHIES who were slain in the Battle of Concord, April 19, 1775.

Broadside, Bloody Butchery by the British Troops [coffin broadside; Lexington & Concord], 1775. The Gilder Lehrman Collection, on deposit at the Pierpont Morgan Library. GLC 4810

Regular Officers." Colonel Isaac Merrill, who mobilized the Amesbury militia, offered the following description of one of the Revolution's opening clashes.

ISAAC MERRILL, APRIL 19, 1775, TO CAPTAIN JOHN CURRIER, GLC 303

[T]his Day I have received intelligence that the ministerial troops under the Command of general Gage did Last evening march out of Boston and marched to Lexington & there Killed a number of our American Soldiers & thence proceed[ed] to Concord Killing and Destroying our men and interest. These [orders] are therefore to Order you forthwith to Mobilize and muster as many of your under officers and Soldiers as you can to meet immediately to Some suitable place: and then to march of[f] forthwith to Concord or Else where as in your Discretion you shall think best to the relief of our Friend[s] and Country....

25 / *"The name of God has been introduced in the pulpits to excite and justify devastation and massacre"*

In British eyes, the Revolution was the work of a small group of demagogues and radicals who plotted with debtors and smugglers to overthrown British rule. This proclamation, issued by the British commander, General Thomas Gage (1721–87), offers a pardon to all Bostonians except John Hancock and Samuel Adams. Ghostwritten by British Lieutenant General John Burgoyne (1722–92), this amnesty proclamation badly backfired. Not only did loyalists fail to flock to the British side, but also many previously apathetic colonists were repelled by the document's patronizing tone. After the battles at Lexington and Concord, the miliitas of Massachusetts and other New England colonies surrounded Boston to tie down the British troops.

THOMAS GAGE, PROCLAMATION OF AMNESTY IN BOSTON TO ALL BUT SAMUEL ADAMS AND JOHN HANCOCK, JUNE 12, 1775, GLC 4781

Whereas the infatuated multitudes, who have long suffered themselves to be conduced by certain well known Incendiaries and Traitors in a fatal progression of crimes against the constitutional authority of the state, have at length proceeded to avowed rebellion; and the good effects which were expected to arise from the patience and leniency of the King's government, have been frustrated, and are now rendered hopeless, by the influence of evil counsels; it only remains for those who are entrusted with supreme rule, as well for the punishment of the guilty, as the protection of the well affected, to prove they do not bear the sword in vain.

The infringements which have been committed upon the most sacred rights of the crown and people of Great Britain are too many to enumerate.... All unprejudiced people...will find upon a transient review, marks of premeditation and conspiracy that would justify the fullness of chastisement.... The authors of the present unnatural revolt never daring to trust their cause, or their actions to the judgements of an impartial public, or even to the dispassionate reflection of their followers, have uniformly placed their chief confidence in the suppression of truth: And while indefatigable and shameless pains have been taken to obstruct every appeal to the interest of the people of America; the grossest forgeries, calumnies and absurdities that ever insulted human understanding, have been imposed upon their credulity. The press, that distinguished appendage of public liberty...has been invariably prostituted to the most contrary purposes.... The name of God has been introduced in the pulpits to excite and justify devastation and massacre....

A number of armed persons, to the amount of many thousands assembled on the 19th of April last and from behind walls, and lurking holes, attacked a detachment of the King's troops, who...unprepared for vengeance, and willing to decline it, made use of their arms only in their own defense. Since that period, the rebels, deriving confidence from impunity, have added insult to outrage; have repeatedly fired upon the King's ships and subjects, with cannon and small arms, have possessed the roads, and other communications by which the town of Boston was supplied with provisions; and with a preposterous parade of military arrangement, they affect to hold the army besieged; while part of their body make daily and indiscriminate invasions upon private property, and with a wantonness of cruelty ever incident to lawless tumult, carry degradation and distress wherever they turn their steps....

In this exigency...I avail myself of the last effort within the bounds of my duty, to spare the effusion [of blood]; to offer, and I do hereby in his Majesty's name, offer and promise, his most gracious pardon to all persons who shall forthwith lay down their arms, and return to the duties of peaceable subjects, excepting only from the benefit of such pardon, Samuel Adams and John Hancock, whose offenses are of too flagitious a nature to admit of any other consideration than that of condign punishment.

26 / *"All Europe is interested in the fate of America"*

In May 1775, shortly after the battles at Lexington and Concord, the Second Continental Congress met in Philadelphia. In mid-June, Congress established the Continental Army and named George Washington (1732–99) commander in chief.

The colonists needed artillery, and in May patriots captured Fort Ticonderoga, a British post in New York, seizing more than a hundred artillery pieces. Meanwhile, back in Boston, the British and the patriots began to occupy hills overlooking the city. On June 17, British forces attacked American positions on Breed's Hill. To save ammunition, the patriots were ordered: "Don't fire until you see the whites of their eyes." After three advances, the British finally dislodged the colonists. The misnamed Battle of Bunker Hill was the bloodiest engagement of the entire war. The British suffered more than 1,000 causalities, 40 percent of the troops involved in the battle. American losses amounted to 411, or 30 percent.

The artillery from Fort Ticonderoga reached the Boston area in late January 1776, enabling patriots to fortify the high ground south of the city. British troops, realizing that they could no longer hold the city, evacuated Boston and sailed to Canada.

In an effort to lure Canada into the rebellion, two American expeditions invaded Canada in the fall of 1775. Both efforts ended in failure, and the Americans retreated to New York.

Mercy Otis Warren (1728–1814) of Plymouth, Massachusetts, was among the most effective advocates of the American cause. She wrote and published many political satires and plays, all published anonymously. After American independence was won, she wrote a three-volume history of the American Revolution, which remains a valuable source of information today.

MERCY OTIS WARREN, AUGUST 24, 1775, TO CATHARINE MACAULAY, GLC 1800.2

At a time when all Europe is interested in the fate of America you will forgive me my Dear Madam if I lay aside the ceremony usually observed…& again call your Attention… to my Last [letter] in which I hinted that the sword was half drawn from the scabbard. Soon after which this people were obliged to unsheathe it to repel the violence offered to individuals & the impotence of an attempt to seize the private property of the subjects of the king of England. And thereby put it out of their power to defend themselves against the Corrupt Ministry of this Court.

You have undoubtedly, Madam, been Apprized of the Consequences of this hostile movement which compelled the Americans to fly to arms in Defense of all that is held dear & sacred among Mankind. And the public papers as well as private accounts have witnessed to the Bravery of the peasants of Lexington & the spirit of freedom Breathed from the Inhabitants of the surrounding Villages. You have been told of the distresses of the people of Boston. Famine & pestilence began to rage in the City [forcing]…most of them to Depart leaving their Effects behind & to quit this Elegant and Convenient Habitation in the Capital & fly back into the Hospitable army of their Brethren in the Country. And the Conflagration of Charlestown [the Battle of Bunker Hill] will undoubtedly Reach each British Ear before this came to your hand. Such instances of wanton Barbarity have been seldom practiced even among the most Rude & uncivilized Nations. The ties of Gratitude which now broken through by the king, troops, in this base tradition greatly enhance their guilt. It was the Inhabitants of that town who prompted by humanity generously opened the door to the routed Gage on the Nineteenth of April and poured Balm into the Wound, of the Exhausted & dying soldiers after their precipitant retreat. Had they observed a different conduct on that Memorable day. Had they assisted in cutting off s[ai]d…retreat it might not have been in the power of General Gage to have wrapped that town in flames & driven out the miserable inhabitants the prey of poverty & despair…. I shall…only give a short account of the present situation of American affairs in the Environs of Boston. We have a well appointed brave and high spirited continental army. Consisting of about twenty-two thousand Men commanded by the accomplished George Washington…of one of the first fortunes in America. A man whose military abilities & public & private virtue, place him in the first class of the Good & Brave & one really of so high a Stamp as to do Honor to Human Nature. This army as it be originally recruited & to be supported & paid at the expense of the United colonies of America. And were Britain powerful & infatuated enough to find out a force sufficient to cut of[f] this little Resolute army…it would exhibit in the field thrice their Number, Ready to avenge the stroke & cut down the justice of Heaven on the Destroyer of the peace, liberty, & happiness of Mankind….

The great Council of America have once more petitioned His Majesty to devise some…Reconciliation. This is a final proof with what Reluctance the progeny of Britain draw forth the sword against their unnatural parent. Both the Ministerial & the American army seem at present to be rather on the defensive as if each were wishing for some Benign Hand to interpage and heal the dreadful contest without letting out the blood from the bosom of their Brethren.

27 / "I offer nothing more than simple facts, plain arguments, and common sense"

"I know not," John Adams wrote in 1806, "whether any man in the world has had more influence on its inhabitants or affairs for the last thirty years than Thomas Paine." After enduring many failures in his native England, Paine (1737–1809), whose father was a Quaker, arrived in Philadelphia in November 1774 bearing invaluable letters of introduction from Benjamin Franklin.

By far the Revolution's most important pamphleteer, Paine exerted enormous influence on the political thinking of the revolutionaries. His pamphlet *Common Sense*, which sold as many as 150,000 copies in the year after it was published in January 1776, demanded a complete break with Britain and establishment of a strong federal union. It was also a powerful attack on the idea of monarchy and hereditary privilege:

> For all men being originally equals, no one by birth could have a right to set up his own family in perpetual preference to all others forever.... [A king is] nothing better than the principal ruffian of some restless gang. Of more worth is one honest man to society and in the sight of God, than all the crowned ruffians that ever lived.

Thomas Paine, Common Sense, 1776, GLC 3777

In the following pages I offer nothing more than simple facts, plain arguments, and common sense....

I have heard it asserted by some, that as America has flourished under her former connection with Great-Britain, the same connection is necessary towards her future happiness, and will always have the same effect. Nothing can be more fallacious than this kind of argument. We may as well assert that because a child has thrived upon milk, that it is never to have meat, or that the first twenty years of our lives is to become a precedent for the next twenty. But even this is admitting more than is true; for I answer... that America would have flourished as much, and probably much more, had no European power taken any notice of her. The commerce by which she hath enriched herself are the necessaries of life, and will always have a market while eating is the custom of Europe.

But she has protected us, say some....We have boasted the protection of Great Britain, without considering, that her motive was *interest* not *attachment*....

This new World hath been the asylum for the persecuted lovers of civil and religious liberty from *every part* of Europe....

As Europe is our market for trade, we ought to form no partial connection with any part of it. It is the true interest of America to steer clear of European contentions, which she never can do, while, by her dependence on Britain, she is made the make-weight in the scale of British politics.

Europe is too thickly planted with Kingdoms to be long at peace, and whenever a war breaks out between England and any foreign power, the trade of America goes to ruin, *because of her connection with Britain*....

There is something absurd, in supposing a Continent to be perpetually governed by an island....

No man was a warmer wisher for a reconciliation than myself, before the fatal nineteenth of April, 1775 [the day of the battles of Lexington and Concord], but the moment the event of that day was made known, I rejected the hardened, sullen-tempered Pharaoh of England for ever; and disdain the wretch, that with the pretended title of FATHER OF HIS PEOPLE can unfeelingly hear of their slaughter, and composedly sleep with their blood upon his soul....

Where, say some, is the king of America? I'll tell you, Friend, he reigns above, and doth not make havoc of mankind like the royal brute of Great Britain... So far as we approve of monarchy...in America the law is king.

A government of our own is our natual right.... Ye that oppose independence now, ye know not what ye do: ye are opening the door to eternal tyranny.... There are thousands and tens of thousands, who would think it glorious to expel from the Continent, that barbarous and hellish power, which hath stirred up the Indians and the Negroes to destroy us....

O! ye that love mankind! Ye that dare oppose not only the tyranny but the tyrant, stand forth! Every spot of the old world is overrun with oppression. Freedom hath been hunted round the Globe. Asia and Africa have long expelled her. Europe regards her like a stranger, and England hath given her warning to depart. O! receive the fugitive, and prepare in time an asylum for mankind.

28 / "The Course of Events naturally turns the thoughts of Gentlemen to the Subjects of Legislation"

By the end of 1775, compromise between Britain and its colonies was becoming a less viable option. Richard Henry Lee (1732–94), a delegate from Virginia to the Second Continental Congress, asked John Adams to help him convince his home state of the need for independence. In response, Adams proposed a plan for a new state government with three branches. This letter offers one example of the way that patriots experimented with new systems of government based on reason and their analysis of human nature as being inevitably inclined toward corruption and the abuse of power unless checked and balanced by competing power. After his return to Congress and with the Massachusetts delegation's agreement, Lee proposed a congressional resolution for independence.

JOHN ADAMS, NOVEMBER 15, 1775, TO RICHARD HENRY LEE, DELEGATE FROM VIRGINIA, GLC 3864

The Course of Events naturally turns the thoughts of Gentlemen to the Subjects of Legislation and Jurisprudence, and it is a curious Problem what Form of Government is most readily & easily adopted by a Colony upon a Sudden Emergence. Nature and Experience have already pointed out the Solution of this Problem, in the choice of Conventions and Committees of Safety. Nothing is wanting in addition to these to make

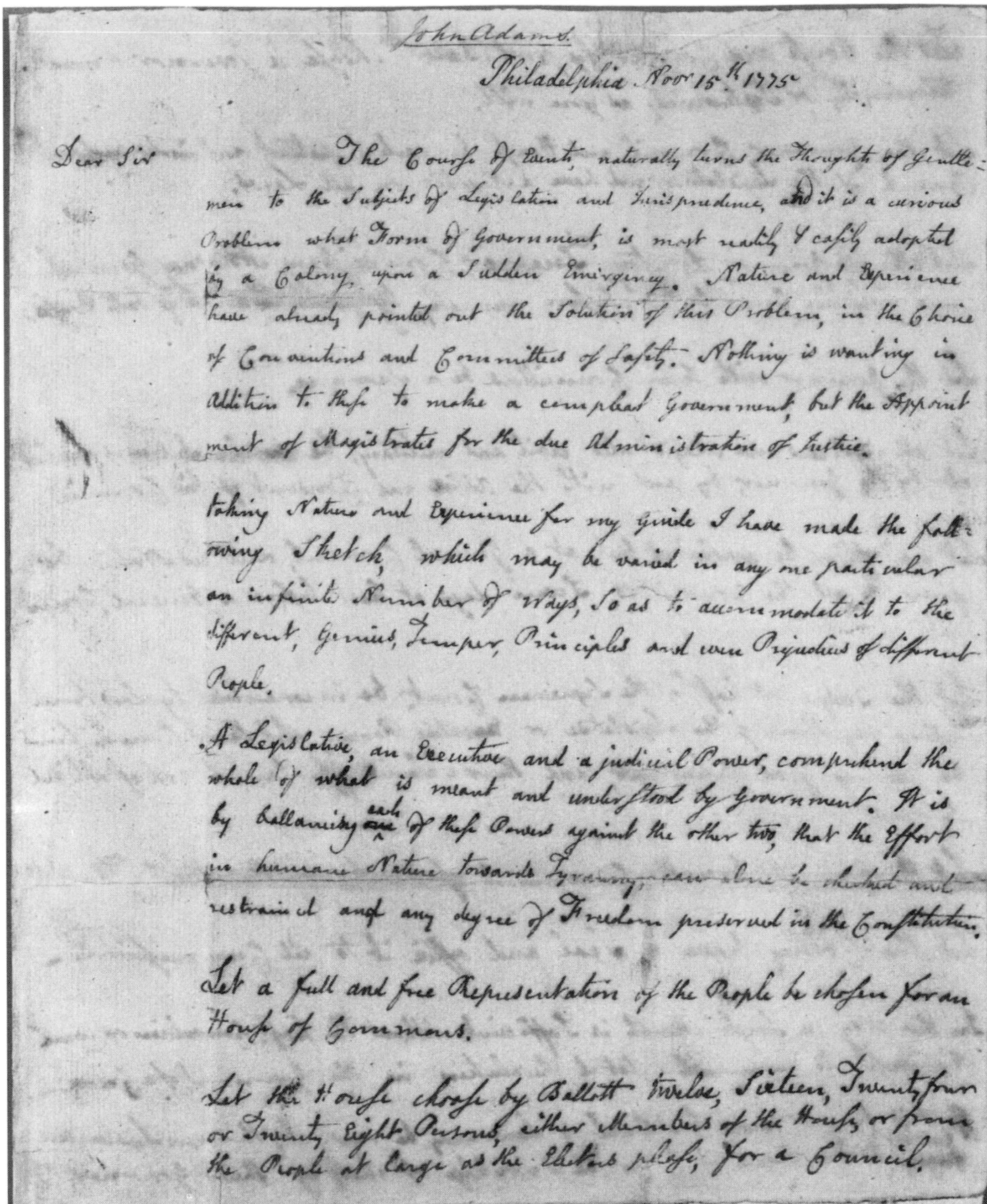

John Adams

Philadelphia Novr 15th. 1775

Dear Sir

The Course of Events, naturally turns the Thoughts of Gentlemen to the Subjects of Legislation and Jurisprudence, and it is a curious Problem what Form of Government, is most readily & easily adopted by a Colony, upon a Sudden Emergency. Nature and Experience have already pointed out the Solution of this Problem, in the Choice of Conventions and Committees of Safety. Nothing is wanting in Addition to these to make a compleat Government, but the Appointment of Magistrates for the due Administration of Justice.

Taking Nature and Experience for my Guide I have made the following Sketch, which may be varied in any one particular an infinite Number of Ways, So as to accommodate it to the different, Genius, Temper, Principles and even Prejudices of different People.

A Legislative, an Executive and a judicial Power, comprehend the whole of what is meant and understood by Government. It is by ballancing each of these Powers against the other two, that the Effort in humane Nature towards Tyranny, can alone be checked and restrained and any degree of Freedom preserved in the Constitution.

Let a full and free Representation of the People be chosen for an House of Commons.

Let the House choose by Ballott twelve, Sixteen, Twenty four or Twenty Eight Persons, either Members of the House, or from the People at Large as the Electors please, for a Council.

John Adams. Autograph letter signed, to Richard Henry Lee, 1775/11/15. The Gilder Lehrman Collection, on deposit at the Pierpont Morgan Library. GLC 3864

a compleat Government, but the Appointment of Magistrates for the due Administration of Justice.

Taking Nature and Experience for my guide I have made the following Sketch, which may be varied in any particular an infinite Number of Ways, So as to accommodate it to the different genius, Temper, Principles and even Prejudices of different People.

A Legislative, an Executive and a judicial Power, comprehend the whole of what is meant and understood by Government. It is by balancing each of these Powers against the other two, that the Effort in human Nature toward Tyranny can alone be checked and restrained and any degree of Freedom preserved in the Constitution. Let a full and free Representation of the People be chosen for an House of Commons.

Let the House choose by Ballot twelve, Sixteen, Twenty four or Twenty eight Persons, either Members of the House, or from the People at Large as the Electors please, for a Council.

Let the House and Council by joint Ballot choose a governor annually, triennially or septennially as you will.

Let the Governor, Council, and House be each a distinct and independent Branch of the Legislature, and have a Negative on all Laws.

Let the Lt. Governor, Secretary, Treasurer, Commissary Attorney General and Solicitor General, be chosen annually, by joint Ballot of both Houses.

Let the Governor with Lower Councilors be a Quorum.

Let all officers and magistrates civil and military be nominated and appointed by the Governor by and with the Advice and Consent of his Council.

Let no officer be appointed but at a General Council, and let Notice be given to all the Councilors, Seven days at least before a General Council.

Let the Judges at least of the Supreme Court, be incapacitated by Law from holding any share of the Legislative or Executive Power, Let their Commissions be during good Behavior, and their salaries after [be the same] and established by law.

Let the Gov[erno]r have the Command of the army, the Militia, &tc.

Let the Colony have a Seal and offer it to all Commissioners.

In this way a single [constitution] is Sufficient without the least Convulsion or Animosity to a total Revolution in the Government of a Colony.

If it is thought more beneficial, a Law made by this new Legislature passing to the People at Large the Privilege of choosing their Governor and Councilors annually....

In adopting a Plan, in some currents similar to this[,] human Nature would appear in its morning glory, asserting its own dignity, pulling down Tyrannies at a single exertion and creating such new [arrangements], as it thinks well calculated to promote its happiness.

As you were the last evening polite enough to ask me for this model, if such a trifle will be of any service to you, or any gratification of curiosity, here you have it....

29 / *"It is not choice...but necessity that calls for Independence"*

Richard Henry Lee (1732–94), writing to a fellow Virginian, calls for American independence, a goal suddenly and effectively popularized in January 1776 by Thomas Paine's anonymous pamphlet *Common Sense*. Lee subsequently introduced the resolution in

Congress "That these United Colonies are, and of right ought to be, free and independent states." Congress appointed a committee—consisting of John Adams, Benjamin Franklin, Thomas Jefferson, Robert Livingston, and Roger Sherman—to draft a declaration of independence in case Lee's resolution was adopted. On July 2, Congress approved Lee's resolution, and two days later adopted the final draft of the Declaration of Independence.

Richard H. Lee, June 2, 1776, to Landon Carter, GLC 3421

It is not choice then, but necessity that calls for Independence as the only means by which foreign Alliances can be obtained; and a proper confederation by which internal pea[ce] and Union may be secured. Contrary to our earnest, early, and repeated petitions for peace, liberty and safety, our enemies press us with war, threaten us with danger and Slavery.

30 / *"Our affairs are hastening fast to a Crisis"*

John Hancock (1738–1793), the President of the Continental Congress, was one of many patriots who feared that the British ministry had embarked on a systemic plan to enslave the colonists by suppressing their liberties and depriving them of their property. In a message to patriots in Maryland, he recounts British hostilities against the colonists, including the recruitment of Hessian mercenaries from Germany, and declares that Americans "are called upon to say, whether they will live Slaves or die Freemen."

The colonists' emphasis on the danger of mass enslavement derived in part from their reading of seventeenth-century English history. According to the Whig interpretation of English history, which was widely popular in the colonies, the pro-Catholic Stuart kings had plotted to impose arbitrary rule and undermine Protestant religion. Only the Glorious Revolution of 1688 had prevented the loss of English liberties. In the year before the American Revolution, many pamphlets and sermons warned the colonists that if they failed to unite against infringements on their liberties, the inevitable result would be a total loss of freedom.

Americans' fears of enslavement took on added meaning from the highly visible example of Negro slavery. The white colonists knew full well what it meant to deprive people of proprety and personal freedom. In 1774, George Washington explained that if the colonists' failed to aggressively assert their rights, then the British ministry "shall make us as tame and abject slaves, as the blacks we rule over with such arbitrary sway."

In a letter to the Massachusetts legislature dated July 6, 1776, two days after the signing of the Declaration of Independence, John Hancock expressed his faith that if Americans defeated British tyranny, they would be freed from all forms of Old World depotism. "We shall be a great happy people totally unfetter[e]d & releas[e]d from the bonds of Slavery," he wrote. "That we may be then free." (GLC 595)

John Hancock, June 4, 1776, to the Convention of Maryland, GLC 639.12

Our affairs are hastening fast to a Crisis; and the approaching Campaign will, in all probability, determine for ever the fate of America.

Such is the unrelenting Spirit which possesses the Tyrant of Britain and his

Parliament, that they have left no Measure unessayed that had a Tendency to accomplish our Destruction. Not satisfied with having lined our Coasts with Ships of War, to starve us into a Surrender of our Liberties, and to prevent us from being supplied with Arms and Ammunition, they are now about to pour in a Number of foreign troops; who from their Want of connections, and those feelings of Sympathy which frequently bind together the different Parts of the same Empire, will be more likely to do the Business of their Masters without Remorse or Compunction.... Should the Canadians and Indians take up Arms against us (which there is too much Reason to fear) we shall then have the whole Force of that Country to contend with, joined to that of Great Britain, and all her foreign Auxiliaries. —In this Situation, what Steps must we pursue?—The Continental Troops alone, are unable to stem the Torrent; nor is it possible at this Day, to raise and discipline men ready to take the Field by the Time they will be wanted....

Should the United Colonies be able to keep their ground this Campaign, I am under no Apprehensions on Account of any future one. We have many Disadvantages at present to struggle with, which Time, and progress in the Art of War will remove.... The Militia of the United Colonies are a Body of Troops that may be depended upon. To their Virtue, their Delegates in Congress now make the most solemn Appeal. They are called upon to say, whether they will live Slaves, or die Freemen. They are requested to step forth in Defense of their Wives, their Children, their Liberty, and every Thing they hold dear. The Cause is certainly a most glorious one; and I hope every Man in the Colony of Maryland is determined to see it gloriously ended, or to perish in the Ruins of it.

In short, on your exertions at this critical Period, together with those of the other Colonies in Common Cause, the Salvation of America now evidently depends. Your Colony, I am persuaded, will not be behind hand. Exert therefore every Nerve to distinguish yourselves. Quicken your Preparations, and stimulate the good People of your government; and there is no Danger, notwithstanding the mighty Armament with which we are threatened, but they will be lead onto Victory, to Liberty and to Happiness.

DECLARING INDEPENDENCE

31 / *"The Christian King of Great Britain [is] determined to keep open a market where MEN should be bought & sold"*

More than a year passed between the outbreak of fighting at the battles of Lexington and Concord and the decision to issue the Declaration of Independence. The major reason for the delay was the high value that the colonists attached to unanimity. While New England, Virginia, and South Carolina were ready to declare independence in 1775, other colonies still hoped that British merchants or the parliamentary opposition would respond to American grievance. Many feared that a full-scale war for independence might give France and Spain the opportunity to expand their New World empires.

In a famous clause that was ultimately deleted from the Declaration of Independence, Thomas Jefferson (1743–1826) cited the African slave trade as one of the

IN CONGRESS, JULY 4, 1776.

The unanimous Declaration of the thirteen united States of America,

When in the Course of human events, it becomes necessary for one people to dissolve the political bands which have connected them with another, and to assume among the powers of the earth, the separate and equal station to which the Laws of Nature and of Nature's God entitle them, a decent respect to the opinions of mankind requires that they should declare the causes which impel them to the separation. —— We hold these truths to be self-evident, that all men are created equal, that they are endowed by their Creator with certain unalienable Rights, that among these are Life, Liberty and the pursuit of Happiness. — That to secure these rights, Governments are instituted among Men, deriving their just powers from the consent of the governed, — That whenever any Form of Government becomes destructive of these ends, it is the Right of the People to alter or to abolish it, and to institute new Government, laying its foundation on such principles and organizing its powers in such form, as to them shall seem most likely to effect their Safety and Happiness. Prudence, indeed, will dictate that Governments long established should not be changed for light and transient causes; and accordingly all experience hath shewn, that mankind are more disposed to suffer, while evils are sufferable, than to right themselves by abolishing the forms to which they are accustomed. But when a long train of abuses and usurpations, pursuing invariably the same Object evinces a design to reduce them under absolute Despotism, it is their right, it is their duty, to throw off such Government, and to provide new Guards for their future security. — Such has been the patient sufferance of these Colonies; and such is now the necessity which constrains them to alter their former Systems of Government. The history of the present King of Great Britain is a history of repeated injuries and usurpations, all having in direct object the establishment of an absolute Tyranny over these States. To prove this, let Facts be submitted to a candid world. —— He has refused his Assent to Laws, the most wholesome and necessary for the public good. —— He has forbidden his Governors to pass Laws of immediate and pressing importance, unless suspended in their operation till his Assent should be obtained; and when so suspended, he has utterly neglected to attend to them. —— He has refused to pass other Laws for the accommodation of large districts of people, unless those people would relinquish the right of Representation in the Legislature, a right inestimable to them and formidable to tyrants only. —— He has called together legislative bodies at places unusual, uncomfortable, and distant from the depository of their public Records, for the sole purpose of fatiguing them into compliance with his measures. —— He has dissolved Representative Houses repeatedly, for opposing with manly firmness his invasions on the rights of the people. —— He has refused for a long time, after such dissolutions, to cause others to be elected; whereby the Legislative powers, incapable of Annihilation, have returned to the People at large for their exercise; the State remaining in the mean time exposed to all the dangers of invasion from without, and convulsions within. —— He has endeavoured to prevent the population of these States; for that purpose obstructing the Laws for Naturalization of Foreigners; refusing to pass others to encourage their migrations hither, and raising the conditions of new Appropriations of Lands. —— He has obstructed the Administration of Justice, by refusing his Assent to Laws for establishing Judiciary powers. —— He has made Judges dependent on his Will alone, for the tenure of their offices, and the amount and payment of their salaries. —— He has erected a multitude of New Offices, and sent hither swarms of Officers to harrass our people, and eat out their substance. —— He has kept among us, in times of peace, Standing Armies without the Consent of our legislatures. —— He has affected to render the Military independent of and superior to the Civil power. —— He has combined with others to subject us to a jurisdiction foreign to our constitution, and unacknowledged by our laws; giving his Assent to their Acts of pretended Legislation: — For Quartering large bodies of armed troops among us: — For protecting them, by a mock Trial, from punishment for any Murders which they should commit on the Inhabitants of these States: — For cutting off our Trade with all parts of the world: — For imposing Taxes on us without our Consent: — For depriving us in many cases, of the benefits of Trial by Jury: — For transporting us beyond Seas to be tried for pretended offences — For abolishing the free System of English Laws in a neighbouring Province, establishing therein an Arbitrary government, and enlarging its Boundaries so as to render it at once an example and fit instrument for introducing the same absolute rule into these Colonies: — For taking away our Charters, abolishing our most valuable Laws, and altering fundamentally the Forms of our Governments: — For suspending our own Legislatures, and declaring themselves invested with power to legislate for us in all cases whatsoever. — He has abdicated Government here, by declaring us out of his Protection and waging War against us. —— He has plundered our seas, ravaged our Coasts, burnt our towns, and destroyed the lives of our people. —— He is at this time transporting large Armies of foreign Mercenaries to compleat the works of death, desolation and tyranny, already begun with circumstances of Cruelty & perfidy scarcely paralleled in the most barbarous ages, and totally unworthy the Head of a civilized nation. —— He has constrained our fellow Citizens taken Captive on the high Seas to bear Arms against their Country, to become the executioners of their friends and Brethren, or to fall themselves by their Hands. —— He has excited domestic insurrections amongst us, and has endeavoured to bring on the inhabitants of our frontiers, the merciless Indian Savages, whose known rule of warfare, is an undistinguished destruction of all ages, sexes and conditions. In every stage of these Oppressions We have Petitioned for Redress in the most humble terms: Our repeated Petitions have been answered only by repeated injury. A Prince, whose character is thus marked by every act which may define a Tyrant, is unfit to be the ruler of a free people. Nor have We been wanting in attentions to our British brethren. We have warned them from time to time of attempts by their legislature to extend an unwarrantable jurisdiction over us. We have reminded them of the circumstances of our emigration and settlement here. We have appealed to their native justice and magnanimity, and we have conjured them by the ties of our common kindred to disavow these usurpations, which, would inevitably interrupt our connections and correspondence. They too have been deaf to the voice of justice and of consanguinity. We must, therefore, acquiesce in the necessity, which denounces our Separation, and hold them, as we hold the rest of mankind, Enemies in War, in Peace Friends. ——

We, therefore, the Representatives of the united States of America, in General Congress, Assembled, appealing to the Supreme Judge of the world for the rectitude of our intentions, do, in the Name, and by Authority of the good People of these Colonies, solemnly publish and declare, That these United Colonies are, and of Right ought to be Free and Independent States; that they are Absolved from all Allegiance to the British Crown, and that all political connection between them and the State of Great Britain, is and ought to be totally dissolved; and that as Free and Independent States, they have full Power to levy War, conclude Peace, contract Alliances, establish Commerce, and to do all other Acts and Things which Independent States may of right do. —— And for the support of this Declaration, with a firm reliance on the protection of divine Providence, we mutually pledge to each other our Lives, our Fortunes and our sacred Honor.

John Hancock

Button Gwinnett
Lyman Hall
Geo Walton.
Wm Hooper
Joseph Hewes,
John Penn
Edward Rutledge 1.
Thos Heyward Junr.
Thomas Lynch Junr.
Arthur Middleton
Samuel Chase
Wm Paca
Thos. Stone
Charles Carroll of Carrollton
George Wythe
Richard Henry Lee
Th Jefferson
Benja Harrison
Thos Nelson jr.
Francis Lightfoot Lee
Carter Braxton
Robt Morris
Benjamin Rush
Benja. Franklin
John Morton
Geo Clymer
Jas. Smith
Geo. Taylor
James Wilson
Geo. Ross
Caesar Rodney
Geo Read
Tho M:Kean
Wm Floyd
Phil. Livingston
Frans. Lewis
Lewis Morris
Richd. Stockton
Jno Witherspoon
Fras. Hopkinson
John Hart
Abra Clark
Josiah Bartlett
Wm Whipple
Saml Adams
John Adams
Robt Treat Paine
Elbridge Gerry
Step. Hopkins
William Ellery
Roger Sherman
Saml Huntington
Wm Williams
Oliver Wolcott
Matthew Thornton

Declaration of Independence exact facsimile on parchment. The Gilder Lehrman Collection, on deposit at the Pierpont Morgan Library. GLC 154.02

examples of British oppression. Jefferson's reference to the king's "prostit[ing] his negative" refers to the English government's repeated vetoes of attempts by colonial legislatures to restrict or halt the importation of slaves. Virginia, especially, had profited from a great natural increase in its slave population and had no desire for a further slave "surplus" or for competition with its own profitable practice of selling slaves to South Carolina and Georgia. Ironically, Jefferson's language reinforced the antislavery myth that Englishmen were "captivating" and forcibly enslaving Africans. In actuality, the vast majority of slaves had been enslaved in the African interior and sold to various African dealers before being finally purchased by Europeans.

Thomas Jefferson, 1776, draft of the Declaration of Independence

He [King George] has waged cruel war against human nature itself, violating its most sacred rights of life & liberty in the persons of a distant people who never offended him, captivating & carrying them into slavery in another hemisphere, or to incur miserable death in their transportation thither. This piratical warfare, the opprobrium of *infidel* powers, is the warfare of the *Christian* King of Great Britain, determined to keep open a market where *MEN* should be bought & sold, he has prostituted his negative for suppressing every legislative attempt to prohibit or to restrain this execrable commerce: and that this assemblage of horrors might want no fact of distinguished die, he is now exciting those very people [slaves in the South] to rise in arms against us, and to purchase that liberty of which *he* has deprived them by murdering the people upon whom *he* also obtruded them: thus paying off former crimes committed against the *liberties* of one people, with crimes which he urges them to commit against the *lives* of another.

Writings of Thomas Jefferson. Collected and edited by Paul Leicester Ford. New York: G.P. Putnam's Sons, 1893, Vol. II, pp. 52–54.

During the spring of 1776, as the historian Pauline Maier has shown, colonies, localities, and groups of ordinary Americans—including New York mechanics, Pennsylvania militiamen, and South Carolina grand juries—adopted resolutions endorsing independence. These resolutions encouraged the Continental Congress to appoint a five-member committee to draft a formal declaration of independence. Thomas Jefferson wrote the initial draft, which was then edited by other members of the committee and by Congress as a whole.

The most radical idea advanced by the American Revolutionaries was the proposition set forth in the Declaration of Independence that "all Men are created equal, that they are endowed by their Creator with certain unalienable Rights, that among these are Life, Liberty, and the pursuit of Happiness." In 1856 Senator Rufus Choate (1799–1859) would dismiss this phrase as "glittering…generalities," prompting the philosopher Ralph Waldo Emerson (1803–1882) to quip, "Glittering generalities? They are blazing ubiquities!"

One of the most important themes in American history involves the repeated effort to extend the meaning of the "inalienable rights" with which Americans are endowed and adopt a more inclusive definition of those who are "created equal." In the decades preceding the Civil War, reformers pictured their efforts to improve the nation's educational system and to abolish slavery as attempts to realize the republican ideals enshrined in the Declaration of Independence.

Proponents of abolition, women's rights, world peace, and other reforms drafted "Declarations of Sentiments" modeled on the wording of the Declaration of Independence. Workingmen's parties in New York and Philadelphia in the 1820s, abolitionists in the 1830s, and advocates of women's rights in 1848 each issued declarations listing a "history of repeated injuries and usurpations" that justified their proposed reforms. Convinced that the sacred principles of the Revolution had been corrupted, reformers sought to revive the spirit of 1776 by exposing a host of abuses that contradicted the nation's revolutionary principles.

SLAVERY AND THE AMERICAN REVOLUTION

The American Revolution had profound effects on the institution of slavery. Several thousand slaves won their freedom by serving on both sides in the War of Independence. As a result of the Revolution, a surprising number of slaves were manumitted, while thousands of others freed themselves by running away. In Georgia alone, five thousand slaves, a third of the colony's prewar total, escaped.

Both the British and the colonists believed that slaves could serve an important role during the Revolution. In April 1775, Lord Dunmore (1732–1809), the royal governor of Virginia, threatened that he would proclaim liberty to the slaves and reduce Williamsburg to ashes if the colonists resorted to force against British authority. In November, he promised freedom to all slaves belonging to rebels who would join "His Majesty's Troops...for the more speedily reducing the Colony to a proper sense of their duty...". Some eight hundred slaves joined British forces, some wearing the emblem "Liberty to the Slaves." The British appeal to slave unrest outraged slaveholders not only in the South but also in New York's Hudson Valley. Later, Sir Henry Clinton (1738–95) promised protection to all slaves who deserted from the rebels. Clinton's promise may well have contributed to the collapse of the British cause in the South. By suggesting that the Revolution was a war over slavery, he alienated many neutrals and even some loyalists.

Meanwhile, an American diplomat, Silas Deane (1737–89), hatched a secret plan to incite slave insurrections in Jamaica. Two South Carolinians, John Laurens (1754–82) and his father, Henry (1724–92), persuaded Congress to unanimously approve a plan to recruit an army of three thousand slave troops in South Carolina and Georgia. The federal government would compensate the slaves' owners and each black would, at the end of the war, be emancipated and receive $50. The South Carolina legislature rejected the plan, scuttling the proposal. In the end, however, and in contrast to the later Latin American wars of independence and the U.S. Civil War, neither the British nor the Americans proved willing to risk a full-scale social revolution by issuing an emancipation proclamation.

32 / *"In the year of our Lord 1775...I entered into the service of the U.S. as a private soldier"*

African-American soldiers served with valor at the battles of Lexington and Bunker Hill. In November 1775, however, Congress decided to exclude blacks from future enlistment out of a sensitivity to the opinion of southern slaveholders. But Lord Dunmore's promise of freedom to slaves who enlisted in the British army led Congress reluctantly to reverse its decision, fearful that black soldiers might join the redcoats.

African Americans played an important role in the Revolution. They fought at Fort Ticonderoga and the Battle of Bunker Hill. A slave helped row Washington across the Delaware. By 1778 many states, including Virginia, granted freedom to slaves who served in the Revolutionary War.

A former slave who fought in the Revolutionary war, Peter Kiteridge, recounts his background to the town officials of Newfield, Massachusetts. Now fifty-eight years of age, with no compensation available for his war injuries, he seeks assistance supporting his wife and four children.

Kiteridge was one of approximately five thousand free blacks and slaves who served in the American army during the Revolution.

Peter Kiteridge, April 6, 1806, to the Selectmen of the Town of Newfield, Massachusetts, GLC 1450.702

Gentlemen

I beg leave to state to you my necessitous circumstances, that through your intervention I may obtain that succour, which suffering humanity ever requires. Borne of African parents...and apprenticed in Boston, from whence I was removed to Roseley and from thence again to Andover into the family of Locerage, with whom as was then the lot of my unfortunate race, I passed the best part of my life as a slave. In the year of our Lord 1775 or 6 and in the twenty fifth of my age I entered into the service of the U.S. as a private soldier wherein I continued five years and contracted a complaint from which I have suffered in a greater or less degree ever since and with which I am now afflicted. After leaving the army to become a sailor for two years I was for some time in Newtown, from whence I went to Natick where I remained for a short time and then removed to Dover whence I was a day labourer during the period of seven years. Eight years past I removed to the place where I now live and have until this time by my labor assisted by the kindness of the neighbouring inhabitants been enabled to support myself and family. At present having arrived at the fifty eight year of my life and afflicted with an unusable arm as I apprehend with incurable diseases where by the labor of my hands is wholly cut off, and it is the only means of my support. My family at this time consists of a wife and four children three of whom are so young as to be unable to support themselves and the time of their mother is wholly occupied in taking care of myself & my little ones—thus gentlemen in this my extremity I am induced to call on you for assistance; not in the character of an inhabitant of the town of Westfield for I have no such claim but as a stranger accidently falling within your borders, one who has not the means of subsistence, and one who must fail through want and disease unless sustained by your care.

33 / *"The Iniquitous Practice of depriving any of their just right to Liberty"*

"How is it," the English essayist Samuel Johnson (1709–84) asked at the start of the Revolution, "that we hear the loudest *yelps* for liberty among the drivers of Negroes?" Many British Tories taunted colonists with the jarring contradiction between their complaints about political oppression and the reality of chattel slavery. The American Revolution underscored the contradiction between a people torn between allegiance to high moral ideals and a base reality of racial domination.

While it would be a mistake to underestimate the strength of slavery during the revolutionary period, there can be no doubt that slavery had begun to arouse concern in new ways. This concern was evident in the Continental Congress's agreement in 1774 to prohibit the importation of slaves; in the founding of the first antislavery society, in Philadelphia in 1775; in Vermont's decision to explicitly exclude slavery in its Constitution of 1777; and Pennsylvania's enactment of the Western Hemisphere's first gradual emancipation act in 1780.

Slavery posed special problems for Quakers, who strove to lead sinless lives. In 1774 the Philadelphia Yearly Meeting forbade Quakers from buying or selling slaves and required masters to free slaves at the earliest opportunity. Two years later, the meeting directed Friends to disown any Quakers who resisted pleas to manumit their slaves. For Quakers, as for many later abolitionists, slavery could never be reconciled with the Golden Rule or with the other bedrock Judeo-Christian precept that God "is no respecter of Persons"—or in other words, that worldly titles, status, and privilege do not matter in the ultimate scheme of things.

Society of Friends, extracts from the minutes of the Yearly Meeting, September 23–28, 1776, GLC 1021

...In this time of Singular Difficulty and tryal...we are unanimous in sentiment that...friends [Quakers] should be particularly vigilant in watchful Christian care over themselves & each other....

And as we have for some years past been frequently concerned to exhort & advise Friends to withdraw from being active in Civil Government...we find it necessary to give our sense & judgment, that if any making Profession with us, do accept or continue in public offices of any kind, either of Profit or Trust, under the present Connections, & unsettled state of public affairs, such are acting therein contrary to the profession, & principles we have ever maintained since we were a religious society....We are United in judgment that such who make religious profession with us and do either openly or by connivance pay any fine, penalty or tax in lieu of their personal services for carrying on the war under the prevailing commotions, or who do consent to, and allow their children, apprentices, or servants to act therein, do thereby violate our Christian testimony and by so doing, manifest that they are not in religious fellowship with us....

We affectionately desire, that Friends may be careful to avoid engaging in any trade or business tending to promote war, and particularly from sharing or partaking of the spoils of war, by buying, or vending [selling] prize goods of any kind....

On the subject of obtaining liberty to the Bondmen among us...a Committee of 32 friends was appointed.... It is earnestly recommended...to persevere in a further close Labour for the Convincement of those professing with us, who yet continue in the Iniquitous Practice of depriving any of their just right to Liberty, and for the exaltation of our Testimony against it, agreeable to the sense of judgment of the said committee....

We the committee appointed to take under our Consideration the deeply affecting case of our oppressed fellow men of the African race and also the state of those who hold them in Bondage, have several times met and heard the concurring sentiments of diverse other friends and examined the reports from the Quarterly meetings, by which it appears that much labor & care hath been extended since the last year for the Convincement of such of our Members who had, or yet have them in possession, many of whom have of late from under hand & seal properly discharged such as were in their position from a State of slavery.

Yet sorrowful it is, that many there are in Membership with us, who, notwithstanding the Labour bestow'd still continue to hold these People as Slaves under the Consideration whereof we are deeply affected, and United in Judgement, that we are loudly called upon to a faithful Obedience to the Injunction of our blessed Lord "to do all Men as we would they should do unto us" and to bear a clear testimony to these truths that "God is no respecter of Persons" and that "Christ died for all Men without distinction," which we earnestly and affectionately entreat may be duly consider'd in the awful and alarming Dispensation, and excite to impartial justice and judgment to black and white, rich and poor.

Under the calming influence of pure love, we do with great unanimity give it as our sense & judgment that quarterly & Monthly Meetings should still speedily unite in further close labor with all such as are slaveholders and have any right of membership with us, and where any members continue to reject the advice of their brethren, and refuse to execute proper instruments of writing for releasing from a state of slavery such as are in their power, or on whom they have any claim, whether arrived to full age or in their minority, and no hopes of the continuance of friends labor being profitable to them that Monthly meetings, after having discharg'd a Christian duty to such should testify their disunion with them....

34 / "To prohibit a great people...from making all that they can of every part of their own produce...is a manifest violation of the most sacred rights of mankind"

In his *Inquiry into the Nature and Causes of the Wealth of Nations*, published in 1776, the Scottish economist Adam Smith (1723–90) argued that the individual pursuit of economic self-interest, unhindered by government interference, would promote economic and social well-being. "It is not from the benevolence of the butcher, the brewer, or the baker, that we expect our dinner," he wrote, "but from their regard to their own interest. We address ourselves, not to their humanity but to their self-love, and never talk to them of our own necessities, but of their advantages. Nobody but a beggar chooses to depend chiefly upon the benevolence of his fellow-citizens." Smith argued that the natural workings of the free market would result in social progress, "as if by an invisible hand."

In his book Smith criticized the British colonial system as a textbook example of the detrimental effects of tariffs, bounties, and other restraints on trade. In arguing in behalf of "hands off" government policies toward the economy and against mercantilism, Smith discussed the economic irrationality of Britain's colonial system, which provided bounties for the production of such items as pitch, tar, rosin, turpentine, hemp, masts, yards, and bowsprits, while imposing a host of prohibitions on the production of steel, hats, woolen goods, and many other products in North America. In many respects, Smith presented in 1776 the economic counterpart to the Americans' revolutionary ideology, envisioning a kind of economic freedom and prosperity that would be as attractive to millions of future American immigrants as the ideals of political freedom and equal rights.

Adam Smith, *An Inquiry into the Nature and Causes of the Wealth of Nations*, 1776, GLC 4740, 5192

The most perfect freedom of trade is permitted between the British colonies of America and the West Indies, both in the enumerated and the non-enumerated commodities. These colonies are now become so populous and thriving that each of them finds in some of the others a great and extensive market for every part of its produce. All of them taken together, they make a great internal market for the produce of one another.

The liberality of England, however, towards the trade of her colonies has been confined chiefly to what concerns the market for their produce, either in its rude state or in what may be called the very first stage of manufacture. The more advanced or more refined manufactures...the merchants and manufacturers of Great Britain choose to reserve to themselves, and have prevailed upon the legislature [Parliament] to prevent their establishment in the colonies, sometimes by high duties, and sometimes by absolute prohibitions.

While Great Britain encourages in America the manufactures of pig and bar iron, by exempting them from duties to which the like commodities are subject when imported from any other country, she imposes an absolute prohibition upon the erection of steel furnaces and slit-mills in any of her American plantations. She will not suffer her colonists to work in those more refined manufactures, even for their own consumption; but insists upon their purchasing of her merchants and manufacturers all goods of this kind which they have occasion for.

She prohibits the exportation from one province to another by water, and even the carriage by land upon horseback or in a cart, of hats, of wools and woolen goods, of the produce of America—a regulation which effectually prevents the establishment of any manufacture of such commodities for distant sale, and confines the industry of her colonists in this way to such coarse and household manufactures as a private family commonly makes for its own use, or for that of some of its neighbors in the same province.

To prohibit a great people, however, from making all that they can of every part of their own produce, or from employing their stock and industry in the way that they judge most advantageous to themselves, is a manifest violation of the most sacred rights of mankind.

Unjust, however, as such prohibitions may be, they have not hitherto been very hurtful to the colonies. Land is still so cheap and, consequently, labor so dear among them that they can import from the Mother Country almost all the more refined or more advanced manufactures cheaper than they could make them for themselves. Though they had not, therefore, been prohibited from establishing such manufactures, yet in their present state of improvement a regard to their own interest would probably have prevented them from doing so. In their present state of improvement those prohibitions, perhaps, without cramping their industry, or restraining it from any employment to which it would have gone of its own accord, are only the impertinent badges of slavery imposed upon them, without any sufficient reason, by the groundless jealousy of the merchants and manufacturers of the Mother Country. In a more advanced state they might be really oppressive and insupportable....

35 / *"Our cause is the cause of God, of human nature & Posterity"*

Toward the end of 1776, when John Jay (1745–1829) made this appeal to the inhabitants of New York, a pall of despair lay upon the American cause. The New York Assembly had fled to Fishkill, New York, to escape the British army. Jay, who himself came from a slaveholding family, declares that New Yorkers face two alternatives: slavery or freedom.

The patriot cause had reached a low point. A British army of thirty thousand opposed an American force of only about eighteen thousand. The patriots suffered a series of demoralizing defeats, and by December 1776, the British had forced Washington and his troops to retreat from New Jersey across the Delaware into Pennsylvania. Desertions depleted the colonial ranks, and on January 1, 1777, one-year enlistments of troops were to expire.

With his forces near collapse, Washington made a bold move. On the night of December 25, 1776, Washington and twenty-four hundred men recrossed the Delaware and marched through the night. The next day, they captured nine hundred Hessian mercenaries. Victory at Trenton and at Princeton on January 3 gave fresh impetus to the colonial cause. An English observer commented: "A few days ago they had given up the cause for lost. Their late successes have turned the scale and now they are all liberty mad again."

John Jay, December 23, 1776, To the inhabitants of the state of New York, GLC 6

At this important Period...the Freedom & Happiness, or the slavery & misery, of the present & future Generations of Americans is to be determined.... It becomes the Duty of the Representatives of a free People to call their attention to this most serious subject, and the more so at a time when their enemies are industriously endeavoring to delude, seduce & intimidate them by false suggestions, artful misrepresentations, & insidious promises of Protection.

The Great God of the universe created you and all men free, & authorized them to establish government for the Preservation of their Rights against oppression & the Security of the Liberty he had given them against the rapacious Hand of Tyranny & lawless Power....

Under the auspices & Direction of divine Providence, your Forefathers removed to the wilds & wilderness of America. By their Industry they made it a fruitful, & by their virtue a happy Country. And we should still have enjoyed a continuance of the Blessings of Peace & Plenty, Had we had not forgotten the source from which these Blessings flowed, & permitted our country to be contaminated by Irreligion & the many shameful tho' fashionable vices which have prevailed among us....

You may remember that the most dutiful Petitions were presented for a Redress of the many grievances to which that King had subjected us not only by the several Assemblies but by the Representatives of all America in general Congress. And you cannot have forgot with what contempt they were rejected....

By our vigorous Efforts and the Goodness of divine Providence, those cruel Invaders [the French] were driven [in] the last Campaign from our country and we flattered ourselves that the signal success of our Arms, the unanimity & spirit of our People, would have induced our Enemies to desist from the further Prosecution of their wicked Designs, and disposed them to Peace. But we had not yet deserved Peace. —Exultation took place of Thanksgiving, and we ascribed that to our own Prowess which was only to be attributed to the great Guardian of the Innocent.

The enemy with greater strength again invade us—invade us not less by their acts than arms. They tell you that if you submit you shall have protection. That their king breathes nothing but Peace, that he will revise (not repeal) all his cruel acts & Instructions, & will receive you into favour. —But what are the Terms on which you are promised Peace? Have you heard of any except absolute, unconditional obedience & servile submission[?] If his professions are honest—if he means not to deceive and cajole you, why are you not informed of the Terms, and whether the Parliament mean to tax you hereafter at their will & Pleasure[.] Upon this & the like Points, these military comm[issione]rs of Peace are silent....

Why if there be one single Idea of Peace in his mind, does he order your Cities to be burned, your country desolated, your Brethren to starve, and languish, & die in Prisons[?] Why If any thing but Destruction, Bloodshed, and Devastation was intended, are the Barbarians of Germany hired and transported near four thousand miles to plunder your Houses—ravish your wives and Daughters, to strip your Infant children, expose whole Families naked, miserable and forlorn, to want, to Hunger, to inclement Skies, and wretched Deaths?...Why do they excite the Savages of the wilderness to murder our inhabitants & exercise cruelties unheard of among civilized nations[?]...Your very Churches bear witness of their Impiety. They hesitate not to use them as stables & Houses for sport & theatrical Exhibitions....

You may be told that your Forts have been taken, your country ravaged, & that your armies have retreated, and therefore that God is not with you. It is true that some Forts have been taken, our country ravaged, and that our Armies have retreated, and that our Maker is displeased with us, but it is also true that the king of Heaven is not like the King of Britain, implacable. If his Assistance be sincerely implored, it will surely be obtained. If we turn from our Sin, he will turn from his anger. Then will our arms be crowned with success....

Amidst all the Dismay and Terror which has possessed some weak minds, let the advantage under which the Americans prosecute this war be considered....

Gun Powder, arms & ammunition are now manufactured in almost all American States in great abundance and our armies will have ample supplies of all military stores. We have more fighting men in America than Great Britain can possibly send into it. Our Trade is free, and every Port of France & Spain affords Protection to our Ships.... By the most authentic accounts from France, we are assured that the people of that Kingdom are ripe for a war with Britain and will not omit the opportunity of extending her commerce and humbling her rival....

Whoever therefore considers the natural strength & advantages of this country, the Distance it is removed from Britain, the obvious Policy of many European Powers, the great supplies of arms & ammunition cheerfully afforded us by the French & Spaniards, the feeble & destitute condition of Britain[:] that she is drained of men & money, & her Trade ruined, her Inhabitants divided, her King unpopular, her ministry execrated, obliged to hire foreign mercenaries to execute her wicked purposes, her Trade ruined, that she is overwhelmed with a monstrous Debt, cut off from the vast Revenue heretofore obtained from Taxes on American produce, its West India Islands in a starving condition, its Ships Taken, its Merchants involved in bankruptcy, their Designs against us wicked, unjust, cruel, contrary to the Laws of God and man & pursued with a spirit unrelenting, implacable, and in a manner barbarous and opposed to the usage of civilized nations—that our cause is the cause of God, of human nature & Posterity....

Remember the long and glorious struggle of the States of Holland with Spain. These states were once been subjected to Spain. Their extent was small, their country poor, their people far from numerous. Spain attempted to enslave them. They dutifully remonstrated against the Design. Their Petitions were treated with contempt, & fire and sword were carried into their country to compel submission. They nobly resolved to be free, they opposed force to force, they declared themselves independent States, and after an obstinate struggle, frustrated the wicked Intentions of Spain....

Rouse, therefore—do your Duty like men and refuse to be persuaded that the divine Providence will permit this Western World to be involved in the Horrors of slavery.

36 / *"It seems their design is, this spring, to spread smallpox thro the country"*

The Continental Congress faced serious problems financing the Revolution. Lacking the power to tax, Congress made assessments of the states, but they provided only limited funds. To pay for the war, the Continental Congress began to issue a national currency known as the continental dollar. Without gold or silver to back the currency, Congress simply printed the money it needed. Rapid inflation resulted. Soon the currency was virtually worthless, prompting the phrase "Not worth a continental." Since the thirteen states continued to print their own paper money, fourteen different kinds of currency were in circulation, contributing to further confusion.

In this letter, Josiah Bartlett (1729–95), a signer of the Declaration of

Independence and governor of New Hampshire, blames the rash of wartime inflation on the efforts of the Revolution's opponents to circulate counterfeit notes.

Historians estimate that about 20 percent of the population were loyalists who supported the British cause. Contrary to the common assumption that most loyalists were wealthy, it now appears that their composition mirrored that of the population as a whole.

Josiah Bartlett, April 21, 1777, to William Whipple (dated Kingstown, Rhode Island), GLC 193

We have lately discovered a most diabolical scheme to ruin the paper currency by counterfeiting it, vast quantities of the Massachusetts bill & ours [in Rhode Island], that are now passing are counterfeit, and so neatly done that it is extremely difficult to discover the difference, we are but newly acquainted with the scheme and have not made all the discovery we hope for. But by what appears at present, it is a Tory plan and one of the most infernal that was ever hatched. There are great numbers of people bound together by the most solemn oaths & imprecations to stand by each other & to destroy the persons who betray them; beside ruining the paper currency it seems their design is, this spring, to spread smallpox thro the country....We have reason to think most of the Tories in New England are in the plan. Last Thursday by agreement Massachusetts & this state seized on a considerable number who are now confined, hope we shall make further discoverys & defeat the plan; no trouble pains or danger will be spared for that purpose....

Since so much money has been found to be counterfeit people begin to be scrupulous of the continental bills and are looking out for marks, but by reason we have no standards of the former emission, we are not able to detect them, if there are any, and I have some reason to suspect there are some & that they came from New-York; I wish you would procure proof sheets of Every Emission & send them forward to be kept in the treasury of this state for that purpose agreeable to a former order of Congress....

We seem to have many difficulties to encounter both from our open & secret enemies within and without, who are meditating our destruction by fraud and deceit as well as open violence. However I trust that by the assistance of that Power who Loves Justices and hates iniquity & oppression the United States will rise Superior to all their Machiavellian plots & schemes and will be soon happy & prosperous, blessed with peace, health & plenty.

37 / *"I hope you will not consider yourself as commander in chief of your own house"*

Wartime conditions thrust new responsibilities on American women. With many husbands absent, women assumed heightened responsibilities for managing family finances and operating family farms and shops. The correspondence between Lucy Knox and her husband, Henry, one of Washington's leading generals, an artillery expert, and his future secretary of war, underscores the disruptive effects of the Revolution on women's lives.

Henry Knox (1750–1806) was only twenty-seven at the time of this letter, and he and his wife had been married only three years. Her family, the Fluckers, were loyalists who had fled Boston. This is the lost father, mother, brother, and sisters she refers to in her letter, illustrating the way that the Revolution divided families. During the awful winter at Valley Forge, Knox was given a leave of absence to visit his wife in Boston. Note how the revolutionary ideology of liberty and equal rights enters into the correspondence.

Lucy Knox, August 23, 1777, to her husband, General Henry Knox, GLC 2437

My dearest friend

I wrote you a line by the last post just to let you know I was alive, which…was all I could then say with propriety for I had serious thoughts that I never should see you again, so much was I reduced by only four days of illness but by help of a good constitution I am surprisingly better today. I am now to answer your three last letters in one of which you ask for a history of my life. It is my love barren of adventure and replete with repetition that I fear it will afford you little amusement. How such as it is I give to you. In the first place, I rise about eight in the morning so late an hour you will say but the day after that is full long for a person in my condition. I presently after sit down to my breakfast, where a page in my book and a dish of tea, employ me alternately for about an hour. When after seeing that family matters go on right, I repair to my work…for the rest of the forenoon. At two o'clock I usually take my solitary dinner where I reflect upon my past happiness. I used to sit at the window watching for my Harry, and when I saw him coming my heart would leap for joy when he was at my own side and never happy apart from me when the bare thought of six months absence would have shook him. To divert Alex's pleas I place my little Lucy by me at table, but the more engaging her little actions are so much the more do I regret the absence of her father who would take such delight in them. In the afternoon I commonly take my chaise and ride into the country or go to drink tea with one of my few friends…I often spend the evening entirely alone, to reflect that the only friend I have in the world is such an immense distance from me to think that he may be sick and I cannot assist him. My poor heart is ready to burst, you who know what a trifle would make me unhappy can conceive what I suffer now. When I seriously reflect that I have lost my father, mother, brother, and sisters entirely lost them I am half distracted…. I have not seen him for almost six months, and he writes me without pointing at any method by which I may ever expect to see him again. Tis hard my Harry indeed it is. I love you with the tenderest the purest affection. I would undergo any hardship to be near you and you will not let me….

The very little gold we have must be reserved for my love in case he should be taken [for ransom]….

[A person] if he understands business he might without capital make a fortune—people here without advancing a shilling frequently clear hundreds in a day, such chaps as Eben Oliver are all men of fortune while persons who have ever lived in affluence are in danger of want and that you had less of the military man about you, you might then after the war have lived at ease all the days of your life, but now, I don't know what you will do, you being long accustomed to command—will make you too haughty for mercantile matters—tho I hope you will not consider yourself as commander in chief of your own house, but be convinced that there is such a thing as equal command.

38 / *"It would be next to impossible for Britain to succeed"*

At first glance, George Washington (1732–99) might seem to be an unlikely choice to lead the Continental Army. His only previous military experience, during the Seven Years' War, had not been particularly successful. He and his men had been ambushed at Pennsylvania and then been forced to surrender Fort Necessity.

During the Revolution, however, Washington proved to be a mature and politically astute leader. Even though he lost more battles than he won, he was nevertheless a brilliant strategist who understood that the key to victory lay not in holding territory but in keeping his forces intact and maintaining his soldiers' morale. He also demonstrated sensitivity toward civilians and loyalists—a sensitivity he exhibits in the following letter.

In September 1777, at Brandywine Creek in southeastern Pennsylvania, a British force came perilously close to defeating Washington's army. A contingent of British troops attacked Washington's forces from behind, surprising the American forces, but Washington and his men managed to retreat. In October, at Germantown, north of Philadelphia, the Americans again had to retreat.

Meanwhile, a British army led by Lieutenant General John Burgoyne (1722–92) had advanced southward from Canada, intending to cut off New England from the other colonies. In October Burgoyne became stranded near Saratoga, New York. Finding himself surrounded, he surrendered. The Americans took nearly six thousand prisoners and large supplies of arms.

John F. Renault. Print, The British surrendering their Arms to Gen: Washington...at York Town [Yorktown], 1819/01/28. The Gilder Lehrman Collection, on deposit at the Pierpont Morgan Library. GLC 5861

The Battle of Saratoga was a major turning point of the war. It encouraged France to recognize American independence and to intervene in the war on the American side. And it convinced Britain to concentrate on conquering the colonies from the south, while protecting its possessions in the West Indies.

George Washington, December 14–15, 1777, to the president of Congress, GLC 5572

...Four thousand men under the command of Lord Cornwallis...were foraging in the neighboring country.... No discrimination marked his proceedings—all property, whether Friends or Foes, that came in their way was seized and carried off....

I learn from Mr Griffin, who has just come from Boston that this gentleman [General Burgoyne] either holds, or professes to hold, very different ideas of our power from what he formerly entertained; that, without reserve, he has said it would be next to impossible for Britain to succeed in her views, and that he should with freedom declare his sentiments accordingly on his arrival in England; and that he seemed to think the recognition of our independence by the King and Parliament an eligible measure, under a treaty of commerce upon a large and extensive scale. How far these professions are founded in sincerity, it is not easy to determine; but if they are, what a mighty change!...

Congress seem to have taken for granted a fact, that is really not so. All the forage for the army has been constantly drawn from Bucks and Philadelphia counties, and those parts most contiguous to the city; insomuch that it was nearly exhausted, and entirely so in the country below our camps. From these, too, were obtained all the supplies of flour, that circumstances would admit of. The millers in most instances were unwilling to grind, either from their disaffection or from motives of fear. This made the supplies less than they otherwise might have been, and the quantity, which was drawn from thence was little, besides what the guards, placed at the mills, compelled them to manufacture. As to stock, I do not know that much was had from thence, nor do I know that any considerable supply could have been had.

I confess I have felt myself greatly embarrassed with respect to a vigorous exercise of military power. An ill-placed humanity, perhaps, and a reluctance to give distress, may have restrained me too far; but these were not all. I have been well aware of the prevalent jealousy of military power, and that this has been considered as an evil, much to be apprehended, even by the best and most sensible among us. Under this idea, I have been cautious and wished to avoid as much as possible any act that might increase it. However, Congress may be assured, that no exertions of mine, as far as circumstances will admit, shall be wanting to provide our own troops with supplies on the one hand, and to prevent the enemy from getting them on the other.... I should be happy, if the civil authority in the several states, through the recommendations of Congress, or their own mere will, seeing the necessity of supporting the army, would always adopt the most spirited measures, suited to the end. The people at large are governed much by custom. To acts of legislation or civil authority they have ever been taught to yield a willing obedience, without reasoning about their propriety; on those of military power, whether immediate or derived originally from another source, they have ever looked with a jealous and suspicious eye.

39 / *"We had...not less than 2898 men unfit for duty, by reason of their being barefoot and otherwise naked"*

In May 1777 Washington had an army of only about 10,000 men, of whom fewer than 7,400 were present and fit for duty. Many were unfree, either indentured servants or slaves who were serving as substitutes for their masters in exchange for a promise of freedom at the war's end. Most long-term soldiers were landless, unskilled, and young, usually in their mid-teens to their mid-twenties. The military also accepted women, who cared for the sick and wounded, cooked, mended clothing, and occasionally served in combat.

Washington's army spent the terrible winter of 1777–78 camped at Valley Forge, about twenty miles north of Philadelphia. Suffering a severe shortage of food, many of the troops also lacked shoes and other clothing. By spring nearly a quarter of the soldiers had died of malnutrition, exposure, or such diseases as smallpox and typhoid fever.

In this letter Washington appeals to New Hampshire to provide supplies for that state's regiments.

George Washington, December 29, 1777, to the state of New Hampshire (dated Valley Forge), GLC 3706

I take the liberty of transmitting you the inclosed return, which contains a state of the New Hampshire Regiments. By this you will discover how deficient, how exceedingly short they are of the complement of men which of right according to the establishment they ought to have. This information, I have thought it my duty to lay before you, that it may have that attention which its importance demands; and in full hope, that the most early and vigorous measures will be adopted, not only to make the Regiments more respectable but compleat. The necessity and expediency of this procedure are too obvious to need Arguments. Should we have a respectable force to commence an early Campaign with, before the Enemy are reinforced, I trust we shall have an Opportunity of striking a favorable and a happy stroke; if we should be obliged to defer it, it will not be easy to describe with any degree of precision, what disagreeable consequences may result from it. We may rest assured, that Britain will strain every nerve to send from Home and abroad, as early as possible, All the Troops it shall be in her power to raise or procure. Her views and schemes for subjugating these states, and bringing them under her despotic rule will be unceasing and unremitted. Nor should we, in my opinion, turn our expectations to, or have the least dependence on the intervention of a Foreign War. Our wishes on this head have been disappointed hitherto and perhaps it may long be the case. However, be this as it may, our reliance should be wholly on our own strength and exertions. If in addition to these, there should be aid derived from a War between the Enemy and any of the European Powers, our situation will be so much the better. If not our efforts & exertions will have been the more necessary and indispensable. For my own part, I should be happy, if the idea of a Foreign rupture should be thrown entirely out of our Scale of politicks, and that it may not have the least weight in our public measures. No bad effects could flow from it, but on the contrary many of a satisfactory nature. At the same time I do not mean that such an Idea ought to be discouraged among the people at large because the event is probable.

There is one thing more to which I would take the liberty of soliciting your most serious and constant attention; to wit, the cloathing of your Troops, and the procuring of every possible supply in your power from time to time for that end. If the several States exert themselves...in this instance, and I think they will, I hope that the Supplies they will be able to furnish in aid of those, which Congress may immediately import themselves, will be equal and competent to every demand. If they do not, I fear, I am satisfied the Troops will never be in a situation to answer the public expectation and perform the duties required of them. No pains, no efforts on the part of the States can be too great for this purpose. It is not easy to give you a just and accurate idea of the sufferings of the Army at large of the loss of men on this account. Were they to be minutely detailed, your feelings would be wounded, and the relation would probably be not received without a degree of doubt & discredit. We had in Camp, on the 23rd Inst. by a Field Return then taken, not less than 2898 men unfit for duty, by reason of their being barefoot and otherwise naked. Besides this number, sufficiently distressing of itself, there are many Others detained in Hospitals and crowded in Farmers Houses for the same causes. In a most particular manner, I flatter myself the care and attention of the States will be directed to the supply of Shoes, Stockings and Blankets, as their expenditure from the common operations and accidents of War is far greater than of any other articles. In a word, the United and respective exertions of the States cannot be too great, too vigorous in this interesting work, and we shall never have a fair and just prospect for success till our Troops (Officers & Men) are better appointed and provided than they are or have been.

40 / "The benevolent overtures of Great-Britain towards a re-union and coalition with her colonies"

In May 1778 General Henry Clinton (1738–95) became commander of chief of British forces. He replaced William Howe (1729–1814), who was occupying Philadelphia. The British ministry ordered Clinton to abandon Philadelphia, go to New York, and dispatch some of his troops to the West Indies. While marching across New Jersey toward New York, patriots attacked neared Monmouth Court House, and Clinton's forces counterattacked. The Battle of Monmouth Court, which ended in a draw, was the last major battle in the North.

France, eager to rebuilt its prestige and power after the humilitating defeat in the Seven Years' War, had secretly aided America with money, arms, and supplies, and then in 1778 entered the war, thanks in part to Benjamin Franklin's successful diplomacy. Spain followed France in 1779, hoping to recover Gibraltar and the Floridas. In May 1780 French Count Rochambeau would land at Newport, Rhode Island, with six thousand troops, who would eventually march south to Yorktown in Virginia.

Alarmed in February 1778 by France's intervention, Lord North sent commissioners to North America with a peace offer, renouncing the right of taxing Americans. But Congress rejected this offer June 17, since with the French alliance, *independence* had become an attainable goal. Clinton subsequently offered amnesty to Americans and argued that only France would benefit from continued warfare. Clinton's proclamation of October 3, 1778, represented Britain's last formal attempt at reconciliation, offering the colonists all they had *originally* wanted.

Sir Henry Clinton, the earl of Carlisle, "Manifesto and Proclamation to the Members of the General Assemblies or Conventions of the several Colonies," October 3, 1778, GLC 5221

Having amply and repeatedly made known to the Congress, and having also proclaimed to the inhabitants of North America in general, the benevolent overtures of Great-Britain towards a re-union and coalition with her colonies, we do not think it consistent either with the duty we owe to our country, or with a just regard to the characters we bear, to persist in holding out offers which in our estimation required only to be known to be most gratefully accepted....

To the members of the Congress then, we again declare that we are ready to concur in all satisfactory and just arrangements for securing to them and their respective constituents, the re-establishment of peace, with the exemption from any imposition of taxes by the Parliament of Great-Britain, and the irrevocable enjoyment of every privilege consistent with that union of interests and force on which our mutual prosperity and the safety of our common religion and liberties depend....

To the General Assemblies and Conventions of the different Colonies...we now separately make the offers which we originally transmitted to the Congress, and we hereby call upon and urge them to meet expressly for the purpose of considering whether every motive, political as well as moral, should not decide their resolution to embrace the occasion of cementing a free and firm coalition with Great-Britain. It has not been, nor is it, our wish, to seek the objects which we are commissioned to pursue by fomenting popular divisions and partial cabals; we think such conduct would be ill-suited to the generous nature of the offers made, and unbecoming the dignity of the King and the State which make them. But it is both our wish and our duty to encourage and support any men or bodies of men in their return of loyalty to our Sovereign and of affection to our fellow-subjects....

The policy as well as the benevolence of Great-Britain have thus far checked the extremes of war when they tended to distress a people still considered as our fellow-subjects, and to desolate a country shortly to become again a source of mutual advantage: but when that country professes the unnatural design not only of estranging herself from us but of mortgaging her self and her resources to our enemies, the whole contest is changed; and the question is, How far Great Britain may by every means in her power destroy or render useless a connexion contrived for her ruin, and for the aggrandizement of France. Under such circumstances the laws of self-preservation must direct the conduct of Great Britain....

WE ACCORDINGLY HEREBY GRANT AND PROCLAIM A PARDON OR PARDONS OF ALL, AND ALL MANNER OF TREASONS...BY ANY PERSON OR PERSONS, OR BY ANY NUMBER OR DESCRIPTION OF PERSONS WITHIN THE SAID COLONIES, PLANTATIONS, OR PROVINCES, COUNSELLED, COM-

MANDED, ACTED OR DONE, ON OR BEFORE THE DATE OF THIS MANIFESTO AND PROCLAMATION.

BENEDICT ARNOLD'S TREASON

41 / *"The story...is indeed shocking to humanity"*

Toward the end of 1780, morale within the Continental Army reached a low point. Troop strength fell to just six thousand, and many officers threatened to resign over unpaid wages and inadequate supplies. In September, one of the frustrated officers—Benedict Arnold (1741–1801)—switched to the British side.

Earlier in the war, Arnold had been one of the country's most respected and successful military leaders. In 1775 he led eleven hundred American soldiers into Canada and suffered a serious leg wound in the unsuccessful American siege of Québec. In 1776 he distinguished himself in an American naval battle on Lake Champlain and played a pivotal role in forcing the British surrender at Saratoga in 1777.

Arnold, however, also suffered severe disappointments. In 1777 he was passed over for promotion, even though he had more seniority than any of the five men Congress named as major generals. The next year, when Arnold was in command in Philadelphia, the executive council of Pennsylvania accused him of using military personnel to perform personal favors. A court-martial cleared Arnold but ordered George Washington to reprimand him.

Angry at his country's ingratitude, Arnold, who was now in command of West Point, agreed to surrender the post to the British commander Sir Henry Clinton. The capture of British major John André, who was carrying papers sent by Arnold to Clinton, exposed Arnold's treachery. Arnold fled to British protection, while André was hanged. Immigrating to England with his wife, Arnold was shocked to find that he was regarded as anything but a hero.

To generations of patriots, Arnold stood as the antithesis of George Washington: Arnold was a man who lacked the moral virtue to resist British offers of £10,000 and a generalship. In the following selection, Edmund Pendleton (1721–1803), a leading Virginia jurist who later served in the Continental Congress and as Virginia's governor, views the uncovering of Arnold's treachery as a sign that God favored the American cause. Thomas Paine held a similar view: "I see so many chances the Treason had of succeeding and every chance opposed by an uncontrived something, that I almost feel myself a Predestinarian."

EDMUND PENDLETON, OCTOBER 17, 1780, TO JAMES MADISON, GLC 99.050

The story we have of Genl. Arnold's corruption is indeed shocking to humanity, & I wish much to know the utmost consequence of the discovery, as they are manifest & proper to be made public, for I know you too well ever to ask you to reveal even to me what your duty, or the interest of the states requires to be kept secret, and I know myself I would not desire it of any one. This I wish to gratify curiosity.... Providence in bringing this secret mischief to light just as it was on the point of completion, has given another instance of its kind interposition in favour of our just cause, which I hope will rouse all its favourers from the apathy from which alone our enemies can hope for success.

THE WAR IN THE SOUTH

42 / *"The loud roaring of our approaching Enemy"*

France's entry into the Revolution in 1778 altered the entire nature of the conflict. No longer was the Revolution simply a conflict between Britain and the United States; the war quickly expanded to include a number of other major European powers. In 1779 Spain joined France, hoping to regain Gibraltar and the Floridas. And in late 1780, Britain declared war on the Netherlands, partly in order to cut off war supplies that were flowing to the Americans from a small Dutch island in the Caribbean.

Having failed to suppress the Revolution in the North, Britain redirected its attention to the South, which it believed would be easier to conquer. The British plan was to secure the major southern seaports at Savannah, Georgia, and Charleston, South Carolina, and to use these ports as bases for inland campaigns and for rallying southern loyalists.

In December 1778 a British force sailed from New York City and easily captured Savannah. Within months, the British army controlled all of Georgia. A joint French and American operation in October 1779 failed to drive the British from Savannah.

Early in 1780, British forces landed near Charleston, South Carolina. This letter, by Henry Laurens (1724–1792), was written as British forces approached the city, which they captured in May, forcing the surrender of about fifty-five hundred American soldiers.

So desperate was the situation that Laurens proposed arming five thousand slaves—a proposal ultimately blocked by the South Carolina legislature. Maintenance of the slave system was more important to the legislators than blocking the British invasion.

HENRY LAURENS, FEBRUARY 14, 1780, TO WILLIAM ELLERY, GLC 110

[F]rom the loud roaring of our approaching Enemy one would think So. Carolina...may be reduced to extreme poverty & other pains & penalties within ten days, but I hope better things & am in no fears save such as arise from considerations of the distresses of Women, Children aged & infirmed persons. For my own part I trust, that, "Although the fig trees shall not blossom, neither shall fruit be in the vines, the labor of the Olive shall fail, & the fields shall yield no meat, the stock shall be cut off from the Lord & there shall be no herd in the stalls, I will rejoice in the Lord I with joy in the God of my Salvation." I have not time to tell you whence I derived this pious Resolution, the sentiments have from youth upwards been strongly impressed upon my mind & appear in full force & vigor whenever danger appears. I pray God to bless you & all my friends in Congress—be assured.

43 / *"A considerable Fleet of the Enemy has arrived within our Capes"*

Few Americans realize that much of the Revolution's bitterest fighting took place in the South. To replace the army that had been captured at Charleston, Horatio Gates

(1728–1806), the hero of Saratoga, assembled raw recruits in Virginia and North Carolina. He then rushed into South Carolina to halt the British advance. Charles, Lord Cornwallis (1738–1805), intercepted Gates's forces outside Camden, South Carolina, and devastated the poorly prepared army.

Buoyed by his victories, Cornwallis advanced toward North Carolina even before he had secured firm control in South Carolina. As soon as Cornwallis's forces began to march, rebel guerrilla bands, led by such legendary figures as the "Swamp Fox" Francis Marion (1732–95), began to attack British loyalists.

In October 1780 an army of frontiersmen defeated one wing of Cornwallis's army at Kings Mountain in northern South Carolina. Without support of his full army, Cornwallis was unable to suppress rebel guerrilla bands, which terrorized British loyalists.

In the fall of 1780, Britain, under Benedict Arnold, invaded Virginia. Thomas Jefferson was serving as governor of Virginia at the time of the invasion. In January 1781 Britain staged a second invasion, which resulted in the capture and burning of Richmond. Jefferson was forced to move the state government to Charlottesville; the state archives were lost, destroyed, or captured. A side expedition raided Jefferson's home at Monticello. Jefferson's governorship would be marred by this debacle during his last days in office.

Interestingly, Jefferson was so eager to secure Virginia's claims to the Ohio country that he had tried to send part of the Virginia militia to the region a few months earlier. The militia units, however, had mutinied and refused to leave Virginia.

THOMAS JEFFERSON, OCTOBER 22, 1780, TO JOHN SMITH, THE COUNTY LIEUTENANT OF FREDERICK, GLC 1636

Certain information being received that a considerable Fleet of the Enemy has arrived within our Capes, and have begun their debarkation I have thought proper with advice of the Council of State, to require one fourth of the Militia of your County to repair immediately to Richmond armed & accoutred in the best manner possible. Let every Man bring his own Blanket. It is not necessary that any field Officer should come with them, as field and General Officers will be provided by the Executive. They are to [be] furnished with provisions by impressing it, as directed by the provision Law, giving the persons from whom they take it, a Certificate of the Article, Price and Purpose, and transmitting to me a List of all such Certificates. I am to request that you lose not a Moments Time in the execution of these Orders.

44 / *"Measures for suppressing the remains of Rebellion"*

British policy in the South was based on several miscalculations. Britain had decided to concentrate its military efforts in the South because it believed it could count on significant support from southern loyalists. The British military, however, failed to provide loyalists with effective protection. In South Carolina, for example, guerrilla bands harassed loyalists who aided British forces.

Britain not only exaggerated the strength of southern loyalism, it also exaggerated the effectiveness of traditional, European-style battle tactics. Despite superior numbers and artillery, the British were extremely vulnerable to guerrilla tactics. The

American militia ambushed supply trains, terrorized loyalists, and thwarted British control over the backcountry. When Cornwallis massed his troops for battle, the soldiers offered ready targets for American sharpshooters.

Finally, the British believed that the fact they had the world's best navy guaranteed they would win the war. They confidently assumed that their navy gave them superior mobility, permitting them to move troops rapidly by sea while American soldiers marched overland. But this advantage, too, proved illusory. While the British could seize coastal cities, they faced punishing popular resistance whenever they ventured into the interior.

After becoming convinced that he could not conquer South Carolina, Cornwallis marched his men to the North Carolina coast and found this to be a highly discouraging experience. In a letter to Sir Henry Clinton, he wrote: "I have experienced the distresses and dangers of marching some hundreds of miles in a country chiefly hostile, without one active or useful friend; without intelligence, and without communication with any part of the country."

In February 1781, when Cornwallis invited loyalists in North Carolina to join his forces, few responded. Convinced that he could not win in the lower South, he retreated to Wilmington, on the coast of North Carolina, and then retreated again to Yorktown, Virginia, on Chesapeake Bay.

CHARLES CORNWALLIS, "A PROCLAMATION," FEBRUARY 20, 1781, GLC 496.023

> Whereas it has pleased the Divine Providence to prosper the operations of His Majesty's Arms, in drawing the Rebel Army out of this Province [North Carolina] and Whereas it is His Majesty's most gracious Wish to rescue the faithful & loyal subjects from the cruel Tyranny under which they have groaned of several years. I have thought proper to issue this Proclamation to invite all such loyal & faithful subjects to repair without loss of time with their arms & ten days Provisions to the Royal headquarters now erected at Hillsborough, where they will meet with the most friendly reception, and I do hereby assure them that I am ready to concur with them in effectual measures for suppressing the remains of Rebellion in this Province & for the establishment of good order & constitutional government.

45 / *"Our affairs have been for some time growing from bad to worse"*

In October 1780 Major General Nathanael Greene (1742–86) replaced Horatio Gates as commander of the American army in the South. Greene proceeded to divide his troops into three smaller forces, one of which worked alongside the rebel guerrilla bands. Greene's plan was to avoid fixed battles, seize outposts and isolated settlements, and let Cornwallis chase the American armies around the countryside. Then, when the British were exhausted, Greene would attack.

In January 1781 one of Greene's armies, led by Brigadier General Daniel Morgan, attacked 1,100 British troops at Hannah Cowpens, in western South Carolina. All but 140 of the British troops were killed, captured, or wounded by American sharpshooters. Two months later, Greene destroyed more than a fourth of Cornwallis's army at Guilford

Court House, North Carolina. Cornwallis claimed victory because the Americans abandoned the battlefield. But as one Briton observed acidly: "Another such victory would destroy the British army."

George Mason (1725–92), who wrote the following letter, was one of the authors of the Virginia Declaration of Rights in 1776, which served as a basis of the Bill of Rights of the U.S. Constitution. Although Mason played an important role in the Constitutional Convention of 1787, he refused to sign the final draft of the Constitution because he objected to compromises over the slavery and tariff questions. Mason was an early advocate of gradual slave emancipation. Here he describes the conflict in South Carolina and Virginia.

GEORGE MASON, JUNE 3, 1781, TO GEORGE MASON, JR., GLC 3256

Your Brother William writes you by this opportunity. He returned some time ago from South Carolina, where he commanded a company of volunteers, 70 fine young hellions from this country. He had a rough campaign of it and has acquired the reputation of a vigilantly good officer and I think is greatly improved by the exhibition. Your brother Thomson has lately returned from a Tour of Militia Duty upon James River [in Virginia], he commanded a platoon, in a pretty close action at Williamsburg & behaved with proper coolness and Integrity. He is now from home, or would have wrote to you.

I have written you very fully lately, upon domestic subjects; but am not able to give you any agreeable public news. Our affairs have been for some time growing from bad to worse. The enemy's fleet commands our Rivers, & puts it in their power to remove their Troops from place to place, when, & where...without opposition, so that we no sooner collect a Force sufficient to counteract them in one part of the country but they shift to another, ravaging, plundering, & destroying everything before them. Our Militia turn out with great Spirit, & have in several late Actions, behaved bravely, but they are badly armed & appointed.

General [Nathanael] Greene, with about 1200 regular Troops & some militia is in South Carolina, where he has taken all the Enemy's Posts, except Charles Town [Charleston]. The Enemy's capital object, at this time, seems to be Virginia. General Philips died lately in Petersburg upon which the Command of the British Troops there devolved upon [Benedict] Arnold, but Lord Cornwallis, quitting North Carolina has since joined Arnold with about 1200 Infantry & 300 Horse, & taken the chief command of their Army in Virginia, now consisting of about 5000 men; they have crossed James River....their light horse having advanced as far as Hanover Court House...& have plundered great part of the adjacent Country. The Marquis de la Lafayette is about twenty miles below Frederickburg, with about 1200 regulars & 3000 Militia, waiting for the arrival of General Wayne, with about 1500 regular troops of the Pennsylvania line. We have had various Accounts of the sailing of the French Fleet, with a Body of Land forces for America; should they really arrive, it would quickly change the face of our Affairs, & infuse fresh Spirits & Confidence; but it has been so long expected in vain, that little credit is now given to Reports concerning it. You know, from your own Acquaintance in this part of Virginia, that the Bulk of the People here are staunch Whigs, strongly attached to the

American Cause, & will assent to the French Alliance yet they grow uneasy & restless & begin to think that our Allies are spinning out the war, in order to weaken America, as well as Great Britain, and thereby leave us, at the end of it, as dependent as possible upon themselves [This distrust of France led the United States to sign a separate peace with Britain at the end of the Revolution]. However unjust this opinion may be, it is natural enough to farmers & planters, burdened with heavy Taxes, & frequently drag'd from their Familys upon military Duty, on the continual Alarms occasioned by the Superiority of the British Fleet. They see their Prosperity daily exposed to Destruction; they see with what Facility the British Troops are removed from one part of the Continent to another, and with what infinite....Fatigue ours are, too late, obliged to follow, and they see too, very plainly, that a strong French Fleet might have prevented all this. If our Allies had a superior Fleet here, I should have no doubt of a favourable issue to the war; but without it I fear we are deceiving both them & ourselves, in expecting we shall be much longer able to keep our people firm in so unequal an opposition to Great Britain.

France surely intends the Separation of the States for ever from Great Britain; but by drawing out the thread too fine & long, it may unexpectedly break in her Hands.

God bless you, my dear child! and grant that we may meet again in your native Country, as Freemen; otherwise, that we may never see each other more, is the Prayer of Your affectionate Father.

46 / "We are told the enemy['s]...superior fleet will soon drive off the French"

Convinced that he could not suppress the rebellion in the Carolinas, Lord Cornwallis retreated to Virginia in 1781. Sir Henry Clinton, fearful of an American attack on his base in New York City, ordered Cornwallis to send part of his army to New York and to take up defensive positions in Virginia. Still confident that he could defeat the rebels, Cornwallis refused to send troops northward and began to build fortifications at Yorktown, along Chesapeake Bay.

Cornwallis's decision to take up positions at Yorktown, on a peninsula formed by Virginia's York and James Rivers, proved to be a disastrous military mistake. A French fleet from the West Indies sailed to Chesapeake Bay, preventing Cornwallis's army from escaping by sea. A force of seventy-eight hundred French peasants, fifty-seven hundred Continental Army soldiers, and thirty-two hundred militia kept Cornwallis from retreating on land. Cornwallis held out for three weeks and then surrendered in October, while a British band played a tune called "The World Turned Upside Down." One quarter of the entire British army in America surrendered at Yorktown.

In a letter written precisely one month before Cornwallis's surrender, before the French and Americans had surrounded the British army, Edmund Pendleton assesses prospects for the future.

EDMUND PENDLETON, SEPTEMBER 10, 1781, TO JAMES MADISON, GLC 99.076

Very little important hath happen'd here, at least that has come to my knowledge, since the great event of the safe arrival of the Fleet & army of our good Ally [France].... It was supported that Earl Cornwallis would on their arrival, have endeavoured to effect an escape to the southward over James River; but whether the precautions taken by the Marquis [Lafayette] to prevent him, or his confidence in his own strength, or in being timely reinforced, influenced his stay, I know not, but so it is that he must now abide his fate at York Town, the French troops having landed at James Town & join'd the Marquis, so as to cut off his passage out of that neck so long as he is deprived of the dominion o'er the waters; and tho' he might cross his army over into Gloucester, where we have a body of militia, he could not that way expect to escape, since tho' they are not strong enough to oppose his army in the field, they might harass their march until a sufficient force could get above them & take them in that neck, but this I think they will not attempt, since by such a step they would immediately sacrifice all their vessels, which at present lie up York River above the town....

We expect here to have a busy autumn, supposing this is to become the seat of war since the Commander in Chief [George Washington] is to honour us with his presence; we are daily in expectation of his arrival by land, tho' we are told the troops come by water down the Bay....We are told that the enemy give out that a superior fleet will soon drive off the French. Of such a fleet at New York, we have various accounts, some say they are 29 sail of the line, others 23 only...; but can they venture to draw all their fleet from New York & leave the French fleet behind them at Rhode Island? I think upon the whole that we must have this army, which will go a good way towards destroying their American forces & give the peace.

47 / *"The designs of the enemy in strengthening Canada, & bending the residue of their force against the West Indies"*

Although Americans often treat their history in isolation from other countries', in fact foreign events have played a shaping role in the American past. After Cornwallis surrendered at Yorktown, Sir Henry Clinton still had sixteen thousand British troops in New York. But British leaders were fearful that they might lose other parts of the British Empire if the American war continued.

During the eighteenth century, the Caribbean, not the thirteen mainland colonies, was the heart of Britain's New World empire. During the early 1700s, the value of exports to England from islands such as Antigua, Barbados, Montserrat, and Jamaica was fourteen times greater than the value from all the colonies north of the Chesapeake combined.

By the end of 1781 the American Revolution had become a global war, with fighting taking place in India, the West Indies, and Florida. In Europe, France and Spain were planning an offensive against Gibraltar. In Britain there was much internal opposition to the American war and even sympathy for the colonists. In April 1782 the British began peace talks with the Americans in Paris, and the two sides agreed to a peace treaty in November. The following letter was written a few weeks before Britain and the United States reached a peace agreement.

Total American war-related deaths were more than twenty-five thousand. About seventy-two hundred Americans were killed in battle. Another ten thousand soldiers died of disease and exposure; approximately eighty-five hundred died in British prison camps; and about fourteen hundred soldiers were reported missing in action. British deaths numbered about ten thousand. To assist soldiers following the war, many states offered aid in the form of bonuses or land. Congress, however, did not agree to provide pensions to soldiers until 1818.

EDMUND PENDLETON, OCTOBER 21, 1782, TO JAMES MADISON, GLC 99.077

The continuance of the negotiation after the last change of ministry, shews they do not care to loose sight of that object, & will probably be serious in it, at the close of this Campaign.... We have nothing to expect pacific to us; but I think their situation & the spirit of the nation will coerce the acknowledgment of American independence.

There is nothing material in the Bill for peace or truce, since it only gives a (perhaps unnecessary) power to the King to make either without anything mandatory—yet it's having lain so long with the Lords, & being passed just at the close of the Session, together with the purging it of the offensive terms *Revolted Colonies*, give it a conciliatory aspect....

I find your opinion coincides with mine as to the designs of the enemy in strengthening Canada, & bending the residue of their force against the West Indies. I hope our allies are prepared there for such an event, so as to disappoint any extraordinary fruits of their plan....

THE ARTICLES OF CONFEDERATION

48 / "'Twas high time the confederation was completed"

In 1781 the thirteen original states ratified the first U.S. constitution, the Articles of Confederation. The Articles served as the new nation's plan of government until the Constitution of the United States was ratified in 1789. In this letter, Edmund Pendleton (1721–1803) urges establishment of a formal compact among the states, and stresses the need for compromise as the only way to obtain union.

Under the Articles of Confederation, the national government was composed of a Congress, which had the power to declare war, appoint military officers, sign treaties, make alliances, appoint foreign ambassadors, and manage relations with Indians. All states were represented equally in Congress, and nine of the thirteen states had to approve a bill before it became law. Amendments required the approval of all the states.

The Articles of Confederation represented an attempt to balance the sovereignty of the states with an effective national government. To protect states' rights, the Articles set strict limits on congressional authority. Under the Articles, the states, not Congress, had the power to tax. Congress could raise money only by asking the states for funds, borrowing from foreign governments, or selling western lands. In addition, Congress could not draft soldiers or regulate trade. There was no provision for national courts or a chief executive.

Equally important, the Articles did not establish a genuinely republican government. Members of the Confederation Congress were selected by state governments, not by the people. Further, power was concentrated in a single assembly, rather than being divided, as in the state governments, into separates houses and branches.

Edmund Pendleton, September 25, 1780, to James Madison, GLC 99.047

I have thought long ago that 'twas high time the confederation was completed, & feared some foreign Powers might entertain from its delay, suspicions of some secret disunion amongst the states, or a latent intention in Congress to keep it open for purposes unworthy of them; I am happy to hear it is resumed & think it becoming & indeed an indispensable duty in this, as in all other Social Compacts, for the contracting members to yield points to each other, in order to meet as near the centre of general good as the different interests can be brought, and did it depend upon my opinion I would not hesitate to yield a very large portion of our back [western] lands to accomplish this purpose.... 12 states were satisfied & agreed to confederate & yet one [Rhode Island] stops the whole business, setting up her judgment in opposition to so many. Yield to her in this, may not she play the same game to gain any future point of interest?

PART SIX

Creating a New Nation

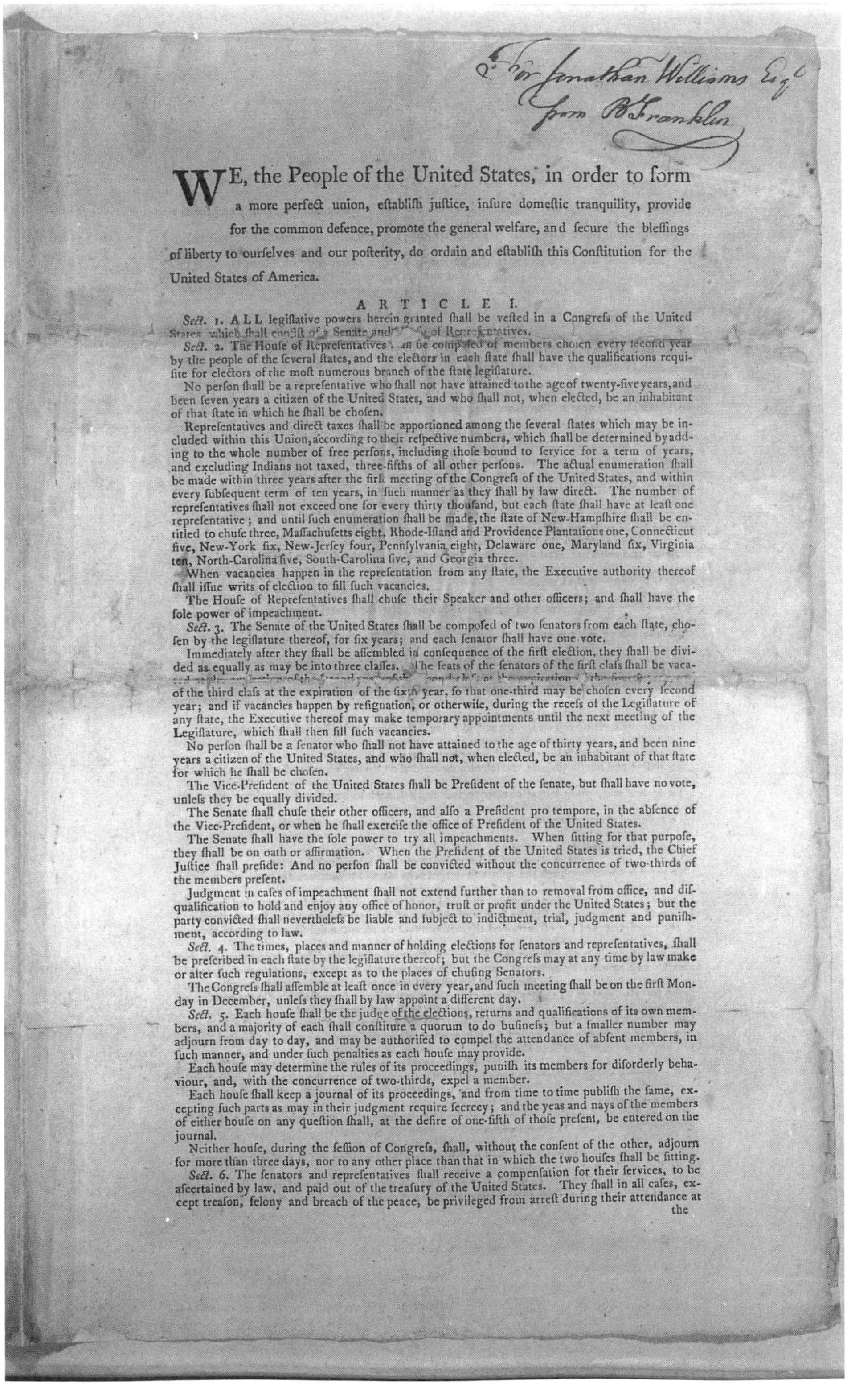

WE, the People of the United States, in order to form a more perfect union, eſtabliſh juſtice, inſure domeſtic tranquility, provide for the common defence, promote the general welfare, and ſecure the bleſſings of liberty to ourſelves and our poſterity, do ordain and eſtabliſh this Conſtitution for the United States of America.

ARTICLE I.

Sect. 1. ALL legiſlative powers herein granted ſhall be veſted in a Congreſs of the United States, which ſhall conſiſt of a Senate and [illegible] of Repreſentatives.

Sect. 2. The Houſe of Repreſentatives ſhall be compoſed of members choſen every ſecond year by the people of the ſeveral ſtates, and the electors in each ſtate ſhall have the qualifications requiſite for electors of the moſt numerous branch of the ſtate legiſlature.

No perſon ſhall be a repreſentative who ſhall not have attained to the age of twenty-five years, and been ſeven years a citizen of the United States, and who ſhall not, when elected, be an inhabitant of that ſtate in which he ſhall be choſen.

Repreſentatives and direct taxes ſhall be apportioned among the ſeveral ſtates which may be included within this Union, according to their reſpective numbers, which ſhall be determined by adding to the whole number of free perſons, including thoſe bound to ſervice for a term of years, and excluding Indians not taxed, three-fifths of all other perſons. The actual enumeration ſhall be made within three years after the firſt meeting of the Congreſs of the United States, and within every ſubſequent term of ten years, in ſuch manner as they ſhall by law direct. The number of repreſentatives ſhall not exceed one for every thirty thouſand, but each ſtate ſhall have at leaſt one repreſentative; and until ſuch enumeration ſhall be made, the ſtate of New-Hampſhire ſhall be entitled to chuſe three, Maſſachuſetts eight, Rhode-Iſland and Providence Plantations one, Connecticut five, New-York ſix, New-Jerſey four, Pennſylvania eight, Delaware one, Maryland ſix, Virginia ten, North-Carolina five, South-Carolina five, and Georgia three.

When vacancies happen in the repreſentation from any ſtate, the Executive authority thereof ſhall iſſue writs of election to fill ſuch vacancies.

The Houſe of Repreſentatives ſhall chuſe their Speaker and other officers; and ſhall have the ſole power of impeachment.

Sect. 3. The Senate of the United States ſhall be compoſed of two ſenators from each ſtate, choſen by the legiſlature thereof, for ſix years; and each ſenator ſhall have one vote.

Immediately after they ſhall be aſſembled in conſequence of the firſt election, they ſhall be divided as equally as may be into three claſſes. The ſeats of the ſenators of the firſt claſs ſhall be vaca- [illegible] of the third claſs at the expiration of the ſixth year, ſo that one-third may be choſen every ſecond year; and if vacancies happen by reſignation, or otherwiſe, during the receſs of the Legiſlature of any ſtate, the Executive thereof may make temporary appointments until the next meeting of the Legiſlature, which ſhall then fill ſuch vacancies.

No perſon ſhall be a ſenator who ſhall not have attained to the age of thirty years, and been nine years a citizen of the United States, and who ſhall not, when elected, be an inhabitant of that ſtate for which he ſhall be choſen.

The Vice-Preſident of the United States ſhall be Preſident of the ſenate, but ſhall have no vote, unleſs they be equally divided.

The Senate ſhall chuſe their other officers, and alſo a Preſident pro tempore, in the abſence of the Vice-Preſident, or when he ſhall exerciſe the office of Preſident of the United States.

The Senate ſhall have the ſole power to try all impeachments. When ſitting for that purpoſe, they ſhall be on oath or affirmation. When the Preſident of the United States is tried, the Chief Juſtice ſhall preſide: And no perſon ſhall be convicted without the concurrence of two-thirds of the members preſent.

Judgment in caſes of impeachment ſhall not extend further than to removal from office, and diſqualification to hold and enjoy any office of honor, truſt or profit under the United States; but the party convicted ſhall nevertheleſs be liable and ſubject to indictment, trial, judgment and puniſhment, according to law.

Sect. 4. The times, places and manner of holding elections for ſenators and repreſentatives, ſhall be preſcribed in each ſtate by the legiſlature thereof; but the Congreſs may at any time by law make or alter ſuch regulations, except as to the places of chuſing Senators.

The Congreſs ſhall aſſemble at leaſt once in every year, and ſuch meeting ſhall be on the firſt Monday in December, unleſs they ſhall by law appoint a different day.

Sect. 5. Each houſe ſhall be the judge of the elections, returns and qualifications of its own members, and a majority of each ſhall conſtitute a quorum to do buſineſs; but a ſmaller number may adjourn from day to day, and may be authoriſed to compel the attendance of abſent members, in ſuch manner, and under ſuch penalties as each houſe may provide.

Each houſe may determine the rules of its proceedings, puniſh its members for diſorderly behaviour, and, with the concurrence of two-thirds, expel a member.

Each houſe ſhall keep a journal of its proceedings, and from time to time publiſh the ſame, excepting ſuch parts as may in their judgment require ſecrecy; and the yeas and nays of the members of either houſe on any queſtion ſhall, at the deſire of one-fifth of thoſe preſent, be entered on the journal.

Neither houſe, during the ſeſſion of Congreſs, ſhall, without the conſent of the other, adjourn for more than three days, nor to any other place than that in which the two houſes ſhall be ſitting.

Sect. 6. The ſenators and repreſentatives ſhall receive a compenſation for their ſervices, to be aſcertained by law, and paid out of the treaſury of the United States. They ſhall in all caſes, except treaſon, felony and breach of the peace, be privileged from arreſt during their attendance at

the

Benjamin Franklin. Document signed, U.S. Constitution. Printed Dunlap & Claypoole ed. inscribed to Jonathan Williams, 1787/09/17. The Gilder Lehrman Collection, on deposit at the Pierpont Morgan Library. GLC 3585

The American Revolution was much more than a war for national independence, such as the sixteenth- and seventeenth-century Dutch wars for independence from Spain. It was also much more than a revolt against taxes and trade regulations. It was truly a *revolution*. It enjoyed widespread popular support and gave rise to a revolutionary ideology, an ideology resting on the ideas of inalienable natural rights, the sovereignty of the people, and government resting on the consent of the governed. It infused our society with a commitment to liberty and equality, which, however compromised it might be in practice, always stands as a reminder of our imperfections.

An antislavery petition presented to the Virginia legislature in 1786 highlighted the radical implications of the revolutionary ideology of liberty and equal rights. This petition declared "that the Glorious and ever memorable Revolution can be Justified on no other Principles but what doth plead with great Force for the emancipation of our Slaves...as the oppression exercised over them exceeds the oppression formerly exercised by Great Britain over these States."

Unlike the French Revolution of 1789 or the Russian Revolution of 1917, the American was not a radical social revolution in which an upper class was overthrown by the lower class. Nevertheless, the Revolution did accelerate social and political changes that were already under way.

The political consequences are easiest to measure. Leaders in post-independence governments tended to be more mobile, less wealthy, and less likely to be connected by marriage and kinship than the generation before the Revolution. For the first time, state assemblies erected galleries to allow the public to watch legislative debates, and newspapers began to report legislative debates.

At the same time, taxation became more progressive, and inheritance laws were reformed, as entail and primogeniture were abolished in all states. (The reform of inheritance laws, however, was partly of symbolic importance, since it applied only to those dying without wills. But since a majority of adult men died without wills, this reform had practical significance as well.)

The Revolution also accelerated certain important social transformations. Important features of the prerevolutionary social order were revised. After the Revolution, systems of apprenticeship and indentured servitude rapidly declined. At the same time, many southern states ended public support for the Anglican Church. Meanwhile, new social roles emerged. A new sort of religious leadership arose: itinerant preachers who depended on charisma for their influence. A new type of political figure also appeared, the professional politician who earned a living from politics.

The Revolution encouraged a new assertiveness among ordinary Americans and stimulated attacks on practices that smacked of aristocracy and special privilege. After a group of former Continental Army officers founded the Society of the Cincinnati to make Congress aware of the needs of veterans, many people denounced the group as an effort to establish an aristocracy, since membership was hereditary.

Urban artisans and small shopkeepers attacked political and economic privilege, contrasting the honest labor of the productive classes with the parasitic lifestyles of speculators and would-be aristocrats. A number of slaves began to petition for their freedom, and many owners manumitted their slaves or allowed their slaves to purchase their own freedom.

1 / *"The Loyalists of this Country are all preparing to leave it to settle in Nova Scotia"*

One of the Revolution's most striking consequences involved the confiscation and auctioning of lands owned by British loyalists, a policy that resulted in wider land distribution. About one hundred thousand loyalists, and many former slaves, left America mainly for Canada or other regions following the Revolution. In the following letter, Brooks Watson, a British merchant, a member of Parliament, a founder of Lloyds of London, a director of the Bank of England, and a Lord Mayor of London, describes loyalist preparations for immigrating to Nova Scotia. Joshua Mauger, the recipient of these letters, was a leading Nova Scotia land owner.

Watson's correspondence offers a loyalist's perspective on the Revolution. In another letter written in 1783, he comments: "The People of this Independent country are run a muck, and will soon become objects of Compassion. The unfortunate People who they are now driving to seek refuge will very soon be envied by the Lawless wretches who now persecute them. In Europe we see the Spirit of Freedom Burning from the flames of Discord as Montesquieu says, but in America, the flames of Discord [are sprouting] from the Seeds of Liberty."

The American War for Independence provided the basis for the establishment of the modern Dominion of Canada. During the Revolution, the maritime provinces, Québec, and the island colonies stood by Britain. During and after the war, tens of thousands of loyalists (including many former slaves liberated by the British army in the South) immigrated to Canada. Some settled in the maritime provinces; others moved to a new province, New Brunswick. Many others moved to Upper Canada, or what would subsequently become Ontario.

Brooks Watson, March 14, 1783, to Joshua Mauger, GLC 3902.030

Here we are without a Line from England since the first of Novem[be]r consequently in total Darkness respecting Peace or War and that at a time the most critical to the Political Interests of the two Countrys, for the power of the Congress is quite broken, nay dissolved, and the people more disposed than ever, during the war, to reconcile with the Mother Country, yet my Commander in Chief without information, without powers.

Coming the Winter my time has been fully employed in settling all my public Accounts, to the end I might be ready to move early in the Spring, this I have completed and am now under orders [as an officer] to hold myself ready to Embark for Nova Scotia...

> The Loyalists of this Country are all preparing to leave it to settle in Nova Scotia.... At least 3000 Souls will Sail hence the beginning of next month, and carry a body of troops with Cannon...and a very considerable property, a like Number will probably sail for St. Johns at the same time. There you see my Dear friend the Province will at least be settled and that with good People of Property, carrying in their Hearts the most settled Love to the Constitution of England, they will form a Barrier against those of opposite principles, and become the envy of all their Neighbors.

NATIVE AMERICANS AND THE AMERICAN REVOLUTION

2 / *"An expedition must be instantly undertaken into the Indian Country"*

Prior to the American Revolution, a surprisingly large number of Native Americans lived among whites. There was a large population of people of mixed ancestry, and many lived in such colonial cities as Philadelphia and Charleston. At the start of the Revolution, Indians in Stockbridge, Massachusetts (Algonquins who originally came from western Long Island and eastern New Jersey), provided minutemen to fight the British.

The Revolution marked an important watershed in the history of Native Americans east of the Mississippi River. Because of their interest in the fur trade and in avoiding costly Indian wars, the British had been eager to prevent rapid settlement of the backcountry and to guarantee Indians the integrity of their hunting grounds. Not surprisingly, Native Americans usually sided with the British during the Revolution.

The American patriots, in contrast, did not need Native Americans in the way either the French or the British had. The patriots were much more interested in rapid western settlement, which resulted in campaigns to subdue and remove tribes on the borders of white settlement. Indeed, such campaigns of removal began during the war itself, as this letter from Thomas Jefferson, then serving as Virginia's governor, makes clear. Jefferson ultimately recommended the expulsion of all borderland Indians.

During the war, many traditional hunting grounds were devastated. British-Indian attacks in the borderlands brought retaliation from American patriots, who destroyed the crops and burned down towns of Indians suspected of being loyal to the British. Many patriots regarded all Indians as disloyal and forced them to migrate westward. The Stockbridge Indians who had provided minutemen were forced to move from Massachusetts to New York. The end of the war brought a westward surge of back-country settlers onto Indian lands.

Thomas Jefferson, April 19, 1780, GLC 5710

> I have heard with much concern of the many murders committed by the Indians...in the neighborhood of Pittsburg[h]. Hostilities so extensive [indicate]...a formidable Combination of that kind of enemy. Propositions have been made for...stations of men as present a safeguard to the Frontiers, but I own they do not appear to me adequate to the object; all experience has proved that you cannot be defended from the savages but by carrying the war home to themselves and striking decisive blows. It is therefore my opinion that instead of putting our Frontier Inhabitants under that fallacious idea of security,

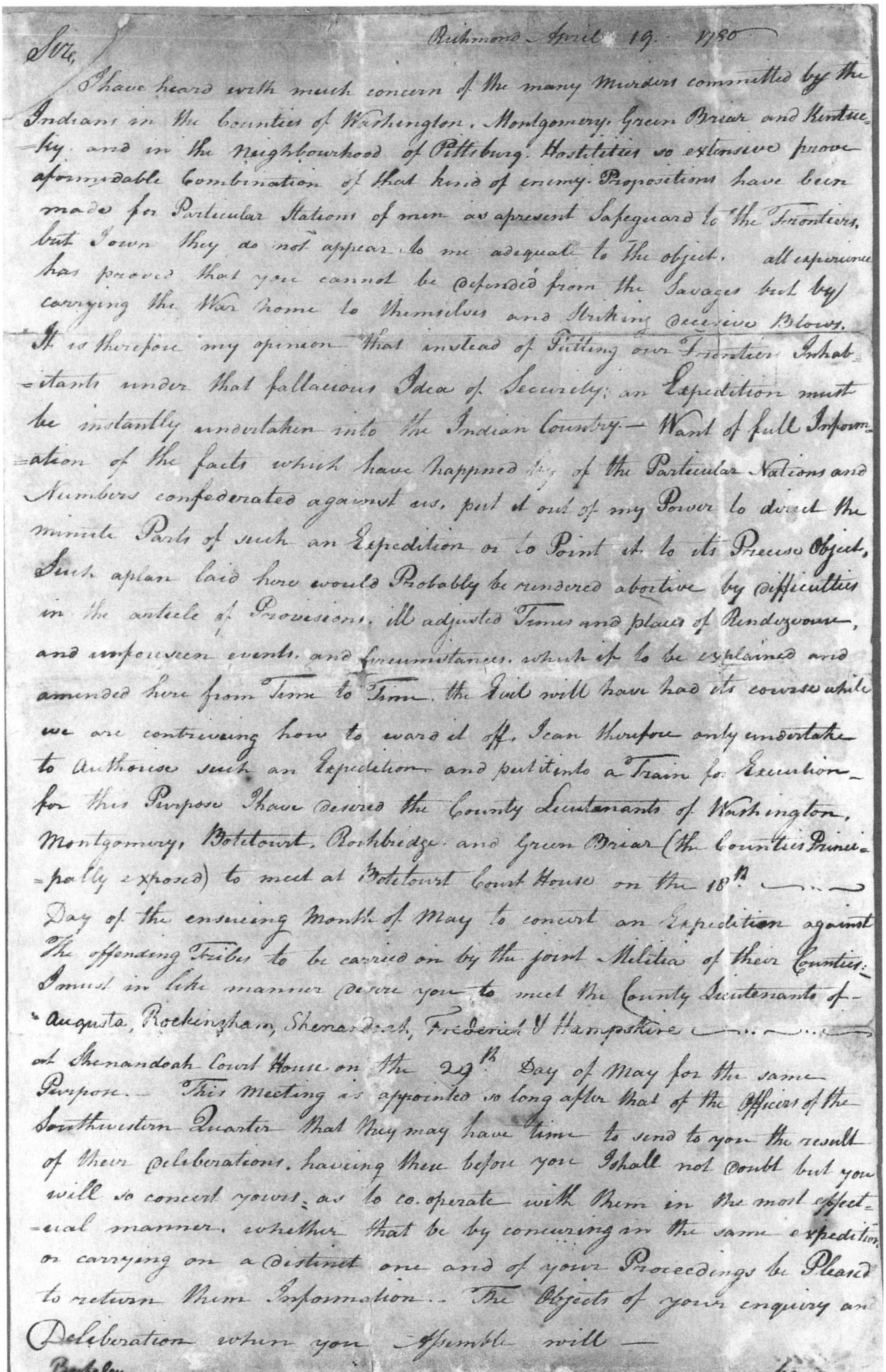
Richmond April 19. 1780

Sir,

I have heard with much concern of the many Murders committed by the Indians in the Counties of Washington, Montgomery, Green Briar and Kentucky and in the Neighbourhood of Pittsburg. Hostilities so extensive prove a formidable Combination of that kind of enemy. Propositions have been made for Particular Stations of men as a present Safeguard to the Frontiers, but I own they do not appear to me adequate to the object. all experience has proved that you cannot be defended from the Savages but by carrying the War home to themselves and Striking decisive Blows. It is therefore my opinion that instead of Putting our Frontier Inhabitants under that fallacious Idea of Security; an Expedition must be instantly undertaken into the Indian Country— Want of full Information of the facts which have happned of the Particular Nations and Numbers confederated against us, put it out of my Power to direct the minute Parts of such an Expedition or to Point it to its Precise Object, Such a plan laid here would Probably be rendered abortive by difficulties in the article of Provisions, ill adjusted Times and places of Rendezvous, and unforeseen events and circumstances. which if to be explained and amended here from Time to Time, the Evil will have had its course while we are contriving how to ward it off. I can therefore only undertake to Authorise such an Expedition and put it into a Train for Execution— for this Purpose I have desired the County Lieutenants of Washington, Montgomery, Botetourt, Rockbridge and Green Briar (the Counties Principally exposed) to meet at Botetourt Court House on the 18th Day of the ensuing Month of May to concert an Expedition against the offending Tribes to be carried on by the joint Militia of their Counties. I must in like manner desire you to meet the County Lieutenants of Augusta, Rockingham, Shenandoah, Frederick & Hampshire at Shenandoah Court House on the 29th Day of May for the same Purpose. This Meeting is appointed so long after that of the Officers of the Southwestern Quarter that they may have time to send to you the result of their deliberations. having these before you I shall not doubt but you will so concert yours, as to co-operate with them in the most effectual manner. whether that be by concurring in the same expedition or carrying on a distinct one and of your Proceedings be Pleased to return them Information.. The Objects of your enquiry and Deliberation when you Assemble will —

Berkeley.

be

Thomas Jefferson. Letter signed, to Co. Lieut. of Berkeley, 1780/04/19. The Gilder Lehrman Collection, on deposit at the Pierpont Morgan Library. GLC 5710

an expedition must be instantly undertaken into the Indian County. Want of full information...put[s] it out of my power to direct the minute parts of such an expedition or to point it to its precise object. Such a plan laid here would probably be rendered abortive by difficulties in the articles of provisions, ill adjusted times and places of rendezvous, and impose unforeseen events and circumstances, which if to be explained and amended from here time to time, the evil will have had its course while we are contriving how to ward it off. I can therefore only undertake to authorize such an expedition and put it into a train for execution....

It might be premature to speak of terms of peace but if events will justify it, the only condition with the Shawnees should be their removal beyond the Mississippi or the [Great] Lakes, and with the other tribes whatever may most effectually secure their observation of the treaty. We have been too diverted by interests of Humanity from enforcing good behavior by severe punishment. Savages are to be curbed by fear only; We are not in a condition to repeat expensive expeditions against them. The business will more be done so as not to have to repeat it again and that instead of making peace on their Application you will only make it after such as shall be felt and remembered by them as long as they are a nation.

THE NEWBURGH CONSPIRACY

3 / *"The behavior of the soldiers in their insult to Congress"*

Following the British surrender at Yorktown, George Washington moved eleven thousand Continental Army soldiers to Newburgh, New York. Resentful at the lack of support they had received during the war and bitter at Congress's failure to compensate them for their wartime sacrifices with back pay and pensions, many officers and soldiers threatened a military uprising. This threat of a military coup—known as "the Newburgh Conspiracy"—was strongly opposed by Washington, who believed that the military needed to be subordinate to civilian authority.

In June 1783, however, a group of armed former Pennsylvania soldiers marched on Philadelphia, surrounded Independence Hall, and demanded back pay. Congress asked the Pennsylvania government for assistance. The state refused, and the humiliated Congress temporarily relocated, first in Princeton, New Jersey, and later in Annapolis, Maryland, and New York City.

EDMUND PENDLETON, JULY 21, 1783, TO JAMES MADISON, GLC 99.119

With your last favor [letter]...came the missing one of June 24th containing the account of the behavior of the soldiers in their insult to Congress.

I wish the conspiracy may be traced to its real source, and the motives truly investigated, when I still think it will not terminate in public good, or the redress of real injury in the Army; the citizens I supposed cannot be well pleased either with the company of their Military visitants, or reflections upon their conduct which made such a visit necessary, and fix'd a stigma on their public character, as wanting either *inclination* or *courage* to support the members of the great National Council, holding Session in their metropolis—perhaps the people might want neither, and the fault was in their rulers in not calling forth exertions. Be this as it may, they do not reason badly who counsel a return to Philadelphia either to prevent unfavourable impressions abroad, or that the great question of fixing the permanent residence of Congress may not be embarrassed, or influenced by temporary convenience.

SLAVERY IN POSTREVOLUTIONARY AMERICA

4 / *"The case of the oppressed blacks commands our attention"*

The Revolution's promise of natural rights and equality carried far-reaching implications for the issue of slavery. In 1777 Vermont adopted the first constitution specifically prohibiting slavery. In 1780 Pennsylvania passed the first gradual emancipation law in the New World. In 1782 Virginia enacted a law (later repealed) allowing voluntary manumission. The 1783 Massachusetts case of *Commonwealth* v. *Jennison* removed judicial sanction from slavery in that state, and judicial decisions also eroded slavery in New Hampshire. In 1784 Connecticut and Rhode Island enacted gradual-emancipation laws, and Congress narrowly rejected Thomas Jefferson's proposal to exclude slavery from all western territories after 1800. In 1787 the Continental Congress prohibited slavery from the territories north of the Ohio River and east of the Mississippi River.

Still, it would be a mistake to underestimate the opposition to slave emancipation in revolutionary America, even in the North. New York did not adopt a gradual-emancipation law until 1799 and New Jersey until 1804.

Two economists have described the gradual-emancipation laws adopted outside of New England as "philanthropy at bargain prices," since the laws required adult slaves to remain in bondage and only freed their children after a period of years, to compensate owners for the costs of raising them. Such laws worked extremely slowly. Slavery did not come to a final end in New York until 1827 and, at the beginning of the Civil War, there were still more slaves in the "free" state of New Jersey than in Delaware, a "slave" state.

In this letter, a prominent Quaker and early American abolitionist explains to a pioneering British Quaker abolitionist how the American Revolution has created political bodies, such as Congress, to which antislavery petitions could be addressed. The Revolution had interrupted the cooperative antislavery efforts of British and American Quakers. This letter from James Pemberton (1723–1808) to James Phillips represents the first postwar effort to reestablish collective or coordinated action. The letter also raises the issue of whether the Quakers should admit African Americans to membership within their own Society of Friends—an issue that would test the Quaker commitment to full racial equality, including racial intermarriage.

JAMES PEMBERTON, NOVEMBER 18, 1784, TO JAMES PHILLIPS IN LONDON (DATED PHILADELPHIA), GLC 4237

I am much obliged by the kindness in sending me the Essays on Slavery, the case of the oppressed blacks commands our attention to move in endeavors for their relief as opportunities are favorable; altho Congress has done as little in consequence of our address as your Parliament has in favor of your Petition, and I conclude on similar motives; An application is now about to be made by Friends to the Legislature of New Jersey on this Subject, and we have reprinted five hundred copies of the Petition of your yearly meeting and the Representation which followed it from your meeting...for general distribution among the people in these States, & the Rulers in particular, a fragment of a letter from T[homas] Day printed in London concise & serious has been reprinted by private procurement in newspapers & otherwise by which it has a general dispersion and will I hope prove useful.

The admission of members into our Religious Society is at all times a matter of weight, a base convincement of the rectitude of our principles and discipline, and a foundation sufficient without satisfactory proof of real conversion, the want of which has been productive of burdens & troubles to meetings in many instances, and in the case of Blacks, considerations of another nature occur which are of great importance, wherein friends here do not agree in sentiment tho religiously affected for the real welfare of those people, the concord of Society therefore requires a mature deliberate consideration of the Subject in a collective capacity, for which no occasion has yet offered and I know of no more than one instance of an application of this sort to any Monthly meeting; while some friends are advocates for an unrestricted admission, others plead if no limitation is proscribed they must become entitled to the privilege of intermarriage, and I believe there are few who would freely consent to introduce such a union in their families which mixture some think would reverse the order of Divine Providence who in his wisdom inscrutable to us has been pleased to form distinction of Colour, for tho[ugh] of one blood he made all nations of men, yet it is also said he has fixed their habitation, which has been changed by avarice & ambition. However when the subject becomes necessary to be religiously discussed, I hope friends will be favored with the true spirit of judgment rightly determined &c.

5 / "[Nothing] will ever prevent me from doing all in my Power to obtain Restitution of the Negroes taken from the Southern States"

During the Revolution, the British army had liberated thousands of slaves in the South, including a third of the slaves in Georgia. A key question in postrevolutionary America was whether slaveholders would receive compensation for those losses.

Written in response to a letter announcing his appointment as American minister to Great Britain, John Adams (1735–1826), writing from France, states that his opposition to slavery would not stand in the way of a staunch defense of southern interests—and firm efforts to win restitution for the freed slaves. Such a position, Adams saw, was a prerequisite for national unity and trust. Adams proceeds to discuss the difficulties and challenges facing an American ambassador who must negotiate with wily and sophisticated European diplomats.

JOHN ADAMS, APRIL 28, 1785, TO ELBRIDGE GERRY, GLC 24

1. It is very true that I have little Admiration of the Philosophical Philanthropy or Equity of the Slave Trade. This Defect however has never prevented, nor will ever prevent me from doing all in my Power to obtain Restitution of the Negroes taken from the Southern States and detained from them in violation of the Treaty. I am not conscious that any Philosophical Speculations upon this subject, have ever influenced my Conduct in this respect, nor do I see that they ought to enter into this Business.

2. In negotiating the Treaty, I was not sensible, nor do I now remember that any of my Colleagues were more anxious than myself respecting the American Debts. There was no difference of Sentiment among us, upon this head that I can recollect. We were all sensible of the hardships upon many Individuals, but it was so much a Point with the British, and a point that would have appeared in the Eyes of the World so much to our disadvantage, to have stood out upon, that We all thought alike upon the Subject.... If you send a Minister to St. James's, he must have an Answer. What it will be, I know not, although I am apprehensive it will be difficult to obtain the Interposition of Government in the matter of Debts. It is clear to me, that the delay desired and proposed, will be at least as advantageous to the British Creditors as to the American Debtors and if government cannot be prevailed with to stipulate, I hope they may be convinced of the Necessity of the Measures taken by the States, and not treat them or consider them as Breakers of the Treaty, and that if the Creditors may be quieted, in the Case of the Negroes it is clear, that they ought to restore every one of them or pay his full value....

In truth I have not cared a Farthing, since the Peace whether I went home or remained in Europe. I have for some time intended to come home at the Expiration of our present commissions...for no Swiss was ever more homesick than I. An arrangement with England to mutual satisfaction so as to prevent War, and consequently prevent the military Gentlemen from creating a European System among us, is all that remains in Europe near my heart. And I am persuaded that a settlement with Spain, harmony with France, and Agreement with all the other Nations of Europe would follow it, of course. This done, the Sooner I get home the better: for altho I am persuaded you must have Ministers, for many years with several Courts I assure you I don't desire nor intend to be long one of them.

6 / "I never mean...to possess another slave by purchase"

In this brief note, written at a time when he owned some 277 slaves, George Washington expresses his hopes for the gradual abolition of slavery. This letter not only reveals Washington's principles and distaste for slavery, but also an outlook shared by many of the founders, including many from the upper South. Many of the new nation's leaders desperately wanted to find gradualistic solutions to America's deepest-rooted problem. In his will, Washington provided for the emancipation of his slaves following his wife's death.

George Washington, September 9, 1786, to John Francis Mercer, GLC 3705

...I never mean (unless some peculiar circumstances should compel me to it) to possess another slave by purchase; it being among my first wishes to see some plan adopted by the Legislature by which slavery in this Country may be abolished by slow, sure & imperceptible degrees.

WHITE SLAVERY

7 / "Congress having...invest[ed] us with full Powers entering into a Treaty...with the...Government of Algiers"

The problem of slavery received a new meaning when white American sailors were enslaved by the so-called Barbary pirates of North Africa. In 1785 the American

Mount Vernon 9th. Sep 1786

Dear Sir,

Your favor of the 20th.
ulto. did not reach me till about the
first inst. — It found me in a fever,
from which I am now but sufficiently
recovered to attend to business. — I
mention this to shew that I had it
not in my power to give an answer
to your propositions sooner. —
With respect to the first.
I never mean (unless some particu
lar circumstances should compel
me to it) to possess another slave
by purchase; it being among my
first wishes to see some plan adop
ted by the legislature by which slavery in this country
may be abolished by slow, sure, &
imperceptable degrees. — With
respect to the 2d, I never did, nor
never intend to purchase a milita
ry certificate; — I see no difference
it makes with you (if it is one of
the funds allotted for the discharge
of my claim) who the the purchaser
is

George Washington ALS, dated Mount Vernon, 9 Sept. 1785. The Gilder Lehrman Collection, on deposit at the Pierpont Morgan Library. GLC 3705

schooner *Maria*, sailing off the coast of Portugal, was boarded by Algerian pirates. Its captain and five crew members were taken prisoner. Then a second American ship, the brig *Dauphin*, was captured, and its fifteen-member crew was taken to Algiers and enslaved. Several Americans were put to work as domestic servants; another was forced to care for the dey of Algiers's lion. Much of the time the hostages were kept in leg irons, chained to pillars, or locked in a rat-infested prison. Six American captives died of bubonic plague. One went insane.

During the late eighteenth century, three small North African states—Algiers, Tripoli, and Tunis—preyed on merchant ships sailing in the Mediterranean, seizing their crews and cargoes and holding both for ransom. Many European countries paid tribute to the Barbary States to ensure that their ships would be unmolested. But America did not. Major powers such as Britain and France tolerated the "Barbary pirates" because they raised the shipping costs of potential competitors, such as Denmark, Holland, Portugal, and the United States.

In a bid to free these white American "slaves," the Continental Congress decided to send John Lamb to negotiate with Dey Mohomet of Algiers for release of Americans prisoners and for safe passage of American ships in the Mediterranean. The dey demanded $3,000 ransom per hostage, twice as much as he asked of other nations. Lamb returned home in 1789 without securing a treaty.

Over the next eight years, Algerian pirates seized more than a hundred hostages from a dozen captured American ships. Finally, in 1795, the United States successfully negotiated for the hostages' release. To gain their freedom, the United States agreed to pay $800,000 plus annual tribute that amounted to about 20 percent of the yearly federal budget.

It was not until 1815 that the United States successfully ended North African piracy. In that year a fleet of ten American ships under the command of Stephen Decatur threatened to bombard Algiers. The threat worked. The North African states agreed to release American prisoners without ransom and to cease all interference with American shipping.

John Adams, U.S. minister to England, cosigned by Thomas Jefferson, U.S. minister to France, October 1, 1785, Instructions to John Lamb, Esq., GLC 345

Congress having been pleased to invest us with full Powers entering into a Treaty of Amity & Alliance with the Dey [the Algerian ruler] & Government of Algiers & it being impracticable for us to attend on them in Person & equally impracticable on account of our separate Stations to receive a Minister from them. We have concluded to effect our object by the intervention of a confidential Person. We concur in wishing to avail the United States of your Talents in the execution of this Business, and therefore furnish you with a Letter to the Dey and Government of Algiers to give a due Credit to your transactions with them....

You will present our letter with the Copy of our full powers, with which you are furnished at such time or times, & in such Manner as you shall think best; as the negotiation & conclusion of a treaty may be a work of time, you will endeavor in the first place to procure an immediate Suspension of Hostilities. You will proceed to negotiate with their Minister the terms of a treaty of Amity & Commerce as nearly as possible conformed to the draught [draft] we give you. Where Alterations, which in your opinion shall not be [of] great importance shall be urged by the other Party, you are at Liberty to agree to them; where they shall be of great importance, & you think they may be accepted, you will ask time to take our Advice & advise with us accordingly, by Letter, or by Courtier as you shall think best: When the Articles shall all be agreed you will sign them in a preliminary form & send them to us by some proper Person for definitive execution.

The whole expense of this treaty, including as well the Expenses of all Persons employed about it, as the presents to the Dey &c. must not exceed 40,000 Dollars & we urge you to use your endeavors to bring them as much below that Sum as you possibly can. And to this End we leave it to your discretion to represent to the Dey Government of Algiers or their Ministers if it may be done with Safety, the particular circumstances of the United States, just emerging from a long & distressing war, with one of the most powerful nations of Europe; which we hope may be an apology if our presents should not be so splendid as those of older & abler Nations....

RELATIONS WITH BRITAIN

8 / *"I have done nothing in the late contest, but what I thought myself...bound to do by...Duty"*

Under the Treaty of Paris of 1783, Britain recognized the independence of the United States and national boundaries extending from the Atlantic coast to the Mississippi River and from the Great Lakes to Florida. Britain also agreed to evacuate military posts on American soil. Nevertheless, the nature of the United States' postwar relationship with Britain remained unclear.

The following two letters offer radically contrasting appraisals of American-British relations. In the following letter, John Adams describes his first audience with King George III. In the next letter, Jefferson offers a more skeptical perspective.

JOHN ADAMS, JUNE 2, 1785, TO SECRETARY OF STATE JOHN JAY, GLC 1538

...[I] address'd myself to his Majesty [George III] in the following words.

Sir

The United States of America, have appointed me their Minister Plenipotentiary to your Majesty, and have directed me to deliver to your Majesty, this Letter, which contains the Evidence of it. It is in obedience to their express Commands that I have the Honour to assure your Majesty of their Unanimous Disposition and desire, to cultivate the most friendly and liberal Intercourse between your Majesty's Subjects and their Citizens and of their best wishes for your Majesty's Health and Happiness and for that of your Royal Family.

The Appointment of a Minister from the United States to your Majesty's Court will form an Epoch in the History of England and of America. I think myself more fortunate than all my fellow Citizens, in having the distinguished Honour, to be the first to Stand in your Majesty's Royal Presence, in a diplomatic Character: and I shall esteem myself the happiest of Men, if I can be instrumental in recommending my Country, more and more to your Majesty's Royal Benevolence and of restoring an entire esteem, confidence and affection, or in better Words, "the old good Nature and the old good Humour" between People who, tho separated by an ocean and under different Governments have the same Language, a similar Religion and kindred Blood. —I beg your Majesty's Permission to add, that although I have sometimes before been entrusted by my country, it was never in my whole Life, in a manner so agreeable to myself.

The King listened to every word I said with dignity, it is true, but with an apparent Emotion. Whether it was the Nature of the Interview, or whether it was my visible Agitation, for I felt more than I did or could express, that touched him, I cannot say, but he was much affected, and answered me with more tremor, than I had spoken with, and said

Sir

The Circumstances of this Audience are so extraordinary, the language you have now held is so extremely proper and the Feelings you have discovered, so justly adapted to the occasion that I must say, that I not only receive with Pleasure, the Assurances of the friendly Dispositions of the United States, but that I am very glad the Choice has fallen upon you to be their Minister. I wish you, Sir, to believe, and that it may be understood in America, that I have done nothing in the late contest, but what I thought myself indispensably bound to do by the Duty which I owed to my people. I will be very frank with you. I was the last to consent to the separation; but the separation having been made, and having become inevitable, I have always said as I say now, that I would be the first to meet the Friendship of the United States as an independent Power. The moment I see such sentiments and Language as yours prevail, and a disposition to give this country the Preference, that moment I shall say let the Circumstances of Language, Religion and blood, have their natural and full Effect....

The King then asked me, whether I came last from France, and, upon my answering in the affirmative, he put on an air of Familiarity, and smiling or rather laughing said "There is an opinion, among some People, that you are not the most attracted of all your Countrymen, to the manners of France." I was surprised at this, because I thought it, an Indiscretion and a descent from his Dignity. I was a little embarrassed, but determined not to deny the Truth on the one hand, nor leave him to infer from it, any attachment to England on the other, I threw off as much Gravity as I could and assumed an air of Gaiety and a Tone of Derision, as far as was decent, and said "That opinion Sir, is not mistaken, I must avow to your Majesty, I have no Attachment but to my own Country." The King replied, as quick as lightning "An honest Man will never have any other."

9 / *"That nation hates us"*

Thomas Jefferson's life was filled with many paradoxes and contradictions. He was a great admirer of urban culture, yet he also denounced cities as sinkholes of corruption. He extolled the yeoman farmer who labored in the earth, yet devoted much of his own life to scientific investigation, politics, and architecture. But the central contradiction of Jefferson's life involved slavery.

Jefferson described slavery as an abomination and a curse that "nursed" the children of masters "in tyranny." His words in the Declaration of Independence were among the most important ideological forces undermining slavery, and yet Jefferson was also a lifelong owner of slaves who harbored "suspicions" of racial inferiority.

In this letter, written three years before the outbreak of the French Revolution, Jefferson offers a vivid description of the differences between France and England, making his own pro-French views clear, despite his praise for England's mechanical ingenuity.

This letter offers a carefully crafted expression of the revolutionary era's ideal of republican virtue. In this letter Jefferson praises frugality and simplicity; yet he would die deeply in debt, debts acquired partly from the construction of his home at Monticello, and the purchase of books, wines, and other expensive luxuries.

Thomas Jefferson, May 4, 1786, to John Page, GLC 2529

I returned but three or four days ago from a two months trip to England. I traversed that country much, and own both town & country fell short of my expectations. Comparing it with this [France], I found a much greater proportion of barrens, a soil in other parts not naturally so good as this, not better cultivated, but better manured, & therefore more productive. This proceeds from the practice of long leases there, and short ones here. The labouring people here [in France] are poorer than in England. They pay about one half their produce in rent, the English in general about a third. The gardening in that country is the article in which it Surpasses all the earth. I mean their pleasure gardening. This indeed was far beyond my ideas. The city of London, tho' handsomer than Paris, is not so handsome as Philadelphia. Their architecture is in the more wretched style I ever saw, not meaning to except America where it is bad, nor even Virginia where it is worse than any other part of America, which I have seen. The mechanical arts in London are carried to a wonderful perfection. But of these I need not speak, because of them my countrymen have unfortunately too many samples before their eyes. I consider the extravagance which has seized them as a more baneful evil than toryism was during the war. It is the more so as the example is set by the best and most amiable characters among us. Would a missionary appear who would make frugality the basis of his religious system, and go thro the land preaching it up as the only road to salvation, I would join his school tho' not generally disposed to seek my religion out of the dictates of my own heart. These things have been more deeply impressed on my mind by what I have heard and seen in England. That nation hates us, their ministers hate us, and their king more than all other men. They have the impudence to avow this, tho' they acknowledge our trade important to them. But they say we cannot prevent our countrymen from bringing that into their laps. A conviction of this determines them to make no terms of commerce with us. They say they will pocket our carrying trade as well as their own. Our overtures of commercial arrangement have been treated with a derision which show their firm persuasion that we shall never unite to suppress their commerce or even to impede it. I think their hostility towards us is much more deeply rooted at present than during the war. In the arts the most striking thing I saw there, new, was the application of the principle of the steam-engine to grist mills. I saw 8. p[ai]r. of stones which are worked by steam, and they are to set up 30 pair in the same house. A hundred bushels of coal a day are consumed at present.

THE CRITICAL PERIOD AND SHAYS' REBELLION

10 / *"This high-handed offence...must tend to subvert all law and government"*

Historians once characterized the 1780s as the "critical period" in American history, when the new nation, saddled with an inadequate system of government, suffered crippling economic, political, and foreign policy problems that threatened its independence. Although it is possible to exaggerate the country's difficulties during the first years of independence, there can be no doubt that the country did face severe challenges.

One problem was the threat of government bankruptcy. The nation owed $160 million in war debts, Congress had no power to tax, and the states rarely sent in more than half of Congress's requisitions. The national currency was worthless. To help pay the government's debts, several members of Congress proposed the imposition of a 5 percent duty on imports. But because the Articles of Confederation required unanimous approval of legislation, a single state, Rhode Island, was able to block the measure.

The country also faced grave foreign policy problems. Spain closed the Mississippi River to American commerce in 1784 and secretly conspired with Westerners (including the famous frontiersman Daniel Boone) to acquire the area that would eventually become Kentucky and Tennessee. Britain retained military posts in the Northwest, in violation of the peace treaty ending the Revolution, and tried to persuade Vermont to become a Canadian province.

The economy also posed serious problems. The Revolution had a disruptive impact, especially on the South's economy. Planters lost about sixty thousand slaves (including about twenty-five thousand slaves in South Carolina and five thousand in Georgia). New British trade regulations—the Orders in Council of 1783—prohibited the sale of many American agricultural products in the British West Indies, one of the country's leading markets, and required commodities to be shipped on British vessels. Massachusetts shipbuilders, who had constructed about 125 ships a year before the war, built only 25 ships a year after the war. Merchants who had purchased large quantities of British goods after the war found it difficult to sell these commodities to hard-pressed Americans. States protected local interests by imposing tariffs on interstate commerce.

Yet for all these problems, it seems clear in retrospect that the 1780s marked a crucial period in the development of the American economy. Output by farmers increased sharply during the 1780s—a remarkable development given the absence of any new farm machinery. Farmers also significantly shifted their investment away from cattle and farm implements to more liquid forms of wealth, such as bonds and mortgages. Meanwhile, a growing number of farm households began to produce goods previously imported from Britain. At the same time, merchants, freed of British trade restrictions, had opened commerce with Asia. But to many Americans, the signs of economic recovery remained faint.

Economic conditions were particularly troubled in Massachusetts. The British Orders in Council of 1783 dealt a severe blow to the state's agricultural, shipping, and shipbuilding trades. Making matters worse, the state legislature had voted to pay off the state's Revolutionary War debt in three years. Between 1783 and 1786, taxes on land rose more than 60 percent.

Desperate farmers in western Massachusetts demanded cuts in property taxes and adoption of stay laws to postpone farm foreclosures. The lower house of the

Massachusetts legislature passed relief measures in 1786, but eastern creditors persuaded the upper house to reject the package.

Local courts started to seize the property, farm implements, and even the furniture and clothing of farmers such as Daniel Shays (1747–1825), a Revolutionary war veteran. In late August 1786, a thousand farmers in Northampton County shut down the county court. Frightened state leaders in Boston appealed for public support. Easterners raised £5000 to send an army led by the former Continental Army general Benjamin Lincoln to suppress the rebellion.

In January 1787 Shays and his followers attacked the federal arsenal at Springfield but were driven off. In early February the army routed the rebels. These setbacks, along with tax relief from the assembly and amnesty for the rebellion's leaders, ended the uprising. Shays' Rebellion, however, held broader significance. It convinced national leaders that only a strong central government could save the republic from chaos.

Governor James Bowdoin, September 2, 1786, GLC 3538

A Proclamation

Whereas information has been given to the Supreme Executive of this Commonwealth, that on Tuesday last, the 29th of August, being the day appointed by law for the sitting of the Court of Common Pleas and Court of General Sessions of the Peace, at Northampton...a large concourse of people, form several parts of that county, assembled at the Court-House...many of whom were armed with guns, swords, and other deadly weapons, and with drums beating and fifes playing, in contempt and open defiance of the authority of this Government, did, by their threats of violence and keeping possession of the Court-House until twelve o'clock on the night of the same day, prevent the sitting of the Court, and the orderly administration of justice in that county:

And whereas this high-handed offence is fraught with the most fatal and pernicious consequences, must tend to subvert all law and government, to dissolve our excellent Constitution, and introduce universal riot, anarchy, and confusion, which would probably terminate in absolute despotism, and consequently destroy the fairest prospects of political happiness, that any people was ever favoured with:

I have therefore thought fit, by and with the advice of the Council, to issue this Proclamation, calling upon all Judges, Justices, Sheriffs, Constables, and other officers, civil and military within this Commonwealth, to prevent and suppress all such violent and riotous proceedings....

And I do hereby, pursuant to the indispensable duty I owe to the good people of this Commonwealth, most solemnly call upon them, as they value the blessings of freedom and independence, which at the expense of so much blood and treasure they have purchased—as they regard their faith, which in the sight of God and the world, they pledged they would not disappoint the hopes, and thereby become contemptible in the eyes of other nations, in the view of whom they have risen to glory and empire—as they would not deprive themselves of the security derived from well-regulated Society, to their lives, liberties, and property; and as they would not devolve upon their children, instead of peace, freedom and safety, a state of anarchy, confusion and slavery....

11 / *"The proportion of debtors run high in this State"*

Benjamin Lincoln (1733–1810), who would soon lead an army into the western part of Massachusetts to put down Shays' Rebellion, assesses the causes and significance of upheaval to his former comrade-in-arms George Washington.

In his letter, Lincoln refers to Washington's decision to resign his membership in the Society of Cincinnati. Many people condemned this organization as "unrepublican" because membership was limited to former Revolutionary War officers and their sons, which made it appear to be both hereditary and elitist.

BENJAMIN LINCOLN, DECEMBER 4, 1786, TO GEORGE WASHINGTON, GLC 1478

I wish your Excellency had not in so decided a manner expressed your determination to retire from the head of the order of Cincinnati. I shall communicate your address to our delegates to the next general meeting and to our State Society.

I have made three trips into the eastern country this year, partly on public & partly on private business...It is a country which abounds with fish of almost every kind and the waters are covered with fowls. The land, will be friendly to the growth of wheat, rye, barley, oats, hemp & flax, but not much so to Indian corn. Indeed I am so pleased with the country that I frequently wish my self there where I might be free from the present noise and tumult but I cannot leave this part of the state at present, for notwithstanding the resolutions I had formed ever to decline entering again into public life I was persuaded by my friend to take the command of the first division of militia in this state. I am now busily employed in organizing it &c. This business which would at all times be a duty {is} especially so now, when the state is convulsed and the hands of government, in some parts of it, are cast off.

I cannot be surprised therefore to hear our Excellency inquire "are your people getting mad? Are we to have the goodly fabric that eight years were spent in rearing pulled over our heads? What is the cause of all the high commotions? When and how will they end?" Although I cannot pretend to give a full and complete answer to them yet I will make some observations which shall involve in them the best answers to the several questions in my power to give.

"Are your people getting mad?" Many of them appear to be absolutely so if an attempt to annihilate our present constitution and dissolved the present government can be considered as evidence of insanity.

"Are we to have the goodly fabric that eight years were spent in rearing pulled over our heads?" There is I think great danger that it will be unless the tottering system shall be supported by arms and even then a government which has no basis than the point of the bayonet, should one be suspended thereon, is so totally different from ye one established at least in ideal, by the different States that if we might have recourse to the sad experiment of arms it can hardly be said that we have supported "the goodly fabric," in this view of the matter it may be "pulled over our heads" this probably will be the case for there doth not appear to be virtue enough among the people to preserve a perfect republican government.

"What is the cause of this commotion?" The causes are too many and too various for me to pretend to trace...them out. I therefore shall only mention of them which appear to be the principal ones among those I may rank the case with which property was acquired, with which credit was obtained, and debts were discharged in the time of the war. Hence people were diverted from their usual industry and economy, a luxurious mode of living crept into vogue and soon that income, by which the expenses of all should as much as possible be limited was no longer considered as having anything to do with the question at what expense families ought to live, or rather which they ought not to have exceeded. The moment the day arrived when all discovered that things were fast returning back into their original channel, that the industrious were to reap the fruits of his own industry, and that the indolent and improvident would soon experience the evils of their own idleness & sloth, very many startled at the idea and instead of attempting to subject themselves to such a line of conduct, which duty to the public, and a regard to their own happiness evidently pointed out, they contemplated how they should evade the necessity of reforming their system and of changing their exorbitant present mode of life. They just complained of commutation, of the weight of the public taxes, of the insupportable debt of the union, of the scarcity of money, and of the cruelty of suffering the private creditors to call for their just dues. This catalogue of complaints was listened to by many. County conventions were formed and the cry for paper money, subject to a depreciation as was declared by some of their public resolves, was the clamour of the day. But notwithstanding instructions to members of the General Court and petitions from different quarters the majority of that body were opposed to the measures. Failing of their point the disaffected attempted, and in many instances succeeded, to stop the courts of law and to suspend the operation of government until they could, by force, sap the foundations of our constitution and bring into the legislature creatures of their own by which they would make a government at pleasure and make it subservient to all their purposes and when an end should be put thereby to public & private debts the agrarian law might follow with ease. In short the want of industry, economy, & common honesty seem to be the causes of the present commotions. It is impossible for me to determine "when and how they will end" as I see little possibility that they will be brought to a period and the dignity of government supported without bloodshed. When a single drop is drawn the most prophetic Spirit will not, in my opinion, be able to determine when it will cease flowing.

The proportion of debtors run high in this State. Too many of them are against the government. The men of property, and the holders of the public securities are generally abettors of our present constitution, but a few of them have been in the field, and it remains quite problematical whether they will in time fully discover their own interests as they shall be induced thereby to lend for a season out of their property for the security of the remainder. If these classes of men should not turn out on a broad scale with spirit and the insurgents should be in the field & keep it [then] our constitutions [will be] overturned and the federal government broken upon by loping off one branch essential to the well being of the whole. This cannot be submitted to by the United States with impunity. They must send force to our aid, when this shall be shall be collected they will be equal to *all* purposes.

The insurgents have now every advantage if we move in force against them[.] We move under the direction of the civil authority and we cannot act but by the direction of it, after the riot act has been read & one hour has elapsed. They may disperse if they think proper, the next day they assemble again in another place and so they may conduct themselves with perfect security from day to day until a favorable moment should offer, those well affected to government are worn out, for the insurgents to commence their attack. Had the last general court declared the disaffected counties in a state of rebellion they would have placed the conflict upon a different footing and the rebels might have been soon crushed. They did not do it, what they will do at their next session, which will be in February next, is quite uncertain. And must remain at present, with the time when & manner how these commotions are to end, concealed form me in the unturned pages of...futurity.

P.S., January 21, 1787

The above observations were made some time since as will appear by the date of them and would have been forwarded at the time had there not then appeared some disposition in the executive to call into example the power delegated for the support of the authority of the government. They have just determined upon the measure and have ordered out four thousand militia and have appointed me to command them and have given me powers to call for such future aid as I may think necessary to effect the objects of my commission. I am thus far on my march toward the disaffected counties, viz. Worcester, Hampshire & Berkshire. It has been given out that *Shays* would stop the court to be holden at Worcester on the 23rd. I think he will not be there tho it is said that he is assembling his troops at different places. If he should not be at Worcester I expect to march the troops to the county of Berkshire to take up the insurgents to give confidence to the well affected and to convince those of an other character how much they have been imposed on when they have been made to believe that no troops would turn out in favor of government.

The gentlemen of property and men of influence have come forth fully on this occasion and have loaned a considerable sum of money to government. I cannot but hope that we shall be able to crush the opposition & that the people will be disposed to submit to government and enjoy undisturbed in [the] future the blessings of it. When ever I mention military matters I feel a responsibility to your excellency and shall when any thing turns up of importance do my self the pleasure to communicate it.

12 / "There are combustibles in every State, which a spark might set fire to"

In a letter to his former Revolutionary war comrade General Henry Knox (1750–1806), Washington offers his view of Shays' Rebellion. This letter epitomizes the perception that severe dangers—from corruption, British intrigue, and popular discontent—threatened all that had been won during the Revolution.

George Washington, December 26, 1786, GLC #2437.53.63

...Lamentable as the conduct of the Insurgents of Massachusetts is, I am exceedingly obliged to you for the advice respecting them;...I feel, my dear Genl. Knox, infinitely more than I can express to you, for the disorders which have arisen in these States. Good God! who besides a tory could have foreseen, or a Briton predicted them! were these people wiser than others, or did they judge of us from the corruption and depravity of their own hearts? The latter I am persuaded was the case, and that notwithstanding the boasted virtue of America, we are far gone in every thing ignoble and bad....

There are combustibles in every State, which a spark might set fire to. In this State, a perfect calm prevails at present, and a prompt disposition to support, and give energy to the federal System is discovered, if the unlucky stirring of the dispute respecting the navigation of the Mississippi [with Spain] does not become a leaven that will ferment, and sour the mind of it....

That G[reat] B[ritain] will be an unconcerned Spectator of the present insurrections (if they continue) is not to be expected. That she is at this moment sowing the Seeds of jealousy and discontent among the various tribes of Indians on our frontier admits of no doubt, in my mind. And that she will improve every opportunity to foment the spirit of turbulence within the bowels of the United States, with a view of distracting our governments, and promoting divisions, is, with me, not less certain. Her first Maneuvers will, no doubt, be covert, and may remain so till the period shall arrive when a decided line of conduct may avail her. Charges of violating the treaty, and other pretexts, will not then be wanting to color overt acts, tending to effect the great objects of which she has long been in labour....We ought not therefore to sleep nor to slumber. Vigilance in watching, and vigour in acting, is, in my opinion, become indispensably necessary. If the powers are inadequate amend or alter them, but do not let us sink into the lowest state of humiliation and contempt, and become a byword in all the earth.

13 / *"A proper arrangement of the militia may be regarded as the foundation of the future glory and power of the United States"*

This plan was written for members of Congress who, like Henry Knox, feared the potential for military dictatorship posed by a regular standing army. Knox's plan reflects basic underlying assumptions regarding republican government. Like many post-Revolutionary era leaders, he was convinced that a large standing army was "hostile to the principles of liberty" and believed that the country should trust to a well-regulated militia instead. Further, Knox believed that human nature would not change in America, but Americans could profit by studying the history and experiences of other people and by instituting government rationally. Yet Knox also believed that a strong military force was essential for ensuring the country's "future glory and power" and shaping the character of the nation's young men.

Henry Knox, A Plan for the General Arrangement of the Militia, Pamphlet, 1786, GLC 4554

The Secretary of United States, for the Department of War, having been ordered by Congress, "to devise a plan for the general regulation of the Militia of the United States, in such manner, as to render it most respectful, and least expensive to the respective states..."; reports that he has considered as extensively, and as maturely as his abilities would admit, the necessity and importance of a national militia. That the various views he has taken of this subject, have convinced him, that a proper arrangement of the militia may be regarded as the foundation of the future glory and power of the United States.

Acting under this impression, he has been anxious to bring forward an institution to form the manners and habits of youth, on principles of true republican magnanimity. And also, to erect on the power, inherent in the people, a durable edifice of national greatness....

Unless a republic prepares itself by proper arrangements to meet those exigencies to which all States are in a degree liable, then its independence is more precarious than the forms of government in which the will of one directs the conduct of the whole, for the defence of the nation....

The exertions of the virtuous citizens of the United States, during the late trying war, deserve the highest praise. Numerous instances of extensive patriotism might be produced, which would vie in lustre with the most splendid actions of antiquity.

But the powerful springs which then impelled to action, having ceased to exist, it may be apprehended that the sweets of peace will cling so close to many citizens, as to produce a supineness of conduct, forgetful of the past, and regardless of future dangers. The effulgence of wealth will dazzle weak minds, and the seducing influence of luxury may introduce a corruption of manners, destructive to a republic.

Hence the wisdom of fixing the public mind on objects of national utility; of forming the manners of the rising generation on principles of republican virtue; of infusing into their minds, that the love of their country, and the knowledge of defending it, are political duties of the most indispensable nature.

The design of the plan herewith submitted, is to establish institutions, which shall in a degree effect the above purposes.... The plan is formed on the following general principles:

1st. That every independent nation ought to possess within itself, the means for its defence.

2d. That is an essential security to a free state, for the great body of the people, to possess a competent knowledge of the military art.

3d. That this knowledge cannot be generally attained, but by establishing efficient institutions for the military education of the youth, and that the knowledge acquired therein, should be diffused through the community by the means of rotation....

Youth is the time, for the state to avail itself of those services which it has a right to demand, and by which it is to be invigorated and preserved; in this season, the passions and affections, are strongly influenced by the splendor of military parade. The impressions the mind receives will be retained through life. The young man will repair with pride and pleasure to the field of exercise, while the head of a family, anxious for its general welfare, and perhaps its immediate subsistence, will reluctantly quit his domestic duties for any length of time.

The habits of industry will be rather strengthened, than relaxed, by the establishment of the annual camps of discipline, as all the time will be occupied by the various military duties. Idleness and dissipation will be regarded as disgraceful, and punished accordingly....

It ought to be a permanent rule, that those who in youth decline or refuse to subject themselves to the course of military education, established by the laws, should be considered as unworthy of public trust, or public honors, and be excluded therefrom accordingly....

NORTHWEST ORDINANCE

14 / *"Neither Slavery nor involuntary Servitude in the said territory"*

Some of the bitterest controversies in post-Revolutionary America involved western land. Connecticut, Georgia, Massachusetts, New York, North and South Carolina, and Virginia insisted that their colonial charters extended their boundaries to the Mississippi River or beyond. Maryland, which had no western land claims, refused to approve the Articles of Confederation unless it received assurance that the other states agreed to yield their claims to the federal government. Between 1781 and 1785 the "landed" states ceded their western land claims to Congress. Virginia ceded the single largest area to the national government. Known as the Northwest Territories, it comprised the present-day states of Illinois, Indiana, Michigan, Ohio, and Wisconsin, as well as part of Minnesota.

In hopes of raising revenue from the sale of western land, Congress passed the Land Ordinance of 1785. It provided for the division of the Northwest Territory into townships, each of which would be subdivided into lots a mile square, or 640 acres. The cost of a single lot was too high—a minimum of $640—to attract buyers. In the end, Congress agreed to sell more than a million acres to a group of New England land speculators, who called themselves the Ohio Company, for fewer than ten cents an acre.

Another source of controversy involved the governance of the western territories. No one yet knew whether the western lands would remain part of the United States or form a separate confederation or whether any states created out of the West would be equal to the original states. Thomas Jefferson in 1784 proposed that the Northwest Territories be divided into ten units and that any one of them could become a state as soon as its population equaled that of the smallest existing state. Many Easterners opposed this proposal, fearing that western states would quickly dominate Congress.

In 1787 Congress adopted the Northwest Ordinance, which provided a model for the organization of future territories. The ordinance gave Congress the power to divide the area into three to five separate territories. Congress would appoint a governor, a secretary, and three judges to govern each territory. When a territory had five thousand free adult males, it could send a nonvoting member to Congress and choose a territorial legislature (whose enactments had to be approved by the congressionally appointed governor). Once a territory had sixty thousand free inhabitants, it could apply for admission as a state, with all the rights of the existing states.

The Northwest Ordinance guaranteed residents' property rights, as well as other rights such as trial by jury and freedom of religion. It also prohibited slavery in the Northwest Territory.

From the outset, the issue of slavery in the western territories was a major source of controversy. When North Carolina and Georgia ceded their western lands to the federal government, they stipulated that slavery be permitted in any territories made out of those lands. In 1784 Jefferson offered a proposal to prohibit slavery in any new state after 1800. The Continental Congress defeated this measure by a single vote. Just six years later, in stark contrast, Congress omitted any mention of slavery when it set up territorial governments in the Southwest.

Even though the prohibition of slavery in the Northwest Ordinance seems clear, it must be emphasized that this provision did not affect slaves already living in the territory and did not prevent some slaveholders from bringing slaves into the Indiana and Illinois territories. In parts of the Old Northwest, there was strong pressure for slavery. In 1802 a convention in Indiana Territory asked Congress to allow slaves to be brought into the region. Later, an indentured-servant act allowed de facto slavery in the territory. It was only in 1823 that Illinois defeated the efforts of a proslavery party. These antislavery victories drew heavily on the precedent of the Ordinance of 1787.

NORTHWEST ORDINANCE, 1787, GLC 1042

Article the Sixth. *There shall be neither Slavery nor involuntary Servitude in the said territory otherwise than in the punishment of crimes, whereof the party shall have been duly convicted;* Provided always, *That any person escaping into the same, from whom labor or service is lawfully claimed in any one of the original States, such fugitive may be lawfully reclaimed and conveyed to the person claiming his or her labor or service as aforesaid.*

CREATING REPUBLICAN GOVERNMENTS

15 / "The...Power of Government of this State is vested in, and must be derived from the People"

The United States was the first modern nation to self-consciously design systems of government reflecting certain fundamental philosophical principles. After the country declared independence in 1776, many states drew up new constitutions that embodied republican ideals.

A basic goal of the new state constitutions was to curb the kinds of abuses that provoked the Revolution. The British had lacked a written constitution; many Americans felt that a written constitution would be harder to violate. To keep state governments from abusing their power, the state constitutions included a bill of rights, which guaranteed certain elemental rights that government could not infringe, such as freedom of the press, freedom of religion, and the right to trial by jury.

The new state constitutions also curbed executive power. Two states—Georgia and Pennsylvania—eliminated the position of governor altogether. The other states prohibited governors from vetoing laws, dissolving the state legislature, and granting land, and sharply limited their power to appoint government officials.

The new state constitutions gave the legislature the most governmental power precisely because legislative assemblies had actively resisted attempts by royal governors and the king's ministers to violate their rights. But because they feared giving too much power to any one governmental body, all the states except Georgia and Pennsylvania divided the state legislature into two branches.

As a symbol that the new state constitutions reflected the sovereignty of the people, the documents were typically drafted by special constitutional conventions rather than by state legislatures. The constitutions were then submitted to the people for approval.

New Hampshire, A Declaration of Rights, and Plan of Government for the State of New-Hampshire, 1779, GLC 3182

Whereas by the tyrannical Administration of the Government of the King and Parliament of Great Britain, this State of New Hampshire with the other United States of America, have been necessitated to reject the British Government and Declare themselves Independent States; all of which is more largely set for the Continental Congress in their Resolution and Declaration of the fourth of July A.D. 1776.

And Whereas it is recommended by the said Continental Congress to each and every of the said United States to establish a form of government most conducive to the welfare thereof. We the Delegates of the said State of New Hampshire chosen for the purpose of forming a permanent plan of Government subject to the review of our Constitutions have composed the following Declaration of Rights, and Plan of Government, and recommend the same to our Constituents for the Approbation.

First, We declare that we the People of the State of New Hampshire are Free and Independent of the Crown of Great Britain.

Secondly. We the People of this State, are entitled to Life, Liberty, and Property; and all other Immunities and Privileges which we heretofore enjoyed.

Thirdly. The common and Statute Laws of England, adopted and used here, and the Law of this State (not inconsistent with the Declaration of Independence) now are, and shall be in force here for the Welfare and good Government of the State, unless the same shall be repealed or altered by the future Legislature thereof.

Fourthly. The whole and entire Power of Government of this State is vested in, and must be derived from the People whereof, and from no other Source whatsoever.

Fifthly. The future Legislature of this State, shall make no Laws to infringe the Rights of Conscience, or any other of the natural unalienable Rights of Men, or Contrary to the Laws of God, or against the Protestant Religion.

Sixthly. The Extent of Territory of this State is, and shall be the same which was under the Government of the late Governor John Wentworth, Esq. Governor of New Hampshire. Reserving nevertheless our claim to the New Hampshire Grants, to...the West of the Connecticut River {Vermont}.

Seventhly, The Right of Trial by Jury in all Cases as heretofore used in this State, shall be preserved inviolate forever.

THE U.S. CONSTITUTION

16 / "The only step of moment taken by Cong[res]s...has been a recommendation of the proposed meeting...for revising the federal articles"

By the Spring of 1787, many national figures believed that the national government needed to be strengthened if the young republic was to survive. The threat of national bankruptcy, Britain's refusal to evacuate military posts in the Northwest Territory, Spanish intrigues on the western frontier, and armed rebellion in western Massachusetts had revealed serious weaknesses in the Articles of Confederation. The only solution, many national leaders were convinced, was to create a central government, led by a strong chief executive, which would be powerful enough to maintain social stability, suppress Indian warfare, negotiate with Britain and Spain, overcome state rivalries, and restrain the democratic tendencies unleashed by the Revolution. A firm union, in turn, would depend on repeated compromises, especially over the explosive issue of slavery.

Of the fifty-five delegates who gathered in Philadelphia in May 1787, a third were Revolutionary War veterans and thirty-four were lawyers. They represented every state except Rhode Island, and were instructed by Congress to propose amendments to the Articles of Confederation. But shortly after deliberations began, the delegates agreed to draft an entirely new plan of government, the Constitution of the United States. The Constitution established not only a confederation of states but also a national government with clear powers to raise taxes, enforce laws, regulate trade, and suppress internal resistance.

In this letter, James Madison (1751–1836), the "father of the Constitution," describes the reasons behind the Continental Congress's decision to endorse revisions of the Articles of Confederation.

James Madison, February 24, 1787, to Edmund Pendleton

...The only step of moment taken by Cong[res]s, since my arrival has been a recommendation of the proposed meeting in May for revising the federal articles. Some of the States, considering this measure as an extra-constitutional one, had scruples ag[ains]t concurring in it without some regular sanction. By others it was thought best that Cong[res]s should remain neutral in the business, as the best antidote for the jealousy of an ambitious desire in them to get more power in their hands. This suspense was at length removed by an instruction from this State to its delegates to urge a Recommendatory Resolution in Congress which accordingly passed a few days ago. Notwithstanding this instruction from N. York, there is room to suspect her disposition not to be very federal, a large majority of her House of delegates having very lately entered into a definite refusal of the impost, and the instruction itself having passed in the State by a casting vote only. In consequence of the sanction given by Cong[res]s, Mass[achuset]ts it is said will send deputies to the Convention, and her example will have great weight with the other N. England States. The States from N. C[arolin]a to N. Jersey inclusive have made their appointments, except Mary[lan]d, who has as yet only determined that she will make them. The gentlemen here from S. C[arolin]a & Georgia, except that those States will follow the general example. Upon the whole therefore it seems probable that a meeting will take place, and that it will be a pretty full one. What the issue of it will be is among the other arcana of futurity and nearly as inscrutable as any of them. In general I find men of reflection much less sanguine as to the new than despondent as to the present System. Indeed the Present System neither has nor deserves advocates; and if some very strong props are not applied, will quickly tumble to the ground. No money is paid into the public Treasury; no respect is paid to the federal authority. Not a single State complies with the requisitions; several pass them over in silence, and some positively reject them. The payments ever since the peace have been decreasing, and of late fall short even of the pittance necessary for the Civil list of the Confederacy. It is not possible that a government can last long under these circumstances. If the approaching convention should not agree on some remedy, I am persuaded that some very different arrangement will ensue. The late turbulent scenes in Mass[achuset]ts & infamous ones in Rhode Island, have done inexpressible injury to the republic character in that part of the U. States; and a propensity towards Monarchy is said to have been produced by it in some leading minds. The bulk of the people will probably prefer the lesser evil of a partition of the Union into three more practicable and energetic Governments. The latter idea I find after long confinement to individual speculations & private circles, is beginning to shew itself in the Newspapers. But tho' it is a lesser evil, it is so great a one that I hope the danger of it will rouse all the real friends of the Revolution to exert themselves in favor of such an organization of the confederacy as will perpetuate the Union, and redeem the honor of the Republican name....

The Writings of James Madison, 1783–1787. (New York: G.P. Putnam's Sons, 1901), Vol. II, pp. 317–20.

17 / *"My opinion of the energetic wants of the federal government are well known"*

Even during his lifetime, George Washington was considered as much a monument as a man. To Americans of the Revolutionary and early national periods, he personified republican virtue. A superb horseman, dignified in appearance, standing well over six feet tall, Washington looked like a military hero. But it was his character that elicited particular admiration, especially his decision at the end of the Revolution in December 1783 to surrender his sword to Congress and return to his plantation at Mount Vernon in Virginia. This decision, wrote the painter John Trumbull (1756–1843) in London in 1784, "excites the astonishment and admiration of this part of the world."

Acutely aware of his reputation for republican virtue, Washington was extremely careful about how he behaved in public. The Constitutional Convention posed genuine quandaries for Washington. He very much hoped for a stronger federal government than the Articles of Confederation could provide, but he also feared that the public might question his motives for participating in the proposed convention. In the end, Washington agreed to serve as president of the Constitutional Convention, and his popularity and prestige helped to secure the Constitution's ratification.

George Washington, February 3, 1787, to Henry Knox, GLC 2437.53.65

My first wish is, to do for the best, and to act with propriety; and you know me too well, to believe that reserve or concealment of any circumstance or opinion, would be at all pleasing to me. The legality of this Constitution I do not mean to discuss, nor how problematical the issue of it may be. That powers are wanting, none can deny.[...] That which takes the strongest course to obtain them, will, in my opinion, under present circumstances, be found best. Otherwise, like a house on fire, whilst the most regular mode of extinguishing it is contending for, the building is reduced to ashes. My opinion of the energetic wants of the federal government are well known; publickly & privately, I have declared it....

DEBATES WITHIN THE CONSTITUTIONAL CONVENTION

18 / "A national government ought to be established consisting of a Supreme Legislature, Judiciary, and Executive"

For three and a half months during a hot, muggy Philadelphia summer, the delegates debated remarkably sensitive issues: among them were whether the national government should be allowed to veto state laws and whether the states should be eliminated altogether. To encourage the delegates to speak candidly, the Constitutional Convention took extraordinary steps to ensure secrecy. Sentries were posted at the doors of Independence Hall, and no copies of the journal were permitted. Delegates were urged to burn their notes.

Nevertheless, some of the notes kept by delegates survive, including those of Pierce Butler (1744–1822) of South Carolina. Here, Butler, a wealthy planter who was also a champion of backcountry interests in South Carolina (calling for greater representation for western interests and moving the state capital westward) summarizes a plan for the new government presented by delegates from Virginia. The Virginia Plan, written by James Madison but presented by Edmund Randolph (1753–1813), proposed a national legislature divided into two houses, the House of Representatives and the Senate. Voters in each state would elect members of the House of Representatives. Under the Virginia Plan, population would determine the number of representatives a state would have in the House.

Under Madison's plan, the House of Representatives would select members of the Senate from candidates suggested by state legislatures. The House would also choose members of the judiciary and a president, who would serve for seven years. Congress would have the power to override state legislation.

Many delegates objected to the authority over state laws that the Virginia Plan gave Congress. Delegates from small states protested that the plan would give larger states too much power in the national government. New Jersey proposed that all states have an equal number of representatives. Under the New Jersey Plan, which strongly resembled the government under the Articles of Confederation, Congress would consist of only one house, to be elected by the state legislatures, not directly by the people.

Delegates rejected both the Virginia and the New Jersey plans. Connecticut delegates offered a compromise proposal that became known as the Connecticut Compromise or the Great Compromise. Like the Virginia Plan, it provided for a Congress with two houses. This plan provided for equal state representation in the Senate, along with representation in proportion to population in the House of Representatives. Voters in each state would elect members of the House of Representatives to two-year terms, while state legislatures would choose senators for six-year terms.

To foster rational debate and to ensure that the people would elect representatives whose outlook transcended narrow local interests, the convention kept the House of Representatives small. The first House had only sixty-five members, fewer than many state legislatures, which meant that representatives had to win support from large constituencies.

Pierce Butler, GLC 819.06

State of the resolutions submitted to the consideration of the House by the honorable Mr. [Edmund] Randolph [of Virginia], as altered, amended, and agreed to in a Committee of the whole House.

1 Resolved that is the opinion of this Committee that a national government ought to be established consisting of a Supreme Legislative, Judiciary, and Executive

2 Resolved that the national legislature ought to consist of two branches.

3 Resolved that the members of the first branch of the national Legislature ought to be elected by

the People of the several States
for the term of three years
to receive fixed stipends by which they may be compensated for the devotion of their time to public service
to be paid out of the National Treasury
to be ineligible to any office established by a particular State or under the authority of the United States (except those peculiarly belonging to the functions of the first branch) during the term of service, and under the national government, for the space of one year after its expiration

4 Resolved that the Members of the second branch of the national Legislature ought to be chosen by

the individual Legislatures
to be of the age of thirty years at least
to hold their offices for a term of years sufficient to ensure their independency namely seven years
to receive fixed stipends, by which they may be compensated for the devotion of their time in public service
to be paid out of the national treasury
to be ineligible to any office established by a particular state, or under the authority of the United States (except those peculiarly belonging to the functions of the second branch) during the term of service, and under the national government, for the space of one year after its expiration

5 Resolved that each branch ought to possess the right of originating acts

6 Resolved that the national Legislature ought to be empowered to enjoy the legislative rights vested in Congress by the confederation—and moreover

to legislate in all cases to which the separate states are incompetent: or in which the harmony of the united States may be interrupted by the exercise of individual legislation
to negative all laws passed by the several States contravening, in the opinion of the national Legislature, the articles of union, or any treaties subsisting under the authority of the union

7 Resolved that the right of suffrage in the first branch of the national Legislature ought

not be according to the rule established in the articles of confederation but according to some equitable ratio of representation, namely, in proportion to the whole number of white and other free citizens and inhabitants, of every age, sex, and condition including those bound to servitude for a term of years, and three fifths of all other persons [slaves] not comprehended in the foregoing description except Indians, not paying taxes in each State

8 Resolved that the right of suffrage in the second branch of the national Legislature ought to be according to the rule established for the first

9 Resolved that a National Executive be instituted to consist of
a Single Person
to be chosen by the National Legislature
for the term of seven years
with power to carry into execution the national laws
to appoint to offices in cases not otherwise provided for
to be ineligible a second time—and
to be removable on impeachment and conviction of malpractice or neglect of duty
to receive a fixed stipend by which he may be compensated for the devotion of his time to public service
to be paid out of the national Treasury

10 Resolved that the national Executive shall have a right to negative any legislative act which shall not be afterwards passed unless by two third parts of each branch of the national Legislature

11 Resolved that a national Judiciary be established to consist of one supreme Tribunal
The Judges of which to be appointed by the second branch of the national Legislature to hold their offices during good behaviour: and to receive, punctually at stated times, a fixed compensation for their services: in which no increase or diminution shall be made, so as to affect the persons actually in office at the time of such increase or diminution

12 Resolved that the national Legislature be empowered to appoint inferior Tribunals

13 Resolved that the jurisdiction of the national Judiciary shall extend to cases which respect the collection of the national revenue; impeachment of any national officers; and questions which involve the national peace and harmony

14 Resolved that provision ought to be made for the admission of states, lawfully arising within the limits of the United States, whether from a voluntary junction of government and territory, or otherwise, with the consent of a number of voices in the national Legislature less than the whole

15 Resolved that provision ought to be made for the continuance of Congress and their authorities and privileges until a given day after the reform of the articles of union shall be adopted: and for the completion of all their engagements

16 Resolved that a republican constitution, and its existing laws, ought to be guaranteed to each state by the United States

17 Resolved that provision ought to be made for the amendments of the articles of union whensoever it shall seem necessary

18 Resolved that the Legislative, Executive, and Judiciary powers within the several states ought to be bound by oath to support the articles of union

19 Resolved that the amendments which shall be offered to the confederation by the Convention, ought at a proper time or times, after the approbation of Congress, to be submitted to an Assembly or Assemblies of representatives, recommended by the several Legislatures, to be expressly chosen by the people to consider and decide thereon

THE THREE-FIFTHS COMPROMISE

19 / *"Three-fifths of all other persons"*

The Constitution was a document based on compromise: between larger and smaller states, between proponents of a strong central government and those who favored strong state governments, and, above all, between northern and southern states. Of all the compromises on which the Constitution rested, perhaps the most controversial was the Three-fifths Compromise, an agreement to count three-fifths of a state's slaves in apportioning representatives, presidential electors, and direct taxes.

The three-fifths figure was the outgrowth of a debate that had taken place within the Continental Congress in 1783. The Articles of Confederation had apportioned taxes not according to population but according to land values. The states consistently undervalued their land in order to reduce their tax burden. To rectify this situation, a special committee recommended apportioning taxes by population. The Continental Congress debated the ratio of slaves to free persons at great length. Northerners favored a four-to-three ratio, while southerners favored a two-to-one or a four-to-one ratio. Finally, James Madison suggested a compromise: a five-to-three ratio. All but two states—New Hampshire and Rhode Island—approved this recommendation. But because the Articles of Confederation required unanimous agreement, the proposal was defeated. When the Constitutional Convention met in 1787, it adopted Madison's earlier suggestion.

The taxes that the Three-fifths Compromise dealt with were "direct" taxes, as opposed to excise or import taxes. It was not until 1798 that Congress imposed the first genuine direct taxes in American history: a tax on dwelling houses and a tax on slaves aged twelve to fifty.

The Three-fifths Compromise greatly augmented southern political power. In the Continental Congress, where each state had an equal vote, there were only five states in which slavery was a major institution. Thus the southern states had about 38 percent of the seats in the Continental Congress. Because of the 1787 Three-fifths Compromise, the southern states had nearly 45 percent of the seats in the first U.S. Congress, which took office in 1790.

It is ironic that it was a liberal northern delegate, James Wilson of Pennsylvania, who proposed the Three-fifths Compromise, as a way to gain southern support for a new framework of government. Southern states had wanted representation apportioned by population; after the Virginia Plan was rejected, the Three-fifths Compromise seemed to guarantee that the South would be strongly represented in the House of Representatives and would have disproportionate power in electing presidents.

Over the long term, the Three-fifths Compromise did not work as the South anticipated. Since the northern states grew more rapidly than the South, by 1820, southern representation in the House had fallen to 42 percent. Nevertheless, from Jefferson's election as president in 1800 to the 1850s, the three-fifths rule would help to elect slaveholding presidents. Southern political power increasingly depended on the Senate, the president, and the admission of new slaveholding states.

U.S. Constitution, Article I, Section 2, GLC 80

Representatives and direct taxes shall be apportioned among the several States which may be included within this Union, according to their respective Numbers, which shall be determined by adding the whole Number of free Persons, including those bound to Service for a Term of Years, and excluding Indians not taxed, three-fifths of all other persons. The actual Enumeration shall be made within three Years after the first Meeting of the Congress of the United States, and within every subsequent Term of ten years, in such Manner as they shall by Law direct. The Number of representatives shall not exceed one for every thirty Thousand, but each State shall have at Least one Representative.... [In 1929 Congress fixed the total number of Representatives at 435; currently there is 1 Representative for about every 519,000 persons.]

20 / "Objections to the Constitution as far as it has advanced"

Over the course of the Constitutional Convention, the delegates devised the fundamental principles that underlie the American framework of government: separation of powers, checks and balances, federalism, and judicial review. The system they created emerged gradually in response to certain deep-rooted concerns. Balancing the framers' republican faith in the people was a fear of direct democracy and the dangers posed by unchecked majorities. And balancing their desire to create an effective national government was a fear that a strong national government with the power to regulate trade and levy taxes would not truly be republican. The challenge the founders faced was to create a national government that would be both strong and effective and republican, a government that would not ultimately degenerate into anarchy or tyranny.

The only recent examples of republicanlike societies—the Netherlands and Switzerland—were small, loosely knit confederations. Many doubted that a it was possible to have a large and diverse republican society with a strong central government. James Madison formulated an answer to this concern: He argued that in a large republic, difficulties of communication and a wide variety of interest groups would make it difficult to form an oppressive majority.

The Constitutional Convention was unable to achieve unanimous agreement on a plan of government. In this selection, Pierce Butler summarizes the objections that Edmund Randolph (1753–1813), a Virginia delegate, raised over the proposed Constitution. Randolph was one of three delegates—the other two were Elbridge Gerry (1744–1814) and George Mason (1725–1792)—who refused to sign the Constitution because they objected to the powers it granted to the federal government.

EDMUND RANDOLPH, AUGUST 30, 1787, GLC 819.18

Objections to the Constitution as far as it has advanced

1st No privilege is given to the House of Representatives, which by the way are too few, in disposition of money; by way of counterbalance to the permanent condition of the Senate in the circumstances of duration, power, & smallness of number.

2d The expulsion of members of the Legislature is not sufficiently checked.

3d The inequality of voices in the Senate is too great.

4th The power of raising armies is too unlimited

5th The sweeping clause absorbs everything almost by constitution.

6th No restriction is made on a Navigation Act and certain regulations of Commerce.

7th The Executive is one.

8th The power of pardon is unlimited.

9th The appointment of officials will produce too great influence in the Executive

10th The jurisdiction of the Judiciary will swallow up the Judiciaries of the States.

11th Duties on exports are forbidden but with the approval of the General Legislature of the U.S.

FUGITIVE SLAVES AND THE CONSTITUTION

21 / "Any person bound to service...[who] shall flee"

The most controversial issues discussed at the Constitutional Convention involved slavery. Among the matters the convention debated was whether states were obligated to return runaway slaves; whether slaves would count in apportioning representation or taxation; whether Congress had the power to abolish or regulate the slave trade from Africa or the West Indies or to regulate the interstate slave trade; and whether Congress had the right to prohibit slavery in the western territories. In the end, the northern delegates' commitment to union proved to be greater than any commitment to weaken slavery.

Pierce Butler of South Carolina proposed that states be required to return fugitive slaves. The provision was adopted without debate, in part because the northern delegates feared that fugitives might create an unemployment problem in the North.

PIERCE BUTLER, GLC 819.17

Wheresoever any person bound to service or labour in any state shall flee into another state, he shall not be thereby discharged from such service or labor: but the legislatures of the several states shall make provision for the recovery of such person[.]

A PROSLAVERY DOCUMENT?

22 / "Mr. L[uther] Martin proposed...to allow a prohibition or tax on the importation of slaves"

During the decades preceding the Civil War, abolitionists bitterly debated whether the Constitution was a proslavery or an antislavery document. Some opponents of slavery, such as William Lloyd Garrison (1805–79), attacked the Constitution as a proslavery document on the grounds that it guaranteed that Congress could not interfere with the African slave trade until 1808; failed to recognize free blacks as citizens; provided for the return of fugitive slaves; and counted slaves as three-fifths of white persons in apportioning representation and taxation, and therefore augmented southern strength in the House of Representatives.

Other abolitionists, however, maintained that the Constitution had strong antislavery implications. They pointed to the provision that stated that Congress could not regulate the slave trade until 1808. They argued that this provision gave Congress the power to prohibit the movement of slaves into the territories or new states and after 1808 into the original states. Further, the Constitution did not bar *states* from closing off the slave trade. Portions of the Constitutional Convention discussion over the slave trade follow.

MAX FARRAND, ED., *The Records of the Federal Convention of 1787*

Slave Imports

[August 21] Mr. L[uther]. Martin [of Maryland] proposed to vary article 7, sect. 4 so as to allow a prohibition or tax on the importation of slaves. First, as five slaves are to be counted as three freemen in the apportionment of representatives, such a clause would leave an encouragement to this traffic. Second, slaves [through danger of insurrection] weakened one part of the Union, which the other parts were bound to protect; the privilege of importing them was therefore unreasonable. Third it was inconsistent with the principles of the Revolution, and dishonorable to the American character, to have such a feature in the Constitution.

Mr. [John] Rutledge [of South Carolina] did not see how the importation could be encouraged by this section [as now phrased]. He was not apprehensive of insurrections, and would readily exempt other states from the obligation to protect the Southern states against them. Religion and humanity had nothing to do with this question. Interest alone is the governing principle with nations. The true question at present is whether the Southern states shall or shall not be parties to the Union. If the Northern states consult their interest, they will not oppose the increase of slaves, which will increase the commodities of which they will become the carriers.

Mr. [Oliver] Ellsworth [of Connecticut] was for leaving the clause as it stands. Let every state import what it pleases. The morality or wisdom of slavery are considerations belonging to the states themselves. What enriches a part enriches the whole, and the states are the best judges of their particular interest. The old Confederation had not meddled with this point, and he did not see any greater necessity for bringing it within the policy of the new one.

Mr. [Charles C.] Pinckney [of] South Carolina can never receive the plan if it prohibits the slave trade. In every proposed extension of the powers of Congress, that state has expressly and watchfully excepted that of meddling with the importation of Negroes. If the states be all left at liberty on this subject, South Carolina may perhaps, by degrees, do of herself what is wished, as Virginia and Maryland already have done....

Mr. [Roger] Sherman [of Connecticut] was for leaving the clause as it stands. He disapproved of the slave trade; yet, as the states were now possessed of the right to import slaves, as the public good did not require it to be taken from them, and as it was expedient to have as few objections as possible to the proposed scheme of government, he thought it best to leave the matter as we find it. He observed that the abolition of slavery seemed to be going on in the United States, and that the good sense of the several states would probably by degrees complete it....

Col. [George] Mason [of Virginia]. This infernal trade originated in the avarice of British merchants. The British government constantly checked the attempts of Virginia to put a stop to it. The present question concerns not the importing states alone, but the whole Union.... Maryland and Virginia, he said, had already prohibited the importation of slaves expressly. North Carolina had done the same in substance. All this would be in vain if South Carolina and Georgia be at liberty to import. The Western people are already calling out for slaves for their new lands, and will fill that country with slaves, if they can be got through South Carolina and Georgia. Slavery discourages arts and manufactures. The poor despise labor when performed by slaves. They prevent the immigration of whites, who really enrich and strengthen a country. They produce the most pernicious effect on manners. Every master of slaves is born a petty tyrant. They bring the judgment of Heaven on a country. As nations cannot be rewarded or punished in the next world, they must be in this. By an inevitable chain of causes and effects, Providence punishes national sins by national calamities. He lamented that some of our Eastern [northeastern] brethren had, from a lust of gain, embarked in this nefarious traffic.... He held it essential, in every point of view, that the general government should have power to prevent the increase of slavery.

Mr. Ellsworth [of Connecticut], as he had never owned a slave, could not judge of the effects of slavery on character. He said, however, that if it was to be considered in a moral light, we ought to go further, and free those already in the country. As slaves also multiply so fast in Virginia and Maryland that it is cheaper to raise than import them, whilst in the sickly rice swamps foreign supplies are necessary, if we go no further than is urged, we shall be unjust towards South Carolina and Georgia. Let us not intermeddle. As population increases, poor laborers will be so plenty as to render slaves useless. Slavery, in time, will not be a speck in our country....

Gen. [Charles C.] Pinckney [of South Carolina] declared it to be his firm opinion that if himself and all his colleagues were to sign the Constitution, and use their personal influence, it would be of no avail towards obtaining the assent of their constituents [to a slave-trade prohibition]. South Carolina and Georgia cannot do without slaves. As to Virginia, she will gain by stopping the importations. Her slaves will rise in value, and she has more than she wants. It would be unequal to require South Carolina and Georgia to confederate on such unequal terms.... He contended that the importation of slaves would be for the interest of the whole Union. The more slaves, the more produce to employ the carrying trade; the more consumption also; and the more of this, the more revenue for the common treasury. He admitted it to be reasonable that slaves should be duried like other imports; but should consider a rejection of the clause as an exclusion of South Carolina from the Union.

Max Farrand, ed., *The Records of the Federal Convention of 1787* (New Haven: Yale University Press, 1911), Vol. II, pp. 364–5, 369–72.

RATIFICATION DEBATES

The question of whether the proposed Constitution was consistent with republican government dominated the ratification debates. The Constitution's critics, who are known as the Anti-Federalists, objected to the new framework of government on several grounds. Some feared that unless senators and representatives were barred from reelection, they would become a corrupt, entrenched oligarchy. Others worried that it would be impossible for two distinct governments—a federal government and state governments—to operate simultaneously over the same territory.

The Anti-Federalists were a disparate group. They included prominent leaders such as Samuel Adams (1722–1803) and Patrick Henry (1736–99) who feared that the Constitution lacked sufficient safeguards to protect the rights of individuals and the states. There were also many ordinary farmers, small shopkeepers, and artisans who feared giving the federal government authority over taxes and commerce. Convinced that republicanism depended on government close to the people, such individuals worried that the Constitution transferred control of local affairs to a remote central government, a government that would be controlled by elites. This was an argument easily exploited by local elites who feared any dwarfing of their own power.

Many concerns were voiced during the ratification debates, including such matters as the length of terms of senators and the president and the danger of a federally controlled military. But the issue that prompted the most concern was the absence of a written Bill of Rights. In Massachusetts, New York, and Virginia, opposition to the proposed Constitution was particularly significant. But because the framers ultimately agreed to add a Bill of Rights, which was actually adopted during the first Congress in 1791, the United States never developed the kind of ongoing anti-constitution tradition that would be found in other countries, such as France.

23 / "To expect...unanimity in points of so great magnitude... was contrary to all experience"

Writing two weeks after the convention of 1787 adopted the Constitution, Benjamin Rush (1746–1813), a signer of the Declaration of Independence and the new nation's leading physician, described the Constitution as a "masterpiece of human wisdom. I now look forward to a golden age in America," he wrote. "The new Constitution realizes every hope of the patriot & rewards every toil of the hero." His only misgiving was that he wished the convention "had gone further, & absorbed more of the power of our State governments."

In the following letter to James Madison, the "Father of the Constitution," the Virginia jurist Edmund Pendleton (1721–1803) offers a careful and candid appraisal of the new Constitution, examining whether it conforms to republican principles of government.

EDMUND PENDLETON, OCTOBER 8, 1787, TO JAMES MADISON, GLC 99.132

To expect individual or even state unanimity in points of so great magnitude and difficulty, was contrary to all experience, and to maintain one's opinion by all the arguments which reason and mental powers afford, is manly & becoming whilst the subject is in agitation & suspense; but to yield to the decision of a majority, when further opposition can have no good, & may produce many bad effects, is not only commendable, but in my opinion an individual duty....

I have read the paper [a critique of the Constitution] with great attention, but without the aid of any judicious friend to confer with; however I mean to trouble you with my thoughts upon it, as they occur, which, tho' I do not flatter myself with a thought that they will be useful to you, will be doing on my part what you seem to have expected, when you did me the honour of sending it.

I began to read it with two impressions on my mind, with which I think every reader of it should set out. 1st. That something was necessary to be done, and that a plan, very far short of perfection, was greatly preferable to our present condition, and which would probably have been considered as desperate, if the Convention had risen without doing anything. 2nd. That in Governments as well as other things, perfection is unattainable, and indeed attempts to approach it, by too much refinement, generally produce more mischief than good. I recollect the very sensible observations of Sir William Temple "That none was ever perfect, or free from very many & just exceptions.... An absolute monarchy ruins the people; one limited endangers the Prince; an aristocracy is subject to emulations of the great, and oppression of the poor; and a democracy to popular tumults & convulsions." His conclusion is "A perfect scheme of government seems as endless and as useless a search as that of the universal medicine or the Philosopher's stone." And mine is that all which human wisdom is capable of on this great occasion is to adopt the form most likely to coincide with the genius of the people to be governed; to preserve the great outlines and fundamentals of that form, and avoid, as far as may be, the natural infirmities, which experience has probed to be annexed to it.

A Republic was inevitably the American form, and its natural danger popular tumults & convulsions. With these in view I read over the Constitution accurately and do not find a trait of any violation of the great principles of the form, all power being derived mediately or immediately from the people; no titles or powers that are either hereditary or of long duration so as to become inveterate.... The people, the origin of power by representation—the [members of the House of Representatives]...are to consist of their immediate choice, and the choice of the Federal Senate and President, seems admirably contrived to prevent popular tumults, as well to preserve the equilibrium expected from balancing power of the three branches. In the power of negation [the President's veto power, which can be overridden by two-thirds vote of both houses of Congress] to the laws, the modification strikes out a happy balance between an absolute negative in a single person, and having no stop & cheque upon laws too hastily passed....

The President is indeed to be a great man, but 'tis only to represent the Federal dignity & power, having no latent prerogatives, any powers but such as are defined & given him by law. He is to be Commander in Chief of the Army & Navy, but Congress are to raise & pay them, and that not for above two years at a time. He is to nominate officers, but Congress must first create the offices & fix them and may discontinue them at pleasure, & he must have the consent of 2/3ds of the Senate to his nomination. Above all his tenure of office is short, & the danger of impeachment a powerful restraint against abuse of office. A political head and that adorned with powder'd hair, seem necessary & useful in government...; and I have observed in the history of the United Netherlands, their affairs always succeeded best, when they allowed their [official] to exercise his Constitutional powers.

I was struck with the objection to the Senate having been made an Executive Council, since having a participation in two branches, they influence laws for recreating unnecessary offices, or giving extravagant salaries to those necessary, & then fill them up with themselves, their families or dependents & thought it best to have the three branches kept wholly distinct from each other, and as an executive council was necessary, I cast about for their formation, & though they might be found in the numbers voted for President, but when I considered that the objection has not force but in the case of a general corruption pervading the whole Legislative & Executive bodies, and that on such a supposition it would admit of no remedy, and what was afforded by new elections or by recurring to revolutionary principles; that in the House of Representatives, as well as the incapacity of members of either House to be appointed to offices created whilst they are members, there are considerable cheques on the Senate; and above all as the considerable expense of this separate Council is saved (and I am more afraid of expense than fraud) I became reconciled to the mode, as an evil which did not admit of a remedy, that would not introduce a greater evil.

The like objection occurs to the Senate's being made the triers upon impeachments, and they therein participate in the judicial powers, and it may be added that in case of impeachment of the President for mal-conduct by their advice, they will be a strange tribunal to judge of it; at the same time it will be objected to as borrowed from the British form and approximating too nearly to the obnoxious power of the Lords. Tho' I do not see any material reason for having taken this trial out of the judiciary course, yet it is really not so exceptional as it at first appears. The mode of prosecution as generally practiced, is not a favorite with me, being generally the engine of party contentions for office, and no matter how seldom practiced. It is in the hands of the House of Representatives, who will not use it in the case supposed, or if they do, and meet the obstruction, may yet resort to the Courts of Justice, as an acquittal would not bar that remedy—the assimilation to the power of the Lords, is too futile to merit notice.

The line between Federal and State powers, the most difficult part of the work, appears to me most happily drawn, and I much applaud that spirit of amity and concession which produced, and which I hope may continue to perfect it. In the regulations of commerce however, I shall hope not to see projects introduced for discouraging foreign trade, or driving us too soon into manufactures, in favor of which our presses have groaned under labour'd nonsense in the course of this summer. Trade & manufactures should both be free, and will make their way in proper time.

The restrictions of paper emissions & unjust tender laws are alone of value sufficient to outweigh all objections to the system. In the exclusive right of coining, I foresee great risque & expense in conveying bullion & money between the seat of Congress & the remote states, over balancing the Federal revenue, which seems the only reason for confining it. When Congress fixed the proportion of alloy, the value of the coin, and other regulations to prevent counterfeits, might not the states have been trusted with coining subject to those rules?

In art. 2 Clause 5th are these words "Nor shall vessels bound *to* or *from* one state, be *obliged* to *enter clear* or pay *duties* in another," which do not appear sufficiently explicit. If it was intended to allow a free trade between the states without entry, clearance or duty, (which does not seem to be meant, tho' the words may bear that construction) will it not tend to defeat all regulations of commerce & revenue? If, as I supposed, it was intended to reach the cases only of casually touching at a state port they were not bound to, or passing through one state to get to their ports in another, (as the vessels of Maryland do thro' ours in navigating Chesapeake) there appears to want words of restriction from trading added to the exemption.

My last criticism you will probably laugh at, tho' it is really a serious one with me. Why require an oath from public officers, and yet interdict all religious tests, their only sanction? Those hitherto adopted have been narrow & illiberal, because designed to preserve established modes of worship; but since a belief of a future state of rewards & punishments, can alone give conscientious obligation to observe an oath, it would seem that test should be required or oaths abolished.

It is time I had done with my trifling observation, with which & a thousand others more material, you had been sufficiently tried at Phil[adelphi]a, I will only add my warmest thanks as an individual to the authors of the work of their labours, & declare my unequivocal acceptance of it, with all it's imperfections.

24 / "We are at the Eve of a Bankruptcy"

In the following document, William Blount (1749–1800), a member of the Constitutional Convention who later served as a U.S. senator from Tennessee, describes the precarious state of the Union in order to convince the North Carolina General Assembly of the necessity of ratifying the new Constitution.

William Blount, December 15, 1787, to the General Assembly of North Carolina, GLC 4842.03

We received the commands of the...General Assembly...to lay before you...the present state and circumstances of the Union.... To describe the present state and circumstances of the Union we may declare in one word that we are at the Eve of a Bankruptcy and of a total dissolution of Government. Since the close of the war there has not been paid into the general Treasury as much money as was necessary for one years interest of the domestic and foreign debt and Congress have been reduced to the dreadful alternative of borrowing principal to pay interest. Our efforts at home to this end were ineffectual. Abroad where we were not known and, where enthusiasm for liberty has enrolled us among the most deserving of mankind, we were more successful. The deception cannot much longer be kept up and unless something can be done before the close of the ensuing year we must cease to be a unified government. Our friends must give us up and we shall become a laughing stock to our enemies. The annual requisitions are so partially attend[ed] to by states that our foreign and domestic embarrassments have accumulated beyond the possibility of being retrieved by other means than the punctual compliance on the part of the States.... The sale of the western land has gone and will go a great way in discharge of our domestic debut. But our foreign debt is increasing and the best way of judging of the probability of soon discharging of it is by our own exertions; in five years we have made one payment something less than forty thousand dollars....

25 / *"We must insist that the Continental Constitution contain a Bill of Rights"*

At the town meeting of Townshend, Massachusetts, Daniel Adams opposed ratification of the Constitution on the grounds that it lacked a Bill of Rights and failed to provide for support of organized religion. Massachusetts ultimately ratified the Constitution in February 1788.

DANIEL ADAMS, DECEMBER 31, 1787, GLC 799

In the Bill of Rights for this Commonwealth it is declared that the happiness of the people & the Preservation of civil government depend upon the piety religion & morality & that the people have a right to invest their Legislature with power to require that provision be made for the public worship of God & the support of protestant teachers & require the attendance of people upon such worship instructions....We must insist that the Continental Constitution contain a Bill of Rights which...shall secure to us our privileges especially our religion.

26 / *"There never was a time when the public Interest required more attention"*

Massachusetts agreed to ratify the Constitution only after receiving assurances that a Bill of Rights would be added to the document. In this speech, Governor John Hancock (1737–93) urges the Massachusetts legislature to ensure that this promise is kept.

JOHN HANCOCK, CA. 1788, DRAFT OF ADDRESS TO MASSACHUSETTS LEGISLATURE AFTER RATIFICATION OF THE CONSTITUTION, GLC 1559

There never was a time when the public Interest required more attention or greater abilities than the present, the first impression of Laws under the Government of the United States will have a strong and lasting influence, those parts of the Constitution which are now vague and indefinite will receive an interpretation from those acts and great Exertions will be required to place the Commerce of the Southern and Northern States upon a proper degree of equality & reciprocity of advantage....

I submit to your Consideration whether you will instruct your Senators and Representatives to attend to the obtaining Amendments in the Constitution of the United States.

You will recollect that when that System was ratified by the Convention of this Commonwealth it was done on the idea that Amendments should be finally effected. The people have well grounded expectations that this important matter will be attended to; for my own part I wish the world to know that *I was sincere* in the part I took on the Subject. I had not, nor will I have any other than plain, open, & undisguised politicks.

I should dread as a great Calamity a new general Convention upon this Business. The forms of Government has pointed out an easy method to procure alterations as

Congress may propose to the Legislatures such Amendment as appear to be necessary, and in this way there can be no hazard, but another Convention might amount to a dissolution of the Government. I feel obliged therefore to urge you to give our Senators and Representatives such positive instructions on this Subject as may look to the peace, security and tranquility of the Union.

27 / "The property, the ability, and the virtue of the State, are almost solely in favor of the constitution"

In this letter to Washington, General Henry Knox discusses the nature of the Constitution's supporters and opponents.

HENRY KNOX, FEBRUARY 10, 1788, TO GEORGE WASHINGTON, GLC 2437

The constitution has labored in Massachusetts exceedingly more than was expected. The opposition has not arisen from a consideration of the merits or demerits of the thing itself, as a political machine, but from a deadly principle levelled at the existence of all government whatever. The principle of insurgency expanded, deriving fresh strength and life from the impunity with which the rebellion of last year was suffered to escape. It is a singular circumstance, that in Massachusetts the property, the ability, and the virtue of the State, are almost solely in favor of the constitution. Opposed to it are the late insurgents, and all those who abetted their designs, constituting four fifths of the opposition. A few, very few indeed, well meaning people are joined to them. The friends of the constitution in that State, without overrating their own importance, conceived that the decision of Massachusetts would most probably settle the fate of the proposition. They therefore proceeded most cautiously and wisely, debated every objection with the most guarded good nature and candor, but took no questions on the several paragraphs, and thereby prevented the establishment of parties. This conduct has been attended with the most beneficial consequences. It is now no secret, that, on the opening of the convention, a majority were prejudiced against it.

28 / "Very extensive Petitions will be laid...against the new Constitution"

After Pennsylvania ratified the Constitution, critics inundated the state assembly with petitions demanding that the vote of the ratification convention be overturned. In Carlisle, Pennsylvania, and several other towns, the Constitution's opponents staged riots, raising the specter of armed insurrection. Walter Stewart (1756?–96), a brigadier general in the Continental Army during the Revolution, discusses opposition to the Constitution in the state and notes that Massachusetts had ratified the Constitution two weeks earlier, in part because of promises that a Bill of Rights would be appended to the document.

WALTER STEWART, FEBRUARY 20, 1788, TO GENERAL WILLIAM IRVINE, A PENNSYLVANIA DELEGATE TO THE CONTINENTAL CONGRESS, GLC 4844

Yesterday our Assembly were to meet and I suppose they will be able to make a House next week. It is expected by the Anti-Federal Party that very extensive Petitions will be laid before them against the new Constitution. I however think they have abated very much in their Warmth since they see Massachusetts have come into it.... And they at last say they think amendments will probably be made. I sincerely hope they will, as it would be a means of reconciling all Party's, and enable us to carry it through; Without them, the opposition will be so powerful as to clog its execution in too great a degree....

I much fear matters will be carried to great lengths against the people concern'd in the riot at Carlisle. I have spoken to many on the subject, some of whom think it would be best to bury the whole in oblivion, whilst others fear the people then might conceive it a want of ability in Government to punish the offenders thus letting the prosecution drop.

29 / *"Congratulations on the acceptance of the new constitution by the State of Massachusetts"*

During the ratification debates, the Constitution's proponents stressed the document's democratic and republican character. Even though the framers had expressed concern during their deliberations over the dangers of democracy and demagoguery, they knew that ratification would fail if the new plan of government was perceived as "aristocratic." In the following letter to Henry Knox, his Revolutionary War comrade-in-arms, George Washington discusses the ratification debates.

George Washington, March 3, 1788, to Henry Knox, GLC 5638

...Congratulations on the acceptance of the new constitution by the State of Massachusetts. Had this been done...by a larger majority, the stroke would have been more severely felt by the antifederalists in other States. As it is, it operates as a damper to their hopes, and is a matter of disappointment and chagrin to them all.

Under the circumstances enumerated in your letters, the favorable decision, which has taken place in that State, could hardly have been expected. Nothing less than the good sense, sound reasoning, moderation, and temper of the supporters of the measure could have carried the question. It will be very influential on the equivocal States. In the two, which are next to convene, New Hampshire and Maryland, there can be no doubt of its adoption, and in South Carolina but little, which will make nine States without a dissentient. The force of this argument is hardly to be resisted by local sophistry. Candor and prudence, therefore, it is to be hoped will prevail; and yet I believe there are some characters among us, who would hazard everything rather than cease their opposition, or leave to the operation of the government the chance of proving the fallacy of their predictions, by which their sagacity and foresight might be impeached.

From the last European intelligence, the political state of affairs in France seems to be in a delicate situation. What will be the issue is not easy to determine; but the spirit, which is diffusing itself, may produce changes in that government, which a few years ago could hardly have been dreamt of.

THE NEW REPUBLIC

30 / *"Feelings not unlike those of a culprit...going to the place of his execution"*

The United States was the first nation in history to institute a periodic national census. Since 1790, the country has tried to count each person every ten years. Taking the nation's first census was an extraordinarily difficult task. The nation's sheer physical

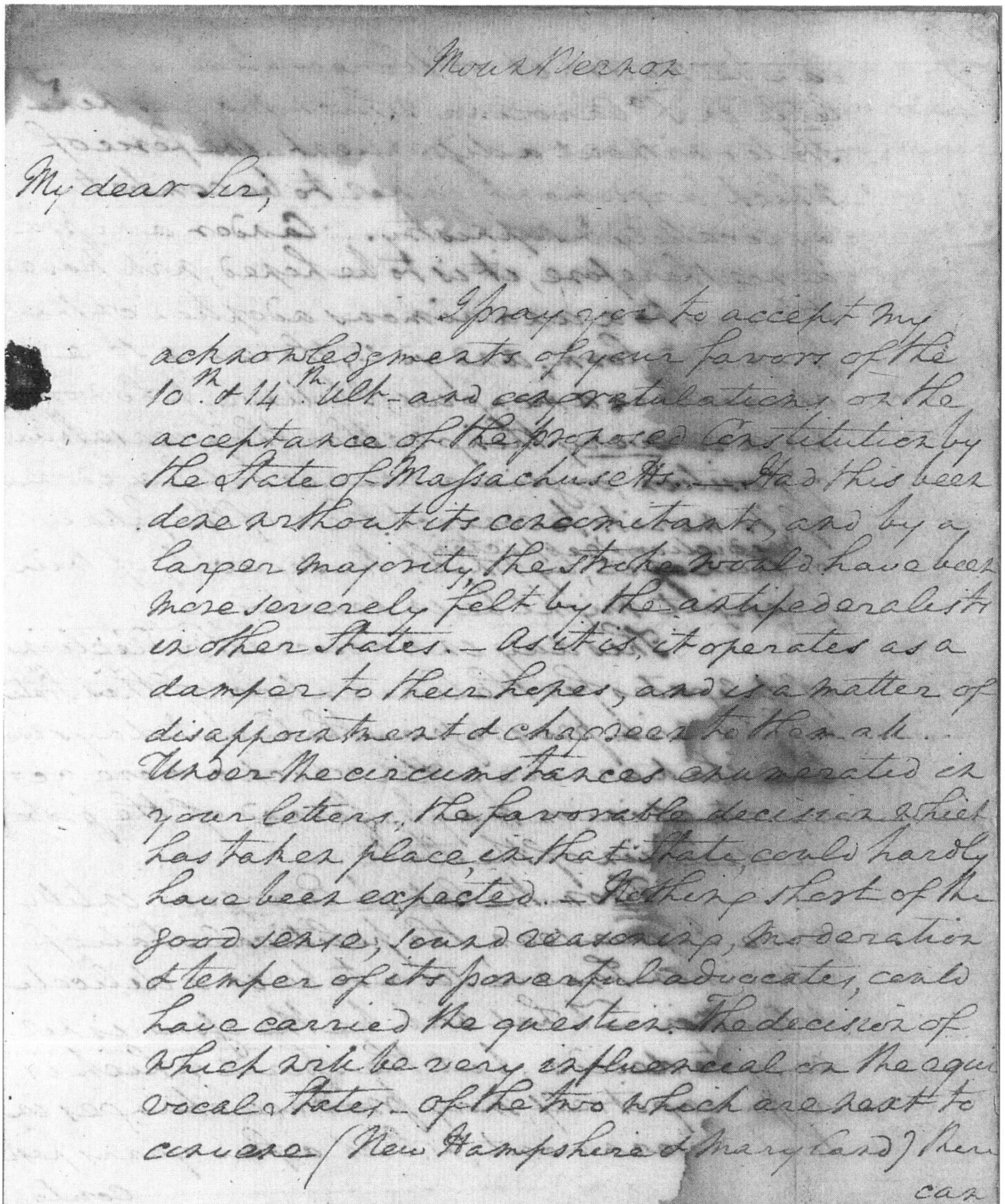

Mount Vernon

My dear Sir,

I pray you to accept my acknowledgments of your favors of the 10th & 14th Ult—and congratulations on the acceptance of the proposed Constitution by the State of Massachusetts.—Had this been done without its concomitants, and by a larger majority, the stroke would have been more severely felt by the antifederalists in other States.—As it is, it operates as a damper to their hopes, and is a matter of disappointment & chagreen to them all.—Under the circumstances enumerated in your letters, the favorable decision which has taken place in that State, could hardly have been expected.—Nothing short of the good sense, sound reasoning, moderation & temper of its powerful advocates, could have carried the question. The decision of which will be very influencial on the equivocal States.—Of the two which are next to convene (New Hampshire & Maryland) there can

George Washington. Autograph letter signed, to Henry Knox, 1788/03/03. The Gilder Lehrman Collection, on deposit at the Pierpont Morgan Library. GLC 5638

size—867,980 square miles—made it difficult to conduct an accurate count. The first census counted 3,929,214 people, about half in the northern states, half in the South. The population was only about a quarter of England's and a sixth of France's size. But it was growing extraordinarily rapidly. Just an estimated 1.17 million in 1750, it would pass 5 million by 1800.

The 1790 census revealed a nation that was still overwhelmingly rural in character. Only two cities (Philadelphia and New York) had more than 25,000 residents each and only 200,000 people lived in the 24 towns and cities with at least 2500 inhabitants. But the urban population, while small, was growing extremely rapidly, especially in the West, where towns like Cincinnati and Louisville were mushrooming in size.

In 1790 most Americans still lived on or near the Atlantic coast. The geographic center of population was on Maryland's Eastern Shore, just a few miles from the ocean. Nevertheless, the West was the most rapidly growing part of the nation. During the 1790s the population of Kentucky and Tennessee increased nearly 300 percent, and by 1800, Kentucky had more people than 5 of the original 13 states.

The 1790s was in many respects the nation's formative decade—economically as well as politically. In 1789, when the new government was launched, there were fewer than 100 newspapers in the country, just 3 banks, and 3 insurance companies. Over the next 10 years American society made tremendous economic advances. Ten times as many corporations, banks, and transportation companies were chartered in the 1790s as in the 1780s. The value of exports climbed from $29 million to $107 million; cotton production rose from 3,000 bales to 73,000 bales. The number of patents issued increased from just three in 1790 to 44 in 1800. The first mechanized factories were built in the country during the 1790s, producing everything from firearms and nails to umbrellas and hats.

Just as he was about to assume office as President, Washington, who longed to return to agricultural pursuits, sent this note to his friend General Henry Knox.

George Washington, April 1, 1789, to Henry Knox, GLC 2437

> My movements to the chair of Government will be accompanied with feelings not unlike those of a culprit who is going to the place of his execution, so unwilling am I, in the evening of a life nearly consumed in public cares to quit a peaceful abode for an ocean of difficulties.

31 / *"We are too poor for Monarchy, too wise for despotism, too... selfish & extravagant for Republicanism"*

The United States was, apart from the Netherlands, the first modern nation to achieve independence as a result of a revolution against colonial rule. Although many colonies in the nineteenth and twentieth centuries followed the United States' example, few were as successful in subsequent economic and political development. Even the United States, however, struggled to establish itself in its first decade under the Constitution.

One problem was to consolidate support among the American people. In 1790 two states, North Carolina and Rhode Island, continued to support the Articles of Confederation. Citizens of Vermont threatened to join Canada.

The new nation also faced severe economic and foreign policy problems. A huge debt remained from the Revolution, and paper money issued during the war was virtually worthless. In addition, there were serious foreign threats to the nation's independence. Britain continued to occupy forts in the Old Northwest, and Spain refused to recognize the nation's southern and western boundaries.

Finally, it was uncertain what place, if any, there would be in the new nation for a formal political opposition. In 1789 there was little acceptance of the idea of a legitimate political opposition organized into a formal party. During the 1790s and early 1800s many groups, including western frontier settlers and prominent New Englanders, threatened to secede from the Union. Commitment to civil liberties and freedom of the press were limited. A question that haunted the new nation was whether it was possible for a stable, republican government to survive.

In this letter, Mercy Otis Warren (1728–1814), sister of the prominent Massachuetts patriot James Otis and herself an important early American historian and writer, assesses the new government's prospects.

Mercy Otis Warren, September 20, 1789, to Catharine Macaulay, GLC 1800.04

It is time we have a government established & Washington at its head. But we are too poor for Monarchy, too wise for despotism, too dissipated selfish & extravagant for Republicanism. It ill becomes an infant government when the foreign & domestic [arrangements] are large & the [finances] small to begin its [government] in all the splendor of Royalty. Should trade be blocked, manufacturing checked, the spirit of agriculture dispersed, & the people almost deprived of the means of subsistence to [meet]...the payment of exorbitant salaries—in order to support the dignity of officers & keep up the ostentatious pomp for which the ambitious have sighed from the moment of the ratification of the articles of confederation. The *computations* may appear small to an ancient monarchy and powerful nation, but the estimated amount began already to cost [so much] that they [the people] are up in arms....

But I leave America to wait the success of her bold experience, and [reflect] a moment with you at the [progressing] revolution in France. Would it not be surprising if that nation should [show] a greater advantage from the spirit of liberty diffused through the continent than the Americans may be able to boast after all their struggle and sacrifice to become a free people. But more of this subject in my next. I dare not yet [be] pessimistic—I only interpret the past and contemplate the probabilities of futility, for so various are the practices, the interests & the principles among us that no human calculation can decide [th]e fate of America.

32 / "Molasses has shipwrecked New England virtue"

The American Revolution bred an exhilarating sense of new possibilities. In the following letter, in which he anticipates the hopes of later abolitionists and temperance (anti-alcohol) reformers, George Clymer (1739–1810), a signer of the Declaration of Independence from Pennsylvania, reveals the extent to which American political leaders viewed government and its taxing authority not merely as an tool for furthering political interests but also as an instrument of soulcraft—a means of moral betterment and character formation. To prevent the nation's republican experiment from unraveling into anarchy, many Americans were convinced that it was necessary to instill within citizens the kind of character, virtue, and moral ideals essential for self-government.

Since rum and molasses were produced by slave labor on West Indian plantations, a tax on alcohol stood out as an antislavery measure.

GEORGE CLYMER, CA. 1789, TO DR. BENJAMIN RUSH, GLC 4769

The impost has not yet taken its complete shape, but enough of it is seen to pronounce upon it, and I am afraid there are some of its features you will not like. Among the expected glories of the Constitution, next to the abolition of Slavery was that of Rum, but molasses has shipwrecked New England virtue and we must look to the day still more distant for the promised blessing—some hope...that a congressional excise will reach the distillations, if not the states must individually defend themselves against the poison.

33 / *"A mortifying consciousness of inferiority"*

Although the American Revolution, unlike the French, the Haitian, the Russian, and the Chinese revolutions, did not result in a root-and-branch transformation of a social order, it did unleash a revolutionary ideology that threw into question many established ideas and customs. One of the Revolution's radical consequences was an emerging consciousness of the disparity between the society's egalitarian ideals and the status of women.

Writing under the pen name "Constantia," Judith Sargent Stevens Murray (1751–1820), the daughter of a wealthy Gloucester, Massachusetts, sea captain and merchant, issued a call in 1790 for equality of the sexes—two years before the pioneering English feminist Mary Wollstonecraft (1759–97) published *A Vindication of the Rights of Woman* (1792). Murray later advocated establishment of female academies not simply to produce "sensible and informed" companions for men but also to prepare young women to support themselves financially.

JUDITH SARGENT STEVENS MURRAY, 1790

Is the needle and kitchen sufficient to employ the operations of a soul...? I should conceive not. Nay, it is a truth that those very departments leave the intelligent principle vacant, and at liberty for speculation. Are we deficient in reason? we can only reason from what we know, and if an opportunity of acquiring knowledge hath been denied us, the inferiority of our sex cannot fairly be deduced from thence...." But our judgment is not so strong—we do not distinguish so well."—Yet it may be questioned, from what doth this superiority...proceed. May we not trace its source in the difference of education, and continued advantages? Will it be said that the judgment of a male of two years old, is more sage than that of a female of the same age? I believe the reverse is generally observed to be true.... How is one [the male] exalted, and the other [the female] depressed, by the contrary modes of education which are adopted! the one is taught to aspire, and the other is early confined and limited.... At length arrived at womanhood, the uncultivated fair one feels a void, which the employments allotted her are by no means capable of filling.... Is she united to a person whose soul nature made equal to her own, education hath set him so far above her, that in those entertainments which are productive of such rational felicity, she is not qualified to accompany him. She experiences a mortifying consciousness of inferiority, which embitters every enjoyment....

Yes, ye lordly, ye haughty sex, our souls are by nature equal to yours; the same breath of God animates, enlivens, and invigorates us....

Judith Sargent Stevens Murray, "On the Equality of the Sexes," *Massachusetts Magazine,* (March and April 1790), pp. 132–35, 223–26.

34 / "The postage of a single letter...amounts almost to a prohibition of communication through the post office"

When President Washington took office, the U.S. government consisted of 75 post offices, a large debt, and an army of just 46 officers and 672 soldiers. There was no federal court system, no navy, no system for collecting taxes, and only the most rudimentary postal service.

To create an efficient postal service—which was essential to promote economic development—Washington appointed Samuel Osgood (1748–1813), of Massachusetts, postmaster general. Osgood, who had been a captain of a company of minutemen at Lexington and Concord, had to carry out his tasks in a single room with two clerks. In this report Osgood discusses the problems and prospects that faced him.

SAMUEL OSGOOD, POSTMASTER'S FIRST REPORT, JANUARY 20, 1790, GLC 1033

In obedience to the orders of the Supreme Executive, I have the honor of laying before you such remarks and observations as have occurred to me, in attending to the department of the post-office....

The existing ordinance for regulating the post-office, though very defective in many things, has not probably ever been put fully in execution; yet the smallness of the revenue arising under the same, may have been the effect of various causes, some of which could not, and others might have been remedied, but not so fully as they may under the present government.

As to the revenue of the post-office, it may be observed, first, that there may be so few letters written, that under the best regulations, it would not amount to any thing considerable; and the dispersed manner of settling the country, may operate powerfully against the productiveness of the post-office....

The amount of revenue will undoubtedly be considerable, if the department is well regulated. If we should form an opinion from a comparative view of the wealth, numbers, and revenue of the post-offices of other countries, it would be, that the post-office of the United States, ought to bring in annually nearly half a million dollars, under similar regulations; whereas the gross receipts in any one year have not exceeded thirty-five thousand dollars; and for the two last years have been at about twenty-five thousand dollars a year....

The great extent of territory over which three millions of people are settled, occasions a great expense in transporting the mail; and it will be found impracticable to accommodate all that wish to be accommodated unless a great proportion of the revenue is given up for this object.

The applications for new post-offices, and new post roads [toll roads], are numerous; cross roads must be established, and of very considerable extent, in order to open a communication with the treasury and revenue officers....

Newspapers, which have hitherto passed free of postage, circulate extensively through the post-offices; one or two cents upon each would probably amount to as much as the expenses of transporting the mail....

The postage of a single letter from Georgia, or rather Savannah, to New-York, is...[thirty-seven cents], which amounts almost to a prohibition of communication through the post-office. If it should be reduced to about fifteen cents, the revenue would not probably be injured by it....

35 / *"The assumption of the debts of the several states... is now under consideration"*

The most pressing problems facing the new government were economic. As a result of the Revolution, the federal government had acquired a huge debt: $54 million, including interest. The states owed another $25 million. Foreign credit was unavailable.

Ten days after Alexander Hamilton (1754–1804) became secretary of the treasury, Congress asked him to report on ways to solve the nation's financial problems. Hamilton immediately realized that he had an opportunity to create a financial program that would embody his political principles. Born in the West Indies, Hamilton never developed the intense loyalty to a state that was common among Americans of the time. He intended to use government fiscal policies to strengthen federal power at the expense of the states and "make it in the immediate interest of the moneyed men to co-operate with government in its support." Such an alliance, in his view, was indispensable for the survival and growth of the United States.

In his "Report on Public Credit," Hamilton proposed that the government assume the entire indebtedness of both the federal government and the states, and retire the old depreciated obligations by borrowing new money at a lower interest rate. This proposal ignited a firestorm of controversy, since the states of Maryland, Pennsylvania, North Carolina, and Virginia had already paid off their war debts and saw no reason why they should be taxed to pay off other states' debts. Others opposed the scheme because it would provide profits to speculators who had bought bonds from Revolutionary War veterans for as little as ten or fifteen cents on the dollar.

For six months, bitter debate raged in Congress, before Hamilton approached Thomas Jefferson with a compromise proposal. In exchange for southern votes on his debt plan, Hamilton promised his support for locating the future national capital on the banks of the Potomac River, the border between two southern states, Maryland and Virginia.

In the following letter Roger Sherman (1721–93), a member of Congress from Connecticut and the author of the Connecticut Compromise at the Constitutional Convention, explains why he supports Hamilton's policy on the debt and outlines the ideal relationship between federal and state governments.

Roger Sherman, March 6, 1790, to Governor Samuel Huntington, GLC 4841

The report of the Secretary [Hamilton] has been under consideration for some time respecting a provision for the national debt. There has been a long debate respecting a discrimination between the Securities in the hands of the original creditors and those which

> have been transferred [i.e., bought up by speculators]—but it was finally decided by a large majority against a discrimination, the motives were that the Securities were by government made transferrable, & payable to the bearer, and therefore the transfer vested the whole property in the purchaser, if there were no fraud or compulsion.... No common market price could be fixed without great inequality & injustice in many instances, and a particular inquiry into the circumstances of every case would be impracticable; besides the public faith had been pledged after the transfers in most of the cases of speculation by issuing new securities to the purchasers in their own names. It was therefore concluded that government could do nothing to impair or alter the contracts consistent with good faith. The assumption of the debts of the several states incurred for the common defense during the late war, is now under consideration. The Secretary of the Treasury has been directed to report what funds can be provided for them in case they should be assumed. His report is contained in one of the enclosed papers. He supposed that sufficient provision may be made for the whole debt, without resorting to direct taxation, if so I think it must be an advantage to all the states, as well as to the creditors. Some have suggested that it will tend to increase the power of the federal government & lessen the importance of the state governments, but I don't see how it can operate in that manner, the constitutions are so framed that the government of the United States & those of the particular states are friendly, & not hostile, to each other, their jurisdictions being distinct, & respecting different objects, & both standing upon the broad basis of the people, will act for *their* benefit in their respective spheres without any interference. And the more strength each have to attain the ends of their Institutions the better for both, and for the people at large.
>
> I have ever been of opinion that the governments of particular States ought to be supported in their full vigour, as the security of the civil & domestic rights of the people more immediately depend on them, that their local interests & customs can be best regulated and supported by their own laws; and the principal advantages of the federal government is to protect the several States in their enjoyment of those rights, against foreign invasion, and to preserve peace, and a beneficial intercourse between each other, and to protect & regulate their commerce with foreign nations.

THE BIRTH OF POLITICAL PARTIES

The framers of the Constitution had not prepared the Constitution with political parties in mind. They associated parties with the corrupt factions that dominated British politics. The founders hoped that the "better sort of citizens," rising above popular self-interest, would debate key issues and reach harmonious consensus regarding how best to legislate for the nation's future. Thomas Jefferson reflected this outlook when he declared in 1789, "If I could not go to heaven but with a party, I would not go there at all."

Despite a belief that parties were evil and that they posed a threat to republican government, leaders in Washington's first administration created the first modern political parties. Divisions first emerged in 1791 over Hamilton's proposals to fund the federal and state debts, to establish a national bank, and to provide government assistance to manufacturing.

On the grounds that Hamilton's fiscal plans threatened his vision of the Republic,

James Madison organized congressional opposition and retained the poet Philip Freneau to edit a newspaper, the *National Gazette*, to warn the populace about Hamilton's designs. Madison and his ally Thomas Jefferson saw in Hamilton's program an effort to establish the kind of patronage society that existed in Britain, with a huge public debt, a standing army, high taxes, and government-subsidized monopolies.

Hamilton responded in kind. He secured John Fenno to publish the *Gazette of the United States*, claiming that his opponents wanted to return the national government to its weak condition under the Articles of Confederation. By 1794 his faction had evolved into the Federalist Party, the first national political party in history capable of nominating candidates, coordinating votes in Congress, staging public meetings, organizing petition campaigns, and disseminating propaganda.

36 / *"[The British] view a war as very possible"*

In this letter, Thomas Jefferson, the nation's first secretary of state, discusses the difficulty of settling unresolved issues with Britain left over from the Revolutionary War. Americans were concerned about two key issues: the evacuation of British forts in the Northwest Territory, and reimbursement for slaves who had been removed from the southern states by Britain during the Revolution. In the fall of 1789 Alexander Hamilton began informal meetings with a representative of Britain, Major George Beckwith, in Québec. In the spring of 1790 President Washington sent Governeur Morris (1752–1816) to England to begin diplomatic negotiations.

The British government acted aloofly toward Morris and did not comply with any of his requests before his departure in September. In early 1790, however, Britain found itself on the verge of war with Spain over conflicting claims in the Pacific Northwest and requested permission for troops to pass through the United States to attack the Spanish possessions of Louisiana and Florida. The situation was ultimately resolved through negotiations, but it made Britain, which was becoming increasingly aware of its diplomatic isolation, realize the importance of establishing good relations with the United States.

Thomas Jefferson, August 12, 1790, to Gouverneur Morris, GLC 4887

Your letter of March 29 to the President of the United States has been duly received. You have placed the proposition of exchanging a Minister {with Britain} on proper ground. It must certainly come from them {from the British ministry} & come in unequivocal form. With those who respect their own dignity so much, ours must not be counted at nought. On their own proposal formally to exchange a minister, we sent them one. They have taken no notice of that and talking agree to exchange one now as if the idea were new. Besides what they are saying to you, they are talking to us thro Quebec; but so informally that they may disavow it when they please. It would only oblige them to make the fortune of the poor Major whom they would pretend to sacrifice. Thro him they talk of a minister, a treaty of commerce *and alliance*. If the object of the latter be honorable, it is useless; if dishonorable, inadmissable. These tamperings prove they view a war as very possible; & some symptoms indicate designs against the Spanish possessions adjoining us. The consequences of their acquiring all the country on our frontier from the St. Croix to the St. Mary's are too obvious to you to need development. You will readily see the dangers which would environ

> [face] us. We wish you therefore to intimate to them that we cannot be indifferent to enterprises of this kind. That we should contemplate a change of neighbors with extreme uneasiness; & that a due balance on our borders is not less desirable to us, than a balance of power in Europe has always appeared to them. We wish to be neutral, and we will be so, *if they will execute the treaty fairly and attempt no conquests adjoining us*. The first condition is just: the 2d imposes no hardship on them. They cannot complain that the other dominions of Spain would be so narrow as not to leave them room enough for conquest.... If the war takes place, we would really wish to be quieted on these two points, offering in return an honorable neutrality. More than this they are not to expect. It will be proper that these ideas be conveyed in delicate and friendly terms; but that they be conveyed if the war takes place; for it is in that case alone, & not till it be begun, that we would wish our disposition to be known. But in no case need they think of our accepting any equivalent for the posts.

37 / *"The expediency of encouraging manufactures in the United States"*

After his debt program was approved, Hamilton's next objective was to create a Bank of the United States, modeled after the Bank of England, to issue currency, collect taxes, hold government securities, regulate the nation's financial system, provide funds in the event of a national emergency, handle government debt payments to foreign and domestic creditors, and make loans to the government and private borrowers. This proposal, like the debt scheme, unleashed a storm of protest.

Critics charged that the bank threatened the nation's republican values by encouraging speculation and corruption. They also contended that the bank was unconstitutional, since the Constitution did not give Congress the power to create a bank. Other grounds for criticism were that the bank would subject America to foreign influences (because foreigners would have to purchase a high proportion of the bank's stock) and give a propertied elite disproportionate influence over the nation's fiscal policies (since private investors would control the bank's board of directors). Despite the bitter opposition of such figures as Jefferson and Madison, Congress succeeded in chartering a Bank of the United States.

The final plank in Hamilton's economic program was a proposal to aid the nation's infant industries. Through high tariffs designed to protect American industry from foreign competition, government bounties and subsidies, and internal improvements of transportation, Hamilton hoped to break Britain's manufacturing hold on America.

The most eloquent opposition to Hamilton's proposals came from Thomas Jefferson, who believed that the growth of manufacturing threatened the values of an agrarian way of life. Hamilton's vision of America's future directly challenged Jefferson's ideal of a nation of farmers communing with nature and maintaining personal freedom by virtue of landownership. Like slaves, Jefferson feared, factory workers would be manipulated by their masters, who would make it impossible for them to think and act as independent citizens.

Although Jefferson and his followers successfully painted Hamilton as an elitist defender of a deferential social order and an admirer of monarchical Britain, in fact Hamilton offered a remarkably modern economic vision based on investment, industry, and expanded commerce. Most strikingly, it was an economic vision with no place for slavery. Before the 1790s, the American economy, North and South, was tied to a transatlantic system of slavery. A member of New York's first antislavery society, Hamilton wanted to reorient the American economy away from slavery and trade with the slave colonies of the Caribbean.

Alexander Hamilton, "Report on Manufactures," 1791, GLC 891

The expediency of encouraging manufactures in the United States, which was not long since deemed very questionable, appears at this time to be pretty generally admitted....

There still are, nevertheless, respectable patrons of opinions, unfriendly to the encouragement of manufactures. The following are, substantially, the arguments, by which these opinions are defended.

"In every country (say those who entertain them) Agriculture is the most beneficial and *productive* object of human industry. This position, generally, if not universally true, applies with peculiar emphasis to the United States, on account of their immense tracts of fertile territory, uninhabited and unimproved....

"To endeavor by the extraordinary patronage of Government, to accelerate the growth of manufactures, is in fact, to endeavor, by force and art, to transfer the natural current of industry, from a more to a less beneficial channel. Whatever has such a tendency must necessarily be unwise. Indeed it can hardly ever be wise in a government, to attempt to give a direction to the industry of its citizens. This under the quicksighted guidance of private interest, will, if left to itself, infallibly find its own way to the most profitable employment....

"If contrary to the natural course of things, an unseasonable and premature spring can be given to certain fabrics, by heavy duties, prohibitions, bounties, or by other forced expedients; this will only be to sacrifice the interests of the community to those of particular classes...."

It ought readily to be conceded, that the cultivation of the earth—as the primary and most certain source of national supply—...has *intrinsically a strong claim to pre-eminence over every other kind of industry*.

But, that it has a title to any thing like an exclusive predilection, in any country, ought to be admitted with great caution....

It might...be observed...that the labour employed in Agriculture is in a great measure periodical and occasional, depending on seasons, liable to various and long intermissions; while that occupied in manufactures is constant and regular, extending through the year....

Manufacturing establishments not only occasion a positive augmentation of the Produce and Revenue of the Society, but...they contribute to rendering them greater than they could possibly be, without such establishments. These circumstances are...additional employment to classes of the community not ordinarily engaged in the business.... The promoting of emigration from foreign Countries.... The furnishing greater scope for the diversity of talents and dispositions which discriminate men from each other.... The creating in some instances a new, and securing in all, a more certain and steady demand for the surplus produce of the soil....

The objections to the pursuit of manufactures in the United States, which next present themselves to discussion, represent an impracticality of success, arising from three causes—scarcity of hands—dearness of labor—want of capital....

With regard to scarcity of hands, the fact itself must be applied with no small qualification to certain parts of the United States. There are large districts, which may be considered as pretty fully peopled....

But there are circumstances...that materially diminish every where the effect of a scarcity of hands. These circumstances are—the great use which can be made of women and children...—the vast extension given by late improvements to the employment of machines, which substituting the Agency of fire and water, has prodigiously lessened the necessity for manual labor....As soon as foreign artists shall be made sensible that the state of things here affords a moral certainty of employment and encouragement—competent numbers of European workmen will transplant themselves, effectually to ensure the success of the design....

The supposed want of Capital for the prosecution of manufactures in the United States is the most indefinite of the objections which are usually opposed to it....

The introduction of Banks....has a powerful tendency to extend the active Capital of a Country. Experience of the Utility of these Institutions is multiplying them in the United States. It is probable that they will be established wherever they can exist with advantage; and wherever, they can be supported, if administered with prudence, they will add new energies to all pecuniary operations.

The aid of foreign Capital may safely, and, with considerable latitude be taken into calculation. Its instrumentality has been long experienced in our external commerce; and it has begun to be felt in various other modes....

There remains to be noticed an objection to the encouragement of manufactures, of a nature different from those which question the probability of success. This is derived from its supposed tendency to give a monopoly of advantages to particular classes at the expense of the rest of the community....

It is not an unreasonable supposition, that measures, which serve to abridge the free competition of foreign Articles, have a tendency to occasion the enhancement of prices...; but the fact does not uniformly correspond with the theory. A reduction of prices has in several instances immediately succeeded the establishment of a domestic manufacture....

But though it were true, that the immediate and certain effect of regulations controlling the competition of foreign with domestic fabrics was an increase of prices, it is universally true, that the contrary is the ultimate effect with every successful manufacture. When a domestic manufacture has attained to perfection, and has engaged in the prosecution of it a competent number of Persons, it invariably becomes cheaper....

There seems to be a moral certainty, that the trade of a country which is both manufacturing and Agricultural will be more lucrative and prosperous, than of a Country, which is, merely Agricultural....

The importation of manufactured supplies seem invariably to drain the merely Agricultural people of their wealth....

Previous to the revolution, the quantity of coin, possessed by the colonies, which now compose the United States, appeared, to be inadequate to their circulation; and their debt to Great Britain was progressive. Since the revolution, the States, in which manufactures have most increased, have recovered fastest from the injuries of the late War, and abound most in pecuniary resources....

It is not uncommon to meet with an opinion that thought the promoting of manufactures may be the interest of a part of the Union, it is contrary to that of another part. The northern & southern regions are sometimes represented as having adverse interests in this respect. Those are called Manufacturing, these Agricultural states; and a species of opposition is imagined to subsist between the Manufacturing and Agricultural interests.

The idea of an opposition between these two interests is the common error of the early periods of every country, but experience gradually dissipates it....

Ideas of a contrariety of interests between the northern and southern regions of the Union, are in the Main as unfounded as they are mischievous. The diversity of Circumstances on which such contrariety is usually predicated, authorizes a directly contrary conclusion. Mutual wants constitute one of the strongest links of political connection....

If the northern and middle states should be the principal scenes of such establishments, they would immediately benefit the more southern, by creating a demand for productions....

38 / *"The contests of European Nations"*

On July 14, 1789, twenty thousand French men and women stormed the Bastille, a hated royal fortress, marking the beginning of the French Revolution. For three years France experimented with a constitutional monarchy. But in 1792 Austria and Prussia invaded France, and French revolutionaries responded by deposing King Louis XVI, placing him on trial, and executing him. A general war erupted in Europe, pitting revolutionary France against a coalition of monarchies, led by Britain. With two brief interruptions, this war lasted twenty-three years.

Many Americans reacted enthusiastically to the overthrow of the king and the creation of a French republic. France appeared to have joined America in a historical struggle against royal absolutism and aristocratic privilege. More cautious gentlemen, however, expressed horror; they viewed the French Revolution as an assault against property and Christianity.

Washington believed that involvement in the European war would weaken the new nation before it firmly established its own independence. The president, however, faced a problem. During the American Revolution, the United States had signed an alliance with France and had won independence as a result of French aid. Washington took the position that while the United States would continue to repay its war debts to France, it would refrain from supporting the French republic. In April 1793 he issued a proclamation of neutrality, stating that the "conduct" of the United States would be "friendly and impartial toward the belligerent parties."

George Washington, March 25, 1793, to Gouverneur Morris (in France), GLC 494

If you, who are at the fountain-head of those great and important transactions, which have lately engrossed the attention of Europe and America, cannot pretend to say what will be their event, surely we, in this distant quarter, should be presumptuous indeed in venturing to predict it. And unwise should we be in the extreme to involve ourselves in the contests of European Nations, where our weight could be but small, tho' the loss to ourselves should be certain. I can however with truth aver, that this country is not guided by such a narrow and mistaken policy, as will lead it to wish the destruction of any nation, under the idea that our importance will be increased in proportion as that of others is lessened. We should rejoice to see every nation enjoying all the advantages that nature & its circumstances would admit, consistent with civil liberty and the rights of other nations. Upon this ground the prosperity of this country would enfold itself every day, and every day it would be growing in political importance.

THE HAITIAN REVOLUTION

39 / *"St. Domingo has expelled all its whites"*

Revolution took on a new meaning when slaves in the French colony of St. Domingue (later Haiti) rose in revolt. The outbreak of the French Revolution led the colony's mulattoes—who were nominally free but deprived of civil rights—to demand full citizenship. In 1791 France granted them citizenship, but the colony's whites then sought to reverse this decision. The mulattoes fomented resistance, and the slaves in the colony's Northern Province rose in mass insurrection, engulfing St. Domingue in race war.

The conflict lasted more than a decade. The whites sought help from the mother country, but found that the new revolutionary government was too busy fighting in Europe to provide much assistance. In 1793 French commissioners proclaimed freedom for the slaves, but upheaval continued. In the later 1790, Pierre-Dominique Toussaint Louverture (1743–1803), a former slave who had long been free and had owned land and slaves himself, succeeded in defeating Spanish, British, and mulatto-French armies. With secret aid from the United States, Toussaint won de facto independence.

In 1801, however, Napoleon (1769–1821) sent a twenty-thousand-man French expeditionary force to Haiti; the force obtained Toussaint's surrender in May 1802. A month later, Toussaint was arrested, transported to France, and imprisoned in a cell in the Jura Mountains, where he died of pneumonia. After his imprisonment by the French, Toussaint declared: "In overthrowing me, you have broken down only the trunk of the tree of liberty for the blacks; it will spring up again from its roots, which are many and deep." Toussaint's prediction proved correct. His successors, aided by guerrilla forces in the mountains and by diseases that enfeebled the French, drove out the rest of the French forces, and in 1804 Jean-Jacques Dessalines declared Haitian independence.

In a note to his daughter, Secretary of State Jefferson reports on the early slave revolt against the French in St. Domingue. Jefferson's claim that all whites had been expelled from Haiti was false. A large British expeditionary force had landed, and many French planters remained.

Thomas Jefferson, December 1, 1793, to Martha Jefferson Randolph

St. Domingo has expelled all its whites, has given freedom to all its blacks and coloured people, and seems now to have taken its ultimate form, and that to which all of the West Indian islands must come.

Thomas Jefferson, December 1, 1793, to Martha Jefferson Randolph, MA 1029 (67).

40 / *"Show no mercy with anyone"*

In the summer of 1802, following Toussaint's imprisonment, rebellion broke out anew in St. Domingue. In the following letter, General Charles Victor Emmanuel LeClerc (1772–1802), the French commander, discusses the problems faced by French troops, but nonetheless speaks confidently of suppressing the revolution. In fact, LeClerc died in November, three months after this letter was written, and in about a year, the Haitians, aided by yellow fever, which devastated the French ranks, defeated the French army.

When the Haitian Revolution ended in 1804, the population had been reduced by half and the economy was in ruins. In one gruesome episode, the French converted a ship, the *Stifler*, into an extermination machine. The French drove blacks into the ship's hold, where they were asphyxiated by noxious fumes.

American responses to the Haitian Revolution shifted radically over time. Under the administration of President John Adams, which was fighting an undeclared naval war with France, the United States signed a treaty with Toussaint, provided his army with arms and provisions, and even transported his troops by sea, allowing the blacks to successfully resist the French and mulatto military. But President Jefferson, who was strongly pro-French and a slaveholder to boot, adopted much more hostile policies toward the Haitian Revolution. He assured the French in 1801 that he would be happy to supply a fleet and help "reduce Toussaint to starvation." He subsequently imposed a total embargo on Haiti.

General Charles Victor Emmanuel LeClerc, August 6, 1802, to Comte de Rochambeau, GLC 4032.00

I have received, Citizen General, your letter with the list of the troubling subjects with which you contend. Show no mercy with anyone that you suspect.... One must be unflinching and inspire great terror; it is the only thing that will suppress the blacks.

General [Antoine] Richepanse has very unwisely reestablished slavery in Guadeloupe. Here and there one sees signs of unrest. A division of boats is addressing the insurrection. Most of the troops of General [Jean-Baptiste] Brunet [who was responsible for Toussaint's arrest] are ill. I have ordered Jacques Dessalines [the black leader who is in a temporary alliance with the French against insurgents] to use the most violent means to frighten the rebels....

Reinforcements have now arrived.... But illness is ravaging the battalion so badly that I am obliged to send almost all back to France....

This insurrection is in its last crisis. By the first month of the revolutionary calendar, with a month of campaigning, all will be over....

Frequently inform me about your position. I need to be informed as often as possible. Use examples of severity to inspire terror.

THE CITIZEN GENET AFFAIR

41 / "You have probably heard of a great misunderstanding between Mr Genet & us"

During 1793 and 1794 a series of explosive controversies divided followers of Hamilton and Jefferson. Washington's administration confronted a French effort to entangle the United States in its war with England, armed rebellion in western Pennsylvania, Indian resistance, and the threat of war with Britain. These controversies intensified party spirit and increased voting along party lines in Congress.

In April 1793, "Citizen" Edmond Charles Genet (1763–1834), a French minister, arrived in the United States and passed out letters authorizing Americans to attack British commercial vessels and Spanish New Orleans. Washington regarded these actions as a clear violation of American neutrality and demanded that France recall its minister. The Genet affair did have an important effect: It intensified party feeling. From Vermont to South Carolina, citizens organized Democratic-Republican clubs to celebrate the triumphs of the French Revolution. Hamilton and his supporters suspected that these societies really existed to stir up grass roots opposition to the Washington administration.

THOMAS JEFFERSON, NOVEMBER 27, 1796, TO THOMAS PINCKNEY, GLC 3730

The [yellow] fever [epidemic] which at that time had given alarm in Philadelphia, became afterward far more destructive than had been apprehended, & continued much longer from the uncommon drought & warmth of the autumn. The 1st day of this month...began the first rains which had fallen for some months. They were copious, & from that moment the...disease terminated most suddenly. The inhabitants who had left the city, are now all returned, & business going on again as briskly as ever....

Our negotiations with the Northwestern Indians have completely failed, so that war must settle our difference. We expected nothing else, & had gone into the negotiations only to prove to all our citizens that peace was unattainable on terms which any one of them would admit.

You have probably heard of a great misunderstanding between Mr Genet & us. On the meeting of Congress it will be made public....We have kept it merely personal, convinced his nation [France] will disapprove him. To them [the French] we have with the utmost assiduity given every proof of inviolate attachment. We wish to hear from you on the subject of M. de la Fayette, tho we know that circumstances [the increasing radicalism of the French Revolution, which put the lives of moderates like Lafayette in danger] do not admit sanguine hopes.

THE WHISKEY REBELLION

42 / "A daring and cruel outrage has been committed"

Political polarization was further intensified by the outbreak of popular protests in western Pennsylvania against Hamilton's financial program. To help fund the nation's debt, Hamilton in 1791 adopted an excise tax on whiskey. On the frontier, because of high transportation costs, the only practical way to sell surplus corn was to distill it into

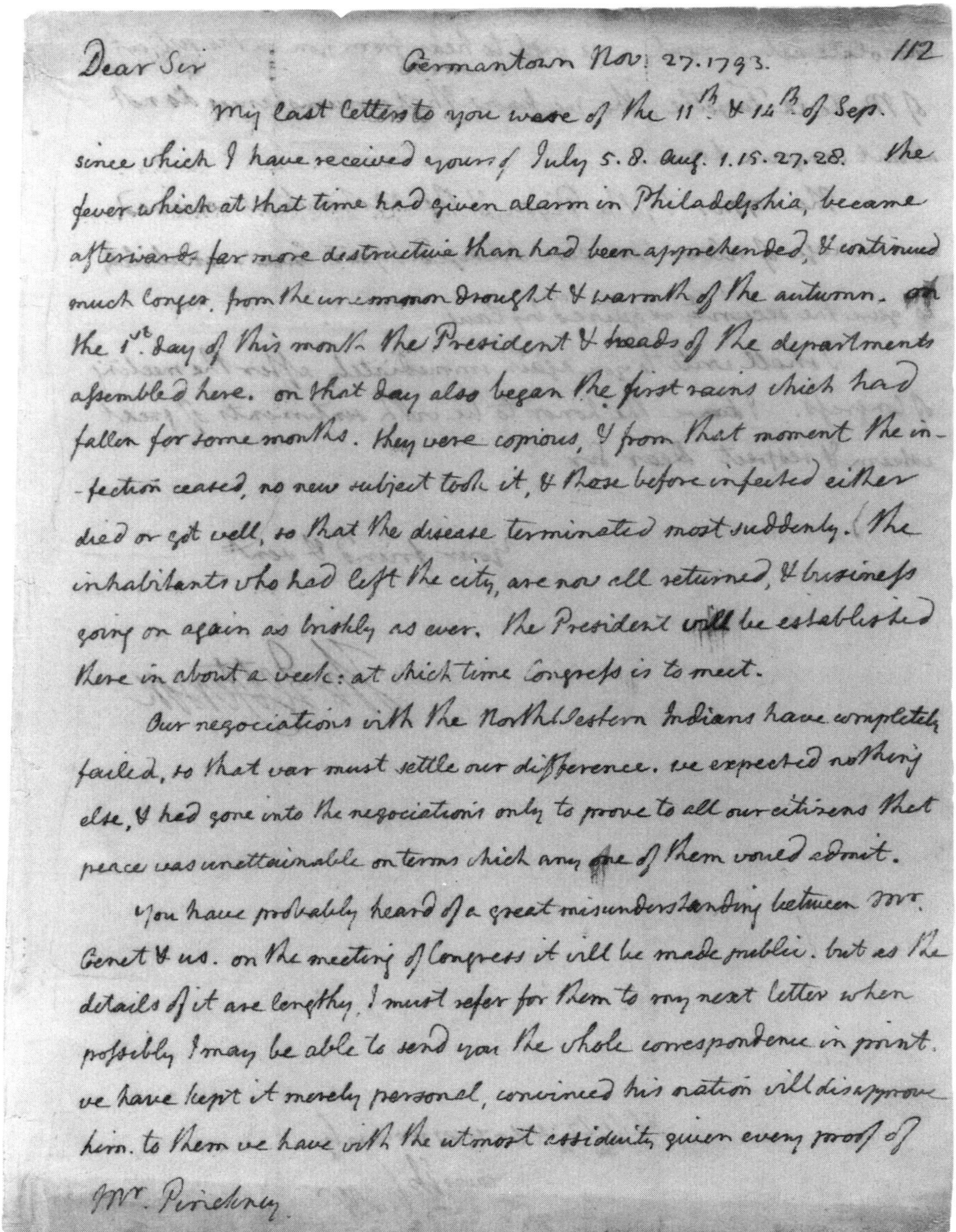
Dear Sir Germantown Nov. 27. 1793. 112

My last letters to you were of the 11th. & 14th. of Sep. since which I have received yours of July 5. 8. Aug. 1. 15. 27. 28. the fever which at that time had given alarm in Philadelphia, became afterwards far more destructive than had been apprehended, & continued much longer, from the uncommon drought & warmth of the autumn. on the 1st. day of this month the President & heads of the departments assembled here. on that day also began the first rains which had fallen for some months. they were copious, & from that moment the infection ceased, no new subject took it, & those before infected either died or got well, so that the disease terminated most suddenly. the inhabitants who had left the city, are now all returned, & business going on again as briskly as ever. the President will be established there in about a week: at which time Congress is to meet.

Our negociations with the NorthWestern Indians have completely failed, so that war must settle our difference. we expected nothing else, & had gone into the negociations only to prove to all our citizens that peace was unattainable on terms which any one of them would admit.

You have probably heard of a great misunderstanding between Mr. Genet & us. on the meeting of Congress it will be made public. but as the details of it are lengthy, I must refer for them to my next letter when possibly I may be able to send you the whole correspondence in print. we have kept it merely personal, convinced his nation will disapprove him. to them we have with the utmost assiduity given every proof of

Mr. Pinckney

Thomas Jefferson. Autograph letter signed, to Thomas Pinckney, 1793/11/27. The Gilder Lehrman Collection, on deposit at the Pierpont Morgan Library. GLC 3730

whiskey. Frontier farmers regarded a tax on whiskey the same way that the colonists had regarded Britain's stamp tax.

By 1794, western Pennsylvanians had had enough. Like the Shays rebels of 1786, they rose up in defense of their property and the right to earn a decent living. Some seven thousand frontier settlers marched on Pittsburgh to stop collection of the tax. Determined to set a precedent for the federal government's authority to enforce laws enacted by Congress, Washington gathered an army of fifteen thousand militiamen to disperse the rebels. In the face of this overwhelming force, the uprising collapsed. Two men were convicted of treason, but later pardoned by the president.

U.S. Congress, July 25, 1794, GLC 981

Gentlemen,

The Governor having received information that a daring and cruel outrage has been committed in the county of Allegheny by a lawless body of armed men, who, among other enormities, attacked and destroyed the house of Gen. Neville on the 17th instant, request, in the most earnest manner, that you will exert all your influence and authority to suppress, within your jurisdiction, so pernicious and unwarrantable a spirit; that you will ascertain, with all possible dispatch, the circumstances of the offence; and that you will pursue, with the utmost vigilance, the lawful steps for bringing the offenders to justice. Every honest Citizen must feel himself personally mortified at the conduct of the rioters, which, particularly if it passes with impunity, is calculated to fix an indelible stigma on the honor and reputation of the state....

43 / *"To resist and prevent the execution of the law...by violence...[is] treason"*

John Barnet was among several Whiskey rebellion participants arrested by federal authorities and tried for treason. His acquittal had profound consequences for the future. As a result of this case, the country adopted a very narrow definition of treason, which was limited to "levying war" against the United States. In the future, treason prosecutions would not be used to silence dissent.

The following selection is drawn from the notes that William Paterson (1745–1806), an associate justice of the U.S. Supreme Court, kept during the trial. Before President Washington named Paterson to the Court, he had served a delegate to the Constitutional Convention and as New Jersey's governor. At the Constitutional Convention, Paterson had introduced the New Jersey Plan, which proposed a federal government consisting of three branches: an executive, a judiciary, and a one-house legislature in which all states would be represented equally.

At the time that Paterson took these notes, he was sitting as a judge on the U.S. Circuit Court of Appeals. Until 1869, U.S. Supreme Court justices also sat as judges on the federal appeals court.

U.S. Supreme Court Associate Justice William Paterson, May 29, 1795, Whiskey Rebellion trial manuscript notes, *U.S. v. John Barnet*, GLC 1114

This brings us to consider the particular case of the p[risone]r at the bar; and to examine how far he was traitorously concerned. The traitorous purpose is a necessary ingredient.

> The mind of the prisoner must be manifested by some overt act, and it is your province, gen[tleme]n, to collect or infer the intention from the testimony laid before you. A person may be present from curiosity or from accident, but if he does not by his conduct indicate a traitorous spirit or intention, he is not to be criminated. If on the other hand it appears, and you are of opinion, that the pris[one]r knew of the object, that it was, to compel the revenue officer by intimidation or force, to resign, to suppress the office of excise, to resist and present the execution of the law, or to procure its repeal by intimidation, by violence, by numbers, by an armed force, and if he willingly embarked and aided in the insurrection, then his guilt rises into treason.

44 / *"Britain has acted unwisely and unjustly"*

For a decade, Britain refused to evacuate forts in the Old Northwest, as promised in the treaty ending the Revolution. Control of those forts impeded white settlement in the Great Lakes region. Frontier settlers believed that British officials at those posts sold firearms to Native Americans, paid money for American scalps, and incited uprisings against white settlers. War appeared imminent when British warships stopped three hundred American ships carrying food to France and France's overseas possessions, seized their cargoes, and forced sailors suspected of deserting from British ships into the British navy. In this letter, the chief justice of the U.S. Supreme Court, John Jay (1745–1829), conveys a sense of how immediate the danger of war seemed.

JOHN JAY, APRIL 9, 1794, TO SALLY JAY, GLC 4011

> The question of war or peace seems to be as much in suspense here [in Philadelphia] as in New York when I left you. I am rather inclined to think that peace will continue, but should not be surprized if war should take place. In the present State of Things it will be back to the ready for the *Latter* Event in *every* Respect....
>
> The aspect of the Times is such, that prudential arrangement calculated on the Prospect of War should not be neglected nor too long postponed. Peace or war appears to me a Question which cannot now be resolved.... There is much Irritation and agitation in this town and in Congress. G. Britain has acted unwisely and unjustly, there is some Danger of our acting intemperately.

45 / *"[Jay's Treaty] excited much uneasiness in the councils of... [the French] government"*

Washington acted decisively to end the crisis with Britain. He sent a three-thousand-troop army under Anthony Wayne (1745–96) to the Ohio country. Wayne's army overwhelmed one thousand Native Americans at the Battle of Fallen Timbers in northwestern Ohio, after destroying every Indian village on their way to the battle. Under the Treaty of Greenville (1795), Native Americans ceded much of the present-day state of Ohio in return for cash and a promise of fair treatment in land dealings.

Washington then sent Chief Justice John Jay (1745–1829) to London to seek a negotiated settlement with the British. Armed with knowledge of Wayne's victory at Fallen Timbers, Jay persuaded Britain to evacuate its forts on American soil. He also got the British negotiators to agree to cease harassing American shipping (provided the ships did not carry contraband to Britain's enemies). In addition, Britain agreed to pay damages for ships it had seized and to permit the United States to trade with western Indians and carry on restricted trade with the West Indies.

Jay failed, however, to win concessions on other American grievances. The treaty said nothing about the British incitement of Native Americans, British searches for deserters on Americans ships, or compensation for slaves carried off by the British during the Revolution.

Debate over Jay's Treaty marked the full emergence of the nation's first party system. Jeffersonian Republicans denounced the treaty as craven submission to British imperial power and a sop to wealthy commercial, shipping, and trading interests. Southerners were particularly vocal in their disapproval because the treaty not only ignored compensation for slaves but also required them to repay prerevolutionary debts owed to British merchants while northern shippers collected damages for ships and cargoes that Britain had seized. In Boston, graffiti appeared on a wall: "Damn John Jay! Damn everyone who won't damn John Jay!! Damn everyone that won't put lights in his windows and sit up all night damning John Jay!!!"

In this letter, James Monroe, who was then serving as American minister to France, observes that Jay's Treaty had produced deep consternation within the French government.

JAMES MONROE, JANUARY 17, 1795, TO JOHN JAY, GLC 4925

English papers were received here containing such accounts of your adjustment with the British administration as excited much uneasiness in the councils of this [the French] government.... At that moment however I was favored with your [letter] of the 25 of Nov[ember] intimating that the contents of the treaty could not be made known until it was ratified, that I might say it contained nothing derogatory to our existing treaties with other powers.... I proceeded therefore to make the best use in my power of the information already given.... I find you consider yourself at liberty to communicate to me the contents of the treaty, and as it is of great importance to our efforts here.... I... resume my original plan of sending a person to you...for that purpose.... [I]n case I should be favored with the communication promised in cypher, it would be impossible for me to comprehend it.... It is necessary however to observe that *as nothing will satisfy this government but a copy of the instrument itself*, and which as our ally it thinks itself *entitled to*, so it will be useless for me to make to it any new communication but short of that.

WASHINGTON'S FAREWELL ADDRESS

46 / *"The immense value of your national Union"*

By 1796 Washington was in a position to retire gracefully. He had avoided war with Britain, pushed the British out of western forts, suppressed Native Americans in the Old Northwest, and opened the Ohio country to white settlement. In a farewell address, published in a Philadelphia newspaper in September 1796, Washington announced his retirement and offered his countrymen "the disinterested warnings of a parting friend." In his address, the president complained bitterly about "the baneful effects of the Spirit of Party" and warned his countrymen against the growth of partisan divisions. In foreign affairs he also warned against long-term alliances. Declaring the "primary interests" of America and Europe to be fundamentally different, he argued that "it is our true policy to steer clear of permanent alliance with any portion of the foreign world."

Among Washington's main themes were the danger that political demagogues would manipulate sectional passions and the importance of subordinating regional interests to the preservation of the Union.

Address of the late General George Washington, September 17, 1796, GLC 2557

...A solicitude for your welfare, which cannot end but with my life...urge me...to offer...the disinterested warnings of a parting friend, who can possibly have no personal motive to bias his counsels....

The Unity of Government which constitutes you one people...is a main Pillar in the Edifice of your real independence...your tranquility at home; your peace abroad.... But as it is easy to foresee, that, from different causes, and from different quarters, much pains will be taken, many artifices employed, to weaken in your minds the conviction of this truth....You should properly estimate the immense value of your national Union to your collective and individual happiness...indignantly frowning upon the first dawning of every attempt to alienate any portion of our Country from the rest, or to enfeeble the sacred ties which now link together the various parts....

The *North*, in an unrestrained intercourse with the *South*...finds in the productions of the latter great additional resources of maritime and commercial enterprise—and precious materials of manufacturing industry.—The *South*, in the same intercourse, benefiting by the agency of the *North*, sees its agriculture grow and its commerce expand....

In contemplating the causes which may disturb our Union, it occurs as a matter of serious concern, that any ground should have been furnished for characterizing parties by *Geographical* discriminations—*Northern* and *Southern*—*Atlantic* and *Western*; whence designing men may endeavor to excite a belief, that there is a real difference of local interests and views....

Towards the preservation of your Government and the permanency of your present happy state, it is requisite, not only that you steadily discountenance irregular oppositions to its acknowledged authority, but also that you resist with care the spirit of innovation upon its principles, however specious the pretexts....

I have already intimated to you the danger of parties in the State, with particular reference to founding them on geographical discriminations. Let me now take a more comprehensive view, and *warn* you, *in the most solemn manner*, against the baneful effects of the Spirit of Party, generally.

This spirit, unfortunately, is inseparable from our nature, having its root in the strongest passions of the human mind. It exists under different shapes, in all governments, more or less stifled, controlled or repressed; but in those of the popular form, it is seen in its greatest rankness, and is truly their *worst enemy*.

The alternate dominion of one faction over another, sharpened by the spirit of revenge, natural to party dissension, which, in different ages and countries, has perpetrated the most horrid enormities, is itself a frightful despotism; but this leads at length to a more formal and permanent despotism. The disorders and miseries which result, gradually incline the minds of men to seek *security and repose* in the absolute power of an Individual....

'T is substantially true, that virtue or morality is a necessary spring of popular government....

Promote, then, as an object of primary importance, institutions for the general diffusion of knowledge. In proportion as the structure of a government gives force to public opinion, it is essentially that public opinion should be enlightened....

Observe good faith and justice towards all Nations. Cultivate peace and harmony with all....

Nothing is more essential than that permanent, inveterate antipathies against particular nations and passionate attachments for others should be excluded.... The Nation, which indulges towards another an habitual hatred or an habitual fondness, is in some degree a slave. It is a slave to its animosity or to its affection, either of which is sufficient to lead it astray from its duty and its interest....

Against the insidious wiles of foreign influence...the jealousy of a free people ought to be *constantly* awake, since history and experience prove that foreign influence is one of the most baneful foes of republic Government....

The great rule of conduct for us, in regard to foreign Nations, is, in extending our commercial relations, to have with them as little *Political* connection as possible....

'T is our true policy to steer clear of permanent alliances, with any portion of the foreign world....

Taking care always to keep ourselves, by suitable establishments, on a respectable defensive posture, we may safely trust to temporary alliances for extraordinary emergencies....

47 / *"Great anxiety prevails...[about] the future President"*

Washington's announcement that he would not seek a third term set the stage for the country's first contested presidential election. The election of 1796 was the first in which voters could choose between two competing parties; it was also the first in which candidates were nominated for vice president. It was a critical test of whether the nation could transfer power through a contested election.

The Federalists chose John Adams, the first vice president, as their presidential candidate, and the Republicans selected Thomas Jefferson. Both parties turned directly to the people, rallying supporters through the use of posters, handbills, and rallies. Republicans portrayed their candidate as "a firm Republican" while they depicted their opponent as "the champion of rank, titles, and hereditary distinctions." Federalists countered by condemning Jefferson as the leader of a "French faction" intent on undermining religion and morality.

In the popular voting, Federalists drew support from New England; Atlantic seaports (including Charleston, South Carolina); commercial, shipping, manufacturing, and banking interests; Congregational and Episcopalian clergy; professionals; and farmers who produced for markets. Republicans attracted votes from the South; backcountry

Baptists, Methodists, and Roman Catholics; small merchants, tradesmen, and artisans; and subsistence farmers.

Adams won the election, despite backstage maneuvering by Alexander Hamilton, who disliked Adams intensely. Hamilton devised a scheme to elect Thomas Pinckney (1750–1828), the Federalist candidate for vice president. Under the electoral system set up by the Constitution, each presidential elector was allowed to vote twice, with the candidate who received the most votes becoming president, while the candidate who came in second was elected vice president. According to Hamilton's plan, southern electors would drop Adams's name from the ballot while still voting for Pinckney, thus electing him president. When New Englanders learned of this plan, they dropped Pinckney from their ballots, ensuring that Adams won the election. When the final votes were tallied, Adams received only three more electoral votes than Jefferson. As a result, Jefferson became vice president.

CHARLES CARROLL, DECEMBER 5, 1796, TO JAMES MCHENRY, GLC 985

It is said upon what foundation I know not neither Adams nor Jefferson will get any votes in S. Carolina. It is confidently assented that Mr. Adams will be elected by a majority of least 3 votes. I have my fears. Should Jefferson be elected or if no election takes place by the Electors, I suppose he will be elected by the present House of Representatives. Great anxiety prevails generally which [man will become] the future President. The friends of the Government dread the election of Jefferson; they fear he will press a very different line of conduct from the present President.... I am confident the great body of the people are attached to the Govern[men]t, approve its measures and wish to remain at peace with all nations.

48 / *"What is more important than a perfect free trade"*

The late eighteenth century was a period of intense anxiety and hope. While the wars of the French Revolution underscored the persistence of bitter national rivalries, there was also a mounting faith that expanded trade and the growth of industry would overcome national differences and usher in an era of peace and prosperity. In this letter to an English correspondent, the inventor Robert Fulton (1765–1815) discusses the economic advantages of free trade, which he regards as a panacea for many of the world's problems. In 1807 Fulton successfully demonstrated the commercial practicality of steam navigation. In that year he sailed a 160-ton side-wheeler, the *Clermont*, 150 miles from New York City to Albany in just thirty-two hours. "Fulton's folly" opened a new era of faster and cheaper water transportation, particularly in the South and the Mississippi River Valley.

ROBERT FULTON, APRIL 14, 1798, GLC 4661.03

I have insisted...that manual labour is true riches, and that there is no true policy but that which tends to multiply the produce of labour, and increase the conveniences of life. I have also asserted that the best means to produce so desirable an effect is by a steady attention to cultivate local advances and encourage home improvements. All this will be better understood on considering the following points. First that all unnecessary war is a waste of manual labor. Second I prove that Foreign oppression and restrictions in trade...are of no advantage to nations but absolutely a loss. It proves that all wars entered for such objects have been unnecessary [and] consequently a waste of manual labour and an injury to society. As a circumstance which is fresh in our memory and well suited to prove the bad application of war or manual labour, I will consider the expense since America [fought for independence from]...England. It is now agreed on all sides that the trade of England has not been diminished by the American independence, nor can it be made to appear that England has lost any one advantage in her commerce by such independence. Consequently the war was unnecessary and millions which it cost England was an actual loss to the nation and burden to the people of at least 6 millions of taxes per year....

From the commencement to the termination of the American War was a space of about 8 years during which time England must have employed in all the departments of War not less than 150 thousand men. This number of Men could with ease construct 2 thousand miles of canal per year at the necessary quantity in about 11 years. Which is not equal to the time spent in the American and present war. It seems almost impossible that an intelligent mind can view this calculation without seeing that home improvement is the real interest of nations and that a free trade will be the consequence of such systems of industry....

What is more important than a perfect free trade in the accomplishment of which a mass of evils will be swept away which have created numerous wars and interrupted the tranquility of nations?... I would ask Englishmen what they are to lose by a free trade?... They will gain perpetual peace with foreign nations, and having the superiority of manufactures they will trade to all countries without interruption, and riches will flow into the England in proportion as her manufactures are superior to that of any other country....

Governors who do not direct their reflections to this end are not only ignorant but wicked, sacrificing the public good to an ignorant ambition which produces nothing but misery with the pity or contempt of thinking and rational men.

THE QUASI-WAR WITH FRANCE AND THE XYZ AFFAIR

49 / *"It would be both just and proper to declare the treaty with France to be void"*

A decade after the Constitution was drafted, the United States faced its most serious international crisis: an undeclared naval war with France. In Jay's Treaty, France perceived an American tilt toward England, especially in the provision permitting Britain to seize French goods from American ships in exchange for financial compensation. France retaliated by launching an aggressive campaign against American shipping, particularly in the West Indies, capturing hundreds of vessels flying the U.S. flag.

Adams attempted to negotiate with France, but the French government refused to receive the American envoy and suspended commercial relations. Adams then called Congress into special session. Determined that the United States not be "humiliated," he recommended that Congress arm American merchant ships, fortify harbors, and expand the army and navy. By a single vote the House of Representatives authorized the president to arm American merchant ships but postponed consideration of the other defense measures.

Adams then sent three commissioners to France to negotiate a settlement. French foreign minister Charles Maurice de Talleyrand (1754–1838) continually postponed official negotiations. In the meantime, three of the minister's emissaries (known simply as X, Y, and Z) said that the only way the Americans could see the minister was to pay a bribe of $250,000 and provide France with a $10 million loan! The indignant American commissioners refused. When word of the "XYZ Affair" became known in the United States, it aroused a popular demand for war. The popular slogan was "millions for defense, but not one cent for tribute."

During the winter of 1798, fourteen American warships backed by two hundred armed merchant ships captured eighty French vessels and forced French warships out of American waters. But the president refused to ask Congress for an official declaration of war. This is why this conflict is known as the quasi-war. In this selection John Jay, now the governor of New York, reflects on the country's tangled relations with France.

In 1800, after seven months of negotiations, diplomats worked out an agreement known as the Convention of 1800. The agreement freed the United States from its alliance with France; in exchange, America forgave $20 million in damages caused by France's illegal seizure of American merchant ships during the 1790s.

John Jay, June 25, 1798, GLC 2528.02

In my opinion it would be both just and proper to declare the treaty with France to be void—but I think it would be more advisable to direct reprisals than to declare war at *present*, for the public mind does not appear to me to be quite prepared for it.... The Jacobin [radical French] leaders will continue to persuade their deluded followers that the [U.S.] Government is chargeable not only with precipitation but with a *desire* to prevent an accommodation which they effect to believe practicable, notwithstanding the treatment of our envoys....

Whenever the mass of our people are convinced that the war would be just, necessary, and *unavoidable*, they will be content that it should be declared, and will support it vigorously, but I doubt whether that conviction however well founded, is as yet so prevailing and general as it ought to be, and as it would be but for the arts practiced to retard and prevent it. To me there seems to be reason to apprehend that there are characters to whom revolution and confiscation would not be disagreeable. Nothing should be omitted to frustrate their endeavors to deceive—everything should be done to inform the People and assist them to see Things as they are. Mr. [Elbridge] Gerry's remaining in France [continuing to negotiate with the French government] is an unfortunate circumstance, it tends to prolong vain hopes—and to cherish old divisions and to create new ones. He was doubtless actuated by the best intentions, but I think he committed a mistake. If both Houses [of Congress] should concur in opinion that a Declaration of War would be *seasonable*, I hope the minority against it, may not be so considerable as to give countenance to a contrary opinion.

50 / *"A profest Democrat...will leave nothing unattempted to overturn the Government of this Country"*

Washington writes to James McHenry (1753–1816), his former secretary of war (and Adams's then current war secretary) to express his concern about the integrity of the army about to be raised in preparation for a possible war with France in the wake of the

XYZ Affair. The letter contains one of Washington's most outspoken statements of distrust of the Democratic-Republican Societies, which had arisen in support of the French Revolution and which the former president had already blamed for inciting the Whiskey Rebellion in 1794. Adams offered Washington command of the provisional army being raised in event of war with France. At first the former president refused the post, but McHenry ultimately persuaded him to accept the appointment.

In this letter, the former president expresses hostility toward the Republicans and supports the Alien and Sedition Acts, an attempt by the Federalist-controlled Congress to suppress political opposition and stamp out sympathy for revolutionary France. These acts gave the president the power to imprison or deport foreigners believed to be dangerous to the United States and made it a crime to attack the government with "false, scandalous, or malicious statements." While the Alien and Sedition Acts represent a low point in the history of American civil liberties, Washington's anger toward the Republicans was in many respects well founded: The Jeffersonians were extraordinarily naive and idealistic in their dealings with Revolutionary France and the Napoleonic regime that was just emerging.

George Washington, September 30, 1798, to Secretary of War James McHenry, GLC 581

I have lately received information, which, in my opinion, merits attention. The brawlers against Government measures, in some of the most discontented parts of this state, have, all of a sudden become silent, and, it is added, are very desirous of obtaining Commissions in the army about to be raised.

This information did not fail to leave an impression upon my mind at the time I received it; but it has acquired strength from a publication I have lately seen in one of the Maryland Gazettes.... The motives ascribed to them are, that in such a situation they would endeavor to divide, & contaminate the army, by artful & seditious discourses, and perhaps at a critical moment, bring on confusion. What weight to give to these conjectures you can judge of, as well as I. But as there will be characters enough of an opposite description, who are ready to receive appointments, circumspection is necessary; for my opinion of the first are, that you could as soon scrub the blackamoor white, as to change the principles of a profest Democrat; and that he will leave nothing unattempted to overturn the Government of this Country. Finding the resentment of the People at the conduct of France too strong to be resisted, they have, in appearance, adopted their sentiments; and pretend that, not withstanding the misconduct of Government have brought it upon us, yet, if an Invasion should take place, it will be found that *they* will be among the first to defend it. This is their story at all Elections, and Election meetings, and told in many instances with effect.

51 / "Liberty without limit...is the worst kind of tyranny"

The Alien and Sedition Acts were so broadly written that hundreds of foreign refugees fled to Europe fearing detention. It was the Sedition Act, which sought to suppress criticism of the government, that produced the greatest fear within the Republican opposition. Federalist prosecutors secured indictments against twenty-five people, mainly Republican editors and printers. Ten people were convicted, one a Republican representative from Vermont.

The most notorious use of the law took place in July 1798. Luther Baldwin, the pilot of a garbage scow, was arrested in a Newark, New Jersey, tavern, on charges of criminal sedition. While cannons roared to celebrate a presidential visit to the city, Baldwin said "that he did not care if they fired through [the president's] arse." For his drunken remark, Baldwin was locked up for two months and fined.

Republicans accused the Federalists of conspiring to subvert fundamental liberties. In Virginia, the state legislature adopted a resolution written by James Madison declaring that states had the right to determine the constitutionality of federal laws and that the Alien and Sedition Acts were unconstitutional. Kentucky's state legislature went farther, adopting a resolution written by Thomas Jefferson that held that the acts were "void and of no force." The Kentucky resolution raised an issue that would grow increasingly important in the years before the Civil War: Did states have the right to declare acts of Congress null and void?

In this charge to the grand juries in Pennsylvania's fifth district, Alexander Addison (1759–1807), president of Pennsylvania's county courts, defends the Sedition Act, arguing that it was necessary to restrain demagoguery.

ALEXANDER ADDISON, PRESIDENT OF FIFTH CIRCUIT OF THE STATE OF PENNSYLVANIA, JANUARY 1799, GLC 4072

It is of the utmost importance to a free people that the full limits of their rights be well ascertained and preserved; for liberty without limit is licentiousness, it is the worst kind of tyranny....

Reputation, character, good name or opinion is a kind of property or possession, which every man who has honestly acquired it, has a right to enjoy. Like any other possession or property, it cannot be taken away from us but by our own act. And not only individuals but especially men in public [offices]...have a right, for the sake of the benefits we receive from them, to reputation, good name and opinion....

The exercise of those faculties of opinion...[must] be limited, so that it never...represent[s] a solemn truth or exercise of religion as false or ridiculous, an established and useful principle or form of government as odious and detestable; a regular or salutary act or motive of the authorities as unlawful [or] pernicious...; or an upright man as corrupt.

The principles of liberty, therefore, the rights of Men, require, that our right of communicating information, as to facts and opinions, be so restrained, as not to infringe the right of reputation.

52 / *"Folly begets folly"*

The following letter by Jefferson offer insights into how a key American political leader and thinker viewed the critical events taking place across the seas: Napoleon's rise to power and the global war between France and Britain. Note the way Jefferson links his domestic concerns about a standing army, a large debt, and suppression of dissent to his assessment of the British-French struggles in Europe and Asia. Despite Napoleon's actions in Egypt, Jefferson sympathizes with the French as fellow republicans. Although he knows about the XYZ Affair, when French officials requested bribes before negotiating with American diplomats, Jefferson sees the flexibility of Minister Talleyrand in a positive light.

THOMAS JEFFERSON, JANUARY 21, 1799, TO JOHN EPPES, HIS SON-IN-LAW, GLC 148

...The additional army to be raised (about 9000 men) will add 2 1/2 millions, & the additional navy proposed by the Secretary 3 millions, so that when they are complete there will be wanting for annual expenses 4 1/2 millions of dollars to be raised by new taxes to which add half a million nearly for the interest of the new loan. The existing taxes are 2 1/2 dollar a head on a population of four millions. With the future they will be 3 3/4 D[ollars] a head. We are now reading [Elbridge] Gerry's communication of what passed between him & Talleyrand after the departure of his colleagues. They show the most anxious desire & earnest endeavors of that government to prevent a breach with us, and Gerry gives it explicitly as his opinion that a just treaty could have been obtained from them [the French] at any time before his departure.... They have opened a loan for money to raise the army & build the navy of 5 millions at 8 percent. So it is that folly begets folly. Every newspaper kills Buonaparte in a different form but the news of London, Vienna & Constantinople is merely fabricated to keep up the spirits of their own people. The last rational accounts from Buonaparte, showed him in a very firm position. I do not believe he was destined to proceed further than Egypt. The London accounts of Irish affairs are thought equally fabulous [Here, Jefferson refers to reports that a French army was about to land in Ireland.]

53 / "Let [the Jeffersonians] set up a broomstick, and call it a true son of Liberty...and it will command their votes in toto!"

In this letter to his former personal secretary, written just five months before his death, former president Washington expresses his concern that the French government was interfering in domestic American politics. He also rejects Federalist pleas that he come out of retirement and run for the presidency in 1800. The growth of partisanship in American politics meant that an individual candidate's character and reputation no longer mattered. If he were nominated for the presidency, Washington was "thoroughly convinced" that he "should draw not a *single* vote from the anti-Federal side."

Early in the morning of December 13, 1799, Washington woke his wife, complaining of severe pains. Over the course of that day and the next, doctors arrived and attempted to ease Washington's pain by applying blisters, administering purges, and bloodletting—removing perhaps four pints of his blood. Medical historians generally agree that Washington needed a tracheotomy (a surgical operation into the air passage), but this was too new a procedure to be risked on the former president, who died on December 14.

During the early weeks of 1800, every city in the United States commemorated the death of the former leader. In Boston, business was suspended, cannons roared, bells pealed, and six thousand people—a fifth of the city's population—stood in the streets to express their last respects for the fallen general. In Washington, D.C., Richard Henry Lee delivered the most famous eulogy. He described George Washington as "first in war, first in peace, and first in the hearts of his countrymen."

GEORGE WASHINGTON, JULY 21, 1799, TO GOVERNOR JONATHAN TRUMBULL OF CONNECTICUT, GLC 5787

No well informed and unprejudiced man, who has viewed with attention the conduct of the French Government since the Revolution in that Country, can mistake its objects, or the tendency of the ambitious projects it is pursuing. Yet, strange as it may seem, a party, and a powerful one too, among us, affect to believe that the measures of it are dictated by a principle of self preservation; that the outrages of which the Directory [the governing body in France] are guilty, proceed from dire necessity; that it wishes to be upon the most friendly & amicable terms with the United States; that it will be the fault of the latter if this is not the case; that the defensive measures which this Country has adopted, are necesary & expensive, but have a tendency to produce the evil which, to deprecate, is mere pretence in the Government; because War with France they say, is its wish; that on the Militia shd. rest our security; and that it is time enough to call upon these, when the danger is imminent, & apparent.

With these, and such like ideas, attempted to be inculcated upon the public mind (aided by prejudices not yet eradicated) and with art and sophistry, which regard neither truth nor decency; attacking every character, without respect to persons, Public or Private, who happen to differ from themselves in Politics, I leave you to decide the probability of carrying such an extensive plan of defence as you have suggested in your last letter, into operation; and in the short period which you supposed may be allowed to accomplish it in.

I come now, my dear Sir, to pay particular attention to that part of your Letter which respects myself....

Let that party [the Jeffersonian Republicans] set up a broomstick, and call it a true son of Liberty, a Democrat, or give it any other epithet that will suit their purpose, and it will command their votes in toto! Will not the Federalists meet, or rather defend their cause on the opposite ground? Surely they must, or they will discover a want of Policy, indicative of weakness & pregnant of mischief, which cannot be admitted. Wherein then would lye the difference between the present Gentlemen in Office, & Myself?

It would be a matter of sore regret to me, if I could believe that a serious thought was turned towards me as his successor; not only as it respects my ardent wishes to pass through the value of life in retirement undisturbed in the remnant of the days I have to sojourn here. Unless called upon to defend my country (which every citizen is bound to do), but on Public ground also; for although I have abundant cause to be thankful for the good health with which I am blessed, yet I am not insensible to my declination in other respects. It would be criminal therefore in me, although it should be the wish of my Countrymen, and I could be elected, to accept an Office under this conviction, which another would discharge with more ability, and this too at a time when I am thoroughly convinced I should not draw a *single* vote from the Antifederal side; and of course, should stand upon no stronger grounds than any other Federal character well supported; & when I should become a mark for the shafts of envenomed malice, and the basest calumny to fire at; when I should be charged not only with irresolution, but with concealed ambition, which wants only an occasion to blaze out, and, in short, with dotage and imbecility.

All this I grant ought to be like dust in the balance, when put in competition with a great public good, when the accomplishment of it is apparent. But as no problem is better defined in my mind than that principle, not men, is now, and will be, the object of contention, and that I could not obtain a *solitary* vote from that Party; that any other respectable Federal character would receive the same suffrages that I should; that at my time of life, (verging towards three score & ten) I should expose myself without rendering any essential service to my Country, or answering the end contemplated; Prudence on my part must arrest any attempt of the well meant, but mistaken views of my friends, to introduce me again into the Chair of Government.

54 / "If Jefferson *and* Burr *come with equal votes...the former ought to be preferred*"

In 1800 the young republic faced another crucial test: whether national leadership could pass peacefully from one political party to another. Once again, the nation faced a choice between John Adams and Thomas Jefferson.

Deep substantive and ideological issues divided the two parties. Federalists feared that Jefferson would reverse all the accomplishments of the preceding twelve years. A Republican president, they thought, would overthrow the Constitution by returning power to the states, dismantling the army and navy, and overturning Hamilton's financial system. The Republicans charged that the Federalists, by creating a large standing army, imposing heavy taxes, and using federal troops and the federal courts to suppress dissent, had shown contempt for the liberties of the American people.

The contest was one of the bitterest in American history. Jefferson's opponents called him an "atheist in religion and a fanatic in politics." They claimed he was a drunkard, an enemy of religion, and the father of numerous mulatto children. Jefferson's supporters called President Adams a warmonger, a spendthrift, and a monarchist who longed to reunite Britain with its former colonies.

The election was extremely close. Because of the three fifths representation of southern slaves, the final outcome hinged on results in New York. Rural New York supported the Federalists, and Republican fortunes therefore depended on voting in New York City. There, Jefferson's running mate, Aaron Burr, created the first modern political organization, complete with ward committees and rallies. Then known as the Tammany Society, this organization would later be known as Tammany Hall. With Burr's help, Republicans won a majority in New York's legislature, which gave the state's twelve electoral votes to Jefferson and Burr.

Jefferson appeared to have won by a margin of eight votes. But a complication arose. Because each Republican elector cast one ballot for Jefferson and one for Burr, the two men received exactly the same number of electoral votes. Under the Constitution, the election was thrown into the Federalist-controlled House of Representatives. Instead of emphatically declaring that he would not accept the presidency, Burr failed to say anything. So Federalists faced a choice: They could elect the hated Jefferson, or they could throw their support to the opportunistic Burr.

In this private letter, Hamilton urges Federalists in the House of Representatives to support Jefferson. Hamilton considers Burr too power-hungry and personally ambitious for public service.

ALEXANDER HAMILTON, DECEMBER 23, 1800, TO HARRISON GRAY OTIS, GLC 496.028

My opinion, after mature reflection, that if *Jefferson* and *Burr* come with equal votes to the House of Representatives, the former ought to be preferred by the Federalists. Mr.

Jefferson is respectably known in Europe—Mr. Burr little and that little not advantageously for a President of the U[nited] States.—Mr. Jefferson is a man of easy fortune.—Mr. Burr, as I believe, is bankrupt beyond redemption unless by some coup at the expense of the public and his habits of expense are such that Wealth he must have at any rate,—Mr. Jefferson is a man of fair character for probity.—Very different ideas are entertained of Mr. Burr by his enemies and what his friends think, you may collect from this anecdote—A lady said to Edward Livingston ironically "I am told Mr Burr will be President. I should like it very well if I had not learned that he is a man without property."—"Let him alone for that," replied Edward,—"If he is President four years, he will remove the objection."—Mr. Jefferson, though too revolutionary in his notions, is yet a lover of liberty and will be desirous of something like orderly Government.—Mr. Burr loves nothing but himself—Thinks of nothing but his own aggrandizement—and will be content with nothing short of permanent power in his own hands.—No compact, that he should make with any passion in his breast except Ambition, could be relied upon by himself.—How then should we be able to rely upon our agreement with him? Mr. Jefferson I suspect will not dare much. Mr. Burr will Dare every thing in the sanguine hope of affecting every thing.

If Mr. Jefferson is likely from predilection for France to draw the country into war on her side—Mr. Burr will endeavor to do it for the sake of creating the means of personal power and wealth.

This portrait is the result of long and attentive observation of a man with whom I am personally well-acquainted and in respect to whose character I have had peculiar opportunity of forming a correct judgment.

By no means, my Dear Sir, let the Federalists be responsible for his Elevation.—In a choice of Evils, let them take the least—Jefferson is in my view less dangerous than Burr.

But we ought—still to seek some advantages from our situation. It may be advisable to make it a ground of exploration with Mr. Jefferson or his confidential friends and the means of obtaining from him some assurances of his future conduct. The three essential points for us to secure is. 1 The continuance of the neutral plan *bona fide* towards the belligerent powers 2 The preservation of the present System of public credit—3 The maintenance & *gradual* increase of our navy. Other matters may be left to take their chance....

55 / *"The votes are even between Jefferson & Burr"*

A lawyer, educator, and mayor of New Haven, Connecticut, for nineteen years, Elizur Goodrich (1761–1849) was a Federalist member of Congress during the critical presidential election of 1800. In the following letter, Goodrich reports on the House of Representatives' protracted efforts to select a president. Jefferson ultimately received the required majority in the House, but not until the thirty-sixth ballot, after Virginia and Pennsylvania had mobilized their state militias and made it clear, in Jefferson's words, "that a legislative usurpation would be resisted by arms."

In his last hours in office in 1801, President John Adams appointed Goodrich collector of the Port of New Haven. The Jeffersonians denounced such "midnight" appointments as a violation of the people's will and promptly removed Goodrich from office.

ELIZUR GOODRICH, JANUARY 1, 1801, TO STEPHEN TWINING, GLC 5754.2

The votes are even between Jefferson & Burr. It will not be a matter of course that Mr. Jefferson be designated, as the probable Man in the minds of the Electors. I apprehend that his majority of States, if he obtains one, will not be very great. Never were men more seriously alarmed than our republican friends. They do not hesitate to say that Mr. Burr is not fit for the office, that it never was their intention.... It is a question of immense importance and ought not to be decided in heat in a passion—or without great deliberation—and as one of them, who are to act on the subject—determining to act on my own best Judgment—to be able to form that opinion correctly. I wish to know what are the impressions of men in general—what say the Democrats—and what are the individual opinions of our respectable federal men. You...will have a good opportunity to learn and I wish you to take a little pain to ascertain the sentiments of some of the Judges, the Bar &c—what say the clergy....

56 / *"Hamilton's schemes to...monopolize power to himself"*

During the 1790s and early 1800s, the United States confronted many of the same problems that have confronted newly independent nations in Africa and Asia in the twentieth century. Like other nations born in anticolonial revolutions, the United States faced severe challenges in building a sound economy, preserving national independence, and providing a place for a legitimate political opposition.

The textbook picture of the past tends to be calm and dispassionate, but in real life, events were confusing and unpredictable. The nation's first two decades under the Constitution were rife with conflict, partisan passion, and threats of disunion and civil war.

In a bitter letter written two years after Vice President Aaron Burr (1756–1836) shot and killed Alexander Hamilton in a duel, former president Adams offers a savage attack on the former treasury secretary's character. Adams draws a comparison between the early years of the new republic and the history of the Roman republic. Adams, like many Americans of the founding generation, believed that the Roman republic, which provided a model for such American institutions as the Senate, had collapsed because of the malevolent designs of scheming men and the public's lack of virtue. He is haunted by a fear that the new American republic is doomed to follow the same fate.

JOHN ADAMS, DECEMBER 4, 1805, TO BENJAMIN RUSH, GLC 747

I am half inclined to be very angry with you for destroying the Anecdotes and Documents you had collected for private Memoirs of the American Revolution. From the Memoirs of Individuals, the true Springs of events and the real motives of actions are to be made known to posterity. The patriots in the history of the world, the best understood, is that of Rome from the time of Marius to the birth of Cicero, and this distinction is entirely owing to Cicero's Letters and Orations. Then we see the true character of the time and the passions of all the actors on the state.... Change the nations and every anecdote will be applicable to us....

The [Roman] triumvirate of Caesar, Pompey and Crassus and the other of Octavius, Anthony and Lapidus, the first formed by Caesar and the last by Octavius, for the purpose of worming themselves into empire...have analogues enough with Hamilton's

I know of no more melancholly Books than Sullys Memoirs and Ciceros Life.

The Triumvirate of Cæsar, Pompey and Crassus, and the other of Octavius Anthony and Lepidus, the first formed by Cæsar and the last by Octavious for the purpose of worming themselves into Empire their Shifts and Turns, their Intrigues and Cabals have Analogy enough with Hamiltons Schemes, to get rid of Washington Adams Jay and Jefferson, and monopolize all Power to him Self. You may introduce Burr and McKean and Clinton into the Speculation if you please, and even Mr Madison. You may pursue the Subject if you think fit— I have not patience for it.

You inquire what passed between W. and Hamilton at York Town? Washington had ordered or was about to order another Officer to take the Command of the Attack upon the Redoubt.— Hamilton flew into a violent Passion and demanded the command of the Party for himself and declared if he had it not, he would expose General Washingtons Conduct in a Pamphlet. Thus you see

Its proper power to hurt each Creature feels
Bulls aim their horns and Asses lift their heels.

Hamiltons Instruments of Offence were Libels, not true Libels according to the New York Doctrine, but Lying Libells.

The Storming of a Redoubt by a Boy, was to be the Coup de Theatre or the Scenery of the Business, to make him afterwards Commander in Chief of the Army and President of Congress, though there is no more qualification for either, in Storming a redoubt, than there would have been in killing a Deer in the Woods. The one proved him a good Partisan the other would have gained him the Reputation of a good Shot: but neither would fit him to command Armies or govern States.

John Adams. Autograph letter signed, to Benjamin Rush, 1805/12/04. p.2. The Gilder Lehrman Collection, on deposit at the Pierpont Morgan Library. GLC 747 schemes to get rid of Washington, Adams, Jay, and Jefferson and monopolize the power to himself.... You inquire what passed between W[ashington] and Hamilton at York Town. Washington had ordered or was about to order another officer to take the command of the attack upon the redoubt. Hamilton flew into a violent passion and demand the command of the party for himself and declared if he had it not, he would expose General Washington's conduct in a pamphlet. Thus you see

Its proper power to hurt each creature feels
Bulls aim their horns and also lift their heels.

Hamilton's instrument of offence were libels, not true libels according to the New York doctrine, but lying libels.

JEFFERSONIAN REPUBLICANISM

Thomas Jefferson's goal as president was to restore the principles of the American Revolution. In his view, a decade of Federalist rule had threatened the nation's republican character. Not only had the Federalists levied oppressive taxes, stretched the provisions of the Constitution, and established a bastion of wealth and special privilege by creating a national bank, they also had subverted civil liberties and expanded the powers of the central government at the expense of the states. A new revolution was necessary, "as real a revolution in the principles of our government as that of 1776 was in its form."

In a letter written in 1810, Jefferson explained why he thought that Federalist measures needed to be reversed. "I have been ever opposed to the party, so falsely called federalists," he wrote, "because I believe them desirous of introducing into our government, authorities hereditary or otherwise independent of the national will. These always consume the public contributions and oppress the people with labour & poverty."

Through his personal conduct and public policies, Jefferson sought to return the country to the principles of republican simplicity, economy, and limited government. To rid the country of aristocratic customs that had prevailed during the administrations of Washington and Adams, he had White House guests shake hands instead of bowing stiffly; he also placed dinner guests at a round table, so that no individual would have a more important seat than any other. Jefferson refused to ride in an elegant coach or host formal dinner parties and balls.

Jefferson believed that presidents should not impose their will on Congress, and consequently he refused to initiate legislation or to veto congressional bills on policy grounds. Convinced that Presidents Washington and Adams had acted like British monarchs by personally appearing before Congress, Jefferson simply sent Congress written messages. Not until the presidency of Woodrow Wilson would another president publicly address Congress and call for legislation.

Jefferson's commitment to republican simplicity was matched by his stress on economy in government. He eliminated taxes on whiskey, houses, and slaves; fired all federal tax collectors; and slashed the army to three thousand soldiers, the navy to six frigates, and foreign embassies to three. His budget cuts allowed him to cut the federal debt by a third, despite the elimination of all internal taxes.

Yet Jefferson did not conceive of government in wholly negative terms. Convinced that ownership of land was the firmest basis of republican government, Jefferson convinced Congress to cut the price of public lands and to extend credit to purchasers to encourage rapid western settlement.

57 / *"The fatal errors which have lost to nations the present hope of liberty"*

After receiving a history of the French Revolution, Jefferson reflects on the meaning and implications of that epochal historical event. During the early 1790s Jefferson had been a strong supporter of the revolution, which he viewed as part of a broader struggle to overthrow monarchical tyranny. In 1793, the year Louis XVI was executed, Jefferson had gone so far as to write that he was willing to see half the earth drenched in blood if this was necessary to bring about human freedom. In retrospect, however, he expresses his misgivings about the revolution's outcome.

Pierre Paganel, the author of *Essai historique et critique sur la Révolution Française* (Paris, 1810), was a member of the Committee of Public Safety and served as secretary to the National Convention. The first edition of his 1810 book was almost completely destroyed by Napoleon's censors. Later, Louis XVII exiled Paganel, who died in 1826, the same year as Jefferson.

THOMAS JEFFERSON, APRIL 15, 1811, TO PIERRE PAGANEL, GLC 4433

I received through Mr Warden the copy of your valuable work on the French revolution, for which I pray you to accept my thanks. That it's sale should have been suppressed is no matter of wonder with me. The friend of liberty is too feelingly manifested, not to give umbrage to its enemies. We read in it, and weep over, the fatal errors which have lost to nations the present hope of liberty, and to reason the fairest prospect of its final triumph over all impostures, civil & religious. The testimony of one who himself was an actor in the scenes he notes, and who knew the true mean between rational liberty, and the frenzies of demagogy, are a tribute of inestimable value. The perusal of this work has given me new views of the causes of failure in a revolution of which I was a witness in its early part, & then augured well of it. I had not means afterwards of observing its progress but the public papers, & their information came thro channels too hostile to claim confidence. An acquaintance with many of the principal characters, & their fate, furnished me grounds for conjectures, some of which you have confirmed, & some corrected. Shall we ever see as free & faithful a tableau of the subsequent acts of this deplorable tragedy? Is reason ever to be amused with the *hochets* [disturbances] of physical sciences, in which she is indulged merely to divert her from solid speculations on the rights of man, and wrongs of his oppressors? It is impossible. The day of deliverance will come, altho' I shall not live to see it. The art of printing secures us against the retrogradation of reason & information, and the examples of its safe & wholesome guidance in government, which will be exhibited thro' the wide spread regions of the American continents, will obliterate in time the impressions left by the abortive experiment of France. With my prayers for the hastening of that auspicious date....

THE JEFFERSONIANS IN POWER

58 / *"The President's inauguration past gave great hopes that he would... council[iate] all parties"*

Beginning in his first day in office, Jefferson sought to demonstrate his administration's commitment to republican principles. At noon, March 1, 1801, clad in clothes of plain cloth, he walked from a nearby boardinghouse to the new U.S. Capitol in Washington, D.C., and took the presidential oath of office. In his inaugural address, he sought to allay fear that he planned a Republican reign of terror. "We are all Republicans," he said, "we are all Federalists." Echoing Washington's Farewell Address, he asked his listeners to set aside partisan and sectional differences. He also laid out the principles that would guide his presidency: a frugal, limited government; reduction of the public debt; respect for states' rights; encouragement of agriculture; and a limited role for government in people's lives.

In the following letter, Elias Boudinot (1740–1821), a leading New Jersey Federalist who had served as president of the Continental Congress, describes the reaction to Jefferson's inaugural address and then comments on recent events in Europe, which hold out the prospects of radical shifts in European power relations. As the letter makes clear, the United States was born during a period of war and revolution, which presented the country with both great opportunities for territorial expansion and grave perils to its political and economic independence.

Elias Boudinot, April 25, 1801, to Jacob Burnet (dated Philadelphia), GLC 5242

We have had little political News—the President's inauguration past gave great hopes that he would pursue such measures, as to council[iate] all parties—but some turnings out & appointments have a little roused the Jealousy of the federalists.... However there seems a prevailing disposition to give the present Administration fair play, and to make no opposition till a full experiment is made.

Great Britain has experienced a great reverse of fortune—Lately she was in league with all the Power of Europe ag[ainst] France—Now all the Power of Europe seem to be leagued ag[ainst] her—The King is again quite insane.—a dreadful scarcity, if not a famine, prevails thru the united Kingdoms. Mr. Pitt has again gained the reins of government, and the Dogs of War are let loose afresh to destroy mankind—France & Spain are invading Portugal, and a deadly stroke at the trade of great Britain, is made by all the northern powers, joined by France and Russia.

Thus it is that the Powers of Europe seem to be overturning, overturning, & will still be overturning till he whose right it is, shall rule....

REPEAL OF THE JUDICIARY ACT OF 1801

When Jefferson took office, not a single Republican served as a federal judge. In Jefferson's view, the Federalists had turned the federal judiciary into a branch of their political party, and intended to use the courts to frustrate Republican plans. The first major political battle of Jefferson's presidency involved an effort to weaken Federalist control of the federal courts.

The specific issue that provoked the president's wrath was the Judiciary Act of 1801, passed by Congress five days before Adams's term as president expired. The law created sixteen new federal judgeships, positions that Adams promptly filled with Federalists. The act also extended jurisdiction of the federal courts over such issues as bankruptcy and land disputes, which were previously the exclusive domain of state courts. Finally, the act reduced the number of U.S. Supreme Court justices effective with the next vacancy, delaying Jefferson's opportunity to name a new Supreme Court justice. Jefferson's supporters in Congress repealed the act in 1802.

JUDICIAL REVIEW

59 / *"To disable the court from deciding constitutional questions"*

When John Marshall (1755–1835) became the nation's fourth chief justice in 1801, the U.S. Supreme Court lacked prestige and public respect. Presidents found it difficult to get people to serve as justices. The Court was considered so insignificant that it held its sessions in a clerk's office in the basement of the Capitol. During the thirty-four years he served as chief justice, John Marshall transformed the Supreme Court into a vigorous third branch of government.

Marshall was born in the foothills of the Virginia's Blue Ridge Mountains in 1755, far from the wealthy tobacco and slave Tidewater region of the state. During the Revolution, he led a company of riflemen and spent the terrible winter of 1777 at Valley Forge. Out of his Revolutionary War experiences he became a staunch nationalist who distrusted state governments, which, he believed, had failed to support the soldiers.

Marshall delivered his first landmark opinion two years after joining the Court. John Adams had appointed a loyal Federalist, William Marbury (1761?–1835), to a judgeship at the very end of his term. Although approved by the Senate, Marbury never received his letter of appointment. When Jefferson became president, Marbury demanded that the new secretary of state, James Madison, issue the commission. Madison refused and Marbury sued, claiming that under Section 13 of the Judiciary Act of 1789, the justices could issue a court order compelling Madison to give him his judgeship.

The case threatened to provoke a direct confrontation between the judiciary and the Republicans. If the Supreme Court ordered Madison to give Marbury the judgeship, the secretary of state was likely to ignore the Court, and Congress might limit the Court's power.

In his opinion in *Marbury* v. *Madison*, Marshall ingeniously expanded the Court's power without directly provoking the Jeffersonians. He conceded Marbury's right to his appointment, but ruled that the Court had no authority to order the secretary of state to act, since the section of the Judiciary Act that gave the Court the power to issue an order was unconstitutional. A landmark in American constitutional history, the decision asserted the power of federal courts to review the constitutionality of federal laws and to invalidate acts of Congress when they are found to conflict with the Constitution. This power, known as judicial review, provides the basis for the important place the U. S. Supreme Court occupies in American life today.

In fact, the Supreme Court did not invalidate another act of Congress for half a century. But the assertion of this power proved enormously controversial. In 1823, Senator Richard M. Johnson (1781–1850) proposed that more than a simple majority of judges must agree in order to declare a law unconstitutional. Here, Justice Marshall responds.

JOHN MARSHALL, DECEMBER 22, 1823, TO HENRY CLAY, GLC 141

That gentleman [Senator Richard M. Johnson], I perceive has moved a resolution requiring a concurrence of more than a majority of all the Judges of the supreme court to decide that a law is repugnant to the constitution....

If Congress should say explicitly that the courts of the Union should never enter into the enquiry concerning the constitutionality of a law, or should dismiss for want of jurisdiction, every case depending on a law deemed by the Court to be unconstitutional, could there be two opinions disputing such an act?....

When we consider the remoteness, the numbers, and the ages of the Judges, we cannot expect that the assemblage of all of them [a unanimous decision]...will be of frequent recurrence. The difficulty of the questions, and other considerations, may often divide those who do attend. To require almost unanimity is to require what cannot often happen, and consequently to disable the court from deciding constitutional questions.

A majority of the court is according to the...common understanding of mankind, as much the court, as the majority of the legislature, is the legislature; and it seems to me that a law requiring more than a majority to make a decision as much counteracts the views of the constitution as an act requiring more than a majority of the legislature to pass a law.

LOUISIANA, EXPANSION, AND DISUNIONIST CONSPIRACIES

60 / *"None but an armed nation can dispense with a standing army"*

In 1795 Spain granted western farmers the right to ship produce down the Mississippi River to New Orleans, where their cargoes of corn, whiskey, and pork were loaded aboard ships bound for the East Coast and foreign ports. In 1800 Spain secretly ceded the Louisiana Territory to France, which closed the port of New Orleans to American farmers. Westerners, left without a port from which to export their goods, exploded with anger. Many demanded war.

The prospect of French control of the Mississippi alarmed Jefferson. Spain held only a weak and tenuous grip on the river, but France was a much stronger power. Jefferson feared the establishment of a French colonial empire in North America, blocking American expansion. The United States appeared to have only two options: diplomacy or war. In response to growing concerns from the western states, Jefferson, with congressional approval, called for the state governors to raise a militia of 80,000 men in preparation for a possible war with France.

THOMAS JEFFERSON, FEBRUARY 2, 1803, GLC 4626

...I take the liberty of urging on you the importance and indispensable necessity of vigorous exertions, on the part of the State Governments, to carry into effect the militia

System adopted by the national legislature, agreeably to the power reserved to the states respectively by the constitution of the United States, and in a manner the best calculated to ensure such a degree of military discipline and knowledge of tactics, as will, under the auspices of a benign providence, render the militia a sure and permanent bulwark of national defence.

None but an armed nation can dispense with a standing army. To keep ours armed & disciplined, is, therefore, at all times, important, but especially so at a moment when rights the most essential to our welfare have been violated, and an infraction of treaty committed without colour or pretext....While, therefore, we are endeavoring, with a considerable degree of confidence, to obtain, by friendly negotiation, a peaceable redress of the injury and effectual provision against its repetition, let us arrange the Strength of the nation, and be ready to do with promptitude and effect whatever a regard to justice and our future security may require.

61 / *"A Governor is placed over us, whom we have not chosen"*

Jefferson sent James Monroe (1758–1831) to France, with instructions to purchase New Orleans and as much as the Gulf Coast as he could for $2 million. Then suddenly circumstances played into American hands. In 1802, French troops seemed to be on the verge of crushing the Haitian Revolution when they were wiped out by mosquitoes carrying yellow fever. "Damn sugar, damn coffee, damn colonies," Napoleon reportedly exclaimed. Without Haiti, the centerpiece of France's American empire, Napoleon had little interest in keeping Louisiana.

Two days after Monroe's arrival, the French finance minister announced that France was willing to sell all of Louisiana, a territory stretching from Canada to the Gulf of Mexico and westward as far as the Rocky Mountains. The negotiators agreed on a price of $15 million. Since the Constitution did not give the president specific authorization to purchase land, Jefferson considered asking for a constitutional amendment. In the end, fearing that Napoleon might change his mind, Jefferson simply sent the agreement to the Senate, which ratified it. In a single stroke, Jefferson doubled the size of the country.

The status of slavery in Louisiana touched off a major debate in Congress. In the treaty of purchase, the federal government recognized the property rights of inhabitants who owned slaves under French and Spanish rule. Congress voted to restrict incoming slaves to the bona-fide property of actual settlers and rejected a motion to limit the bondage of incoming slaves to one year.

The following document expresses the grievances of French settlers in Louisiana after it was annexed by the United States.

PIERRE DERBIGNEY, MEMORIAL PRESENTED BY THE INHABITANTS OF LOUISIANA TO THE CONGRESS OF THE UNITED STATES, WASHINGTON: SAMUEL H. SMITH, 1804, GLC 4571

We the subscribers, Planters, Merchants and other inhabitants of Louisiana respectfully approach the Legislature of the United States with a memorial of our rights, [and] a remonstrance against certain laws which contravene them....

Without any agency in the events which have annexed our country to the United

States, we yet considered them as fortunate, and thought our liberties secured even before we knew the terms of the cession. Persuaded that a free people would acquire territory only to extend the blessings of freedom, that an enlightened nation would never destroy those principles on which its government was founded, and that their Representatives would disdain to become the instruments of oppression, we calculated with certainty that their first act of sovereignty would be a communication of all the blessings they enjoyed.... It was early understood that we were to be American citizens: this satisfied our wishes, it implied every thing we could desire, and filled us with that happiness which arises from the anticipated enjoyment of a right long withheld. We knew that it was impossible to be citizens of the United States without enjoying personal freedom, protection for property, and above all the privileges of free representative government, and did not therefore imagine that we could be deprived of those rights....

With a firm persuasion that these engagements would be soon fulfilled, we passed under your jurisdiction with a joy bordering on enthusiasm.... Even the evils of a military and absolute authority were acquiesced in, because it indicated an eagerness to complete the transfer, and place beyond the reach of accident the union we mutually desired. A single magistrate vested with civil and military, with executive and judiciary powers, upon whose laws we had no check, over whose acts we had no control, and from whose decrees there is no appeal, the sudden suspension of all those forms to which we had been accustomed, the total want of any permanent system to replace them, the introduction of a new language into the administration of justice, the perplexing necessity of using an interpreter for every communication with the officers placed over us, the involuntary errors, of necessity committed by judges, uncertain by what code they are to decide, wavering between the civil and the common law, between the forms of the French, Spanish and American jurisprudence, and with the best intentions unable to expound laws of which they are ignorant...these were not slight inconveniences...but we submitted with resignation....

We pray leave to examine the law for erecting Louisiana.... This act does not "incorporate us in the Union," that it vests us with none of the "Rights," gives us no advances and deprives us of all the "immunities" of American citizens....

A Governor is to be placed over us, whom we have not chosen, whom we do not even know, who may be ignorant of our language, uninformed of our institutions, and who may have no connections with our Country or interest in its welfare.

The Governor is vested with all executive, and almost unlimited legislative power; for the law declares that "by and with the advice and consent of the legislative body he may change, modify and repeal the laws," &c. But this advice and consent will no doubt in all cases be easily procured, from the majority of a council, selected by the President or Governor, and dependent on him for their appointment and continuance in office, or if they should prove refractory, the power of prorogation frees him from any troublesome interference, until a more prudent selection at the end of the year, shall give him a council better suited to his views; the true legislative power then is vested in the Governor alone, the Council operates as a cloak, to conceal the extent of his authority, to screen him from the odium of all unpopular acts, to avoid all responsibility and give us the faint semblance of a representative assembly, with so few of its distinguishing features....

Taxation without representation, an obligation to obey laws, without any voice in their formation, the undue influence of the executive upon legislative proceedings, and a dependent judiciary, formed, we believe, very prominent articles in the list of grievances complained of by the United States, at the commencement of their glorious contest for freedom; the opposition to them, even by force, was deemed meritorious and patriotic, and the rights on which that opposition was founded were termed fundamental, indefeasible, self-evident, and eternal; they formed, as your country then unanimously asserted, the only rational basis on which government could rest....

These were the sentiments of your predecessors, were they wrong?... No, they were not wrong!...

Are truths, then so well founded, so universally acknowledged, inapplicable only to us? Do political axioms on the Atlantic, become problems when transferred to the shores of the Mississippi? or are the unfortunate inhabitants of these regions the only people who are excluded from those equal rights, acknowledged in your Declaration of Independence, repeated in the different state constitutions, and ratified by that, of which we claim to be a member?... Liberty? Self-government? Independence? and a participation in the advantages of the Union? If these were offered to us as the reward of a certain term of patience and submission, though we could not acquiesce in the justice of the procedure, we should have some consolation in our misfortunes; but no manifestation of what awaits us at the expiration of the law, is yet made....

We know not with what view the territory North of the 33d degree has been severed from us....If this division should operate so as to prolong our state of political tutelage, on account of any supposed deficiency of numbers, we cannot but consider it as injurious to our rights, and therefore enumerate it among those points of which we have reason to complain....

There is one subject however extremely interesting to us, in which great care has been taken to prevent any interference even by the Governor and Council, selected by the President himself. The African trade is absolutely prohibited, and severe penalties imposed on a traffic free to all the Atlantic states, who choose to engage in it, and as far as relates to procuring the subjects of it from other states, permitted even in the territory of the Mississippi.

It is not our intention to enter into arguments that have become familiar to every reasoner on this question. We only ask the right of deciding it for ourselves, and of being placed in this aspect on an equal footing with other states. To the necessity of employing African labourers, which arises from climate, and the species of cultivation, pursued in warm latitudes, is added reason in this country peculiar to itself. The banks raised to restrain the waters of the Mississippi can only be kept in repair by those whose natural constitution and habits of labour enable them to resist the combined effects of a deleterious moisture, and a degree of heat intolerable to whites; this labour is great, it requires many hands and it is all important to the very existence of our country....

Another subject...of great moment to us, is the sudden change of language in all the public offices and administration of justice. The great mass of the inhabitants speak nothing but the French: the late government was always careful in their selection of officers, to find men who possessed our language and with whom we could personally communicate...their judicial proceedings were indeed in Spanish; but being carried on altogether by writing, translations were easily made; at present for the slightest communication an interpreter must be procured.... That free communication so necessary to give the Magistrate a knowledge of the people, and to inspire them with confidence in his administration, is by this means totally cut off....

We therefore respectfully pray that so much of the law mentioned above as provides for the temporary government of this country, as divides it into two territories, and prohibits the importation of slaves, be repealed.

62 / *"Saw immense herds of buffalo today"*

To gather information about the geography, natural resources, and people of Louisiana, and to establish territorial claims to the trans-Mississippi West, Jefferson dispatched an expedition, led by his private secretary, Meriwether Lewis (1774–1809), and William Clark (1770–1838), a Virginia-born military officer.

Lewis and Clark led some thirty soldiers and ten civilians on one of history's great adventures. The Lewis and Clark expedition has been likened to the first trip to the moon, except that unlike the astronauts, Lewis and Clark were out of contact with their countrymen for two years. With the assistance of Sacagawea (1787?–1812), a Shoshoni Indian, who served as an interpreter, and Toussaint Charbonneau, a French-Canadian trapper, the expedition traveled up the Missouri River to the Rockies and then on to the Pacific Ocean. The expedition helped establish American claims to the Pacific Northwest and encouraged an expansionist spirit that later became known as "Manifest Destiny."

MERIWETHER LEWIS, 1805, GLC 4051

Tuesday, Mary 14th, 1805

Some fog on the [Missouri] river this morning, which is a very rare occurrence. The country much as it was yesterday with this difference that the bottoms are somewhat wider: passed some high black bluffs. Saw immense herds of buffalo today, also elk deer wolves and antelopes.... Capt. Clark walked on shore and killed a very fine buffalo cow. I felt an inclination to eat some veal and walked on shore and killed a very fine buffalo calf and a large wolf, much the whitest I had seen, it was quite as white as the wool of the common sheep. One of the party wounded a brown bear very badly, but being alone did not think proper to pursue him. In the evening the men...discovered a large brown bear lying in the open grounds about 300 paces from the river, and six of them went out to attack him, all good hunters. They took the advantage of a small eminence which concealed them and got within 40 paces of him unperceived. Two of them reserved their fires as had been previously concerted, the four others fired nearby at the same time and put each his bullet through him, two of the balls passed through the bulk of both lobes of his lungs. In an instant this monster ran at them with open mouth. The two who had reserved their fires discharged their pieces at him as he came towards them. Both of them struck him, one only slightly and the other fortunately broke his shoulder. This however only retarded his motion for a moment. The men unable to reload their guns took to flight, the bear pursued and had very nearly overtaken them before they reached the river. Two of the party betook themselves to a canoe and the others separated and concealed themselves among the willows, reloaded their pieces, each discharged his piece at him as they had an opportunity. They struck him several times again but the guns served only to direct the bear to them. In this manner he pursued the two of them separately so close that they were obliged to throw away their guns and pouches and throw themselves into the river altho' the bank was nearly twenty feet perpendicular. So enraged was this animal that he plunged into the river only a few feet behind the second man he had compelled [to] take refuge in the water, when one of those who still remained on shore shot him through the head and finally killed him. They then took him on shore and butchered him when they found eight balls had passed through him in different directions. The bear being old the flesh was indifferent, they therefore only took the skin and fleece, the latter made us several gallons of oil.

63 / *"I am anxious to see the Progress of Burr's Tryal"*

Anger over the acquisition of Louisiana led some Federalists to consider secession as a last resort to restore their party's former dominance. One group of Federalist congressmen plotted to establish a "Northern Confederacy" that would consist of New Jersey, New York, the New England states, and Canada. Alexander Hamilton repudiated this scheme, and the conspirators turned to Vice President Aaron Burr. In return for Federalist support in his campaign for the governorship of New York, Burr was to swing the state into the confederacy. Burr was badly beaten, in part because of Hamilton's opposition. Incensed, Burr challenged Hamilton to the duel in which the Federalist leader was fatally wounded.

As a result of the duel, Burr was ruined as a politician. New Jersey and New York indicted the vice president on murder charges; the charges were later quashed. The desperate Burr then became involved in a conspiracy for which he would be tried for treason.

In the spring of 1805, Burr and James Wilkinson (1757–1825), the military governor of Louisiana, hatched an adventurous scheme, the exact nature of which remains unknown. The British minister was told that for $500,000 and British naval support, Burr would separate the states and territories west of the Appalachians from the Union and create an empire with himself as head.

In the fall of 1806, when Burr and some 60 conspirators traveled down the Ohio River toward New Orleans, Wilkinson betrayed the former vice president. He sent a letter to Jefferson describing a "deep, dark, wicked, and widespread conspiracy...to seize New Orleans, revolutionize the territory, and carry an expedition against Mexico." Burr fled, but was apprehended and tried for treason, with Chief Justice John Marshall presiding. Under the Constitution, each act of treason must be attested to by two witnesses. The prosecution was unable to meet this strict standard, and Burr was acquitted.

Was Burr guilty of conspiring to separate the West? Probably not. The prosecution's case rested on the unreliable testimony of co-conspirator Wilkinson, who was a spy in the pay of Spain. It appears that Burr was planning an unauthorized military attack on Mexico, then under the control of Spain. The dream of creating an "empire for liberty" appealed to many Americans who feared that a European power might seize Spain's New World colonies unless Americans launched a preemptive strike. Hamilton himself had aspired to raise a huge army to invade and conquer Spanish territories. To the end of his life, Burr denied he had plotted treason against the United States.

In this letter, former president Adams expresses his interest in the outcome of Burr's treason trial.

JOHN ADAMS, SEPTEMBER 1, 1807, TO DR. BENJAMIN RUSH, GLC 4879

I am anxious to see the Progress of Burr's Tryal: not from any Love or hatred I bear the man, for I cannot say that I feel either.... But I think Something must come out of the Tryal, which will strengthen or weaken our Confidence in the General Union. I hope something will appear to determine clearly whether any foreign Power has or has not been tampering with our Union.... [Burr's actions] could be instigated only by his own ambitious avarice or Revenge. But I hope his Innocence will be made to appear, and that he will be fairly acquitted....

SLAVERY AND RACE IN JEFFERSONIAN AMERICA

The most deep-seated contradiction in American history lies in the jarring discrepancy between the American creed, with its emphasis on the inalienable right to freedom, justice, and opportunity for all, and the reality of slavery and racial discrimination. Jefferson himself embodied this contradiction. He hated slavery, yet he freed only eight of his almost two hundred slaves during his lifetime and in his will. He had no apprehensions about whites intermarrying with Indians, but expressed "great aversion" to miscegenation between blacks and whites.

His words in the Declaration of Independence posed a deep ideological challenge to slavery. Yet in his *Notes on the State of Virginia*, he expressed his "suspicions" that African Americans were biologically and intellectually inferior to whites. In one of his most abhorrent phrases, he wrote: "But never yet could I find that a black had uttered a thought above the level of plain narration; never saw even an elementary trait of painting or sculpture. In music they are more generally gifted than the whites."

64 / *"The Abolition of Slavery must be gradual"*

In response to two abolitionists, who had sent him an antislavery pamphlet by a Quaker reformer, Warner Mifflin (1745–98), President Adams expresses his views on slavery, the dangers posed by abolitionists (who at the time were mostly Quakers and unpopular religious radicals), and emancipation. This letter is particularly revealing in what it discloses about Adams's sense of priorities.

In his letter, Adams mistakenly concludes that slavery was an institution in decline. The 1790 census counted almost seven hundred thousand slaves. According to the census of 1800, the year before Adams wrote this letter, that number had grown to almost nine hundred thousand.

JOHN ADAMS, JANUARY 24, 1801, TO GEORGE CHURCHMAN AND JACOB LINDLEY, GLC 921

Although I have never sought popularity by animated Speeches or inflammatory publications against Slavery of the Blacks, my opinion against it has always been known...and never in my life did I own a Slave. The Abolition of Slavery must be gradual and accomplished with much caution and Circumspection. Violent means and measures would produce greater violations of Justice and Humanity than the continuance of the practice. Neither...[of you], I presume, would be willing to venture on exertions which would probably excite Insurrection among the Blacks to rise against their Masters.... There are many other evils in our Country which are growing, (Whereas the practice of slavery is fast diminishing) and threaten to bring punishment on our Land, more immediately than the oppression of the blacks. That Sacred regard to Truth in which you and I were educated, and which is certainly taught and enjoyed from on high seems to be vanishing from among us. A general Dereliction of Education and Government. A general Debauchery as well as dissipation, produced by pestilential philosophical Principles of Epicurus infinitely more than by Shews and theatrical Entertainments. These are in my opinion more serious and threatening Evils, than even the Slavery of the Blacks, hateful as that is.

I might even add that I have been informed that the condition of the common sort of White People in some of the Southern states particularly Virginia, is more oppressed, degraded and miserable than that of the Negroes.... I wish you success in your benevolent Endeavours to relieve the distresses of our fellow Creatures, and shall always be ready to co-operate with you, as far as my means and Opportunities can reasonably be expected to extend.

65 / *"[The slaves in question] are not felons"*

The Haitian Revolution inspired a slave insurrection in Virginia in 1800, known as Gabriel's Rebellion. This event terrified Jefferson.

In this letter to the U.S. minister to Britain, President Jefferson proposes that a group of insurgent slaves be deported to West Africa under the auspices of the Sierra Leone Company, an English abolitionist organization that had established Freetown as a home for former slaves. The slaves were accused of conspiring with Gabriel (1775–1800) to attack Richmond, seize the arsenal, and kill white residents. About thirty of the accused conspirators were executed.

Gabriel's stated basis for the attempted rebellion was the Declaration of Independence, a point that was not lost on its principal author. Tacitly recognizing that slaves could be motivated by the same ideals that had inspired the American colonists to revolt against their British masters, Jefferson told Rufus King to assure the Sierra Leone Company that the rebel slaves were not criminals, but men aspiring for freedom.

Negotiations with the Sierra Leone Company were unsuccessful, and most of the accused conspirators were sold as slaves to Spanish and Portuguese colonies. For Jefferson, Gabriel's Rebellion reinforced his view that race war could be avoided only if emancipation were tied to expatriation—what came to be called colonization.

Thomas Jefferson, July 13, 1802, to Rufus King, MA 1239

[The slaves in question] are not felons, or common malefactors, but persons guilty of what the safety of society, under actual circumstances, obliges us to treat as a crime, but which their feelings may represent in a far different shape. They are such as will be a valuable acquisition to the settlement already existing there, and well calculated to cooperate in the pace of civilization.

66 / *"At no period since the slave-trade was prohibited, have all our citizens abstained from...[this] traffic"*

It is a striking historical irony that some slaveholders were at the forefront of efforts to suppress the African slave trade. While partly reflecting humanitarian motives, efforts to restrict the slave trade also expressed a variety of economic and political interests.

For example, in 1774, the First Continental Congress prohibited the importation of slaves into the United States and banned American participation as a way of asserting the colonists' economic independence and attaching the moral stigma of slavery to Britain. In 1787 South Carolina temporarily prohibited the slave trade to prevent debtors from purchasing slaves rather than repaying creditors. Some Virginians feared that continued imports threatened to reduce their slaves' value and diminish the profitable export of Virginia's surplus slaves to the Deep South and West.

The invention of the cotton gin in 1792 had stimulated demand for slaves to raise short-staple cotton. By 1825, field hands, who brought $500 apiece in 1794, were worth $1,500.

James Madison, who was serving as secretary of state at the time he wrote this letter, regarded the African slave trade as America's original sin, but anticipated horrendous upheavals if slaves were emancipated.

JAMES MADISON, CIRCULAR LETTER RE: ACT TO FURTHER PROTECT AMERICAN SEAMEN, APRIL 9, 1803, GLC 515

> It has unfortunately happened, that at no period since the slave-trade was prohibited, have all our citizens abstained from a traffic, deemed worthy of the anxious solicitude of Congress to restrain, as manifested in the several highly penal laws passed on the subject, and alike discountenanced by the regulations of every state in the Union. Now when peace has turned the attention of several nations of the settlement and extension of their colonies, there is danger of the evil increasing, and I must recommend earnestly to the Consuls, especially to those in America, to exert a steadfast vigilance respecting all such infractions of the laws, which may be attempted and to report them, with due precision, to the Department of State.

67 / *"Every consideration of justice, humanity, and safety, forbids that any more Negroes should be brought into your state"*

Georgia, as we have seen, was the only colony that ever attempted to outlaw slavery. As early as 1750, however, the colony's settlers had acquired slaves despite the efforts of Georgia's trustees and the British government to stop them. Because of Georgia's late start in establishing a plantation economy, there were only thirty-five hundred slaves (out of a total population of ninety-six hundred) in 1760.

Demand for slaves soared during the 1760s and 1770s. Delegates from Georgia vehemently opposed the First Continental Congress's prohibition on slave imports, and by the early and mid-1790s Georgia was the only state still legally importing slaves.

In 1793, however, in response to the Haitian Revolution, Georgia excluded slave imports from the West Indies and Spanish Florida; and in 1798 Georgia prohibited all further slave imports, partly out of a fear of slave revolts.

In 1803 the neighboring state of South Carolina reopened the African slave trade and legally imported some forty thousand African slaves between 1803 and 1808. The state law barred slaves from the West Indies (for fear that they might lead slave revolts) and required slaves imported from other states to be of "good character; and have not been concerned in any insurrection." The decision to reopen the Atlantic slave trade, motivated by the growing demand for cotton after the invention of the cotton gin and the opening of fresh lands for slavery in Louisiana, shocked the nation and produced a move in Congress to abolish the Three-fifths Compromise.

The following letter describes the mounting controversy over slavery. The letter's author, William Few (1748–1828), was a signer of the Constitution from Georgia who moved to New York in 1799. This letter's recipient, Edward Telfair (1735–1807), served several terms as Georgia's governor.

WILLIAM FEW, JUNE 30, 1804, TO EDWARD TELFAIR, GLC 4842.05

...Is there one person of understanding & reflection among you who will not admit that every consideration of justice, humanity, and safety, forbids that any more Negroes should be brought into your state, and yet it is well known that the avarice of your citizens, and the rage for acquiring that property has broke through all legal restrictions, and in violation of law and every principle of policy and expediency they are carrying on that diabolical and injurious traffic, and hastening those evils in their nature most dreadful, which seems to demand every exertion to retard or prevent it. Trust not on your Eastern friends for aid, if you do not enforce righteous measures for your own safety; they will laugh at your calamity and seek for profit by your misfortunes. Already they begin to resist that principle in the Constitution which admits the Negroes of the Southern States to increase the number of Representatives in the Congress of the United States. A motion has been brought forward in the Legislature of Massachusetts to instruct their Members of the Senate...to move for an amendment...so as to apportion the number of Representatives according to the number of free men in the United States....

68 / *"Establish an impregnable rampart of Slaveholding power, under the false batteries of democracy"*

In 1804, Federalist senator Timothy Pickering (1745–1829) called for a constitutional amendment apportioning each state's representation in the House of Representatives solely on the basis of the number of freeman. Such an amendment would have overturned the Three-fifths Compromise and greatly reduced the number of slave state representatives.

While Federalists, during the first years of the nineteenth century, attacked the three-fifths clause as a source of Republican power, they hesitated to directly challenge the institution of slavery itself. Their descendants, however, would assume a leading role in the antislavery campaign.

Few politicians would play a more important role in generating popular support for antislavery than John Quincy Adams (1767–1848). It is striking that as early as 1804, Adams was already thinking in terms of a "Slaveholding power"—a small group of large slaveowners who would stop at nothing to expand southern political power and expand the territory opened to slavery.

The only son of a president to become president himself, Adams was a first-hand participant in many critical events in American politics from the 1780s to the 1840s. In his youth he dined with George Washington and was regarded by Thomas Jefferson as a son. At 14, he served as secretary to an American diplomat in Russia. During a political career that stretched more than half a century, he served as minister to the Netherlands, Prussia, Britain, and Russia; secretary of state; a senator from his native Massachusetts; and, after an unhappy term as president, a nine-term representative.

His parents demanded great things from him. "You come into life with advantages which will disgrace you if your success is mediocre," his father warned him, and if he failed, it "will be owing to your own *Laziness*, *Slovenliness*, and *Obstinacy*," Adams would achieve his greatest success not as president, but as the scourge of the southern Slave Power and its efforts to annex Texas, gag discussion of the slavery issue in Congress, and foment war with Mexico. A Virginia member of Congress called him "the acutest, the astutest, the archest enemy of Southern slavery that ever existed."

John Quincy Adams, July 17, 1804, to Uriah Tracy, senator from Connecticut, GLC 4754

...I have long thought it an important error, of many good and distinguished men among us, that they are too ready to indulge that love of ease and domestic comfort—Too ready to withdraw from the field of public action.... This love of retirement and domestic pleasures, has in this state kept in confinement to their chimney corners, numbers of men, who ought to stand forth the guardians of the public interest, and the guides of our public opinions—It is the only thing which can possibly hazard the steadiness of our politics—I hope they will even resist the dangers of this drowsy opiate....

You will have seen by the proceedings in our Legislature that a serious alarm has of late been so active at the seat of government to establish an impregnable rampart of Slaveholding power, under the false batteries of democracy—The Senators of the State in Congress are instructed to propose and endeavour to effect an amendment of the Constitution so that the representation in the National House of Representatives may be a representation of freeman—I believe this alteration must be made, and I have no doubt it will be effected whenever those states can be United in its favour.... If this great majority of the numbers, wealth, and strength of the Country can be made to harmonize in the pursuit of an object so obviously just in itself, and so clearly important to them I cannot doubt but they will obtain it—This however must be the work of Time and of chance perhaps more than of anything else.

THE AMERICAN EAGLE, THE FRENCH TIGER, AND THE BRITISH SHARK

69 / *"Seamen who are not British subjects...shall be exempt from impressments"*

The European war pitting an alliance of monarchies led by Britain against Napoleonic France was a source of immense profits for Americans, who, John Adams quipped, lined their pockets while Europeans slit each other's throats. As citizens of a neutral nation, Americans were able to trade with both Britain and France, but such trade encouraged retaliation. Here John Marshall refers to one form of retaliation: the British practice of "impressment." The British navy, desperate for sailors, claimed the right to stop neutral ships on the high seas, remove seamen alleged to be British subjects, and impress them into the British navy. By 1811 nearly ten thousand American sailors had been forced into the British navy.

JOHN MARSHALL, SEPTEMBER 20, 1800, INSTRUCTIONS WRITTEN AS SECRETARY OF STATE TO RUFUS KING, U.S. MINISTER TO BRITAIN (PRIOR TO MARSHALL'S APPOINTMENT TO THE U.S. SUPREME COURT), GLC 2539

The United States therefore require positively, that their seamen who are not British subjects, whether born in America, shall be exempt from impressments. The case of British subjects, whether naturalized or not, is more questionable; but the right even to impress them is denied.

70 / "Nearly the whole of the American Commerce... will fall under the destructive operation of the [British] order"

Opportunities for American merchants and shippers to make quick profits in Europe evaporated in 1805 when an English court ruled (in the *Essex* case) that U.S. ships could not carry cargo from French colonies to France. Britain then began to blockade American ports, intercept American ships, and confiscate cargoes bound for France.

In 1806 and 1807 Napoleon tried to ruin Britain's economy by cutting off its trade with Continental Europe. His "Continental System" ordered the seizure of any neutral ship that visited a British port, paid British duties, or allowed itself to be searched by a British vessel.

Britain retaliated by issuing an order-in-council forbidding trade with French ports and other ports under French control. U.S. shipping was caught in the crossfire. By 1807 France had seized five hundred American ships and Britain a thousand.

The order-in-council was the brainchild of British abolitionist James Stephen (1758–1832), whose hidden agenda included an attack on illegal slave ships using the American flag as protection. Stephen understood that American ships supplied Caribbean slave colonies with provisions of all sorts and that ships engaged in the African slave trade were flying the American flag.

The following letter by Secretary of State James Madison condemns the British order-in-council as a violation of America's rights as a neutral nation.

JAMES MADISON, MARCH 29, 1807, TO DAVID M. ERSKINE, BRITISH MINISTER TO THE UNITED STATES, GLC 1096

In this view of the order, it demands on the part of the United States, the most serious attention, both to its principle, and to its operation.

With respect to its *principle*, it will not be contested that a retaliation by one nation, on its enemy, which is to operate thro' the interest of a nation not an enemy essentially require not only that the injury inflicted should be limited by the measure of injury sustained, but...should be preceded by an unreasonable failure of the neutral party, in some mode or other, to put an end to the inequality wrongfully produced....

The United States...are bound by justice to their interests, as well as by respect for their rights, to consider the British order as a ground for serious complaint and remonstrance....

The necessity of presenting the subject in its true light, is strengthened by the *operation* which the British order will have on a vast proportion of the entire commerce of the United States.... It cannot be overlooked that the character and course of nearly the whole of the American Commerce, with the ports of Europe, other than of Great Britain, will fall under the destructive operation of the order. It is well known that the Cargoes exported from the United States frequently require that they be disposed of partly, at one market, and partly at another. The return Cargoes are still more frequently collected at different ports, and not infrequently at ports different from those receiving the outward Cargoes. In this circuitous voyage, generally consisting of several links, the interest of the undertakers materially requires also either a trade or a freightage, between the ports visited in the circuit. To restrain the vessels of the United States therefore from their legitimate and customary mode of trading with the Continent of Europe, as is contemplated by the order, and to compel them, on one hand, to dispose of the whole of their Cargo at a port which may want but a part, and on the other hand to seek the whole of their returns at the same port, which may furnish but a part, or perhaps no part of the articles wanted, would be a proceeding as ruinous to our commerce, as contrary to our essential rights.

71 / *"War? or No War? That is the question"*

Outrage over the British practice of impressment reached a fever pitch in 1807, when the British man-of-war *Leopard* fired three broadsides at the U.S. naval frigate *Chesapeake*, which had refused to stop at the order of the *Leopard*'s commander. The blasts killed three American sailors and wounded eighteen more. British authorities then boarded the American ship and removed four sailors, only one of whom was a British subject.

The country clamored for war. Even some Federalists joined in the anti-British outcry. Said one, "Without substantial reparation for the crying offense against our honor, rights and independence, we must go to war." "Never," wrote President Jefferson, "since the battle of Lexington have I seen this country in such a state of exasperation."

In this letter, former president Adams discusses the clamor for war and the irony of Americans, who were unconcerned about fugitive slaves, being almost obsessively concerned about fugitive British sailors. Note how Adams parodies the voice of "a zealous Republican," attacking, as he was contantly attacked, a "Monarchical, Anti-republican administration."

JOHN ADAMS, SEPTEMBER 1, 1807, TO DR. BENJAMIN RUSH, GLC 4879

War? or No War? That is the question. Our Monarchical, Anti-republican administration conceal from us, the People, all that Information which I a zealous Republican was always prompt to communicate.... If an express stipulation is demanded...that our Flag on board Merchant as well as Ships of War shall protect all British subjects; Deserters from their Navy and all others, I will apprehend the English will not agree to it....

> Prudence would dictate that our government should forbid all its Naval offices to recruit a Deserter from any Nation, in any case; and if the President has not the power to enact it, Congress should enact it. But our People have such a Predilection for Runaways of every description except Runaway Negroes that I suppose Congress would think it too unpopular to abridge this right of man. How we will get out of this Scrape I know not...tho' I carry the Principle by the Law of Nations, to as great an extent as Mr. Jefferson does. If the English fly into a Passion and with or without declaring War Seize every ship and Cargo we have at Sea, I don't believe our present Congress would declare War against them. I am sure they cannot consistently, with their avowed system...defend Nothing but our Farms....

THE DAMBARGO OF 1807

In a desperate attempt to stave off war, for which it was ill prepared, and win respect for America's neutral rights, the United States imposed an embargo on foreign trade. Convinced that American trade was vital to European industry, Jefferson persuaded Congress in late 1807 to adopt a policy of "peaceable coercion": a ban on all foreign shipping and exports.

Jefferson regarded the embargo as an idealistic experiment and a moral alternative to war. The president was not a doctrinaire pacifist, but he had long advocated economic coercion as an instrument of diplomacy. Now he had a chance to put his ideas into practice.

The embargo was an unpopular and costly failure. It hurt the American economy far more than the British and the French, and resulted in widespread smuggling. Without the European export market, warehouses were crammed with huge stockpiles of unsold grain and cotton. Farm prices fell sharply, and shippers suffered. Without the lucrative wartime trade, nearly thirty thousand sailors found themselves jobless. The embargo resuscitated the Federalist Party, which regained power in several New England states and made substantial gains in the congressional elections of 1808. After reading the president's embargo order, the New York Federalist Gouverneur Morris (1752–1816) quipped that Jefferson "seems to be out of his wits. If I am not mistaken, this session will, according to the vulgar phrase, do him over."

72 / *"The only honorable expedient for avoiding war"*

Jefferson believed that Americans would cooperate with the embargo out of patriotism. Instead, smuggling flourished, particularly through Canada. To enforce the embargo, Jefferson took steps that infringed on his most cherished principles: individual liberties and opposition to a strong military. He had to mobilize the army and navy to enforce the blockade, and in April 1808 he declared the Lake Champlain region of New York, along the Canadian border, in a state of insurrection.

Early in 1809, three days before Jefferson left office, Congress repealed the embargo. In effect for fifteen months, it had exacted no political concessions from either France or Britain. But it had produced economic hardship, evasion of the law, and political dissension at home.

In this broadside, the president defends the embargo as "the only honorable expedient for avoiding war."

THOMAS JEFFERSON, CA. 1808, BROADSIDE SIGNED TO ELIOT BROWN, JR., OF STOCKBRIDGE, GLC 115.01

I have duly received the address of that portion of the citizens of Stockbridge [Massachusetts] who have declared their approbation of the present suspension of our commerce, and their dissent from the representation of those of the same place who wished its removal. A division of sentiment was not unexpected. On no question can a perfect unanimity be hoped, or certainly it would have been on that between war and embargo, the only alternatives presented to our choice; for the general capture of our vessels would have been war on one side, which reason and interest would repel by war and reprisal on our part.

Of the several interests composing those of the United States, that of manufactures would of course prefer to war, a state of non-intercourse, so favorable to their rapid growth and prosperity. Agriculture, although sensibly feeling the loss of market for its produce, would find many aggravations in a state of war. Commerce and navigation, or that portion which is foreign, in the inactivity to which they are reduced by the present state of things, certainly experience their full share in the general inconvenience: but whether war would to them be a preferable alternative, is a question their patriotism would never hastily propose. It is to be regretted, however, that overlooking the real sources of their sufferings, the British and French Edicts, which constitute the actual blockade of our foreign commerce and navigation, they have, with too little reflection, imputed them to laws which have saved them from greater, and have preserved for our own use our vessels, property and seamen, instead of adding them to the strength of those with whom we might eventually have to contend.

The Embargo, giving time to the belligerent powers to revise their unjust proceedings and to listen to the dictates of justice, of interest and reputation, which equally urge the correction of their wrongs, has availed our country of the only honorable expedient for avoiding war: and should a repeal of these Edicts supersede the cause for it, our commercial brethren will become sensible that it has consulted their interests, however against their own will. It will be unfortunate for their country if, in the mean time, these, their expressions of impatience, should have the effect of prolonging the very suffering which have produced them, by exciting a fallacious hope that we may, under any pressure, relinquish our equal right of navigating the ocean, go to such ports only as others may prescribe, and there pay the tributary exactions they may impose; an abandonment of national independence and of essential rights revolting to every manly sentiment: While these Edicts are in force, no American can ever consent to a return of peaceable intercourse with those who maintain them.

73 / *"Jefferson expired and Madison came to Life last night"*

Distressed by the embargo's failure, Jefferson looked forward to his retirement from the presidency. "Never," he wrote, "did a prisoner, released from his chains, feel such relief as I shall on shaking off the shackles of power."

The problem of American neutrality now fell to Jefferson's handpicked successor, James Madison. A quiet and scholarly man who secretly suffered from epilepsy, "the Father of the Constitution" brought a keen intellect and a wealth of experience to the presidency. As Jefferson's secretary of state he had kept the United States out of the Napoleonic wars and was committed to using economic coercion to force Britain and France to respect America's neutral rights. In this letter, former president Adams notes Madison's ascension to the presidency.

JOHN ADAMS, MARCH 4, 1809, TO BENJAMIN RUSH, GLC 639.01

Jefferson expired and Madison came to Life last night.... I pity poor Madison. He comes to the helm in such a storm as I have seen in the Gul[f] Stream, or rather such as I had to encounter in the Government in 1797. Mine was the worst however, because he has a great Majority of the officers and Men attached to him.

THE ROAD TO WAR

In 1809 Congress replaced the failed embargo with the Non-Intercourse Act, which reopened trade with all nations except Britain and France. Violations of American neutrality continued, and a year later Congress replaced the Non-Intercourse Act with a new measure, Macon's Bill No. 2. This act reopened trade with France and Britain. But it stated that if either Britain or France agreed to respect America's neutral rights, the United States would immediately stop trade with the other nation.

Napoleon seized on this policy to entangle the United States in his war with Britain. In 1810 he announced repeal of all French restrictions on American trade. Even though France continued to seize American ships and cargoes, President Madison snapped at the bait. In 1811 he cut off trade with Britain and recalled the American minister.

For nineteen months Britain went without American trade, but gradually economic coercion worked. Food shortages, mounting unemployment, and increasing inventories of unsold manufactured goods led Britain to end its trade restrictions (although not the policy of impressment). But it was too late; President Madison had already persuaded Congress to declare war.

Why did the United States declare war on Britain in 1812? Resentment at British interference with American rights on the high seas was the most loudly voiced grievance. If British trade restrictions and impressment were the primary motivations for war, why then did the prowar majority in Congress come largely from the South and the western frontier, and not from northeastern shipowners and sailors? Representatives from western and frontier states voted 65 to 15 for war, while representatives from New England, New York, and New Jersey voted 34 to 14 against war.

Northeastern Federalists regarded war with Britain as a grave mistake. They believed that the United States could not challenge British naval supremacy and that the government could not finance a war without bankrupting the country. Southerners and westerners, in contrast, were eager to avenge British actions that mocked American sovereignty. Many blamed British trade policies for depressing agricultural prices. War with Britain also offered another incentive: clearing western lands of Indians and adding Canada and Spanish-controlled lands in Florida and Texas to the United States.

74 / *"Open Mexico to the political influence of the U.S."*

Decades before the phrase "Manifest Destiny" was coined, James Madison harbored ambitions for westward expansion. In 1811 the southwestern frontier was in a state of ferment. The collapse of the Spanish government after Napoleon's invasion opened the door to revolution in Mexico. The United States took advantage of Spanish weakness by seizing West Florida in 1811.

In 1812 and 1813 Madison secretly had William Shaler (1778–1833), a trader, support efforts by Mexicans and Americans to overthrow the Spanish government in Texas. The briefly established Texas Republic collapsed in August 1813. Shaler was engaged in the China trade in the 1790s; traded furs on the Northwest Coast at the turn of the century; and lived in Hawaii in 1803 and 1804. After serving as a U.S. special agent in Havana, and fomenting revolution in Texas, he served as a peace negotiator during the War of 1812.

Shaler served as Madison's eyes and ears on the southwestern frontier. In the following extracts from his letters, he reports on the opportunities and risks facing the United States in the Southwest.

William Shaler, GLC 5246.01, 5246.02, 5246.03

Letter 50 to James Monroe, May 2, 1812:

I understand that they are persons of respectable character and fortune in Upper Louisiana, who had gone into New Mexico with a view of opening a trade with that country...they report the province to be almost defenseless, and the disposition to insurrection to be universal...the practicality of such a scheme is the general topic of conversation.

Letter 64 to James Monroe, October 5, 1812:

[American influence is] growing into an irresistible torrent that will sweep the crazy remains of the Spanish government from the Internal Provinces, and open Mexico to the political influence of the U.S. and to the talents and enterprize of our citizens...."

THE "WAR HAWKS"

Weary of Jefferson's and Madison's pacifistic policy of economic coercion, voters in 1810 swept 63 of 142 representatives from Congress and replaced them with young Republicans that Federalists dubbed "War Hawks." These second-generation Republicans avidly supported national expansion and national honor. They elected Henry Clay (1777–1852), a representative from frontier Kentucky, Speaker of the House on his very first day in Congress.

Staunchly nationalist and rabidly anti-British, the young Republicans regarded the Napoleonic Wars in Europe as an unparalleled opportunity to defend national honor, assert American interests, and conquer Canada and Spanish territory in Florida and the Southwest.

In a letter written in the spring of 1812, John Quincy Adams, a son of the former president, predicts that war would have a profound, and he hoped favorable, impact on the American national character. "That we should be destined to enjoy a perpetual Peace, however ardently humanity may desire it, cannot reasonably be expected," he wrote. "If War is not the natural State of human Society at all times, it is that of the age upon which we have fallen."

75 / *"An immense majority of the people are...averse from a conflict... menacing ruin to themselves"*

Although Congress voted strongly in favor of war, the country entered the conflict deeply divided. Many New Englanders were appalled by the thought of becoming allies of Napoleon and of the nation that had indulged in the Reign of Terror. Not only would many New Englanders refuse to subscribe to war loans, but some merchants actually shipped provisions that Britain needed to support its army. In the following selection, a committee of citizens in Boston denounces the drift toward war.

[J.C. Jones], June 11, 1812, GLC 2880

THE Committee appointed by the Town of Boston to take into consideration the present alarming state of our public affairs, and report what measures in their opinion it is proper for the Town to adopt, at this momentous crisis,

RESPECTFULLY REPORT,

THAT...while the temper and views of the national administration are intent upon war, an expression of the sense of this Town, will, *of itself*, be quite ineffectual, either to avert this deplorable calamity, or to accelerate a return of peace. But believing, as we do, that an immense majority of the people are invincibly averse from a conflict equally unnecessary, and menacing ruin to themselves and their posterity; convinced, as we are, that the event will overwhelm them with astonishment and dismay; we cannot but trust that a general expression of the voice of the people would satisfy Congress that those of their Representatives who have voted in favor of war, have not truly represented the wishes of their constituents; and thus arrest the tendency of their measures to this extremity.

But should this be hopeless, it will enable the people to combine their operations in order to produce, by constitutional means, a change of men and measures, and rescue the Nation from ruin. From the commencement of the system of commercial restrictions, the Inhabitants of this Town (inferior we trust to none in ardent patriotism and attachment to the Union) have appeared to render themselves obnoxious to the national administration, and its partisans in this State, by their foresight and predictions of the utter inefficacy, destructive operation, and ultimate tendency of this unprecedented and visionary scheme. They could discern in it nothing but a deliberate sacrifice of their best interests, and a conformity to the views of France, with whose system it cooperates, and whose approbation it receives; and hostility to Britain, whose interests it wounds, and whose resentment it was calculated to excite. It was for the national government to determine, whether the decrees and aggressions of the belligerent powers (which commenced with the European war) would probably demand of the national honor, retaliation and resistance; or whether the peculiar character of the war, and relative situation of our country, would justify a suspension of our resentment, and an adherence to our pacific policy. In the one case, the years which have elapsed should have been occupied in warlike preparations, which now have been imposing and formidable.

In the other event, it was the dictate of sound policy, to protest against the predatory systems which have annoyed our commerce, and still to have pursued it by all practicable means. But government has adopted neither of these courses. It has not prepared to vindicate our commercial rights upon the Ocean, where alone they are assailed; nor has it permitted the merchant to indemnify himself in any measure for the loss of that commerce which is interrupted, by a participation in that which is left. But by a strange and infatuated policy, under the pretense of resisting the invasion of maritime rights, it has debarred its own Citizens from the use of the Ocean; and professing to avenge the injuries sustained from France and England, it has aggravated them by its own measures. The Decrees of France, the Edicts of England, and the Acts of Congress, though intended to counteract each other, constitute in effect, *a triple league* for the annihilation of American commerce; and our own government, as if weary of waiting for a lingering dissolution, hastens to dispatch the sufferer, by the finishing stroke of a British war.

Had the policy of government been inclined towards resistance to the pretensions of the belligerents, by open war, there could be neither policy, reason, or justice in singling out Great Britain as the exclusive object of hostility. If the object of war is merely to vindicate our honor, why is it not declared against the first aggressor? If the object is defence and success, why is it to be waged against the adversary most able to annoy, and least likely to yield? Why, at the moment when England explicitly declares her Orders in Council repealed whenever France shall rescind her Decrees, is the one selected for an enemy, and the other courted as a conqueror? These inquiries lead us into contemplations too painful to indulge, and too serious to express....

But under the present circumstances, there will be...no chance for success, no hope of national glory, no prospect but of a war against Britain, in aid of the common enemy of the human race; and in the end an inglorious peace, in which our ally will desert our interest, and act in concert with our enemy, to shackle and restrain the commerce of our infant empire, by regulations in which they will find a common interest....

Therefore Resolved, That under existing circumstances, the inhabitants of this Town most sincerely deprecate a war with Great Britain, as extremely injurious to the interests and happiness of the people, and peculiarly so, as it necessarily tends to an alliance with France, thereby threatening the subversion of their liberties and independence. That an offensive war against Great Britain *alone* would be manifestly unjust; and that a war against both the belligerent powers would be an extravagant undertaking, which is not required by the honour or interest of the nation.

76 / "The friends of Peace, Commerce and Liberty...are hourly rising"

A Boston newspaper editorializes against Madison's war policy.

Columbian Centinel, BOSTON, SEPTEMBER 5, 1812, GLB 327.01

The Prospect Before Us

The Madisonian interest is daily decreasing like a rope of sand, while the friends of

Peace, Commerce and Liberty in all quarters are hourly rising like a pyramid of granite. Facts are stubborn things.

A gentleman lately from a tour through the eastern part of Massachusetts (Maine) gives the following result of his observation: Every thing wears the aspect of decay and grief. It is truly melancholy to see the dismantled state of the shipping; to view the ruin of the merchants—the poverty of the mechanics. No business, except here and there in the refitting of some paltry privateer. This state of inactivity and wretchedness has already greatly injured good morals, those guardian angels of order and happiness. Nor are the baneful effects of the unjust and unnecessary War confined to the seaboard. The country is equally impoverished. No...sale for their lumber, and other products. Without money or credit, and generally in debt for the necessaries of life—and the prospects of harvest very scant. A land, or other heavy taxes (which *must* be laid) to support an unpopular War, is only necessary to complete their ruin! But amid this darksome gloom there is a *light* coming forth, thank God! which cheers the heart of despondency—the light of Truth and Justice;—and whilst a Federalism is stretching forth her renovating hand, Democracy is "vanishing into air, thin air." The voice of the People will continue to be loud and deep; and the War-Makers be whelmed in confusion and contempt.

77 / *"Our Northern & Western Armies seemed to be doomed to misfortune and Disgrace"*

The United States was woefully unprepared for war. The army consisted of fewer than seven thousand soldiers; the navy, of fewer than twenty vessels.

The American strategy called for a three-pronged invasion of Canada and heavy harassment of British shipping. The attack on Canada, however, was a disastrous failure. At Detroit, two thousand American soldiers surrendered to a much smaller British and Indian force. An attack across the Niagara River, near Buffalo, New York, resulted in nine hundred American prisoners of war when the New York State militia refused to provide support. Along Lake Champlain, a third army retreated into U.S. territory after failing to cut undefended British supply lines. By the end of 1812, British forces controlled key forts in the Old Northwest, including Detroit and Fort Dearborn, the future site of Chicago.

In this excerpt, Benjamin Tallmadge (1754–1835), who had served as a colonel during the Revolution and as an agent for the Ohio Company, a land acquisition company, comments on the U.S. army's deplorable condition.

BENJAMIN TALLMADGE, NOVEMBER 29, 1812, TO JAMES MCHENRY, GLC 3342

The House have passed a Bill raising the wages of Privates in the Army to Eight Dollars, & the non commissioned Officers accordingly—It also authorizes the Enlistment of Minors...& secures from arrest Debtors of any magnitude or Amo[un]t who will fly to the American Standard....

Our Northern & Western Armies seem to be doomed to misfortunate and Disgrace.

78 / *"The great & immortal Jackson, leads the valiant & daring sons of Tennessee to victory & to glory"*

In 1813 the United States suffered new failures. In January an American army advancing toward Detroit was defeated and captured in the swamps west of Lake Erie. In April Americans staged a raid on what is now Toronto, where they set fire to the two houses of the provincial parliament. This act brought British retaliation in the burning of Washington, D.C. Only a naval victory at the Battle of Lake Erie in September 1813 raised American spirits.

In early 1814, prospects for an American victory dimmed. In the spring, Britain defeated Napoleon in Europe, freeing 18,000 battle-tested British troops to invade the United States. The British launched three separate invasions: in upstate New York, the Chesapeake Bay, and New Orleans. Outnumbered more than three to one, American forces repelled Britain's northern invasion at Niagara and Lake Champlain.

In a second attempt to invade the United States, Britain landed four thousand soldiers on the Chesapeake Bay coast. This force then marched on Washington, where untrained soldiers lacking uniforms and standard equipment protected the capital. In August 1814 the British humiliated the nation by capturing and burning Washington, D.C. Britain's next objective was Baltimore. To reach the city, British warships had to pass the guns of Fort McHenry, manned by 1,000 American soldiers. British warships began a twenty-five-hour bombardment of the fort, but the Americans repulsed the attack with only 4 soldiers killed and 24 wounded. One observer, Francis Scott Key (1779–1843), a young lawyer detained on a British ship, was so moved by the American victory that he wrote the words to "The Star-Spangled Banner," the song destined to become the country's national anthem, on the back of an envelope.

The country still faced severe threats in the South. In 1813 the Creek Indians, encouraged by the British, attacked American settlements in present-day Alabama and Mississippi. In one incident known as the "Massacre at Fort Mims," near Mobile, 553 American men, women, and children were killed. Frontiersmen from Georgia, Mississippi, and Tennessee, led by Major General Andrew Jackson (1767–1845), retaliated and succeeded in defeating the Creeks in March 1814 at the Battle of Horseshoe Bend. The following letter, by Tennessee senator Ephraim Hubbard Foster (1795?–1854), refers to both the massacre and the Battle of Horseshoe Bend.

EPHRAIM HUBBARD FOSTER, APRIL 8, 1814, TO WILLIAM GRAHAM, GLC 2804

I should not have this soon thrown myself in your presence but that had not the glorious and transporting news of the victory of the 27th attained by the unconquerable arms of Tennessee reached us yesterday evening. I hasten my friend to lay the account before you, that your heart may feel all the pleasant sensations, my own does at this moment. How pleasing is the thought, that while in the North everything means the face of discomforture, & disgrace, the American colours wave triumphant in the South. While [Generals] Wilkinson, Hampton, & Harrison are either lying inactive, or moving to no purpose but to their shame, the great & immortal Jackson, leads the valiant & daring sons of Tennessee to victory & to glory.

More than once has he laid the savage beneath the rod of his victory. More than once he made the mistaken beings feel the valor of his arms.... Behold, behold, my dear friend behold the blow he struck 27th March. [The battle that effectively ended the

Creek War} More than 800 prostrate Indians atone for the loss of the brave Major Montgomery & his dead fellow soldiers. More than 2000 atone for the slaughter at Fort Mims and I am transported beyond conception. Did you ever read of the like. Will the like ever take place again. Yes. Yes. Headed by the Genl. the true Genl. Jackson. Our soldiers must conquer. The 27th of March, will ever be a jubilee in the annuls of Tennessean warfare....

Before this time General Jackson has set out for the Hickory ground.... In a few days more we hope to hear he has added another plume to the name of Tennessee. May the great gods continue unto him his former successes. May he go on conquering & to conquer until not one enemy shall dare show himself in the south.

I am somehow so elevated above myself that I can not talk on any other subject. My Graham, I am proud of being a Tennessean. Yes I am.

79 / *"The proceedings at Hartford have excited much anxiety"*

Many Federalists believed that the War of 1812 was fought to aid Napoleon in his struggle against Britain. Some opposed the war by refusing to pay taxes, boycotting war loans, and refusing to furnish troops. In December 1814, delegates from New England gathered in Hartford, Connecticut, where they recommended a series of constitutional amendments to restrict Congress's power to wage war, regulate commerce, and admit new states. The delegates also supported a one-term presidency (to break the grip of Virginians on the office) and abolition of the Three-fifths Compromise, and talked of seceding if they did not get their way. In this message, Madison's secretary of state, James Monroe, expresses concern over the Hartford Convention and fear that New England Federalists might seize the federal armory at Springfield, Massachusetts.

JAMES MONROE, TO AN UNKNOWN RECIPIENT, JANUARY 11, 1815, GLC 5280

Confidential

...The proceedings at Hartford have excited much anxiety, as likely to embarrass the measures of the Government, and by the countenance they have afforded the enemy to prolong the war, if they should not lead into worse consequences. General Swartout has been authorised to take measures, in case they should be necessary, for the security of the arms at Springfield {Massachusetts}.... I trust that any evil which may be contemplated, however great, will be defeated.

80 / *"The war...on our part, is entirely defensive"*

A leading national newspaper discusses the Hartford Convention, Britain's war aims, the possibility that American forces at New Orleans can rebuff a British invasion, and African Americans' participation in the war effort.

Niles Weekly Register, BALTIMORE, JANUARY 28, 1815, GLB 327.02

New England Convention

It is universally known that the causes for which we declared war are no obstruction to peace. The practice of blockade and impressment having ceased by the general pacification of Europe, our government is content to leave the principle as it was—referring to the settlement to some future arrangement or the common opinion of the civilized world—or in reserving the right again to resist both, or either, if repeated, hereafter....

Having, as before observed, and for the reasons stated, proffered peace on the terms that we stood upon before the war was declared, we have no further business in hostility, than such as is purely defensive; while that of Great Britain is to humble or subdue us. The war, on our part, has become a contest for life, liberty and property—on the part of our enemy, of revenge or ambition. No matter for what cause it was waged—such is the principle of its duration; and one might have thought that such a state of things would have united the whole people to repulse the enemy. But alas! it certainly appears that the more outrageous he is, the more impudent are the jacobins to distract the measures of government and enkindle the spirit of party.... When I hear a man clamor for peace, ardently desired by all—I ask him how he would proceed to obtain it—what he would do that our ministers at Ghent are not authorized to do? I have put these questions to several, and never got an answer but once; when the jacobin said, he would get it by changing the president.... I am not, perhaps, the most ardent admirer of Mr. Madison—I have thought that other men might be found better fitted for the times in which we live, (though I know that many of the faults attributed to him, justly belong to congress; whose half-way measures at the last, and disgraceful waste of time in the present session, had nearly brought the country to ruin.)—Yet were he to me the most offensive of beings, I would not sacrifice the freedom of choice in the people, or violate the provisions of the constitution to "depose him"...and though I might vote against him myself, I can hardly conceive any danger that I would not encounter to support him in his legal authority, against the dictation, or power of a foreign nation....

The war then, on our part, is entirely defensive—and the enemy wages it with a degree of barbarity unknown to their history of modern times. He allies himself with the savages—he allies himself with Negro slaves—he would desolate the frontiers with the tomahawk, and give up the interior to all the horrors that exterminated the white population of St. Domingo. He avows his object, to "destroy all places assailable".... What then are we to do? Are we to encourage him by divisions among ourselves—to hold out the hope of a separation of the states and a civil war—to refuse to bring forth the resources of the country against him.... I did think that in a defensive war—a struggle for all that is valuable—that all parties would have united. But it is not so—every measure calculated to replenish the treasury or raise men is opposed as though it were determined to strike the "star spangled banner" and exalt the bloody cross. Look at the votes and proceedings of congress—and mark the late spirit (now, perhaps, "laid" for a time) that existed in Massachusetts, and see with what unity of action every thing has been done to harass and embarrass the government. Our loans have failed; and our soldiers have wanted their pay, because those who had the greater part of the monied capital covenanted with each other to refuse its aid to the country. They had a right, legally, to do this; and perhaps, also, by all the artifices of trade or power that money gave them, to oppress others not of their "stamp" and depress the national credit—but history will shock posterity by detailing the length to which they went to bankrupt the republic....

With a perfect knowledge of these transactions, how could Great Britain be better encouraged to persevere in the war, to "cripple us for fifty years"...? Dive et impera [divide and conquer] is the everlasting principle of arbitrary power.... The English have talked of the inordinate ambition of Napoleon Bonaparte—Villainous hypocrites!—all that Bonaparte attempted in Europe was but a type of what they themselves had done in Asia, where they boast of from sixty to eighty millions of slaves. What the "detestable Napoleon" did was angelic, compared with their deeds in India.... Such are the monsters that set themselves up as the preservers of the religion, the liberty and the morals of the world!....

"In union there is strength," and were our people united, the war would immediately end; or be prosecuted with different success.

If the negotiations at Ghent shall not have very considerably advanced before the news of the "Hartford convention" reaches the cabinet of London, I am clearly of opinion, that they will be suspended, or shuffled off, until the proceedings are known; for nothing is more evident than that the war is prosecuted for revenge or ambition; and what, under heaven, is so well calculated to aid it, as the ideas that were held out as to the objects of that assembly—"to withhold the resources of the N[ew] E[ngland] States and make a separate peace?" It is indubitable that she regards us with envy and hate. Our manufacturers and commerce, the glory of our little navy and the steady valor of our army, excite horrid sensations in her bosom.... "Westward the course of empire takes its way;" and she is quite jealous of the prosperity of the United States....

To conclude—why does the war continue? It is not the fault of the government—we demand no extravagant thing. I answer the question, and say—*it lasts because Great Britain depends on the exertions of her "party" in this country to destroy our resources, and compel "unconditional submission."*

Thus the war began, and is continued, by our divisions.

State of the War

We are yet without definite intelligence from New-Orleans. The news will probably arrive *this day*, that will, at least, relieve our suspense....

One letter says that Jackson engaged them with only about 2000 men—he had about 9000 then under his command—it also says that the British had not been able to land their artillery, and expresses an idea that the whole of them would be made prisoners that day—that is, December 24.

The whole British force is variously stated by the prisoners at from 7 to 15,000 men—the probable number is 6000, commanded by major-general Keane.

Such is the substance of our intelligence. We think New-Orleans is safe, and anticipate the details of a glorious victory—if it has fallen, it has been dearly purchased.

On Sunday the 18th Dec. General Jackson reviewed the militia of the city....
To the Embodied Militia.

Fellow citizens and soldiers!

...Long strangers to the perils of war, you have embodied yourselves to face them with the cool countenance of veterans—and with motives of disunion that might operate on weak minds, you have forgotten the difference of language and the prejudices of national pride, and united with a cordiality that does honor to your understandings as well as to your patriotism. Natives of the United States! They are the oppressors of your infant political existence, with whom you are to contend—they are the men your fathers conquered whom you are to oppose. Descendants of Frenchmen! natives of France! they are English, the hereditary, the eternal enemies of your ancient country, the invaders of that you have adopted, who are your foes. Spaniards! remember the conduct of your allies at St. Sebastians, and recently at Pensacola, and rejoice that you have an opportunity of avenging the brutal injuries inflicted by men who dishonor the human race.

Fellow citizens, of every description! remember for what and against whom you contend. For all that can render life desirable—for a country blest with every gift of nature—for property, for life—for those dearer than either, your wives and children—and for liberty, without which country, life, property, are no longer worth possessing; as ever the embraces of wives and children become a reproach to the wretch who could deprive them by his cowardice of those invaluable blessings. You are to contend for all this against an enemy whose continued effort is to deprive you of the least of these blessings—who avows a war of vengeance and desolation, carried on and marked by cruelty, lust, and horrors unknown to civilized nations.

Thomas L. Butler
To the Men of Color
Soldiers—From the shores of Mobile I collected you to arms—I invited you to share in the perils and to divide the glory of your white countrymen. I expected much from you, for I was not uninformed of those qualities which must render you so formidable to an invading foe—I knew that you could endure hunger and thirst, and all the hardships of war—I knew that you loved the land of your nativity, and that, like ourselves, you had to defend all that is most dear to man—-but you surpass my hopes. I have found in you, united to those qualities, that noble enthusiasm which impels to great deeds.

81 / "A treaty of peace was received last night"

Ironically, American and British negotiators in Ghent, Belgium, signed a peace treaty ending the war two weeks before the Battle of New Orleans. A war-weary Britain agreed to return to conditions that existed before the war. Left unmentioned in the peace treaty were the issues over which Americans had supposedly fought the war—impressment, naval blockades, and the British orders in council. In this letter, President Monroe announces the Treaty of Ghent.

JAMES MONROE, TO CHARLES EVERETT, FEBRUARY 18, 1815, GLC 5568

I have the pleasure to inform you that a treaty of peace was received last night by Mr. Carroll from Ghent, which was signed on the 24 of Dec. It is perfectly honorable to the U States. It is short, and little more than a treaty of *peace*. Nothing like concession is made on any point.

It is highly honorable to our country to have maintained its ground, singly, against G. Britain, & to have forced her to such a peace. This contest has been glorious to the U

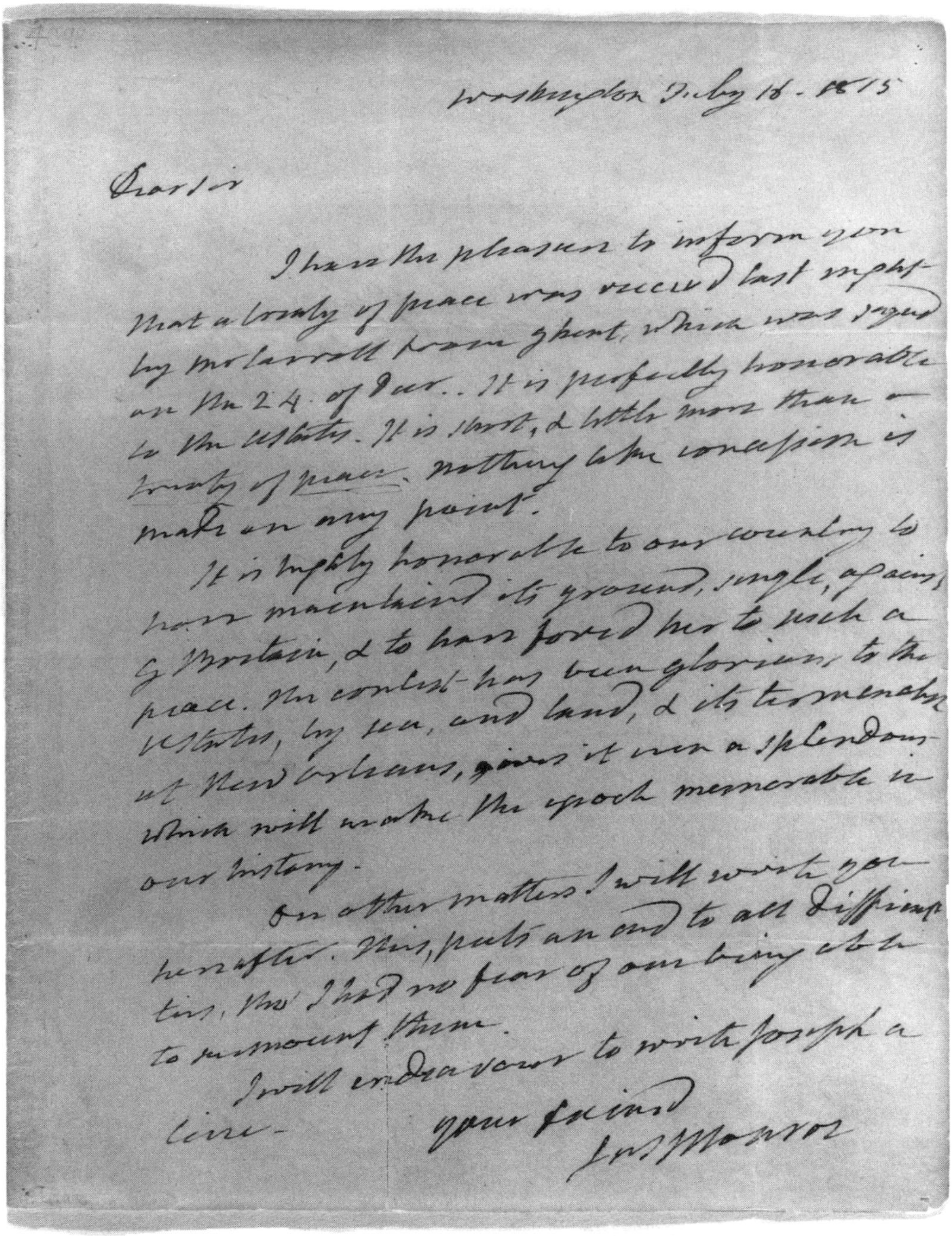
Washington Feby 18 - 1815

Dear Sir

I have the pleasure to inform you that a treaty of peace was receiv'd last night by Mr Carroll from Ghent, which was signed on the 24. of Dec. It is perfectly honorable to the UStates. It is short, & little more than a treaty of peace. nothing like concession is made on any point.

It is highly honorable to our country to have maintain'd its ground, single, against G Britain, & to have forc'd her to such a peace. The contest has been glorious to the UStates, by sea, and land, & its termination at New Orleans, gives it even a splendour which will make the epoch memorable in our history.

On other matters I will write you hereafter. This, puts an end to all difficulties, tho' I had no fear of our being able to surmount them.

I will endeavour to write Joseph a line—

your friend

Jas Monroe

James Monroe. Autograph letter signed, to Charles Everett, 1815/02/18. The Gilder Lehrman Collection, on deposit at the Pierpont Morgan Library. GLC 5568

States, by sea and land, & its triumph at New Orleans, give it even a splendour which will make the epoch memorable in our history.

82 / "The British naval Commanders...have carried away from the United States all the slaves they have taken"

Although often treated as a minor footnote to the Napoleonic Wars, the War of 1812 was crucial for the United States. It effectively destroyed the eastern Indians' ability to resist American expansion. A coalition of Native Americans was defeated at the Battle of Tippecanoe in Indiana in 1811, and the Creek Indians were defeated in the South by General Andrew Jackson. Abandoned by their British allies, Native Americans reluctantly ceded most lands north of the Ohio River and in southern and western Alabama to the U.S. government.

The war greatly strengthened America's position relative to Spain in the South and Southwest. It allowed the United States to solidify control over the lower Mississippi River and the Gulf of Mexico. Although the United States did not succeed in conquering Canada or defeating the British Empire, it had fought the world's strongest power to a stalemate. Spain recognized the significance of this fact and in 1819 abandoned Florida and agreed to an American boundary running to the Pacific Ocean.

The Federalist Party never recovered from its opposition to the war. The proposals of the Hartford Convention became public knowledge at the same time as the Treaty of Ghent and the American victory at New Orleans. Euphoria over the war's end led many people to brand the Federalists as traitors. The party never recovered from this stigma.

Finally, the war produced profound changes in New England. As a result of the war, New England importing and exporting was in ruins, and wealthy New Englanders reinvested their resources in manufacturing. Further, with its dominant political party discredited, New Englanders found new ways to influence national policy. In the future, New England would engage in far-reaching campaigns of moral reform intended to make its values the nation's values.

In this letter, John Quincy Adams (1767–1848), a son of the former president and America's minister to Britain, discusses the defiance of the terms of the Treaty of Ghent by British officers.

John Quincy Adams, as minister to Great Britain, August 31, 1815, to William Eustis, as minister to the Hague, GLC 3626

The British naval Commanders, in defiance of the Treaty of Ghent, have carried away from the United States all the slaves they have taken—There was no certainty that Michillimakinac [a naval base in Michigan] had been restored—The Agents and Traders were instigating the Indians in the North, and a British Officer posted in Florida was doing the same thing with the Creeks—Our fishing vessels had been turned away, and warned, to twenty leagues from the coast—The British Packet had been seized at New-York for an attempt to smuggle goods—At the same time the Cabinet here have been determined to increase their naval Armaments on the Lakes of Canada—And the Ministerial Gazettes are marked with strong symptoms of hostili-

> ty—The language held here is temperate, and full of conciliatory professions—But when the affairs of France shall be settled to their satisfaction (which I think will be soon) I expect a change of tone....

CLEARING THE LAND OF INDIANS

Native Americans were the biggest losers in the War of 1812. The defeat of the Shawnees in the Old Northwest and of the Creeks in the Old Southwest destroyed any hopes of an alliance of northern and southern Indians. No longer would the Indians have a European ally capable of slowing the advance of white Americans.

The end of the War of 1812 ignited a great debate over Indian policy. Bitter disputes erupted over whether the Indians should be subject to state law; whether the United States should continue to treat Indian tribes as sovereign units; and whether the goal of government policy should be to remove Indians from the lands east of the Mississippi River or to force them to adopt the customs and religion of the dominant culture.

83 / *"Introduce among the several Indian Nations...the arts of civilization"*

Beginning with Thomas Jefferson's presidency, two conflicting Indian policies—assimilation and removal—governed treatment of Native Americans. The assimilation policy encouraged Indians to adopt white American customs and economic practices. The government provided financial assistance to missionaries in order to Christianize and educate Native Americans and convince them to adopt single-family farms. Proponents defended assimilation as the only way Native Americans could survive in a white-dominated society. By the 1820s the Cherokees, who lived in northwestern Georgia, had demonstrated a remarkable capacity to adapt to changing conditions while maintaining their tribal heritage. Sequoyah, a leader of these people, developed a written alphabet. Soon the Cherokees opened schools, established churches, built roads, operated printing presses, and even adopted a constitution asserting sovereignty over their homeland.

In this letter, Henry Dearborn (1751–1829), Jefferson's secretary of war, outlines a program for teaching Indians the "arts of civilization."

HENRY DEARBORN, JULY 8, 1803, TO CALLENDER IRVINE, MA 6016

> The Government considers it a very important object to introduce among the several Indian Nations within the United States the arts of civilization—to induce the men to engage in agriculture and the raising of stock, and to convince the women of the benefits they would derive from a knowledge of the domestic arts and manufactures.

84 / *"They would have...been amalgamated with us within no distant period of time"*

Thomas Jefferson came to regard the assimilationist program as a failure. In this letter, he laments the failure of his "benevolent plan" to educate Indians—and attributes the failure to British policy.

Thomas Jefferson, December 6, 1813, to Baron Alexander von Humboldt, Heineman ms. 188. The Dannie and Hettie Heineman Collection

They would have mixed their blood with ours, and been amalgamated and identified with us within no distant period of time.... They [the British] seduced the greater part of the tribes within our neighborhood, to take up the hatchet against us, and the cruel massacres they have committed on the women and children of our frontiers taken by surprise, will oblige us now to pursue them to extermination, or drive them to new seats beyond our reach.... The confirmed brutalization, if not the extermination, of this race in our America is therefore to form an additional chapter in the English history of the same colored man in Asia, and of the brethren of their own color in Ireland and wherever else Anglo-mercantile cupidity can find a two-penny interest in deluging the earth with human blood.

85 / "The warriors of that village was [sic] with me fighting the battles of our country"

In December 1817 President James Monroe authorized General Andrew Jackson to lead a punitive expedition against the Seminole Indians in Florida, who used the Spanish colony as a jumping off point for raids on settlements in Georgia. The Seminoles actually consisted of several groups, including Muskogee-speaking Creek Indians, Mikawuki-speakers, and fugitive slaves.

Jackson was assisted in his Florida expedition by a Creek people from southwestern Georgia known as the Chehaws. While Chehaw men had fought in Florida, the Georgia state militia killed Chehaw villagers—an act condemned by Jackson in the following letter. Acting on reports of attacks on white settlers by other Creeks, the state militia, under Captain Obed Wright, attacked and burned a Chehaw village, killing at least seven Indians. Captain Wright was eventually imprisoned for this attack, but later escaped and disappeared. This fascinating document underscores the complexity of relations between whites and Indians, the state and federal governments, and state militia and national army authorities.

Andrew Jackson, May 4, 1818, to Governor William Rabun of Georgia, GLC 782.11.01

I have this moment received by express the letter of Genl. Glascock...detailing the base, cowardly and inhuman attack on the old women and men of the Chehaw Villages, whilst the warriors of that *village* was [*sic*] with me fighting the battles of *our* country against the common enemy, and at a time too when undoubted testimony had been obtained and was in my possession...of their innocence of the charge of killing Leigh & other Georgians at Cedar Creek.

That a Governor of a State should assume the right to make war against an Indian tribe in perfect peace with and under the protection of the United States, is assuming a responsibility, that I trust you will be able to excuse to the government of the United States, to which you have to answer, and through which I had so recently passed, promising the aged that remained at home my protection and taking the warriors with me on the campaign is as unaccountable as strange. But it is still more strange that there could exist within the U. States as cowardly a monster in human shape, that could violate the sanctity of a flag when borne by any person, but more particularly when in the hands of a superannuated Indian chief worn down with age. Such base cowardice and murderous conduct as this man's action affords has not its parallel in history, and shall meet with its merited punishment.

You Sir as Governor of a State within my Military Division have no right to give a military order whilst I am in the field, and this being an open and violent infringement of the treaty with the Creek Indians[,] Capt. Wright must be prosecuted and punished for this outrageous murder, & I have ordered him to be arrested and confined in irons until the pleasure of the President of the United States is known upon the subject. If he has left Hartford before my order reaches him, I call upon you as Governor of Georgia to aid in carrying into effect my orders for his arrest and confinement, which I trust will be afforded, and Capt. Wright brought to condign punishment for this unprecedented murder.... This act will to the last ages fix a stain upon the character of Georgia.

MISSIONARY WORK AND INDIAN POLICY

86 / "I had the pleasure of being introduced to the principal Chief of the Potawatamie Indians"

One major goal of American missionaries was to Christianize and assimilate Native Americans, to make them, as one missionary put it, "English in their language, civilized in their habits, and Christian in their religion." Yet missionary work among Native Americans was largely unsuccessful. By 1829 only about fifteen hundred Native Americans had been converted to Christianity.

In the following letter to his children, William Dickson, a missionary among Illinois Indians, discusses his work.

William Dickson, May 28, 1834, to George and Cyrus Dickson, GLC 3383

A line from your affectionate Father, who is now 7 or 800 miles from you in a strange and a far western land I trust will not be unacceptable. I left home on the 5 day of this month and am now seated in the Town of Ottawa [Illinois] 80 miles south west of Chicago. I will give you a short account of my journey.... We traveled in a light wagon and brought our saddles with us. Some part of the road was somewhat difficult, however we got along very well we traveled through part of Penna, the length way of Ohio & Michigan and across the end of Indiana. We are now about 100 miles into the state of Illinois, and I must say that I believe we are in the Garden of America—the Country from Chicago to this place is at least 3/4 Prairie, in some places as far as the eye can see it is nothing but a beautiful field covered with grass, which is now about 6 or 8 inches high waving with the wind. The soil is rich and the most of the ground is rolling with an abundance of beautiful springs, the streams run rapid, the timber is rather scarce, but lime stone & sand stone for building is plenty....

I was no little astonished when I came here to find that God had established a church in this almost entirely new country.... There is also a Sabbath School and a Temperance Society.

At Chicago I had the pleasure of being introduced to the principal Chief of the Potawatamie Indians, and I had a long talk with him, in regard to his people, the conversation was very interesting, he seemed to cast off all reserve and gave his opinion freely as to the best plan to Christianize the Indians, he says it never can be done until white men are prevented from taking the Strong Water (liquor) among them, and he likewise said that the wicked traders had done more to destroy his people than the bad spirit had—and when I told him that Congress had passed a law prohibiting all men from taking liquor across the Mississippi, he rejoiced as he said his nation was about to remove west of that river. I gave him my views respecting the Indians and the best way to cultivate their morals. He said it was the best way he had ever heard of, which was to settle near them and bring their children among ours, and teach them to read and to labor, and deal honestly with them and give them no whisky. He said it would not be long until the old ones would die off, and the young ones would become good. I told them it was my intention to visit some of the tribes near the Mississippi. He expressed a great deal of gratitude, and said he was wishing to do all in his power to forward my wishes, he gave me a reference to Keokuk, the principal chief of the Sauks, who he said I would find at their village on the west bank of the Mississippi....

87 / *"We beg the President...to hear us patiently"*

The alternative to the assimilation policy was Indian removal. First suggested by Thomas Jefferson as the only way to ensure the survival of Indian cultures, the removal policy sought to encourage Native Americans to migrate westward to lands where they could live free from white harassment. In 1825 President James Monroe set before Congress a plan to resettle all eastern Indians on tracts in the West where whites would not be allowed to live.

Under Presidents Andrew Jackson and Martin Van Buren (1782–1862), federal Indian policy emphasized removal. A dispute between the Cherokee Nation and the state of Georgia encouraged the shift toward removal. After the Cherokees adopted a constitution asserting sovereignty over their land, the state of Georgia abolished tribal rule and claimed that the Cherokees fell under its jurisdiction. The discovery of gold on Cherokee land triggered a land rush, and the Cherokees sued to keep whites from encroaching on their territory. In two important cases, *Cherokee Nation* v. *Georgia* in 1831 and *Worcester* v. *Georgia* in 1832, the U.S. Supreme Court ruled that states could not pass laws conflicting with federal Indian treaties and that the federal government had an obligation to exclude white intruders from Indian lands. Angered, Jackson is said to have exclaimed: "John Marshall has made his decision; now let him enforce it."

Emboldened by the Supreme Court decisions, the Cherokees resisted Jackson's efforts to get them to sell all tribal lands in exchange for new lands in Oklahoma and Arkansas. The federal government bribed a faction of the tribe to leave Georgia in exchange for transportation costs and $5 million, but most Cherokees held out until 1838, when the army evicted them from their land. (Both before and after removal,

Cherokee traditionalists assassinated a number of Cherokees who cooperated with white missionaries and government officials.)

In this letter, John Ross (1790–1866), the principal leader of the Cherokee Nation, and other Cherokees, petition President Van Buren for claims against the government during the removal of Cherokee from western Georgia to Oklahoma. Nearly four thousand people, a quarter of the Cherokee population, perished of malnutrition, exposure, and cholera on the eight-hundred-mile trek from Georgia to the newly established Indian territory west of the Mississippi.

John Ross, August 14, 1840, to Martin Van Buren, GLC 2856

We will not occupy the time of the President...to hear our nation speak of the injuries under which they suffer from the course pursued toward us, their representatives, and themselves, from the time of the formation of our new constitution of Government up till the present moment.

Yet we cannot forbear to say, in sorrow and not in anger, that while information has been constantly received from those either at enmity with us and gross officers of the U.S. whose previous course was not that of friends, we have been denied the privilege of conference or representation in the exclusion of our principal delegates from the chambers of the Secretary of War and hence have been prevented from giving these explanations and establishing facts which would have relieved us from the imputations so harshly cast upon us....

We beg the President, "the Great Father of the Cherokee," to hear us patiently. Many hundreds of moons have passed since the Cherokee and the white man first began to speak with one another, and we call upon the "talking leaf," the record of your nation, to show that ever the chief of our nation told a lie about money. We have been stubborn, as you may call it, and irreconcilable to our removal from the consecrated and "lonely beds" of our fathers. We have the bitter anguish of a "wounded spirit" longing to drop a burning tear on our desecrated hearth stone—ere we passed away to an unknown land, but who until now has ever accused us of fault....

On the 3d Sept. Genl Scott aware of the uncommon drought—the impossibility of getting water—the suffocating dust of the road. He said to John Ross "how in the name of God Mr. Ross do your people expect to get along?" Mr. Ross replied "General, that is not for us to hesitate about—we are under a pledge and will fulfill it, trusting to God to protect us"—The response of General Scott was one which called for the heartfelt gratitude of the nation. "Mr. Ross I have not been sent here to be a murderer of the Cherokees. I call a halt, a halt, until there is such time as your people can get water...."

88 / *"Prevent those people from cultivating the soil"*

A number of tribes resisted removal. In the Old Northwest, the Sauk and Fox Indians fought the Black Hawk War to recover ceded tribal lands in Illinois and Wisconsin, announcing that they had not understood the implications of the treaty transferring title to their land. The U.S. army and the Illinois militia ended the resistance by wantonly killing nearly five hundred Fox and Sauks who were trying to retreat across the Mississippi River.

In 1832 in Florida, a number of Seminole leaders had signed a treaty under which they agreed to leave Florida for Indian Territory in Oklahoma. Other Seminoles refused to recognize the treaty and took refuge in the Florida Everglades. In the Second Seminole War, the military spent seven years putting down resistance at a cost of $20 million and fifteen hundred casualties, and even then succeeded only after the treacherous act of seizing the Seminole leader Osceola during peace talks.

In the following letter, a future president, Zachary Taylor (1784–1850), discusses the campaign against the Seminoles. He failed to pacify the Seminoles and was relieved of duty at his own request.

Zachary Taylor, March 25, 1838, GLC 5284

I regret to hear of the recent murders committed near Fort Lauderdale, & am satisfied you have fixed on the real perpetrators, the Seminoles, which shows conclusively that no reliance can be placed on their promises or engagements, could the perpetrators of the act be gotten hold of, they ought to be put to death in some way as a terror to others of their nation....

If determined to do so they can avoid you or anyone else for years, by keeping in or near the everglades.... If this war cannot not now be closed in a few months or measurably so by negotiations through the agency of the chiefs you have employed for that purpose, it may continue for many years, in that event a small but efficient force should carry it on, barely sufficient to prevent those people from cultivating the soil, & cutting off their supplies of clothing & ammunition, which must be done by mounted troops, aided by a few revenue cutters properly arranged around the peninsula, and a small force of Inf[antr]y judiciously stationed along the frontier or among exposed white settlers, to protect them from the attacks & degradations of the enemy; a war of this kind if properly conducted would after a while drive the whole of the Indians from the country, & could be carried on with a moderate expenditure of life & treasure.

PART SEVEN

Antebellum America

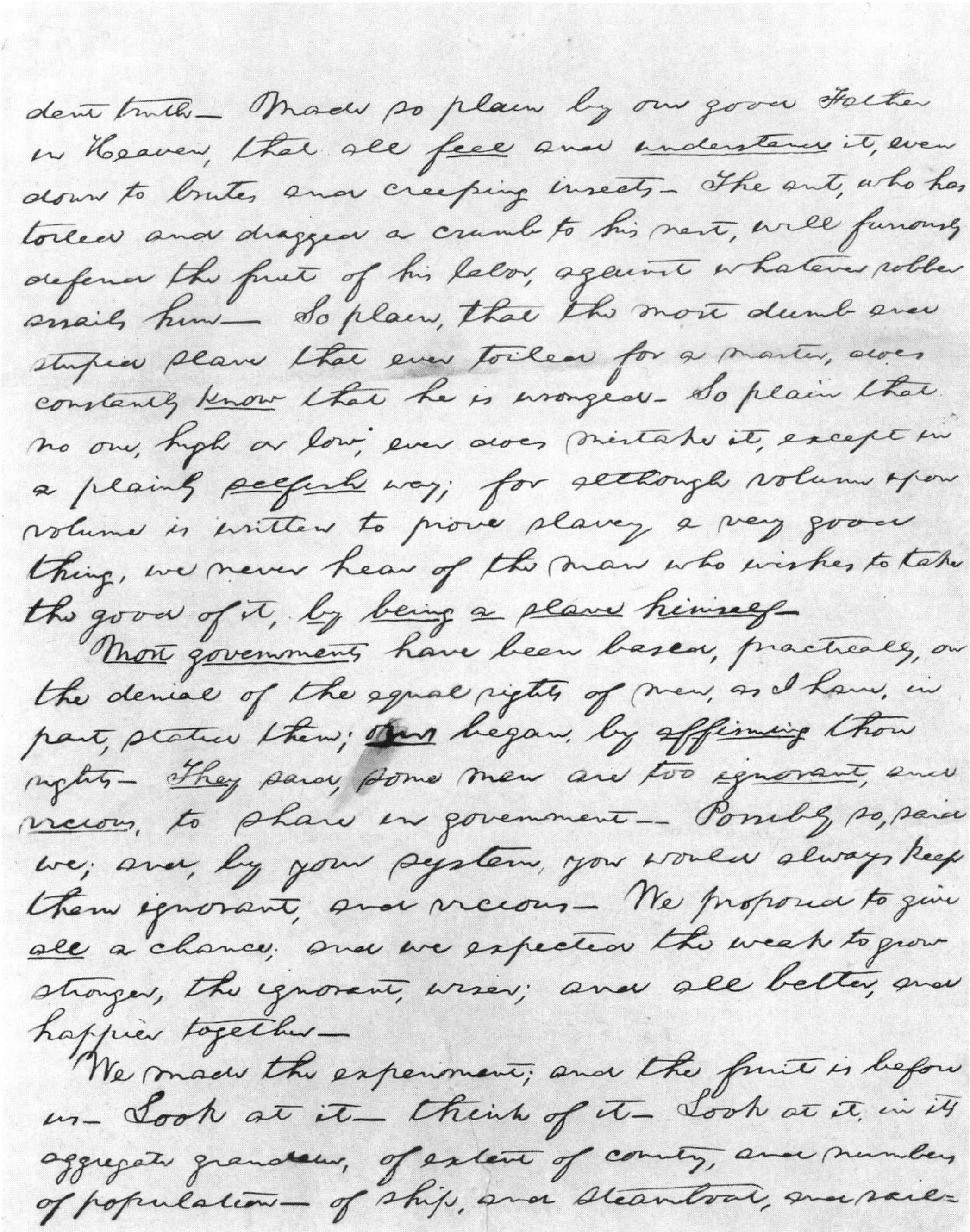

dent truth— Made so plain by our good Father in Heaven, that all *feel* and *understand* it, even down to brutes and creeping insects— The ant, who has toiled and dragged a crumb to his nest, will furiously defend the fruit of his labor, against whatever robber assails him— So plain, that the most dumb and stupid slave that ever toiled for a master, does constantly *know* that he is wronged— So plain that no one, high or low, ever does mistake it, except in a plainly *selfish* way; for although volume upon volume is written to prove slavery a very good thing, we never hear of the man who wishes to take the good of it, by *being a slave himself*—

Most governments have been based, practically, on the denial of the equal rights of men, as I have, in part, stated them; *ours* began, by *affirming* those rights— *They* said, some men are too *ignorant*, and *vicious*, to share in government— Possibly so, said we; and, by your system, you would always keep them ignorant, and vicious— We proposed to give *all* a chance; and we expected the weak to grow stronger, the ignorant, wiser; and all better, and happier together—

We made the experiment; and the fruit is before us— Look at it— think of it— Look at it, in its aggregate grandeur, of extent of country, and numbers of population— of ship, and steamboat, and rail-

Abraham Lincoln. Autograph fragment of a speech, [ca.1858]. The Gilder Lehrman Collection, on deposit at the Pierpont Morgan Library. GLC 3251

The year 1815 marked the beginning of the first modern "postwar" era. The conclusion of the Napoleonic Wars brought an end to half a century of global war and revolution and the start of a new period of nationalism and rapid economic growth. For Americans, the end of the War of 1812 unleashed a new spirit of nationalism, the rapid growth of cities and industry, and a quickening of expansion westward.

During the early nineteenth century, and especially after the War of 1812, American society was profoundly transformed. These years witnessed rapid economic and territorial expansion; the extension of democratic politics; the spread of evangelical revivalism; the rise of the nation's first labor and reform movements; the growth of cities and industrial ways of life; radical shifts in the roles and status of women; and deepening sectional conflicts that would bring the country to the verge of civil war.

Before 1812, westward expansion had proceeded slowly. In 1800, two-thirds of the nation's population still lived within fifty miles of the Atlantic seaboard. Buffalo and Rochester, New York, did not exist. Kickapoos, Miamais, Wyandots, and other Native American peoples populated the area that would become Illinois, Indiana, Michigan, and Wisconsin, while Cherokees, Chickasaws, Choctaws, and Creeks considered the future states of Alabama and Mississippi their homes. Thomas Jefferson predicted in 1803 that it would be a thousand years before settlers occupied all the region east of the Mississippi River.

It took Americans a century and a half to expand as far west as the Appalachian Mountains, a few hundred miles from the Atlantic coast. It took another fifty years to push the frontier to the Mississippi River. By 1830 fewer than one hundred thousand pioneers had crossed the Mississippi. But by 1850 Americans had pushed the edge of settlement all the way to Texas, the Rocky Mountains, and the Pacific Ocean.

Between 1815 and 1840 a political revolution occurred in the United States. Property qualifications for voting and officeholding were abolished, voting by voice was eliminated, voter participation skyrocketed, and a new party system emerged, with grassroots organization and support in all parts of the nation.

The early nineteenth century also saw an outpouring of religious faith that was so massive it has acquired its own name, the Second Great Awakening. Religious faith helped to inspire the first movements in American history to educate the deaf and the blind, care for the mentally ill, reform criminals, build public schools, and extend equal rights to women.

The early nineteenth century marked the emergence of a new economic order in the North. Commercial agriculture replaced subsistence agriculture. Household production was supplanted by centralized manufacturing outside the home. And nonagricultural employment began to overtake agricultural employment. By 1860 nearly half of the North's population made a living outside the agricultural sector, including growing numbers of wage-earning women, who found jobs as schoolteachers, factory hands, and writers.

By the late 1850s many Americans viewed the North and South as two distinct civilizations, each with its own distinctive values and ideals: one increasingly urban and industrial, the other committed to slave labor. Although the two sections shared many of the same ideals, ambitions, and prejudices, they had developed along diverging lines. In increasing numbers, Northerners identified their society with progress and believed that slavery was an intolerable obstacle to innovation, self-improvement, and commercial and economic growth. A growing number of Southerners, in turn, regarded their rural and agricultural society as the true embodiment of republican values. The great question before the nation was whether it could continue to exist half slave, half free.

SHIFTS IN SENSIBILITY: FAMILY, GENDER ROLES, RELIGION, AND THE RISE OF HUMANITARIANISM

THE EMERGENCE OF THE REPUBLICAN FAMILY

Few people think that they are making history when they go about the daily business of their lives—caring for children, conversing with a spouse, deciding to have children, decorating a house, or going to church. But history is not something made exclusively by "great men." It is also made by ordinary people in the everyday course of their lives. Some of the most dramatic cultural transformations—such as the emergence of the modern middle-class family—occurred not as the result of cataclysmic public events, but by the actions of countless individuals in their daily lives.

During the late eighteenth and early nineteenth centuries, many aspects of private life were transformed. Instead of making cloth and clothing at home, families began to buy them. Instead of hand-milling grains, families began to buy processed grains. Kerosene lamps replaced candles as a source of light; coal replaced wood as fuel; friction matches replaced crude flints. Even poorer families began to cook their food on cast-iron cookstoves. Middle-class families planted lawns around their homes, and began to furnish their homes with mirrors, curtains, upholstered chairs, carpets, desks, and bookcases. Communities added steeples to churches, and built the first modern rural "park" cemeteries, replacing crowded urban church graveyards.

The most far-reaching change, however, took place in peoples' sensibilities: in their moral outlooks and sense of self. An eighteenth-century ideal of order and restraint gave way to a "romantic" insistence on the importance of personal feelings, love and affection, and piety.

Classical republican thought tended to view politics and civic engagement as essential to human fulfillment. But increasingly, middle-class Americans began to emphasize the care and rearing of children, marital companionship, and religion as what gave life its meaning and importance. There was a greater emphasis attached to romantic love as the basis for marriage, growing idealization of marital affection, greater tolerance for divorce as a solution to unhappy marriages, and more stress placed on child nurture as the key to rearing proper republican citizens.

A flood of novels and advice books appeared in the late eighteenth century that told readers that love was superior to property as a basis for marriage; that marriage should be based on affection and friendship; that parental example was more effective than physical coercion in governing children; and that the ideal parent sought to cultivate children's natural talents and abilities through love. At the same time, Americans began to self-consciously limit births, so that parents could devote increased attention to each child. In 1800 the typical American mother gave birth to seven or more children. By 1850 that figure had fallen by half.

1 / *"Now is your time to lay a foundation for future usefulness"*

Middle-class family roles underwent a profound change during the late eighteenth and early nineteenth centuries. During the colonial era, the family was conceived of as a patriarchal unit under the authority of the father. Childrearing manuals were addressed to fathers, not mothers. In cases of divorces, fathers were almost automatically awarded custody. When young men corresponded with their family from school or an apprenticeship, they addressed their letters to their father.

Many pieces of evidence contribute to an image of colonial patriarchy. Fathers had a legal right to determine which men could court their daughters and a legal responsibility to give or withhold consent to their children's marriages. Husbands generally addressed letters to their wives with condescending terms such as "Dear Child," while

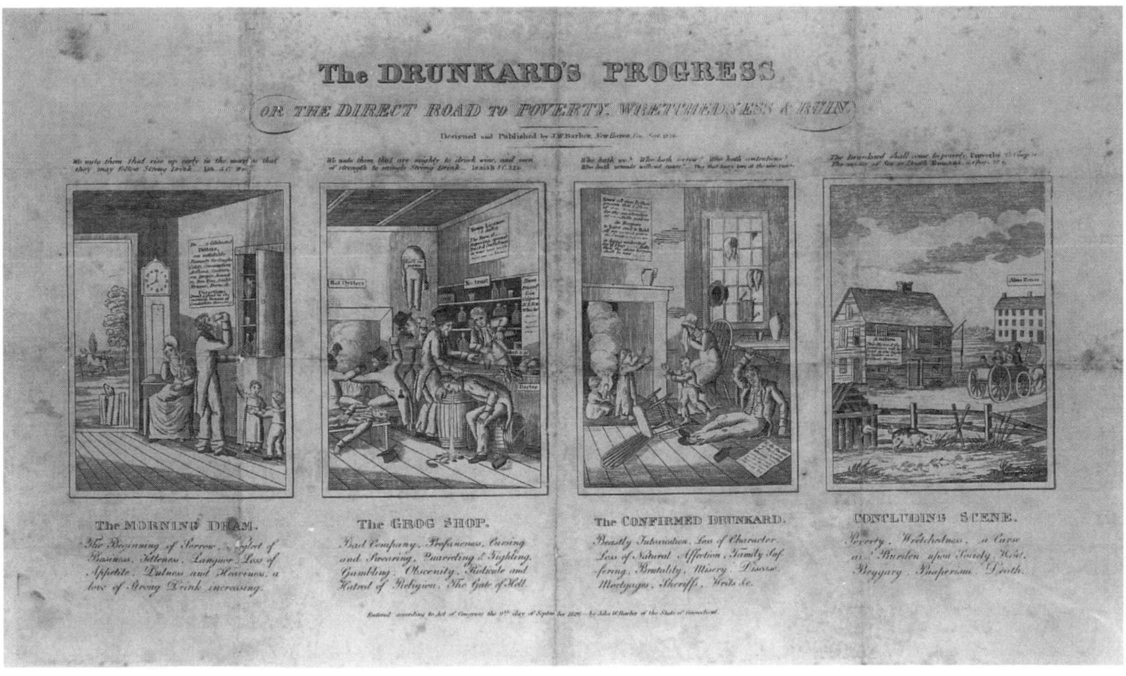

John W. Barber. Broadside, The drunkard's progress, or the direct road to poverty, wretchedness, & ruin, 1826. The Gilder Lehrman Collection, on deposit at the Pierpont Morgan Library. GLC 6025

women addressed their husbands as "Mister" and signed their letters "your faithful and obedient Wife." A symbol of male dominance was the fact that the father sat in an armchair while other family members sat on benches or stools.

Paternal authority in the colonial family rested on a father's control of land. During the late eighteenth and early nineteenth centuries, changes in the economy altered men's family role. The home and the workplace grew increasingly distant. More and more, men left home each day to go to work, while their wives stayed home. Many middle-class women began to make child nurture and household management a self-conscious vocation, while men began to view themselves as economic providers. At the same time, the older idea of a patriarch controlling the details of his children's lives gave way to a very different ideal: of a father preparing his children for independence.

In the following letter, William Ellery (1727–1820), a signer of the Declaration of Independence from Rhode Island, offers paternal advice to his son who was attending an early private college-preparatory school, Washington Academy. Apparently a delightful man, Ellery combines affection and an occasional quirkiness in his letters to his son. It is noteworthy that a friend named his own son after Ellery. William Ellery Channing (1780–1842) became a leader of American Unitarianism and inspired many social reformers as well as a group of thinkers known as the American Transcendentalists.

William Ellery, January 16, 1803, GLC 2300.02

Now is your time to lay a foundation for future usefulness. Time past cannot be recalled. Therefore, my son, exert yourself, and let not your hours run to waste, without improvement.... I do not mean that you should be always at your books; for, as the old proverb justly observes, all work and no play makes a dull boy. Exercise is necessary to health, and health gives vigor to the Soul, but exercise ought not to be pursued to the neglect of learning. Avoid card playing, it is worse than a useless amusement. It, besides being a waste of time, is too apt to produce jangling [nerves], and to sour the temper. Don't forget to read the Bible. You will find in that too much neglected book the best rules of living, and by an attention to it with the assistance of the Divine Spirit you will become wise unto everlasting Salvation.

REPUBLICAN MOTHERHOOD

2 / *"Dear children! I tremble for you"*

A new division of household labor emerged in the late eighteenth and early nineteenth centuries that provided the basis for a novel conception of women's roles. While increasing numbers of middle-class men viewed themselves as their family's breadwinner and provider, a growing number of women considered themselves responsible for nurturing their children's character and making their home a sanctuary from the corruptions of the outside world.

Precisely because women were barred from participating in the "masculine sphere" of business and politics, they could see themselves as untainted by the materialism and the self-seeking of public life. According to the ideal of "republican motherhood" that flourished in the late eighteenth and early nineteenth centuries, women were models of piety and virtue who were responsible for shaping society's moral and intellectual character.

During the early nineteenth century, this conception of women as purer and more moral than men sanctioned unprecedented efforts by women to reform the public sphere. Women provided much of the grassroots support for campaigns to establish public schools and asylums for the mentally ill, to abolish slavery, and to suppress such forms of male vice as heavy drinking, gambling, and prostitution. One of the earliest forms of women's activism was the founding of maternal associations, which disseminated new ideas about childrearing and provided childcare for impoverished working mothers. In the following selection, Susan Mansfield Huntington (1791–1823), one of the founders of the Boston Maternal Association, underscores the growing self-consciousness with which mothers approached child nurture.

SUSAN MANSFIELD HUNTINGTON, APRIL 4, 1815

April 4 [1815] It appears to me that three simple rules...would make children's tempers much more amiable than we generally see them. *First*. Never to give them any thing improper for them, because they strongly and passionately desire it: and even to withhold proper things, until they manifest a right spirit. *Second*. Always to gratify every reasonable desire, when a child is pleasant in its request; that your children may see that you love to make them happy. *Third*. Never to become impatient and fretful yourself, but proportion your displeasure exactly to the offence. If parents become angry, and speak loud and harsh, upon every slight failure of duty, they may bid a final adieu to domestic subordination, unless the grace of God interposes to snatch the little victims of severity from destruction. I feel confident...that although more children are injured by excessive indulgence than by the opposite fault, yet the effects of extreme rigor are the most hopeless. And the reason is, associations of a disagreeable nature...are the strongest....

For my own part, I find myself falling so far short, that I am, sometimes, overwhelmed with the distressing apprehension of erroring fatally. Dear children! I tremble for you, when I reflect how dangerous is the path in which you are to tread, and how difficult the task of directing you in safety.

Benjamin B. Wisner, ed., *Memoirs of the Late Mrs. Susan Mansfield Huntington* (Boston: Crocker & Brewster, 1826), pp. 127–29.

3 / *"I have felt...a sense of my obligations to God"*

When Alexander Hamilton was asked why the framers of the Constitution had omitted the word "God" from the document, he reportedly replied: "We forgot." Few of the nation's founders were devoutly religious. They were gentlemen of the Enlightenment, who valued rational inquiry and rejected religious enthusiasm. Thomas Jefferson's views were not unusual among the founders. He considered himself a Christian and called the teaching of Jesus Christ "the most perfect and sublime that has ever been taught by man." At the same time he apparently did not believe in Christ's divinity or in the authenticity of biblical miracles.

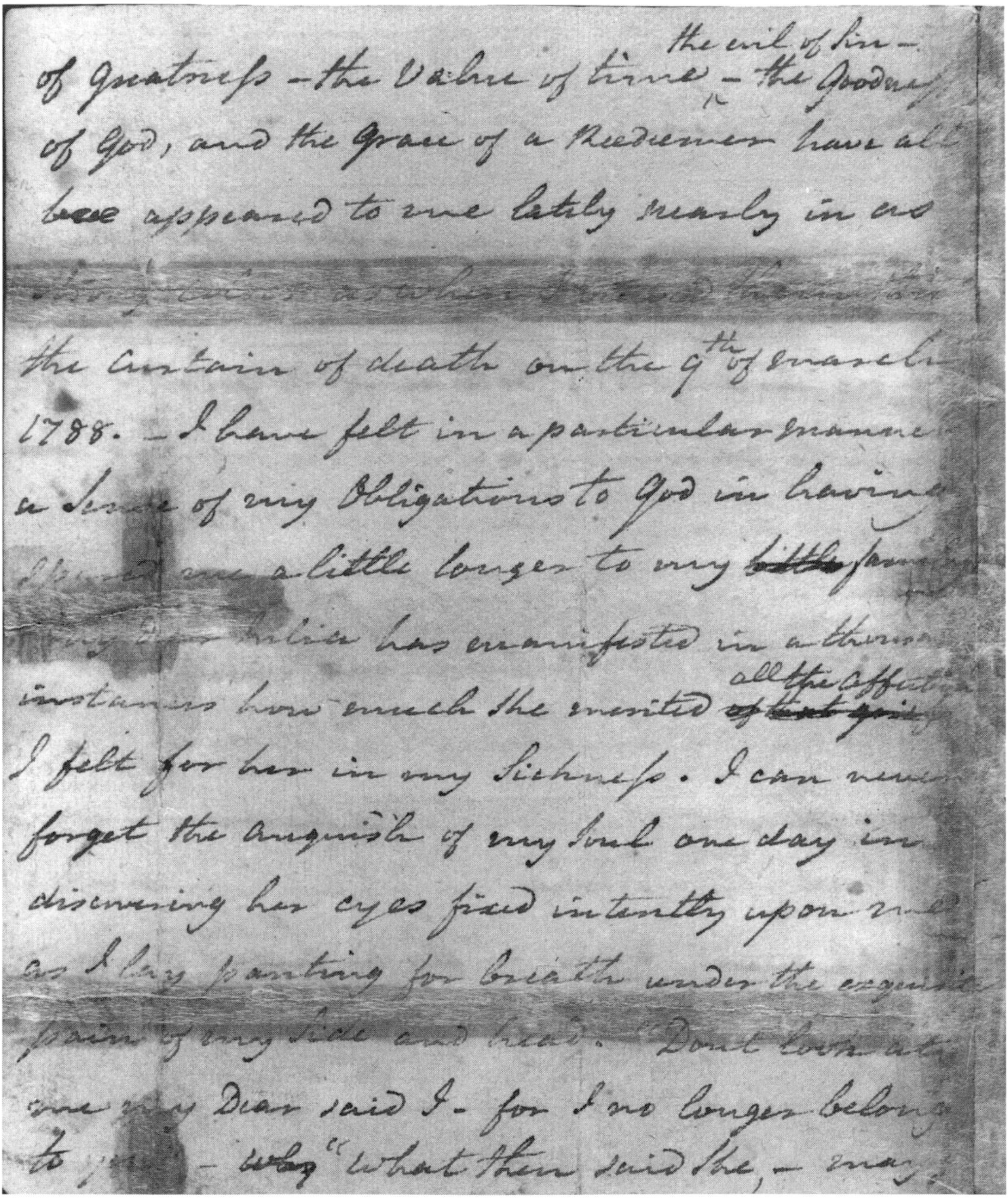
of greatness — the Value of time — the evil of sin — the Goodness
of God, and the Grace of a Redeemer have all
~~bee~~ appeared to me lately nearly in as
[illegible]
the Curtain of death on the 9th of March
1788. — I have felt in a particular manner
a Sense of my Obligations to God in having
spared me a little longer to my ~~little~~ family
my dear Alice has manifested in a thousand
instances how much she merited ~~of that grief~~ all the affection
I felt for her in my Sickness. I can never
forget the anguish of my soul one day in
discovering her eyes fixed intently upon me
as I lay panting for breath under the exquisite
pain of my side and head. Don't look at
me my Dear said I — for I no longer belong
to you — ~~why~~ "what then said she, — may

Martin Van Buren. Document signed, Orders for transport of the Amistad captive (c/s John Forsyth), 1840/01/07. The Gilder Lehrman Collection, on deposit at the Pierpont Morgan Library. GLC 5508.011

During the 1790s, however, alarm over irreligion and secularism mounted, particularly after leaders in revolutionary France abolished Christianity and the worship of God. Open expressions of religious commitment became more pronounced. Benjamin Rush (1746–1813), the author of the following letter, was America's most distinguished physician. Here he views benevolence toward other human beings as the highest expression of religious sentiment.

Benjamin Rush, March 9, 1790, to his sister Polly Stockton, GLC 5508.011

This is the anniversary of the favorable issue of that illness in which you bore so distinguished a part as a friend and a nurse two years ago. Many of the ideas of that memorable period have lately been familiar to me. The vanity of wealth, the littleness of greatness, the value of time, the evil of Sin, the goodness of God, and the grace of a redeemer have all appeared to me lately nearly…as [clearly] as when I viewed them through the curtain of death…. I have felt in a particular manner a sense of my obligations to God in having spared me a little longer to my family….

I have lately been much delighted in reading twelve of Mr. [John] Wesley's sermons bound up in the American Magazine. In one of these he describes the rise and progress of Christianity in the human heart in a collection of circles. The outside one includes "Attendance upon public worship." The second, "Acts of piety towards God, such as prayer, praise, and a conformity to the ordinances of the Gospel." The third includes "Acts of charity and mercy to our fellow creatures." The fourth includes "Holy tempers such as…humility—gentleness—self-denial—purity—forgiveness and love of enemies, and the like….

In contemplating this ingenious acc[oun]t of the rise and progress of religion in the soul, we are struck with our duties to our fellow creatures being placed within and above the outward duties to God. How great is the love of God to his distressed children, when he dispenses with the duties to himself in their favor, and admits of an act of charity to a fellow creature as a more acceptable offering to himself, than prayer or praise.

RELIGIOUS LIBERALISM AND EVANGELICAL REVIVALISM

Two significantly different trends transformed American Protestantism during the late eighteenth and early nineteenth centuries: religious liberalism and evangelical revivalism. Religious liberalism was an emerging humanitarian form of religion that rejected harsh Calvinist doctrines of original sin and predestination. Its preachers stressed the basic goodness of human nature and each individual's capacity to follow Christ's example by cultivating proper moral attitudes and behavior. Religious liberals tended to reject literal interpretations of the Bible and instead emphasized the importance of reason in interpreting Scripture. They also rejected the orthodox boundaries of the Trinity, and, denying the divinity of Jesus Christ, instead viewed him as a moral model all humanity should strive to emulate.

Another important current in late eighteenth and early nineteenth-century American Protestantism can be found in the enthusiastic religious revivals that swept the nation. These revivals sought to awaken Americans to their need for religious rebirth and redemption. The term "evangelical" refers to a belief that all people must recognize their depravity and worthlessness, repent of their sins, and undergo a conversion *experience* and a rebirth of religious feeling. Two key terms in the revivalists' vocabulary were "ability" and "decision." In their eyes, all people had the ability to open their heart to the Holy Spirit and to decide whether they would submit to God's will.

4 / *"It is more than forty years, since...I renounced the Calvinistic Scheme"*

In 1783, the president of Yale College, Ezra Stiles (1727–95), predicted that three religious denominations—the Congregationalists, the Episcopalians, and the Presbyterians—would dominate the new nation's religious life. His prediction proved to be entirely wrong. A number of older denominations quickly expanded—notably the Baptists, Catholics, and Methodists—and a host of new denominations arose, radically reshaping the religious landscape—Disciples of Christ, Mormons, and separate African-American churches.

Unitarianism, the epitome of religious liberalism, was one of many new religious denominations to appear in the early nineteenth-century United States. Few religious denominations exerted a stronger influence on American intellectual life, through such figures as the poets William Cullen Bryant (1794–1878), Henry Wadsworth Longfellow (1807–82), and James Russell Lowell (1819–91) and the historian Francis Parkman (1823–94), or contributed as many prominent antebellum reformers, including Dorothea Dix (1802–87), a crusader on behalf of the mentally ill; Samuel Gridley Howe (1801–76); a staunch advocate for the blind; and the educational reformer Horace Mann (1796–1859).

A bitter theological conflict, known as the Unitarian Controversy, divided early nineteenth-century New England Congregationalists. This conflict pitted theological conservatives who emphasized human depravity against religious liberals who denied there was a scriptural basis for a belief in predestination or original sin. In this letter, Timothy Pickering (1745–1829), a Federalist political leader and secretary of state under President John Adams, mentions his shift away from orthodox Calvinism to Unitarianism.

TIMOTHY PICKERING, JANUARY 6, 1816, TO JAMES MCHENRY, GLC 4835

It is more than forty years, since, with strong conviction, I renounced the Calvinistic Scheme, in which I had been educated, as utterly incompatible with the perfections of the Deity. But it was not till a later period that the doctrine of the Trinity (which I had never heard controverted in the pulpit) employed my thoughts...and induced me...to reject this dogma, liberalise the creed of Calvin. It has since been the essential article of my faith and practice, to worship only *One God*, who sent his son to be Savior of the World.

DISESTABLISHMENT

5 / "Any person may separate from one...Religious Society and join another"

In 1833 Massachusetts became the last state to end state support for churches. Nine years earlier, the state had adopted a measure allowing officially recognized religious societies, not only the official Congregationalists, to assess taxes on all church members.

Religious revivals, in part, were a reaction to the disestablishment of churches. Deprived of tax revenue, Protestant ministers held revivals to ensure that America would remain a God-fearing nation. The popularity of revivals also reflected many Americans' hunger for an emotional religion that downplayed creeds and emphasized conversion. Revivals met a growing need for a sense of community and communal purpose. At a time of increasing mobility and mounting commercialism, revivals offered an antidote to secularism, materialism, and individualism.

To some extent, revivals transcended class lines, but they had particular appeal to distinct social groups. In the South, revivals attracted the dispossessed, slaves as well as yeoman whites. In the North, it was the aspiring and upwardly mobile groups, especially in thriving market towns and new western cities. Middle-class women, in particular, joined the revivals in large numbers.

The revivals left an indelible imprint on antebellum American culture. The rituals of evangelical religion—the camp meeting, the dramatic conversion experience, and mass baptisms along rivers and creeks—were truly distinctive American experiences before the Civil War. When Lincoln, in the Gettysburg Address and his second inaugural address, spoke about a bloody sacrifice, rebirth, collective punishment, and national mission, his words carried haunting echoes of revivalist sermons.

Columbian Centinel, Boston, April 28, 1824, GLB 327.03

Laws of Massachusetts, "An Act respecting Public Worship and Religious Freedom"

...Any person may separate from one Parish or Religious Society and join another, either of the same or of a different denomination, by filing with the Clerk of the Society...a certificate of the fact....

No citizen of this Commonwealth, being a member of any Religious Society in the Commonwealth, shall be assessed or liable to pay any tax for the support of Public Worship, or other Parochial charges, to any Parish, Precinct, or Religious Society whatever, other than to that of which he is a member.

ORIGINS OF THE AMERICAN REFORM TRADITION

The early nineteenth century witnessed enormous efforts to improve society through reform. Inspired by the revolutionary ideals of the Declaration of Independence, by the Enlightenment faith in reason, and, above all, by liberal and evangelical religious ideals, reformers launched unprecedented campaigns to assist the handicapped, rehabilitate criminals and prostitutes, curb the drinking of alcohol, guarantee women's rights, and abolish slavery. Our modern systems of free public schools, prisons, and hospitals for the mentally ill are all legacies of this first generation of reformers.

Reformers had many different reasons for wanting to change American society. Some hoped to remedy the distresses created by social disorder, violence, and widening class divisions. Others found motivation in a religious vision of a godly society on earth.

Many reformers believed that the American Revolution had inaugurated a new epoch in human history. The success of the Revolution, the rapid growth in church membership, and the quickening pace of technological and scientific progress convinced many Americans that the United States was the New Israel destined to lead the world to the millennium, the establishment of God's kingdom on earth.

American reform passed through a series of overlapping phases. The earliest reformers sought to persuade Americans to adopt more godly personal habits. They set up associations to battle profanity and Sabbath-breaking, to place a Bible in every home, to provide a religious education for the children of the poor, and to curb the widespread heavy drinking of hard liquor. By discouraging drinking, gambling, and encouraging observance of the Sabbath, moral reformers hoped to "restore the government of God."

Beginning in the 1820s a new phase of reform—social reform—spread across the country, directed at such problems as crime, illiteracy, and poverty. Reformers sought to solve these problems by creating new institutions to deal with them—including prisons, public schools, and asylums for the deaf, the blind, and the mentally ill.

During the 1830s a third phase of reform—radical reform—emerged. Radical reformers sought national regeneration by eliminating African-American slavery and racial and sexual discrimination and by creating ideal communities to serve as models for a better world.

DUELING

6 / *"Dueling is a mode of settling certain points of honour...by single combat"*

Early nineteenth century Americans did not view sin as a metaphysical abstraction. Religious leaders taught that sin was concrete. High living, moral indifference, and preoccupation with worldly and commercial matters—all these were denounced as manifestations of human depravity. After Aaron Burr killed Alexander Hamilton in a duel, a growing number of reformers denounced dueling as a sin, a relic of a more barbaric stage in human history. In the future, later reformers would not only denounce drinking and slavery as capital sins, but also would repudiate all forms of force and violence.

In a letter to his son, William Ellery condemns dueling.

WILLIAM ELLERY, NOVEMBER 5, 1805, TO HIS SON GEORGE WANTON ELLERY, GLC 2300.13

You are about to write a composition on dueling, and I...wish that I could assist you composing those final lines....

Dueling is a mode of settling certain points of honour, as they are called, by single combat.... It was introduced into Europe at a barbarious period, a period when property was not decided by judicial combat, when it was absurdly imagined that the Deity would always give victory in favor of right. Both these practices [are inconsistent] with the Christian religion.... The party who killed his adversary...is...guilty of murder, & expressly forbidden by the eighth commandment in the Decalogue [the Ten Commandments] and sound reason can never admit what God has prohibited & Judicial combats have long since been pushed aside and for the sake of religion, reason and humanity, the infamous practice of dueling ought to be reprobated with universal contempt.

EDUCATION

7 / *"The school was large, and the pupils rather ungovernable"*

Of all the ideas advanced by antebellum reformers, none was more original than the principle that all children should be educated to their fullest capacity at public expense. Reformers viewed education as the key to individual opportunity and the creation of an enlightened and responsible citizenry. Reformers also believed that public schools could serve as an effective weapon in the fight against juvenile crime and as an essential ingredient in the assimilation of immigrants.

At the beginning of the nineteenth century, the United States enjoyed the world's highest literacy rate—approximately 75 percent. Apprenticeship was a major form of education, supplemented by private academies for the affluent and charity schools for the poor. But the growth of urban slums and the breakdown of the apprenticeship system resulted in gangs of uneducated juveniles roaming city streets.

The campaign for public schools began in earnest in the 1820s, when religiously motivated reformers advocated public education as an answer to poverty, crime, and deepening social divisions. At first, many reformers championed Sunday schools as a way to "reclaim the vicious, to instruct the ignorant, and secure the observance of the Sabbath." But soon reformers began to call for establishment of free, tax-supported public school systems, improved school curricula, and state-supported teacher training. Public schools were the products of widespread efforts at the local level. In this selection, two New England teachers describe the condition of education on the eve of school reform.

ACCOUNT OF FIRST NEW ENGLAND TEACHER, AUGUST 1831

Ten years ago I was called to superintend a district school...in Connecticut.... The school had usually been under the care of a male instructor four or five months in the winter, and a female as many months in the summer, with a vacation in the spring, and another in the fall, of from one to two months each. The instructors had been changed often; few of them ever taught two seasons in succession. The school was large, and the pupils rather ungovernable.... No one remaining in the school more than four or five months, little could be done, except assisting the pupils in recalling what they had forgotten during the previous long vacation, inculcating new laws, and perhaps introducing some new school-book....

School was commenced precisely at 9 a.m., and 1 p.m., throughout the year....

The greatest number I ever had...was about sixty, and this only during a very short period of the winter; the school averaged forty four throughout the year.... Many pupils had a mile to walk, and some nearly two....

When I entered the school, there were fifty scholars under five years of age. The greater part were under four, and several only about three.... I stoutly maintained, that no child ought to be sent to school under five years of age. But the parents insisted on sending them, and I was obliged to submit. To meet the exigency, means were provided at the schoolhouse for allowing them to sleep occasionally during the hot weather....

Account of second New England teacher, October 1831

The school house stood...at the junction of four roads, so near the usual track of carriages, that a large stone was set up at the end of the building to defend it from injury. Except in the dry season the ground is wet, permitting small collections of water on the surface....The spot is peculiarly exposed to the bleak winds of winter; nor are there at present any shade trees near, to shelter the children from the scorching rays of the summer's sun during their recreations.... Neither is there any such thing as an outhouse of *any kind*, not even a wood shed.

The size of the building was twenty two feet long, by twenty broad.... Around three sides of the room, were connected desks arranged so that when the pupils were sitting at them, their faces were towards the instructor and their backs towards the wall. Attached to the sides of the desks nearest the instructor, were benches for small pupils. The instructor's desk and chair occupied the centre. On this desk were stationed a rod or ferule [a cane]; sometimes both....

The windows were five in number....They were situated so low in the walls, as to give full opportunity to the pupils to see every traveller as he passed, and to be easily broken....

The school was not unfrequently broken up for a day or two for want of wood in former years; but since they have used a smaller fire place, this occurrence has been more rare. The instructor or pupils were, however, sometimes compelled to cut or saw it, to prevent the closing of the school.... The [school]house was frequently cold and uncomfortable.... Frequently too, we were annoyed by smoke....

The ventilation of the school room, was as much neglected as its temperature; and its cleanliness, more perhaps than either.... There were...no arrangements made for cleaning feet at the door, or for washing floors, windows, &c....

Instructors have usually boarded in the families of the pupils. The compensation has varied from seven to eleven dollars a month for males; and from sixty two and a half cents to one dollar a week for females....

American Annals of Instruction, Vol. II (August and October 1831), pp. 380–83, 468–72.

8 / "An uniform system of weights and measures"

In 1776 Thomas Paine wrote words that would continue to inspire future generations of Americans: "We have it within our power to begin the world anew." This idea, that the United States had the power to reorder the world on a more rational and moral basis, would inspire many efforts at reform. One of the most interesting involved attempts to fashion a system of weights and measures appropriate to a modern society.

In 1793 revolutionary France introduced a new system of weights and measures: the metric system. In fact, France did not fully embrace the metric system until the 1830s. In 1819, the House of Representatives asked Secretary of State John Quincy Adams to recommend a system of measurement for the new American republic. Two years later he issued his report, which recognized the strengths of the metric system but recommended against it.

Adams argued in behalf of the English system of weights and measures, in part because it had been perfected by hundreds of years of practical experience and partly because it used units of measurement based on the human body. An inch, Adams noted, was about the length of a knuckle; a yard represented the length of an extended arm; and a mile represented the distance the ground remained visible before it passed over the horizon (which is why a mile was sometimes called an "eye"). All that government should do, in Adams's view, was to ensure the accuracy and uniformity of customary measurements.

JOHN QUINCY ADAMS, 1821, REPORT UPON WEIGHTS AND MEASURES, GLC 4045

Since the establishment of our national independence, we have partaken of that ardent spirit of reform, and that impatient longing for uniformity, which have so signally animated the two nations from which we descended [Greece and ancient Israel]. The Congress of the United States have been as earnestly employed in the search of an uniform system of weights and measures....

France and Great Britain are the only nations of modern Europe who have taken much interest in the organization of a new system, or attempted a reform for the avowed purpose of uniformity. The proceedings in those two countries have been numerous, elaborate, persevering, and, in France especially, comprehensive, profound and systematic....

During the conquering period of the French Revolution, the new system of French weights and measures was introduced into those countries which were united to the empire. Since the severance of those countries from France, it has been discarded, excepting in the kingdom of the Netherlands....

In England, from the earliest records of parliamentary history, the statute books are filled with ineffectual attempts of the legislature to establish uniformity. Of the origin of their weights and measures, the historical traces are faint and indistinct: but they have had, from time immemorial, the pound, ounce, foot, inch and mile, derived from the Romans, and through them from the Greeks, and the yard...a measure of Saxon origin, derived, like those of the Hebrews and the Greeks, from the human body....

The philosophers and legislators of Britain have...despised the primitive standards assumed from the stature and proportions of the human body.... They tasked their ingenuity and their learning to find, in matter or motion, some immutable standard of linear measure, which might be assumed as the single universal standard from which all measures and all weights might be derived....

After a succession of more than sixty years of inquiries and experiments, the British parliament have not yet acted in the form of law. After nearly forty of the same years of separate pursuit of the same object, uniformity, the Congress of the United States has shown the same cautious deliberation: they have yet authorized no change of the existing law....

If that universal uniformity, so desirable to human contemplation, be an obtainable perfection, it is now attainable only by the adoption of the new French system....

This system approaches to the ideal perfection of uniformity applied to weights and measures; and, whether destined to succeed, or doomed to fail, will shed unfading glory upon the age in which it was conceived, and upon the nation by which its execution was attempted.... In the progress of its establishment, it has often been brought in conflict...with the habits, passions, prejudices, and necessities of man.... But if man upon earth be an improvable being; if that universal peace, which was the object of a Saviour's mission...if the Spirit of Evil is, before the final consummation of things, to be cast down from his dominion over men, and bound in the chains of a thousand years, the foretaste here of man's eternal felicity; then this system of common instruments, to accomplish all the changes of social and friendly commerce, will furnish the links of sympathy between the inhabitants of the most distant regions....

It results, however, from [a] review of the present condition of the French system in its native country...that the time has not arrived at which so great and hazardous experiment can be recommended, as that of discarding all our established existing weights and measures, to adopt and legalize those of France in its stead....

COLONIZATION

9 / *"They neither enjoyed the immunities of freemen, nor... the incapacities of slaves, but partook...of both"*

By the early nineteenth century, the emancipation of slaves in the northern states and the outlawing of the African slave trade nourished the optimistic view that slavery was a dying institution. In 1787 the Confederation Congress barred slavery from the Old Northwest. The number of slaves freed by their masters in the Upper South rose dramatically during the 1780s and 1790s. By 1804 nine states north of Maryland and Delaware had either freed their slaves or adopted gradual-emancipation plans. Both the United States and Britain in 1808 outlawed the African slave trade. In 1791, a religious leader predicted that within fifty years it will "be as shameful for a man to hold a Negro slave, as to be guilty of common robbery or theft."

Yet a belief that blacks and whites could not coexist as free and equal citizens encouraged futile efforts at deportation and overseas colonization. In 1817 a group of prominent ministers and politicians formed the American Colonization Society to resettle free blacks in West Africa. Many of these colonizationists were confident that a successful colony of free black settlers in Africa would encourage planters to voluntarily emancipate their slaves, and create a group of black missionaries who would spread Christianity in Africa. In this way, colonizationists hoped not only to end slavery but also to expiate the nation's guilt.

With some aid from federal and state governments the American Colonization Society sent a party of blacks to the British colony of Sierra Leone, and beginning in

1822, to the newly founded colony of Liberia. The colonization project was bitterly opposed, however, by many American free blacks and by slaveholders in the Deep South, who saw the American Colonization Society as a Trojan horse for abolitionists. Deprived of significant federal support in the late 1820s and viciously attacked by radical abolitionists in the 1830s, colonization remained a kind of vague ideal that attracted disillusioned black leaders in the 1850s and that still appealed to Abraham Lincoln early in the Civil War.

"A View of Exertions Lately Made for the Purpose of Colonizing the Free People of Color of the United States, in Africa, or Elsewhere," Washington, D.C., 1817, GLC 5181

Soon after the commencement of the present session of Congress the expediency of colonizing free people of colour became a subject of consideration with many gentlemen of respectability from the different states. The propriety of such a measure could it be carried into effect, was generally admitted. It was thought that a design of such importance so intimately connected with the best interest of the citizens of the U. States, and promising at the same time to improve and meliorate that class of the community for which provision was to be made, should not be abandoned without a vigorous effort to carry it into execution.

The formation of a colonization society was therefore proposed.... The following preamble and resolution were approved by the House of Delegates of [Virginia]....

Whereas the General assembly of Virginia have repeatedly sought to obtain an asylum, beyond the limits of the United States, for such persons of color, as have been, or might be, emancipated under the laws of this commonwealth, but have hitherto found all their efforts frustrated, either by the disturbed state of other nations, or domestic causes equally unpropitious to its success.

They now avail themselves of a period when peace has healed the wounds of humanity, and the principal nations of Europe have concurred, with the government of the U. States, in abolishing the African slave trade, (a traffic, which this commonwealth, both before and since the revolution, zealously sought to terminate) to renew this effort....

[Henry] Clay said...that class, of the mixt population of our country was in a peculiar situation. They neither enjoyed the immunities of freemen, nor were they subject to the incapacities of slaves, but partook in some degree of the qualities of both. From their condition, and the unconquerable prejudices resulting from their color, they never could amalgamate with the free whites of this country. It was desirable, therefore, both as it respected them, and the residue of the population of the country, to drain them off. Various schemes of colonization had been thought of, and a part of our own continent, it was thought by some, might furnish a suitable establishment for them. But for his part Mr. Clay said he had a decided preference for some part of the coast of Africa. There ample provision might be made for the colony itself, and it might be rendered instrumental to the introduction, into that extensive part of the globe, of the arts, civilization and Christianity. There was a peculiar, a moral fitness in restoring them to the lands of their fathers. And if, instead of the evils and sufferings which we had been the innocent cause of inflicting upon the inhabitants of Africa, we can transmit to her the blessings of our arts, our civilization and our religion, may we not hope that America will extinguish a great portion of that moral debt which she has contracted to that unfortunate continent?

10 / *"The existence of distinct and separate castes... is an inherent vice in the composition of society"*

The president of the American Society for Colonizing the Free People of Color, Bushrod Washington (1762–1829), who served as an associate justice on the U.S. Supreme Court from 1798 to 1829, defends colonization as a way to spread the blessing of Christianity and modern technology.

BUSHROD WASHINGTON, "MEMORIAL OF THE PRESIDENT AND BOARD OF MANAGERS OF THE AMERICAN SOCIETY FOR COLONIZING THE FREE PEOPLE OF COLOR OF THE U.S.," JANUARY 14, 1817, GLC 5181

It is now reduced to be a maxim, equally approved in philosophy and practice, that the existence of distinct and separate castes, or classes, forming exceptions to the general system of policy adapted to the community, is an inherent vice in the composition of society; pregnant with baneful consequences, both moral and political and demanding the utmost exertion of human energy...to remedy or remove it....

It may be reserved for our government, (the first to denounce an inhuman and abominable traffic, in the guilt and disgrace of which most of the civilized nations of the world were partakers) to become the honorable instrument, under Divine Providence, of conferring a still higher blessing upon the large and interesting portion of mankind...by demonstrating that a race of men, composing numerous tribes, spread over a continent of vast and unexplored extent, fertility, and riches; known to the enlightened nations of antiquity; and who had yet made no progress in the refinements of civilization; from whom history has preserved no monuments of arts or arms: that even this, hitherto, ill-fated race, may cherish the hope of beholding at last the orient star revealing the best and highest aims and attributes of man.

11 / *"No adequate provision...was made for the shelter and comfort of the people"*

A few African Americans supported African colonization in the belief that it provided the only alternative to continued degradation and discrimination. Paul Cuffe (1759–1817), a Quaker sea captain who was the son of a former slave and an Indian woman, led the first experiment in colonization. In 1815 he transported 38 free blacks to Sierra Leone, and devoted thousands of his own dollars to the cause of colonization.

Virtually all the leading white abolitionists were colonizationists before calling for the immediate emancipation of slaves. But by 1830, abolitionists such as William Lloyd Garrison (1805–79) had begun to denounce colonization as a wholly impractical solution to the slavery problem. Each year the nation's slave population rose by roughly 50,000. But in 1830 the American Colonization Society persuaded just 259 free blacks to immigrate to Liberia, bringing the total number of African Americans colonized in Africa to only 1400. Nevertheless, it is possible to exaggerate the impracticality of colonization, since *more than* 50,000 Africans were being carried every year, most of them illegally, to the New World.

The biggest problems that the American Colonization Society faced, aside from finance and opposition from free blacks, were disease and morality, as the following letter points out. In this selection, the Board of Managers of the American Colonization Society describes a disastrous attempt to resettle free blacks along the coast of Africa.

E. B. Caldwell and the Board of Managers of the American Colonization Society, October 27, 1826, GLC 5181

The Board of Managers of the American Colonization Society have to discharge a painful duty in laying before the...republic the distressing intelligence received from the coast of Africa. The following extract of a letter, from a correspondent in London is the latest information obtained....

"You will probably have heard...of the fatal calamity which has been permitted to befall Mr. Bacon and most of his *white* companions on the coast of Africa, in their benevolent undertaking for the welfare of their fellow creatures. It is another of that class of Providential dispensations which repeats, with a loud voice, 'Be still; and know that I am GOD;" but which should never be permitted to discourage human efforts.... [Five white colonization society agents died of disease and] 15 out of 82 people of color had also died...."

At present we would request our friends not to be discouraged. The Board lament the unfortunate issue of their first efforts; but they had no right to calculate upon the absence of those disasters and disappointments which attend all human affairs, and which are ordered or permitted to attend them for purposes, the wisdom and goodness of which, though we may not see, we cannot doubt. We lament, also, the loss sustained by the Society and our country, and the cause of humanity, in the deaths of those who so freely offered themselves in the service of God, and for the good of man, to toil and suffering and death. They have "entered into their rest, and their works do follow them" and we trust they have obtained "the prize of their high calling;" and their example and their fate, we rejoice to know, instead of deterring, has encouraged others to assume their posts.... Could we believe that the climate of the coast of Africa was such as to forbid all hope of settlement, we should be ready to abandon our purpose, and look elsewhere for a more safe asylum; but the circumstances that have occurred there do not, in our judgment, any further prove such a fact than similar instances during the late season in our own country....

The rains were at hand, and no adequate provision, we think it probable, was made for the shelter and comfort of the people. The zeal and activity of the agents, in providing for this state of things, we have no doubt, increased their exposure and danger. Against all these disadvantages, we hope to be better able to guard for the future. It is also worthy of particular remark, that the mortality amongst our people should by no means be imputed to the situation selected for our first settlement. On the contrary, we have every reason to presume that the fatal diseases were contracted by them either on board the vessels, to which they appear to have been a good deal confined on a sickly coast; or at such temporary abodes on shore as were resorted to for shelter, until the necessary arrangements could be completed for obtaining a grant of the lands contemplated as the site of our intended settlements.... We are pleased to discover that the free colored people of this country are not intimidated; numbers of the most respectable and intelligent of that population are renewing their entreaties to be sent out this Fall; and agents well qualified have already offered themselves to lead them. With these views and encouragements, the Board of Managers propose to send out one or two vessels in the course of the next month....

POSTWAR NATIONALISM AND DIVISION

The end of the War of 1812 resulted in a burst of nationalistic fervor. The economic program adopted by Congress, including a new national bank and a protective tariff, reflected the growing feeling of national unity. The U.S. Supreme Court also promoted the spirit of nationalism by establishing the principle of federal supremacy.

But this same period also witnessed the emergence of new political divisions as well as growing sectional animosities. Whether the spirit of nationalism or the spirit of sectionalism would triumph was the great question that would dominate American politics over the next four decades.

12 / *"We were embarked in the same sacred cause of liberty"*

Early in the summer of 1817, as a conciliatory gesture toward the Federalists who had opposed the War of 1812, President James Monroe embarked on a goodwill tour through the Northeast and what is now the Midwest. Everywhere Monroe went, citizens held parades and banquets in his honor. In Federalist Boston, a crowd of forty thousand welcomed the Republican president. A Federalist newspaper called the times "the era of good feelings."

James Monroe (1758–1831) was the popular symbol of the era of good feelings. His life embodied much of the history of the young republic. He had joined the Continental Army in 1776 and spent the terrible winter of 1777–78 at Valley Forge. He had been a member of the Articles of Confederation Congress and performed double duty as secretary of state and secretary of war during the War of 1812.

The last president to don the fashions of the eighteenth century, Monroe wore his hair in a powdered wig and favored knee breeches, long white stockings, and buckled shoes. His political values, too, were those of an earlier day. Like George Washington, he hoped for a country without political parties, governed by leaders chosen on their merits. So great was his popularity that he won a second presidential term by an electoral college vote of 231 to 1.

Here Monroe replies to an address of the Massachusetts Society of the Cincinnati, an organization of surviving Revolutionary War officers.

James Monroe, July 4, 1817, Speech to Massachusetts Society of the Cincinnati, GLC 69

No approbation can be more dear to me than that of those with whom I had the honour to share the common toils and perils of the war for our independence. We were embarked in the same sacred cause of liberty, and we have lived to enjoy the reward of our common labors. Many of our companions-in-arms fell in the field before our Independence was achieved, and many less fortunate than ourselves lived not to witness the perfect fulfillment of their hopes in the prosperity and happiness of our country. You do but justice to yourselves in claiming the confidence of your country, that you can never desert the standard of freedom. You fought to obtain it in times when men's hearts & principles were severely tried, and your public sacrifices and honorable actions are the best pledges of your sincere and devoted attachment to our excellent Constitution. May your children never forget the sacred duties devolved on them, to preserve the inheritance so gallantly acquired by their fathers. May they cultivate the same manly patriotism, the same disinterested friendship, and the same political integrity which has distinguished you, and thus united in perpetuating that social concord and public virtue on which the future prosperity of our country must so essentially depend. I feel most deeply the truth of the melancholy suggestion, that we shall probably meet no more. While, however, we remain in life, I shall continue to hope for your countenance and support, so far as my public conduct may entitle me to your confidence; and in bidding you farewell, I pray a kind Providence long to preserve your valuable lives for the honour and benefit of our country.

1818 AND 1819: WATERSHED YEARS IN AMERICAN HISTORY

History textbooks tend to be organized by topics; sections on politics are followed by sections on foreign affairs or geographic expansion. One problem with such an approach is that it offers no sense of how events interrelate.

There are, however, certain defining moments in American history when underlying connections between events do become clear. These moments, commonly called historical "watersheds" or "turning points," mark a symbolic end to one era in American history and the beginning of another. The years 1818 and 1819 represent a watershed in American history. With the advantage of hindsight, it is apparent that these years brought an end to the era of the country's founders and inaugurated a new era committed to rapid economic growth and geographical expansion.

By 1818 the world of the nation's founders had quite literally come to a close. In that year, fewer than 10 percent of the country's population could personally remember the Revolutionary struggle for independence. The Revolutionary generation's commitment to simplicity and virtue and its vision of a natural aristocracy commanding deference from the people was rapidly giving way to a commitment to rapid geographic and economic expansion and free market capitalism—and also to humanitarian reform as a way to solve the problems encountered by the victims of social change.

What were some of the events of 1818 and 1819? These years saw the emergence of a new liberal religious denomination, American Unitarianism, which rejected orthodox Calvinist ideas of original sin and predestination. At the same time, religious liberals opened an asylum for the deaf and the blind in Hartford, Connecticut, inaugurating a new notion of institutionalized humanitarian care for the handicapped.

A series of seemingly disconnected events that took place in 1818 and 1819 illustrates a growing commitment to rapid growth. In foreign affairs, these years saw the seizure of Florida from Spain as well as the establishment of American claims to territory all the way to the Pacific Ocean.

In the realm of constitutional law, the U.S. Supreme Court issued two landmark decisions that played a crucial role in encouraging economic development and expanding the powers of Congress. In *Dartmouth* v. *Woodward* the Court promoted business growth by holding that contracts were sacred and inviolable, denying that states had the right to alter or impair contracts unilaterally, and declaring that corporations possess all the rights of a private person. In *McCullough* v. *Maryland* the Court ruled that the words of the Constitution should be construed broadly and loosely and that Congress had broad powers to do whatever was "necessary and proper" to carry out its constitutional functions.

The years 1818 and 1819 also saw the emergence of political divisions and deepening sectional rivalries that would dominate the country's politics for the next forty years. An economic depression known as the Panic of 1819, which was the country's first experience with the boom-and-bust cycles of modern capitalism, left a lasting imprint on American politics and provoked bitter division over questions of banking and tariffs. Simultaneously, the expansion of slavery west of the Mississippi River into Missouri provoked a bitter sectional crisis, which foreshadowed future disputes over the expansion of slavery into the western territories.

How might one tie these seemingly unrelated events together? By weakening Spain and igniting wars of independence throughout Spanish America, the Napoleonic Wars had opened the way to rapid U.S. territorial expansion. In the name of safeguarding national security and individual opportunity, the United States moved aggressively to acquire new territory. Yet as early as 1819 it was already clear that economic and geographical growth ignited profound political divisions, particularly over the westward expansion of slavery and government's role in promoting and regulating the economy.

THE SECOND BANK OF THE UNITED STATES

13 / *"The Bank bill has passed"*

Originally the Republican Party stood for limited government, states' rights, and a strict interpretation of the Constitution. By 1815, however, the party had adopted former Federalist positions on a national bank, protective tariffs, a standing army, and national roads.

The severe financial problems created by the War of 1812 led to a wave of support for the creation of a second national bank. The demise of the first Bank of the United States just before the war had left the nation ill equipped to deal with the war's financial demands. To finance the war effort, the government borrowed from private banks at high interest rates. To make matters worse, the U.S. government was unable to redeem millions of dollars deposited in private banks. Soldiers, army contractors, and government security holders went unpaid, and the Treasury temporarily went bankrupt.

Supporters of a second national bank argued that it would provide a safe place to deposit government funds and be a convenient mechanism for transferring money between states. Supporters also claimed that a national bank would promote monetary stability by regulating private banks. Opposition to a national bank came largely from private banking interests and traditional Jeffersonians, who considered a national bank to be unconstitutional and a threat to republican government.

In this selection, John F. Lovett (1761–1818), a Federalist representative from New York, describes the bank as a concentration of unaccountable power inappropriate in a republican society.

JOHN F. LOVETT, MARCH 14, 1815, GLC 4309

Exhausted in a seven hours sitting, I can but [write] a word.

We are over the Rubicon—*The Bank bill has passed*...

This is an evil hour, from stocks constructed I know not how, and *stacked* I know not in what manner, have we constructed the *Trojan Horse*, and given commission to unite against the Republic. I make good prize of *every thing* for 20 years; after that period, the *Commander* & *Crew* will get their commission received to *do just what they please*, and no questions asked....

14 / *"The expediency of taxing the United States Bank"*

After a second national bank was chartered, legislators in several states sought to restrict the bank's operations by imposing a tax on the bank notes of banks not chartered by their state. One state that considered levying such a tax was Pennsylvania. In the following letter, Jonathan Roberts (1771–1854), a Republican senator from Pennsylvania, defends the bank. During the Missouri Crisis of 1819 and 1820, Roberts proposed legislation that would have prevented the introduction of any more slaves into Missouri.

JONATHAN ROBERTS, JANUARY 16, 1818, TO DOCTOR TOBIAS SILLON OF THE PENNSYLVANIA ASSEMBLY, HARRISBURG, GLC 4309

I think I have seen a motion made in your behalf to inquire into the expediency of taxing the United States Bank and branches in the state. What feelings prevail on this subject I know not. I should regret the proposition should be entertained. I regret the motion has been agitated. It must...[en]danger...the Union. The Bank of the United States was a measure of and is a sensible necessity. Till now we had no real [national] currency.... The bank has to struggle against stupendous difficulties but has been of immense benefit already. Such a measure [the imposition of a tax on its notes] cannot be undertaken without affecting its credit.... It [the bank] has established branches liberally to accommodate the public all of which...are an expense. An immense Bonus & benefit of subscription has been obtained from it by this government for the benefit of all. If full proportion of burden has been imposed upon it I doubt if any state Bank has contributed more to the revenue. But I can not enlarge on this subject. I think a little reflection will discover the evil with which the proposition is fraught. You will excuse these remarks, they are made in the freedom of friendship. If they be different from your ideas I hope you will let them pass as they are offered.

MCCULLOUGH V. MARYLAND

15 / "The Judgment of the Supreme Court... in the case of McCullough agst. the State of Maryland"

In a direct attack on the new national bank, Maryland actually imposed a tax on its bank notes. The bank sued in federal court, and in 1819 the U.S. Supreme Court rendered its decision in the landmark case of *McCullough* v. *Maryland,* which established the constitutionality of the second bank of the United States and denied states the right to exert an independent check on federal authority.

In his decision, Chief Justice John Marshall dealt with two fundamental questions. The first was whether the federal government had the power to incorporate a bank. The justices said that the answer to this question was yes, because the Constitution granted Congress implied powers to do whatever was "necessary and proper" to carry out its constitutional powers—in this case, the power to manage a currency. The second question was whether a state had the power to tax the notes issued by the bank. The court said no, ruling that the Constitution had created a new government with sovereign power over the states.

Here, the "Father of the Constitution" criticizes the Court's decision, fearing that Marshall's broad construction of "necessary and proper" means will open the way to unlimited kinds of legislative tyranny.

JAMES MADISON, SEPTEMBER 2, 1819, TO JUDGE SPENCER ROANE, GLC 2945

I have rec[eive]d your favor [letter]...enclosing a copy of your observations on the Judgment of the Supreme Court of the U.S. in the case of McCulloch agst. the State of Maryland, and I have found their latitudinary mode of expounding the Constitution combated in them with the ability and the force which were to be expected.

It appears to me as it does to you that the occasion did not call for the general and abstract doctrine interwoven with the decision of the particular case. I have always supposed that the meaning of a law, and for a like reason, of a Constitution so far as it depends on Judicial interpretation, was to result from a course of particular decisions, and not those from a previous and abstract comment on the subject. The example in this instance tends to reverse the rule and to forego the illustration to be derived from a series of cases actually occurring for adjudication....

But what is of most importance is the high sanction given to a latitude in expounding the Constitution which seems to break down the landmarks extended by a specification of the powers of Congress, and to substitute for a definite connection between means and ends, a Legislative discretion as to the former to which no practical limit can be assigned. In the great system of political economy having for its general object the national welfare, every thing is related immediately or remotely to every other thing; and consequently a power over any one thing, if not limited by some obvious and precise affinity, may amount to a power over every other.... The British Parliament in collecting a revenue from the commerce of America found no difficulty in calling it either a tax for the regulation of trade, or a regulation of trade with a view to the tax as it suited the argument or the policy of the moment.

Is there a Legislative power in fact, not expressly prohibited by the Constitution, which might not, according to the doctrine of the Court, be exercised as a means of carrying into effect some specified power!

Does not the Court also relinquish by their doctrine, all control on the Legislative exercise of unconstitutional powers?... Suppose Congress should, as would doubtless happen, pass unconstitutional laws not to accomplish objects not specified in the Constitution, but the same laws as means expedient, convenient or conducive to the accomplishment of objects entrusted to the Government; by what handle should the Court take hold of the cases?...

It was anticipated I believe by few if any of the friends of the Constitution, that a rule of construction would be introduced as broad & as pliant as what has occurred.... There is certainly a reasonable medium between expounding the Constitution with the strictness of a penal law, or other ordinary Statue, and expounding it with a laxity which may vary its essential character; and encroach on the local sovereignties with w[hi]ch it was meant to be reconcilable.

ACQUIRING FLORIDA

16 / *"Different hordes of people...have violated our laws... and have committed every kind of outrage"*

A critical foreign policy issue facing the United States after the War of 1812 was the fate of Spain's New World Empire. In 1808 Napoleon deposed Spain's king, and Spain's New World colonies took advantage of the situation to fight for their independence. These revolutions aroused enormous sympathy in the United States. But this unrest also raised American fear that European powers might put down the revolutions and restore monarchical order in the Spanish Empire.

President Monroe's initial objective was to secure the nation's southern border. A particular source of concern was Spanish Florida. In December 1817 Monroe authorized Andrew Jackson to attack the Seminole Indians in Florida. Jackson proceeded to destroy their villages, overthrow the Spanish governor, and execute two British citizens, whom he accused of inciting the Seminoles to commit atrocities against Americans. Instead of apologizing for Jackson's conduct, President Monroe, in the following message, defended the Florida raid as a legitimate act of self-defense and informed Spain that it would either have to police Florida effectively or cede it to the United States. In 1819 Spain transferred Florida to the United States, and the U.S. government agreed to honor $5 million in damage claims by Americans against Spain.

James Monroe, November 16, 1818, GLC 5569

Throughout the whole of those provinces [the Floridas], to which the Spanish title extends, the government of Spain has been scarcely felt. Its authority has been confined almost exclusively to the walls of Pensacola, and St. Augustine within which only small garrisons have been maintained. Adventurers from every country, fugitives from justice, & absconding slaves, have found an asylum there. Several tribes of Indians, strong in the number of their warriors, remarkable for their ferocity, and whose settlements extend to our limits, inhabit those provinces. These different hordes of people, connected together, disregarding on the one side, the authority of Spain, and protected, on the other, by an imaginary line, which separates Florida from the United States, have violated our laws, prohibiting the introduction of slaves, have practiced various frauds, on our revenue, and have committed every kind of outrage, on our peaceable citizens, which their proximity to us, enabled them to perpetuate....

This country had, in fact, become the theatre, of every species of lawless adventure.... The Indian tribes have constituted, the effective force in Florida. With these tribes...adventurers had formed, at an early period, a connection, with a view to avail themselves of that force, to promote their own projects of accumulation & aggrandizement. It is to the interference of some of these adventurers, in misrepresenting the claims, and titles, of the Indians, to land, and in practicing, on their savage propensities, that the Seminole war were principally to be traced. Men who thus connect themselves with Savage communities, and stimulate them to war, which is always attended on their part with acts of barbarity the most shocking, deserve to be viewed in a worse light than the Savages. They would certainly have no claim, to an immunity from the punishment, which according to the rules of warfare practiced by the Savages, might justly be inflicted on the Savages themselves.

If the embarrassments of Spain, prevented her from making an indemnity to our citizens, for so long a time, from her treasury, for the loss of spoliation, and otherwise, it was always in her power, to have provided it, by the cession of this territory. Of this, her government has been repeatedly apprized, and the cession was the more to be anticipated, as Spain must have known, that in ceding it, she would, in effect, cede what had become of little value to her, and would likewise relieve herself, from the important obligation, secured by the treaty of 1795....

There is nevertheless a limit, beyond which this spirit of amity & forbearance, can, in no instance, be justified.... The right of self defence never ceases. It is among the most sacred; and alike necessary, to nations & to individuals. And whether the attack be made by Spain, herself or by those who abuse her power, its obligation is not the less strong....

In authorizing Major General [Andrew] Jackson to enter Florida, in pursuit of the Seminoles, care was taken not to encroach on the rights of Spain.... The Commanding general was convinced that he should fail in his object, that he should in effect accomplish nothing, if he did not deprive those Savages of the resource on which they had calculated, and of the protection on which they had relied in making the war....

Experience has clearly demonstrated that independent Savage communities, cannot long exist within the limits of a civilized population. The progress of the latter, almost invariably, terminated in the extinction of the former, especially of the tribes belonging to our portion of this hemisphere, among whom loftiness of sentiment, and gallantry in action, have been conspicuous. To civilize them, & even to prevent their extinction, its seems to be indispensable, that their independence as communities should cease; & that the control of the United States over them, should be complete & undisputed. The hunter state, will then be more easily abandoned, and recourse will be had to the acquisition & culture of land, & to other pursuits tending to dissolve the ties, which connect them together as a savage community and to give a new character to every individual.

THE MONROE DOCTRINE

17 / *"The American continents...are henceforth not to be considered... for future colonization by any European powers"*

The United States feared European intervention not only in Florida, but also in the Pacific Northwest and in Latin America. In 1821 Russia claimed control of the entire Pacific coast from Alaska to Oregon and closed the area to foreign shipping. This development coincided with rumors that Spain, with the help of its European allies, was planning to reconquer its former Latin American colonies.

European intervention threatened British as well as American interests. Not only did Britain have a flourishing trade with Latin America, which would decline if Spain regained its New World colonies, it also had claims to territory in the Oregon country of the Pacific Northwest. In 1823 British foreign minister George Canning (1770–1827) proposed that the United States and Britain jointly announce their opposition to further European intervention in the Americas.

Secretary of State John Quincy Adams opposed a joint declaration. He convinced President Monroe to make a unilateral declaration of American policy, which has since become known as the Monroe Doctrine. He announced that the Western Hemisphere was henceforth closed to further European colonization. Monroe also said that the United States would not interfere in internal European affairs.

For much of the nineteenth century, the United States lacked the military strength to prevent European intervention in the New World. But since European meddling threatened British as well as American interests, the Monroe Doctrine was enforced by the Royal Navy. Nevertheless, for the American people, the Monroe Doctrine was a proud symbol of American hegemony in the Western Hemisphere. Unilaterally, the United States had defined its rights and interests in the New World.

JAMES MONROE, MESSAGE TO CONGRESS, DECEMBER 2, 1823, GLC 4824

The occasion has been judged proper for asserting, as a principle in which the rights and interests of the United States are involved, that the American continents, by the free and independent condition which they have assumed and maintain, are henceforth not to be considered as subjects for future colonization by any European powers....

The citizens of the United States cherish sentiments the most friendly in favor of the liberty and happiness of their fellow-men on that side [the European side] of the Atlantic. In the wars of the European powers in matters relating to themselves we have never taken any part, nor does it comport with our policy so to do. It is only when our rights are invaded or seriously menaced that we resent injuries or make preparation for our defense. With the movements in this hemisphere we are of necessity more immediately connected, and by causes which must be obvious to all enlightened and impartial observers. The political system of the allied powers is essentially different in this respect from that of America.... We owe it, therefore, to candor and to the amicable relations existing between the United States and those powers to declare that we should consider any attempt on their part to extend their system to any portion of this hemisphere as dangerous to our peace and safety. With the existing colonies or dependencies of any European power we have not interfered and shall not interfere. But with the Governments who have declared their independence and maintained it, and whose independence we have, on great consideration and on just principles, acknowledged, we could not view any interposition for the purpose of oppressing them, or controlling in any other manner their destiny, by any European power in any other light than as the manifestation of an unfriendly disposition toward the United States. In the war declared between those new Governments and Spain we declared our neutrality at the time of their recognition, and to this we have adhered, and shall continue to adhere, provided no change shall occur which, in the judgment of the competent authorities of this Government, shall make a corresponding change on the part of the United States indispensable to their security....

Our policy in regard to Europe, which we adopted at an early stage of the wars which have so long agitated that quarter of the globe, nevertheless remains the same, which is not to interfere in the internal concerns of any of its powers; to consider the government *de facto* as the legitimate government for us; to cultivate friendly relations with it, and to preserve those relations by a frank, firm, and manly policy, meeting in all instances the just claims of every power, submitting to injuries from none.

THE MISSOURI CRISIS

18 / *"The great question which now agitates the nation"*

In 1819 a financial panic swept across the United States. Unemployment mounted, banks failed, mortgages were foreclosed, and agricultural prices fell by half. The panic unleashed a storm of popular protests. Many debtors agitated for "stay laws" to delay repayment of debts and for the abolition of debtors' prisons. Manufacturing interests called for increased protection from foreign imports, while many Southerners blamed high tariffs for reducing the flow of international trade. The panic also led to demands for the democratization of state constitutions, an end to restrictions on voting and office-holding, and hostility toward banks and other "privileged" corporations.

In the midst of the panic, a crisis over slavery erupted with stunning suddenness. It was, Thomas Jefferson wrote, like "a firebell in the night." The crisis was ignited by Missouri's application for statehood, and it involved the status of slavery west of the Mississippi River. East of the Mississippi, the Ohio River formed a boundary between slave states and free states. West of the Mississippi, there was no clear line demarcating the boundary between free and slave territory.

Representative James Tallmadge (1778–1853) of New York provoked the crisis in February 1819 by introducing an amendment that would prohibit the *further* introduction of slaves into Missouri and provide for the emancipation of the children of slaves at age twenty-five. Voting along ominously sectional lines, the House approved this very moderate amendment, but the Senate defeated it.

Compromise ultimately resolved the crisis. In 1820 Congress voted to admit Missouri as a slave state. To preserve the sectional balance, it also voted to admit Maine, previously a part of Massachusetts, as a free state, and to prohibit the formation of any slave states within the Louisiana Purchase north of 36° 30' north latitude.

Southerners won a victory in 1820, but they paid a high price. While many states would eventually be organized from the Louisiana Purchase north of the compromise line, only two (Arkansas and part of Oklahoma) would be formed from the southern portion. If the South was to defend its political power against an antislavery majority, it had but two options in the future. It would either have to forge new political alliances with the North and West, or it would have to acquire new territory in the Southwest—inevitably reigniting northern opposition to the further expansion of slavery.

The era of good feeling ended on a note of foreboding. Sectional antagonism, Jefferson wrote, "is hushed, indeed, for the moment. But this is a reprieve only.... A geographical line, coinciding with a marked principle...will never be obliterated; and every new irritation will mark it deeper and deeper." John Quincy Adams agreed. The Missouri Crisis, he declared, is only the "title page to a great tragic volume."

In this letter, John Tyler (1790–1862), a future president from Virginia who was then serving in the House of Representatives, reflects on the meaning of the Missouri Crisis.

John Tyler, February 14, 1820, to Appeals Court Judge Spencer Roane, GLC 5646

The great question which now agitates the nation is one well calculated to elicit sensibility and feeling—About the nature of the power which is attempted to be exercised by Congress you and myself cannot fail to agree in pronouncing it a bold and daring assumption—-warranted neither by the constitution or the principles of justice. My intention is to represent to you as accurately as may be the actual posture of affairs in relation to it. Maine and Missouri are both before us as applicants for admission into the Union—The Maine Bill pass'd our house unincumbered but on the motion of Mr. Barbour of the Senate, was refer'd to a select committee who amended it by annexing a Bill for the admission of Missouri—The amendment has so far [been] unsuccessfully oppos'd by the advocates of restriction—but a proposition to inhibit the further introduction of slaves as a condition of admission has been propos'd—and has been negatived in that Body. This majority against the restriction however has been obtained by votes from non-slaveholding states. A proposition has been or will be made to incorporate in the same bill a provision extending the inhibition to the territories north of a given degree of latitude and a majority in the Senate will I have every reason to believe without aid from the slave holding states be found to support the measure. It is then probable that the bill thus amended will come down to the house of Representatives. But its fate with us is more uncertain. Those or a majority of those who are advocates of restriction will vote for no Bill which shall permit Missouri to come in to the Union unrestricted and believing as I do with almost all the South that the restriction on the Territories is unjust not to say unconstitutional, we shall also vote against the Bill because of its containing that provision. Thus the great probability is that the Bill from the Senate will be lost and that neither Missouri nor Maine will be admitted. When the game is over another will be play'd—a joint resolution restricting the territories will pass our house and the Senate, and if approv'd by the President, will become a law. This being general in its terms will not only embrace, as has been imagined, the territory north of Missouri, but Missouri itself, it remaining a territory and Arkansas also. I do not believe however that a regulation of this character would meet with the countenance from the president. This opinion is not founded on any authentic information, but is more properly the creature of hope raised up with confidence in the firmness of Mr. Monroe. Be that as it may Missouri will not become a state at this or the next session nor to speak candidly do I believe that she will for the next ten years by the voluntary assent of the North and North West unless she will abandon the struggle for sovereignty and submit to conditions. The non slave holding States now have the majority of us and that majority will be increased at the next census—In what then does our present safety consist? In nothing but the firmness of the President. I am told that he has not committed himself in any way, but has declared his opinion to be made up and that nothing earthly shall shake him or cause him to waver....

For myself permit me to add that I have planted myself on the constitution and the principles of right, and that I will not yield an inch of ground to any power on earth. A crisis like the present requires stout hearts and resolute minds, and altho' we may regret the approach of the storm, it becomes us to meet it like men.

19 / *"A...deliberate sanction seems to be... given to the continuance of domestic slavery"*

During the Missouri Crisis, northeastern reformers, for the first time, sought to mobilize public opinion against the westward expansion of slavery. The vehemence of anti-Missouri feeling is apparent in an editorial that appeared in the *New York Advertiser*: "THIS QUESTION INVOLVES NOT ONLY THE FUTURE CHARACTER OF OUR NATION, BUT THE FUTURE WEIGHT AND INFLUENCE OF THE FREE STATES. IF NOW LOST—IT IS LOST FOREVER."

Compromise was possible in 1820 because most Northerners were apathetic about the exclusion of slavery from Missouri, and opponents of slavery were disunited. The Panic of 1819 consumed public attention. Congregationalist and Presbyterian church members from the Northeast led the drive to restrict slavery in Missouri, provoking widespread hostility from an anticlerical and anti-Federalist opposition.

The Pennsylvania Abolition Society had been the first organization in world history committed to the cause of eradicating human slavery. Though traditionally conservative in approach, the society now cautiously threatens to join in a movement of national disunion if Congress continues to sanction the expansion of slavery.

Meeting of the Pennsylvania Society for Promoting the Abolition of Slavery and Improving the Condition of the African Race, held on the 13th day of April, 1820, GLC 777

This Society views with deep concern, the result of the late proceedings of Congress in respect to the formation of a new state in the territory of Missouri.

A solemn and deliberate sanction seems to be thereby given to the continuance of domestic slavery, within the limits of a nation, whose original separation from Great Britain, was, professedly, founded on the abhorrence of slavery in every form, and whose toleration of it in their general constitution, was only excused by an imperious state necessity.

At a period when such a plea cannot be urged; when the Christian powers of Europe are actively cooperating in preventing the continuance of the slave trade from Africa; when almost every other public act, and profession of public opinion, emanating from our own government, conveys the impression of abhorrence of its existence, to open a new mart for this unnatural traffic, and with facilities of transfer not restrained but indirectly invited and protected, to stamp a constitutional perpetuity on its principles appears to us equally inconsistent and unjust.

Yet the power to form a state, without a restriction in these respects by Congress, has been declared, and however it may be regretted, must be submitted to, until some constitutional remedy shall be obtained.

It remains to be seen, whether the virtue of the inhabitants, when collected to form their constitution as a state, will not supply what Congress has decided not to require as a preliminary condition to the formation of their constitution; whether their own sense of justice, their own attachment to the sound principles of political and civil liberty, their own perception of the real interests of their country, will not lead them to present to Congress a constitution, from whose face this odious feature shall be expressly and forever excluded, and thus establish by voluntary and honourable compact, what they might from other motives reject as a condition imposed on them.

If this hope should fail, another remains. It will rest with the legislature of the United States, whether they will receive into their bosom a new member, who has neglected or disclaimed the opportunity and the honour of approaching the Union with a constitution truly republican, unstained by the infusion of a principle inconsistent with the purity and freedom that can alone consolidate, ennoble and perpetuate our country; and to this we earnestly and respectfully invite the future attention of our representatives....

We deem this a proper occasion to declare, that with a deep conviction that slavery is inconsistent with moral principle, national interest, and above all, with the Christian dispensation; we never have sought to raise our opposition to it above the constitutional barriers intended to surround and protect our country. To the constitutional powers of the Legislature of the United States, to avert and to remove evils, we have always looked with confidence and satisfaction. Holding, as we do, the union of the states, as the great basis of their prosperity and happiness, we shall be among the last of the members of this free nation to abandon it; and we shall wait until the heavy pressure of the evils which might have been prevented or remedied, by the due and proper exercise of those powers, shall compel us to submit to its termination. That period will we cordially hope never arrive.

20 / *"It is not a moral question, but one merely of power"*

Jefferson wrote the following letter at a crucial turning point in the history of slavery. Cotton cultivation was spreading extremely rapidly into the Old Southwest—Mississippi, Alabama, Louisiana, and Arkansas—a development that coincided with the decline of the West Indies, once America's major market for all kinds of exports, and the portentous clash between North and South over admitting Missouri as a slave state. In this letter to Lafayette, the principal author of the Declaration of Independence advances the specious argument that the movement of slaves to the western territories offered the best solution to slavery. This hope of "diffusing" the black slave population to the west and toward Mexico, as a means of solving the problems of slavery and racial coexistence, drew increasing support from the Upper South.

Thomas Jefferson, December 26, 1820, to Gilbert du Motier, the marquis de Lafayette, MA 54

The boisterous sea of liberty indeed is never without a wave, and that from Missouri is now rolling towards us; but we shall ride over it as we have all others.... It is not a moral question, but one merely of power....

All know that permitting the slaves of the South to spread in the West will not add one being to that unfortunate condition, that it will increase the happiness of those existing, and by spreading them over a larger surface, will dilute the evil everywhere and facilitate the means of getting finally rid of it, an event more anxiously wished by those on whom it presses than by the noisy pretenders to exclusive humanity.

SLAVERY AND SECTIONALISM

21 / *"The policy of liberating the slaves in the W. Indies"*

Pressure to abolish slavery within the British Empire was already mounting in Britain in the mid-1820s. This effort would achieve success in 1833, when Britain emancipated 780,000 slaves, paying £20 million compensation to their owners and requiring the former slaves to work for a term as "apprentices."

In an effort to assist opponents of the African slave trade, the United States came close to agreeing in 1824 to allow Britain to search the ships of American slave traders. In this letter, President Monroe explains the agreement. By defining the slave trade as piracy, British ships would be allowed to stop and board American slave trading vessels, without arguments over sovereignty or affronts to American shipping. The measure was defeated, however, in the Senate.

Monroe was a sincere enemy of the African slave trade and was more liberal on the slavery issue than many historians have thought. Yet in this letter he expresses the clear view that emancipation in the British colonies would provide a dangerous precedent for the future. This document is valuable for suggesting that slavery was the supreme political issue in the United States, even if discussion was largely suppressed. The United States failed to attend a hemispheric conference on slavery and other matters in Panama in 1824, the year this letter was written.

JAMES MONROE, MAY 20, 1824, APPARENTLY TO A MEMBER OF CONGRESS, GLC 969

I hear that the convention lately concluded with G[reat]. B[ritain]., whereby the crime of piracy, is attached to the slave trade, is in danger of being rejected, as Congress made that trade, piratical, by law, and the H[ouse] of R[representatives] recommended it, by a resolution, which passed almost unanimously, to the Executive, to endeavour, by negotiation & treaty, with other powers, to make the trade piracy by the law of nations, the rejection of this convention, would in my opinion, produce very serious mischief. I hear with deep concern, that some of our estimable friends, to the South, are opposed to it, but on what grounds I know not. The British government wished, to adopt, & make general, a different plan, that is, to extend the right of search, which is a belligerent right, to a time of peace, & to board vessels on that principle. We feared that this right thus sanctioned, would be subject to abuse, in the hands of the superior naval power, and therefore declined it. Under the authority of Congress, we went further; the trade was made piratical, and the right of entry would rest on the crime, which it became the law of nations would be common to all....

As to the motives imputed to Mr. Canning [the British prime minister], of acceding to our project, to sustain himself in England, admit the fact, & what the consequences? The Wilberforce party [the British abolitionists] are pushing the policy of liberating the slaves in the W. Indies, to which Mr. Canning [the prime minister] is opposed. By adopting our treaty, and making the trade piratical, he showed to that party, that he was as averse to the trade as they were, altho' he was not willing to disturb the existing state in the Colonies, & ruin the people there. Which of the parties, the Wilberforce or ministerial, ought we to strengthen, or in other words, ought we to promote the emancipation of slaves in the W. Indies, or the retaining things in their present state there? In every light that I can view the subject, I should consider the rejection of this treaty as the most dangerous measure.

22 / *"We have the wolf by the ear & feel the danger of holding or letting loose"*

Thomas Jefferson was of two minds about slavery. He viewed the institution as a crime, an abomination, and a wasteful, dangerous, and immoral system of labor. Yet at the same time, he feared that emancipation, in the absence of colonization, would result in race war. In his 1783 draft of a new Virginia constitution, he called for freedom for all slave children born after 1800; and in 1784 and again 1800 he called for excluding slaves from the western territories. But he never defended the Northwest Ordinance prohibition on slavery; he failed to oppose those who wanted to take slaves into Louisiana or even into Indiana; and late in life, when younger Virginians sought his blessings for liberating their slaves, he refused to encourage them.

Jefferson's letter to the popular poet Lydia Sigourney (1791–1865), "the sweet singer of Hartford," encapsulates his ambivalent attitude toward slavery and suggests how his conviction that blacks and whites could not coexist equally paralyzed him from taking effective steps against slavery. In 1820 he had expressed this thought in more famous wording: "We have the wolf by the ears; and we can neither hold him, nor safely let him go. Justice is in one scale, and self-preservation in the other."

In the very year that Jefferson wrote this letter he also presented his only detailed plan for abolishing slavery. Jefferson proposed emancipating slave children, "leaving them, on due compensation, with their mothers, until their services are worth their maintenance, then putting them to industrious occupations, until a proper age for deportation" to the West Coast of Africa, Haiti, or some other asylum. He suggested that the cost of this plan could be paid for by selling lands taken from the Indians. "The separation of infants from their mothers," Jefferson wrote, "would produce some scruples of humanity. But it would be straining at a gnat, and swallowing a camel." In 1824 Jefferson was eighty-one.

THOMAS JEFFERSON, JULY 18, 1824, TO LYDIA SIGOURNEY, MA 6014

> I am not apt to despairing, yet I see not how we are to disengage ourself from that deplorable entanglement, we have the wolf by the ear & feel the danger of holding or letting loose.... I shall not live to see it but those who come after us will be wiser than we are, for light is spreading and man improving. To that advancement I look, and to the dispensations of an all-wise and all-powerful providence to devise the means of effecting what is right.

23 / "John Harris is a Citizen of the United States of America"

The antebellum period, which witnessed the extension of the right to vote and hold public office to all white men, was also a period when free blacks faced increasing restrictions on their freedom.

After the Revolution, slaveowners had freed thousands of slaves, while other slaves freed themselves by fleeing to freedom in the midst of wartime disruption. In Louisiana, a large free black creole population had emerged under French rule, and in South Carolina a much smaller creole population had arrived from Barbados. The number of free blacks in the Deep South increased rapidly with the arrival of thousands of light-colored mulattoes from Haiti.

Free blacks varied profoundly in status. Most lived in poverty, but in a few cities such as New Orleans, Charleston, and Baltimore, some worked as skilled carpenters, shoemakers, tailors, and millwrights. In the Lower South, a few free blacks achieved high occupational status and actually bought slaves. One of the wealthiest was William Ellison, the son of a slave mother and a white planter. Ellison learned how to make cotton gins and at age twenty-six bought his freedom with his overtime earnings. At the time of his death he owned sixty-three slaves worth more than $100,000. In the South, free people of color occupied an uneasy middle ground between the dominant whites and the mass of slaves. Some distanced themselves from blacks who remained in slavery; other identified with slaves and took the lead in establishing separate black churches.

Although free blacks comprised no more than 3.8 percent of the population of any northern state, they faced mounting legal, economic, and social discrimination. They were denied the right to serve on juries or to testify against whites. They were prohibited from marrying whites and were relegated to segregated jails, cemeteries, asylums, and schools. All but four New England states denied them the right to vote. By the 1830s they began to suffer heightened competition from white immigrants in the skilled trades and even in such traditional occupations as domestic service.

Whether African Americans were legally citizens of the United States was a controversial issue in the decades before the Civil War. The following document, issued by the state of Massachusetts, formally recognizes the citizenship rights of John Harris, a free black, who currently lived in the city of Salem, and as a black sailor faced the danger of being imprisoned if his ship landed in South Carolina, where, following the exposure of the Denmark Vesey conspiracy, all free blacks were seen as a threat to public security.

Ezekiel Savage, October 23, 1824, GLC 4289

> ...John Harris...is a Citizen of the United States of America, born in the City of Alexandria State of Virginia, that he is a free colored man, now residing in said Salem and never has been under allegiance to any foreign Prince or States. He is five feet six inches high, thirty two years of age, black complexioned.... And I do hereby Certify, that the Act of the Congress of the United States, "for the relief and protection of American Seamen" not having made provision for Persons of Colour to obtain Certificates of Citizenship at the Custom Houses; this is granted to show that the said John Harris is a Citizen of the United States of America, and ought to be respected accordingly, in his Person and Property, at all times by Sea and Land in the Prosecution of his lawful concerns.

THE UNDERGROUND RAILROAD

24 / *"The master & mistress...treated her with great severity, so much so as to induce some of the friends of Freedom... to assist her in making her escape"*

About a thousand slaves permanently escaped slavery each year. Most runaways fled only a short distance. Slaves might hide in nearby swamps to escape punishment or sale. Many ran away to visit spouses or children. Groups of slaves sometimes ran away to protest overwork or cruel punishment. While masters often offered rewards for the return of runaways, sometimes they used ads to plead or bargain with a fugitive. Those fugitives who were trying to escape slavery did not necessarily flee northward. Many headed toward Florida or to the Great Dismal Swamp in Virginia and North Carolina, where they established "maroon" colonies. Others hid with free blacks in southern cities.

For the most part, those fugitives who fled northward could not depend on an organized system of underground railroad stations to ferry them to freedom. Most runaways had to rely on their own wits. They had to borrow or forge passes, devise disguises, locate hiding places, or stow away on boats or trains. Nevertheless, some abolitionists such as Levi Coffin (1798–1877), William Still (1821–1902), and Harriet Tubman (1820–1913), actively assisted fugitives. The following letter by a Rhode Island Quaker, Edward Lawton of Newport, describes the efforts to help a female slave escape her cruel owner and asks Thomas Evans, a Philadelphia druggist, to help prevent the woman's recapture.

> EDWARD LAWTON, MAY 22, 1825, TO THOMAS EVANS, GLC 5800
>
> In the summer of 1822 or 23, a person by the name of Anthony Barklay, or Barclay came from the south to spend the summer here accompanied by his Family in which was included a black girl held by him as a slave. Although professing great suavity of manners and much apparent kindness the master & mistress of this girl treated her with great severity, so much so as to induce some of the friends of Freedom in this place to assist her in making her escape from such intolerable and cruel servitude. She has been pursued by her master with the most implacable determination and there is reason to fear that if he should succeed in recovering her that her persecutions would be redoubled. Thus far the exertions of her friends have been successful in withholding her from his grasp, but information has reached here that Barclay will be here soon (perhaps this day) that he is still determined to recover his slave, and it is also known that many persons who are not to be trusted, nay many who are seeking to betray her are possessed of the leading circumstances of her present condition and only want his arrival to disclose them to him. She has been residing in the Family of Nathaniel Hathaway in New Bedford, whose wife was Anna Shoemaker of Philadelphia, who is on a visit among her connections there and has the girl with her. I am unacquainted with the persons mentioned but have the information from an undoubted source in New Bedford by a Letter received this morning. The object of this letter is obviously to obtain for this unfortunate, and I am informed, very deserving girl, the speedy and effectual protection which her case demands, and which will I presume be a sufficient apology for this hasty address from an entire stranger.

THE RISE OF THE SECOND PARTY SYSTEM

25 / *"I believe their existence to be salutary"*

Following the War of 1812, American politics was still dominated by deference. Voters generally deferred to the leadership of local elites or leading families. Political campaigns tended to be relatively staid affairs. Direct appeals by candidates for support were considered in poor taste.

By later standards, election procedures were undemocratic. Most states imposed property and taxpaying requirements on the white adult males, who alone had the vote.

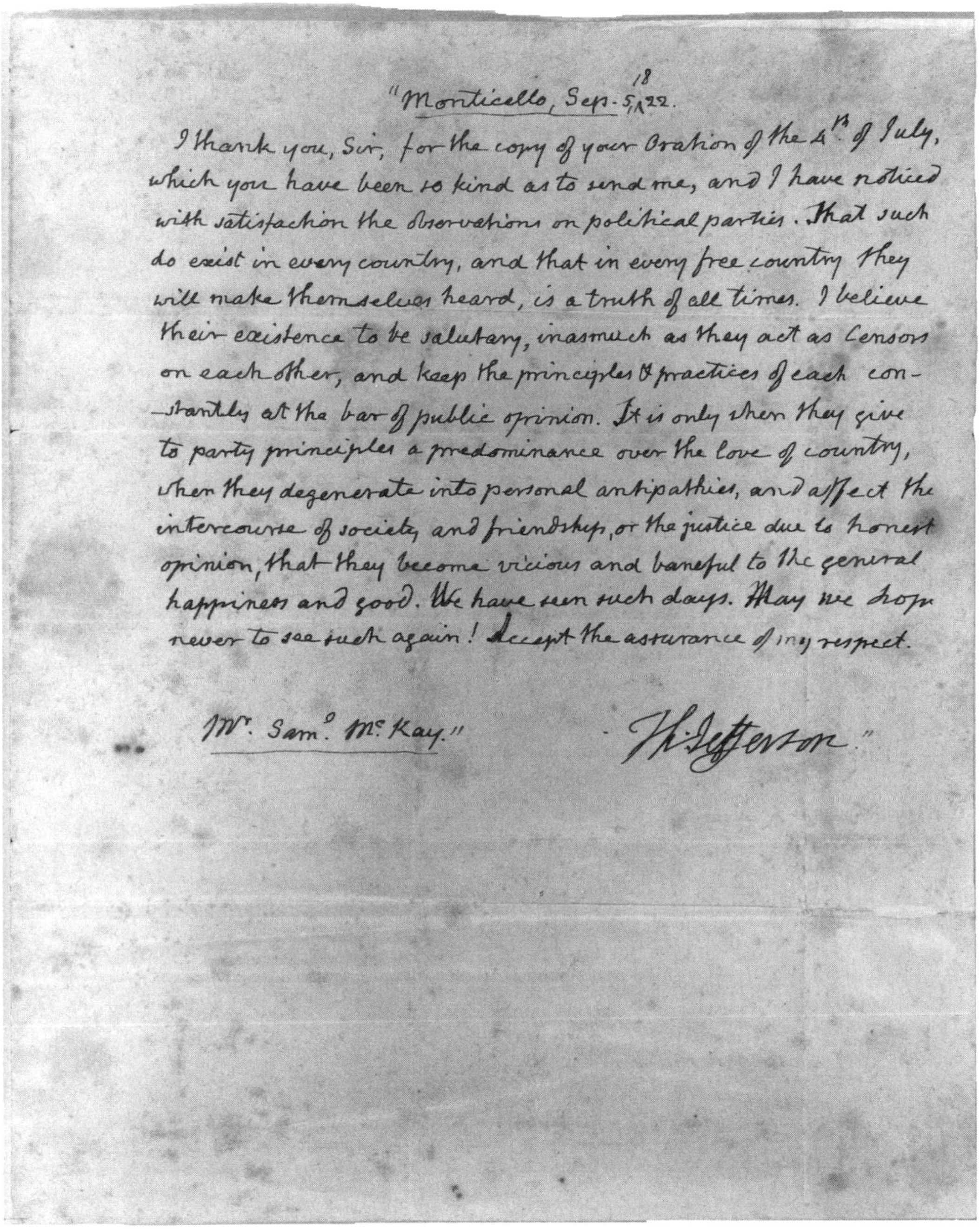

"Monticello, Sep. 5. 1822.

I thank you, Sir, for the copy of your Oration of the 4th of July, which you have been so kind as to send me, and I have noticed with satisfaction the observations on political parties. That such do exist in every country, and that in every free country they will make themselves heard, is a truth of all times. I believe their existence to be salutary, inasmuch as they act as Censors on each other, and keep the principles & practices of each constantly at the bar of public opinion. It is only when they give to party principles a predominance over the love of country, when they degenerate into personal antipathies, and affect the intercourse of society, and friendship, or the justice due to honest opinion, that they become vicious and baneful to the general happiness and good. We have seen such days. May we hope never to see such again! Accept the assurance of my respect.

Mr. Saml. McKay."

Th: Jefferson."

Thomas Jefferson. Autograph letter signed, to Samuel McCay, 1822/09/05. The Gilder Lehrman Collection, on deposit at the Pierpont Morgan Library. GLC 639.14

Voting was conducted by voice. Presidential electors were generally chosen by state legislatures. Given the fact that citizens had only the most indirect say in the election of a president, it is not surprising that voting participation was generally low, amounting to less than 30 percent of adult white males.

By 1840, voting participation had reached unprecedented levels. Nearly 80 percent of adult white males went to the polls. A major reason for the expanded electorate was the replacement of the politics of deference and leadership by elites with a new two-party system. By the mid-1830s two national political parties with marked philosophical differences, strong organizations, and wide popular appeal competed in virtually every state. Professional party managers used partisan newspapers, speeches, parades, and rallies to mobilize popular support.

In 1789 Jefferson had declared, "If I could not go to heaven but with a party, I would not go there at all." In the following letter he reverses his early opposition to parties and argues that two political parties are essential to a functioning democracy.

THOMAS JEFFERSON, SEPTEMBER 5, 1822, TO SAMUEL MCCAY, GLC 639.14

I believe their existence to be salutary inasmuch as they act as Censors on each other, and keep the principles & practices of each constantly at the bar of public opinion. It is only when they give to party principles a predominance over the love of country, when they degenerate into personal antipathies, and affect the intercourse of society and friendship, or the justice due to honest opinion, that they become vicious and baneful to the general happiness and good. We have seen such days. May we hope never to see such again!

26 / "The same parties exist now which existed before"

In this letter, Thomas Jefferson reports on the nature of partisan politics in the United States during the early 1820s. After the War of 1812 the nation had reverted to a period of one-party government in national politics. The decline of the Federalist Party had created the illusion of national political unity, but, as Jefferson observes, appearances were deceptive. Without the discipline imposed by competition with a strong opposition party, the Republican Party began to fragment into cliques and factions. In this letter Jefferson maintains that while the Federalist Party as a formal political organization had disappeared, its ideas and principles persisted.

The letter's recipient, the Marquis de Lafayette (1757–1834), had sailed from France to America in 1777 and helped the colonists win independence. He was instrumental in persuading France to send military aid to the colonists and served as a major general in the Continental Army. He also played a leading role in the early stages of the French Revolution. In 1824 Lafayette returned to America and received a hero's welcome from a grateful public. Congress voted that $200,000 and a township in Florida be given him.

THOMAS JEFFERSON, OCTOBER 28, 1822, TO GILBERT DU MOTIER, THE MARQUIS DE LAFAYETTE, MA 54

The papers tell you there are no parties now. Republicans and federalists forsooth are all amalgamated. This, my friend, is not so. The same parties exist now which existed

> before. But the name of Federalist was extinguished in the battle of New Orleans; and those who wore it now call themselves republicans. Like the fox pursued by the dogs, they take shelter in the midst of the sheep. They see that monarchism is a hopeless wish in this country, and are rallying anew to the next best point, a consolidated government. They are therefore endeavoring to break the barriers of state rights, provided by the constitution, against a consolidation.

27 / *"I zealously supported the emancipation ticket"*

Over time, local and personal political factions coalesced into a new political party system. Three critical factors contributed to the creation of the second party system. The first was the financial Panic of 1819, which resulted in demands for elimination of property qualifications for voting; calls for new state constitutions; and political divisions over such issues as debt relief, banking and monetary policy, and tariffs.

A second source of party formation was southern alarm over the slavery debates in Congress in 1819 and 1820. Many southern leaders feared that the Missouri Crisis might spark a realignment in national politics along sectional lines. Many Southerners sought political alliances with the North. As early as 1821, Virginia Republicans opposed to high tariffs, a national bank, and federally funded internal improvements had begun to form a loose alliance with Senator Martin Van Buren of New York and the Republican faction he commanded.

A third major source of political division was the selection of a presidential candidate. The Virginia dynasty of presidents, a chain that had begun with Washington and included Jefferson, Madison, and Monroe, was at its end in 1824. Traditionally, the Republican Party candidate was selected by a caucus of the party's members of Congress. At the 1824 caucus the members chose William H. Crawford (1772–1834), a Georgian and Monroe's secretary of the treasury. But not all Republicans supported this method of nominating candidates and therefore refused to participate.

When Crawford suffered a stroke and was left partially disabled, four other candidates emerged: Secretary of State John Quincy Adams; John C. Calhoun of South Carolina; Andrew Jackson, the hero of the Battle of New Orleans and victor over the Creeks and Seminoles; and Henry Clay, the Kentuckian Speaker of the House.

In this letter Clay assesses his chances for election and describes his stand on slavery and emancipation over the preceding twenty-five years. As the president and most famous leader of the American Colonization Society, Clay's views on slavery remained ambiguous.

Henry Clay, August 28, 1823, to Thomas J. Wharton, GLC 509

> Certainly it would have been more auspicious to my interests that the popular demonstrations made in Pennsylvania in favor of Genl. Jackson should have been given my support! But the next best thing to have happened is that which has already occurred....
>
> The papers at Cincinnati, the principal point of unavailing opposition to me in Ohio, have begun to assume a friendlier tone and do harmonize more with the residue of

that State. In short, every where in the West my ground is not only maintained, but there is a sensible & sure progress making in my prospects. My cause, perhaps, feels the want of some well established democratic press in the large cities to sustain it, as suggested by you, but this disadvantage is less, in consequence of the very great division among the presses there, and the reciprocal abuse which is so copiously lavished upon their respective favorites. Will not the moderate portion of the community, disgusted with those who are, at the same time, the objects of unmerited calumny and undeserved eulogy, finally rather concentrate their votes upon one who has been held up neither to their delectation nor idolatry?...

On the matter of fact, respecting the part which I played on the question of Gradual Emancipation, debated in this state [Kentucky] many years ago, on which you desire information, I am sorry that I am not able to transmit you any from the record. All that I can communicate is preserved now by tradition, but is known to hundreds within and without this state. In 1798 and 1799 the question of a new Convention to amend and alter our State Constitution afflicted & divided this State. One of the grounds upon which it was supported and approached was that of introducing a provision similar to what is contained in your Abolition act, for the gradual emancipation of slaves. I took the side of a new Convention, and that of gradual emancipation. We carried the question of Convention, and then came on, in the year 1799, the election of members to it. Emancipation & antiemancipation tickets were formed. The greatest animation every where prevailed. I was then about 23, too young to be a member of the Convention; but I zealously supported the emancipation ticket, in all circles, public descriptions and news papers....We were opposed by...John Breckenridge, then the most powerful & prominent Citizen of this State.... The slave interest was too predominant for us and we were beaten at the elections, but in several important ones, we lost by very small majorities. My opinion is unchanged. I advised the Delegate from Missouri to strive to get a provision inserted in the Constitution of that State for gradual emancipation. The expediency of the measure, I think depends, in some degree, upon the relative proposition of the two races existing in any State in which it may be proposed. Here my opinion was and is that the African portion of the community is not so large as to make any hazard to the purity & safety of Society by a gradual and prepared emancipation of the offspring. However, should my friends think it useful to make any public allusion to the incident I have been relating, in my early life, perhaps it would not be proper to refer to present opinions, lest it should be said that these result from sinister motives.

THE ELECTION OF 1824

28 / "I think it certain that the election will come into the H[ouse] of R[epresentatives]"

In the following letter, Clay predicts that the presidential election of 1824 will be decided by the House of Representatives. In the election, Jackson received the greatest number of votes both at the polls and in the electoral college, followed by Adams, Crawford, and then Clay. But Jackson failed to win the constitutionally required majority of the electoral votes.

As provided by the Twelfth Amendment of the Constitution, the election was thrown into the House of Representatives, which was required to choose from among the top three vote-getters in the electoral college. There, Clay persuaded his supporters to vote for Adams, commenting acidly that he did not believe "that killing two thousand five hundred Englishmen at New Orleans" was a proper qualification for the presidency. Adams was elected on the first ballot.

A Philadelphia newspaper charged that Adams had made a secret deal to obtain Clay's support. Three days later, Adams's nomination of Clay as secretary of state seemed to confirm the charge of a "corrupt bargain." Jackson was outraged, since he could legitimately argue that he was the popular favorite. The general exclaimed, "The Judas of the West [Clay] has closed the contract and will receive the thirty pieces of silver."

HENRY CLAY, MARCH 6, 1824, TO DR. J.D. GODMAN, GLC 1028

I think it certain that the election will come into the H[ouse] of R[epresentatives].

Pennsylvania having decided for Genl. Jackson, I think it most probable that Mr. Adams and the Genl. will be two of the three highest who will be carried into that house.

If I should obtain the vote of New York, I shall also be one of those three, and the highest of them.

If Mr. Crawford should obtain it, he will enter the House and I shall be left out of it unless I can counterbalance the vote of Genl. Jackson by a support derived from some eastern state.

In respect to the dispositions of New York, you are probably well informed in Philadelphia. Here the belief is that the real contest in that state is between Mr. Adams and me.

If I enter the H. of R. no matter with what associates my opinion is that I shall be elected.

If Mr. Adams, Mr. Crawford and Gen. Jackson should happen to be the three highest, I think Mr. Adams will be elected.

The states of Ohio, Kentucky, Indiana, Illinois, Missouri and Louisiana, according to indisputable information received here, remain unshaken in their determination to support me. Virginia prefers me next to Crawford. South Carolina is balanced between Genl. Jackson and me. My opinions on the Tariff will probably occasion me the loss of that state. It is a little remarkable that, while those opinions subject me to certain & positive loss to the South, they bring me no corresponding gain in other quarters....

My present belief is that Mr. Adams, Genl Jackson and myself will be the three highest who will enter the H. of R. And the number of votes respectively which we may have will depend mainly upon the decision of N. York. If that decision should be against Mr. Crawford I think his friends will abandon him and make their secondary choice, which I have reason to think will, as to most of them, be for me.

29 / "Roads and Canals are among the most essential means of improving the condition of the Nation"

John Quincy Adams was one of the most brilliant men to occupy the White House. A deeply religious man, he read the Bible at least three times a day—once in English, once in German, and once in French. He was fluent in seven languages, including Greek and Latin.

But Adams, like his father, lacked the political and personal skills necessary to win support for his programs. His adversaries mockingly described him as a "chip off the old iceberg." But his problems did not arise exclusively from his temperament. His misfortune was to serve as president at a time of growing partisan divisions. The Republican Party had split into two distinct camps. Adams and his supporters, known as the National Republicans, favored a vigorous federal role in promoting economic growth, while the Jacksonian Democrats demanded a limited government and strict adherence to laissez-faire principles.

In this letter, Adams observes that throughout his political career he believed that the central government was responsible for maintaining what has come to be called the nation's infrastructure.

JOHN QUINCY ADAMS (AS SECRETARY OF STATE), MAY 6, 1824, TO JOHN MCLEAN, COMMISSIONER OF THE GENERAL LAND OFFICE, GLC 1727

Conformably to your desires, I enclose herewith a copy of the Resolution moved by me in the Senate of the United States on the 23d. of February 1807. in relations to internal improvements....

This was I believe the first Resolution ever offered in Congress, contemplating a *general system* of internal improvement....

The question of the power of Congress, to authorize the making of internal improvements, is, in other words, a question, whether the people of this Union, in forming their social compact, avowedly for the purpose of promoting their general welfare, have performed their work in a manner so ineffably stupid, as to deny themselves the means of bettering their own condition. I have too much respect for the intellect of my country to believe it. The first object of human association is the improvement of the condition of the associates—Roads and Canals are among the most essential means of improving the condition of the Nation, and a People which should deliberately by the organization of its authorized power, deprive itself of the faculty of multiplying its own blessings, would be as wise as a Creator, who should undertake to constitute a human being without a Heart.

POWER AND IDEOLOGY IN JACKSON'S AMERICA

In the election of 1828, "J.Q. Adams who can write" squared off against "Andy Jackson who can fight." Jackson's followers charged that Adams was an "aristocrat" who had obtained office as a result of a "corrupt bargain." Adams's supporters called the general a slave trader, a gambler, and a backwoods buffoon who could not spell more than one word out of four correctly.

The Jackson campaign was the first to appeal directly for voter support through a professional political organization. Jackson supporters set up a network of newspapers and campaign committees and erected hickory poles, Jackson's symbol. Twice as many voters cast ballots in 1828 as in 1824, four times as many as in 1820. Jackson won a resounding victory, sweeping every state in the South and West as well as Pennsylvania and part of New York. Jackson's victory symbolized a shift in power to the West.

In certain respects the new president was truly a self-made man. He was the first president born west of the Appalachians and the first to be born in a log cabin. Orphaned at an early age, he had volunteered to fight in the Revolution when he was thirteen. But although Jackson would gain a reputation as the champion of the common people, in Tennessee he was allied by marriage, business, and political ties to the state's elite. As a land speculator, cotton planter, and attorney, he accumulated a large personal fortune and more than a hundred slaves. His candidacy for the presidency was initially promoted by speculators, creditors, and elite leaders in Tennessee who hoped to exploit the general's popularity to fend off challenges to their dominance of state politics.

As president, Jackson espoused an ideology that stressed the common people's virtue, intelligence, and capacity for self-government. He also expressed disdain for the "better classes," which claimed "a more enlightened wisdom" than common people. Endorsing the view that a fundamental conflict existed between working people and the "nonproducing" classes of society, Jackson and his supporters promised to remove any impediments to the ordinary citizens' opportunities for economic improvement.

Nowhere were the Jacksonian ideals of openness and opportunity made more concrete than in Jackson's embrace of the spoils system and the political nominating convention. In his first annual message to Congress, Jackson argued that public offices should be rotated among party supporters in order to help the nation achieve its republican ideals. Performance in office, he maintained, required no special intelligence or training, and rotation in office would ensure that the government did not develop a class of corrupt civil servants set apart from the people. Jackson defended the party nominating convention as a way to ensure that candidates reflected the people's will.

In office, Jackson greatly enhanced the power and prestige of the presidency. He used the veto power more often than all previous presidents and used it in such a way that he succeeded in representing himself as the champion of the people against special interests in Congress. In addition, his skillful use of patronage and party organization and his successful manipulation of public symbols helped create the nation's first modern political party with truly national appeal.

Jackson's veto of the Maysville Road Bill, a proposal to fund a road entirely within Henry Clay's Kentucky, offers an example of the president's techniques. Jackson denounced the bill as a flagrant example of government favoritism that provided benefits to a privileged minority at the public's expense.

NULLIFICATION AND THE BANK WAR

30 / *"[The tariff] has divided the country into two great geographical divisions"*

During Jackson's presidency, tariff and banking policies dominated national politics. Compared to the issues that dominated British politics during the same years—slave emancipation, factory regulation, and assistance to the poor—the issues Americans fought over might seem less important. Nevertheless, vital interests were at stake, relat-

MONUMENTAL INSCRIPTIONS!

These Inscriptions, compiled from authentic sources, but principally from Official Documents, communicated by the Department of War to *Congress*, on the 25th of January, 1828, are, in this form, submitted to the serious consideration of the American People, under the firm conviction, that the facts embodied in them, ought to, and will, produce a cool and deliberate examination of the qualifications, from Nature and Education, of General ANDREW JACKSON, for the high Civil Station to which he aspires, and to attain which he electioneers with a boldness and pertinacity, unexampled in this Republic. If he shall be found guilty of having ILLEGALLY AND WANTONLY SHED THE BLOOD OF HIS COUNTRYMEN AND FELLOW SOLDIERS, ENTRUST NOT THE LIBERTY AND HAPPINESS OF THIS MOST FREE AND MOST HAPPY COUNTRY TO HIS KEEPING.

THESE MARBLE WALLS
Enclose the remains of
EDWARD LINDSEY,
He was one of the Six Militia men,
Who, with others, yielding to the general opinion,
That the legal period of their service had expired,
Returned to their Homes.
Jealous of his Reputation,
He voluntarily returned to Camp, on hearing that *doubts*
Were entertained as to the propriety of his departure.
For this he was
WITH FIVE OTHER AMERICANS,
Shot to Death
After the usual forms of a Military trial.
BY THE ORDERS OF
GENERAL ANDREW JACKSON,
This cruel deed was executed
On the 21st February, 1815.

Humanity, weeping over deeds which
Sully the lustrous fame of one whose Military renown
Would otherwise have been dear to our country,
Has prompted its citizens
To erect this Tablet,
ON THE FOURTH OF JULY,
1828.

WHATEVER WAS MORTAL
OF
HENRY LEWIS,
Reposes within these bounds.
In the Creek War he gallantly met the Savage foe
and conquered.
Believing that his second tour of duty had expired,
He left the camp and returned to his home,
Where learning that he might have erred in so doing,
And anxious to preserve his dearly earned fame,
He willingly sought the camp again, and offered to do his duty,
If yet legally bound.
For this temporary absence he was arrested, tried, convicted;
And by the orders of
GENERAL ANDREW JACKSON,
SHOT TO DEATH.
His sympathising Brethren in arms, detailed for the execution
of this revolting sentence,
Sought to miss the gallant Youth.
His life fled not at the first fire, humanity labored
for its preservation,
Whilst he anxiously prayed to live, only that he might
wipe away the foul stain.
He died in Extreme Agony on the evening
of the
21st February, 1815.

THIS MONUMENT,
Erected by numerous freemen of these United States
will perpetuate their respect for the Virtues
of a Brave Militia Man:
Whilst it manifests to the world that the
renown of a Military Hero,
Can never be permitted to render them
insensible either to his Cruelties
or to their Rights.

ERECTED JULY 4, 1828.

HERE LIE
THE MORTAL REMAINS
OF
David Morrow,
A BRAVE
And conscientious soldier in the Militia of the
Creek War.
His term of service had expired,
And he returned to his home justified by the officers of every grade.
Fearing that his legal tour of duty had possibly not expired,
He voluntarily returned to Camp,
EXPRESSED GREAT CONTRITION FOR HIS ERRORS,
If any had been committed,
And thereupon received from his General
A WRITTEN PARDON.
He was nevertheless Arrested, Tried, and
SHOT TO DEATH,
BY THE ORDERS OF
GEN. ANDREW JACKSON,
On the 21st February.
1815.

Oh! reader whoever you are,
Let not the splendour of Military renown,
Blot out from your indignant recollection
this bloody deed,
DONE BY A HERO.

The Mites of Widows and Orphans,
Have contributed to raise this Slab,
to the memory of a brave man,
On the 4th July, 1828.

HERE LIES
JACOB WEBB,
Of Poor and Humble Parentage,
And without Education; yet he fostered the
Virtues of Patriotism and Bravery.
He faithfully served as a private in the Militia during
the Creek War.
He served for Three Months,
And believing that to be the period for which he had been drafted
Reposing in the judgment of others,
(The soundness of which has since been ascertained,)
He sought his paternal roof,
But soon returned to camp, on being informed that his Tour
of duty had possibly not expired.
After the usual formalities of a Military trial, he was
SHOT TO DEATH
BY THE ORDERS OF
General Andrew Jackson,
On the 21st February, 1815.

The remembrance of this horrid deed remains,
though thirteen years have passed away.
The People of these United States,
Who love *Discipline* tempered with *Humanity*,
Have erected this Monument
In vindication of the fair fame of a poor but
faithful Militia man.
And in the hope that when war shall again assail
their country our honest Yeomanry,
May not be deterred by this example of a
Hero's recklessness of human life.
*If the Hero has been cruel, the Country
has been just.*

ERECTED JULY 4, 1828.

SACRED
TO THE MEMORY OF
JOHN HARRIS.
He was a
*Preacher of the Gospel of Christ to the Heathen
in the Wilderness.*
His temporal substance was destroyed by Fire.
TO EARN BREAD
For a Wife and Nine Children, he entered as a
SUBSTITUTE
In the Militia during the Creek War.
He sought information from his Colonel as to his legal Tour of Duty.
IT WAS WITHHELD FROM HIM.
He was instructed by his Officers that his Tour of duty would
Expire on the 20th September;
On that day he surrendered his musket to his Captain,
Took from him a receipt for it,
Departed from Camp, and
Returned to the wretched hovel which contained his family.
Fearing that he might have erred, he
VOLUNTARILY RETURNED TO CAMP,
And offered to do duty, if he had mistaken his rights.
FOR THESE ACTS HE WAS
Arrested, Tried, and by the Orders
of
GEN. ANDREW JACKSON,
SHOT TO DEATH
On the 21st of February, 1815.
Having only Four Days Notice of his fate,
During which time,
He busied himself in writing to his
AFFLICTED WIFE,
Counseling her, and urging her to bring up his
Nine Children in the love and fear
of
THE LORD.

An outraged country, erects this Monument
July 4, 1828.

THIS
MARBLE CELL
CONTAINS THE MOULDERING REMAINS
OF THE GALLANT
DAVID HUNT,
He was the Son of a Soldier of the Revolution.

A Volunteer in the Creek War,
He faithfully served his country, until his Tour of Duty had expired,
When he left the Camp,
And returned to the home of his Brave Parent;
Where learning that his tour of duty had possibly not expired,
He returned to Camp and to his Duty,
The Veteran Father saying,
"Go my Son, I am sure no harm can come to you;
I too have been a soldier, and under
WASHINGTON
A soldier returning to duty which he had left
in error, always found mercy."
*But the Son never more saw the face of his
Venerable Father!*
He was Arrested, Tried, and
Shot to Death
AT FOUR DAY'S NOTICE,
BY ORDER OF
GEN. ANDREW JACKSON,
On the 21st February, 1815.

The Militia of his Native State, erected
this simple slab to his Memory
on the 4th of July, 1828.

MOURNFUL TRAGEDY;

Or, the death of Jacob Webb, David Morrow, John Harris, Henry Lewis, David Hunt and Edward Lindsey—six militia men, who were condemned to die, the sentence approved by Major General Jackson, and by his order the whole six shot.

O! did you hear that plaintive cry
Borne on the southern breeze?
Saw you John Harris earnest pray
For mercy, on his knees?

Low to the earth he bent, and pray'd
For pardon from his chief;
But to his earnest prayer for life
Jackson, alas! was deaf.

"Spare me," he said, "I mean no wrong,
"My heart was always true:
"First for my country's cause it beat,
"And next, great chief, for you.

"We thought our time of service out—
"Thought it our right to go;
"We meant to violate no law,
"Nor wish'd to shun the foe.

"Our officers declar'd that we
"Had but three months to stay;
"We serv'd those three months faithfully,
Up to the latest day.

"No one suspects intended wrong;
The judgment only err'd
"In such a case, O noble Chief,
"Let mercy's voice be heard.

"At Home an aged mother waits
"To clasp her only son;
"A wife, and little children—this arm
Alone depend upon.

"Cut me not off from those dear ties,
"So soon from life's young bloom:
"O 'tis a dreadful thing to die,
"And moulder in the tomb!

"Sure mercy is a noble gem
"On every Chieftain's brow;
"More sparkling than a diadem—
"O exercise it now."

'Twas all in vain, John Harris' prayer,
'Tis past the soul's belief!
Hard as the flint was Jackson's heart;
He would not grant relief.

He order'd Harris out to die,
And five poor fellows more!
Young, gallant men, in prime of life,
To welter in their gore!!

Methinks I hear the muffled drum,
And see the column move;
Lo here they come—how sad their looks:
Farewell to life and love!

See six black coffins rang'd along—
Six graves before them made;
Webb, Lindsey, Harris, Lewis, Hunt,
And Morris kneel'd and pray'd.

They kneel'd, & pray'd & tho't of home,
And all its dear delights—
The deadly tubes are levell'd now—
The scene my soul affrights!

Sure he will spare! Sure Jackson yet
Will all reprieve but one—
O hark! those shrieks! that cry of death
The dreadful deed is done!

All six militia men were shot:
And O! it seems to me
A dreadful deed—a bloody act
Of needless cruelty.

Andrew Jackson. Broadside, Monumental Inscriptions! [Anti-Jackson tombstone broadside naming men killed], 1828/07/04. The Gilder Lehrman Collection, on deposit at the Pierpont Morgan Library. GLC 1825

ing to such fateful questions as equality of opportunity, the balance of sectional power, and the proper role of government in the economy.

In 1828, before Jackson's election, a new law, which became known as the Tariff of Abominations, raised tariffs as high as 50 percent of the price of European goods. The tariff, Southerners objected, was essentially a tax on their region to assist northern manufacturers. In an unsigned essay, Vice President John C. Calhoun argued that a single state might overrule or "nullify" a federal law within its own territory, until three quarters of the states had upheld the law as constitutional. South Carolina decided not to implement the doctrine of nullification, but to wait and see what attitude the next president would adopt toward the tariff.

Jackson revealed his position at a Jefferson Day dinner in April 1830. Fixing his eyes on Vice President Calhoun, the president expressed his sentiments with this toast: "Our Union: It must be preserved." Calhoun responded to Jackson's challenge and offered the next toast: "The Union, next to our liberty, most dear. May we always remember that it can only be preserved by distributing equally the benefits and burdens of the Union."

An article in a Connecticut newspaper presents Calhoun's views on the tariff question.

Connecticut Herald, AUGUST 30, 1831, GLB 282

Mr. Calhoun's Sentiments

It would be in vain to conceal that it [the tariff] has divided the country into two great geographical divisions, and arrayed them against each other, in opinion at least, if not interests also, on some of the most vital of political subjects; on its finance, its commerce, and its industry; subjects calculated above all others...[to place] the sections in question in deep and dangerous conflict.... If there be any point to which the...weaker of the two sections is unanimous, it is that its prosperity depends, in a great measure, on free trade, light taxes, economical and as far as possible, equal disbursements of the public revenue, and an unshackled industry, elevating them to pursue whatever may appear most advantageous to their interests....

The stronger [states], in order to maintain their superiority, giving a construction to the instrument [the Constitution] which the other believes would convert the General Government into a consolidated, irresponsible government, with the total destruction of liberty; and the weaker, seeing no hope of relief from such assumption of powers, turning its eye to the reserved sovereignty of the States, as the only refuge from oppression....

We are fast approaching a period very novel in the history of nations, and bearing directly and powerfully on the point under consideration—the final payment of a long standing funded debt....When it arrives, the Government would find itself in possession of a surplus revenue of 10,000,000 or 12,000,000 of dollars, if not previously disposed of....

The honest and obvious course is, to prevent the accumulation of the surplus in the treasury, by a timely and judicious reduction of the imposts; and thereby leave the money in the pockets of those who made it, and from whom it cannot be honestly nor constitutionally taken unless required by the fair and legitimate wants of the Government....

Every duty imposed for the purpose of protection, is not only unequal, but also unconstitutional.

31 / *"Disunion, by armed force, is TREASON"*

In 1832, in an effort to conciliate the South, Jackson proposed a lower tariff. Revenue from the existing tariff (together with the sale of public lands) was so high that the federal debt was quickly being paid off. In fact, on January 1, 1835, the U.S. Treasury had a $440,000 surplus. The new tariff was somewhat lower than the Tariff of 1828, but still maintained the principle of protection. In protest, South Carolina's fiery "states' righters" declared both the Tariff of 1832 and the Tariff of 1828 null and void. To defend nullification, the state legislature voted to raise an army.

Although President Jackson owed his election to the presidency to southern slaveholder votes, he was an ardent Unionist who was willing to risk civil war to defy South Carolina's nullification threats. In the proclamation that follows, Jackson declared nullification illegal and became the first president to declare the Union indissoluble. He then asked Congress to empower him to use force to execute federal law; Congress promptly enacted a Force Act. Privately, Jackson threatened to "hang every leader...of that infatuated people, sir, by martial law, irrespective of his name, or political or social position." He also dispatched a fleet of eight ships and a shipment of five thousand muskets to a federal installation in Charleston harbor.

Andrew Jackson, December 10, 1832, Proclamation, GLC 1863,

Whereas a convention assembled by the State of South Carolina, have passed an ordinance by which they declare, "That the several acts...of Congress...for the imposing of duties and imposts on the importation of foreign commodities...are unauthorized by the Constitution of the United States and violate the true meaning and intent thereof, and are null and void, and have no law" nor binding on the citizens of that State....

And...the said ordinance declares that the people of South Carolina...have said that they will consider any act passed by Congress abolishing or closing the ports of the said State...as inconsistent with the longer continuance of South Carolina in the Union....

And whereas the said Ordinance prescribes on the people of South Carolina a course of conduct in direct violation of their duty as citizens of the United States, contrary to the laws of their country, subversive of its constitution, and having for its object the destruction of the Union.... To preserve this bond of our political existence from destruction, to maintain inviolate this state of national honor and prosperity, and to justify the confidence my fellow-citizens have reposed in me, I, Andrew Jackson, President of the United States, have thought proper to issue this my PROCLAMATION, stating my views of the Constitution and laws applicable to the measures adopted by the Convention of South Carolina....

The Ordinance is founded not on the...right of resisting acts which are plainly unconstitutional and too oppressive to be endured; but on the strange position that one State may not only declare an Act of Congress void, but prohibit its execution.... It is true, they add, that to justify this abrogation...it must be palpably contrary to the constitution; but it is evident that to give the right of resisting laws of that description, coupled with the uncontrolled right to decide what laws deserve that character, is to give the power of resisting all laws. For, as by the theory, there is no appeal, the reasons alleged by the State, good or bad, must prevail....

I consider then the power to annul a law of the United States, assumed by one State, INCOMPATIBLE WITH THE EXISTENCE OF THE UNION, CONTRADICTED EXPRESSLY BY THE LETTER OF THE CONSTITUTION, UNAUTHORIZED BY ITS SPIRIT, INCONSISTENT WITH EVERY PRINCIPLE ON WHICH IT WAS FOUNDED, AND DESTRUCTIVE OF THE GREAT OBJECT FOR WHICH IT WAS FORMED....

The law in question was passed under a power expressly given by the Constitution, to lay and collect imposts.... The Constitution has given expressly to Congress the right of raising revenue and of determining the sum the public exigencies will require. The States have no control over the exercise of this right, other than that which results from the power of changing the Representatives who abuse it, and thus procure redress....

On such expositions and reasonings the Ordinance grounds not only an assertion of the right to annul the laws of which it complains, but to enforce it by a threat of seceding from the Union if any attempt is made to execute them.

This right to secede is deduced from the nature of the Constitution, which they say is a compact between sovereign States, who have preserved their whole sovereignty, and therefore are subject to no superior: that because they made the compact, they can break it, when, in their opinion, it has been departed from by the other states. Fallacious as this course of reasoning is, it enlists State pride, and finds advocates in the honest prejudices of those who have not studied the nature of our Government sufficiently to see the radical error on which it rests.

The people of the United States formed the Constitution, acting through the State Legislatures in making the compact, to meet and discuss its provisions, and acting in separate conventions when they ratified those provisions; but the terms used in its construction show it to be a government in which the people of all the States collectively are representative. We are ONE PEOPLE in the choice of the President and Vice President. Here the States have no other agency than to direct the mode in which the votes shall be given.... The people, then, and not the States, are represented in the Executive branch....

When chosen, they [members of the House of Representatives] are all representatives of the United States, not representatives of the particular State from which they come. They are paid by the United States, not by the State; nor are they accountable to it for any act done in the performance of their legislative functions; and however they may in practice, as it is their duty to do, consult and prefer the interests of their particular constituents when they come in conflict with any other partial or local interest, yet it is their first and highest duty, as representatives of the United States, to promote the general good.

The Constitution of the United States, then, forms a government, not a league, and whether it be formed by compact between the States, or in any other manner, its character is the same. It is a government in which all the people are represented, which operates directly on the people individually, not upon the States—they retained all the power they did not grant. But each State having expressly parted with so many powers as to constitute jointly with the other States a single Nation, cannot from that period possess any right to secede, because each secession does not break a league, but destroys the unity of a Nation, and any injury to that unity is not only a breach which would result from the contravention of a compact, but it is an offence against the whole Union....

No one fellow citizens, has a higher reverence for the reserved rights of the States than the Magistrate who now addresses you.... The States, severally have not retained their entire sovereignty. It has been shown that in becoming parts of a nation, not members of a league, they surrendered many of their essential parts of sovereignty. The right to make treaties—declare war—levy taxes—exercise exclusive judicial and legislative powers—were all of them functions of sovereign power. The States then, for all these important purposes, were no longer sovereign. The allegiance of their citizens was transferred in the first instance to the Government of the United States—they became American citizens, and owed obedience to the Constitution of the United States and to laws made in conformity with the powers it vested in Congress.... Treaties and alliances were made in the name of all. Troops were raised for the common defence. How then, with all these proofs that under all changes of our position we had, for designated purposes and with defined powers, created national Governments—how it is, that the most perfect of those several modes of union, should now be considered as a mere league that may be dissolved at pleasure? It is an abuse of terms....

Fellow citizens of my native State! let me not only admonish you, as the first Magistrate of our common country, not to incur the penalty of its laws, but use the influence that a Father would over his children whom he saw rushing to certain ruin.... You are free members of a flourishing and happy union. There is no settled design to oppress you.—You have indeed felt the unequal operation of the laws which may have been unwisely, not unconstitutionally, passed; but that inequality must necessarily be removed. At the very moment when you were madly urged on to the unfortunate course you have begun, a change in public opinion has commenced. The nearly approaching payment of the public debt, and the consequent necessity of a diminution of duties, had already produced a considerable reduction, and that too on some articles of general consumption to your State....

If your leaders could succeed in establishing a separation, what would be your situation? Are you united at home—are you free from the apprehension of civil discord, with all its fearful consequences? Do our neighboring republics, every day suffering some new revolution or contending with some new insurrection—do they excite your envy?.... The laws of the United States must be executed. I have no discretionary power on the subject—my duty is emphatically pronounced in the Constitution. Those who told you that you might peaceably prevent their execution, deceived you—they could not have been deceived themselves. They know that a forcible opposition could alone prevent the execution of the laws, and they know that such opposition must be repelled. Their object is disunion: but be not deceived by names: disunion, by armed force, is TREASON....

32 / *"I recognize no ALLEGIANCE, as paramount to that which the citizens of South Carolina owe to the State of their birth"*

In Congress, Henry Clay, the "Great Pacificator," who had engineered the Compromise of 1820, worked feverishly to reduce South Carolina's sense of grievance. In less than a month he persuaded Congress to enact a compromise tariff with lower levels of protection.

Although South Carolina regarded Jackson's forceful actions as "the mad rages of a driveling dotard," the state legislature backed down, rescinding the ordinance nullifying the federal tariff. As a final gesture of defiance, however, the state adopted an ordinance nullifying the Force Act.

In 1831 and 1832 South Carolina stood alone. No other southern state yet shared its fear of federal power or its militant desire to assert the doctrine of states' rights. South Carolina's anxiety had many causes. Declining cotton prices (from thirty-one cents a pound in 1818 to eight cents a pound in 1831) and a growing concern about the future of slavery transformed the state from a supporter of economic nationalism into the nation's most aggressive advocate of states' rights. Increasingly, economic grievances fused with concerns over slavery. In 1832 the Palmetto State was one of just two states whose population was made up of a majority of slaves (Mississippi was the other). Events throughout the hemisphere made South Carolinians desperately uneasy about slavery's future. In 1831 and 1832 militant abolitionism had erupted in the North; slave insurrections had erupted in Southampton County, Virginia, and in Jamaica; and Britain was moving to emancipate all the slaves in the British Caribbean.

By using the tariff as a focus of their grievances, South Carolina found an ideal way to debate the question of state sovereignty without debating the morality of slavery. Following the Missouri Compromise debates, in 1822, a slave insurrection led by Denmark Vesey, a free black who was familiar with antislavery speeches made in Congress during the Missouri debates, was uncovered in Charleston. In 1832 South Carolinians did not want to stage debates in Congress that might bring the explosive slavery issue to the fore and possibly incite another slave revolt.

A leading South Carolina newspaper reprinted the inaugural address of Governor Robert Y. Hayne (1791–1839), which presented the state's view of the nullification crisis.

Governor Robert Y. Hayne, *Columbia Telescope Extra*, December 13, 1832, GLC 2890

In the great struggle in which we are engaged, for the preservation of our rights and liberties, it is my fixed determination to assert and uphold the SOVEREIGN AUTHORITY OF THE STATE, and to enforce by all the means that may be entrusted to my hands, her SOVEREIGN WILL. I recognize no ALLEGIANCE, as paramount to that which the citizens of South Carolina owe to the State of their birth, or their adoption....

South Carolina, after ten years of unavailing petitions and remonstrances, against a system of measures on the part of the Federal Government, which in common with the other Southern States—she has repeatedly declared, to be founded in USURPATION, utterly subversive of the rights, and fatal to the prosperity of her people,—has in the face of the world PUT HERSELF UPON HER SOVEREIGNTY, and made the solemn declaration that this system shall no longer be enforced within her limits. All hope of a redress of this grievance, from a returning sense of justice on the part of our oppressors, or from any probable change in the policy of the Government, having fled, nothing was left for South Carolina, but to throw herself upon her reserved rights, or to remain for ever in a condition of "Colonial vassalage." She has, therefore, resolved to stand upon her rights, and it is for her sister States, now, to determine, what is to be done in this emergency. She has announced to them her anxious desire that this controversy shall be amicably adjusted, either by a satisfactory modification of the Tariff, or by a reference of the whole subject to a convention of all the States. Should neither of these reasonable propositions be acceded to, then she will feel herself justified before God and Man, in firmly maintaining the position she has assumed, until some other mode can be devised, for the removal of the difficulty. South Carolina is anxiously desirous of living at peace with her brethren; she has not the remotest wish to dissolve the political bonds which have connected her with the great American family of Confederated States. With Thomas Jefferson, "she would regard the dissolution of our Union with them, as one of the greatest of evils—but not the greatest,—there is one greater: SUBMISSION TO A GOVERNMENT WITHOUT LIMITATION OF POWERS;" and such a government she conscientiously believes will be our portion, should the system against which she is now struggling, be finally established as the settled policy of the country. South Carolina is solicitous to preserve the Constitution as our fathers framed it—according to its true spirit, intent, and meaning, but she is inflexibly determined never to surrender her reserved rights, not to suffer the Constitutional compact to be converted into an instrument for the oppression of her citizens....

A confederacy of sovereign states, formed by the free consent of all, cannot possibly be held together, by any other tie than mutual sympathies and common interest. The unhallowed attempt to cement the union with the blood of our citizens, (which if successful would reduce the free and sovereign States of this confederacy to mere dependent provinces) South Carolina has solemnly declared, would be regarded by her, as absolving her "from all further obligation to maintain or preserve her political connexion with the people of the other States." The spirit of our free institutions, the very temper of the age, would seem to forbid the thought of an appeal to force, for the settlement of a constitutional controversy. If, however, we should be deceived in this reasonable expectation—South Carolina, so far as her means extend, stands prepared to meet danger, and repel invasion, come from what quarter it may....

If after making those efforts due to her own honor and the greatness of the cause, she is destined utterly to fail, the bitter fruits of that failure, [will fall] not to herself alone, but to the entire South, nay to the whole union.... The speedy establishment, on the ruins of the rights of the states, and the liberties of the people, of a great CONSOLIDATED GOVERNMENT, "riding and ruling over the plundered ploughman and beggared yeomanry" [Jefferson's words] of our once happy land—our glorious confederacy, broken into scattered and dishonored fragments—the light of liberty extinguished, never perhaps to be resumed—these—these will be the melancholy memorials of that wisdom, which saw the danger while yet at a distance, and of that patriotism, which struggled gloriously to avert it....

33 / *"The union between Mr. Clay & Calhoun"*

The Jacksonians made a great effort to persuade voters to identify their cause with Thomas Jefferson and their opponents with Alexander Hamilton. A radical Jacksonian made the point bluntly: "The aristocracy of our country...continually contrive to change their party name," wrote Frederick Robinson. "It was first Tory, then Federalist, then no party, then amalgamation, then National Republican." In point of fact, however, Hamilton's son was a leading Jackson adviser!

Despite his reputation as the president of the common man, Jackson's policies did little to help small farmers, artisans, and working people. Indeed, many historians now believe that notwithstanding his opposition to nullification, slaveholders were the chief beneficiaries of Jackson's policies. His Indian removal policy opened new lands for slavery in the rich cotton lands of the Old Southwest, and his view of limited government forestalled federal interference with slavery.

In this letter to James A. Hamilton (1788–1878), Jackson offers his view of the underlying political motives behind the nullification controversy. In 1840 Hamilton abandoned the Democratic Party and supported the Whig presidential candidate, William Henry Harrison. During the Civil War, Hamilton was an early proponent of slave emancipation as a war measure.

ANDREW JACKSON, FEBRUARY 23, 1833, TO JAMES A. HAMILTON, GLC 5176

I have been I may say, literally, pressed with business from sunrise to 12 at night.... The papers will have given you the union between Mr. Clay & Calhoun & how strange their position [is]. Nullification cannot be recognized as a peaceful & constitutional measure, and the American system of M[r.] Clay being on the wane, a union between these two extremes are formed, and I have no doubt that the people will duly appreciate the motives which have led to it. I have good reason to be gratified, content even, with my own course as I find these men are obliged to adopt it, to give peace & harmony to the union....

34 / *"A metallic currency to meet the wants of the labouring class"*

The major political issue of Jackson's presidency was his war against the Second Bank of the United States. To understand this battle, it is necessary to recognize that the banking system was wholly different than it is today. The federal government coined only a limited supply of hard money and printed no paper money at all. The principal source of circulating currency was private commercial banks (of which there were 329), chartered by the various states. The notes they issued promised to pay gold or silver upon demand, but they were backed by a limited amount of precious metal and they fluctuated greatly in value.

In 1816 the federal government had chartered the Second Bank of the United States in an effort to control the notes issues by state banks. By demanding payment in gold or silver, the national bank could discipline overspeculative private banks. But the bank was unpopular for various reasons. Private banks resented its privileged position in the banking industry. Some blamed it for causing the Panic of 1819. Others resented its political influence.

In 1832 Henry Clay, Daniel Webster, and other Jackson opponents, seeking an issue for that year's presidential election, passed a bill rechartering the bank. The bank's charter was not due to expire until 1836, but Clay and Webster wanted to force Jackson to take a clear pro bank or antibank position.

Jackson vetoed the bill in a forceful message that condemned the bank as a privileged "monopoly" created to make "rich men...richer by act of Congress." The bank, he declared, was "unauthorized by the Constitution, subversive of the rights of the States, and dangerous to the liberties of the people." In the presidential campaign of 1832 Clay tried to make an issue of the bank veto, but Jackson swept to an easy second-term victory, defeating Clay by 219 electoral votes to 49.

Jackson interpreted his reelection as a mandate to undermine the bank still further. In September 1833 he ordered his treasury secretary to divert $11 million in federal revenues from the Bank of the United States to selected state banks, which came to be known as "pet" banks. The treasury secretary and his successor resigned rather than carry out the president's order. It was only after Jackson appointed a second new secretary that his order was implemented. Jackson's decision to divert federal deposits prompted his adversaries in the Senate to formally censure his actions as arbitrary and unconstitutional.

The bank's president, Nicholas Biddle (1786–1844), responded to Jackson's actions by reducing loans and calling in debts. Over six months, the bank reduced loans by nearly $10 million to pressure Jackson into approving a new charter. "The Bank...is trying to kill me," the president declared, "but I will kill it." The following letter deals with the economic panic that followed Biddle's decision to call in loans, and Jackson's decision to prohibit all bank notes worth less than $5.

Andrew Jackson, March 14, 1834, to Moses Dawson, GLC 1736

> The panic is fast subsiding and like other panics must end in leaving society in a more pure state. The cowards fly, and the corrupt & infected portion of our country will fail, and leave our country in a more healthy condition, by giving us, in time, a metallic currency to meet the wants of the labouring class of the community by putting down the circulation of notes under five dollars and in time, under twenty dollars.... The tyrant [the Second Bank of the United States] is chained & must expire at the end of its charter.

35 / *"My great dread is a Civil War"*

Jackson's decision to divert funds from the bank drew strong support from many businesspeople who believed that the bank's destruction would increase the availability of credit. Jackson, however, hated all banks. Based partly on his unpleasant personal experience with debt, Jackson believed that the only sound currencies were gold and silver. The president launched a crusade to replace all bank notes with hard money. In the

Specie Circular of 1836 he prohibited payment for public lands with anything but gold or silver.

Initially, land sales, canal construction, cotton production, and manufacturing boomed following Jackson's decision to divert federal funds from the bank. At the same time, inflation increased dramatically; prices rose 28 percent in three years. Then in 1837, just after the election of Jackson's handpicked successor, Democrat Martin Van Buren, a deep financial depression struck the country. Not until the mid-1840s would the country fully recover from the effects of the Panic of 1837.

In this letter, David Crockett (1780–1836), the famous frontier hero and an anti-Jackson member of Congress from Tennessee, attacks Jackson's withdrawal of government funds from the Bank of the United States and calls the president a tyrant ruled by personal ambition. Crockett blamed the economic panic on Jackson and his war on the bank. In 1835 pro-Jackson forces defeated Crockett's reelection bid.

David Crockett, April 4, 1834, to John Drurey, GLC 931

I will now give you a history of the times at headquarters {Washington, D.C.}. We are still engaged in debating the great question of the removal of the {federal government's} deposits {from the Bank of the United States}. This question has consumed almost the whole of the session {of Congress}.... The Senate took the vote last week on Mr. Clay's Resolutions {on the administration's decision to divert federal funds from the bank}. First resolution was that the Secretary's reasons were insufficient, and was not satisfactory to the Senate and the other was that the President {Jackson} has violated the Laws and the Constitution. The first resolution was adopted 28 to 18 and the Second by a vote of 27 to 19.... This was the vote of the Senate and I hope the vote may be taken in the House next week. It will be a close vote. Both parties claim the victory. I am still of {the} opinion that the House will adopt similar Resolutions to that of the Senate. My reasons for these opinions is that in so large and intelligent body of men called Honourable men cannot violate principle so much as for a majority to vote for a measure that every man that knows anything must acknowledge is contrary to the laws and Constitution. I have conferred with some of our own numbers that has acknowledged that the act was not right, that Jackson had not a friend in Congress but was sorry that the act was done, but that they must sustain their party. This is what may be called forsaking principle to follow party. This is what I hope ever to be excused from. I cannot nor will not forsake principle to follow after any party and I do hope there may be a majority in Congress that may be governed by the same motive....

I do consider the question now before Congress is one of deep interest to the American people. The question is whether we will surrender up our old long and happy mode of government and take a despot. If Jackson is sustained in this act we say that the will of one man shall be the law of the land. This you know the people will never submit to. I do believe nothing keeps the people quiet at this time only the hope that Congress will give some relief to the Country. We have had memorials from more than three hundred thousand people praying for the restoration of the deposits and a revival of the Charter of the United States Bank. They state that the manufactures have all stopped and dismissed their hands and that there is men, women and children ro[a]ming over the country offering to work for their victuals. You know that such a state of things cannot be kept quiet long. This has never been the case before since previous to the old war [the War of 1812]. The people petitioned in vain...and at length we knew what followed and...my great dread is a Civil War. I do consider the South Carolina question [the nullification controversy] nothing to compare with the present moment. We see the whole circulatory medium of the Country deranged and destroyed and the whole commercial community oppressed and distressed.... Just to gratify the ambition of one man [Jackson] that he may [w]reck his vengeance on the United States Bank. And for what? Just because it refused to lend its aid in upholding his party. The truth is he is surrounded by a set of imps...that is willing to sacrifice the country to promote their own interest....

I have no doubt of the people getting their eyes open yet in time to defeat the little political Judas, Martin Van Buren.... Never was the money of Rome more compleat on the hands of Caesar than the whole purse of the nation is at the time in the hands of our President Jackson.... He is now in possession of both sword and purse. Caesar said to the secretary of Rome give me the money and the secretary said no person have a right to ask that but the Roman Senate and Caesar said to him that it would be as easy for Caesar to take your life as to will it to another. With that the Secretary knowing that Caesar had all power he stepped aside and Caesar took the money. How was it with Andrew Jackson when he asked Mr. Duane to remove the deposits and he refused & he was then dismissed and a more pliable one appointed and the act is done and I believe they are sorry for it. No man knows where the money of the Country is. Congress has no control over it. This is a new scene in our political history.

36 / *"I will go to the Wilds of Texas"*

In this selection, Crockett complains of Jackson's sway with American voters, calling them "Volunteer Slaves," and announces his plans to leave the United States and move to Texas.

DAVID CROCKETT, DECEMBER 25, 1834, TO CHARLES SCHULTZ, GLC 1162

I wrote you a short time ago and as I have caught a leisure moment I will write again although I can add but little.... The western & southern men dare not to sustain Jackson in his mad Caesar [-like rages] and when they refuse all the blood in the nation will be let loos[e] on them.

The time has come that virtue is expected to be transferable and as negotiable as a promissory note...in these days of glory and Jackson and reform &c. [L]ittle Van [Martin van Buren] set in his chair and looks as Sly as a red fox and I have no doubt but that he thinks Andrew Jackson has full power to transfer the people of these United States at his will and I am afraid that a majority of free Citizens will submit to it and Say amen. Jackson done it, it is right. If we judge by the past, we can reach no other calculations.

I have almost given up the ship as lost, I have gone so far as to declare that if Martin Van Buren is elected that I will leave the United States for I never will live under

> his Kingdom. [B]efore I will submit to his government I will go to the Wilds of Texas. I will consider that government a Paradise to what this government will be. I never will...submit to his government[.] In fact at this time our Republican Government has dwindled almost into insignificance, our boasted land of liberty have almost bowed to the yoke of Bondage our happy days of Republican principles are near at an end when a few is to transfer the many[.] This is Van Buren principles. There is more slaves in New York and Pennsylvania than there is in Virginia and South Carolina and they are the meanest kind of slaves; they are volunteer slaves....

POLITICAL DEMOCRATIZATION AND THE DORR WAR

37 / *"Choice of those who make and administer laws is a Natural Right"*

The most significant political innovation of the early nineteenth century was the abolition of property qualifications for voting and officeholding. Following the English principle that voters had to have a stake in the community, the American colonies generally required citizens to own a certain minimum amount of land to qualify to vote. Aspirants for public office were required to meet higher property qualifications. In South Carolina, a representative had to own at least five hundred acres of land and ten slaves. A number of colonies also imposed a religious test. In Connecticut, New Hampshire, New Jersey, and Vermont, no atheist, Jew, or Roman Catholic could hold public office.

By 1860, however, only two states, Rhode Island and South Carolina, still imposed property qualifications for voting, while another five states—Delaware, Georgia, Massachusetts, North Carolina, and Pennsylvania—restricted voting to male taxpayers. All other states and territories had adopted universal white manhood suffrage—a sharp contrast to England, which only with Reform Bill of 1832 gave most middle-class men the right to vote.

In most states, the transition from property qualifications to universal white manhood suffrage occurred gradually, without violence, and with surprisingly little dissension. In Rhode Island, however, the issue provoked an episode known as the "Dorr War." In the 1830s Rhode Island still operated under a royal charter granted in 1663, which restricted suffrage to landowners and their eldest sons. The charter lacked a bill of rights and grossly underrepresented growing industrial cities, such as Providence, in the state legislature. By 1841, just 11,239 of 26,000 adult males were qualified to vote.

In 1834, Thomas W. Dorr (1805–54), a Harvard-educated attorney, launched a campaign to draft a new state constitution and repeal voting restrictions. In 1841 Dorr organized an extralegal convention to frame a new constitution and abolish voting restrictions. The state's governor declared Dorr and his supporters guilty of insurrection, proclaimed a state of emergency, and called out the state militia. Dorr tried unsuccessfully to capture the state arsenal at Providence. He was arrested, found guilty of high treason, and sentenced to life imprisonment at hard labor. To appease popular resentment, the governor then pardoned Dorr, and Rhode Island adopted a new constitution.

Thomas W. Dorr, "An Address to the People of Rhode Island, from the Convention Assembled at Providence on the 22nd Day of February and Again on the 12th Day of March, 1834, to Promote the Establishment of a State Constitution," GLC 4162

Fellow Citizens,

We desire...to disclaim, in the outset, any design or desire of offering the slightest disrespect to the memory, or the character of our predecessors, who first established that scheme of government, into which we are now anxious to carry the work of reformation. If any pride of ancestry may be indulged in this country, the people of Rhode Island may honorably exult in those noble forefathers, who abandoned their native home, and again, their adopted land, and encountered the dangers of a savage wilderness, for the sake of that great experiment of Religious Liberty, in the blessings of which we all participate....

Nor is the business, fellow-citizens, in which we are engaged, a mere narrow party-affair, got up to promote the sordid views of personal aggrandizement. The aspect of our assembly, composed, as it is, of men of all the political divisions in the State, affords sufficient evidence to the contrary....

We begin by inquiring whether it be consistent with the spirit of the Declaration of American Independence, and becoming the character of Rhode Island Republicans, any longer to acknowledge the charter of a British King as a Constitution of civil government?...

The Charter is further essentially defective in having affixed a certain Representation to each town for all time to come; thus making no provision for the changes that might happen.... The town of Jamestown, for instance, sends one Representative to every 18 freemen...and the city of Providence but one Representative to every 275 freemen.... An inequality of representation like this is too unjust to be much longer tolerated.... This inequality of representation has had the effect of placing the majority of the qualified voters in this State, under the control of the minority....

Strange as it is, the State of Rhode Island, so far famed for Religious liberty, seems to have become insensible to the claims of Political liberty. It is the only State in this great Republican Confederacy in which the People have not limited the power of their Legislature by a written Constitution; the only State in the Union in which the People suffer a fair and equal representation of their interests to be defeated by a *rotten borough system*....

We contend then *That a participation in the choice of those who make and administer laws is a Natural Right; which cannot be abridged nor suspended any farther than the greatest good of the greatest number imperative requires*....

It is...objected to the doctrine of a natural right of suffrage, that Minors and Females are excluded from political privileges.... The restriction upon minors does not conflict in the least with any natural right; it acknowledges their rights, and only decides the period at which they shall commence and be exercised....

With regard to the exclusion of women from the exercise of political power, we are far enough from denying to them the possession of natural rights. It is well known that they formerly exercised the elective franchise in one of the States of this Union—New

Jersey; and now that they have ceased to do so, the suspension of their rights rests, not upon any decree of mere force, but upon a just consideration of the best good of society, including that of the sex itself. Their own assent, it should be added, confirms this arrangement of their natural protectors; and being fully aware that the dignity and purity of their sex, character and example would be soon impaired in the conflicts of party strife, they have wisely consented to forego the nominal exercise of political power, and to rule mankind by the only absolute authority which is consistent with their greatest happiness....

Are those citizens who by an extension of suffrage would be admitted to vote, such a class of persons as are unfitted by their character to participate in the political privileges which they claim? We wish this question to be fairly met. Enough has been said in vague and general terms, about "unwholesome citizens," "persons not to be safely trusted," "without property and vicious"—about "protecting the sound part of the community against those who have nothing at stake in society."... Let those who use this language come out and say, if they will venture the assertion, *that the body of traders and mechanics, and professional men, and sons of landholders, are the base and corrupt persons who are aimed at in these sweeping denunciations.*

PARTY COMPETITION AND THE RISE OF THE WHIGS

38 / "We are now in the midst of a higher political excitement than I have ever yet witnessed"

During the thirty-two years following Andrew Jackson's election to the presidency, the Democratic Party controlled the White House all but eight years. It would be a mistake, however, to assume that the Jacksonians faced no effective opposition. Although it took a number of years for Jackson's opponents to coalesce into an effective national political organization, by the mid-1830s the Whig Party was able to battle the Democrats on almost equal terms throughout the country, especially on the state and local levels.

The Whigs, a coalition united by their hatred of Jackson and his "usurpations" of congressional and judicial authority, took their name from the seventeenth-century English Whigs, who had defended English liberties against the pro-Catholic Stuart kings.

In 1836 the Whigs ran three regional candidates against Martin Van Buren. The party strategy was to follow the example of 1824 and throw the election into the House of Representatives, where the Whigs would unite behind a single candidate. But Van Buren easily defeated all his Whig opponents.

In 1840 William Henry Harrison (1773–1841), who had crushed an Indian coalition at the Battle of Tippecanoe in Indiana in 1811, received the Whigs' united support. The 1840 presidential campaign was one of the most exciting and colorful in American history. Although Harrison was college-educated and brought up on a plantation with two hundred slaves, his Democratic opponents had dubbed him the "log cabin" candidate who was happiest on his backwoods farm sipping hard cider. Harrison's supporters enthusiastically seized on this image and promoted it in a number of colorful ways. They distributed barrels of hard cider, passed out campaign hats and placards, and mounted log cabins on floats.

The Whig campaign brought many innovations to the art of electioneering. For the first time, a presidential candidate spoke out on his own behalf. Harrison's backers also coined the first campaign slogans: "Tippecanoe and Tyler, too," "Van, Van is a used-up man." While defending their man as the "people's candidate, the Whigs heaped an avalanche of personal abuse on his Democratic opponent. They accused President Martin Van Buren of eating off of golden plates and lace tablecloths and drinking French wines.

The Harrison campaign provided a number of effective lessons for future politicians, notably an emphasis on symbols and imagery over ideas and substance. Fearful of alienating voters, the political convention that nominated Harrison adopted no party platform. Harrison himself said nothing during the campaign about his principles or proposals. He followed the suggestion of an adviser that he run on his military record and offer no indication "about what he thinks now, or what he will do hereafter."

In 1840 voter turnout was the highest it had ever been in a presidential election: Nearly 80 percent of eligible voters cast ballots. The log cabin candidate won a landslide victory in the electoral college. In the following selection, James Buchanan (1791–1868), a future Democratic president, comments on the 1840 presidential campaign.

JAMES BUCHANAN, JUNE 29, 1840, TO HENRY A. MUHLENBERG, U.S. MINISTER TO THE COURT OF AUSTRIA, GLC 2919

We are now in the midst of a higher political excitement than I have ever yet witnessed; and it extends over every portion of the Union. The Whigs are perfectly confident of electing Harrison, & they even begin to talk about who shall be the members of his Cabinet. Their exertions have been prodigious, and at one period many of our friends began to be alarmed for the result. The opposition at one time confidently hoped to carry Pennsylvania, in consequence of the threatened division in our ranks in relation to the indulgence given to the Bank. This division has been entirely healthy, at least so far as regards M[artin] Van Buren, & the Democracy of the Keystone will move in solid & irresistible column at the Presidential election.... I cannot see how it is possible to defeat Mr. Van Buren. We calculate with much confidence that he will receive every vote south of the Potomack & Ohio, with the exception of Kentucky & possibly Louisiana. We have at least an equal chance for New York & Ohio. Instead of avowing any great principles for the regulation of their conduct, the Whigs endeavored to raise a hurrah all over the Country in favor of their military chieftain. They have built Log Cabins & drunk hard cider every where. This senseless clamor of Log Cabins & hard cider is an insult to the understandings of the people & is everywhere beginning to react with tremendous force against its authors. The hard cider will become sour vinegar, unless I am greatly mistaken, before the end of the dog days. Still it cannot be denied that the hard times & low prices have done their cause much good. I repeat, I entertain little fear of the result.

ANTEBELLUM REFORM: THE SHIFT TO IMMEDIATISM

39 / *"The fatal consequences of Intemperance"*

During the 1820s and 1830s evangelical reformers launched a series of crusades to eradicate sin and make the nation live up to Christian values—campaigns to suppress urban prostitution, enforce the Christian Sabbath, and curb the drinking of hard liquor. In initiating these crusades, evangelicals devised the methods and tactics that would later be used in more radical reforms to abolish slavery and win women's rights.

In the decades before the Civil War the campaign against liquor was the key unifying reform, drawing support from middle-class Protestants, skilled artisans, clerks, shopkeepers, free blacks, and Mormons as well as from many conservative clergy and Southerners who were otherwise hostile to reform. Called the temperance movement, the antebellum crusade against hard liquor in fact advocated "intemperance"—teetotal abstinence from all alcohol.

In part, the rise of temperance agitation represented a response to an upsurge in heavy drinking. By 1820 the typical adult male consumed more than 7 gallons of absolute alcohol a year (compared to about 2.8 gallons today). Consumption had risen markedly since farmers distilled corn to make cheap whiskey, which could be transported more easily than bulk corn.

But the rise of the temperance movement was not simply a response to increased drinking. As the following excerpts from a temperance broadside reveal, the movement reflected broader concerns that alcohol led to economic waste, polluted youth, created crime and poverty, and led men to physically abuse their wives.

"A Mirror for the Intemperate," 1830, GLB 200

Extract from the dying Declaration of Nicholas Fernandez, who, with nine others, were executed in front of Cadiz Harbor in December, 1829, for Piracy and Murder.

"Parents into whose hands this my dying declaration may fall will perceive that I date the commencement of my departure from the paths of rectitude and virtue, from the moment when I become addicted to the habitual use of ardent spirits—and it is my sincere prayer that if they value the happiness of their children—if they desire their welfare here, and their eternal well being hereafter, that they early teach them the fatal consequences of Intemperance!"

40 / *"Men of wealth and respectability, who...throw their influence into the scale of intemperance"*

In its earliest stages, the campaign against drinking drew support from local elites, who associated drinking with the breakdown of the hierarchical social order of the eighteenth century. Typical of the early temperance organizations was the Massachusetts Society for the Suppression of Intemperance, founded in 1813 by gentlemen upset by the spread of social disorder and disrespect for society's upper classes. The goals of the early organizations were quite limited, stressing self-control rather than abstinence and opposing only distilled, not fermented, alcohol. The Massachusetts Society actually served wine at its meetings.

The evangelical revivals of the 1820s transformed temperance into a mass movement. Many reformers were particularly critical of moderate drinking, which helped keep saloons and distilleries in business and set a bad example for those susceptible to alcohol's attractions.

J. Kitredge, extract from "An Address Delivered Before the Temperance Society of Plymouth, N.H.," July 4, 1829

There are opposers among us! men of wealth and respectability, who encourage the use of spirituous liquors and throw their influence into the scale of intemperance. There is, after all, a numerous class of what are called temperate, moderate drinkers, who love rum, and must have it. They do more hurt than the drunkard. They have influence. He has none. They try to make rum-drinking respectable; he cannot.

But they are all alike, the drunkard and the drinker. They are but different species of the same genus. Temperate, moderate drinkers; temperate, moderate slavedealers; temperate, moderate gamblers; temperate, moderate sinners, all alike. It is the drinking which is wrong. Drunkenness is but a higher degree of the same crime. These temperate, moderate drinkers are training themselves and their children to the highest order of drunkards. They are learning the trade, they are serving the apprenticeship, and they uphold and encourage the drunkard....

41 / "30,000 to 50,000 individuals...become sots every year"

For evangelicals, drinking and abstinence were visible symbols of sin, repentance, and the practical power of the gospel. Abstinence, sometimes mislabeled "temperance," was a test of humanity's power to improve itself spiritually and morally.

Edward Hitchcocks, professor of chemistry and natural history, Amherst College, extract "An Essay on Alcoholic and Narcotic Substances, as Articles of Common Use."

"As to any permission given in the Bible to use ardent spirit, I remark, that the whole Bible contains not a syllable concerning ardent spirit: and for this reason, that it was not known to exist, till about nine hundred years after Christ, when it was brought to light by an Arabian chemist, in the process of distillation.

"Let us now inquire, whether the principles of the Bible demand total abstinence. These principles require us to avoid temptation. Now from 30,000 to 50,000 individuals in our land become sots every year by moderate drinking; for this is the number annually required to fill up the vacancies occasioned by death in the ranks of intemperance.

"The great law of Christian benevolence requires us to love our neighbor as ourselves, and that *whatsoever we would that men should do to us, we must do even so to them.* What, then is that man doing to others who refuses to abstain entirely from the alcoholic and narcotic substances?...

"By his example, he contributes to uphold a practice, which brings an annual expense upon his fellow countrymen, of more than 100,000,000 of dollars; and thus to reduce to extreme poverty and wretchedness, from 50,000 to 100,000 families; and not less than 150,000 individuals to pauperism. And to shut up 50,000 men annually in the debtor's prison: And to send out 90,000 murderers, robbers, incendiaries,

> thieves, and the like to make havoc in society: And to render from 300 to 500 thousand citizens habitual drunkards: And annually to make a draft upon the temperate part of the community, for thirty or fifty thousand recruits, to fill up the wasting ranks of drunkenness: And to pour out upon the land, such a flood of corruption and profligacy, as seriously to degrade, and threaten with utter ruin, her social, intellectual, political, and moral character.

ABOLITION AND SLAVERY

By 1830 it was clear that the nation had reached a dead end on the issue of slavery. Colonization was a failure. During the 1820s the number of slaves had increased by half a million and the institution had extended into western Georgia, Alabama, Mississippi, Louisiana, and even Texas, still a part of Mexico.

Racial warfare seemed to pose a serious threat. During the 1830s white mobs repeatedly attacked blacks in urban ghettos and burned African American neighborhoods to the ground. In 1829 David Walker (1785–1830), a secondhand clothing dealer in Boston, issued an *Appeal to the Colored Citizens of the World*, a militant pamphlet calling for insurrection if whites failed to abolish slavery and treat blacks equally. Two years later, Nat Turner led a slave insurrection in southern Virginia; and in that same year, one of the bloodiest slave revolts in history erupted in Jamaica.

Yet if racial warfare seemed to be one possibility, emancipation seemed to be another. In 1833, after prolonged debate, the British Parliament adopted a gradual emancipation measure that established an apprenticeship plan to prepare nearly eight hundred thousand slaves for freedom. The success of Britain's abolitionists offered an important lesson to American opponents of slavery: Emancipation required a massive mobilization of public opinion.

The nation's most famous abolitionist was the Massachusetts-born William Lloyd Garrison (1805–79). In 1829, the twenty-four-year-old Garrison denounced colonization as a cruel hoax designed to promote the racial purity of the North while doing nothing to end slavery in the South. Following in the steps of British radicals, he called for "immediate emancipation"—the immediate and unconditional release of slaves from bondage without compensation to slaveowners.

By 1838 there were thirteen hundred antislavery societies in the North, with more than one hundred thousand members. These local groups mounted a massive publicity campaign to proclaim the sinfulness of slavery. They distributed a million pieces of abolitionist literature and gathered two million names in an 1838–39 petition campaign.

42 / *"How is it with the slave?"*

William Lloyd Garrison, the symbol of immediate abolition, had firsthand knowledge of poverty. His father, a sailing master, had abandoned his family when Garrison was three years old. Having little formal schooling, Garrison educated himself while he worked as a printer's apprentice. He then supported himself as a journalist and editor of a weekly reform newspaper. Garrison's former master described his apprentice as "a diligent student" with "an ardent temperament and warm imagination" and "unshaken courage," but also "hasty, stubborn, and dogmatic."

This letter by Garrison refers to his imprisonment for criminal libel. In the *Genius of Universal Emancipation*, an antislavery newspaper, Garrison had accused a merchant of transporting seventy-five slaves from Baltimore to New Orleans and declared that the man should be "SENTENCED TO SOLITARY CONFINEMENT FOR LIFE." In Baltimore Garrison was found guilty and fined $50 plus court costs. Unable to pay, Garrison was confined in prison for seven weeks before Arthur Tappan (1786–1865), a New York merchant and philanthropist, provided the money for his release.

WILLIAM LLOYD GARRISON, JULY 14, 1830, TO EBENEZER DOLE, GLC 4516

I have found the minds of the people strangely indifferent to the subject of slavery. Their prejudices were invincible—stronger, if possible, than those of slaveholders. Objections were stated on every hand; apologies for the abominable system constantly saluted my ears; obstacles were industriously piled up in my path. The cause of this callous state of feeling was owing to their exceeding ignorance of the horrors of slavery. What was yet more discouraging, my best friends—without an exception—besought me to give up the enterprise, and never to return to Baltimore! It was not my duty (they argued) to spend my time, and talents, and services, where persecution, reproach and poverty were the only certain reward. My scheme was visionary—fanatical—unattainable. Why should I make myself an exile from home and all that I held dear on earth, and sojourn in a strange land, among enemies whose hearts were dead to every noble sentiment?—&c. &c. &c. I repeat—*all were against my return*. But I desire to thank God, that he gave me strength to overcome this selfish and pernicious advice. Opposition served only to increase my ardor, and confirm my purpose.

But how was I to return? I had not a dollar in my pocket, and my time was expired. No one understood my circumstances. I was too proud to beg, and ashamed to borrow. My friends were prodigal of pity, but of nothing else. In the extremity of my uneasiness, I went to the Boston Post office, and found a letter from my friend [Benjamin] Lundy, enclosing a draft for $100, from a stranger—yourself, as a remuneration for my poor, inefficient services in behalf of the slaves! Here Providence had again signally interfered in my behalf. After deducting the expenses of travelling, the remainder of the above named sum was applied to discharging a few of the debts incurred by the unproductiveness of the *Genius*.

As I lay on my couch one night, in jail, I was led to contrast my situation with that of the poor slave. Ah! dear sir, how wide the difference! In one particular only, (I said,) our conditions are similar. He is confined to the narrow limits of a plantation—I to the narrow limits of a prison-yard. Farther all parallels fail. My food is better and more abundant, as I get a pound of bread and a pound of meat, with a plentiful supply of pure water, *per diem*. I can lie down or rise up, sit or walk, sing or declaim, read or write, as fancy, pleasure or profit dictates. Moreover, I am daily cheered with the presence and conversation of friends;—I am constantly supplied with fresh periodicals from every section of the country, and, consequently, am advertised of every new and interesting occurrence. Occasionally a letter greets me from a distant place, filled with consolatory

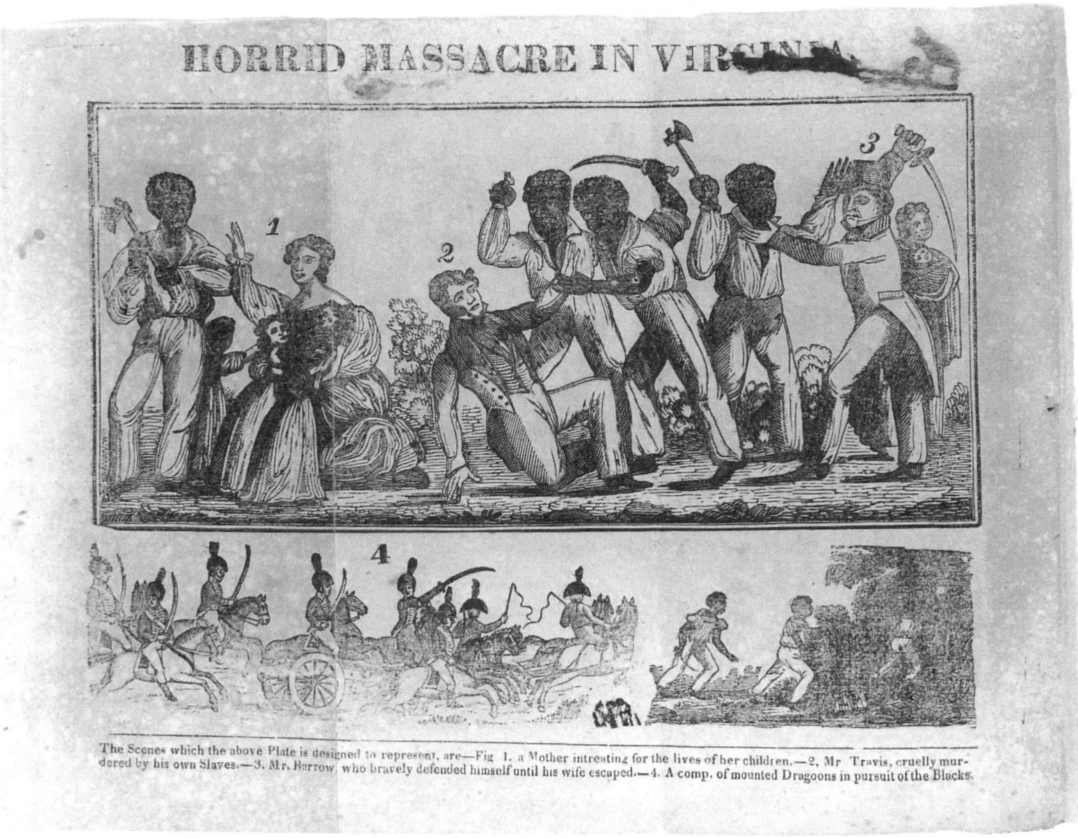

Samuel Warner. Book, Authentic and impartial narrative…massacred by blacks! [Turner slave uprising], 1831. The Gilder Lehrman Collection, on deposit at the Pierpont Morgan Library. GLC 4548

expressions, tender remembrances, or fine compliments. If it rain, my room is a shelter; if the sun flame too intensely, I can choose a shady retreat; if I am sick, medical aid is at hand.—Besides, I have been charged with a specific offence—have had the privilege of a trial by jury, and the aid of eminent counsel—and am here ostensibly to satisfy the demands of justice. A few months, at the longest, will release me form my captivity.

Now, how is it with the slave? He gets a peck of corn (occasionally a little more) each week, but rarely meat or fish. He must anticipate the sun in rising, or be whipped severely for his somnolency. Rain or shine, he must toil early and late *for the benefit of another*. If he be weary, he cannot rest—for the lash of the driver is flourished over his drooping head, or applied to his naked frame; if sick, he is suspected of laziness, and treated accordingly. For the most trifling or innocent offence, he is felled to the earth, or scourged on his back till it streams with blood. Has he a wife and children, he sees them as cruelly treated as himself. He may be torn from them, or they from him, at any moment, never again to meet on earth. Friends do not visit and console him: *he has no friends*. He knows not what is going on beyond his own narrow boundaries. He can neither read nor write. The letters of the alphabet are caballistical to his eyes. A thick darkness broods over his soul. Even the "glorious gospel of the blessed God," which brings life and immortality to perishing man, is as a sealed book to his understanding. Nor has his wretched condition been imposed upon him for any criminal offence. He has not been tried by the laws of his country. No one has stepped forth to vindicate *his* rights. He is made an abject slave, simply because God has given him a skin not colored like his master's; and Death, the great Liberator, alone can break his fetters!

43 / *"Slavery is undoubtedly a manifest violation of the rights of man"*

Henry Clay favored colonization as the only workable solution to slavery—a position that would later be embraced by one of Clay's ardent admirers, Abraham Lincoln (1809–65). In this letter Clay spells out the kind of cautious antislavery position that Garrison began denouncing in 1831.

HENRY CLAY, MAY 19, 1831, TO JOHN SWITZER, GLC 3725

I received your letter of the 6th inst. requesting my opinion on certain questions stated by you in respect to the African portion of our population. I have not time to discuss these at large and must therefore confine myself to a brief reply, upon the condition, suggested by yourself that my letter shall not be a subject of publication....

The question of emancipation, immediate or prospective, as a public measure, appertains, in my opinion, exclusively to the several States, each judging and asking for itself, in which slavery exists. More than thirty years ago I was in favor of the adoption in K[entucky] of a system similar to that which, at the insistence of [Benjamin] Franklin had been previously sanctioned by Penn[sylvani]a. I have never ceased to regret that the decision of this State was adverse to the plan.

Slavery is undoubtedly a manifest violation of the rights of man. It can only be justified in America, if at all, by necessity. That it entails innumerable mischiefs upon our Country I think is quite clear. It may become dangerous in particular parts of the Union. But the slaves can never, I think, acquire permanent ascendancy in any part.

Congress has no power, as I think, to establish any system of emancipation, gradual or immediate, in behalf of the present or any future generation. The several states alone, according to our existing institutions, are competent to make provision on that subject, as already intimated.

NAT TURNER'S INSURRECTION

44 / *"Disagreeable rumors have reached this city of an insurrection of the slaves in Southampton County"*

It was a basic tenet of the proslavery argument that slaves were docile, contented, faithful, and loyal. In fact, there is no evidence that the majority of slaves were contented. Many slaves who did not rebel directly made their masters' lives miserable through a variety of indirect protests against slavery, including sabotage, stealing, malingering, murder, arson, and infanticide.

Four times during the first thirty-one years of the nineteenth century, slaves attempted major insurrections. In 1800 a twenty-four-year-old Virginia blacksmith named Gabriel led a march on Richmond. The plot failed when a storm washed out the road to Richmond, giving the Virginia militia time to arrest the rebels. White authorities executed Gabriel and 25 other conspirators.

In 1811 Charles Deslondes, a free mulatto from Haiti, and 180 to 500 slaves marched on New Orleans. Slaveowners retaliated by killing 82 blacks and placing the heads of 16 leaders on pikes.

In 1822 Denmark Vesey, a former slave who had been born in Africa, lived in St. Domingue (Haiti), and purchased his freedom after winning a lottery, devised a plan to take over Charleston, South Carolina, on a summer Sunday when many whites would be vacationing outside the city. Before the revolt could take place, however, a domestic slave informed his master. The authorities proceeded to arrest 131 blacks and to hang 37.

The most famous slave revolt took place nine years later, in Southampton County in southern Virginia, where in 1830 there were 6,573 whites, 1,745 free blacks, and 7,756 slaves. On August 22, 1831, Nat Turner (1800–1831), a Baptist preacher, led a small group of fellow slaves into the home of his master, Joseph Travis, and killed the entire Travis household. By August 23 Turner's force had increased to 60 to 80 slaves, joined by at least 4 free blacks, and had killed more than 50 whites, mostly women and children. The local militia counterattacked and killed about 100 blacks. Twenty more slaves, including Turner, were later executed. The following published accounts document Turner's insurrection.

Constitutional Whig, RICHMOND, AUGUST 23, 1831

Disagreeable rumors have reached this city of an insurrection of the slaves in Southampton County, with loss of life, in order to correct exaggerations, and at the same time to induce all salutary caution, we state the following particulars.

An express from the Hon. James Trezevant states that an insurrection had broken out, that several families had been murdered, and that the Negroes were embodied, requiring a considerable military force to reduce them....

Serious danger, of course, there is none. The deluded wretches have rushed on assured destruction....

We understand that the insurrection in Southampton is little more than the irruption of 150 or 200 runaway slaves from the Dismal Swamp, incited by a spirit of plunder and rapine. It will be quickly suppressed.

45 / *"Without any cause or provocation"*

Richmond Enquirer, AUGUST 30, 1831, EXTRACT OF "A LETTER FROM JERUSALEM, VA., 24TH AUGUST, 3 O'CLOCK."

A fanatic preacher by the name of Nat Turner (Gen. Nat Turner) who had been taught to read and write, and permitted to go about preaching in the country, was the bottom of this infernal brigandage. He was artful, impudent, and vindictive, without any cause or provocation, that could be assigned. He was the slave of Mr. Travis. He and another slave of Mr. Travis a young fellow, by the name of Moore, were two of the leaders.... And by importunity or threats they prevailed upon about 20 others to cooperate in the scheme of massacre.... They were mounted to the number of 40 or 50; and with knives and axes—knocking on the head, or cutting the throats of their victims.... But as they went from house to house, they drank ardent spirits—and it is supposed, that in consequence of their being intoxicated, or from mere fatigue, they paused in their murderous career about 12 o'clock on Monday.

A fact or two, before we continue our narrative. These wretches are now estimated to have committed *sixty-one murders*! Not a white person escaped at all the houses they visited except *two*....

Early on Tuesday morning, they attempted to renew their bloody work. —They made an attack upon Mr. Blunt, a gentleman who was very unwell with the gout, and who instead of flying determined to brave them out. He had several pieces of firearms, perhaps seven or eight, and he put them into the hands of his own slaves, who nobly and gallantly stood by him. They repelled the brigands—killed one, wounded and took prisoner (Gen. Moore), and we believe took a third who was not wounded at all....

The militia of Southampton had been most active in ferreting out the fugitives from their hiding places.... But it deserves to be said to the credit of many of the slaves whom gratitude had bound to their masters, that they had manifested the greatest alacrity in detecting and apprehending many of the brigands.... It is said that from 40 to 50 blacks were in jail—some of whom were known to be concerned with the murders, and others suspected. The courts will discriminate the innocent from the guilty.

It is believed that all the brigands were slaves—and most, if not all these, the property of kind and indulgent masters. It is not known that any of them had been the runaways of the swamps and only one of them was a free man of color....

Nat, the ringleader, who calls himself General, pretends to be a Baptist preacher—a great enthusiast—declares to his comrades that he is commissioned by Jesus Christ, and proceeds under his inspired directions—that the late singular appearance of the sun was the sight for him, etc., etc., is among the number not yet taken. The story of his having been killed at the bridge, and of two engagements there, is ungrounded. It is believed he cannot escape.

"The Banditti," *Richmond Enquirer,* August 30, 1831, Vol. 28, p. [2].

46 / "Doomed...in this 'Land of Liberty' to a state of cruel bondage!"

This volume was copyrighted just one month after the revolt took place.

SAMUEL WARNER, *Authentic and Impartial Narrative of the Tragical Scene Which was Witnessed in Southampton County...when Fifty-Five of its Inhabitants (mostly women and children) were inhumanely Massacred by the Blacks!*, 1831, GLC 4548

Horrid Massacre

In consequence of the alarming increase of the Black population at the South, fears have been long entertained that it might one day be the unhappy lot of the whites, in that section, to witness scenes similar to those which but a few years since, nearly depopulated the once flourishing island of St. Domingo of its white inhabitants—but, these fears have never been realized even in a small degree, until the fatal morning of the 22d of August last, when it fell to the lot of the inhabitants of a thinly settled township of Southampton county (Virginia) to witness a scene horrid in the extreme!—when FIFTY FIVE innocent persons (mostly women and children) fell victims to the most inhuman barbarity.

The melancholy and bloody event was as sudden and unexpected, as unprecedented for cruelty—for many months previous an artful black, known by the name of Nat Turner, (a slave of Mr. Edward Travis) who had been taught to read and write, and who hypocritically and the better to enable him to effect his nefarious design, assumed the character of a Preacher, and as such as sometimes permitted to visit and associate himself with many of the Plantation Negroes, for the purpose (as was by him artfully represented) of christianizing and to teach them the propriety of their remaining faithful and obedient to their masters; but, in reality, to persuade and to prepare them in the most sly and artful manner to become the instruments of their slaughter!—in this he too well succeeded, by representing to the poor deluded wretches the Blessings of Liberty, and the inhumanity and injustice of their being forced like brutes from the land of their nativity, and doomed without fault or crime to perpetual bondage, and by those who were not more entitled to their liberty than themselves!—and he too represented to them the happy effects which had attended the united efforts of their brethren in St. Domingo, and elsewhere, and encouraged them with the assurance that a similar effort on their part, could not fail to produce a similar effect, and not only restore them to liberty but would produce them wealth and ease!...

Yet we cannot hold those entirely blameless, who first brought them from their native plains—who robbed them of their domestic joys—who tore them from their weeping children and dearest connections, and doomed them in this "Land of Liberty" to a state of cruel bondage!...

To remove this stain from the American people the energies of justice, the life of virtue, and the sacred obligations of principle must be brought into operation. We have already said that all men are born equal—that they are endowed by their Creator with certain unalienable rights, among which are life, LIBERTY and the pursuit of happiness. But do we mean by the term ALL MEN, to be understood those of a white complexion only, and that nature has denied, or the Creator withheld, from those of other shades, the rights which have been contended for?... The colonization scheme of which we have heard at Washington, was opened to the public with feeling and pathetic acknowledgments that Africans were men and that from us they had a right to look for justice. Hence it cannot be denied, they are literally and in fact included in our bill of rights, nor can we be exonerated from the charge of tyranny until by our solemn act we place them in full possession of those rights which are claimed for ourselves, and which are consistent with the principles of our excellent government. While we believe it to have been the object and compatible with the views of the framers of our constitution, to "form a perfect union, establish justice and secure the blessing of liberty to ourselves and our posterity" we cannot admit that they ever intended to entail upon the sons of Africa the chains of perpetual slavery!—and we rejoice that we have it in our power to say that the reputation of the New-England States (as well as that of New-York, New-Jersey and Pennsylvania) is no longer tarnished with this foul stain—her humane and Philanthropic sons have wisely burst asunder the chains of bondage and set the captive free!

Samuel Warner, *Authentic and Impartial Narrative of the Tragical Scene Which was Witnessed in Southampton County...when Fifty-five of its Inhabitants (mostly women and children) were inhumanely Massacred by the Blacks!* (New York: Warner & West, 1831), pp. 5–38.

47 / *"What we have long predicted...has commenced its fulfillment"*

On January 1, 1831, William Lloyd Garrison founded *The Liberator*, a militant abolitionist newspaper that was one of the country's first publications to demand an immediate end to slavery. On the front page of the first issue he defiantly declared: "I will not equivocate—I will not excuse—I will not retreat a single inch—AND I WILL BE HEARD." Incensed by Garrison's proclamation, the state of Georgia offered a $5,000 reward to anyone who brought him to that state for trial.

Turner's rebellion, which occurred just nine months after *The Liberator* began publication, prompted this editorial.

The Liberator, September 3, 1831

The Insurrection

What we have long predicted,—at the peril of being stigmatized as an alarmist and declaimer,—has commenced its fulfillment. The first step of the earthquake, which is ultimately to shake down the fabric of oppression, leaving not one stone upon the other, has been made. The first drops of blood, which are but the prelude to a deluge from the gathering clouds, have fallen....

Read the account of the insurrection in Virginia, and say whether our prophecy be not fulfilled....

True, the rebellion is quelled. Those of the slaves who were not killed in combat have been secured, and the prison is crowded with victims destined for the gallows!... You have seen, it is to be feared, but the beginning of sorrows. All the blood which has been shed will be acquired at your hands. At your hands alone? No—but at the hands of the people of New-England and of all the free states. The crime of oppression is national. The South is only the agent in this guilty traffic. But, remember! the same causes are at work which must inevitably produce the same effects; and when the contest shall have again begun, it must be a war of extermination....

Ye accuse the pacific friends of emancipation of instigating the slaves to revolt.... The slaves need no incentive at our hands. They will find in their stripes—in their emaciated bodies—in their ceaseless toil—in their ignorant minds...in your speeches and conversations, your celebrations, your pamphlets, your newspapers—voices in the air, sounds from across the ocean, invitations to resistance above, below, around them! What more do they need....

For ourselves, we are horror-struck at the late tidings. We have exerted our utmost efforts to avert the calamity. We have warned our countrymen of the danger of persisting in their unrighteous conduct. We have preached to the slaves the pacific precepts of Jesus Christ. We have appealed to christians, philanthropists and patriots, for their assistance to accomplish the great work of national redemption through the agency of moral power—of public opinion—of individual duty. How have we been received? We have been threatened, proscribed, vilified and imprisoned.... If we have been hitherto urgent, and bold, and denunciatory in our efforts—hereafter we shall grow vehement and active with the increase of danger. We shall cry, in trumpet tones, night and day,—Wo to this guilty land, unless she speedily repents of her evil doings! The blood of millions of her sons cries aloud for redress! IMMEDIATE EMANCIPATION can alone save her from the vengeance of Heaven, and cancel the debt of ages!

The Liberator, September 3, 1831, Vol. I, p. 143.

48 / *"Any scheme of abolition...so soon after the Southampton tragedy, would...appear to be the result of the...massacre"*

During the late eighteenth century, the South was unique among slave societies in its openness to antislavery ideas. In Delaware, Maryland, and North Carolina, Quakers freed more than fifteen hundred slaves. Scattered Presbyterian, Baptist, and Methodist ministers condemned slavery as a sin "contrary to the word of God."

By the 1830s, however, the South's openness to antislavery ideas had ended. State legislatures adopted laws suppressing criticism of slavery. White Southerners stopped referring to the institution as a necessary evil and instead began to defend slavery as a positive good. By the 1840s a new, more explicitly racist rationale for slavery had emerged.

Only once, in the wake of Nat Turner's insurrection, did a southern state openly debate the possibility of ending slavery. These debates in the Virginia legislature in January and February 1832 ended with the defeat of proposals to abolish slavery. In the following selection, Thomas R. Dew (1802–46), an influential professor of political economy at the College of William and Mary, discusses the legislative debate. Dew's predecessors at William and Mary, George Wythe (1726–1806) and St. George Tucker (1752–1827), had abhorred slavery.

Thomas R. Dew, "Review of the Debate in the Virginia Legislature," 1832

...In our Southern slave-holding country, the question of emancipation has never been seriously discussed in any of our legislatures, until the whole subject, under the most exciting circumstances, was, during the last winter, brought up for discussion in the Virginia Legislature, and plans of partial or total abolition were earnestly pressed upon the attention of that body. It is well known, that during the last summer, in the county of Southampton in Virginia, a few slaves, led on by Nat Turner, rose in the night, and murdered in the most inhuman and shocking manner, between sixty and seventy of the unsuspecting whites of that county. The news, of course, was rapidly diffused, and with it consternation and dismay were spread throughout the State, destroying for a time all feeling of security and confidence; and even when subsequent development had proved, that the conspiracy had been originated by a fanatical Negro preacher, (whose confessions proved beyond a doubt mental aberration,) and that this conspiracy embraced but few slaves, all of whom had paid the penalty of their crimes, still the excitement remained, still the repose of the Commonwealth was disturbed,—for the ghastly horrors of the Southampton tragedy could not immediately be banished from the mind—and *Rumour,* too, with her thousand tongues, was busily engaged in spreading tales of disaffection, plots, insurrections, and even massacres, which frightened the timid and harassed and mortified the whole of the slave-holding population. During this period of excitement, when reason was almost banished from the mind, and the imagination was suffered to conjure up the most appalling phantom, and picture to itself a crisis in the vista of futurity, when the overwhelming numbers of the blacks would rise superior to all restraint, and involve the fairest portion of our land in universal ruin and desolation, we are not to wonder, that even in the lower part of Virginia, many should have seriously inquired, if this supposed monstrous evil could not be removed from our bosom. Some looked to the removal of the free people of colour by the efforts of the Colonization Society, as an antidote to all our ills. Some were disposed to strike at the root of the evil—to call on the General Government for aid, and by the labors of *Hercules*, to extirpate the curse of slavery from the land. Others again, who could not bear that Virginia should stand towards the Central Government (whose unconstitutional action she had ever been foremost to resist), in the attitude of a suppliant, looked forward to the legislative action of the State as capable of achieving the desired result. In this state of excitement and unallayed apprehension, the Legislature met, and plans for abolition were proposed and earnestly advocated in debate.

Upon the impropriety of this debate, we beg leave to make a few observations. Any scheme of abolition proposed so soon after the Southampton tragedy, would necessarily appear to be the result of the most inhuman massacre. Suppose the Negroes, then, to be really anxious for their emancipation, no matter on what terms, would not the extraordinary effect produced on the legislature by the Southampton insurrection, in all probability, have a tendency to excite another? And we must recollect, from the nature of things, no plan of abolition could act suddenly on the whole mass of slave population in the State. Mr. Randolph's was not even to commence its operation until 1840. Waiting then, one year or more, until the excitement could be allayed and the empire of reason could once more have been established, would surely have been productive of no injurious consequences; and, in the mean time, a Legislature could have been selected which would much better have represented the views and wishes of their constituents on this vital question. Virginia could have ascertained the sentiments and wishes of other slave-holding States, whose concurrence, if not absolutely necessary, might be highly desirable, and should have been sought after and attended to, at least as a matter of State courtesy. Added to this, the texture of the Legislature was not of that character calculated to ensure the confidence of the people in a movement of this kind.... It appears...that the Legislature was composed of an unusual number of young and inexperienced members, elected in the month of April previous to the Southampton massacre, and at a time of profound tranquility and repose, when of course the people were not disposed to call from their retirement their most distinguished and experienced citizens.

"Review of the Debate in the Virginia Legislature of 1831 and 1832" (Richmond: Printed by T.W. White, 1832)

49 / *"Cease to send that paper to this office"*

The abolitionists mistakenly believed that the public—North and South—would easily embrace antislavery arguments. Having labored in earlier movements aimed at moral regeneration, the abolitionists assumed that they could swiftly persuade ministers and other community leaders that slavery was a moral evil. Instead, they encountered a harsh public reaction in both the North and the South.

Mobs often led or instigated by "gentlemen of property and standing"—including many prominent bankers, judges, lawyers, merchants, and physicians—attacked the homes and businesses of abolitionist merchants, destroyed abolitionist printing presses, disrupted antislavery meetings, and attacked black neighborhoods. The reason: Abolitionists represented a direct challenge to the authority of local elites, appealing beyond them to the young, women, and free blacks. Enraged by reports that abolitionists advocated racial amalgamation or intermarriage, convinced that they were dupes of a sinister British plot to undermine democracy, crowds pelted abolitionists with eggs and even stones. In view of such public anger and hostility, it is remarkable that more abolitionists were not killed or seriously injured.

On November 7, 1837, the abolitionist movement acquired its first martyr when an anti-abolitionist mob in East Alton, Illinois (across from St. Louis), murdered the Rev. Elijah P. Lovejoy (1802–37), an abolitionist editor and crusader against intemperance and "popery," after setting his printing presses on fire. In the following letter, Lovejoy refers to the hostility he encountered.

Elijah P. Lovejoy, January 30, 1835, to Elijah Peck, GLC 2448.08

As the "Pioneer" [a local newspaper] seems disposed to use language in reference to myself and my friends which I deem altogether uncalled for, and as I feel that, in my present situation, it is necessary I should, as far as may be, avoid all causes and occasions of irritation I must request that you will cease to send that paper to this office, as I have no wish to see it.

50 / *"What is the actual condition of the slaves in the United States?"*

One third of the South's population labored as slaves. Apologists for slavery asserted the slaves were rarely whipped, that marriages were seldom broken by sale, that public opinion protected slaves from cruelty, and that slaves enjoyed a higher standard of living, a better diet, superior housing, and greater life expectancy than many free workers in the North and Europe.

Historians and economists still disagree sharply over the condition of slaves in the American South. There can be no doubt that slave living conditions were often appalling. In strictly material terms, however, many southern slaves may have probably been better off than slaves in the West Indies or Brazil and most miners and factory workers in the early industrial economies. Nevertheless, even if most southern slaves enjoyed a better diet and material standard of life than most industrial workers in England, Europe, and even parts of the North, slavery remained a morally intolerable evil no matter how "well treated" slaves might be.

The complexities and uncertainties of the debate over slaves' living standards are underscored by the contradictory evidence about diet and nutrition. On the one hand, it seems clear that slaves in the United States and even the Caribbean were substantially taller and probably healthier than West African kin. On the other hand, we also know that slave infants and children suffered extremely high death rates. Half of all slave infants died during the first year of life, twice the rate of white babies. And while death rates fell for those who survived their first year, it remained about twice the white rate. As a result of high infant and child mortality, the average life expectancy of a slave at birth was just twenty-one or twenty-two years, compared to forty to forty-three years for whites.

Read and Ponder THE FUGITIVE SLAVE LAW!

Which disregards all the ordinary securities of PERSONAL LIBERTY, which tramples on the Constitution, by its denial of the sacred rights of Trial by Jury, *Habeas Corpus*, and Appeal, and which enacts, that the Cardinal Virtues of Christianity shall be considered, in the eye of the law, as CRIMES, punishable with the severest penalties,—*Fines and Imprisonment.*

***Freemen of Massachusetts*, R E M E M B E R, That Samuel A. Elliott of Boston, voted for this law, that Millard Filmore, our whig President *approved* it and the Whig Journals of Massachusetts sustain them in this iniquity.**

Section 1. That persons who have been, or may hereafter be, appointed Commissioners, in virtue of any act of Congress, by the Circuit Courts of the United States, and who in consequence of such appointments, are authorized to exercise the powers that any justice of the peace or other magistrate of any of the United States may exercise in respect to offenders for any crime or offence against the United States, by arresting, imprisoning or bailing the same under and by virtue of the thirty third section of the act of the fourth of September seventeen hundred and eighty-nine, entitled "An act to establish judicial courts of the United States," shall be and are hereby authorized and required to exercise and discharge all the powers and duties conferred by this act.

Sec. 2 And be it further enacted. That the Superior Court of each organized Territory of the United States shall have the same power to appoint commissioners to take acknowledgments of bail and affidavits and to take depositions of witnesses in civil causes which is now possessed by the circuit court of the United States; and all commissioners who shall hereafter be appointed for such purposes by the superior court of any organized Territory of the United States, shall possess all the powers and exercise all the duties conferred by law upon the commissioner appointed by the circuit courts of the United States for similar purposes, and shall moreover exercise and discharge all the powers and duties conferred by this act.

Sec. 3. And be it further enacted, That the circuit courts of the United States, and the superior courts of each organized Territory of the United States, shall, from time to time, enlarge the number of commissioners with a view to afford reasonable facilities to reclaim fugitives from labor, and to the prompt discharge of the duties imposed by this act.

Sec. 4. And be it further enacted, That the commissioners above named shall have concurrent jurisdiction with the judges of the circuit and district courts of the United States, in their respective circuits and districts within the several States, and with the judges of the territories, severally and collectively, in term time and vacation; and shall grant certificates to such claimants, upon satisfactory proof being made with authority to take and remove such fugitives from service or labor, under the restrictions herein contained, to the State or Territory from which such persons may have escaped or fled

Sec. 5. And be it further enacted, that it shall be the duty of all marshalls and deputy marshalls to obey and execute all warrants and precepts issued under the provisions of this act, when to them directed; and should any marshall or deputy marshall refuse to receive such warrant or other process when tendered, or to use all proper means diligently to execute the same, he shall, on conviction thereof, be fined in the sum of $1,000, to the use of such claimant, on motion of the claimant, by the circuit or district court for the district of such marshall; and after arrest of such fugitive by said marshall, or his deputy, or whilst at any time in his custody under the provisions under this act, should such fugitive escape, whether with or without the assent of such marshall or his deputy, such marshall shall be liable on his official bond to be prosecuted for the benefit of such claimant for the full value of the service or labor of said fugitive, in the State, Territory or district whence he escaped; and the better to enable the said commissioners, when thus appointed, to execute their duties faithfully and efficiently; in conformity with the requirements of the Constitution of the United States and of this act, they are hereby authorized and empowered, within their counties respectively, to appoint, in writing under their hands, any one or more suitable persons, from time to time, to execute all such warrants and other process as may be issued by them in the lawful performance of their respective duties, with authority to such commissioners or the persons to be appointed by them to execute process as aforesaid, to summon and to call to their aid the bystanders or posse comitatus of the proper county, when necessary to insure a faithful observance of the clause of the constitution referred to, in conformity with the provisions of this act; and ALL GOOD CITIZENS are hereby commanded to aid and assist in the prompt and efficient execution of this law whenever their services may be required, as aforesaid for that purpose; and said warrant shall run and be executed by said officers anywhere in the State, within which they are issued.

Sec. 6. And be it further enacted. That when a person held to service or labor in any State or Territory of the United States has heretofore or shall hereafter escape into another State or Territory of the United States, the person or persons to whom such service or labor may be due, or his, her, or their agent or attorney, duly authorized, by power of attorney, in writing, acknowledged and certified under the seal of some legal officer or court of the State or Territory in which the same may be executed, may pursue and reclaim such fugitive person, either by procuring a warrant from some one of the courts judges or commissioners aforesaid, of the proper circuit, district, or county, for the apprehension of such fugitive from service or labor, or by seizing and arresting such fugitive, where the same can be done without process, and by taking, or causing such person to be taken, forthwith before such court, judge or commissioner, whose duty it shall be to hear and determine the case of such claimant in a SUMMARY MANNER; and upon satisfactory proof being made, by disposition or affidavit, in writing, to be taken and certified by such court, judge, or commissioner, or by other satisfactory testimony, duly taken and certified by some court, magistrate, justice of peace, or other legal officer authorized to administer an oath and take depositions under the laws of the State or Territory from which such persons owing a service or labor may have escaped, with a certificate of such magistracy or other authority, as aforesaid, with the seal of the proper court or officer thereto attached, which seal shall be SUFFICIENT TO ESTABLISH THE COMPETENCY OF THE PROOF, AND WITH PROOF, ALSO BY AFFIDAVIT, of the identity of the person whose service or labor is claimed to be due as aforesaid that the person so arrested does in fact owe service or labor to the person, or persons claiming him or her, in the State or Territory from which such fugitive may have escaped as aforesaid, and that said person escaped to make out and deliver to such claimant, his or her agent or attorney a certificate setting forth the substantial facts as to the service or labor due from such fugitive to the claimant, and of his or her escape from the State or Territory in which such service or labor was due, to the State or Territory in which he or she was arrested with authority to such claimant or his or her agent or attorney, to use such reasonable force and restraint as may be necessary, under the circumstances of the case, to take and remove such fugitive person back to the State or Territory from whence he or she may have escaped as aforesaid. IN NO TRIAL OR HEARING UNDER THIS ACT SHALL THE TESTIMONY OF SUCH ALLEDGED FUGITIVE BE ADMITTED IN EVIDENCE; and the certificates in this and the first section mentioned, shall be conclusive of the right of the person or persons in whose favor granted, to remove such fugitive to the State or Territory from which he escaped, and shall prevent all molestation of said person or persons by any process issued by any court, judge, magistrate, or other persons whomsoever.

Sec. 7. And be it further enacted. That any person who shall knowingly and willingly obstruct, hinder or prevent such claimant, his agent, or attorney, or any person or persons lawfully assisting him, her, or them from arresting such a fugitive from service or labor, either with or without process, as aforesaid; or shall rescue, or attempt to rescue, such fugitive from service or labor, from the custody of such claimant, his or her agent or attorney, or other person or persons lawfully assisting as aforesaid when so arrested, pursuant to the authority herein given and declared; or shall aid, abet, or assist such a person so owing service or labor as aforesaid, directly or indirectly to escape from such claimant, his agent or attorney, or other person or persons legally authorized as aforesaid; or SHALL HARBOR or CONCEAL such fugitive, so as to prevent the discovery and arrest of such person, after notice or knowledge of the fact that such person, was a fugitive from service or labor as aforesaid, shall, for either of said offences be subject to a fine not exceeding one thousand dollars, and imprisonment not exceeding six months, by indictment and conviction before the district court of the United States for the district in which such offence may have been committed, or before the proper court of criminal jurisdiction, if committed within any one of the organized territories of the United States; and shall moreover forfeit and pay, by way of civil damages to the party injured by such illegal conduct, the sum of ONE THOUSAND DOLLARS FOR EACH FUGITIVE SO LOST, as aforesaid to be recovered by action of debt, in any of the district or territorial courts aforesaid, within whose jurisdiction the said offence may have been committed.

Sec. 8. And be it further enacted, That the marshalls, their deputies, and the clerks of said district and territorial courts, shall be paid for their services the like fees as may be allowed to them for similar services in other cases, and where such services are rendered exclusively in the arrest, custody and delivery of the fugitive to the claimant, his or her agent or attorney, or where such supposed fugitive may be discharged out of custody for the want of sufficient proof as aforesaid, then such fees are to be paid in the whole by such claimant, his agent or attorney; and in all cases where the proceedings are before a commissioner, he shall be entitled to a fee of ten dollars in full for his services in each case, upon the delivery of said certificate to the claimant, his or her agent or attorney; or a fee of five dollars in cases where proof shall not in the opinion of such commissioner, warrant such certificate and delivery, inclusive of all services incident to such arrest and examination, to be paid, in either case, by the claimant, his or her agent or attorney. The person or persons authorized to execute the process to be issued by such commissioners for the arrest and detention of fugitives from service or labor, aforesaid, shall also be entitled to a fee of five dollars each for each person he or they may arrest and take before any such commissioners as aforesaid, at the instance and request of such claimant, with such other fees as may be deemed reasonable by such other additional services as may be necessarily performed by him or them; such as attending at the examination, keeping the fugitive in custody, and providing him with food and lodging during his detention, and until the final determination of such commissioner; and in general for performing such other duties as may be required by such claimant, his or her attorney or agent, or commissioner in the premises, such fees to be made up in conformity with the fees usually charged by the officers of the courts of justice within the proper district or county, as near as may be practicable, and paid by such claimants, their agents or attorneys, whether such supposed fugitive from service or labor, be ordered to be delivered to such claimants by the final determination of such commissioners or not.

Sec. 9. And be it further enacted, That upon affidavit made by the claimant of such fugitive his agent or attorney, after such certificate has been issued, that he has reason to apprehend that such fugitive will be rescued by force from his or their possession before he can be taken beyond the limits of the State in which the arrest is made, it shall be the duty of the officer making the arrest, to retain such fugitive in his custody, and to remove him to the State whence he fled, and there to deliver him to said claimant, his agent or attorney. And to this end the officer aforesaid is hereby authorized and required to employ so many persons as he may deem necessary, to overcome such force, and to retain them in his service so long as circumstances may require. The said officer and his assistants, while so employed, to receive the same compensation, and to be allowed the same expenses as are now allowed by law for transportation of criminals, to be certified by the judge of the district within which the arrest is made, and PAID OUT OF THE TREASURY OF THE UNITED STATES.

Sec. 10. And be it further enacted, That when any person held to service or labor in any State or Territory, or in the District of Columbia, shall escape therefrom, the party to whom such service or labor shall be due, his, her, or their agent or attorney may apply to any court of record therein, or judge thereof in vacation, and make satisfactory proof to such court of the escape aforesaid, and that the person escaping owed service or labor to such party. Whereupon the court shall cause a record to be made of the matters so proved, and also a general description of the person so escaping, with such convenient certainty as may be, and a transcript of such record authenticated by attestation of clerk and seal of the said court being produced in any other State, Territory or District in which the person so escaping may be found, and being exhibited to any judge, commissioner or other officer authorized by the law of the United States to cause persons escaping from service or labor to be delivered up, shall be held and taken to be full and conclusive evidence of the fact of escape, and that the service or labor of the person escaping is due to the party in such record mentioned. And upon the production by the said party of other and further evidence, if necessary, either oral or by affidavit, in addition to what is contained in the said record of the identity of the person escaping, he or she shall be delivered to the claimant. And the said court, commissioner, judge or other person authorized by this act to grant certificates to claimants of fugitives shall upon the production of the record, and other evidences aforesaid, grant to such claimant a certificate of his right to take any person identified and proved to be oweing service or labor as aforesaid, which certificate shall authorize such claimant to seize or arrest and transport such persons to the State or Territory from which he escaped, Provided,

That nothing herein contained shall be construed as requiring the production as a transcript of such record as evidence as aforesaid. But in its absence the claim shall be heard and determined upon other satisfactory proof, competent in law.

HOWELL COBB,
Speaker of the House of Representatives.
WILLIAM R. KING,
President of the Senate protempore.
Approved September 18, 1850.

MILLARD FILLMORE.

Read and Ponder the Fugitive Slave Law, broadside. The Gilder Lehrman Collection, on deposit at the Pierpont Morgan Library. GLC 1862

THIRTY DOLLARS
REWARD.

RAN away, on the 22d of Auguſt laſt, *a handſome Negro Lad,* named

ARCH,

ABOUT twenty years of age---the property of the Subſcriber---of a yellow complexion, talks ſenſible and artful, but *if* cloſe examined is apt to tremble; he is rather under the ſize *of* a man, active-made, with ſmall legs, and has a ridge, or ſcar on the back of his neck. He had on and took with him, a new Ruſſia-ſheeting ſhirt, an old Iriſh linen, and an old country linen ditto, a pair *of* old black everlaſting breeches, a pair *of* oznabrig trouſers, and an old hat, though he probably will part *from* his cloaths, and procure others *if* an opportunity offers.

I live in Maryland, near Frederick-Town, and will pay the above Reward, if the ſaid fellow be taken *Sixty* miles, or any further diſtance *from* home; or a *Half Dollar* per mile, *for* any diſtance under, in caſe he be ſecured in any goal, ſo that I get him again; and if brought home reaſonable charges, by.

IGNATIOUS DAVIS.

Frederick-County, September 7, 1791.

Frederick-Town: Printed by JOHN WINTER.

Broadside, Thirty Dollars Reward... "handsome Negro lad" [$30, runaway slave named Arch], 1791/09/07. The Gilder Lehrman Collection, on deposit at the Pierpont Morgan Library. GLC 3157

It appears that the high infant and child death rate was at least partly a result of a diet lacking sufficient protein, thiamine, niacin, calcium, magnesium, and vitamin D. As a result, slave children often suffered from night blindness, abdominal swellings, swollen muscles, bowed legs, skin lesions, and convulsions.

Theodore Dwight Weld (1803–1892), a leading abolitionist, published *American Slavery As It Is* to document abuses under slavery.

Theodore Dwight Weld, *American Slavery As It Is: Testimony of a Thousand Witnesses*, New York (New York: American Anti-Slavery Society, 1839), pp. 7–10, 1839, GLC 5119

Reader, you are empaneled as a juror to try a plain case and bring in an honest verdict. The question at issue is not one of law, but of fact—"What is the actual condition of the slaves in the United States?" A plainer case never went to a jury. Look at it. Twenty seven hundred thousand persons in this country, men, women, and children, are in slavery. Is slavery, as a condition for human beings, good, bad, or indifferent?...

Two millions seven hundred thousand persons in these States are in this condition. They are made slaves and are held such by force, and by being put in fear, and this for no crime!...

As slaveholders and their apologists are...flooding the world with testimony that their slaves are kindly treated; that they are well fed, well clothed, well housed, well lodged, moderately worked, and bountifully provided with all things needful for their comfort, we propose—first, to disprove their assertions by the testimony of a multitude of impartial witnesses, and then to put slaveholders themselves through a course of cross-questioning which shall draw their condemnation out of their own mouths. We will prove that the slaves in the United States are treated with barbarous inhumanity; that they are overworked, underfed, wretchedly clad and lodged, and have insufficient sleep; that they are often made to wear round their necks iron collars armed with prongs, to drag heavy chains and weights at their feet while working in the field, and to wear yokes, and bells, and iron horns; that they are often kept confined in the stocks day and night for weeks together, made to wear gags in their mouths for hours or days, have some of their front teeth torn out or broken off, that they may be easily detected when they run away; that they are frequently flogged with terrible severity, have red pepper rubbed into their lacerated flesh, and hot brine, spirits of turpentine, &c., poured over the gashes to increase the torture; that they are often stripped naked, their backs and limbs cut with knives, bruised and mangled by scores and hundreds of blows with the paddle, and terribly torn by the claws of cats, drawn over them by their tormenters; that they are often hunted with blood hounds and shot down like beasts, or torn in pieces by dogs; that they are often suspended by the arms and whipped and beaten till they faint, and when revived by restoratives, beaten again till they faint, and sometimes till they die; that their ears are often cut off, their eyes knocked out, their bones broken, their flesh branded with red hot irons; that they are maimed, mutilated, and burned to death over slow fires.... We will establish all these facts by the testimony of scores and hundreds of eye witnesses, by the testimony of *slaveholders* in all parts of the slave states, by slaveholding members of Congress and of state legislatures, by ambassadors to foreign courts, by judges, by doctors of divinity, and clergy men of all denominations, by merchants, mechanics, lawyers and physicians, by presidents and professors in colleges and professional seminaries, by planters, overseers and drivers.

NARRATIVE AND TESTIMONY OF SARAH M. GRIMKÉ

51 / "I left my native state on account of slavery"

Daughter of a justice on the South Carolina Supreme Court, Sarah M. Grimké (1792–1873), along with her sister Angelina (1805–79), left South Carolina, joined the Quakers, and spoke out vehemently against slavery. In this selection, Grimké describes how her abhorrence of slavery led her to leave her native state. Later she became an early proponent of women's rights. Her volume *Letters on the Condition of Women and the Equality of the Sexes*, one of the first modern statements of feminist principles, denounced the injustice of lower pay and denial of equal educational opportunities for women. It also expressed outrage that women were "regarded by men, as pretty toys or mere instruments of pleasure" and were taught to believe that marriage is "the *sine qua non* of human happiness and human existence."

Sarah M. Grimké, in Weld, *American Slavery As It Is*, pp. 22–24, GLC 5119

As I left my native state on account of slavery, and deserted the home of my fathers to escape the sound of the lash and the shrieks of tortured victims, I would gladly bury in oblivion the recollection of those scenes with which I have been familiar; but this may not, cannot be.... I feel impelled by a sacred sense of duty, by my obligations to my country, by sympathy for the bleeding victims of tyranny and lust, to give my testimony respecting the system of American slavery....

A handsome mulatto woman, about 18 or 20 years of age, whose independent spirit could not brook the degradation of slavery, was in the habit of running away: for this offence, she had been repeatedly sent by her master and mistress to be whipped by the keeper of the Charleston work-house. This had been done with such inhuman severity, as to lacerate her back in the most shocking manner; a finger could not be laid between the cuts. But the love of liberty was too strong to be annihilated by torture; and as a last resort, she was whipped at several different times, and kept a close prisoner. A heavy iron collar, with three prongs projecting from it, was placed round her neck, and a strong and sound front tooth was extracted, to serve as a mark to describe her, in case of escape.... These outrages were committed in a family where the mistress daily read the scriptures, and assembled her children for family worship....

As I was traveling in the lower country in South Carolina...my attention was suddenly arrested by an exclamation of horror from the coachman, who called out, "Look there, Miss Sarah, don't you see?"—I looked in the direction he pointed, and saw a human head stuck up on a high pole. On inquiry, I found that a runaway slave, who was outlawed, had been shot there, his head severed from his body, and put upon the public highway, as a terror to deter slaves from running away.

52/ "Privations of the Slaves"

"Privations of the Slaves," in Weld, *American Slavery As It Is*, pp. 35–36, 40–1, 43, GLC 5119

I. Food

We begin with the *food* of the slaves, because if they are ill treated in this respect we may be sure that they will be ill treated in other respects, and generally in a greater degree. For a man habitually to stint his dependents in their food, is the extreme of meanness and cruelty, and the greatest evidence he can give of utter indifference to their comfort....

Hon. Robert Turnbull, a slaveholder of Charleston, South Carolina: "The subsistence of the slaves consists, from March until August, of corn ground into grits, or meal, made into what is called *hominy*, or baked into corn bread. The other six months they are fed upon the sweet potato. Meat, when given, is only by way of *indulgence or favor*...."

The Maryland Journal and Baltimore *Advertiser,* May 30, 1788: "A single peck of corn a week, or the like measure of rice, is the ordinary quantity of provision for a hard-working slave; to which a small quantity of meat is occasionally, though rarely, added...."

"The common allowance of food in the penitentiaries, is equivalent to one pound of meat, one pound of bread, and one pound of vegetables per day. It varies a little from this in some of them, but it is generally equivalent to it." First Report of the American Prison Discipline Society....

II. Labor.

Philemon Bliss, Esq., a lawyer of Elyria, Ohio, who lived in Florida in 1834 and 1835. "During the cotton-picking season they usually labor in the field during the whole of the daylight, and then spend a good part of the night in ginning and baling. The labor required is very frequently excessive, and speedily impairs the constitution."

Mr. Cornelius Johnson, of Farmington, Ohio, who lived in Mississippi a part of 1837 and 1838. "It is the common rule for the slaves to be kept at work fifteen hours of the day, and in the time of picking cotton a certain number of pounds is required of each. If this amount is not brought in at night, the slave is whipped, and the number of pounds lacking is added to the next day's job....

III. Clothing.

Wm. Ladd, Esq. of Minot, Maine, recently a slaveholder in Florida. "They were allowed two suits of clothes a year, viz. one pair of trowsers with a shirt...for summer, and for winters, one pair of trowsers, and a jacket of Negro cloth, with a beige shirt and a pair of shoes. Some allowed hats, and some did not; and they were generally, I believe, allowed one blanket in two years. Garments of similar materials were allowed the women."

Mr. Lemuel Sapington, of Lancaster, Pa., a native of Maryland, and formerly a slaveholder. "Their clothing is often made by themselves after night, though sometimes assisted by the old women, who are no longer able to do out-door work; consequently it is harsh and uncomfortable. And I have very frequently seen those who had not attained the age of twelve years go naked."

IV. Dwellings.

Mr. George W. Westgate, member of the Congregational Church in Quincy, Illinois, who has spent a number of years in slave states. "On old plantations, the Negro quarters are of frame and clapboards, seldom affording a comfortable shelter from wind or rain; their size varies from 8 to 10, to 10 by 12, feet, and six or eight feet high; sometimes there is a hole cut for a window, but I never saw a sash, or glass in any. In the new country, and in the woods, the quarters are generally built of logs, of similar dimensions."

Mr. Cornelius Johnson, a member of the Christian Church in Farmington, Ohio. Mr. J. lived in Mississippi in 1837–8. "Their houses were commonly built of logs, sometimes they were framed, often they had no floor, some of them have two apartments, commonly but one; each of these apartments contains a family. Sometimes these families consisted of a man and his wife and children, while in other instances persons of both sexes, were thrown together without any regard to family relationship."

TESTIMONY OF ANGELINA GRIMKÉ

53 / *"It would be utterly impossible to recount the...ways... the heart of the slave is continually lacerated"*

In 1838 Angelina Grimké (1805–79) became the first white woman abolitionist to violate the taboo against speaking to mixed audiences of men and women, provoking condemnation from many northern ministers who believed that she had violated the religious principle of separate spheres for men and women. Here she recounts her memories of slavery.

ANGELINA GRIMKÉ, IN WELD, *American Slavery As It Is*, PP. 52–57, GLC 5119

I will first introduce the reader to a woman of the highest respectability—one who was foremost in every benevolent enterprise.... This lady used to keep cowhides, or small paddles (called "pancake sticks") in four different apartments in her house; so that when she wished to punish, or to have punished, any of her slaves, she might not have the trouble of sending for an instrument of torture. For many years...her slaves, were flogged every day.... But the floggings were not all; the scoldings and abuse daily heaped upon them all, were worse: "fools" and "liars," "sluts" and "husseys," "hypocrites" and "good-for-nothing creatures" were the common epithets which her mouth was filled, when addressing her slaves, adults as well as children....

Only two meals a day are allowed the house slaves—the first at twelve o'clock.... As the general rule, no lights of any kind, no firewood—no towels, basins, or soap, no tables, chairs, or other furniture, are provided.... Chambermaids and seamstresses often sleep in their mistresses' apartments, but with no bedding at all....

Persons who own plantations and yet live in cities, often take children from their parents as soon as they are weaned, and send them into the country; because they do not want the time of the mother taken up by attendance upon her own children, it being too valuable to the mistress.... Parents are almost never consulted as to the disposition to be made of their children; they have as little control over them, as have domestic animals over the disposal of their young. Every natural and social feeling and affection are violated with indifference; slaves are treated as though they did not possess them.

Another way in which the feelings of slaves are trifled with and often deeply wounded, is by changing their names; if, at the time they are brought into a family, there is another slave of the same name; or if the owner happens, for some other reason, not to like the name of the new comer.... Indeed it would be utterly impossible to recount the multitude of ways in which the heart of the slave is continually lacerated by the total disregard of his feelings as a social being and a human creature.

54 / *"General Testimony to the Cruelties Inflicted Upon Slaves"*

"GENERAL TESTIMONY TO THE CRUELTIES INFLICTED UPON SLAVES," IN WELD, *American Slavery As It Is*, PP. 64, 91, GLC 5119

The Rev. John H. Curtiss, a native of Keep Creek, Norfolk county, Virginia, now a local preacher of the Methodist Episcopal Church in Portage Co., Ohio, testifies as follows:—

"In 1829 or 30, one of my father's slaves was accused of taking the key to the office and stealing four or five dollars; he denied it. A constable by the name of Hull was called; he took the Negro, very deliberately tied his hands, and whipped him till the blood ran freely down his legs. By this time Hull appeared tired, and stopped; he then took a rope, put a slip noose around his neck, and told the Negro he was going to kill him, at the same time drew the rope and began whipping: the Negro fell; his cheeks looked as though they would burst with strangulation. Hull whipped and kicked him, till I really thought he was going to kill him...."

Most of our readers are familiar with the horrible atrocities perpetrated in New Orleans, in 1834, by a certain Madame La Laurie, upon her slaves.... The New Orleans Mercantile Advertiser says: "Seven poor unfortunate slaves were found—some chained to the floor, others with chains around their necks, fastened to the ceiling; and one poor man, upwards of sixty years of age, chained hand and foot, and made fast to the floor, in a kneeling position. His head bore the appearance of having been beaten until it was broken, and the worms were actually to be seen making a feast of his brains!! A woman had her back literally cooked (if the expression may be used) with the lash; the very bones might be seen projecting through the skin."

55 / *"I take this opportunity of writing to you"*

Under southern law, slaves were considered chattel property. Like domestic animals, they could be bought, sold, leased, inherited, and physically punished. Slaves were prohibited from owning property, testifying against whites in court, or traveling without a pass. Partially in response to abolitionist attacks on slavery, southern legislatures enacted laws setting minimum standards for housing, food, and clothing. These statutes, however, were difficult to enforce.

Slave marriages lacked legal sanction, and as a result, slave families were extremely vulnerable to separation. The most conservative estimates indicate that at least 10 to 20 percent of slave marriages were severed by sale. Even more common was the sale of slave children. Well over a third of slave children grew up in households from which one or both parents were absent.

Even in instances in which marriages were not broken by sale, slave spouses often resided on separate plantations, owned by different individuals. On large plantations, one slave father in three had a different owner from his wife and could only visit his family at his master's discretion. On smaller holdings divided ownership occurred even more frequently. Just a third of the children on farms with fifteen or fewer slaves lived in a two-parent family.

In the following letter, an unidentified slave writes to his mother to inform her that he will soon be forced to leave Virginia.

SLAVE LETTER BY AN UNIDENTIFIED SLAVE, OCTOBER 8, 1859, TO HIS MOTHER, GLC 226

I take this opportunity of writing to you to let you know that I am still in Alexandria [Virginia]. I expect to start about next Tuesday. There is a young lady here that I am very much taken with and I think that my Master will buy her and take her out with us.... I do not think I can leave Virginia without carrying out a Virginia wife with me.... If I succeed in my undertakings I will send you all the good news when I get home....

A PROSLAVERY NEW YORKER

56 / *"The abolitionist...[should] pay attention to his own affairs"*

One of the most perplexing and hotly disputed historical questions is why, given the abolitionists' public image as fanatics, did their doctrines ultimately prevail? The following letter reveals one former New Yorker's harshly negative view of abolition.

E.W. Taylor, January 25, 1837, to J. Wilbur, GLB 76

I care not what people at the North think, for I am *now* a regular *Southerner*....

And men, like the abolitionist...[who goes] about meddling with other Peoples' affairs...[should] pay attention to his own affairs, & let his neighbor alone. As long as those *professed* to be *Christians*, are...by their influence...producing discord & discontent—rebellion, insurrection, & division, it [emancipation] will never take place. If these matters are going to be [agitated it will]...lead to the separation of the Union.... [I] feel as though I could plunge the dagger to the heart almost of a brother in such a glorious cause—it would be for *Liberty, Liberty*.... I heard of an incident the other day of one of your fraternity suddenly changing his views with regard to slavery. A minister from the North, he was spending the winter in a Southern city and when he could, made known his sentiments. In the course of time he was introduced to a young lady of much beauty, but more property in Plantation slaves amounting to $116,000. All at once his feelings suddenly changed, he ranted against northern abolitionists & northerners generally, the result of it is he's just got the gal & what he likes better the slaves, & I bet $100,000 dole, thus in less than a year, and he will have slaves of his own blood. Now such men I detest. I abhor them, & I must say that I cordially think that these and hundreds of others at the north who are now accusing the southern slaveholder of *cruelty* thus would jump to do as this minister has done.

FROM ANTISLAVERY TO WOMEN'S RIGHTS

57 / "Mere circumstances of sex *does not give to man higher rights... than to women"*

During the 1830s a growing number of female abolitionists became convinced that women suffered legal and economic disabilities similar to those facing enslaved African Americans. Not only were women denied the right to vote and hold public office, they also had no access to higher education and were excluded from most professional occupations. American law accepted the principle that a wife had no legal identity apart from her husband. She could not sue, she could not make a legal contract, nor could she own property. She was not permitted to control her own wages or gain custody of her children in case of separation or divorce.

In this selection, Angelina Grimké explains how the struggle against slavery sensitized female abolitionists to other, more subtle forms of bondage and coercion.

Angelina Emily Grimké, letter XII, October 2, 1837, *Letters to Catherine E. Beecher*

The investigation of the rights of the slave has led me to a better understanding of my own. I have thought the Anti-Slavery cause to be the high school of morals in our land—the school in which *human rights* are more fully investigated, and better understood and taught, than in any other.... Human beings have *rights*, because they are *moral* beings: the rights of *all* men grow out of their moral nature; and as all men have the same moral nature, they have essentially the same rights. These rights may be wrested from the slave, but they cannot be alienated.... Now if rights are founded in the nature of our moral being, then the *mere circumstances of sex* does not give to man higher rights and responsibilities, than to women.... To suppose that it does, would be to break up utterly the relations, of the two natures...exalting the animal nature into a monarch, and humbling the moral into a slave....

The regulation of duty by the mere circumstance of sex, rather than by the fundamental principle of moral being, has led to all that multifarious train of evils flowing out of the anti-christian doctrine of masculine and feminine virtues. By this doctrine, man has been converted into the warrior, and clothed with sternness...whilst woman has been taught to...sit as a dollar arrayed in "gold, and pearls, and costly array," to be admired for her personal charms, and caressed and humored like a spoiled child, or converted into a mere drudge to suit the convenience of her lord and master.... This principle has given to man a charter for the exercise of tyranny and selfishness, pride and arrogance, lust and brutal violence.... Instead of being a helpmeet to man, as a companion, a co-worker, an equal; she has been a mere appendage of his being, an instrument of his convenience and pleasure, the pretty toy with which he whiled away his leisure moments, or the pet animal whom he humored into playfulness and submission....

Dost thou ask me, if I would wish to see woman engaged in the contention and strife of sectarian controversy, or in the intrigues of political partizans? I say no! never—never. I rejoice that she does not stand on the same platform which man now occupies in these respects; but I mourn, also, that he should thus prostitute his higher nature, and vilely cast away his birthright.

Angelina Emily Grimké, Letter XII, *Letters to Catherine E. Beecher* (Boston: I. Knapp, 1838), pp. 114–21

58 / *"The American Anti-Slavery [Society]... divided when women were put among its officers"*

A public debate over the proper role of women in the antislavery movement led to the first organized movement in history for women's rights. By the mid-1830s more than a hundred female antislavery societies had been created, and women abolitionists were circulating petitions, editing abolitionist tracts, and organizing antislavery conventions. At the 1840 annual meeting of the American Anti-Slavery Society in New York, abolitionists split partly over the question of whether women abolitionists could participate in the leadership of the antislavery organization. Moderates, including Arthur Tappan (1786–1865) and Lewis Tappan (1788–1873), two wealthy antislavery philanthropists, withdrew from the organization and formed the American and Foreign Antislavery Society.

The American Anti-Slavery Society proceeded to elect Abigail Kelly Foster (1810?–87) to its business committee and named three women delegates—Foster, Lucretia Mott (1793–1880), and Elizabeth Cady Stanton (1815–1902)—as delegates to a World Anti-Slavery Convention in London. These women were then relegated to seats in a balcony on the grounds that their participation would offend British public opinion.

Responding to queries from Harriet Robinson (1825–1911), who was writing a book on Massachusetts in the Woman Suffrage Movement, Foster recalled the split in the American Anti-Slavery Society over the role of women.

ABIGAIL KELLEY FOSTER, MARCH 9, 1881, TO HARRIET ROBINSON, GLC 2076

It was the American Anti-Slavery [Society] that was divided when women were put among its officers, tho' it was not divided till a year after the first appointment which was that of a woman on a committee to examine and report on the publications of the American A.S. Society in 1839 at its annual meeting in May. In 1840 a woman [Foster herself] was elected on the business committee, and then a minority of the Society withdrew and formed another society.

59 / *"How many truly harmonious households have we now?"*

In 1848 Lucretia Mott (1793–1880) and Elizabeth Cady Stanton (1815–1902) organized the first women's rights convention in history, at Seneca Falls, New York. Participants drew up a declaration of sentiments that opened with the phrase "All men and women are created equal." Modeled after the Declaration of Independence, the document proclaimed that "the history of mankind is a history of repeated injuries and usurpations on the part of man toward woman, having in direct object the establishment of an absolute tyranny over her." After listing a long string of inequities—including the double standard of sexual morality and the denial of the right to vote, to enter the professions, and to obtain a college education—it held that man "has endeavored in every way that he could, to destroy her confidence in her own powers, to lessen her self-respect, and to make her willing to lead a dependent and abject life."

Among the resolutions adopted by the convention, only one was not ratified unanimously—that women be granted the right to vote. Of the sixty-six women and thirty-four men who signed the declaration of sentiments—including the black abolitionist Frederick Douglass (1817–95)—only two lived to see the ratification of the women's suffrage amendment to the Constitution seventy-two years later.

Stanton, who had married the abolitionist Henry Brewster Stanton in 1840 in a ceremony without the word "obey," insisted that the *Declaration of Sentiments* include a demand for woman suffrage. Portions of her address to the women's rights convention follow.

ELIZABETH CADY STANTON, "ADDRESS DELIVERED AT SENECA FALLS," JULY 19, 1848

We are assembled to protest against a form of government, existing without the consent of the governed—to declare our right to be free as man is free, to be represented in the government which we are taxed to support, to have such disgraceful laws repealed as give man the power to chastise and imprison his wife, to take the wages which she earns, the property which she inherits, and in case of separation, the children of her love; laws which make her the mere dependent on his bounty....

And, strange as it may seem to many, we now demand our right to vote according to the declaration of the government under which we live.... To have drunkards, idiots, horse-racing, rumselling rowdies, ignorant foreigners, and silly boys fully recognized, while we ourselves are thrust out from all the rights that belong to citizens, it is too grossly insulting to the dignity for woman to be longer quietly submitted to....

One common objection to this movement is, that if the principles of freedom and equality which we advocate were put into practice, it would destroy all harmony in the domestic circle. Here let me ask, how many truly harmonious households have we now?... The only happy households we see now are those in which husband and wife share equally in counsel and goverment. There can be no true dignity or independence where there is subordination to the absolute will of another, no happiness without freedom.

Elizabeth Cady Stanton, "Address Delivered at Seneca Falls," *Address Delivered at Seneca Falls and Rochester, New York* (New York: Robert J. Johnson Printers, 1870)

60 / *"The isolated household is a source of innumerable evils"*

By the 1840s and 1850s hundreds of religious and secular communities in Indiana, Massachusetts, New York, Ohio, Tennessee, and Texas had experimented with alternate forms of family organization and sexual practices. Some of these "utopian communities" were inspired by a religious faith that the Second Coming of Christ was imminent; others were a product of an Enlightenment faith in reason and the shaping power of environment. Many utopians argued that conventional conceptions of gender roles stultified women's intellect and constricted their development; that monogamous marriage distracted individuals from broader social obligations; and that children needed to have contact with more than two adults and to take part in the world of work.

Among the communities that tried to emancipate women from household and childrearing responsibilities and to elevate them to positions of equality with men were twenty-five inspired by the French theorist Charles Fourier (1772–1837). The coiner of the word "feminism," Fourier hoped to eliminate poverty and alienation by creating self-sufficient communities known as "phalansteries" in which each person would own a share of the property. This excerpt from a Fourierist newspaper describes the movement's attitude toward the nuclear family.

The Phalanx, February 8, 1844

When we say that the isolated household is a source of innumerable evils, which Association alone can remedy, the mind of the hearer sometimes rushes to the conclusion that we mean to destroy the home relations entirely.... When, too, we say, that the existing system of Education is wholly wrong, it is feared that we design some violence to the parental sentiment, or that...we would give children "wholly up to the care of others, when only a mother can bear and forbear with a child, and yet love it."...

The isolated household is wasteful in economy, is untrue to the human heart, and is

> not the design of God, and therefore it must disappear, but the domestic relations are not so, however they may have been falsified and tarnished by what man has mixed with them. Of these relations the present position of woman is an essential part, and she can be raised out of that position only by purging them of what is alien to their essential character. Now, as we think, the pecuniary dependence which society establishes for women, is one of the most hurtful of these foreign elements, and we do not doubt that with its removal we shall see social relations generally rise to a degree of truth and beauty, which they cannot at present attain. In the progress of society we see that the position of woman is a hinge on which all other things seem more or less to turn. In the savage state she is the drudge and menial of man; in the barbarous state she is his slave and plaything, and in the civilized state she is as you confess, his "upper servant." Society rises with the degree of freedom it bestows on woman, and it is only by raising her to "integral independence," and making her as she should be, and as God made her, the Equal of Man, though not by making her precisely the same as man as some mistaken reformers have wished, the world can be saved....
>
> Very many women find other employments more attractive than the care of their children, and consequently the children receive comparatively little attention from them. Now, this seems to me to show the plan of Nature, who does not form every woman to take care of children, but only a certain proportion of women. You will, perhaps, say that these are not good mothers, and that they *ought* to discharge so interesting an office. But is not this to substitute for the method of nature certain notions which you have formed for yourself, and which Nature does not at all recognize?

The Phalanx (February 8, 1844) Vol. I, p. 318.

MANIFEST DESTINY

In 1845 John L. O'Sullivan (1813–95), editor of the *Democratic Review*, referred in his magazine to America's "manifest destiny to overspread the continent allotted by Providence for the free development of our yearly multiplying millions." The idea that America had a special destiny to stretch across the continent motivated many Americans to dream big dreams and migrate west. "We Americans," wrote the novelist Herman Melville, "are the peculiar, chosen people—the Israel of our time." Aggressive nationalists invoked manifest destiny to justify Indian removal, war with Mexico, and American expansion into Texas, California, the Pacific Northwest, Cuba, and Central America. More positively, the idea also inspired missionaries, farmers, and pioneers who dreamed only of transforming plains and fertile valleys into farms and small towns.

GONE TO TEXAS

American settlement in Texas began with the encouragement of first the Spanish, and then the Mexican, governments. In 1821, Spanish authorities gave Moses Austin (1761?–1821), a bankrupt fifty-nine-year-old Missourian, permission to settle three hundred families in Texas. Spain welcomed American settlers for two reasons—to provide a buffer against Indians and illegal U.S. settlers who were already moving into East Texas, and to develop the land, since only thirty-five hundred Mexicans had settled in Texas (which was part of the Mexican state of Coahuila y Tejas).

Moses Austin soon died, but his son Stephen (1789–1836) carried out his dream of colonizing Texas. By 1830 there were sixteen thousand Americans in Texas. These colonists refused to learn the Spanish language, maintained separate schools, conducted most of their trade with the United States, and brought slaves to Texas in violation of Mexican law. To assert its authority over the colonists, the Mexican government reaffirmed its constitutional prohibition against slavery, established a chain of military posts occupied by convict soldiers, restricted trade with the United States, and decreed an end to further American immigration.

These actions might have provoked revolution, but in 1832 General Antonio López de Santa Anna (1794–1876) became Mexico's president, and American colonists hoped he would make Texas a self-governing state, separate from the much more populous Coahuila. In 1834, however, Santa Anna overthrew Mexico's constitutional government, abolished state governments, and made himself dictator. When Stephen Austin went to Mexico City to try to settle the Texans' grievances, Santa Anna imprisoned him for a year.

61 / "The...violations of the constitutional rights of the people... have compelled us to arm in self-defense"

On November 3, 1835, American colonists in Texas adopted a constitution and organized a temporary government but voted overwhelmingly against declaring independence. A majority of colonists hoped to attract the support of Mexican liberals in a joint effort to depose Santa Anna and restore power to the state governments, hopefully including a separate state of Texas.

While holding out the possibility of compromise, the Texans prepared for war. In the middle of 1835, scattered local outbursts erupted against Mexican rule. The provisional government elected Sam Houston (1793–1863), a former Tennessee governor and close friend of Andrew Jackson, to lead whatever military forces he could muster.

In this letter, Austin seeks to justify the Texas Revolution and discusses the Texans' efforts to recruit soldiers in the American South.

Stephen F. Austin, February 16, 1836, to General John M. McCalla, GLC 1161

The revolutions and usurpations and violations of the constitutional rights of the people of Texas by the Mexican Govt. have compelled us to arm in self-defense—ours is a *war of independence*—our object is a total & everlasting separation from Mexico and to form a new and independent republic, or to become a part of these U.S.—we shall be satisfied with either....

We have an organized provisional govt. in operation, an army on the frontier and four armed schooners to protect our coasts.

Gen. Santana *{sic}* is however preparing to invade us in the Spring with all the forces he can collect. The main contest will probably take place in April & we shall then need all the aid we can procure in men and money. Col T.D. Owings late of the U.S.

UNANIMOUS

DECLARATION OF INDEPENDENCE,

BY THE

DELEGATES OF THE PEOPLE OF TEXAS,

IN GENERAL CONVENTION,

AT THE TOWN OF WASHINGTON,

ON THE SECOND DAY OF MARCH, 1836.

WHEN a government has ceased to protect the lives, liberty, and property of the people, from whom its legitimate powers are derived, and for the advancement of whose happiness it was instituted; and so far from being a guarantee for their inestimable and inalienable rights, becomes an instrument in the hands of evil rulers for their oppression. When the Federal Republican Constitution of their country, which they have sworn to support, no longer has a substantial existence, and the whole nature of their government has been forcibly changed, without their consent, from a restricted Federative Republic, composed of Sovereign States, to a consolidated Central Military despotism, in which every interest is disregarded but that of the army and the priesthood, both the eternal enemies of civil liberty, the ever ready minions of power, and the usual instruments of tyrants. When, long after the spirit of the constitution has departed, moderation is at length so far lost by those in power, that even the semblance of freedom is removed, and the forms themselves of the constitution discontinued, and so far from their petitions and remonstrances being regarded, the agents who bear them are thrown into dungeons, and mercenary armies sent forth to force a new government upon them at the point of the bayonet.

When, in consequence of such acts of malfeasance and abduction on the part of the government, anarchy prevails and civil society is dissolved into its original elements, in such a crisis, the first law of nature, the right of self preservation, the inherent and inalienable right of the people to appeal to first principles, and take their political affairs into their own hands in extreme cases, enjoins it as a right towards themselves and a sacred obligation to their posterity to abolish such government, and create another in its stead, calculated to rescue them from impending dangers, and to secure their welfare and happiness.

Nations, as well as individuals, are amenable for their acts to the public opinion of mankind. A statement of a part of our grievances is therefore submitted to an impartial world, in justification of the hazardous but unavoidable step now taken, of severing our political connection with the Mexican people, and assuming an independent attitude among the nations of the earth.

The Mexican Government, by its colonization laws, invited and induced the Anglo American population of Texas to colonize its wilderness under the pledged faith of a written constitution, that they should continue to enjoy that constitutional liberty and republican government to which they had been habituated in the land of their birth, the United States of America.

In this expectation they have been cruelly disappointed, inasmuch as the Mexican nation has acquiesced in the late changes made in the government by General Antonio Lopez Santa Ana, who having overturned the constitution of his country, now offers, as the cruel alternative, either to abandon our homes acquired by so many privations, or submit to the most intolerable of all tyranny, the combined despotism of the sword and the priesthood.

It hath sacrificed our welfare to the state of Coahuila, by which our interests have been continually depressed through a jealous and partial course of legislation, carried on at a far distant seat of government, by a hostile majority in an unknown tongue, and this too, notwithstanding we have petitioned in the humblest terms for the establishment of a separate state government, and have, in accordance with the provisions of the national constitution, presented to the general congress a republican constitution, which was, without a just cause, contemptuously rejected.

It incarcerated in a dungeon, for a long time, one of our citizens, for no other cause but a zealous endeavour to procure the acceptance of our constitution and the establishment of a state government.

It has failed and refused to secure, on a firm basis, the right of trial by jury, that palladium of civil liberty and only safe guarantee for the life, liberty, and property of the citizen.

It has failed to establish any public system of education, although possessed of almost boundless resources, (the public domain;) and although it is an axiom in political science, that unless a people are educated and enlightened, it is idle to expect the continuance of civil liberty, or the capacity for self government.

It has suffered the military commandants, stationed among us, to exercise arbitrary acts of oppression and tyranny, thus trampling upon the most sacred rights of the citizen, and rendering the military superior to the civil power.

It has dissolved, by force of arms, the state congress of Coahuila and Texas, and obliged our representatives to fly for their lives from the seat of government, thus depriving us of the fundamental political right of representation.

It has demanded the surrender of a number of our citizens, and ordered military detachments to seize and carry them into the interior for trial, in contempt of the civil authorities, and in defiance of the laws and the constitution.

It has made piratical attacks upon our commerce by commissioning foreign desperadoes, and authorizing them to seize our vessels and convey the property of our citizens to far distant parts for confiscation.

It denies us the right of worshipping the Almighty according to the dictates of our own conscience, by the support of a National Religion, calculated to promote the temporal interest of its human functionaries, rather than the glory of the true and living God.

It has demanded us to deliver up our arms, which are essential to our defence—the rightful property of freemen—and formidable only to tyrannical governments.

It has invaded our country both by sea and by land, with the intent to lay waste our territory, and drive us from our homes; and has now a large mercenary army advancing, to carry on against us a war of extermination.

It has, through its emmissaries, incited the merciless savage, with the tomahawk and scalping knife, to massacre the inhabitants of our defenceless frontiers.

It has been, during the whole time of our connection with it, the contemptible sport and victim of successive military revolutions, and hath continually exhibited every characteristic of a weak, corrupt, and tyrannical government.

These, and other grievances, were patiently borne by the people of Texas, until they reached that point at which forbearance ceases to be a virtue. We then took up arms in defence of the National Constitution. We appealed to our Mexican brethren for assistance: our appeal has been made in vain; though months have elapsed, no sympathetic response has yet been heard from the interior. We are therefore forced to the melancholy conclusion, that the Mexican people have acquiesced in the destruction of their liberty, and the substitution therefor of a military government; that they are unfit to be free, and incapable of self government.

The necessity of self preservation, therefore, now decrees our eternal political separation.

We, therefore, the deligates, with plenary powers, of the people of Texas, in solemn convention assembled, appealing to a candid world for the necessities of our condition, do hereby resolve and DECLARE, *that our political connection with the Mexican nation has forever ended, and that the people of Texas, do now constitute a* FREE, SOVEREIGN, *and* INDEPENDENT REPUBLIC, *and are fully invested with all the rights and attributes which properly belong to independent nations; and, conscious of the rectitude of our intentions, we fearlessly and confidently commit the issue to the decision of the supreme Arbiter of the destinies of nations.*

RICHARD ELLIS, *President.*

C. B. STEWART, THOMAS BARNETT.	*Austin.*
JAS. COLLINSWORTH, EDWIN WALLER, ASA BRIGHAM, J. S. D. BYROM.	*Brazoria.*
FRANCISCO RUIS, ANTONIO NAVARO, JESSE B. BADGETT.	*Bexar.*
WILLIAM D. LACY, WILLIAM MENIFEE.	*Colorado.*
JAMES GAINES, W. CLARK, JR.,	*Sabine.*
JOHN FISHER, MATT. CALDWELL,	*Gonzales.*
WILLIAM MOTLEY,	*Goliad.*
L. DE ZAVALA,	*Harrisburgh.*
STEPH. H. EVERITT, GEORGE W. SMITH,	*Jasper.*
ELIJAH STAPP,	*Jackson.*
CLAIBORNE WEST, WILLIAM B. SCATES,	*Jefferson.*
M. B. MENARD, A. B. HARDIN,	*Liberty.*
BAILEY HARDIMAN,	*Matagorda.*
J. W. BUNTON, THOS. J. GAZELEY, R. M. COLEMAN,	*Mina.*
ROBERT POTTER, THOMAS J. RUSK, CH. S. TAYLOR, JOHN S. ROBERTS,	*Nacogdoches.*
ROBERT HAMILTON, COLLIN MCKINNEE, ALB. H. LATTIMER,	*Red River.*
MARTIN PARMER, E. O. LEGRAND, STEPH. W. BLOUNT,	*San Augustin.*
SYD. O. PENNINGTON, W. CAR'L CRAWFORD,	*Shelby.*
JAMES POWER, SAM. HOUSTON, DAVID THOMAS, EDWARD CONRAD,	*Refugio.*
JOHN TURNER,	*San Patricio.*
B. BRIGGS GOODRICH, G. W. BARNETT, JAMES G. SWISHER, JESSE GRIMES,	*Washington.*

Printed by Baker and Bordens, San Felipe de Austin.

Unanimous Declaration of Independence, bull broadside. The Gilder Lehrman Collection, on deposit at the Pierpont Morgan Library. GLC 2559

Army has engaged to train two regiments in Kentucky to be called the Kentucky legions and must see the privilege of old friendships so far as to elicit your aid in our cause—a more just and holy one never existed in any country, and it is one which pertains to the interests of the people of the U.S. & especially the western country. Texas ought to be *American*. The tranquility of Louisiana requires it. The cause of liberty, of freedom of conscience, & of civilization, most correctly demand it. This state [Tennessee] & Alabama, & Mississippi have formed many companies who have marched and are preparing to march. I hope that Kentucky will not be behind them.

62 / *"The people of Texas, do now constitute a FREE, SOVEREIGN, AND INDEPENDENT REPUBLIC"*

On March 2, 1836, Texas formally declared itself independent of Mexico. Earlier, a band of some 300 Texans captured Mexico's military headquarters in San Antonio, and Santa Anna had begun to march north with 7000 soldiers (an army filled with raw recruits, including many Indians who spoke and understood little Spanish). Sam Houston ordered Texans to abandon San Antonio, but a group of rebels decided to defend the town and make their stand at an abandoned Spanish mission, the Alamo.

For twelve days, Mexico forces laid siege to the Alamo. On March 6, four days after Texas declared independence, Mexican troops scaled the mission's walls; 183 defenders were killed, including several Mexicans who had fought for Texas independence, and their oil-soaked bodies were set on fire outside the Alamo.

Republic of Texas, March 2, 1836, Unanimous Declaration of Independence, GLC 2559

[The Mexican] government has ceased to protect the lives, liberties, and property of the people, from whom its legitimate powers are derived, and for the advancement of whose happiness it was instituted; and so far from being a guarantee for their inestimable and inalienable rights [has] become an instrument in the hands of evil rulers for their oppression.... We, therefore,...DECLARE, our political connection with the Mexican nation has forever ended, and that the people of Texas, do now constitute a FREE, SOVEREIGN, and INDEPENDENT REPUBLIC....

63 / *"We...have news that St. Anna has been taken by the Texans"*

Two weeks after the defeat at the Alamo, 350 Texans surrendered to Mexican forces near Goliad with the understanding that they would be treated as prisoners of war. Instead, Santa Anna ordered the men shot.

After the defeats at the Alamo and Goliad, volunteers from the American South flocked to Sam Houston's banner. On April 21, 1836, his army of fewer than 800 men surprised and utterly defeated Santa Anna's army as it camped out on the San Jacinto River, east of present-day Houston. The next day, Houston's army captured Santa Anna himself and forced him to sign a treaty granting Texas its independence, a treaty that was never ratified by the Mexican government because it was acquired under duress.

For most Mexicans in Texas, defeat meant that they would be relegated to second-class social, political, and economic status. The new Texas constitution denied citizenship and property rights to those who failed to support the revolution. All persons of Hispanic ancestry were considered in the "denial" category unless they could prove otherwise. Consequently, many Mexican landowners fled the region.

The following letter reports the news that the Texans had taken Santa Anna prisoner at the Battle of San Jacinto.

E.G. Fisk, May 22, 1836, to his sister (dated New Orleans), GLC 765

> We one day have news that St. Anna has been taken by the Texans and next day contradicted, but I believe the general opinion seems to be that he is really a prisoner. We have not had any mail from New York for nearly a week as its passage has been wholly obstructed by the rising of the Indians in Alabama and Georgia. The last news we had from Columbus Geo[rgia] was that from 4 to 5000 people had abandoned their homes and fled to that town for protection.... The authorities compel every person who is able to carry a gun to turn out twice in each day to drill and make them take turns standing guard. All is alarm and confusion in all the frontier settlements....
>
> Since the foregoing was written Genl. Houston has arrived in this city, the Commander in Chief of the Texan army confirmed the news of the capture of Santa Anna & entire destruction of the Mexicans. They have 2000 prisoners among which are 40 officers all the principal men in Mexico. Gen. Houston has come here for Surgical aid being badly wounded in the battle of 21st of April which resulted in the capture of Santa Anna and his entire army. The Texians were 650...and the force under St. Anna amounted to 1700 and subsequently another division descended.... The whole Mexican force that invaded Texas amounted to 7000 and the whole force Genl. Houston had in the field has not at any one time amounted to more than 700 or 800 men, and has entirely destroyed this immense army. Who will say after this anything is impossible with Americans.

TEXAS ANNEXATION

64 / *"Annexation...would risk a war with Mexico"*

Texas had barely won its independence when it decided to become a part of the United States. A referendum held soon after the Battle of San Jacinto showed Texans favoring annexation by a vote of 3,277 to 93.

The annexation question became one of the most controversial issues in American politics in the late 1830s and early 1840s. The issue was not Texas but slavery. The admission of Texas to the Union would upset the sectional balance of power in the U.S. Senate, just as the admission of Missouri had threatened to do fifteen years earlier. In 1838 the elderly John Quincy Adams, now a member of the House of Representatives, staged a twenty-two-day filibuster that blocked annexation.

At this point, proslavery Southerners began to popularize a conspiracy theory that would eventually bring Texas into the Union as a slave state. In 1841 John Tyler, an ardent defender of slavery, succeeded to the presidency on the death of William Henry Harrison. Tyler argued that Britain was scheming to annex Texas and make it a haven for runaway slaves. According to this theory, British slave emancipation in the West

Indies had been a total economic disaster, and Britain hoped to undermine southern slavery by turning Texas into a British satellite state. In fact, British abolitionists, greatly worried that Texas might revive and stimulate the slave trade, were working to convince Texas to outlaw slavery in exchange for British foreign aid.

In the following fragment from one of his speeches, John Quincy Adams denounces proposals to annex Texas.

JOHN QUINCY ADAMS, CA. 1842–1843, SPEECH FRAGMENT, GLC 567

...Annexation, had been put off with a sort of Return Jonathan refusal. He had been told with Solemnity of face that there was a *doubt* of the Constitutional power of Congress and the President to accept the proposal and moreover that they could not think of it *now* because it would risk a war with Mexico, and violate the sacred Faith of Treaties. But Mr. Jefferson had shewn how a Constitutional Camel could be Swallowed for the sake of Louisiana by palates accustomed to strain at a gnat, and the Chairman of the late Committee of Foreign Affairs professed his readiness to swallow another for the sake of Texas. And as to the war with Mexico, one President had told Congress seven months before that it would be *justifiable*, and his successor, even while alleging this pretence of War and the Sacred Faith of Treaties, was about to tell Congress not only that he himself agreed with his Predecessor that War would have been justifiable the Winter before, but that...both Houses of Congress had been of the same opinion, and that it was now not only more justifiable but indispensable because the last magnanimous Appeal to the Justice and the fears of Mexico, heralded by a Courier from that Department of State, with the indulgence of one week for an answer, had totally failed.

65 / *"It would be far better for this country that Texas should remain an independent State"*

A future Democratic president from Pennsylvania, James Buchanan (1791–1868), expresses reservations about the annexation of Texas but also voices fear about the possibility that Texas would fall under Britain's sway.

JAMES BUCHANAN, FEBRUARY 3, 1844, TO EDWARD D. GAZZAM, GLC 2104

It is *highly probable* that the question for the admission of Texas into the Union may force itself or rather be forced upon the consideration of congress before the close of the present session. In my judgment it would be far better for this country that Texas should remain an independent State if this were possible. But suppose that this cannot be, & that it should be satisfactorily established, that we must either admit it or see it pass under the dominion of Great Britain; —what ought then to be done? This is the question & a very grave question it is. It may be a choice of evils; but which is the least? I should be glad, if, at your leisure, you would favor me with your views upon this subject, as well as inform me, what, in your opinion, would be the wishes of the people of Western Pennsylvania. Can any evils which might result from its admission be equal to those which would most probably result from having Great Britain our neighbour along our Southwestern frontier?

66 / *"The annexation of Texas is a great offense against humanity"*

In the spring of 1844, an annexation treaty with Texas failed to gain the required two-thirds majority for Senate ratification. The Texas question became the major political issue in the presidential campaign of 1844. Democratic candidate James Knox Polk (1795–1849) was a strong supporter of annexation, and his victory encouraged Tyler to try to annex Texas again. This time, Tyler submitted the measure in the form of a resolution, which required only a simple majority of both houses. Congress narrowly approved the resolution in 1845, making Texas the twenty-eighth state.

Abiel Abbot (1765–1859), a prominent northern clergyman and writer, expresses his dismay at Congress's vote in favor of Texas annexation.

ABIEL ABBOT, MARCH 11, 1845, GLC 2765

The annexation of Texas is a great offense against humanity & a monstrous transgression of the law of God. It is a violation of the constitution of the U. States. Had either of the senators of N[ew] H[ampshire] voted against the measure the resolution would not have passed. Oh, shame for N[ew] H[ampshire]. The State is not a republic; it is governed by an oligarchy.... Moral principle is divorced from politics—partyism has devoured patriotism, human rights & put conscience to sleep.

67 / *"In our Mountain home we feel not the withering... influence of political...despotism"*

Pioneers migrated West for many reasons—some were driven by hope of economic betterment, others by an urge for adventure. The Mormons moved west for a different reason—to escape religious persecution.

In the history of religion, few stories are more dramatic than that of the Mormons. It is a story with the haunting biblical overtones of divine revelations, of persecution and martyrdom, of an exodus two-thirds of the way across a continent, and of ultimate success in establishing a thriving religious society in a desert.

The Mormon church had its beginnings in upstate New York in 1823, when Joseph Smith (1805–44), a farmer's son, said he received revelations about a set of buried golden plates containing a lost section from the Bible. Smith later published the text as the *Book of Mormon*.

Because Smith said that he had conversed with angels and received revelations from the Lord, local authorities threatened to indict him for blasphemy. He and his followers responded by moving to Ohio, then to Missouri. There, proslavery mobs attacked the Mormons, accusing them of inciting slave insurrection. Fifteen thousand Mormons fled Missouri after the governor proclaimed them enemies who "had to be exterminated, or driven from the state."

In 1839 the Mormons resettled along the eastern bank of the Mississippi River in Nauvoo, Illinois, which soon grew into the second-largest city in the state. In exchange for Mormon votes, the state legislature awarded Nauvoo a special charter that made the town an autonomous city-state, complete with its own two thousand-man militia.

But troubles arose again. In 1844 dissidents attacked Smith for trying to become "king or lawgiver to the church." On Smith's orders, city officials destroyed the dissidents' printing press. Under the protection of the Illinois governor, Smith and his brother were confined in a jail. A mob broke into Smith's cell, shot him and his brother, and threw their bodies out of a second-story window.

Why did the Mormons seem so menacing? Many frontier settlers felt threatened by the communalism of the Mormon Church. By voting and controlling land as a bloc, the Mormons seemed to have an unfair advantage in the struggle for wealth and power. Mormonism was also denounced as a threat to fundamental values, since Mormons insisted that the *Book of Mormon* was Holy Scripture, equal in importance to the Bible. Rumors of polygamy also stirred opposition. While the Mormons did not publicly acknowledge their practice of polygamy until they had settled in Utah, they then contended that the Bible permitted the practice as a way to absorb single and widowed women into their communities and to restore the patriarchal Old Testament family.

After Smith's murder, a new leader emerged, who led them to a new Zion at the Great Salt Lake. Brigham Young (1801–77) began his career as an carpenter, printer, and glazier. As governor of the Mormon state of Deseret and later of Utah, he oversaw the building of Salt Lake City and 186 other communities. He also supervised church-owned businesses and cooperative irrigation projects, which made large-scale agriculture possible in the arid Great Basin.

In this letter to a non-Mormon sympathizer, Young describes the Mormon Zion and comments on the deepening sectional crisis. Three years after Young wrote this letter, public outrage over polygamy and Washington's concern over Young's defiance of federal judges led President James Buchanan to send an army of twenty-five hundred to force the Mormons to obey federal law. This episode ended in 1858, when the Mormons accepted a new governor and Buchanan issued a general pardon.

Brigham Young, June 29, 1854, to Thomas Kane, GLC 3888

As regards the [building of a western] railroad, you well remarked "the best business Congress has met upon in our time." A subject truly worthy of the enterprise of the nation, upon which I myself think Congress could much better employ their time, than discussing the merits or demerits of a question, however it may be determined upon will assuredly only set afloat existing compromises and leave the question of slavery upon the same basis which existed previously to their adoption....

In our Mountain home we feel not the withering sources of influence of political or even fashionable despotism. We breathe free air, drink from the cool mountain stream, and feel strong in the free exercise of outdoor life. I have traveled on several hundred miles this season among the native tribes, to conciliate their hostile feelings, and cause them to become friends. I have found the satisfaction of having been eminently successful, and peace again smiles upon all our settlements, and that too without a resort to arms.

MOUNTING SECTIONAL ANTAGONISMS

68 / *"The stake in the question is your right to petition, your freedom of thought and action"*

In the mid-1830s northern mobs attacked abolitionists and disrupted their meetings. Over the next decade, however, growing numbers of Northerners grew increasingly sympathetic toward the antislavery cause. One key episode contributing to a shift in public opinion was a fight over the receipt of abolitionist petitions in Congress between 1836 and 1844.

Popular petitioning played a crucial role in pressuring Parliament to emancipate British slaves in 1833. American abolitionists initially assumed that "moral suasion" could shame Southerners into freeing their slaves. The failure of moral suasion lent a growing importance to antislavery political action, especially in petitioning Congress to restrict the interstate slave trade and the admission of new states.

During the early 1830s the American Anti-Slavery Society began to distribute petitions calling on Congress to abolish slavery in the District of Columbia. Upon submission to the House of Representatives, the petitions were referred to the Committee on the District of Columbia. In the spring of 1836, however, the House (with the support of northern Democrats) adopted the notorious "gag rule," which required that all petitions dealing with slavery "be laid on the table and that no further action whatever shall be laid thereon."

Former president John Quincy Adams, who had been elected to the House of Representatives in 1836, led opposition to the gag rule. He denied that he was an abolitionist; rather, he argued that the gag rule violated the constitutional right to petition—a right that extended even to slaves. In February 1837 Adams caused a near riot in the House when he submitted a petition purportedly from twenty-two slaves.

Adams's opponents unsuccessfully attempted to strip him of his chairmanship of a congressional committee and twice unsuccessfully tried to censure him. But such efforts had the effect of convincing growing numbers of Northerners that the southern "slave power" threatened civil liberties. Thanks to Adams's efforts, the gag rule was finally suspended in 1844.

John Quincy Adams, March 3, 1837, to the Inhabitants of the 12th Congressional District, GLC 639.05

I presented twenty petitions, all of which were laid on the table without being read, though in every instance I moved for the reading, which the Speaker [James K. Polk] refused to permit—from his decision I took in every case an appeal, and the appeal was in every case laid on the table....

[Adams describes a petition from Fredericksburg, Virginia, that] purported to be from twenty-two *slaves*.... I had suspicions that [it]...came really from the hand of a master, who had prevailed upon his slaves to sign it—that they might have the appearance of imploring the members from the North to cease offering petitions for their emancipation which could have no other tendency than to aggravate the burden of their servitude and of being so impatient under the operation of the petitions in their favour, as to pray that the Northern members who should persist in presenting them should be expelled....

But the petition, avowedly coming from slaves, though praying for my expulsion from the House if I should persevere in presenting abolition petitions, opened to my examination and enquiry a new question, or at least a question which had never occurred to me before, and which I never should have thought of starting upon speculation, namely, Whether the right to petition Congress, could in any case be exercised by slaves? And after giving to the subject all the reflection of which I was capable, I came to the conclusion, that however doubtful it might be whether slaves could petition Congress for anything incompatible with their condition as slaves, and with their subjection to servitude, yet that for all other wants, distresses and grievances incident to their nature as men and to their relations as members, degraded members as they may be, of this community, they do enjoy the right of petition; and that if they enjoyed the right in any case whatsoever, there could be none in which they were more certainly entitled to it, than that of deprecating the attempts of deluded friends to release them from bondage; a case in which they alone could in the nature of things speak for themselves, and their masters could not possibly speak for them....

But after getting these two questions to the satisfaction of my own mind, there remained another. With what temper they would be received in a house, the large majority of which consisted of slave-holders, and of their political Northern associates, whose mouthpieces had already put forth their feelers to familiarize the freeman of the North with the fight of a representative expelled from his seat for the single offence of persisting to present abolition petitions. I foresaw that the very conception of a petition from slaves, would dismount all the slave-holding philosophy of the House, and expected it would produce an explosion, which would spend itself in wind. Without therefore presenting or offering to present the petition, I stated to the Speaker that I had such a paper in my possession, which I had been requested to present, and enquired whether it came within the Resolution of the 18th of January. Now the Speaker decided that under that order, no such paper should be read.... The Speaker...horrified at the idea of receiving and laying on the table a petition from slaves, said that in a case so novel and extraordinary he felt himself incompetent to decide and must take the advice and direction of the House....

If I had stated that I had a petition from sundry persons in Fredericksburg, relating to slavery, without saying that the petitioners were, by their own avowal, slaves, the paper must have gone upon the table; but the discovery would soon have been made, that it came from slaves, and there the tempest of indignation would have burst upon me, with tenfold fury, and I should have been charged with having fraudulently introduced a petition from slaves, without letting the House know the condition of the petitioners.

To avoid the possibility of such a charge, I put the question to the Speaker, giving him notice that the petition purported to come from slaves, and that I had suspicions that it came from another, and a very different source. The Speaker after failing in the attempt to obtain possession of the paper, referred my question to the House for decision, and there ensued a scene of which I propose to give an account, in a subsequent address,

> entreating you only to remember, if what I have said, or may say to you hereafter on this subject [slavery] should tax your patience, that the stake in the question is your right to petition, your freedom of thought and of action, and the freedom in Congress of your Representative.

69 / *"I am no advocate of slavery...but"*

Franklin Pierce (1804–69) was the first "doughface" president. He was, in the popular phrase, "a northern man with southern principles." In this letter, the future president offers his views on slavery and argues that abolition was delaying emancipation in the more northern parts of the South. After his election to the White House in 1852, Pierce, a New Hampshire Democrat, tried to unite the country with an aggressive program of foreign expansion he called "Young America." He sought to annex Hawaii, purchase Cuba, expand American influence in Honduras and Nicaragua, and acquire new territory from Mexico. Many Northerners suspected that Pierce's real goal was the acquisition of new territory for slavery.

> Franklin Pierce, March 18, 1838, to Rev. D.W. Burroughs, GLC 2634
>
> I am no advocate of slavery. I wish it had no existence upon the face of the Earth, but as a public man, I am called upon to act in relation to an existing state of things.... [T]he violent course of the Abolitionists at the North has postponed the emancipation of the coloured population in Maryland, Kentucky & Virginia many & many a long year.... It should be remembered, that there are but two methods by which domestic slavery at the South can possibly be abolished. It can only be accomplished by the consent and agency of the Southern people themselves or by revolution. Would you recommend overturning the Constitution by a civil war, which carry ruin & desolation to every portion of this Country and probably result in the extermination of the coloured population upon this Continent?

70 / *"It will do more to unite...the slaveholding states than can be effected by anything else"*

Beginning in the 1830s the South developed a new and aggressive sense of "nationalism" rooted in its sense of regional distinctiveness and its perception that it was ringed by enemies. More and more, the South began to conceive of itself as the true custodian of America's revolutionary heritage.

At the same time, slaveowners became more outspoken in their defense of slavery. On the Senate floor in 1837, Calhoun pronounced slavery "a good—a positive good" and set the tone for future southern proslavery arguments. White Southerners argued that slavery was a beneficial institution that created a hierarchical society superior to the leveling democracy of the North. The defense of slavery led to a hostility toward all social reforms. The South, said one South Carolina scientist, "was the breakwater which is to stay that furious tide of social and political heresies now setting toward us from the shores of the old world."

Shortly after the War of 1812, John Quincy Adams described John C. Calhoun as being "above all sectional and factious prejudices more than any other stateman of this

Union." But by the late 1830s, the "sentinel of the South" was the country's leading exponent of states' rights. In 1816, when he was an American nationalist and relatively unconcerned about threats to slavery, Calhoun had introduced a proposal for federal aid for road and canal construction. "Let us," he exclaimed, "bind the republic together with a perfect system of roads and canals. Let us conquer space."

Before the introduction of railroads, most western commerce flowed southward along the Mississippi River. The growth of rail transportation shifted western trade in an eastward direction—strengthening ties between the West and the Northeast. In the following letter, Calhoun advocates southern railroad construction as a way to unite the slaveholding states.

JOHN C. CALHOUN, JUNE 15, 1838, TO DAVID HUBBARD, GLC 2320.01

I have long seen the vast superiority of the [railroad] route through Georgia to the Tennessee, over the one...to the Ohio; and at an early period, I proposed, with all my might, the very one that you so strongly recommended, and for similar reasons, but in vain. I however, should not despair, and by continually urging the Georgia route, have so far succeeded, that the Charleston & Cincinnati rail road company have purchased out the Charleston...railway, with the view of uniting with the Augusta & Athens; and finally of uniting with the Tennessee River through that line.... I suppose you know that Georgia has undertaken to make a rail road from the Chattahoochie to the Tennessee River.... A resolution has already proposed for a careful survey of the Tennessee river, with the view to its improvement.

I take the deepest interest in the work, not only in a commercial but a practical point of view. It will do more to unite...the slaveholding states than can be effected by anything else; this will change not only the commercial [affairs] but the politics of the Union.

71 / *"The slave holding states*...**retained** *the complete control of slavery within their boundaries"*

Two years before he was elected president, William Henry Harrison (1773–1841) argued for the sovereign independence of states and insisted that slavery is a matter for the states alone to consider. His position on the inability of the federal government to interfere in any way with slavery in the existing states is an expression of what historians term "the federal consensus." This was the widespread assumption, shared by most radical abolitionists as well as by lawyers and judges, that the Constitution left the issue of slavery to the states and prohibited the federal government from interfering with the institution in states where it already existed.

It was this consensus that made the question of slavery in the territories so urgent and vital. Even Abraham Lincoln assumed that the central government could never tamper with slavery in the states. Hence it took an act of rebellion to finally justify limited emancipation as a war measure.

WILLIAM HENRY HARRISON, OCTOBER 12, 1838, TO JOHN B. DILLON, GLC 2946

I have come to the determination from necessity to decline giving my opinion too indiscreetly upon political subjects for publication. Had I not adopted this rule I would have to sacrifice my business (necessary to the support of my very large family) & devote myself entirely to political writing. But as you tell me that you are about publishing a pamphlet on the subject of slavery I will as a friend give you my opinion upon one constitutional principle in relation to which either you or I may greatly err. No one I think can understand the character of our particular Government without having it impressed upon his mind that our Union is a Union of Sovereign Independent States & that in every particular where power is not expressly surrendered by that instrument to the General Government it is retained by the states and that in the relations to matters so retained they are as completely Sovereign & independent of the Genl. Government and of each other as are France and Great Britain. You seem to suppose that an Article in the Constitution not having been inserted in it, the General Govt would have the complete power over the slavery question in the states. The slave holding states (of which there were at that time 9 out of 13) did not wish to have such an article inserted. They *retained* the complete control over the subject of slavery within their own boundaries by *not surrendering* it. All that they wished to have inserted in the Constitution related to the subject was that where their slaves fled from them & sought refuge in other states that they should be delivered upon their application. When...you say that "an early and amicable acquaintance of the question is desirable," it cannot refer to slavery *in other states* but may with propriety refer to the District of Columbia, within which the power of Legislation is expressively given to Congress. But no law which that body can pass may in any way effect the right which the slave holding states claim over their slaves any more than Congress can pass a law to change the general rules of elections in the states or define the period when minors are to be freed from the control of their parents. To do either would change the whole character of the Government and realise the dread of large portions of the ablest statesmen in our country at the period of the adoption of the Constitution that it would end first in a consolidation & then in a despotism which latter could only be averted by preserving the independence of the states.... The citizens of the free States have the right as individuals to give their opinion to their brethren in Slave States upon the subject of Slavery.... [B]ut they have no power whatever to control them upon any of these subjects....

Give them your opinions then upon the former subjects but I can tell you that however able your appeal to them [the slaveholding states] may be on the abstract question if you assume the *right* of control over the subject either for the US (except as to the District of Columbia) the free states authorities or yourself individually it *may* do no harm but will certainly do no good.

I repeat that I wrote to you mainly as a friend & not by any means for publication.

72 / "The combination of Northern labour and Southern capital to suppress the right of Petition"

In 1837 Adams began to send reports on congressional affairs to a local newspaper, the *Quincy Patriot*. In this letter he refers to a duel in which a proslavery Kentucky member of Congress, William Graves (1805–48), killed a Maine representative, Jonathan Cilley (1802–38). After the incident took place—the two men stood a hundred yards apart and shot at each other four times with rifles—Adams persuaded Congress to pass a law outlawing dueling in the District of Columbia.

John Quincy Adams, September 21, 1838, "To the Editor of the *Quincy Patriot*," GLC 3707

At the second session of the 24th and the first and second sessions of the 25th or present Congress, great numbers of petitions and Remonstrances addressed to the House of Representatives of the United States, were committed to my charge from the citizens of other Districts, the Commonwealth, and from other States of the Union....

The great mass of the petitions from constituents to the Representative body have...the following purport.

1. Praying for the abolition of slavery and the traffic in slaves, within the District of Columbia

2. For the abolition of slavery and the slave trade in all the Territories of the United States

3. For the prohibition of the slave trade between the several States and Territories of the Union

4. Against the admission into the Union of any new State, the Constitution of which recognizes...the institution of domestic slavery

5. Against the admission of Texas into the Union

6. Against the fraudulent treaty...and imploring mercy for the perishing remnants of the Indian tribes...

7. Remonstrances to the House of Representatives against the Resolutions of 18 January and 21 December 1837 [the gag rule]

8. Concerning the fatal duel and demanding some act of Congress for the suppression of the practice between its members

Of these eight classes of Petitions large numbers...were presented to the House by me.

Upon the duel, from three to four weeks of the time of the House were consumed in a struggle to turn the whole transaction into a political electioneering Engine, to blacken all the individuals concerned in the Tragedy on one side, and to whitewash those on the other—A Bill to suppress as far as possible the practice of duelling among the members actually passed the Senate and was referred to the duel Committee in the House—They did not report it back to the House till it was extorted from them, and never made the slightest effort even to call it up for consideration. It may be taken up at the next Session, and feeble and inefficient as it is, would at least have the good effect of bearing the solemn testimony of Congress against a practice congenial only to the moral code of Slavery.

All the other classes of those Petitions were without being read considered laid on the table.... To this universal extinction of the Constitution, the only exception has been enjoyed by the Petitioners against the admission of Texas and they only...because four State Legislatures of the South had passed Resolutions, earnestly urging the annexation on the express ground of fortifying the peculiar Institutions of the South and strengthening the feeble knees of slavery—It was this interposition of State Legislatures Thirsting for Texas, which burst open the doors of discussion upon the blessings of Slavery, so long and so perniciously... barred by Northern labour and Southern capital against all freedom of debate in the Representative Hall of the American People....

> The slaveholding portion...were as tenacious of the freedom of debate and as anxious for their right of reply as the truest believer in the self-evident truths of the Declaration of Independence....
>
> I offered a Resolution to the House requiring...a complete list of all the Petitions...treated at the last three sessions. But the combination of Northern labour and Southern capital to suppress the right of Petition and the freedom of debate, unwilling to expose to the world the extent of their Success and the blushing honors of that triumph, refused to entertain that motion. Nor can I find it in my heart to blame the tacit confession implicit by this refusal that this Catalogue of Petitioners spurned from the doors of the North American Congress, would have exhibited amazement of Mankind and to the contempt of after ages the most melancholy document that ever issued from the successors of that band of Patriots who but three score and two years since promulgated from the State House in Philadelphia the Declaration of Independence.

THE *AMISTAD* AFFAIR

73 / *"However unjust...the slave trade may be, it is not contrary to the law of nations"*

In June 1839, 52 African captives revolted as they were being transported on the Spanish schooner Amistad from Havana to Guanaja, Cuba. Led by Joseph Cinqué, a Mende from the Sierra Leone region of West Africa, the rebels ordered two surviving Spaniards to sail the ship eastward to Africa. The crew sailed eastward during the day, but veered northwestward at night, hoping to encounter a British ship patrolling for vessels engaged in the illegal slave trade or to reach a friendly port.

Four months earlier, the Africans had been illegally shipped to Cuba; a third of the captives died along the way. During the 1830s, Cuba, the world's leading sugar producer, imported over 180,000 slaves in violation of a law prohibiting the importation of slaves from Africa after 1820.

In late August, the U.S.S. Washington seized the Amistad near the Long Island coast. When the Amistad was captured, there were 39 African men and four children on board. A hearing was held in New London, Connecticut, and the Africans were charged with mutiny, murder, and piracy. They were then sent to New Haven, where the adults were placed in a jail cell, 20 by 30 feet in size. For 18 months, the Amistad rebels remained confined to their cell. Spectators paid 12 and a half cents to look at them.

Abolitionists quickly took up the cause of the Amistad rebels. They insisted that since the Africans had been illegally imported into Cuba and were free at the time that they entered U.S. waters, the rebels should be released from jail. The district court judge found on their behalf, but President Martin Van Buren (who came from a Dutch-American family that had once held slaves in New York and who was desperate to maintain southern support for his reelection bid) ordered the case appealed to the Supreme Court.

The Amistad Affair case raised critical issues of law and justice: whether captives had a right to rebel against their captors and whether American courts have jurisdiction over crimes committed outside this country. In September 1939 letter, William S. Holabird (1794?–1855), the U.S. district attorney in Connecticut and a staunch Jacksonian Democrat, informed the Van Buren administration that there was no legal basis for returning the Africans to Spanish authorities in Cuba. He argued that the United States had no right to try the Africans because their rebellion had taken place on a Spanish vessel on the open sea and involved only Spanish subjects.

Weakened by the disastrous economic Panic of 1837, President Van Buren feared that the Amistad case would shatter his support in the South. The administration rejected the district attorney's argument and pressed ahead with the case.

In fact, Van Buren's administration intentionally mistranslated Spanish documents in a desperate effort to mislead the court about whether it was legal to import slaves into Cuba. President Van Buren also ordered a ship to take the rebels to Cuba before the District Court could render its verdict. Both attempts to obstruct justice failed.

In the following legal brief, John Forsyth, Martin Van Buren's Secretary of State, rejects the argument that since the Atlantic slave trade was illegal under U.S. and Spanish law, the Africans on the Amistad had been illegally held captive. If the courts had accepted Forsyth's argument and returned the captives to Cuba, the rebels would almost certainly have been executed.

In a ruling that stunned the Van Buren administration, the District Court ruled that since the Amistad rebels had been born free, they could not be treated as property, and must be returned to Africa. The district attorney appealed the verdict to the Circuit Court, which upheld the District Court's decision. The case then went to the U.S. Supreme Court.

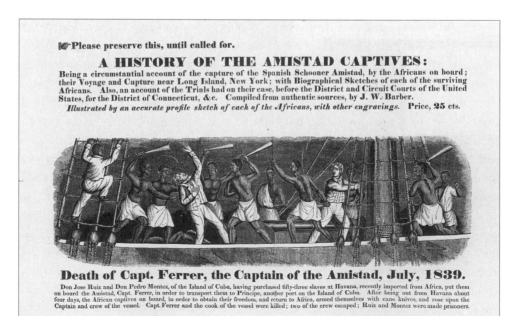

☞Please preserve this, until called for.

A HISTORY OF THE AMISTAD CAPTIVES:

Being a circumstantial account of the capture of the Spanish Schooner Amistad, by the Africans on board; their Voyage and Capture near Long Island, New York; with Biographical Sketches of each of the surviving Africans. Also, an account of the Trials had on their case, before the District and Circuit Courts of the United States, for the District of Connecticut, &c. Compiled from authentic sources, by J. W. Barber.

Illustrated by an accurate profile sketch of each of the Africans, with other engravings. **Price, 25 cts.**

Death of Capt. Ferrer, the Captain of the Amistad, July, 1839.

Don Jose Ruiz and Don Pedro Montez, of the Island of Cuba, having purchased fifty-three slaves at Havana, recently imported from Africa, put them on board the Amistad, Capt. Ferrer, in order to transport them to Principe, another port on the Island of Cuba. After being out from Havana about four days, the African captives on board, in order to obtain their freedom, and return to Africa, armed themselves with cane knives, and rose upon the Captain and crew of the vessel. Capt. Ferrer and the cook of the vessel were killed; two of the crew escaped; Ruiz and Montez were made prisoners.

History of the Amistad Captives. The Gilder Lehrman Collection, on deposit at the Pierpont Morgan Library. GLC 4295

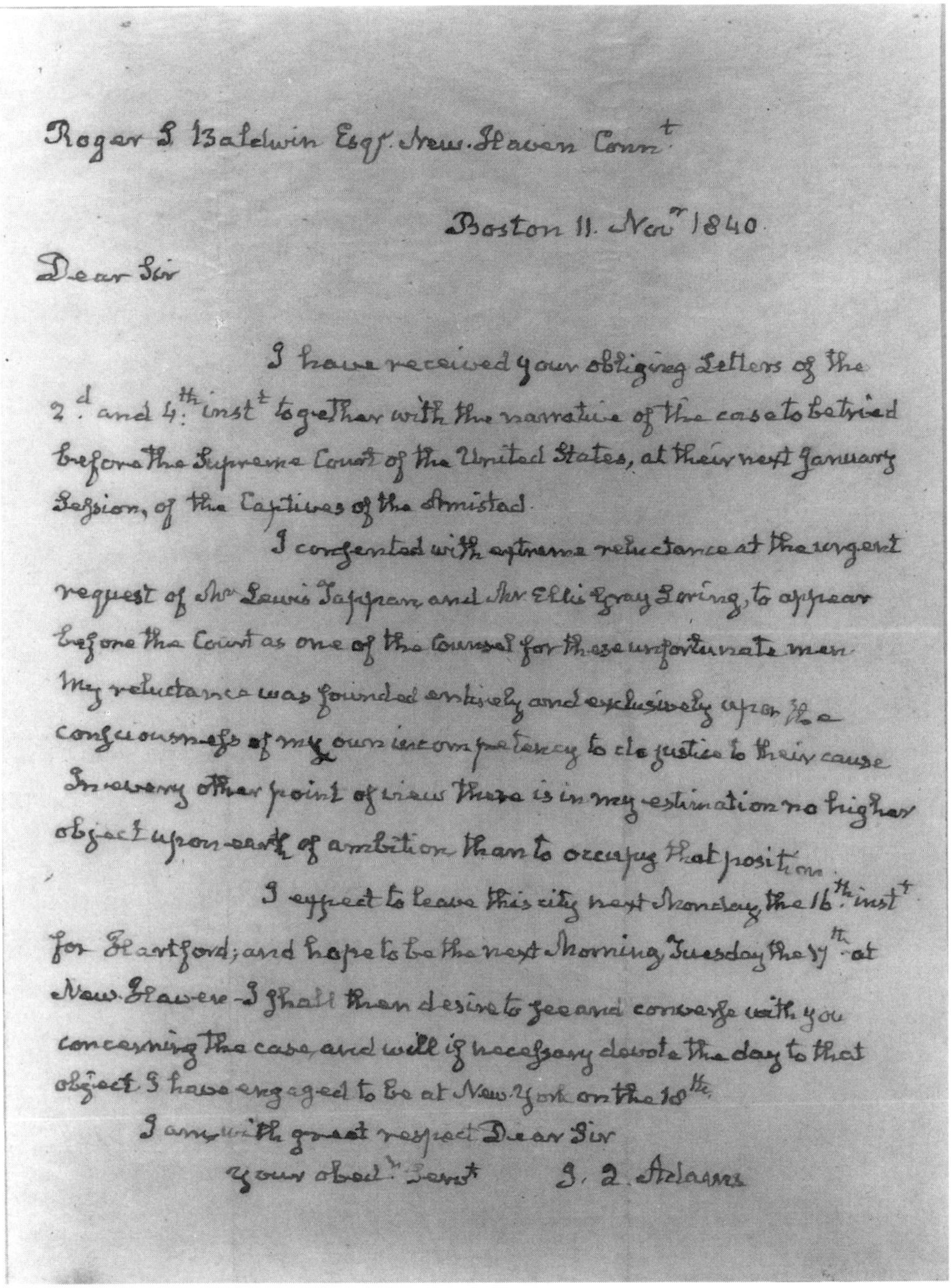

Roger S. Baldwin Esqr. New Haven Connt.

Boston 11. Novr. 1840.

Dear Sir

I have received your obliging Letters of the 2d. and 4th. instt. together with the narrative of the case to be tried before the Supreme Court of the United States, at their next January Session, of the Captives of the Amistad.

I consented with extreme reluctance at the urgent request of Mr. Lewis Tappan and Mr. Ellis Gray Loring, to appear before the Court as one of the Counsel for these unfortunate men. My reluctance was founded entirely and exclusively upon the consciousness of my own incompetency to do justice to their cause. In every other point of view there is in my estimation no higher object upon earth of ambition than to occupy that position.

I expect to leave this city next Monday, the 16th. instt. for Hartford; and hope to be the next Morning, Tuesday the 17th. at New-Haven - I shall then desire to see and converse with you concerning the case, and will if necessary devote the day to that object. I have engaged to be at New-York on the 18th.

I am with great respect Dear Sir

Your obedt. Servt. J. Q. Adams

John Q. Adams. Autograph letter signed, to Roger S. Baldwin, 1840/11/11. The Gilder Lehrman Collection, on deposit at the Pierpont Morgan Library. GLC 582

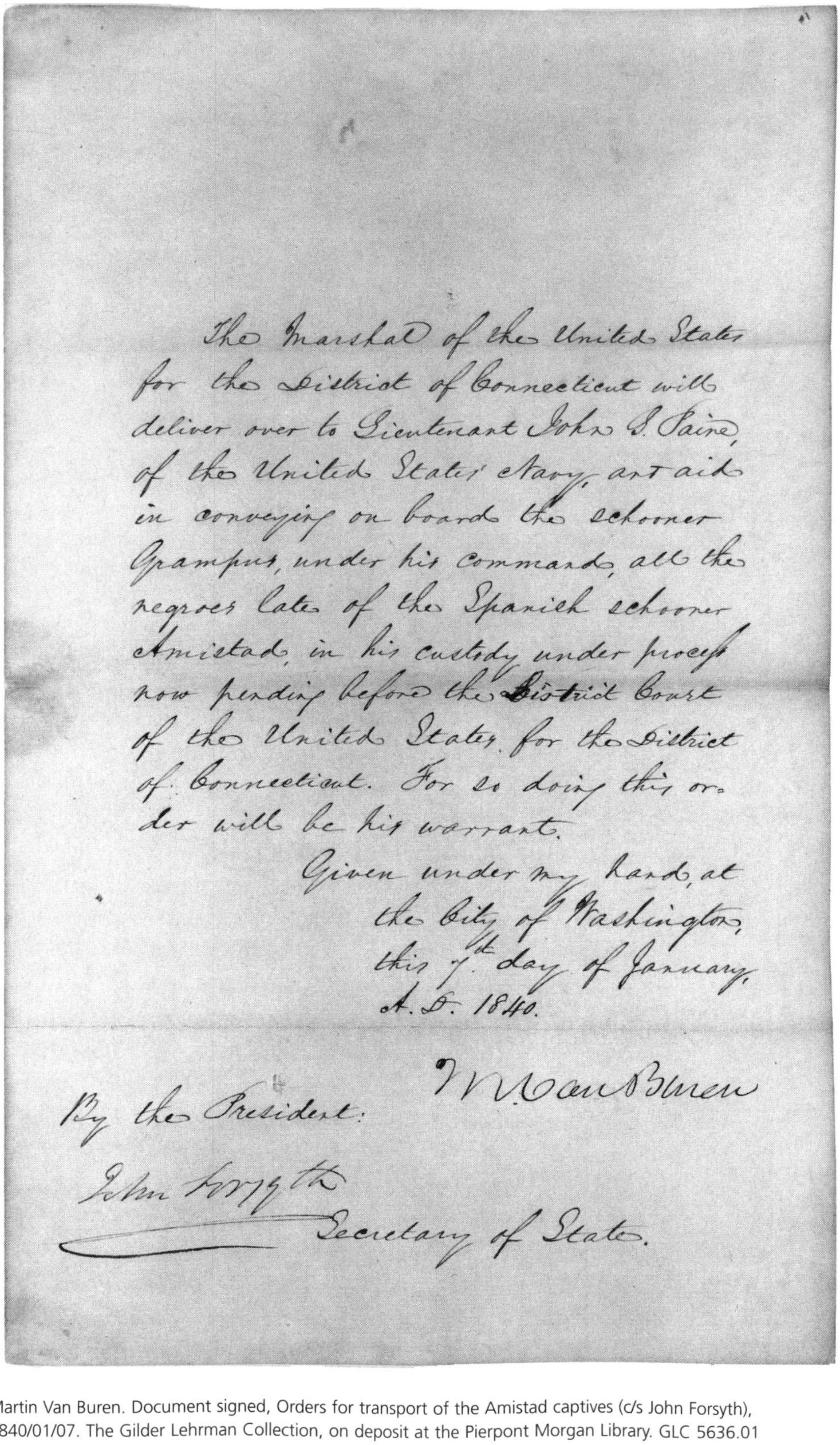
The Marshal of the United States
for the District of Connecticut will
deliver over to Lieutenant John S. Paine,
of the United States Navy, and aid
in conveying on board the schooner
Grampus, under his command, all the
negroes late of the Spanish schooner
Amistad, in his custody under process
now pending before the District Court
of the United States for the District
of Connecticut. For so doing this order will be his warrant.

Given under my hand, at
the City of Washington,
this 7th day of January,
A.D. 1840.

M. Van Buren

By the President:

John Forsyth
Secretary of State.

Martin Van Buren. Document signed, Orders for transport of the Amistad captives (c/s John Forsyth), 1840/01/07. The Gilder Lehrman Collection, on deposit at the Pierpont Morgan Library. GLC 5636.01

John Forsyth, Secretary of State, 1839

...It is true, by the treaty between Great Britain and Spain, the slave trade is prohibited to the subjects of each; but the parties to this treaty or agreement are the proper judges of any infraction of it, and they have created special tribunals to decide questions arising under the treaty; nor does it belong to any other nation to adjudicate upon it, or to enforce it.... In the case of the Antelope, (10 Wheaton, page 66), this subject was fully examined, and the opinion of the Supreme Court of the United States establishes the following points:

1. That, however unjust and unnatural the slave trade may be, it is not contrary to the law of nations.

2. That having been sanctioned by the usage and consent of almost all civilized nations, it could not be pronounced illegal, except so far as each nation may have made it so by its own acts or laws; and these could only operate upon itself, its own subjects or citizens; and, of course, the trade would remain lawful to those whose Government had not forbidden it.

3. That the right of bringing in and adjudicating upon the case of a vessel charged with being engaged in the slave trade, even where the vessel belongs to a nation which has prohibited the trade, cannot exist. The courts of no country execute the penal laws of another....

In the case now before me, the vessel is a Spanish vessel, belonging exclusively to Spaniards, navigated by Spaniards, and sailing under Spanish papers and flag, from one Spanish port to another. It therefore follows, unquestionably, that any offence committed on board is cognizable before the Spanish tribunals, and not elsewhere.

These two points being disposed of—1st. That the Government of the United States is to consider these Negroes as the property of the individuals in whose behalf the Spanish minister has put up a claim; 2d. That the United States cannot proceed against them criminally;—the only remaining inquiry is, what is to be done with the vessel and cargo? the Negroes being part of the latter.

...The claimants of these Negroes have violated none of our laws.... They have not come within our territories with the view or intention of violating the laws of the United States.... They have not introduced these Negroes into the United Sates for the purpose of sale, or holding them in servitude within the United States.... It therefore appears to me that this subject must be disposed of upon the principles of international law and the existing treaties between Spain and the United States....

These Negroes are charged with an infraction of the Spanish laws; therefore, it is proper that they should be surrendered to the public functionaries of that Government, that if the laws of Spain have been violated, they may not escape punishment....

These Negroes deny that they are slaves; if they should be delivered to the claimants, no opportunity may be afforded for the assertion of their right to freedom. For these reasons, it seems to me that a delivery to the Spanish minister is the only safe course for this Government to pursue.

Africans Taken in the Amistad (U.S. 26th Cong., 1st Sess., H. Exec. Doc. 185 (New York: Blair & Rives, 1840), 57–62.

74/ *"All we want is make us free"*

The Amistad Affair took place at a critical moment in the history of the antislavery movement. By 1839, abolitionists had failed in their efforts to end slavery through moral suasion. Northern mobs, often instigated by "gentlemen of property and standing," disrupted abolitionist meetings and destroyed antislavery printing presses. The House of Representatives had adopted the "gag rule," automatically tabling antislavery petitions. The Amistad case offered a opportunity for abolitionists to dramatize the illegal violence in which slavery originated and the discrepancy between slavery and American ideals of natural rights. The affair helped shift the abolitionist movement away from moral suasion to new methods of political and legal agitation that would arouse thousands of Northerners against slavery's immoralities.

Among the Amistad captives were four African children. One, a boy named Kale, who was just eleven years old in 1841, learned English very quickly. When the rebels heard that John Quincy Adams would represent them before the Supreme Court, they selected Kale to write the following letter to the former president.

KALE TO JOHN QUINCY ADAMS, JAN. 4, 1841.

I want to write a letter to you because you love Mendi people, and you talk to the grand court. We want to tell you one thing. Jose Ruiz [one of the two surviving whites on the Amistad] say we born in Havana, he tell lie. We stay in Havana 10 days and 10 nights. We stay no more. We all born in Mendi—we no understand the Spanish language. Mendi people been in America 17 moons. We talk American language a little, not very good. We write every day; we write plenty letters. We read most all time. We read all Matthew, and Mark, and Luke, and John, and plenty of little books. We love books very much. We want you to ask the Court what we have done wrong. What for Americans keep us in prison. Some people say Mendi people crazy, Mendi people dolt, because we no talk American language. American people no talk Mendi language. American people crazy dolts? They tell bad things about Mendi people and we no understand. Some men say Mendi people very happy because they laugh and have plenty to eat. Mr. Pendelton [the jailer] come and Mendi people all look sorry because they think about Mendiland and friends we no see now. Mr. Pendelton say we feel anger and white men afraid of us. Then we no look sorry again. That's why we laugh. But Mendi people feel bad. O, we can't tell how bad. Some people say, Mendi people no have souls. Why we feel bad, we no have no souls? We want to be free very much.

Dear friend Mr. Adams, you have children, you have friends, you love them, you feel very sorry if Mendi people come and take all to Africa. We feel bad for our friends, and our friends all feel bad for us. Americans not take us in ship. We were on shore and Americans tell us slave ship catch us. They say we make you free. If they make us free they tell truth, if they not make us free they tell lie. If America give us free we glad, if they no give us free we sorry—we sorry for Mendi people little, we sorry for America people great deal because God punish liars. We want you to tell court that Mendi people no want to go back to Havana, we no want to be killed. Dear friend,

> we want you to know how we feel. Mendi people think think, think. Nobody know. Teacher, he know, we tell him some. Mendi people have got souls. We think we know God punish us if we tell lie. We never tell lie; we speak the truth, What for Mendi people afraid? Because they have got souls. Cook say he kill, he eat Mendi people—we afraid—we kill cook. Then captain kill one man with knife, and cut Mendi people plenty. We never kill captain if he no kill us. If Court ask who bring Mendi people to America, we bring ourselves. Ceci hold the rudder. All we want is make us free, not send us to Havana. Send us home. Give us Missionary. We tell Mendi people Americans spoke truth. We give them good tidings. We tell them there is one god. You must worship him. Make us free and we will bless you and all Mendi people will bless you, Dear friend Mr. Adams.

Simon Baldwin, "The Captives of the Amistad," papers of the New Haven-Colony Historical Society, Vol. IV (1888), pp. 354–55.

75 / *"I appear…on…behalf of thirty-six individuals, the life and liberty of every one…depend on…this court"*

Abolitionists persuaded former President John Quincy Adams to represent the Amistad rebels before the U.S. Supreme Court. Adams accepted the invitation, stating that "there is in my estimation no higher object upon earth…than to occupy that position."

Adams, the son of one of America's founders, was the only surviving statesman who had been on close terms with Washington, Jefferson, Madison, and Monroe. In a nine-hour closing argument extending over two days, the 74-year-old Adams contended that the Africans had "vindicated their own right of liberty" by executing "the justice of Heaven" upon a "private murder, their tyrant and oppressor." He used the Amistad case to illustrate the federal government's complicity with slavery and the discrepancy between slavery and American ideals of natural rights. Associate Justice Joseph Story, who wrote the majority opinion, described Adams's summation as "an extraordinary argument…extraordinary…for its power, [and] for its bitter sarcasm…."

A majority of the Justices were Southerners, including Chief Justice Roger B. Taney. But one Southerner was too ill to participate in the case and another died of a heart attack during the trial. In the end, the Court ruled that the Africans had exercised the right of self-defense since they had been illegally transported as slaves from Africa to Cuba. As it turned out, private donors returned thirty-five surviving rebels to Sierra Leone almost a year after the Court ruling. While this outcome signified an extraordinary victory for black and white abolitionists, and for John Quincy Adams in particular, the Supreme Court made it clear that the *Amistad* case was highly exceptional and that slaves in general had no right to rebel or escape their bondage.

Cinqué, the revolt's leader, returned to his Mende homeland only to find his village destroyed as a result of a war with a neighboring people. Apparently his wife and children were sold into slavery during this conflict, and he never saw them again. He later worked as an interpreter for the American Missionary Association.

"Argument of John Quincy Adams, Before the Supreme Court of the United States, in the Case of the United States, Appellants, vs. Cinque, and Others, Africans, Captured in the Schooner *Amistad,* Delivered on February 24, and March 1, 1841," GLC 3809

...I appear here on the behalf of thirty-six individuals, the life and liberty of every one of whom depend on the decision of this Court.... Three or four of them are female children, incapable, in the judgment of our laws, of the crime of murder or piracy, or, perhaps, of any other crime. Yet, from the day when the vessel was taken possession of by one of our naval officers, they have all been held as close prisoners, now for the period of eighteen long months....

The Constitution of the United States recognizes the slaves, held within some of the States of the Union, only in their capacity of persons—persons held to labor or service in a State under the laws thereof—persons constituting elements of representation in the popular branch of the National Legislature—persons, the migration or importation of whom should not be prohibited by Congress prior to the year 1808. The Constitution no where recognizes them as property. The words slave and slavery are studiously excluded from the Constitution. Circumlocutions are the fig-leaves under which the parts of the body politic are decently concealed. Slaves, therefore, in the Constitution of the United States are persons, enjoying rights and held to the performance of duties....

The persons aforesaid, described as slaves, are Negroes and persons of color, who have been transported from Africa in violation of the laws of the United States.... The Court should enable the United States to send the Negroes home to Africa...in pursuance of the law of Congress passed March 3, 1829, entitled "An act in addition to the acts prohibiting the slave-trade."...

The President...signed [an] order for the delivery of MEN to the control of an officer of the navy to be carried beyond sea.... The District Judge, contrary to all [the] anticipations of the Executive, decided that the thirty-six Negroes...brought before the Court...were FREEMEN; that they had been kidnapped in Africa; that they did not own...Spanish names;...that they were not correctly described in the passport, but were new Negroes...fully entitled to their liberty.

Well was it for the country—well was it for the President of the United States himself that he paused before stepping over this Rubicon!... The indignation of the freemen of Connecticut, might not tamely endure the sight, of thirty-six free persons, though Africans, fettered and manacled in their land of freedom, to be transported beyond the seas, to perpetual hereditary servitude or to death, by the servile submission of an American President to the insolent dictation of a foreign minister....

[President Van Buren informed his subordinates that] if the decree of the Judge should be in our favor, and you can steal a march upon the Negroes by foreclosing their right of appeal, ship them off without mercy and without delay: and if the decree should be in their favor, fail not to enter an instantaneous appeal to the Supreme Court where the chances may be more hostile to self-emancipated slaves.

Was ever such a scene of Lilliputian trickery enacted by the rulers of a great, magnanimous, and Christian nation? Contrast it with that act of self-emancipation, by which the savage, heathen barbarians Cinqué and Grabeau liberated themselves and their fellow suffering countrymen from Spanish slave traders, and which the Secretary of State...denominates lawless violence.... Cinqué and Graveau are uncooth and barbarous names. Call them Harmodius and Aristogiton, and go back for moral principle three thousand years to the fierce and glorious democracy of Athens. They too resorted to lawless violence, and slew the tyrant to redeem the freedom of their country....

I said, when I began this plea, that my final reliance for success in this case was on this Court as a court of JUSTICE; and in the confidence this fact inspired, that, in the administration of justice, in a case of no less importance than the liberty and the life of a large number of persons, this Court would not decide but on a due consideration of all the rights, both natural and social, of everyone of these individuals.... I have avoided, purposely avoided...a recurrence to those first principles of liberty which might well have been invoked in the argument of this cause. I have shown that [the *Amistad*'s crew members]...were acting at the time in a way that is forbidden by the laws of Great Britain, of Spain and of the United States, and...that these Negroes were free and had a right to assert their liberty....

On the 7th of February, 1804, now more than thirty-seven years past, my name was entered, and yet stands recorded, on both the rolls, as one of the Attorneys and Counsellors of this Court.... I stand before the same Court, but not before the same judges—nor aided by the same associates—nor resisted by the same opponents. As I cast my eyes along those seats of honor and public trust, now occupied by you, they seek in vain for one of those honored and honorable persons whose indulgence listened then to my voice. Marshall—Cushing—Chase—Washington—Johnson—Livingston—Todd—Where are they?...Gone! Gone! All gone!... In taking, then, my final leave of this Bar, and of this Honorable Court, I can only ejaculate a fervent petition to Heaven, that every member of it may go to his final account with as little of earthly frailty to answer for as those illustrious dead....

76 / *"No action of mine can...contribute...to the abolition of Slavery"*

Five years after the *Amistad* affair, and a year after the House of Representatives ended the gag rule, John Quincy Adams expresses his resignation about the possibility of further actions against slavery, such as the abolition of slavery within the District of Columbia. Not until April 1862, long after Adams's death, did Congress pass an act providing for compensated emancipation of "persons held to service or labor in the District of Columbia."

In 1836 Adams had warned the South that if a war was fought in the South, the government would abolish slavery. "From the instant your slave-holding states become a theater of war—civil, servile, or foreign," he predicted, "—from that instant the war powers of the Constitution extend interference with the institution of slavery in every way that it can be interfered with."

In 1846, a year after he wrote the following letter, Adams suffered a paralytic stroke. He recovered sufficiently to return to Congress, but in February 1848, as he rose from his House desk to denounce the Mexican War, he suffered another stroke. As he collapsed, a fellow House member caught him. The stricken former president, too ill to be moved from the Capitol, was carried to the Speaker's office, where he died two days later. The country's last tangible political link with the world of the founders was gone.

JOHN QUINCY ADAMS, JULY 15, 1845, TO ARTHUR TAPPAN, GLC 3891

It would be far more agreeable to me, to concur in opinion with you upon the controverted principles connected in the abolition of Slavery, than to differ with you; but it is a case in which my judgement depends not upon will. —My opinion is that Slavery never will be abolished in the District of Columbia otherwise than it has been abolished in Pennsylvania, New York, and other States—*prospectively*—. Two years ago, I offered to the House Resolutions to that effect. The House refused to receive them and the leading abolitionists declared their explicit disapprobation of them.

Since that time...I have concluded that no action of mine can in the present state of things contribute either to the abolition of Slavery in general, or to its extinguishment in the District of Columbia. Believing as I do that this great revolution in the history and condition of man upon the earth will be accomplished by the will of his maker, and through means provided by him in his good time, I have felt the obligation to act my part in promoting it so far as any exertion on my part may be cheered by his smile of approbation inseparable from success. But when I find my opinions...conflicting with the deliberate judgement and purpose of both parties in this great controversy, I feel the finger of Heaven pressing upon my lips and dooming me to silence and inaction. I consult the *sortes biblicae* {the words of the Bible}, and read that when David proposed to build a Temple to the Lord, the prophet, speaking from the inspiration of his own mind, approved his design and exhorted him to carry it into execution. But when reposing upon his pillow, the Lord appeared to him in vision, and commanded him to go to David and tell him, to build a Temple to the Lord, but that *he* was not the chosen instrument to accomplish that great undertaking, but that it was to await the halcyon age reserved for the wisest of mankind, Solomon, his son.

POLITICAL ANTISLAVERY

77 / *"We have pursued slavery...into all its hiding places"*

Antislavery agitation provoked a harsh public reaction in the North as well as in the South. States debated gag laws to suppress antislavery agitation, and the U.S. postmaster general refused to deliver antislavery tracts to the South.

Abolitionists never expected such a reaction. "When we first unfurled the banner of *The Liberator*, William Lloyd Garrison wrote, "we did not anticipate that...the free states would voluntarily trample under foot all order, law and government, or brand the advocates of universal liberty as incendiaries." This harsh response produced division within the antislavery movement.

At the 1840 annual meeting of the American Anti-Slavery Society in New York, abolitionists split over such questions as women's right to participate in the administration of the organization and the advisability of nominating abolitionists as independent political candidates. Garrison won control of the organization, and his opponents promptly walked out. From this point on, no single organization could speak for abolitionism.

Some abolitionists, led by Garrison, moved in a radical direction. They questioned whether the Bible represented the word of God, withdrew from membership in established churches that condoned slavery, refused to vote, and called for voluntary dissolution of the Union. In 1854 Garrison attracted widespread notoriety by publicly burning a copy of the Constitution, which he called "a covenant with death and an agreement with hell."

Other abolitionists looked to politics as the answer to ending slavery and in 1840 founded the Liberty Party for that purpose. Under the leadership of Arthur and Lewis Tappan, wealthy New York businessmen, and James G. Birney, a former slaveholder, the Liberty Party called on Congress to abolish slavery in the District of Columbia, end the interstate slave trade, and cease admitting new slave states to the Union. The party also sought the repeal of local and state laws in the North that discriminated against free blacks. The Liberty Party nominated Birney for president in 1840, but gathered fewer than seventy-one hundred votes in its first campaign.

Gerrit Smith (1797–1874), a leading abolitionist and a wealthy New York landowner, gave away thousands of acres of land to African-American and white workers, to allow them to set up farms. In this selection he reports on the 1840 campaign.

Gerrit Smith, Report from the County of Madison [New York], ca. 1840

Election Day is past!—and now, in behalf of the friends of the slave in the County of Madison and State of New-York, I declare to you, that we "have fought a good fight—have kept the faith." We have "fought" earnestly, strenuously, untiringly. We have "kept" the whole antislavery "faith." We have stood up for all its righteous and glorious principles; and have stood by each other. We have pursued slavery, hotly and unsparingly, into all its hiding places, whether in the Church or in the State. We have dealt impartially with proslavery demagogues, and proslavery ministers, and proslavery schools, and proslavery churches—and unmasked them all.

At an early day, the duty of voting for the slave was felt by a few persons in this County. Our first systematic effort to get votes for him was in 1837. By means of much toil—of much riding, and writing, and speaking—we induced about fifty of the inhabitants of the County to vote that year upon anti-slavery principles.

In the year 1840, the year of the organization of the Liberty Party, about 230 anti-slavery votes were cast in this county....

In common with the great body of abolitionists, I had not, at this time [1839], given up my reliance on the interrogation-system [of asking Democratic and Whig candidates their stand on slavery]. But, very soon after, a train of thought passed through my mind, leaving the conviction that this reliance should be given up.... I saw now, for the first time, and I was surprised that I had not seen it before, that no National party in this country, whether ecclesiastical or political, is, so long as the system of American slavery endures, to be trusted on the question of slavery. It was now evident to me, that every such party is necessarily proslavery—and that it is so from the simple reason that the South, making slavery her paramount interest, will abide in no party, will come into no party, save on the condition that such party shall not attack slavery. Some may say that the Liberty Party is a National Party, and is, therefore, involved in my condemnation of all National Parties. To this I reply—that it is, in its hopes and objects, a National Party: but that, until the South has come into it, which cannot be until she has let go of slavery, it cannot be an *actual* National Party....

78 / *"The Liberty party is what its enemies reproachfully call it—'a one idea party'"*

In the presidential election of 1844, opponents of slavery were faced with a dilemma: whether to vote for the Whig candidate Henry Clay, or support the Liberty Party candidate, James G. Birney, and possibly throw the election to the Democratic nominee James Knox Polk, an ardent supporter of territorial expansion. In 1844 the Liberty Party polled some sixty-two thousand votes—nine times as many votes as it had received four years earlier—and captured enough votes in Michigan and New York to deny Clay the presidency. In this letter to a leading New York Whig (and later Republican) politician, Gerrit Smith explains why he refused to support the Whig Party.

GERRIT SMITH, JANUARY 1, 1845, TO WILLIAM H. SEWARD, GLC 4717

I am of the number of those who believe that you mistake the "instincts" and character of the Whig party. Were I to regard it in the light in which you do, I should eagerly join it. Not my preference for an Independent Treasury to a National Bank; nor my preference for absolute free trade to either high or low tariffs; nor my conviction, that Government has no more right to make railroads and canals for the people, than it has to make hats and coats for them; would hold me back from joining it. These, which are regarded by most men as mere money questions, are but "as the small dust of the balance," when compared with the question of inalienable, unchangeable personal rights. I am so much of "a one idea man," that I go with the party which goes with the slave, go that party as it may on these inferior questions. To the Whig party, as *you* would have it, I should, as an abolitionist, make little objection. But I cannot consent to substitute your imaginations of its present, or your anticipations of its future, character, for what it really, and now, is....

I am amazed and sorrowful, that this party [the Liberty Party], should be held up as hypocritical, jesuitical, traitorous to the slave, and unprincipled, because it would not vote for Mr. Clay, and because it would pursue just such a course as it always said it would, and as consistency, truth, and decency required it should. It is not enough that, by means of the basest deceptions and boldest forgeries, the Liberty party was defrauded of not less than fifteen or twenty thousand votes. They, who thus defrauded it, are now pursuing it with a spirit envenomed by the consciousness of their cruel, deep, and causeless injuries of it....

That Mr. Clay is a slaveholder, is reason sufficient why the Liberty party could not vote for him. Not to vote for a slaveholder, in any circumstances, or under any temptations, has, from the first, been one of its cardinal and unanimously received doctrines. Though it may be taken as a confession of its narrow mindedness, I am, nevertheless, free to admit, that the Liberty party is what its enemies reproachfully call it—"a one idea party." Its sole object, its sole effort, is to abolish slavery....

It is said that Mr. Clay was opposed to the annexation of Texas. It is enough, however, to justify the opposition of the Liberty party to him, that he remained a slavery [defender]....

It is said, too, that however objectionable Mr. Clay might have been to the abolitionists, they should have voted for him, inasmuch as the party, whose candidate he was, is opposed to the annexation of Texas and to slavery; and inasmuch, moreover, as its rival party is in favor of both. Be assured, that I am not offended when the worst character is given to the Democratic party. A guiltier party there never was. It consented to vote for James K. Polk, when it well knew that its corrupt and corrupting masters nominated him for no other reason than his being in favor of the extension and perpetuity of American slavery....

THE FREE SOIL PARTY

79 / *"The Whig and Democratic candidates... are the shameless tools of the slave-power"*

In 1848 antislavery Democrats and Conscience Whigs (in contrast to Cotton Whigs) merged with the Liberty party to form the Free Soil Party. Unlike the Liberty Party, which was dedicated to slavery's abolition and equal rights for blacks, the Free Soil Party narrowed its demands to the abolition of slavery in the District of Columbia and the exclusion of slavery from the federal territories. The Free Soilers also wanted a homestead law to provide free land for western settlers, high tariffs to protect American industry, and federally sponsored internal improvements.

The Free Soil Party nominated Martin Van Buren as its presidential candidate, even though Van Buren had supported the gag rule that had quashed consideration of abolitionist petitions while he was president. In the following letter, Gerrit Smith discusses Van Buren's nomination. In the election of 1848 Van Buren polled 291,000 votes, enough to split the Democratic vote and throw the election to the Whig candidate, Zachary Taylor.

Gerrit Smith, August 15, 1848, to J.K. Ingalls, editor of the *Landmark*, 4717.14

I hardly need say, that I am deeply interested in the present movement against the extension of slavery; and that I infinitely prefer the election of the candidates, who are identified with it, to the election of the Whig and Democratic candidates. Gen. [Zachary] Taylor and Gen. [Lewis] Cass are proslavery candidates. Mr. Van Buren and Mr. Adams are antislavery candidates. The former are the shameless tools of the slave-power. The latter bravely resist it.

It is true, that, among all the persons, whom there was the least reason to believe the Buffalo Convention [of the Free Soil Party] would nominate for President, Mr. Van Buren was my preference. He was my preference, because I believed he would obtain a much larger vote than any of the others; and, that his nomination would go much farther than that of any of the others toward breaking up the great political parties, which, along with the ecclesiastical parties, are the chief shelters and props of slavery.

But it is not true that I shall vote for Mr. Van Buren. I can vote for no man for President of the United States, who is not an abolitionist; for no man, who votes for slaveholders, or for those, who do; for no man, whose understanding and heart would not prompt him to use the office, to the utmost, for the abolition of slavery. And, let me here confess, that I am not of the number of those, who believe, that the Federal Government has no higher power over slavery than to abolish it in the District of Columbia, and to abolish the inter-State traffic in human beings. On the contrary, I claim that this Government has power, under the Constitution, to abolish every part of American slavery, whether without, or within, the States; and that it is superlatively guilty against God and man for refusing thus to use it. The still higher ground do I take, that no man is fit for President of the United States, who does not scout the idea of the possibility of property in man, and who does not insist, that slavery is as utterly incapable of legalization, as is murder itself. Why is it not? Is it not as bad as murder? Is not, indeed, murder itself one of the elements in that matchless compound of enormous crimes?... There should be no surprise, that, from the day this Nation came into being until the present day, no white man has, in any one of the Southern States, been put to death, under the laws, for the murder of a slave....

THE MEXICAN WAR

Fifteen years before the United States plunged into the Civil War, it fought a war against Mexico that added half a million square miles of territory to the United States. Not only was it the first American war fought almost entirely outside the United States, it also was the first American war to be reported, while it happened, by daily newspapers. A controversial war that bitterly divided public opinion, it also was the war that gave young officers such as Ulysses S. Grant (1822–85), Robert E. Lee (1807–70), Thomas ("Stonewall") Jackson (1824–63), William Tecumseh Sherman (1820–91), and George McClellan (1826–85) their first experience in a major conflict.

The underlying cause of the war was the inexorable movement of American pioneers into the Far West. As Americans marched westward, they moved into land claimed by Mexico, and inevitably Mexican and American interests clashed. The immediate reason for the conflict was the annexation of Texas. Mexico had refused to recognize Texan independence and warned the United States that annexation would be tantamount to a declaration of war. In early 1845, when Congress voted to annex Texas, Mexico cut off diplomatic relations but took no further action.

President James Knox Polk told his commanders to prepare for the possibility of war. He ordered American naval vessels in the Gulf of Mexico to position themselves outside Mexican ports. Secretly, he warned the Pacific fleet to prepare to seize ports along the California coast, which was then part of Mexico, in the event of war. Anticipating a possible Mexican invasion of Texas, he dispatched American forces in Louisiana to Corpus Christi.

In the fall of 1845 the president sent an envoy to Mexico with a proposal to end the dispute peacefully. The United States offered to cancel all damage claims by American citizens for losses during Mexico's years of political turmoil and to pay $5 million if Mexico recognized the Rio Grande as Texas's southwestern boundary (Mexico and Spain had defined the Texas boundary 130 miles northward). The United States also offered up to $5 million for the Mexican province of New Mexico (which included Nevada and Utah and parts of four other states) and up to $25 million for California. Polk was anxious to acquire California because he had been led to believe that Mexico was about to cede California to Britain as payment for outstanding debts.

The Mexican government, already incensed over the annexation of Texas, refused to negotiate. Polk ordered Brigadier General Zachary Taylor to march three thousand troops from Corpus Christi to "defend the Rio Grande." In March 1846 Taylor and his men set up a camp along the Rio Grande, directly across from the Mexican city of Matamoros.

On April 25 a Mexican cavalry unit crossed the Rio Grande and clashed with a small American squadron, forcing the Americans to surrender after the loss of several lives. Polk used this episode as an excuse to declare war. "Hostilities may be considered to have commenced," Taylor wrote to President Polk.

Hours before he received word of the skirmish, Polk and his cabinet had already decided to press for war. On May 11 Polk asked Congress to acknowledge that a state of war already existed. "Mexico," the president announced, "has passed the boundary of the United States, has invaded our territory and shed American blood on American soil." Congress responded with a declaration of war.

80 / *"The Wilmot Proviso will shake that body to its center"*

American strategy was based on a three-pronged attack. Colonel Stephen Kearny (1794–1848) had the task of securing New Mexico, while naval forces under Commodore John D. Sloat (1781–1867) blockaded California, and General Zachary Taylor (1784–1850) invaded Tamaulipas, in present-day northern Mexico. In fewer than two months, Kearny marched his seventeen-hundred-man army more than a thousand miles, occupied Santa Fe, and declared New Mexico's eighty thousand inhabitants American citizens. In California's Sacramento Valley, American settlers revolted even before reliable reports of war had arrived. By January 1847 U.S. naval and ground forces brought California under American control. Meanwhile, the main U.S. army under Taylor took Matamoros and Monterrey.

Although the American invasion of Mexico's northernmost provinces was completely successful, the Mexican government refused to surrender or negotiate. Switching strategies, President Polk ordered General Winfield Scott (1786–1866) to invade central Mexico from the sea, at Veracruz on the Gulf of Mexico, to march inland, and capture Mexico City. Zachary Taylor was in Monterrey when he heard reports that Scott's army had captured the Mexican capital. In this letter Taylor, a Louisiana slaveholder who had never voted in a presidential election, discusses early American military successes, the possibility that he might be nominated for the presidency, and an explosive controversy that had erupted in Congress over the Wilmot Proviso. The proviso, an amendment to a military appropriation bill to prohibit slavery from any territory acquired from Mexico, ultimately passed the House of Representatives but was defeated in the Senate.

ZACHARY TAYLOR, OCTOBER 19, 1847, TO SURGEON R.C. WOOD (DATED NEAR MONTERREY, MEXICO), GLC 529.05

I have not heard any of the particulars as regards...Scott's taking possession of the City of Mexico. All we have heard relative to that affair is that he was in quiet possession of that piece & that the Mexican army had dispersed; I presume there will hardly be another battle; that Santa Anna had gone no one knew where, in the direction of the Pacific, & it was supposed he would leave this country; this is Mexican views & Mexican conjecture.... I presume atrocity of some kind or other will grow out of our taking the city & laying it under contribution [occupation], which the Mexicans say has been done, & should they acquiesce in considerable [loss] of territory, it will produce great strife in the streets, when atrocity is laid before that body for their action. The Wilmot Proviso will shake that body to its center... but I hope some compromise will be entered into between the two parties slavery & anti slavery which will have the effect of allying violent passions on both sides, which will have the effect of perpetuating...or shortening the Union....

It is to me a matter of perfect indifference whether I am ever elected [as president] or not. I do not intend any party shall use me as a convenience; if drafted I intend to stand aloof, & let Whigs and Democrats [use] this matter in their own way.... Depend on it there will be great changes in the complexion of political affairs between now & the end of this next session of Congress; the Whigs as a party between ourselves I look upon as doomed.... I am gratified I took the position I did, which was not to be the exclusive candidate of any party; & if I am elected at all, it will be by a union of a portion of Whig Democrat and native votes. At any rate I am occupying a position & shall continue to do so. I hope that if not elected, I shall neither be mortified or disappointed.

81 / "This people have been conceived in sin &... have been degraded by oppression"

Persifor Smith (1798–1858), General Winfield Scott's second-in-command, provides a firsthand account of the capture of Mexico City. On April 18, 1847, at a mountain pass near Jalapa, a nine-thousand-man American force met thirteen thousand Mexican troops, and in bitter hand-to-hand fighting forced the Mexicans to flee. As Scott's army pushed on toward Mexico City, it stormed a Mexican fortress at Contreras and then routed a large Mexican force at Churubusco. For two weeks, from August 22 to September 7, Scott observed an armistice to allow the Mexicans to consider peace proposals. When negotiations failed, Scott's six thousand remaining men attacked El Molino del Rey and stormed Chapultepec, a fortified castle guarding Mexico City's gates.

GENERAL PERSIFOR SMITH, OCTOBER 26, 1847, TO JUDGE R.W. NICHOLS, GLC 5128

Think of our astonishing campaign, with 8800 bayonets we came down the mountain and first saw this much vaunted valley. Near 300 miles from all our resources, in the midst of a population of eight millions of people, every valley a fortress accessible only through passes which nature seems to have constructed purposely to exclude the approach of a stranger; 32,000 men in front; a city of 180,000 inhabitants situated in the centre of a marsh (formerly a lake) fortified by two lines of works, approachable only by a few narrow causeways, full of wealth, provisions and all the means necessary to support war, ready for every need of their army, the enemy perfectly acquainted with every foot of ground while we could know nothing beyond our own lines, every battery & position they occupied actually *encumbered* with heavy artillery which you *know* they excel in serving. One half of our troops raw, (the law under which they were raised is not yet eight months old) and all somewhat suffering from the change of climate, weigh all this and you will be able to do justice in your own mind to the skill of the commander and the invincible energy of the troops.

Imagine yourself on a battlefield overtopped by the snow covered Popocatépetl & Ixtachuatl [volcanoes], which ages since belched up the misshapen rocks among which you are struggling, now rushing on with the bayonet you carry [into] a half church half fortress & find yourself in one of the first edifices founded by Cortez and on the spot from which he so often looked at the doomed city.... Here where our contending batteries are disputing the possession of an open space...and finally while standing in the grand Plaza you watch the Stars & Stripes climbing the flag-staff to wave over the "Halls of the Montezumas" you are treading on the spot cursed by the unnatural rites of human sacrifice, and before you stands, built into the wall of the cathedral...the wonderful...Calendar of that mysterious people [the Aztecs], hinting darkly, by the astonishing knowledge of Astronomy its calculations displays, at a remote origin among the nations of the East.

In the pride and exultation of success, we fancy ourselves the real proprietors of all the unexplored treasures of Mexican history hidden as they are...we felt that the unknown wonders of the migrations, adventures & conquests of the former masters of this Soil, & the romantic story of Cortez & his captains all now belong to us. God forbid! that we should have any title to the ages of cruelty, oppression, & then anarchy that have succeeded him.

In all our adventures here, I do not recollect a moment when every man was not full of confidence if I except the evening of the 19th of August when [one commander]... went back to tell Gen. Scott...that the effort to turn the enemy's position was hopeless, & advise[d] him to withdraw the troops....

In the meantime Santa Anna came out from the city with 12000 men about 5000 of them cavalry, and took position fronting me. I had 2800 men, no artillery, and not even an officer was mounted. Valencia [a Mexican commander] had 7000 men about 2000 of them cavalry & 22 pieces of cannon many of them heavy....

In seventeen minutes (I looked at my watch to time it) they were entirely defeated, 700 killed 1300 prisoners & the rest dispersed to the mountains, 21 pieces of cannon & 700 mules with their loads of ammunition captured, more generals and colonels than I ever saw before in my life at a time were among the prisoners. You never saw so splendid a sight as our charge on the works....

We might undoubtedly have entered the city...but Gen. Scott knew the Government & People of the United States ardently desired peace, that if we entered the city the government would disperse & a state of anarchy would follow that would prevent all Negotiation,

PROCLAMACION.

EL Gral. en Géfe de las fuerzas Americanas á los habitantes de *Tamaulipas Nuevo Leon y Coahuila.*

Cuando las tropas Americanas primeramente pasaron la Frontera y entraron en los susodichos Departamentos erá con la intencion, como publicamente os fuè declarado, de no hacer la Guerra à los ciudadadanos pacificos del pais, pero si; al Gobiern Central de la Republica, con la mira de conseguir lo mas pronto posible una paz honrosa

El que subscribe fué autorizado por su Gobierno de hacer Leva ó exigir tributos de los pueblos, para la mantencion de su Ejercito; pero desinclinado de echar el duro peso de la Guerra, sobre los, quienes con pocas excepciones habian manifestado una disposicion neutral, él se ha continuado desde el principio de pagar puntualmente y liberalmente por todos los socorros que han sido extraidos para auxiliar su tropa.

El ha usado todo empeño para que la Guerra no pesára sobre los Ciudadanos de estos Departmentos, y habia esperado por estos medios, haber logrado vuestro confianza y asegurado vuestro neutralidad en la contienda actual entre su Gobierno y el de Mejico; pero con sentimiento le es forzoso decir, que su bondad no ha sido apreciada pero ha sido correspondido con hechos de hostilidad y rapiña.

Los Ciudadanos del pais en lugar de continuar pacificamente sus ocupaciones en sus hogares, han con partidos armados en los caminos, puesto emboscadas, y debajo la direccion y con el sosten de las tropas del Gobierno han destriudo *Trenes* de carros, asesinando carruageros con circunstancias de atrocidad que son vergonzosas a la humanidad,

Las vidas, de los que han sido tan facinerosamente asesinados, no las puedan ser restablecidas; pero el que subscribe exigirá de los ciudadanos del pais una indemnisacion por la perdida, causada por la destruccion de los *Trenès* y el pilláge de lo contenido. Para el efecto, se formará por los Oficiales á quines corresponde, una estimacion de todo la perdida; esta perida; se ha de hacer buena en dinero efectivo ó en los productos del pais por la comunidad en general de los Departamentos de Tamaulipas y Nuevo Leon, cada distrito ó juzgado pagando su justa proporcion; y es cosa de esperar, que los Ricos pagarán su cuota cavalmente.

El que subscribe invoca à todos los buenos ciùdadanos, de continuar absolutament neutral, y no dar cara â los partidos que infestan el pais, con el objeto, solo; de matar y robar. Es su mayor deseo, de continuar la misma politica que siempre se ha observado, y se espera que la conducta de los pueblos, sera tal, que no hallarà dificultad en hacerlo.

Z. TAYLOR, Genl. Mayor del Ejercito Americano.

Quartel General, en Monterey, Marzo 22 de 1847.

[Onslow & Gee, *Printers.*]

Zachary Taylor. Broadside, Proclamation. [Spanish], 1847/03/22. The Gilder Lehrman Collection, on deposit at the Pierpont Morgan Library. GLC 4943

and while we *threatened* to take the city the fear of losing it would be one of the strongest motives to treat [negotiate], while as soon as we were in it and that blow no longer to be dreaded they would have no motive for any sacrifice of their prejudices. Although that brilliant conclusion of the day's work was within his power he sacrificed his own ambition for the general good & allowed an armistice for the purpose of negotiation. The corruption among their leading men who live on the public suffering was too strong for any little sense of public interest or virtue among them & after a few days having recovered from their first fright they thought our desire for peace was in reality a fear of their last effort, and as they had not kept the terms of the armistice in one particular, Gen. Scott put an end to it.... On the 12th we bombarded Chapultapec [a fortress outside of Mexico City] & the next morning took it & following up our success, Gen. Quitman with whose division I was serving entered the city just after one p.m. During the night the enemy abandoned it & the next morning at 7 a.m. we had the flag hoisted on the National Palace....

This people have been conceived in sin & born in iniquity. For ages the millions have been degraded by oppression and the few corrupted by unbridled power. Their whole moral character is debased, they have no self respect & are therefore incapable of self government; having no conscience within, they are guilty of any vice they think they can screen from punishment, and now all being alike base they naturally encourage each other's degradation. The best people in the country look on any reform as hopeless without the restraint & example of others and so actually seek to prolong the war with the view of benefiting by the example we give them even as conquerors. The immense crowd of office holders civil as well as military who have hitherto lived on the revenues & exactions of the government, are struggling to perpetuate the abuses by which they exist, and now that their very nationality is at stake the Congress which was to have met...is not yet a quorum. If two weeks more go by without the government being organized I do not think a peace can be made for years, and I believe indeed that they will cease to exist except as little quarrelsome, disorderly States....

Don't let any of my letter get into the paper.

82 / *"The citizens of the country have... encouraged ambushes"*

Despite the capture of their capital, the Mexicans refused to surrender. Belligerent civilians attacked army supply wagons, and guerrilla fighters harassed American troops. In Mexico City and in Mexico's northern provinces hostile crowds staged demonstrations in the streets, and snipers fired shots and hurled stones and broken bottles from the tops of flat-roofed Mexican houses. Zachary Taylor issued the following proclamation in an attempt to impose order.

ZACHARY TAYLOR, "PROCLAMATION," MARCH 22, 1847 [TRANSLATED FROM SPANISH], GLC 4943

PROCLAMATION

The Chief General of the American Forces

to the Inhabitants of Tamaulipas, Nuevo Leon and Coahuila.

When the American troops first crossed the frontier and entered the said districts, it was with the intention not to make war against the peaceful citizens of the country, but instead, with the aim of finding an honorable peace as quickly as possible....

The author [of this proclamation] was authorized by his government to make a levy or require tribute from the local communities in order to maintain his army. But disinclined to throw the heavy weight of the war on those who, with few exceptions, have manifested a neutral disposition, he has continued, from the beginning, to pay punctually and liberally for all the supplies that have been extracted in order to aid his troops.

He has made the greatest effort so that the war will not weigh heavily upon the citizens of those districts, and had hoped through these means to have enjoyed your confidence and assured your neutrality in the current dispute between his Government and that of Mexico. But with regret he is forced to say that his generosity has not been appreciated but has been met with acts of hostility.

Instead of continuing their business peacefully in their hearths, the citizens of the country have distributed arms in the roadways and encouraged ambushes [of U.S. forces]. Under the direction and with the support of the government, they have destroyed wagon trains and assassinated drivers in atrocious circumstances that are shameful to humanity.

The lives of those who have been so wickedly assassinated cannot be restored; but the author requires that the citizens of the country indemnify the losses caused by the destruction of the trains and the pillaging of their contents. Towards that end, an estimate will be made by the authorities of the entire loss. This loss must be made good in cash or in products of the country by the general community in the Districts of Tamaulipas and Nuevo Leon, each judicial district paying its fair share. And it is hoped that the rich will pay their proper share.

The author calls on all good citizens to remain absolutely neutral and not give aid to the partisans who infest the country with the sole object of killing and robbing.

83 / *"We are not furnished with a uniform"*

During the first few weeks following the declaration of war, a frenzy of prowar hysteria swept the country. Some 200,000 men responded to a call for 50,000 volunteers. Novelist Herman Melville (1819–91) observed, "a military ardor pervades all ranks.... Nothing is talked about but the halls of the Montezumas."

But from the war's beginning, a small but highly visible group of intellectuals, clergymen, pacifists, abolitionists, and Whig and Democratic politicians denounced the armed conflict. They considered it an expansionist power ploy dictated by an aggressive southern slaveocracy intent on acquiring more slave states to balance the northern free states in the U.S. Senate. *The Liberator*, risking the charge of treason, expressed open support for the Mexican people: "Every lover of Freedom and humanity throughout the world must wish them the most triumphant success."

As soldiers' letters exposed the hardships and savagery of life on the front, public enthusiasm for the war waned. Troops complained that their food was "green with slime." Diarrhea, amoebic dysentery, measles, and yellow fever ravaged the American soldiers. Seven times as many Americans died of disease and exposure as died of battlefield injuries. Of the 90,000 Americans who served in the war, only 1,721 died in action.

Another 11,155 died from disease and exposure to the elements. This soldier's letter provides a graphic account of duty in central Mexico.

WELLINGTON G. BURNETT, APRIL 4, 1848, TO HIS PARENTS, GLC 155.01

Cuernavaca, Mexico

I enlisted on the 19th of March [1847] in Dayton Ohio, under Capt Edward Ring who was recruiting a company for the fifteenth infantry. We arrived at Vera Cruz on the 4th of May and left the beach on the 3rd of June. On the 5th we had a fight with Guerrillas at Tohmas our party being commanded by Lieut Colonel McIntosh. We lost 64 men killed and wounded. We could not ascertain the loss of the enemy. We arrived at the National Bridge on the 10th of June and had another battle. Gilson was right when he said I had been in four hard fought battles. I am a duty Sergt. in Co. E fifteenth infantry. When I enlisted I said nothing about a noncommissioned office. But there is one thing I can say and that is although the noncommissioned offices were first out filled by those who were so low as to ask for them, I filled the first vacancy without asking for it. My companions will tell you that I learned the drill quicker than any man in the Com[pany] and that I always volunteered on any Hazardous enterprize. I hesitated to tell you that I had been in any battles or that I was a Sergt. out of modesty—I think this extreme modesty was entirely uncalled for towards a parent but my constitution is such that I cannot help it. I have not tasted a drop of intoxicating drinks since I left home. Our living is principally bread and beef. Coffee sugar rice or beans. Vinegar, salt are also furnished, and soap to wash our clothes. Our rations are not as good as at home in time of peace. We are not furnished with a uniform suit, in this country. But we shall get pay for it in money when we are discharged. The term of my enlistment is during the war. My pay is 13 dollars a month. I have not signed the two last pay rolls therefore there is four months pay due me besides 27 dollars which I foolishly lent. But I am glad it was when I was young as I shall profit by the lesson. You spoke of a Lieutenancy. I enlisted as a private as my greatest wish being to do my duty as a good soldier, but if my friends think I am deserving of a commission and are successful in getting it for me I shall accept it with the greatest pleasure. If unsuccessful, I thank them for their kindness. And it will not hurt my feeling in the least as I never expected such an honor!

84 / "The close of my congressional career"

A freshman Whig congressman from Illinois named Abraham Lincoln (1809–65) lashed out against the war, calling it immoral, proslavery, and a threat to the nation's republican values. He introduced a resolution demanding that President Polk identify the spot where the Mexicans had "invaded our territory and shed blood on American soil." One of Lincoln's constituents branded him "the Benedict Arnold of our district," and he was denied renomination.

Lincoln was a staunch advocate of Henry Clay's American System, which emphasized government support for education; "internal improvements," mainly better transportation; and economic development. Lincoln was also a firm believer in the superiority of the North's system of free labor, which, he was convinced, had produced a society that offered unprecedented economic opportunity. "I am not ashamed to confess," he declared, "that twenty-five years ago I was a hired laborer, mauling rails, at work on a flatboat—just what might happen to any poor man's son." But in the free states, a young man knew that "he can better his condition" because "there is no such thing as a freeman being fatally fixed for life, in the condition of a hired laborer." Lincoln's commitment to a system of free labor, mobility, and economic opportunity was the main reason he adamantly opposed slavery: "I want every man to have the chance—and I believe a black man is entitled to it—in which he *can* better his condition."

In this letter to David B. Campbell, an Illinois lawyer who served as mayor of Springfield, Lincoln prepares for his retirement from Congress.

ABRAHAM LINCOLN, JUNE 27, 1848, TO DAVID B. CAMPBELL, GLC 965

As one of my votes on the origin of the Mexican war, and my speech on the subject, had been the object of loco foco [radical Democratic] assault, tell Judge Logan I am much obliged to him for his vindication of me. No fair-minded, sensible man can take any other view of the matter.

I have been making an internal improvement speech, of which I will send you a copy when it shall be printed. I do not expect it will interest the people much, in the midst of the political excitement, immediately preceding a presidential election—but, the subject, being one of great and permanent interest, particularly to our district, I felt it a duty to say something about it. I shall seek an opportunity to make one *political*—Taylor—speech before the end of the session, since that will be about the close of my congressional career.

THE ESCALATING CONFLICT OVER SLAVERY

Although America's conflict with Mexico is overshadowed by the Civil War, in fact the Mexican War had far-reaching consequences for the nation's future. It increased the nation's size by a third, but it also reignited the question of slavery in the western territories. Even before the war began, the poet and philosopher Ralph Waldo Emerson had predicted that the United States would "conquer Mexico, but it will be as the man who swallows the arsenic which will bring him down in turn. Mexico will poison us."

Before the Mexican War, the major political issues dividing Americans were questions of tariffs, banking, internal improvements, and land. After the outbreak of war, a new issue dominated politics—whether the West would be free soil. This question burst into the public spotlight in the summer of 1846 when Congressman David Wilmot (1814–68), a Pennsylvania Democrat, introduced an amendment to a military appropriations bill, known as the Wilmot Proviso, forbidding slavery in any territory acquired from Mexico. The amendment passed the House twice but was defeated in the Senate.

Until December 1848 the issue of slavery in the Mexican cession seemed academic. Most Americans considered the acquired territory a wasteland filled with "broken mountains and dreary desert." Then, in his Farewell Address, Polk electrified Congress with news that gold had been discovered in California—and suddenly the slavery issue was inescapable.

In 1849, eighty thousand people arrived in California, only seven hundred of whom were women. Within a year, California's population had swollen from fourteen thousand to one hundred thousand. California's application for admission to the Union as a free state in 1849 threatened to upset the sectional balance of power in the Senate. If California was admitted as a free state, there would be sixteen free states and only fifteen slave states.

Henry Clay, the "Great Pacificator," once again appealed to Northerners and Southerners to place national patriotism ahead of sectional loyalties. He believed that compromise could be effective only if it addressed all the issues dividing the sections. He proposed that California be admitted as a free state; that territorial governments be established in New Mexico and Utah without any restrictions on slavery; that Texas relinquish claims to land in New Mexico in exchange for federal assumption of Texas's unpaid debts; that Congress enact an enforceable fugitive slave law; and that the slave trade—but not slavery—be abolished in the District of Columbia.

THE COMPROMISE OF 1850

85 / *"What kind of settlement of the slavery question will be made I cannot tell"*

Clay's proposal ignited an eight-month debate in Congress and led John C. Calhoun to threaten southern secession. He warned the North that the only way to save the Union was to "cease the agitation of the slave question," concede "to the South an equal right" to the western territories, return runaway slaves, and accept a constitutional amendment that would protect the South against northern violations of its rights.

Opposition to compromise was fierce. Whig president Zachary Taylor argued that California, New Mexico, Oregon, Utah, and Minnesota should all be admitted to statehood before the slavery question was addressed—a proposal that would have given the North a ten-vote majority in the Senate. In July 1850 northern and southern senators opposed to the very idea of compromise joined ranks to defeat Clay's plan. The following letter reveals just how uncertain the future of Clay's compromise proposals appeared.

David R. Atchison, April 5, 1850, GLC 5574

Calhoun is dead, therefore his want of popularity will be no longer in our way. Our old friend Genl. [Lewis] Cass has been released from his instructions to vote for the Wilmot proviso; indeed that proposition I think is dead. What kind of settlement of the slavery question will be made I cannot tell.

But California will be admitted as a state, governments for the territories without the proviso, a fugitive Slave Bill, etc.

86 / *"The Compromise Bill is not a pro-Slavery measure"*

James Shields (1806–79), who served as a senator for three different states—Illinois, Minnesota, and Missouri—as well as governor of Oregon Territory, once challenged Abraham Lincoln to a duel. In this letter he criticizes the view that the compromise was a proslavery measure.

In June, when Shields wrote this letter, compromise appeared to be dead. Then with unexpected suddenness the outlook abruptly changed. In July 1850 President Taylor died of gastroenteritis, five days after taking part in a Fourth of July ceremony celebrating the building of the still unfinished Washington Monument. Taylor's successor was Millard Fillmore, a fifty-year-old New Yorker who was an ardent supporter of compromise.

In Congress leadership passed to Stephen Douglas (1813–61), a Democratic senator from Illinois. Douglas abandoned Clay's strategy of gathering all issues into a single omnibus bill. Instead he introduced Clay's proposals one at a time. In this way he was able to gather support from varying coalitions of Whigs and Democrats on each issue.

SENATOR JAMES SHIELDS OF ILLINOIS, JUNE 22, 1850, TO JOHN CHATHEN, GLC 3170

I find you fall into a slight error which pervades most of the Northern papers. Clay is not a pro-Slavery man. He is as strongly and certainly as sincerely opposed to the extension of slavery as Col. [Thomas Hart] Benton. The question which divides them, independent of personal views is, whether certain measures which both are for will be passed jointly or severally. You have fallen into a slight mistake on another point. The Compromise Bill is not a pro-Slavery measure. It is opposed most violently by the South, and it will be beat by the South—and not least because they consider it a virtual enactment of the Wilmot provision—as it is—but what will turn up after it is beat God only knows.

87 / *"Read and Ponder the Fugitive Slave Law!"*

The most divisive element in the Compromise of 1850 was the Fugitive Slave Law, which permitted any African American to be seized and sent South solely on the affidavit of anyone claiming to be his or her owner. As a result, free blacks were in danger of being placed in slavery. The law also stripped runaway slaves of the right to a jury trial and the right to testify in their own defense. The law further stipulated that accused runaways stand trial in front of special commissioners, not a judge or a jury, and that the commissioners be paid $10 if a fugitive was returned to slavery but only $5 if the fugitive was freed—a provision that many Northerners regarded as a bribe to ensure that any black accused of being a runaway would be found guilty (the provision was justified by the supposed costs involved). And finally, the law required all U.S. citizens to assist in the capture of escapees.

READ AND PONDER THE FUGITIVE SLAVE LAW!, CA. 1850, GLC 1862

Read and Ponder the Fugitive Slave Law!

Which disregards all the ordinary securities of PERSONAL LIBERTY, which tramples on the Constitution, by its denial of the sacred rights of Trial by Jury, Habeas Corpus, and Appeal, and which enacts, that the Cardinal Virtues of Christianity shall be considered, in the eye of the law, as CRIMES, punishable with the severest penalties,—Fines and Imprisonment....

Sec. 5 And be it further enacted, that it shall be the duty of all marshals and deputy marshals to obey and execute all warrants and precepts issued under the provision of this act, when to them directed; and should any marshal or deputy marshal refuse to receive such warrant...he shall...be fined in the sum of $1,000...and ALL GOOD CITIZENS are hereby commanded to aid and assist in the prompt and efficient execution of this law whenever their services may be required....

Sec. 6. And be it further enacted. That when a person held to service or labor in any State or Territory of the United States has heretofore or shall hereafter escape into another State or Territory...the persons to whom such service or labor may be due...may pursue and retain such fugitive persons, either by procuring a warrant from one of the courts, judges or commissioners...or by seizing and arresting such fugitive, where the same can be done without process, and by taking...such person...before such court, judge or commissioner, whose duty it shall be to hear and determine the case of such claimant in a summary manner, and upon satisfactory proof being made, by disposition or affidavit in writing, to be taken and certified by such court...a certification of such magistrate...shall be SUFFICIENT TO ESTABLISH THE COMPETENCY OF THE PROOF, AND WITH PROOF, ALSO BY AFFIDAVIT, of the identity of the person whose service or labor is claimed to be due.... IN NO TRIAL OR HEARING UNDER THIS ACT SHALL THE TESTIMONY OF SUCH ALLEGED FUGITIVE BE ADMITTED IN EVIDENCE....

Sec. 7. And be it further enacted. That any person who shall knowingly and willingly obstruct, hinder or prevent such claimant, or agent, or attorney, or any person or persons lawfully assisting him...or shall aid, abet, or assist such a person so owning service or labor...directly or indirectly to escape...or SHALL HARBOR or CONCEAL such fugitive...shall, for either of said offences be subject to a fine not exceeding one thousand dollars, and imprisonment not exceeding six months.

88 / *"Live and Die freemen"*

The Fugitive Slave Law kindled widespread outrage in the North and converted thousands of Northerners to the free-soil doctrine that slavery should be barred from the western territories. "We went to bed one night old-fashioned, conservative, compromise, Union Whigs," wrote a Massachusetts factory owner, "and waked up stark mad Abolitionists." Eight northern states attempted to invalidate the law by enacting "personal liberty" laws that forbade state officials from assisting in the return of runaways and extending the right of a jury trial to fugitives.

The free black communities of the North responded defiantly to the 1850 law. Some formed vigilance committees to protect blacks from hired kidnappers who were searching the North for runaways. Some fifteen thousand free blacks, convinced that they could never achieve equality in the United States, immigrated to Canada, the Caribbean, and Africa after the adoption of the Fugitive Slave Law.

In the following selection, Robert C. Nell, a freeman of color in Boston, denounces the Fugitive Slave Law.

Robert C. Nell, "Declaration of Sentiments of the Colored Citizens of Boston on the Fugitive Slave Bill!!!," 1850, GLC 5345

The Fugitive Slave Bill, (exhibited in its hideous deformity at our previous meeting,) has already in hot haste commenced its bloody crusade o'er the land, and the liability of ourselves and families becoming its victims at the caprice of Southern men-stealers, imperatively demands an expression, whether we will tamely submit to chains and slavery, or whether we will, at all and every hazard, Live and Die freemen.

The system of American slavery, the vilest that ever saw the sun, is a violation of every sentiment of Christianity and the antipodes of every dictate of humanity.—The slaveholder's pretention to a claim on human property, are of no more weight than those of the midnight assassin or the pirate on the high seas. "God made all men FREE,—free as the birds that cleave the air or sing in the branches...."

The Massachusetts Bill of Rights declares that ALL MEN are born free and equal, and have certain natural, essential and inalienable rights, among which may be reckoned the right of enjoying and defending their liberties.

The example of the Revolutionary Fathers in resisting British oppression, throwing the tea overboard in Boston Harbor, rather than submit to a three-penny tax, is the most significant one to us, when Man is likely to be deprived of his God-given liberty....

The American people glory in the struggle of 1776, and laud the issues of those who made the bloody resistance to tyranny. The battle cry of Patrick Henry of Virginia—"GIVE ME LIBERTY, OR GIVE ME DEATH"—and that of General Warren, "MY SONS SCORN TO BE SLAVES," are immortalized, and we are proud in not being an exception to that inspiration. It warms our hearts, and will nerve our right arms, to do all and suffer all for Liberty.

The laudation and assistance volunteered by the United States to the Poles and Greeks, and South Americans in their struggles for freedom,—the recent manifestations of sympathy with...the oppressed of Italy, and with Kossuth and his band of noble Hungarians, are so many incentives to the victims of Republican American despotism, to manfully assert their independence, and martyr-like, DIE freemen, rather than LIVE slaves....

Resolved, That in view of the imminent danger, present and looked for, we caution every colored man, woman and child, to be careful in their walks through the highways and byways of the city by day and doubly so, if out at night....

Resolved, That any Commissioner who would deliver up a fugitive slave to a Southern highwayman, under this infamous and unconstitutional law, would have delivered up Jesus Christ to his persecutors for one-third of the price that Judas Iscariot did....

Resolved, That though we gratefully acknowledge that the mane of the British Lion affords a nesting place [in Canada] for our brethren in danger from the claws of the American Eagle, we would, nevertheless, counsel against their leaving the soil of their birth, consecrated by their tears, toils and perils, but yet to be rendered truly, the "land of the free and the home of the brave." The ties of consanguinity, bid ALL remain who would lend a helping hand to the millions now in bonds. But at all events, if the soil of Bunker Hill, Concord and Lexington is the last bulwark of liberty, we can nowhere fill more honorable graves....

89 / *"Momentarily liable to be seized by the strong arm of government"*

Across the North during the 1850s, free blacks staged protests against segregated churches, schools, and public transportation. In New York and Pennsylvania, free blacks launched petition drives for equal voting rights. African churches offered sanctuary to

DECLARATION OF SENTIMENTS

—OF THE—

COLORED CITIZENS OF BOSTON,

ON THE FUGITIVE SLAVE BILL!!!

Per adjournment, the Friends of Freedom rallied at Belknap Street Church, on Friday Evening, October 5th, 1850, a vast concourse, including Fugitives and their Friends were in attendance,—the organization was completed as follows:—

LEWIS HAYDEN, *President.*
JOHN T. HILTON, WILLIAM CRAFTS, HENRY WATSON, *Vice Presidents.*
WILLIAM C. NELL, ISAAC H. SNOWDEN, *Secretaries.*

The President stated that the present was an adjourned meeting from that of last Monday, and trusted the Vigilant Friends had come prepared for definite action on the Fugitive Slave Bill. Though the people were Seventeen Million Strong, he trusted to influences, such as might emanate from these meetings for its Nullification,—the party were now augmenting who knew their rights, and knowing, dare maintain them.

Robert Morris, Esq., called for the Report of the Committee, which was submitted by William C. Nell, as follows:

The Fugitive Slave Bill, (exhibited in its hideous deformity at our previous meeting,) has already in hot haste commenced its bloody crusade o'er the land, and the liability of ourselves and families becoming its victims at the caprice of Southern men-stealers, imperatively demands an expression, whether we will tamely submit to chains and slavery, or whether we will, at all and every hazard, Live and Die freemen.

The system of American slavery, the vilest that ever saw the sun, is a violation of every sentiment of Christianity and the antipodes of every dictate of humanity.—The slaveholder's pretensions to a claim on human property, are of no more weight than those of the midnight assassin or the pirate on the high seas. "God made all men Free,—free as the birds that cleave the air or sing on the branches,—free as the sunshine that gladdens the earth,—free as the winds that sweep over sea and land,—free at his birth,—free during his whole life,—free to-day,—this hour—this moment."

The Massachusetts Bill of Rights declares that ALL MEN are born free and equal, and have certain natural, essential and inalienable rights, among which may be reckoned the right of enjoying and defending their liberties.

The example of the Revolutionary Fathers in resisting British oppression, throwing the tea overboard in Boston Harbor, rather than submit to a three-penny tax, is a most significant one to us, when Man is likely to be deprived of his God-given liberty.

Among the incidents of that seven years' struggle for liberty, and to which the page of impartial history bears record, is the fact that the first Martyr in the attack on residents was a colored man. Crispus Attucks by name, who fell in State Street on the 5th of March, 1770. In that conflict, as also in the war of 1812, colored Americans were devoted and gallant worshippers at Freedom's shrine; and pre-eminently at New Orleans, they were warranted in believing that when the victory was achieved, they, as all who fought should, would be invited to the banquet. But lo! the white man's banquet has been held, and loud peals to liberty have reached the sky above; but the colored American's share has been to stand outside and wait for the crumbs that fell from Liberty's festive board. And to cap the climax at this advanced hour of the nation's prosperity, and the spread over all Christendom of a sentiment of liberty, fraternity and equality, the colored man, woman and child, bond and nominally free, are hunted like partridges on the mountain, if their hearts aspire for freedom.

The American people glory in the struggle of 1776, and laud the names of those who made the bloody resistance to tyranny. The battle cry of Patrick Henry of Virginia—"GIVE ME LIBERTY, OR GIVE ME DEATH,"—and that of General Warren, "MY SONS SCORN TO BE SLAVES," are immortalized, and we are proud in not being an exception to that inspiration. It warms our hearts, and will nerve our right arms, to do all, and suffer all for Liberty.

The laudation and assistance volunteered by the United States to the Poles and Greeks, and South Americans in their struggles for freedom,—the recent manifestations of sympathy with the Blouses of Paris,—the oppressed of Italy, and with Kossuth and his band of noble Hungarians, are so many incentives to the victims of Republican American despotism, to manfully assert their independence, and martyr-like, DIE freemen, rather than LIVE slaves; confirming also, our pre-determined resolution to abide the issue made with us by the slave power—counting our lives not worth preserving at the expense of our liberties.

In connection with what has been previously adopted, the committee would submit the following preamble and resolutions:

Whereas, the Fugitive Slave Bill is unconstitutional, and in direct conflict with the higher law enjoined by our Saviour, "whatsoever ye would that men should do unto you, do you even so to them."

Whereas, from time immemorial, unrighteous enactments have been nullified by all who feared God rather than men; by Moses the deliverer of Israel, against wicked Pharaoh, and Daniel who welcomed incarceration in a den of Lions, rather than perjure his own soul in obedience to the tyrant's mandate.

Whereas, St. Paul expressly declares that he who will not provide for his own household, is an infidel, having denied the faith.

Whereas, the history of nations attest numerous instances where the gallows stake and gibbet have been welcomed when security of life and limb might have been purchased by obedience to inhuman statutes.

Whereas, Thousands in the land from every class and profession in life, without exception, are eagerly registering their vows to oppose this infamous enactment, at whatever cost of money, reputation or life.

Whereas, Sustained as we are, by examples of Mosaic and Christian practice, and from the history of civil society from the earliest ages; encouraged by the voices of our brethren from the East and the West, from the North, and even the tyrant's domain, the bloody South (where many true hearts beat for freedom). But above all, and independent of any suggestions, counsels or examples, guided by our own promptings for the freedom of ourselves and families, (by which we mean, of course, all those in any way exposed to danger from the slave power) and believing that Resistance to tyrants is obedience to God, we are now

Resolved, To organize a League of Freedom, composed of all those who are ready to resist this law, rescue and protect the slave, at every hazard, and who remember that

"Whether on the scaffold high,
Or in the battle's van,
The fittest place where Man can die,
Is where he dies for Man."

Resolved, That in view of the imminent danger, present and looked for, we caution every colored man, woman and child, to be careful in their walks through the highways and byways of the city by day, and doubly so, if out at night, as to WHERE they go—HOW they go—and WHO they go with; to be guarded on side, off side and all sides; as watchful as Argus with his hundred eyes, and as executive as was Briareus, with as many hands; if seized by any one, to make the air resound with the signal-word, and as they would rid themselves of any wild beast, be prompt in their hour of peril.

Resolved, That any Commissioner who would deliver up a fugitive slave to a Southern highwayman, under this infamous and unconstitutional law, would have delivered up Jesus Christ to his persecutors for one-third of the price that Judas Iscariot did.

Resolved, That in the event of any Commissioner of Massachusetts being applied to for remanding a fugitive, we trust he will emulate the example of Judge Harrington, of Vermont, and "be satisfied with nothing short of a bill of sale from the Almighty."

Resolved, That though we learn that bribes have already been offered to our Judiciary to forestall their influence against the panting fugitive, we would not attempt any other effect, than to remind said officers that

"Man is more than Constitutions—
He'd better rot beneath the sod,
Than be true to Church and State
And doubly false to God;"

that should he, in the emergency obey God rather than the devil, by letting the oppressed go free, he will have done his part in wiping out from the escutcheon of Massachusetts the foul stain inflicted by Daniel Webster in promoting, and Samuel A. Eliot in voting for this Heaven-defying law.

Resolved, That though we gratefully acknowledge that the mane of the British Lion affords a nestling place for our brethren in danger from the claws of the American Eagle, we would, nevertheless, counsel against their leaving the soil of their birth, consecrated by their tears, toils and perils, but yet to be rendered truly, the "land of the free and the home of the brave." The ties of consanguinity, bid ALL remain who would lend a helping hand to the millions now in bonds. But at all events, if the soil of Bunker Hill, Concord and Lexington is the last bulwark of liberty, we can nowhere fill more honorable graves.

Resolved, That we do earnestly express the hope that the citizens of Boston will rally in Faneuil Hall, and send forth in the ear of all christendom their opinion of the infamous Fugitive Slave Bill, and of their intention to DISOBEY its decrees; their voice, uttered in the Cradle of Liberty, will assure us as nothing else can, whether they are to be reckoned on the side of liberty or slavery—whether they will vouchsafe to us their aid, or will assist the manthief in hurling us and our little ones into interminable bondage.

Resolved, That this meeting would invite the clergymen in this city and vicinity to dedicate a day or part thereof, in presenting to their people by prayer and sermon, their Christian duty to the flying fugitive, and also in according to requisitions of this atrocious Bill.

Resolved, That as in union is strength, and in this crisis a combination of power is all-important, this meeting recommend the calling of a New England Convention of the friends of Liberty to operate against the Fugitive Law, and to devise ways and means for consolidating their resources here on the soil.

Resolved, That the doings of this and preceding meeting be published for wide circulation.

The report was accepted, and the resolutions adopted by a unanimous vote.

John T. Hilton, in an eloquent and earnest speech advocated the resolutions—remarking that twenty-five years ago he eulogized, as the greatest talent in the country, Daniel Webster for his efforts on Plymouth Rock on the slavery question, and he regretted exceedingly that that talent should have been used in favor of the odious bill. He was no longer to be trusted by the friends of liberty, for he had done more evil, and committed more sin than a thousand such men as the late Professor Webster ever did. This speaker concluded his remarks which were listened to with marked attention, by saying that when his services should be wanted in defence of their rights, he would desire no greater office than to lead them on to battle and to victory.

Joshua B. Smith, hoped no one in that meeting would preach *Peace*, for as Patrick Henry said, "*There is no Peace.*" He narrated with much feeling the increased consternation of his much loved friend—a Fugitive Slave. Since the passage of this infernal bill a near relative of his claimant having been repeatedly seen skulking around his place of business, evidently anticipating the hour of successful seizure, but that he had done his utmost to dispel the agitation of his friend, bidding him at the outset show himself a man,—*If Liberty is not worth fighting for it is not worth having.* He advised every fugitive to arm himself with a revolver—if he could not buy one otherwise to sell his coat for that purpose. As for himself, and he thus exhorted others, he should be kind and courteous to all, even the slave dealer, until the moment of an attack upon his liberty. He should not be taken ALIVE, but upon the slave catcher's head be the consequences. When he could not live here in Boston a FREEMAN, in the language of Socrates, "*He had lived long enough.*" Mr. Smith in conclusion made a demonstration of one mode of defence, which those who best know him say would be exemplified to the *hilt*.

Robert Johnson proclaimed that the meeting was largely composed of ACTORS, and not speakers merely, they were men of over-alls—men of the wharf—those who could do heavy work in the hour of difficulty. He administered a timely caution to the women, who, in pursuit of washing and other work, visited the hotels and boarding houses, that they should be on the constant look-out for the Southern slave catcher or the *Northern accessory*, and as they valued their liberty be prepared for any emergency. [This word to the *wise* women and others, was greeted with lively demonstrations; some remarking that the spirit exhibited by the women some years since, in a slave rescue from the Supreme Court, was yet alive and ready for action.] He would have it a well understood point in our creed of vigilance, in no case to be ourselves the aggressors; in this it was all important to be cautious; we will not go to the depots or elsewhere after the slave hunter, but when he rushes upon our buckler—*kill him.*

Dr. Dan'l Mann spoke of the present state of affairs as affecting us all, white men as well as colored, and detailed many liabilities to which the Fugitive Slave Bill exposed both. He was opposed to war and the spirit of war, but the existing crisis was one that superceded the ordinary, scruples:

"Though space and law the Stag we lend
Ere hound we slip or bow we bend,
Who cares now, WHERE or WHEN
The prowling Fox is trapped or slain!"

R. B. Rogers—would have the Fugitive and his friends remember that it was with the United States Government they were to contend, and that their position in resisting this obnoxious law was that of *Rebels*,—a name however which he did not hesitate to accept, if loyality to the constitution made him false to humanity. He urged the colored people to strive in securing the moral strength of the community in their favor as a potent lever for their enlargement; but would nevertheless assure them that in the event being forced upon them of a personal contest for Liberty, *God was their helper.*

Mr. Garrison—Though a non-resistant himself and determined with the help of God to live and die such, would yet call upon all to be consistent with their own principles, reminding them that William Tell, and George Washington were among the glorious names in the world's annals of patriotic devotion to the shrine of Liberty; but after all, the fugitives in this city and elsewhere would be more indebted to the moral power of public sentiment than by any display of physical resistance. In appreciation of their resolution, invoking the religious sentiment in behalf of the poor fugitive, he would submit an address to the clergy;—its reading was called for and produced a marked sensation upon the meeting, and on motion was unanimously incorporated with the minutes. Mr. Garrison also read an extract from Rev. Henry Ward Beecher's late tribute for the fugitive, pledging himself in a characteristic manner to succor and defend him at every conceivable sacrifice. The applause which this demonstration received would have abundantly convinced its noble hearted author that his proffered aid had not fallen upon ungrateful soil;—many prayers ascended to the fugitives' God, for blessings upon him who would thus commit himself unreservedly for the victims of American Slavery.

Father Hanson—would tell our oppressors that in condemning resistance on the part of the colored people, they were denouncing the examples of Washington and Jefferson, and all Martyrs of Liberty. He concurred with Mr. Garrison and others in a reliance upon moral power, but the meeting well understood that in a crisis for *Liberty or Death*, the speaker would not be quietly led like a lamb to the slaughter.

Charles List, Esq.,—was glad that the fugitives were prepared to defend themselves, and that they solicited a Faneuil Hall meeting of Boston citizens, where they may learn whether their lives and liberties can be secured in the land of the Pilgrim Fathers, or whether men catchers may make hunting grounds of the streets of Boston, driving them at the approach of an inclement season to seek in a foreign land, that safety and refuge from oppression which they cannot find here at home.

Wm. G. Allen being called upon declined in favor of C. C. Briggs, of Vermont, the fugitives' friend, Mr. Briggs responded in thoughts that breathed and words that burned for Liberty; testifying to his pride in being a son of the Green Mountain State, where the sentiments of the people had rendered unnecessary any law relative to slavery. He would yield to no man in efforts to befriend and protect the victim of this inhuman law; and though he would caution all against any injudicious movements by way of resistance, yet he could not but express the opinion that those who would not defend, to the death, their Wives, Sisters and Families from the slave hunter were totally unworthy of a position in civil society.

Rev. Elijah Grisson urged calling upon the Mayor, and police authorities of Boston for defence. [This was generally opposed, knowing that the city officers were not required by the law to arrest the fugitive, and believing that the police force were not at all ambitious of hunting slaves, the appeal was negatived by an overwhelming vote.]

Charles Lenox Remond—having received word of the meeting at his home in Salem left in express haste to be present and though at a late hour, in obedience to a hearty call, gave vent to one of his best efforts; his zeal to reach the meeting, and his liberty inspiring eloquence was loudly and gratefully appreciated. He alluded to the fact that the infamous provisions of the Slave Bill made all colored persons fugitives, imposing on them the necessity of unceasing vigilance. Numbers are nothing in a good cause;

"Thrice armed is he who hath his quarrel just."

The idea of leaving our homes and firesides was in every sense a mistaken one; the Old Bay State should be our Canada. Boston is the Thermopylæ of the anti-slavery cause. Let us be ready in the trial hour to insure its analogy with that classic spot rendered so illustrious by Leonidas and his Spartan Band, or like the more modern but not less significant—Bunker Hill. The history of our country's struggles for Liberty had never been disgraced by a *colored* Arnold; if then we have not proved traitors to the white man, in God's name shall we not prove true to ourselves? He believed that the Fugitive Slave Law had been enacted in great part at the instance of the hand maid of slavery, the Colonization Society in the wicked hope that the fear of being recaptured into bondage would move the colored man to emigrate to Liberia. But this feature only made the whole more damnable, and was to be opposed at all and every point. After rebuking the colored people for lack of anti-slavery character, he declared that he would not yield to any institution or individual that would abridge his liberties or his efforts for the fugitive, and was happy in believing that the colored citizens of Boston would do their whole duty and defend themselves.

Dr. Bowditch moved a general circulation among the masses of the address to the clergy.

The meeting was further addressed by Messrs. Spear, Pierce, Pickett, and others.

On motion the Address to the Clergy was adopted by acclamation and ordered to be published.

After a hymn of Liberty the gathering separated mutually pledging, as did Hannibal, "*Eternal Hostility to Slavery!*"

LEWIS HAYDEN, *President.*
WILLIAM C. NELL, *Secretary.*

Address to the Clergy of Massachusetts.

We, the trembling, prescribed and hunted fugitives from chattel slavery, now scattered through the various towns and villages of Massachusetts, and momentarily liable to be seized by the strong arm of government, and hurried back to stripes, tortures and a bondage, "one hour of which is fraught with more misery than ages of that which your fathers rose in rebellion to oppose,"—most humbly, importunately, and by the mercies of Christ, implore you at this distressing crisis, to "lift up your voices like a trumpet" against the Fugitive Slave Bill, recently adopted by Congress, and designed for our sure and immediate re-enslavement.

You claim, in a special sense, to be witnesses for God — the ambassadors of Him who came to bind up the broken-hearted, to proclaim liberty to the captives, and the opening of the prison to them that are bound. As you would be clear of the blood of all men, it is for you to give to the down-trodden and the oppressed your deepest sympathies, and to hold up to reprobation those who "frame mischief by a law." It is for you to declare the supremacy of the eternal law of God over all human enactments, whether men will hear or forbear.

After years of unrequited labor, of enforced degradation, of unutterable and inconceivable misery, we have succeeded in making our escape from the Southern house of bondage, and are now attempting to lead quiet and peaceable lives in this Commonwealth, and by expanding our faculties and cultivating our moral nature, to "glorify God in our bodies and spirits, which are His." By the recent law of Congress, it is made a highly criminal act to shelter us from the slave-hunter, or to refuse to participate in our capture, at the command of the appointed Commissioners.

Now, therefore, by the solemn injunction of a Christian apostle, "Remember them that are in bonds as bound with them," we implore you, from your pulpits to denounce that iniquitous law!

By the command of Christ, "Whatsoever ye would that men should do to you, do ye even so to them," denounce the law!

By all the horrors and iniquities compressed into that system of slavery, which Wesley has justly styled "the sum of all villainies," denounce the law!

By the cherished memories of Pilgrim Fathers and Revolutionary Sires, denounce the law!

By your warm approval of your country's Declaration of Independence, denounce the law!

By your belief in the scriptural affirmation, that by one God are we all created, and that he "hath made of one blood all nations of men to dwell on all the face of the earth," denounce the law!

By all the woes and warnings pronounced by the prophets against those who refuse to hide the outcast, and bewray him that wandereth—who decree unrighteous decrees, and write grievousness which they have prescribed, to turn aside the needy from judgment—denounce the law!

Thus will you exalt the Christian religion, oppose the mightiest obstacle that stands in the way of human redemption, exert such a moral influence as shall break the rod of the oppressor, secure for yourselves the blessings of those who are ready to perish, and hear the thrilling declaration in the great day of judgment, "Inasmuch as ye did it unto one of the least of these, my brethren, ye did it unto me."

Printed at No. 98 Hanover Street...Boston.

Broadside, Declaration of sentiments of the colored citizens of Boston…, 1850. The Gilder Lehrman Collection, on deposit at the Pierpont Morgan Library. GLC 5345

runaways, and black "vigilance" groups in cities such as New York and Detroit battled slave-catchers who sought to recapture fugitive slaves.

At a meeting of the free persons of color in Boston, former slaves issue an appeal to the clergy of Massachusetts to condemn the Fugitive Slave Law.

DECLARATION OF SENTIMENTS OF THE COLORED CITIZENS OF BOSTON ON THE FUGITIVE SLAVE BILL!!!, 1850, GLC 5345

We, the trembling, prescribed and hunted fugitives from chattel slavery, now scattered through the various towns and villages of Massachusetts, and momentarily liable to be seized by the strong arm of government, and hurried back to stripes, tortures and a bondage, "one hour of which is fraught with more misery than ages of that which your fathers rose in rebellion to oppose,"—most humbly, importunately, and by the mercies of Christ, implore you at this distressing crisis, to "lift up your voices like a trumpet" against the Fugitive Slave Bill, recently adopted by Congress, and designed for our sure and immediate re-enslavement....

After years of unrequited labor, of enforced degradation, of unutterable and inconceivable misery, we have succeeded in making our escape from the Southern house of bondage, and are now attempting to lead quiet and peaceable lives in this Commonwealth, and by expanding our faculties and cultivating our moral nature, to "glorify God in our bodies and spirits, which are His." By the recent law of Congress, it is made a highly criminal act to shelter us from the slave-hunter, or to refuse to participate in our capture, at the command of the appointed Commissioners.

Now, therefore, by the solemn injunction of a Christian apostle, "Remember them that are in bonds as bound with them," we implore you, from your pulpits to denounce that iniquitous law!

90 / "We pour out upon the Fugitive Slave Law the fullest measure of our contempt and hate and execration"

By the 1850s a growing number of Northerners had come to believe that an aggressive southern slave power had seized control of the federal government and threatened to subvert republican principles. Some were convinced that the slave power had dispossessed Indians from their homelands and fomented revolution in Texas and war with Mexico to expand the South's slave empire. At the same time, an increasing number of Southerners believed that antislavery radicals dominated northern politics and would "rejoice" in the race war and racial amalgamation that would surely follow emancipation.

At an anti-Fugitive Slave Law meeting held in 1851 in Syracuse, New York, Gerrit Smith and the famous fugitive slave and abolitionist Frederick Douglass drafted resolutions against the new law.

FREDERICK DOUGLASS AND GERRIT SMITH, ANTI-FUGITIVE SLAVE LAW MEETING, SYRACUSE, NEW YORK, JANUARY 7–9, 1851, 4717.16

1st. Resolved, that we pour out upon the Fugitive Slave Law the fullest measure of our contempt and hate and execration; and pledge ourselves to resist it actively, as well as passively, and by all such means, as shall, in our esteem, promise the most effectual resistance.

2d. Resolved, that they who consent to be the agents of Southern oppressors for executing this law, whether as Commissioners or Marshals, or in any other capacity, are to be regarded as kidnappers and land-pirates.

3d. Resolved, that it is our duty to peril life, liberty, and property, in behalf of the fugitive slave, to as great an extent as we would peril them in behalf of ourselves.

4th. Resolved, that obviously and grossly Unconstitutional as is this Law, nevertheless this is not the chief reason why we condemn and defy it:—for equally, whether they are Constitutional or Unconstitutional, we do condemn and defy all laws, which insult Him, who is above all Constitutions, and which, aiming not to protect, but to destroy, rights, are, therefore, to be regarded as no laws.

5th. Resolved, that horrible as is this law, we must bear in mind, that it is but a perfectly natural and not at all to be wondered at exaction of slavery; and that, hence our first and great work is to get rid, not of the law, but of slavery—as it would be our first and great work to pursue and kill the mad-dog, instead of pausing, until we had effected the cure of one of his bites.

6th. Resolved, that between corrupt politics on the one hand and corrupt churches on the other—between the politicians and parties, who enacted this Law, and the priests who are preaching its enforcement—there is no hope for this Nation, unless it shall very speedily be brought to prefer honesty to knavery, both in its religious teachers and civil rulers.

7th. Resolved, that, were the current religion of this country to be exchanged for rank infidelity, the abolition of slavery would be comparatively easy.

8th. Resolved, that when the immortal writer of the Declaration of Independence said: "If we do not liberate the enslaved by that generous energy of our own minds, they must, they will, be liberated by the awful process" of St. Domingo Emancipation, he uttered words, which there is but too much reason to believe are rapidly approaching their fulfillment.

9th. Resolved, that inasmuch as sound principles and sound teachers are as indispensable in our Institutions of Learning, as in our pulpits, we rejoice to know, that, under the progress of antislavery sentiment, there are already several Colleges in our country, which are opened to colored students; and that there are two of these in which colored students find themselves emphatically at home. There are Oberlin College in Ohio, and Central College in New York—in the latter of which there is a colored Professor.

10th. Resolved, that, inasmuch as every National party in this Nation must, because it is a National party, spare, if not indeed, positively favor, slavery, it follows, that whoever belongs to the Whig or Democratic party, or to any ecclesiastical National party, does, however unwillingly or unwittingly, give his influence and support to slavery.

11th. Resolved, that the time has come, and had long ago come, for gathering a Northern political party, which shall be both determined and able to carry out the principles of the Federal Constitution and the principles of humanity and religion, in overthrowing the base and bloody system of American slavery, and in establishing a righteous Civil Government....

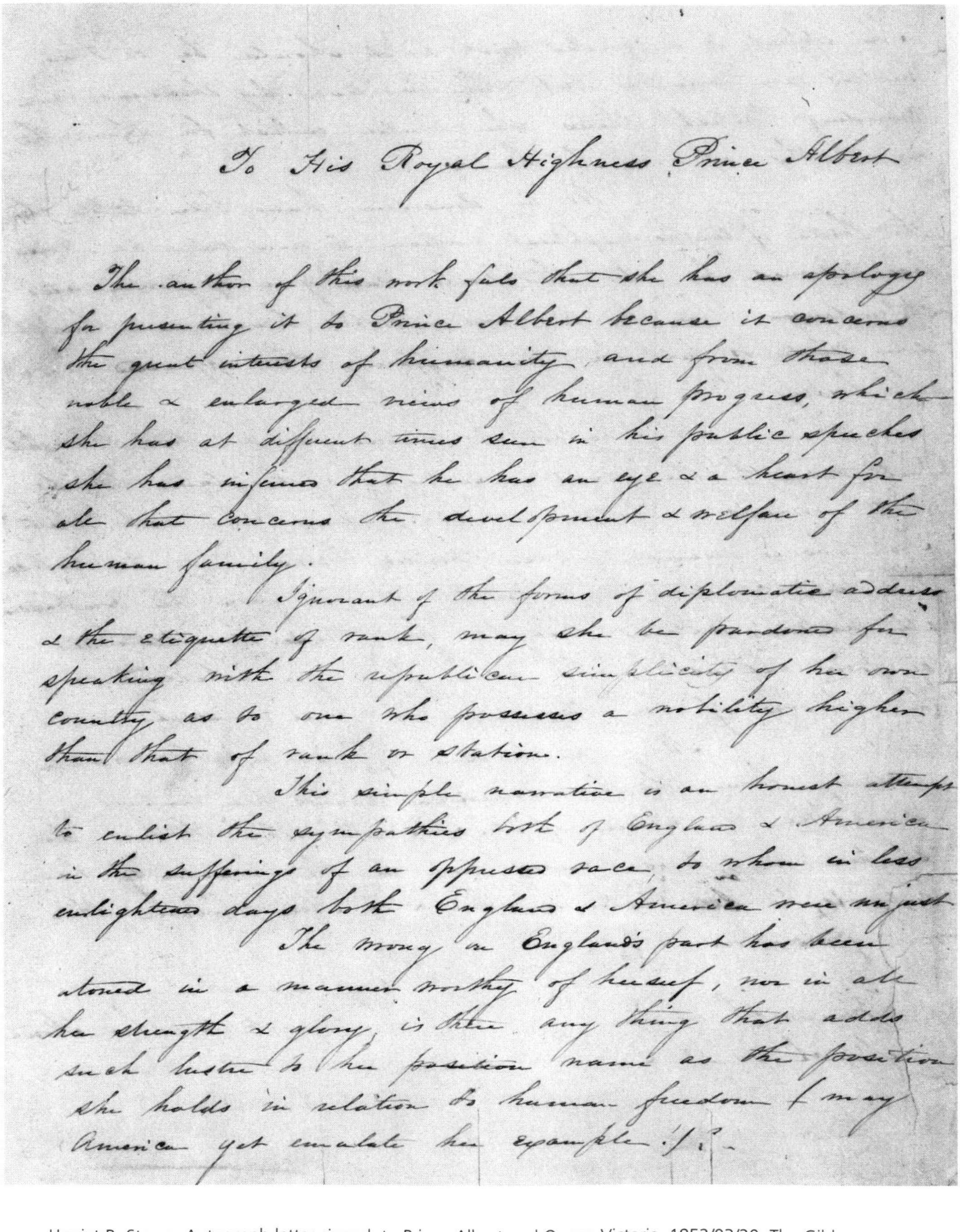
To His Royal Highness Prince Albert

The author of this work feels that she has an apology for presenting it to Prince Albert because it concerns the great interests of humanity, and from those noble & enlarged views of human progress, which she has at different times seen in his public speeches she has inferred that he has an eye & a heart for all that concerns the development & welfare of the human family.

Ignorant of the forms of diplomatic address & the etiquette of rank, may she be pardoned for speaking with the republican simplicity of her own country as to one who possesses a nobility higher than that of rank or station.

This simple narrative is an honest attempt to enlist the sympathies both of England & America in the sufferings of an oppressed race, to whom in less enlightened days both England & America were unjust.

The wrong on England's part has been atoned in a manner worthy of herself, nor in all her strength & glory is there any thing that adds such lustre to her possession name as the position she holds in relation to human freedom (may America yet emulate her example!)

Harriet B. Stowe. Autograph letter signed, to Prince Albert and Queen Victoria, 1852/03/20. The Gilder Lehrman Collection, on deposit at the Pierpont Morgan Library. GLC 1585

91 / *"This simple narrative is an honest attempt to enlist... sympathies...in the sufferings of an oppressed race"*

One northern moderate who was repelled by the Fugitive Slave Law was Harriet Beecher Stowe (1811–96), a forty-one-year-old mother of six from Maine. Stowe had learned about slavery while living in Cincinnati, Ohio, across the Ohio River from slaveholding Kentucky. Her book—one of the first works to show an African American as a hero—placed slavery into a religious framework deeply meaningful to nineteenth-century Americans. The book quickly became one of the best-selling novels of all time.

The novel describes two parallel stories of redemption and deliverance. Tom, who is sold down the river to the brutal Simon Legree, ultimately achieves spiritual salvation, while George and Eliza Harris achieve physical freedom. By awakening Northerners to the fact that slaves suffered just as the ancient Hebrews suffered bondage in Egypt, Stowe created a heightened awareness of slavery's moral evil.

Stowe was a member of one of early nineteenth-century America's most influential families. Her father, Rev. Lyman Beecher (1775–1863), was a major figure in the shift from the established churches of the colonial period to the new era of denominational competition—and from the doctrines of original sin and predestination to new notions of *human agency*, which regarded sin as voluntary rather than predetermined. After the disestablishment of Connecticut's Congregational Church in 1818, Beecher became an advocate of reform and revivals as ways to combat barbarism and infidelity and ensure personal piety and public morality.

On its first day of publication in 1852, Stowe sent a copy of *Uncle Tom's Cabin* to Prince Albert and Queen Victoria. Slavery had been abolished throughout the British Empire in 1833, and Stowe holds Britain up as a model for Americans.

HARRIET BEECHER STOWE, MARCH 20, 1852, TO HIS ROYAL HIGHNESS PRINCE ALBERT, GLC 1585

This simple narrative is an honest attempt to enlist the sympathies of both England & America in the sufferings of an oppressed race, to whom in less enlightened days both England and America were unjust. The wrong on England's part has been atoned in a manner worthy of herself, nor in all her strength & glory, is there any thing that adds such lustre to her name as the position she holds in relation to human freedom (may America yet emulate her example!)[.]

MASS IMMIGRATION

92 / *"Most...who died of ship-fever were delirious"*

During the summer of 1845, a "blight of unusual character" devastated Ireland's potato crop, the basic staple in the Irish diet. A few days after potatoes were dug from the ground, they turned into a slimy, decaying, blackish "mass of rottenness." Dysentery, typhus, and lice soon spread through the countryside. Observers reported seeing children crying with pain, looking "like skeletons." Masses of bodies were buried without coffins, a few inches below the soil.

Over the next ten years, 750,000 Irish died and another 2 million left their homeland. Freighters offered fares as low as $17 between Liverpool and Boston and New York—fares subsidized by English landlords eager to be rid of the starving peasants. In 1847, 40,000—20 percent—of the emigrants perished at sea. "If crosses and tombs could be erected on water," wrote the U.S. commissioner for immigration, "the whole route of the emigrant vessels...would long since have assumed the appearance of a crowded cemetery."

At the beginning of the nineteenth century, just 5,000 immigrants arrived in the United States a year. During the 1840s, 1.7 million immigrants entered the country when harvests all across Europe failed, and reached 2.6 million in the 1850s. Most immigrants came from Ireland, Germany, and Scandinavia, pushed from their homelands by famine, political unrest, and the destruction of traditional handicrafts by factory enterprise, and pulled by the promise of political freedom and economic opportunity. This selection provides a detailed account of an eight-week voyage from Liverpool to New York in the winter of 1847 and 1848.

William Smith, *An Emigrant's Narrative,* 1850

The day advertised for sailing was the 12th of [November 1847], but in consequence of not having got in the cargo, which consisted of pig iron and earthen-ware, we were detained ten days...and one day to stop a leak.... The immigrants...having left Ireland a week, some a fortnight, before the day fixed for sailing, this detention of eleven days was severely felt by those poor creatures, many of them having consumed half of their provisions, without the means of obtaining more.... On Friday, November 26, 1847, we set sail....

[A] storm commenced[;] it rained so heavily the whole day we could not make a fire on deck to cook our victuals with....

About midnight, a number of boxes and barrels broke loose...breaking the water cans and destroying everything capable of being destroyed by them.... In a few minutes the boxes and barrels broke to atoms, scattering the contents in all directions—tea, coffee, sugar, potatoes, pork, shorts, trowsers, vests, coasts, handkerchiefs &c., &c. were mingled in one confused mass. The cries of the women and children was heart-rending; some praying, others weeping bitterly, as they saw their provisions and clothes (the only property they possessed) destroyed. The passengers being sea sick, were vomiting in all parts of the vessel....

We had been at sea four weeks.... I felt sure...that however good the motives were which induced the captain to take a southerly passage, that the dreadful scourge, the ship fever, (which was already on board our ship) would be increased by it; an opinion...verified by the number of cases and deaths increasing....

Most of those who died of ship-fever were delirious, some a day, others only a few hours previous to death....

When we had been at sea a month, the steward discovered the four hogsheads [for water], by oversight or neglect, had not been [filled]. On the following morning...our water was reduced from two quarts to one quart per day for an adult and one pint for a child.... My provisions were consumed, and I had nothing but ship allowance to subsist upon, which was scarcely sufficient to keep us from perishing, being only a pound of sea-biscuit (full of maggots) and a pint of water.... I was seized with the ship-fever; at first I was so dizzy that I could not walk without danger of falling; I was suffering from a violent pain in my head, my brains felt as if they were on fire, my tongue clove to the roof of my mouth and my lips were parched with excessive thirst....

This disastrous voyage...[came] to an end, after an absence of exactly eight weeks from the shores of my native land, (the day we arrived at Staten Island being Friday, the 21st of January, 1848). My whole lifetime did not seem so long as the last two months appeared to me....

William Smith, *An Emigrant's Narrative, or a Voice from the Steerage* (New York: W. Smith, 1850), pp. 1–34

THE KNOW-NOTHINGS AND THE DISINTEGRATION OF THE SECOND-PARTY SYSTEM

93 / *"I am not a Know-Nothing"*

As late as 1850 the two-party system was, to all outward appearances, still healthy. Both the Democrats and the Whigs were able to attract support in every section, and neither party was able to win more than 53 percent of the presidential vote. Then, in the space of just five years, the two-party system disintegrated in response to two issues: foreign immigration and the reemergence of the issue of slavery expansion.

A massive wave of immigration from Ireland and Germany after 1845 led to an outburst of antiforeign and anti-Catholic sentiment. Between 1846 and 1855 three million foreigners arrived in America. Nativists—ardent opponents of immigration—capitalized on deep-seated Protestant antagonism toward Catholics and working-class fear of economic competition from cheaper immigrant labor. Nativists charged that Catholics were responsible for a sharp increase in poverty, crime, and drunkenness, and were subservient to a foreign leader, the pope.

In 1849, native-born Protestant workingmen formed a secret fraternal organization, "The Order of the Star-Spangled Banner," which became the nucleus of a new political party known as the Know-Nothing Party or the American Party. The party received its name from the fact that, when members were asked about the party's workings, they were supposed to reply, "I know nothing."

The Know-Nothings attracted support not only from nativists but also from large numbers of northern free soilers and southern Whigs. By 1855 the party had captured control of all New England except Vermont and Maine and was the dominant opposition party to the Democrats in New York, Pennsylvania, Maryland, Virginia, Tennessee, Georgia, Alabama, Mississippi, and Louisiana. The party platform included a twenty-one-year residency period before immigrants could become citizens and vote, limitations on officeholding to native-born Americans, and restrictions on the sale of liquor.

One Northerner who spoke out against the Know-Nothings was Abraham Lincoln, who eloquently argued that the party's nativist platform was a violation of the country's republican principles.

Abraham Lincoln, letter to Joshua F. Speed, August 24, 1855

I am not a Know-Nothing. How could I be? How can any one who abhors the oppression of Negroes be in favor of degrading classes of white people? Our progress in degeneracy appears to me pretty rapid. As a nation we began by declaring "all men are created equal." We now practically read it, "all men are created equal, except Negroes." When the Know-Nothings get control, it will read "all men are created equal, except Negroes, and foreigners, and Catholics." When it comes to this I should prefer emigrating to some country where they make no pretense of loving liberty—to Russia, for example, where despotism can be taken pure and without the base alloy of hypocrisy.

The *Writings of Abraham Lincoln,* ed. Arthur Brooks Lapsley (New York: G.P. Putnam, 1905), Vol. II, pp. 242–47.

94 / *"We work now to overturn the Slave-Power"*

By 1856 the Know Nothing Party was in decline. Northern workers felt more threatened by the slave power than by the pope and Catholic immigrants, while fewer Southerners were willing to support a party that ignored the expansion of slavery. Nevertheless, the Know-Nothings left an indelible mark on American politics. The movement eroded loyalty to the national political parties, fatally weakened the Whig Party, and undermined the political system's capacity to contain the divisive issue of slavery.

In this letter, Salmon P. Chase (1808–73), a leading Ohio politician, argues that opponents of slavery must ensure that their cause is not neutralized or deflected by the Know-Nothing movement.

Salmon P. Chase, January 26, 1856, to Judge A. Lankey Latty, GLC 11

We work now to overturn the Slave-Power. For that we want the Union of all Liberty loving men, native or foreign born. While engaged in that work there can be no proscription. When that work shall be accomplished either there will be no proscribers or they will be powerless for evil. At this moment I believe that there are few of the Americans who went with us last fall, who desire any extension of the naturalization terms or who would not readily and zealously sustain any good man for office of real Republican principles without reference to the accident of birth.

AMERICA AT MIDCENTURY

So much stress is placed on the deepening sectional conflict during the late 1840s and early 1850s that it is easy to forget that other important events were occurring simultaneously. Take, for example, the year 1848. Not only was this the year that the Treaty of Guadalupe Hidalgo ended the Mexican War, increasing the nation's size by a third, it was also a year of tremendous immigration from Ireland and Germany; the year that the first women's rights convention was held, at Seneca Falls, New York; and the year that gold was discovered at Sutter's Mill in California.

Other events were also taking place at midcentury that carried far-reaching implications for the future. A series of scientific breakthroughs occurred in about 1848: the development of symbolic logic in mathematics and the discoveries of valency in chemistry, of germ transmission in physiology, and of the principle of conservation of energy in thermodynamics. This period also saw stunning technological innovations, including the vulcanization of rubber, the invention of the Bessemer process for manufacturing steel, and the development of the first synthetic dyes and practical calculating machines. The mid-nineteenth century also witnessed profound innovations in political thinking. In 1848 John Stuart Mill published his *Treatise on Political Economy*, a classic statement of modern liberal principles; Herbert Spencer published *Social Statics*, which anticipated Social Darwinist thinking; and Karl Marx and Friedrich Engels issued the *Communist Manifesto*. Most important of all, in terms of biological science and human self-understanding, Charles Darwin worked throughout the 1850s perfecting his revolutionary *Origins of Species*, which he finally published in 1859. The outlines of the major political, economic, and philosophical controversies of the next century were already becoming apparent.

The mid-nineteenth century marked a scientific, technological, and intellectual watershed. In Europe and the United States there was mounting anxiety over which groups would benefit from the tremendous increases taking place in economic productivity and wealth. Across Europe, 1848 was a year of revolution, "the springtime of peoples." Yet most of the revolutionary uprisings of that year were violently suppressed, making 1848 "the turning point where Europe did not turn." The failure of revolutionary change ensured that economic modernization would take place within the context of existing nationalistic rivalries and the old social order. A key question facing the United States at midcentury was whether the plantation South—like the European aristocracy—would share equally in the nation's economic and territorial growth.

At the risk of oversimplification, it is possible to identify three fundamental social and economic processes that were transforming Western societies at midcentury. One involved the economic and political integration of frontier regions into expanding nation-states. In Argentina, Australia, Russia, South Africa, and the American West, one sees simultaneous efforts to explore, conquer, and settle frontier regions, efforts that entailed the wholesale removal or even extermination of aboriginal peoples.

A second fundamental process involved basic shifts in the recruitment and deployment of labor. Throughout the Western world, archaic forms of labor, including New World slavery and Eastern European serfdom, came under attack as morally and economically retrogressive. Britain abolished slavery in its colonies in 1833, and France and Denmark followed in 1848. By midcentury, New World slavery was confined to Brazil, Cuba, Puerto Rico, several small Dutch colonies, and the American South. Efforts to eradicate the Atlantic slave trade were intensifying.

A third key transformation involved the extension across the Western world of the agricultural and industrial revolutions that had begun in Britain. During the mid-nineteenth century, the modernization of agriculture pushed tens of millions of peasants and farmers off the land and into the booming industrial cities in Europe and across the oceans to Australia, Argentina, Brazil, Chile, and the United States.

What is distinctive about American history is that each of these processes occurred within the same national boundaries simultaneously. The intersection of these three processes carried profound political ramifications. For example, the influx of millions of Catholic immigrants from Ireland and Germany disrupted the political system and made it less capable of containing the explosive issue of slavery. Meanwhile, in the face of mounting criticism that slavery was economically and morally backward, southern slaveholders were eager to vindicate slavery as a progressive and Christian institution.

For both slaveholders and a growing number of Northerners, the western frontier became the testing ground for conflicting visions of America's destiny and mission. For many eastern workers, the West was a prime symbol of opportunity. However unrealistic pioneering might be in practice, a free-labor West was a symbol that wage laborers could move westward and start over. For southern slaveholders, the West was a potent symbol of whether the South would share in the nation's growth. The West was also the key to southern political power. If slavery failed to expand westward, then the South would lose its political leverage and would become, in one southern politician's words, "the inferior, the Bondsman in fact, of the North."

REVIVAL OF THE SLAVERY ISSUE

95 / *"The Democrats are undisguised open servants of the slave-power"*

In 1854 Congress passed legislation that reordered the political landscape. The Kansas-Nebraska Act revived the issue of slavery's expansion, divided the Democratic Party, destroyed the Whig Party, and created the Republican Party. Ironically, the author of this legislation was Senator Stephen A. Douglas, the man who had pushed the Compromise of 1850 through Congress and sworn that he would never make another speech on the slavery question.

Douglas proposed that the area west of Iowa and Missouri, which had been set aside as a permanent Indian reservation, be opened to white settlement and to the eventual construction of a transcontinental railroad based in Chicago. Douglas had sought this objective since 1844, but southern congressmen had objected because this territory was located in the northern half of the Louisiana Purchase, where the Missouri Compromise prohibited slavery. To forestall southern opposition, Douglas's bill ignored the Missouri Compromise and provided that the slavery issue be resolved by "popular sovereignty." When the territory was admitted to statehood, it could enter the Union "with or without slavery" as its "constitution may prescribe."

Southern senators insisted that Douglas add a clause specifically repealing the Missouri Compromise. Douglas relented. In its final form, his bill created two territories, Kansas and Nebraska, and declared the Missouri Compromise "inoperative and void." With solid support from southern Whigs and Democrats and the votes of half of the northern Democrats, the measure passed.

In this letter, Gerrit Smith mistakenly concludes that the Whigs will benefit from the act. In fact, its passage radically realigned party support. In both the North and the

South, conservative Whigs joined the Democrats, while Whigs and Democrats with free-soil sentiments repudiated their elected representatives. The chief beneficiary of these defections was a new political organization, the Republican Party.

GERRIT SMITH, NOVEMBER 1, 1854, TO WILLIAM GOODELL, GLC 4717.20

What a godsend to the Whigs was the Nebraska bill! All of them in the free States arrayed themselves against it. This was, it is true, a cheap way of making themselves abolitionists. But, that it made them really such was what they insisted on, in the ears of the credulous and silly abolitionists. I am sorry that I have to call them credulous and silly. But, alas, too many have proved themselves to be such. The Whigs now claimed with more plausibility and effect than ever, that no other antislavery organization than the Whig party is necessary; and that this party is clearly entitled to the votes of all who sympathize with the slave.... But in that mass there is a very radical little handful, who are slow to believe in the abolition character of Whig party, even after all that the Nebraska occasion has done to improve such character. They are slow to attribute a genuine abolition to the party, that insulted and vilified them, because they would not vote for the slaveholder, Henry Clay; to the party, that elected the slaveholder, General Taylor; to the party, whose Millard Fillmore signed the diabolical fugitive slave bill....

I would say, in this connexion, that I think no better of the Democrats than I do of the Whigs. The Democrats are undisguised open servants of the slave-power: and, hence, I need say nothing to guard abolitionists against seductive and misleading influences, in that quarter....

96 / *"This state can be made certain for Frémont"*

No previous piece of legislation passed by Congress had more far-reaching political consequences than the Kansas-Nebraska Act. The act's opponents denounced it as "a gross violation of a sacred pledge" and part of a secret plot "to exclude from a vast unoccupied region, immigrants from the Old World and free laborers from our own States, and convert it into a dreary region of despotism inhabited by masters and slaves."

In almost every northern state, protest groups joined together and adopted the name "Republican." A combination of diverse elements, the Republican Party favored the exclusion of slavery from the western territories. It contained antislavery radicals, free soilers, political abolitionists, Whigs, Jacksonian Democrats, nativists opposed to foreign immigration, and antislavery immigrants.

In the fall of 1854 the new party contested congressional elections for the first time and won 46 seats in the House of Representatives. It included a number of men, such as William H. Seward (1801–72) of New York, who believed that African Americans should receive full civil rights, including the right to vote. But the new party also attracted many individuals like Abraham Lincoln, who favored African-American colonization as the only workable solution to slavery. Despite their differences, all these factions believed that the western territories should be saved for free labor.

In June 1856 the Republican Party held its first national convention, in Philadelphia, nominating the dashing young explorer and Mexican War hero John C.

Frémont (1813–90) for president. A romantic figure who had led more than a dozen major explorations of the Rocky Mountains and the Far West, he had played a critical role in refuting the myth that the West was a "great American desert," "wholly unfit for cultivation." Instead he had depicted the West as a paradise of plenty.

In the presidential campaign, the Democrats described Frémont as a "black abolitionist" who would destroy the Union, while Know-Nothings called him a "papist" (since his wife was Catholic and he sent his children to a Catholic school). Despite these attacks, the Republicans made an extraordinarily impressive showing. Eleven free states voted for Frémont. If only two more states had voted in his favor, the Republicans would have won their first campaign in a presidental election.

Gideon Welles, an organizer of the Republican Party and editor of the Republican newspaper the *Hartford Evening Press*, later served as secretary of the navy under Presidents Lincoln and Johnson. In this letter he discusses Frémont's prospects in the 1856 campaign against the Democrat James Buchanan and the Know-Nothing Millard Fillmore. "Free labor, free soil, free men, Frémont" was the Republican slogan.

Gideon Welles, July 12, 1856, to James F. Babcock, GLC 2128

Whatever of good was to be accomplished by the American party [the Know-Nothings] has been effected, and it has ceased to be useful. I have no idea that it has ever been so formidable in numbers as has been generally supposed; but of those who have been connected with it, a very long proposition, in my opinion four-fifths, wish the whole thing abandoned.... It is mortifying and disgraceful to witness our state [Connecticut] put in jeopardy by the offensive & narrow exclusiveness of these feeble, mischief makers—feeble in mind and feeble in numbers.

If our papers would take a firm and manly stand, the whole difficulty would be ended. It is not necessary to attack them, or have any controversy with them but to ignore them.

The truth is, most of the papers that have connected themselves with the American party have lost, in a degree, their independence, and are afraid to offend even the abuses of the order. But the order is no longer formidable, and would pass into insignificance but for the press over which they exercise this arbitrary control. The few leaders...humbug the public, making the editors the servile tools of their mischievous purposes....

This state can be made certain for Frémont, and placed in a condition to sustain the cause of freedom for years, unless prevented by the bad conduct of the few leaders of the American party, who in their selfish purposes, would sacrifice the great principles in issue.... The time is short—the season is busy—no efficient organization can be perfected, and the cause is embarrassed & put in jeopardy to gratify Americans, at the expense and on the popularity of the rising feeling for Frémont & the cause. The people are not with them—public sentiment is disregarded—and they could do nothing, if the public press was faithful to public opinion, instead of being subservient to the little intriguers who are trifling with great questions and grave subjects....

My impression is that a general convention of all "the friends of Frémont and Freedom" should be called....

97 / *"The people of Kansas...are suffering at the hands of the Federal Administration and the Missouri ruffians"*

Because the Kansas-Nebraska Act stated that the future status of slavery in the territories would be decided by popular vote, antislavery Northerners and proslavery Southerners competed to win the region for their own section. Since Nebraska was too far north to attract slaveowners, Kansas became the arena of sectional conflict. For six years, proslavery and antislavery factions fought in Kansas as popular sovereignty degenerated into violence.

Even before the 1854 act passed, Eli Thayer (1819–99), a Worcester, Massachusetts, businessman, organized the New England Emigrant Aid company to promote migration of New Englanders to Kansas to "vote to make it free." Alarmed by rumors that the Emigrant Aid Society had raised $5 million to make Kansas a haven for runaway slaves, proslavery Missourians formed "Sons of the South" to "repel the wave of fanaticism which threatens to break upon our border."

In May 1855 Kansas held a territorial election. Although only fifteen hundred men were registered to vote, six thousand ballots were cast, many by proslavery "border ruffians" from Missouri. As a result, a proslavery legislature was elected. This body passed laws stipulating that only proslavery men could hold public office or serve as jurors and imposed five years' imprisonment on anyone questioning the legality of slavery in Kansas.

Free soilers called the election a fraud and held their own convention, which drew up a constitution prohibiting slavery in Kansas and barring free blacks from the territory. When Congress convened in January 1856, it was confronted by two rival governments in Kansas. President Franklin Pierce threw his support behind the proslavery legislature and asked Congress to admit Kansas as a slave state.

In a speech, Gerrit Smith discusses the New England Emigrant Aid Society and the efforts of free soilers to make Kansas a free territory.

Gerrit Smith, March 13, 1856, Kansas meeting, Albany, New York, GLC 4717.25

I deeply regret that Mr. [Eli] Thayer...has not yet arrived. He is the President of the New England Emigrant Aid Society.... I have, since coming into this Hall, been permitted to read a communication...just received from Missouri. We learn from this communication, that they have actually begun to organize Emigrant Aid Societies in that State also. But how different are they from the New England Society! A Missouri Society offers a large bounty to those, who will become actual inhabitants of Kansas, provided expressly however that they are "proslavery." The New England Society, on the contrary, gives no bounty to any. It gives information and advice impartially to all, who wish to emigrate to Kansas, and it builds mills and hotels in Kansas for the equal accommodation of all, be they proslavery or antislavery. Surely it is with an ill grace, that they, who see nothing wrong in one of these Missouri Societies, should impute officiousness and unfairness to the New England Society.

But to my society. I will say nothing just now of the repeal of the Missouri Compromise, except to say, that the repeal was very perfidious and very wicked. And but little need be said on this occasion of the doctrine of "squatter sovereignty." That doctrine is absurd, because inasmuch as a Territory belongs to the whole people of the United States, they the whole people are bound to govern it. It is not competent for them to abdicate, and to leave to a handful what belongs to all....

The people of Kansas went to that surpassingly fertile and beautiful portion of the earth to find homes for themselves.—They then undertook to make a government for themselves. But a parcel of unmitigated and desperate scoundrels in Missouri...were determined, that the people of Kansas should not make a government for themselves. They, these scoundrels, would make it for them. Accordingly they marched into Kansas. I say marched—for, in many cases, they entered Kansas in a military conquering style, with drums beating and flags flying. They took possession of the ballot-boxes, and elected whom they would. Instead of a Kansas government, a Missouri or border ruffian government was set up in Kansas. That a government, brought into being in this way, should enact the most diabolical and infamous statutes, is not to be wondered at. A specimen of these statutes is that, which makes it a penitentiary offence to express an opinion against the rightfulness of slaveholding. The border ruffians now insisted, that the people of Kansas should obey these statutes, and be loyally subject to the government, which had been forced upon them. The people of Kansas could but refuse. To have yielded would have been to prove themselves to be little less base than their oppressors. It was now, that these oppressors marched an army into Kansas to enforce subjection. But...their whiskey gave out—and with it their courage. Moreover, what they heard of a new kind of rifle in the hands of the brave men of Kansas—a kind invented by one Sharp—produced a great quaking among them. At any rate, so it was, that they marched back again. All this time the Federal Administration—the powers at Washington—had done nothing, and said nothing, openly. Beyond doubt, however, they were all this time countenancing and encouraging the outrages, of which we have spoken. And now when the terror-stricken border ruffians had fallen back, the Administration came forward with its messages, and proclamations, and threats. I will not say, that it came forward to embolden the ruffians to a fresh invasion; nor to take their place: but I will say, that it came forward to do their work—the work of compelling submission to this foreign and ruffian people to govern themselves—even the handful that might be scattered over a broad National territory. In their eyes the chief glory of the Nebraska Bill was this doctrine. But now this slavery-serving Administration trampled this doctrine under foot, and utterly repudiated in practice what it had so ardently clung to in theory. For now it demanded in the name of all the military power of the nation, that the people of Kansas should submit to a government, not chosen by themselves, but forced upon them by others....

Such then is the unhappy condition to which the people of Kansas are reduced—such the wrongs, which they are suffering at the hands of the Federal Administration and the Missouri ruffians. And the sole terms on which these combined powers will consent to let the people of Kansas remain in Kansas—nay, will consent to let them live—is that they shall acknowledge this impudent and abominable despotism, which has been set up on their soil, and that they shall pollute their souls by perjury, and debase and extinguish their manhood by submitting to whatever their oppressors may lay upon them....

BLEEDING KANSAS

98 / *"We feel more, & more certain that Kansas will be a Free State"*

In Kansas, violence broke out over rival land claims, town sites, railroad routes, and, most dangerous of all, the question of slavery. In one episode, a proslavery grand jury indicted members of the free-soil government for high treason, and eight hundred proslavery men marched into Lawrence, Kansas, to arrest the leaders of the antislavery government. The posse burned the local hotel, looted a number of houses, destroyed two antislavery printing presses, and killed one man.

John Brown (1800–1859), a Connecticut-born abolitionist, announced that the time had come "to fight fire with fire" and "strike terror in the hearts of proslavery men." In reprisal for the "sack of Lawrence," he and six companions dragged five proslavery men and boys from their beds at Pottawatomie Creek, Kansas, split open their skulls with a sword, cut off their hands, and laid out their entrails.

A war of revenge erupted in Kansas. Columns of proslavery Southerners ransacked free farms while they searched for Brown. At Osawatomie, proslavery forces attacked Brown's headquarters, leaving a dozen men dead. Before it was over, guerrilla warfare in Kansas left two hundred dead.

Six months after leaving for Kansas and six months before the attack at Pottawatomie Creek, John Brown wrote the following letter to his father, describing the deepening crisis over slavery in Kansas.

> JOHN BROWN, DECEMBER 5, 1855, TO HIS FATHER, OWEN BROWN, GLC 2454
>
> I feel very thankful for the interest you *still take* in the different members of my numerous Family, & for all your efforts to do them good in things *spiritual & temporal*.... As I become a little more acquainted with this part of the Territory I think quite favorably of it; & I would by no means advise those of my friends who are here to leave in search of a better country. We feel more, & more certain that Kansas will be a Free State. At this moment there is quite an excitement here growing out of a report of the Murder of a young Free Stater man by a Missourian. Large numbers on *both sides* are said to be in Arms near Lawrence; & some anticipate a Bloody fight. We do not seem to get direct information of the true state of matters there; & I think of going immediately there to learn the facts in the case. The distance is about 35 Miles. I will endeavour to give you a more full account of the matter; if there should be much of it. I have no time fixed in my own mind as yet *for my return*; & have no thought of leaving before some time in the Spring....

BLEEDING SUMNER

99 / *"The liberty of white as well as black...will become a name only"*

On May 19, 1856 two days before the "sack of Lawrence"—Senator Charles Sumner (1811–74) of Massachusetts began a two-day speech in which he denounced "The Crime Against Kansas." Sumner charged that there was a southern conspiracy to make Kansas a slave state, and proceeded to argue that a number of southern senators, including

Andrew Butler (1796–1857) of South Carolina, stood behind this conspiracy. Launching into a bitter personal diatribe, Sumner accused the elderly Senator Butler of taking "the harlot, Slavery," for his "mistress."

Two days later, Butler's nephew, Congressman Preston Brooks (1819–57) of South Carolina, entered a nearly empty Senate chamber determined to "avenge the insult to my State." Sighting Sumner at his desk, Brooks charged at him and began striking the Massachusetts senator over the head with a cane. He swung repeatedly and so hard that the cane broke into pieces.

Although it took Sumner three years to fully recover from his injuries and return to his Senate seat, he promptly became a martyr to the cause of freedom in the North, where a million copies of his "Crime Against Kansas" speech were distributed. In the South, Brooks was hailed as a hero. Merchants in Charleston bought the congressman a new gold-headed cane, inscribed "Hit him again." A vote to expel Brooks from Congress failed because every southern representative but one voted against the measure. Instead, Brooks was censured. He promptly resigned his seat and was immediately reelected.

While recuperating from head injuries, Sumner wrote the following note describing his belief that the slave power was seeking to make slavery a national institution.

SENATOR CHARLES SUMNER, DECEMBER 20, 1856, TO HENRY E. REES, GLC 1574.02

> You are right in your present sentiments against slavery. Unless this atrocious interest is checked the liberty of white as well as black in our country will become a name only.

THE DRED SCOTT DECISION

100 / "The right of property in a slave is distinctly and expressly affirmed in the Constitution"

In March 1857, the U.S. Supreme Court answered a question that Congress had evaded for decades: whether Congress had the power to prohibit slavery in the territories. The case originated in 1846, when a Missouri slave, Dred Scott, sued to gain his freedom. Scott argued that while he had been the slave of an army surgeon he had lived for four years in Illinois, a free state, and Wisconsin, a free territory, and that his residence on free soil had erased his slave status.

All nine justices rendered separate opinions, but Chief Justice Roger B. Taney (1777–1864) delivered the opinion that expressed the position of the court's majority. His opinion represented a judicial defense of the most extreme proslavery position. The chief justice made two sweeping rulings. The first was that Scott had no right to sue in federal court because neither slaves *nor* free blacks were citizens of the United States. At the time the Constitution was adopted, the chief justice wrote, blacks had been "regarded as beings of an inferior order" with "no rights which the white man was bound to respect." (In fact, some states did recognize free blacks as taxpayers and citizens at the time the Constitution was adopted.)

Second, Taney declared that any law excluding slaves from the territories was a violation of the Fifth Amendment prohibition against the seizure of property without due process of law. The Missouri Compromise was unconstitutional, he announced, because it prohibited slavery in the Louisiana Purchase north of 36° 30'.

The Dred Scott decision was a major political miscalculation. In its ruling, the Court sought to solve the slavery controversy once and for all. Instead, the Court intensified sectional strife, undercut possible compromise solutions to the issue of slavery's expansion, and weakened the moral authority of the judiciary.

Roger B. Taney, Dred Scott Decision, 1857, GLC 1259

Mr. Chief Justice Taney delivered the opinion of the Court....

In the opinion of the Court the legislation and histories of the times, and the language used in the Declaration of Independence, show that neither the class of persons who had been imported as slaves nor their descendants, whether they had become free or not, were then acknowledged as a part of the people nor intended to be included in the general words used in that memorable instrument....

They had for more than a century before been regarded as beings of an inferior order and altogether unfit to associate with the white race, either in social or political relations; and so far inferior that they had no rights which the white man was bound to respect; and that the Negro might justly and lawfully be reduced to slavery for his benefit. He was bought and sold and treated as an ordinary article of merchandise and traffic whenever a profit could be made by it. This opinion was at that time fixed and universal in the civilized portion of the white race....

No one, we presume, supposes that any change in public opinion or feeling, in relation to this unfortunate race, in the civilized nations of Europe or in this country should induce the Court to give to the words of the Constitution a more liberal construction in their favor than they were intended to bear when the instrument was framed and adopted....

And upon a full and careful consideration of the subject, the Court is of the opinion that, upon the facts stated in the plea in abatement, Dred Scott was not a citizen of Missouri within the meaning of the Constitution of the United States and not entitled as such to sue in its courts....

We proceed...to inquire whether the facts relied on by the plaintiff entitle him to his freedom....

The act of Congress, upon which the plaintiff relies, declares that slavery and involuntary servitude, except as a punishment for crime, shall be forever prohibited in all that part of the territory ceded by France, under the name of Louisiana, which lies north of thirty-six degrees thirty minutes north latitude and not included within the limits of Missouri. And the difficulty which meets us...is whether Congress was authorized to pass this law under any of the powers granted to it by the Constitution....

As there is no express regulation in the Constitution defining the power which the general government may exercise over the person or property of a citizen in a territory thus acquired, the Court must necessarily look to the provisions and principles of the

Constitution, and its distribution of powers, for the rules and principles by which its decisions must be governed.

Taking this rule to guide us, it may be safely assumed that citizens of the United States who migrate to a territory...cannot be ruled as mere colonists, dependent upon the will of the general government, and to be governed by any laws it may think proper to impose....

For example, no one, we presume, will contend that Congress can make any law in a territory respecting the establishment of religion...or abridging the freedom of speech or of the press....

These powers, and others...are...denied to the general government; and the rights of private property have been guarded with equal care....

An act of Congress which deprives a citizen of the United States of his liberty or property, without due process of law, merely because he came himself or brought his property into a particular territory of the United States...could hardly be dignified with the name of due process of law.

The powers over person and property of which we speak are not only not granted to Congress but are in express terms denied and they are forbidden to exercise them.... And if Congress itself cannot do this...it could not authorize a territorial government to exercise them....

It seems, however, to be supposed that there is a difference between property in a slave and other property....

Now...the right of property in a slave is distinctly and expressly affirmed in the Constitution. The right to traffic in it, like an ordinary article of merchandise and property, was guaranteed to the citizens of the United States, in every state that might desire it, for twenty years. And the government in express terms is pledged to protect it in all future time if the slave escapes from his owner. This is done in plain words—too plain to be misunderstood. And no word can be found in the Constitution which gives Congress a greater power over slave property or which entitles property of that kind to less protection than property of any other description....

Upon these considerations it is the opinion of the Court that the act of Congress which prohibited a citizen from holding and owning property of this kind in the territory of the United States north of the line therein mentioned is not warranted by the Constitution and is therefore void; and that neither Dred Scott himself, nor any of his family, were made free by being carried into this territory; even if they had been carried there by the owner with the intention of becoming a permanent resident.

THE GATHERING STORM

In 1858 Senator William H. Seward (1801–72) of New York examined the sources of the sectional conflict. Some people, he said, thought the conflict was "accidental, unnecessary, the work of interested or fanatical agitators, and therefore ephemeral." He believed that these people were wrong. The roots of the conflict went far deeper. "It is an irrepressible conflict," Seward declared, "between opposing and enduring forces."

As the 1850s closed, the dominant question of American political life was whether the nation's leaders could find a peaceful way to resolve sectional differences.

101 / *"The value of all the property...in seven slave States... is less than the real and personal estate...in...New York"*

In 1857 Hinton Rowan Helper (1829–1909), the son of a western North Carolina farmer, published one of the most politically influential books ever written by an American, *The Impending Crisis of the South*. The book argued that slavery was incompatible with economic progress. Using statistics drawn from the 1850 census, Helper maintained that by every measure the North was growing far faster than the South and that slavery was the cause of the South's economic backwardness.

Helper's thesis was that slavery was inefficient and wasteful, that it impoverished the South, degraded labor, inhibited urbanization, thwarted industrialization, and stifled progress. A rabid racist, Helper accompanied his call for abolition with a demand for colonization. He concluded with a call for nonslaveholders to overthrow the South's planter elite. During the 1860 presidential campaign, the *New York Tribune* distributed five hundred copies of the book a day, considering it the most effective propaganda against slavery ever written. Many Southerners burned it, fearful that it would divide the white population.

HINTON ROWAN HELPER, *The Impending Crisis of the South*, 1857, GLC 267.074

The value of all the property, real and personal, including slaves, in seven slave States, Virginia, North Carolina, Tennessee, Missouri, Arkansas, Florida, and Texas, is less than the real and personal estate, which is unquestionably property, in the single state of New York. Nay, worse; if eight entire slave States, Arkansas, Delaware, Florida, Maryland, Missouri, Mississippi, Tennessee and Texas, and the District of Columbia—with all their hordes of human merchandise—were put up at auction, New York could buy them all, and then have one hundred and thirty-three millions of dollars left in her pocket! Such is the amazing contrast between freedom and slavery, even in a pecuniary point of view. When we come to compare the North with the South in regard to literature, general intelligence, inventive genius, moral and religious enterprises, the discoveries in medicine, and the progress in the arts and sciences, we shall in every instance, find the contrast equally great on the side of Liberty.

It gives us no pleasure to say hard things of the Old Dominion, the mother of Washington, Jefferson, Henry, and other illustrious patriots, who, as we shall prove hereafter, were genuine abolitionists; but the policy which she has pursued has been so utterly inexcusable, so unjust to the non-slaveholding whites, so cruel to the Negroes, and so disregardful of the rights of humanity at large, that it becomes the duty of every one who makes allusion to her history, to expose her follies, her crimes, and her poverty, and to publish every fact, of whatever nature, that would be instrumental in determining others to eschew her bad example....

Non-slaveholders of the South! farmers, mechanics and workingmen, we take this occasion to assure you that the slaveholding politicians whom you have elected to offices of honor and profit, have hoodwinked you, trifled with you, and used you as mere tools for the consummation of their wicked designs. They have purposely kept you in ignorance, and have, by molding your passions and prejudices to suit themselves, induced you to act in direct opposition to your dearest rights and interests. By a system of the grossest subterfuge and misrepresentation, and in order to avert, for a season, the vengeance that will most assuredly overtake them ere long, they have taught you to hate the lovers of liberty, who are your best and only true friends. Now, as one of your own number, we appeal to you to join us in our earnest and timely effort to rescue the generous soil of the South from the usurped and desolating control of these political vampires. Once and forever, at least so far as this country is concerned, the infernal question of slavery must be disposed of; a speedy and absolute abolishment of the whole system is the true policy of the South—and this is the policy which we propose to pursue. Will you aid us, will you assist us, will you be freemen, or will you be slaves!...

In our opinion, an opinion which has been formed from data obtained by assiduous researches, and comparisons, from laborious investigation, logical reasoning, and earnest reflection, the causes which have impeded the progress of the South, which have dwindled our commerce, and other similar pursuits, into the most contemptible insignificance; sunk a large majority of our people in galling poverty and ignorance, rendered a small minority conceited and tyrannical, and driven the rest away from their homes; entailed upon us a humiliating dependence on the Free States; disgraced us in the recesses of our own souls, and brought us under reproach in the eyes of all civilized and enlightened nations—may all be traced to one common source, and there find solution in the hateful and horrible word, that was ever incorporated into the vocabulary of human economy—Slavery!....

Our soul involuntarily, but justly we believe, cries out for retribution against the treacherous, slavedriving legislators, who have so basely and unpatriotically neglected the interests of their poor white constituents and bargained away the rights of posterity. Notwithstanding the fact that the white non-slaveholders of the South are the majority, as five to one, they have never yet had any part or lot in framing the laws under which they live. There is no legislation except for the benefit of slavery, and slaveholders. As a general rule, poor white persons are regarded with less esteem and attention than Negroes, and though the condition of the latter is wretched beyond description, vast numbers of the former are infinitely worse off....

The lords of the lash are not only absolute masters of the blacks, who are bought and sold, and driven about like so many cattle, but they are also the oracles and arbiters of all non-slaveholding whites, whose freedom is merely nominal, and whose unparalleled illiteracy and degradation is purposely and fiendishly perpetuated....

102/ "'A house divided against itself cannot stand'"

The critical issues dividing the nation—slavery versus free labor, popular sovereignty, and the legal and political status of African Americans—were brought into sharp focus during the 1858 campaign for U.S. senator from Illinois. The campaign pitted a little-known lawyer from Springfield named Abraham Lincoln against Senator Stephen A. Douglas, the front-runner for the Democratic presidential nomination in 1860.

Lincoln had been born in 1809 and had grown up on the wild Kentucky and

Indiana frontiers. At age twenty-one he moved to Illinois, where he worked as a clerk in a country store, became a local postmaster and lawyer, and served four terms in the lower house of the Illinois General Assembly. A Whig in politics, he was elected in 1846 to the House of Representatives, but his stand against the Mexican War made him too unpopular to win reelection. After the passage of the Kansas-Nebraska Act in 1854, Lincoln reentered politics, and in 1858 the Republican Party nominated him to run against Douglas for the Senate.

Lincoln accepted the nomination with the famous biblical words "A house divided against itself cannot stand." Lincoln proceeded to argue that Douglas's Kansas-Nebraska Act and the U.S. Supreme Court's Dred Scott decision were part of a conspiracy to make slavery lawful "in all the States, old as well as new—North as well as South." The following fragment, which dates from before the June 1858 Republican convention, offers an early formulation of the ideas that Lincoln advanced in his "house divided" speech.

ABRAHAM LINCOLN, CA. 1858, GLC 2533

Why, Kansas is neither the *whole*, nor the *tithe* of the real question.

"A house divided against itself cannot stand."

I believe this government can not endure permanently half slave, and half free.

I expressed this belief a year ago; and subsequent developments have but confirmed me.

I do not expect the Union to be dissolved. I do not expect the house to fall; but I *do* expect it will cease to be divided. It will become *all* one thing, or *all* the other. Either the opponents of slavery will arrest the further spread of it, and put it in the course of ultimate extinction; or its advocates will push it forward till it shall become alike lawful in *all* the states, old, as well as new. Do you doubt it? Study the Dred Scott decision, and then see, how little, even now, remains to be done.

That decision may be reduced to three points. The first is, that a Negro can not be a citizen. That point is made in order to deprive the Negro in every possible event, of that provision of the U.S. Constitution which declares that: "The *citizens* of each State shall be entitled to all privileges and immunities of citizens in the several States."

The second point is, that the U.S. constitution protects slavery, as property, in all the U.S. territories, and that neither congress, nor the people of the territories, nor any other power, can prohibit it, at any time prior to the formation of State constitutions.

This point is made, in order that the territories may safely be filled up with slaves, *before* the formation of State constitutions, and thereby to embarrass the free state [sentiment and enhance the chances of slave constitutions being adopted.]

[The third point decided is that the voluntary bringing of Dred Scott into Illinois by his master, and holding him here a long time as a slave, did not operate his emancipation—and did not make him free.]

103 / *"We never hear of the man who wishes to...[be] a slave himself"*

In the following fragment from a longer speech, Abraham Lincoln reflects on the conflict between slavery and the nature of republican government and expresses his faith in improvement and progress and his vision of the American dream: that all people are entitled to the fruits of their own labor.

Abraham Lincoln, ca.1857–1858, GLC 3251

The ant, who has toiled and dragged a crumb to his nest, will furiously defend the fruit of his labor, against whatever robber assails him. So plain, that the most dumb and stupid slave that ever toiled for a master, does constantly *know* that he is wronged. So plain that no one, high or low, ever does mistake it, except in a plainly *selfish* way; for although volume upon volume is written to prove slavery a very good thing, we never hear of the man who wishes to take the good of it, by being a slave himself.

Most governments have been based practically, on the denial of the equal rights of men, as I have, in part, stated them; *ours* began, by *affirming* those rights. *They* said, some men are too *ignorant*, and *vicious*, to share in government. Possibly so, said we; and by your system, you would always keep them ignorant and vicious. We propose to give *all* a chance, and we expect the weak to grow stronger, the ignorant, wiser; and all better, and happier together.

We made the experiment; and the fruit is before us. Look at it. Think of it. Look at it, in all its aggregate grandeur, of extent of country, and numbers of population, of ship, and steamboat, and rail[road.]

104 / "Mr. Buchanan is a very weak man in the two Houses of Congress"

In September 1857 proslavery forces in Kansas, meeting in Lecompton, drafted a constitution that would bring Kansas into the Union as a slave state. Recognizing that a proslavery constitution would be defeated in a fair election, proslavery delegates offered voters a referendum on whether they preferred "the constitution with slavery" or "the constitution without slavery." In either case, however, the constitution guaranteed property rights in slaves. Free soilers boycotted the election, and as a result "the constitution with slavery" was approved by a six thousand-vote margin.

President James Buchanan—recognizing the Democratic Party's dependence on southern support—accepted the proslavery Lecompton constitution as a satisfactory application of the principle of popular sovereignty. He then asked Congress to admit Kansas as the sixteenth slave state.

Stephen Douglas, though an ardent Democrat, considered the Kansas election a travesty of the principle of popular sovereignty. The Illinois senator broke with the administration and joined with the Republicans in an attempt to defeat the Lecompton constitution.

After a rancorous debate, the Senate passed a bill admitting Kansas as a slave state under the Lecompton constitution. The House rejected this measure and instead substituted a compromise, which allowed Kansans to vote on the proslavery constitution. As a thinly veiled bribe to encourage ratification, the bill offered Kansas a huge grant of public lands if it approved the Lecompton constitution. While federal troops guarded the polls, Kansas voters overwhelmingly rejected the proslavery constitution.

The bloody battle for Kansas had come to an end. Free soilers took control of the territorial legislature and repealed Kansas's territorial slave code. Without legal safeguards for their slave property, slaveowners quickly left the territory. The census of 1860 found just two slaves in Kansas.

But the nation would never be the same. To antislavery Northerners, the Lecompton controversy showed that the slave power was willing to resort to violence, fraud, and intimidation to force slavery on a free people.

In this letter, Andrew Johnson (1808–75), a leading border state politician and future president, offers a candid appraisal of President James Buchanan and assesses Stephen Douglas's future within the Democratic Party.

ANDREW JOHNSON, JANUARY 23, 1858, TO D. J. PATTERSON, GLC 324

Mr. Buchanan is a very weak man in the two Houses of Congress. In fact there seem to be very few devoted to the fortunes of the Administration. As yet there are none willing to come up and make any sacrifice for it. Mr. Buchanan does not attach men to him personally and has no strength outside of the...party organization. I am inclined to think though that he has much more strength through the country than he has in Congress, and it is not detected enough there to make the Members stand close up to call his measures. In regard to democratic measures generally he is entirely too cautious with a pretty fair proportion of [the organization]. He needs will and decision of character while he seems to have a good deal of it in conversation, but he is timid and hesitating in practice. I hope that there will be a much better feeling in Congress and the country in regard to the administration. Douglas' move has angered the Administration some: but I think it will pass off and in the end do him Douglas more harm than the Democratic party. If Douglas intended to bolt and I think he did, he could not have selected a better time than he did for the party.

He was of the opinion that he could make the [move] and identify himself with the antislavery feeling of the north and at the same time hold on to his strength in the South, but instead of doing this he has failed in both and as the thing stands he is perfectly flat. He is a dead cock in the pit.

105 / *"The Democratic Party has become so startlingly wicked"*

By 1858 a growing number of Northerners believed that two fundamentally antagonistic civilizations had evolved in the nation, one dedicated to freedom, the other opposed. They had come to believe that their society was locked in a life-or-death struggle with an aggressive slave power that had seized control of the federal government and imperiled the liberties of free people. Declared the *New York Tribune*: "We are not one people. We are two peoples. We are a people for Freedom and a people for Slavery. Between the two, conflict is inevitable." At the same time, an increasing number of Southerners expressed alarm at the growth of antislavery and antisouthern sentiment in the North.

This broadside, titled *Astounding Disclosures!!*, underscores the political polarization that was taking place as the 1850s drew to a close.

ROBERT GOODENOW, *Astounding Disclosures!*, AUGUST 18, 1858, GLC 4714

What will the Pirate Democracy do next?

The Democratic Party has become so startlingly wicked, and its crimes and outrages so frequent and enormous, that active efforts are now being made...to turn the attention from the *corrupt* and *putrid* carcass, to the imaginary faults of the Republican Party. But the effort will prove vain, indeed. They can no more turn attention from their *crimes* and *villainy*, than they can fly from themselves.

Despised, defeated, overthrown, *routed everywhere* in the FREE STATES; finding nothing but reproaches and despair in their own hearts, they turn, and with a courage rendered desperate by debauchery, charge upon the vagaries of their own corrupt fancy!...

A party which has more capital invested in human flesh than in any other twenty articles of Commerce in our whole country;—a party which makes *men for the market* and *women for the harem*, as we raise sheep for the shambles. A party which would render the piracies of...[Captain] Kidd respectable by re-opening the Slave Trade, with all the soul-sickening horrors of the "middle passage!" A party which would *rob* weak and powerless Spain of the Island of Cuba, for the purpose of bringing a million of Slaves into the confederacy, and giving it the control of the vast National Councils! A party which would open our vast territories to this vile and withering curse.... A party that tried to make Kansas the burial place of liberty, that Slavery might flourish upon its gravel. A party which cheered on the assassin, who, with wood from dishonored soil, struck down, in the Senate House, Charles Sumner, "Liberty's chosen Senator," WHICH FOUL AND MURDEROUS ACT WAS DEFENDED UPON THE HILLTOPS.... A party which openly defends ballot-box stuffing.... A party which stigmatizes the yeomanry and laboring men of the North as "mudsills and greasy mechanics!"....

106 / *"Mr. Lincoln stands on the Old Whig Platform, with Clay and Webster"*

For four months in 1858, Abraham Lincoln and Stephen Douglas crisscrossed Illinois, traveling nearly ten thousand miles and participating in seven face-to-face debates before crowds of up to fifteen thousand. During the course of the debates, Lincoln and Douglas presented two sharply contrasting views of the problem of slavery. Douglas argued that slavery was a dying institution that had reached its natural limits and could not thrive where climate and soil were inhospitable. He asserted that the problem of slavery could be resolved if it was treated as a local problem.

Lincoln, on the other hand, regarded slavery as a dynamic, expansionist institution, hungry for new territory. He argued that if Northerners allowed slavery to spread unchecked, slaveowners would make slavery a national institution and would reduce all laborers, white as well as black, to a state of virtual slavery.

Douglas's strategy in the debates was to picture Lincoln as a fanatical "Black Republican" and "amalgamationist" whose goal was to foment civil war, emancipate the slaves, and make them the social and political equals of whites. Lincoln denied he was a radical. He said that he supported the Fugitive Slave Law and opposed any interference with slavery in the states where it already existed. He also said that he was not in favor "of bringing about the social and political equality of the white and black races."

Abraham Lincoln, 1858, *Facts for the People... The Political Record of Stephen A. Douglas*, ca. 1858, LLSP0003

Lincoln Stands on the Old Whig Platform

The following are Douglas'[s] Questions and Lincoln's Answers at Freeport:

Question 1. "I desire to know whether Lincoln to-day stands as he did in 1854 in favor of the unconditional repeal of the fugitive slave law?"

Answer. I do not now, nor ever did, stand in favor of the unconditional repeal of the fugitive slave law.

Q. 2. "I desire him to answer whether he stands pledged to-day, as he did in 1854, against the admission of any more slave States into the Union, even if the people want them?"

A. I do not now, nor ever did, stand pledged against the admission of any more slave States into the Union.

Q. 3. "I want to know whether he stands pledged against the admission of a new State into the Union, with such a Constitution as the people of that State may see fit to make."

A. I do not stand pledged against the admission of a new State into the Union, with such a Constitution as the people of that State may see fit to make.

Q. 4. "I want to know whether he stands to-day pledged to the abolition of slavery in the District of Columbia?"

A. I do not stand to-day pledged to the abolition of slavery in the District of Columbia.

Q. 5. "I desire him to answer whether he stands pledged to the prohibition of the slave trade between the different States."

A. I do not stand pledged to the prohibition of the slave trade between the different States.

Q. 6. "I desire to know whether he stands pledged to prohibit slavery in all the Territories of the United States, North as well as South of the Missouri Compromise line."

A. I am impliedly, if not expressly, pledged to a belief in the right and duty of Congress to prohibit slavery in all the United States Territories.

Q. 7. "I desire him to answer whether he is opposed to the acquisition of any new Territory unless slavery is first prohibited therein."

A. I am not generally opposed to honest acquisition of territory; and in any given case I would, or would not oppose such acquisition, accordingly as I think such acquisition would or would not agitate the slavery question among ourselves.

Mr. Lincoln stands on the Old Whig Platform, with Clay and Webster....

107 / "Why can't this Union endure permanently, half slave and half free?"

In 1858 it seemed conceivable that Stephen Douglas might assume leadership of an extremely moderate, mainstream antislavery cause. During the debates Lincoln sought to portray Douglas as indifferent to the moral evil of slavery and therefore disqualified from leading an antislavery coalition.

Abraham Lincoln, *Facts for the People...The Political Record of Stephen A. Douglas*, ca. 1858, LLSP0003

Lincoln on the "Ultimate Extinction" of Slavery, Extract from Mr. Lincoln's Jonesboro speech, delivered September 15, 1858:

...[Stephen Douglas] says, "Why can't this Union endure permanently, half slave and half free?" I have said that I supposed it could not, and I will try, before this new audience, to give briefly some of the reasons for entertaining that opinion. Another form of the question is, "Why can't we let it stand as our fathers placed it?" That is the exact difficulty between us. I say that Judge Douglas and his friends have changed them from the position in which our fathers originally placed it. I say in the way our fathers originally left the slavery question, the institution was in the course of ultimate extinction, and the public mind rested in the belief that it *was* in the course of ultimate extinction. I say when this government was first established it was the policy of the founders to prohibit the spread of slavery into the new territories of the United States, where it had not existed. But Judge Douglas and his friends have broken up that policy and placed it upon a new basis by which it is become national and perpetual. ALL I HAVE ASKED OR DESIRED ANYWHERE IS, THAT IT SHOULD BE PLACED BACK AGAIN UPON THE BASIS THAT THE FATHERS OF OUR GOVERNMENT ORIGINALLY PLACED IT UPON. I have no doubt that it *would* become extinct, for all time to come, if we but re-adopted the policy of the fathers by restricting it to the limits it has already covered—restricting it from the new territories....

108 / "Senator Douglas contends that the Territorial Legislatures may lawfully evade the Constitution"

The debates reached a climax at Freeport on August 27, 1858. There, Lincoln asked Douglas to reconcile the Dred Scott decision, which allowed slaveowners to take slavery into the western territories, with popular sovereignty. Could the residents of a territory "in any lawful way" exclude slavery prior to statehood? Douglas replied that the residents of a territory could exclude slavery by refusing to pass laws protecting slaveholders' property rights. "Slavery cannot exist a day or an hour anywhere," he declared, "unless it is supported by local police regulations." Any way he answered, Douglas was certain to alienate northern free soilers or proslavery southerners.

Abraham Lincoln, *Facts for the People...The Political Record of Stephen A. Douglas*, ca. 1858, LLSP0003

What the Southern Papers Say. The Louisville *Journal* on Douglas and Lincoln—Opinion of the Home Organ of Henry Clay.

The Louisville *Journal* has received Douglas['s] Freeport speech, and to the Senator's new averment that slavery may be kept out of the Territories by the refusal of the local Legislatures to pass laws for its protection, in spite of the authoritative mandate of the Constitution and the Supreme Court, thus replies:

...According to Senator Douglas, the Territorial Legislatures, though prohibited by the Constitution from abolishing slavery within their respective jurisdictions, may lawfully abstain from enforcing the rights of slaveholders, and so extinguish the institution by voluntary neglect. In other words, Senator Douglas contends that the Territorial Legislatures may lawfully evade the Constitution by deliberately omitting to protect the rights which it establishes. He holds that the people of the Territories may lawfully abolish slavery indirectly, though the Constitution forbids them to abolish it or prohibit it directly. It is impossible to conceive of squatter sovereignty in a more contemptible shape than this. It is the scurviest possible form of the scurviest of all possible heresies. A refinement, moreover, is added to the enormity of the fact that the Dred Scott Decision, to which Senator Douglas constantly parades his allegiance expressly precludes the whole thing. The opinion of the Court in that case denies the right of Territorial Legislatures to refuse protection to slavery as distinctly as it denies the right to abolish or prohibit it.... Senator Douglas in publicly espousing it [the doctrine that territories can exclude slavery by refusing to pass legislation protecting the institution], goes several lengths beyond the most intense and passionate Republicans in the whole North. He rushes in where Mr. Lincoln and his colleagues scorn to tread.... If slavery is to be prohibited in the Territories by legislation at all, let it be done by the people of the United States, and not by the first handful of nomadic settlers in the Territories themselves.... Abolition itself as respects the Territories, has never, in its highest fury, assumed such radical ground as Douglas took in his Freeport speech. [The abolitionist William Lloyd] Garrison, with all his fanatical and demoniacal hatred of slavery, has never in his whole life uttered an opinion at once so insulting and injurious to the South. The force of unscrupulous Northern demagogism seems spent in this last expedient of the unscrupulous little demagogue of Illinois....

109 / *"Douglas "Don't Care"'*

The sharpest difference between Lincoln and Douglas involved the civil rights of African Americans. Douglas was unable to conceive of blacks as anything but inferior to whites, and he was unalterably opposed to Negro citizenship. "I want citizenship for whites only," he declared. Lincoln said that he, too, was opposed to granting free blacks full civil rights. But he insisted that black Americans were equal to Douglas and "every living man" in their right to life, liberty, and the fruits of their own labor.

ABRAHAM LINCOLN, *Facts for the People...The Political Record of Stephen A. Douglas*, CA. 1858, LLSP0003

Douglas Says Slavery is a Civilized and Christian Institution.

"At that day the Negro was looked upon as being of an inferior race. All history has proved that in no part of the world, or the world's history, had the Negro ever shown himself capable of self-government, and it was not the intention of the founders of this government to violate that great law of God which made the distinction between the white and the black man. *That distinction is plain and palpable, and it has been the rule of civilization and Christianity the world over, that whenever any one man or set of men were incapable of taking care of themselves, they should consent to be governed by those who are capable of managing their affairs for them*" [Douglas's Springfield grand jury speech, June 12, 1857]

Douglas "Don't Care."

"It is none of my business which way the slavery clause (in Kansas) is decided. I

CARE NOT WHETHER IT IS VOTED DOWN OR VOTED UP" [Douglas's speech in the Senate, December 9, 1857]

Lincoln on the "Equality" of the Races. We present the following extract from Mr. Lincoln's speech at Charleston [in southern Illinois] on the 18th of September [1858], as a sufficient reply to the silly twaddle of the Douglasites about his favoring the doctrine of Negro equality:

While I was at the hotel to-day an elderly gentleman called upon me to know whether I was really in favor of producing a perfect equality between the Negroes and white people. [great laughter] While I had not proposed to myself on this occasion to say much on that subject yet as the question was asked me, I thought I would occupy perhaps five minutes in saying something in regard to it. I will say then that I am not, nor ever have been in favor of bringing about in any way the social and political equality of the white and black races [applause]—that I am not nor ever have been in favor of making voters or jurors of Negroes, nor of qualifying them to hold office, nor to intermarry with white people, and I will say in addition to this that there is physical difference between the white and black races which I believe will for ever forbid the two races living together on terms of social and political equality. And inasmuch as they cannot so live, while they do remain together, there must be the position of superior and inferior. I, as much as any other man, am in favor of having the superior position assigned to the white race. I say, upon the occasion, I do not perceive that because the white man is to have the superior position the black should be denied everything. I do not understand that because I do not want a Negro woman for a slave, I must necessarily want her for a wife. [cheers and laughter.].... I have never had the least apprehension that I or my friends would marry Negroes if there was no law to keep them from it [laughter], but as Judge Douglas and his friends seem to be in apprehension that they might, if there were no law to keep them from it (roars of laughter), I give him the most solemn pledge that I will, to the very last, stand by the law of this state, which forbids the marrying of white people with Negroes. [continued laughter and applause].

110 / *"I have said that I do not understand the Declaration to mean that all men are created equal in all respects"*

In the final balloting in 1858, Republicans actually outpolled the Democrats. But the Democrats had gerrymandered voting districts so skillfully that they kept control of the state legislature, which at the time elected U.S. senators. Although Lincoln lost in 1858, his battle with Stephen Douglas had catapulted Lincoln into the national spotlight and made him a serious presidential possibility in 1860. As he himself noted, his defeat was "a slip and not a fall."

To understand Lincoln's attitude toward civil rights in its own terms, it is essential to understand that he drew a distinction, like many Republicans, between "social" rights and "economic" and "political" rights. Lincoln denied any intention of achieving full "social" rights for African Americans, such as the right to associate with whites in the private sphere. But he did believe that black Americans were entitled to full protection of their right to the fruits of their labor.

During Reconstruction, following the Civil War, the Republican Party insisted on full public rights for African Americans—such as the right to vote, to sue in court, and to gain equal access to public accommodations, such as railway cars—while denying that they were committed to equal social rights. Yet even this narrow conception of formal legal equality would be overturned in 1883, when the U.S. Supreme Court struck down the Civil Rights Act of 1875 on the grounds that access to public accommodations was a private right, not a public right, and that Congress lacked the power to forbid discrimination in streetcars and theaters.

In this speech, Lincoln traces the development of his attitudes toward slavery and equality, and expresses his conviction that the southern slave power was engaged in a conspiracy to nationalize slavery and strip whites as well as blacks of their civil rights.

Abraham Lincoln, speech delivered in Springfield, Saturday Evening, July 17, 1858, GLC 2955

Although I have ever been opposed to slavery, so far I rested in the hope and belief that it was in the course of ultimate extinction. For that reason, it had been a minor question with me. I might have been mistaken; but the whole public mind, that is the mind of the great majority, had rested in that belief up to the repeal of the Missouri Compromise [in 1854, as part of the Kansas-Nebraska Act]. But upon that event, I became convinced that either I had been resting in a delusion, or the institution was being placed on a new basis—a basis for making it perpetual, national and universal. Subsequent events have greatly confirmed me in that belief. I believe that [Kansas-Nebraska] bill to be the beginning of a conspiracy for that purpose.... So believing, I thought the public mind will never rest till the power of Congress to restrict the spread of it [slavery] shall again be acknowledged and exercised on the one hand, or on the other, all resistance be entirely crushed out....

Mr. [Preston] Brooks, in one of his speeches, when they were presenting him canes, silver plate, gold pitchers and the like, for assaulting Senator [Charles] Sumner [of Massachusetts], distinctly affirmed his opinion that when this Constitution was formed, it was the belief of no man that slavery would last to the present day.

He said, what I think, that the framers of our Constitution placed the institution of slavery where the public mind rested in the hope that it was in course of ultimate extinction. But he went on to say that the men of the present age, by their experience, have become wiser than the framers of the Constitution; and the invention of the cotton gin had made the perpetuity of slavery a necessity in this country....

My declarations upon this subject of Negro slavery may be misrepresented, but can not be misunderstood, I have said that I do not understand the Declaration to mean that all men are created equal in all respects. They are not our equal in color; but I suppose that it does mean that all men are equal in some respects; they are equal in their right to "life, liberty, and the pursuit of happiness." Certainly the Negro is not our equal in color—perhaps not in many other respects; still, in the right to put into his mouth the bread that his own hands have earned, he is the equal of every other man, white or black. In pointing out that more has been given you, you can not be justified in taking away the little which has been given him. All I ask for the Negro is that if you do not like him, let him alone. If God gave him but little, that little let him enjoy.

When our Government was established we had the institution of slavery among us. We were in a certain sense compelled to tolerate its existence. It was a sort of necessity. We had gone through our struggle and secured our own independence. The framers of the Constitution found the institution of slavery amongst their other institutions at the time. They found that by an effort to eradicate it, they might lose much of what they had already gained. They were obliged to bow to the necessity. They gave power to Congress to abolish the slave trade at the end of twenty years. They also prohibited it in the Territories where it did not exist. They did what they could and yielded to the necessity for the rest....

One more point.... I expressed my belief in the existence of a conspiracy to perpetuate and nationalize slavery.... I showed the part Judge Douglas had played in the string of facts, constituting to my mind the proof of that conspiracy. I showed the parts played by others.

I charged that the people had been deceived into carrying the last Presidential election, by the impression that the people of the Territories might exclude slavery if they chose, when it was known in advance by the conspirators, that the Court was to decide that neither Congress nor the people could so exclude slavery.... I charge him with having been a party to that conspiracy and to the deception for the sole purpose of nationalizing slavery.

HARPERS FERRY

111 / *"My father and two brothers...went down to Harper's Ferry"*

Until the Kansas-Nebraska Act, abolitionists were averse to the use of violence; they hoped to use moral suasion and political legislation to end slavery. By the mid-1850s the abolitionists' aversion to violence had begun to fade. On the night of October 16, 1859, violence came, and John Brown and his followers were its instruments.

Brown's plan was to capture the federal arsenal at Harpers Ferry, Virginia, and arm slaves from the surrounding countryside. His long-range goal was to drive southward into Tennessee and Alabama, raiding federal arsenals, inciting slave insurrections, and creating in the mountains maroon communities or refuges for escaped slaves. Failing that, he hoped to ignite a sectional crisis that would destroy slavery.

In the following letter, one of Brown's daughters, who was fifteen in 1859, reflects back on her memories of the preparations for the raid.

Annie Brown Adams, December 15, 1887, to Garibaldi Ross, GLC 3007.03

My father and two brothers, Owen and Oliver, John Henry Kagi and Jerry G. Anderson went down to Harper's Ferry some time in June to prepare for and get a place that would be quiet and secluded where they could receive their freight and men. They rented Kennedy Farm situated about five miles north of Harper's Ferry as that seemed in all respects perfectly adapted to their purpose.... It was far enough from neighbors to seclude us, in a quiet woodsy place, less than a half mile from the foot of the Blue Ridge Mountains in Maryland, about two miles from Antietam and six miles from Sharpsburg—afterwards noted battlegrounds during the War....

After my father had selected his place, he found out...that he would be obliged to have some woman to help him, to stand between him and the curiosity of outsiders.... So he sent Oliver back to North Elba after Mother and I. Never dreaming that Mother would not go. Oliver's girl wife, Martha and I went back with him. Martha was sixteen and I was fifteen years old then....

I will first describe John Brown, not the one the world knew, but my father as I knew him. He was very strict in his ideas of discipline. We all knew from our earliest infancy that we *must* obey him....

We commenced housekeeping at Kennedy Farm sometime in July.... Our family at that time consisted of six persons.... Then followed the rest—one, two three and four at a time. These last arrivals all came secretly by way of Chambersburg, Father, and some of the rest going there with a light covered wagon, in which they rode or else walked a part of the way. They would hide in the woods and come in to the house before daylight in the morning or else after dark at night. They all lived upstairs over the dining room, coming down at their meals, and at any time that there was no strangers or visitors about....

112 / "I deny every thing but...a design on my part to free Slaves"

At eight o'clock, Sunday evening, October 16, Brown led a party of approximately twenty-one men into Harpers Ferry where they captured the lone night watchman and cut the town's telegraph lines. Encountering no resistance, Brown's men seized the federal arsenal, an armory, and a rifle works. Brown then sent out several detachments to round up hostages and liberate slaves.

But his plan soon went awry. As news of the raid spread, angry townspeople and local militia companies cut off Brown's escape routes and trapped his men in the armory. Two days later, U.S. Marines commanded by Colonel Robert E. Lee arrived. Brown and his men took refuge in a fire engine house. Lee's marines stormed the engine house and rammed down its doors. Five of Brown's party escaped, ten were killed, and seven, including Brown himself, were taken prisoner.

A week later, Brown was put on trial in a Virginia court, even though his attack had occurred on federal property. He was found guilty of treason, conspiracy, and murder, and was sentenced to die on the gallows. The trial's high point came at the very end when Brown was allowed to make a five-minute speech, which helped convince many Northerners that this grizzled man of fifty-nine was a martyr to the cause of freedom.

Address of John Brown to the Virginia Court...[printed for C.C. Mead and for sale at *The Liberator's* office]; undated but probably December 2, 1859, GLC 5508.051

I have, may it please the Court, a few words to say.

In the first place, I deny every thing but what I have already admitted, of a design on my part to *free Slaves*. I intended, certainly, to have made a clean thing of that matter, as I did last winter, when I went into Missouri, and there took Slaves, without the snapping of a gun on either side, moving them through the country, and finally leaving them in Canada. I desired to have done the same thing again, on a much larger scale. *That was all I intended.* I never did intend murder, or treason, or the destruction of property, or to excite or incite Slaves to rebellion, or to make insurrection.

I have another objection, and that is, that it is *unjust* that I should suffer such a penalty. Had I interfered in the manner, and which I admit has been fairly proved,—for I admire the truthfulness and candor of the greater portion of the witnesses who have testified in this case,—had I so interfered in behalf of the Rich, the Powerful, the Intelligent, the so-called Great, or in behalf of any of their friends, either father, mother, brother, sister, wife, or children, or any of *that class*, and suffered and sacrificed what I have in this interference, *it would have been all right*. Every man in this Court would have deemed it an act worthy a reward, rather than a punishment.

This Court acknowledges too, as I suppose, the validity of the LAW OF GOD. I saw a book kissed which I suppose to be the BIBLE, or at least, the NEW TESTAMENT, which teaches me that, "All things whatsoever I would that men should do to me, I should do even so to them." It teaches me further, to "Remember them that are in bounds, as bound with them." I endeavored to act up to that instruction. I say I am yet too young to understand that God is any *respecter of persons*. I believe that to have interfered as I have done—in behalf of His despised poor, was not wrong but RIGHT.

Now if it is deemed necessary that I should forfeit my life for the furtherance of the ends of justice and MINGLE MY BLOOD FURTHER WITH THE BLOOD OF MY CHILDREN, and with the blood of millions in this slave country whose rights are disregarded by wicked, cruel, and unjust enactments—I submit; so LET IT BE DONE.

Let me say one word further: I feel entirely satisfied with the treatment I have received on my trial. Considering all the circumstances, it has been more generous than I expected; but I feel no consciousness of guilt. I have stated from the first what was my *intention*, and what was not. I never had any design against the liberty of any person, nor any disposition to commit treason, or excite Slaves to rebel, or make any general insurrection. I never encouraged any man to do so, but always discouraged any idea of that kind.

Let me say something, also, in regard to the statements made by some of those who were connected with me. I hear that it has been stated by some of them, that I have induced them to join me; but the contrary is true. I do not say this to injure them, but as regarding their weakness. Not one but joined me of his own accord, and the greater part at their own expense. A number of them I never saw and never had a word of conversation with, till the day they came to me, and that was for the purpose I have stated. Now I have done.

113 / *"The boys met their fate very cheerful"*

Aaron D. Stevens, one of the Harpers Ferry raiders, was sentenced to hang on the scaffold March 16, 1860. Before his execution, he wrote the following letter to one of Brown's daughters.

AARON D. STEVENS, JANUARY 5, 1860, TO ANNIE BROWN, GLC 3007.01

...I am quite cheerful & happy, never felt better in my life. It made me feel rather sad, to part with my companions, but I think they are in a better land, and that is a great comfort to me.

I was in the same room with your Father, he was very cheerful all the way through, & appeared as happy on the morning of his execution as I ever saw him. Watson was shot about a half minute before me, this was Monday about eleven o'clock, & he lived until Wednesday morning. I had a very hard time of it, for about four or five weeks, but I am as well now as ever, except my face is paralyzed on one side, which prevents me from *laughing* on that side, and my jaw bone was thrown out of place and my teeth do not meet as they did before, which prevents me from chewing any thing very fine....

The boys met their fate very cheerful. I cannot tell when I shall be tried, but I think in two or three weeks.

114 / "The old Union-saving machinery will... be put in motion again"

John Brown was executed on December 2, 1859. Across the North, church bells tolled, flags flew at half mast, and buildings were draped in black bunting. Ralph Waldo Emerson compared Brown to Jesus Christ and declared that his death made "the gallows as glorious as the cross."

Prominent northern Democrats and Republicans, including Stephen Douglas and Abraham Lincoln, spoke out forcefully against Brown's raid and his tactics. Lincoln denounced Brown's raid as an act of "violence, bloodshed, and treason that deserved to be punished by death" (although he also had some surprisingly empathetic words to say about Brown). But southern whites refused to believe that politicians such as Lincoln and Douglas represented the true opinion of most Northerners. These men condemned Brown's "invasion," observed a Virginia senator, "only because it failed."

This newspaper article suggests the growing confidence of antislavery forces in the North.

"Free Press—Free Speech—Free Soil—Free Men," *Paterson Daily Guardian*, November 22, 1859, GLB 327.06

Howling Dervishes

The late elections having demonstrated that the Opposition of the North are abundantly able to elect a President, we may as well prepare for a stormy session of Congress and a prodigious foaming of slaveholders. To be sure, the people of the country are pretty well used to the raw-head-and-bloody-bone tactics of these gentlemen, but we shall be surprised if they do not outdo all they have ever done in this line, between now and next November. We counsel our readers, in advance, to prepare their minds for such shrieks from the howling Dervishes of our politics as they have never yet heard. A specimen card, a sample of cargo has, to be sure, been on the bulletin board since the advent of John Brown, and by his small specimen we can measure the great things to come. In the attempt to get up a terror in this quarter over the proceedings of Mr. Brown, we have witnessed both the ludicrous and the atrocious—Party spite and falsehood and imposition never attempted anything more foul than to implicate the leading Republicans in the proceedings at Harper's Ferry. But the spasm of detraction has been brief. The engineers of falsehood and alarm did the best they could in the space of time which they had to work in. But it must be remembered that the period was brief. The whole thing was over almost as soon as it was begun, and the actors are now only laughed at for their pains, or denounced for the audacity of their villainy....

Considering the results of last week, it would seem that, if ever a party fairly earned a claim to the title of the "unterrified" it is the Republicans. They gather round their standard in such numbers as to put to flight every suspicion that either calumny or threats can drive them from their convictions or their post, either now or hereafter. Yet the old Union-saving machinery will all be put in motion again, just as though the people could be frightened and just as though they could be driven from their purpose....

We may look for Special Conventions and General Conventions, for State action and the action of States united. In a word, we may look for a copious supply of thunder and lightning on wheels always ready to be carted out at just these special and prodigious conjectures that the managers may be able to create.

115 / *"We have a warm time here with the Southern fire eaters"*

John Brown's raid convinced many white Southerners that a majority of Northerners wished to free the slaves and incite race war. Southern extremists, known as "fire eaters," told large crowds that the raid on Harpers Ferry was "the first act in the grand tragedy of emancipation, and the subjugation of the South in bloody treason." Increasingly, Southerners believed that secession was the South's only option. A Virginia newspaper noted that there were "thousands of men in our midst who, a month ago, scoffed at the idea of a dissolution of the Union as a madman's dream, but who now hold the opinion that its days are numbered."

In this letter, William Windom (1827–91), a Republican who served as a U.S. representative and a senator from Minnesota, comments on the mood in the nation's capital, and suggests that southern threats of disunion are simply a negotiating ploy, a reenactment of similar bluffs made during the Missouri Crisis, the nullification crisis, and the Crisis of 1850.

William Windom, December 10, 1859, to Edward R. Parry et al., GLC 2799

We have a warm time here with the Southern fire eaters. They [are] so anxious...in the House...to kindle anew the fires of agitation and sectionalism, that they could not wait until the organization [of the leadership], but for a full week have delayed the business of the Country, for the purpose of making inflammatory, disunion Speeches. They openly avow their determination (in case of the Election of a Rep[ublican]. President) to dissolve the Union, that sentiment is loudly cheered from the "plug uglies" [anti-Republican gangs] of this City—who fill the galleries. Never until I came to a thoroughly Democratic district, did I hear a disunion Sentiment advanced or cheered but here both are very common. The whole thing is Simply a renewal of the old longtime threats—which have so long brought upon...the weak kneed gentlemen of the North. It is again having the same effect and in many parts of the Country the old *fossils* are calling "Union Meetings" for the purpose of propitiating the South. You will notice by the papers news the Republicans have all (or nearly all) kept silent thus far, and have not answered any of the Speakers. This is done by an understanding among our party for the purpose of affecting the organization as seen as terrible and for the purpose of showing to the Country who are really the slavery agitators.

116 / *"Witness the growing distrust with which the people of the North and South begin to regard each other"*

By 1860, slave labor was becoming an exception in the New World, confined to Brazil, Cuba, Puerto Rico, some small Dutch colonies, and the South. In all of those areas, except the South, slavery could not long survive the ending of slave importations from Africa, since the slave populations had a skewed sex ratio and were unable to naturally reproduce their numbers.

Within the South itself, slavery was sharply declining in the Upper South, and slave ownership was becoming concentrated in fewer hands. Whereas a third of southern whites owned slaves in 1850, a decade later the proportion had dropped to one quarter. In Missouri between 1830 and 1860, the proportion of slaves in the population fell from 18 percent to 10 percent; in Kentucky, from 24 to 19 percent; and in Maryland, from 23 to 13 percent.

By 1860, southern leaders were eager to vindicate slavery, to demonstrate that it was moral, progressive, and not out of step with the times. *Cotton Is King* represented an attempt to refute arguments such as those of Hinton Rowan Helper. The book's essays, written by leading southern politicians, attorneys, and theologians, argued that slavery was a humane and truly Christian institution, economically productive and justified by Scripture.

E.N. Elliott, ed., *Cotton Is King and Pro-Slavery Arguments* (Augusta, Ga.: Pritchard, Abbott & Loomis, 1860) pp. iii-vii, GLC 5115

There is now but one great question dividing the American people, and that, to the great danger of the stability of our government, the concord and harmony of our citizens, and the perpetuation of our liberties, divides us by a geographical line. Hence, estrangement, alienation, enmity, have arisen between the North and South....

Witness the growing distrust with which the people of the North and South begin to regard each other; the diminution of Southern travel, either for business or pleasure, in the Northern States; the efforts of each section to develop its own resources, so as virtually to render it independent of the other; the enactment of "unfriendly legislation," in several of the States, towards other States of the Union, or their citizens; the contest for the exclusive possession of the territories, the common property of the States; the anarchy and bloodshed in Kansas;...the existence of the "underground railroad," and of a party in the North organized for the express purpose of robbing the citizens of the Southern States of their property;...the attempt to circulate incendiary documents among the slaves in the Southern states;....and finally, the recent attempt to excite, at Harper's Ferry, and throughout the South, an insurrection, and a civil and servile war, with all its attendant horrors.

All these facts go to prove that there is a great wrong somewhere, and that a part, or the whole, of the American people are demented, and hurrying down to swift destruction....

Under the Jewish law, a slave might be beaten to death by his master, and yet the master go entirely unpunished, unless the slave died outright under his hand. Under the Roman law, slaves had no rights whatever, and were scarcely recognized as human beings; indeed, they were sometimes drowned in fish-ponds, to feed the eels. Such is not the labor system among us.... The true definition of the term, as applicable to the domestic institution in the Southern States, is as follows: Slavery is the duty and obligation of the slave to labor for the mutual benefit of both master and slave, under a warrant to the slave of protection, and a comfortable subsistence, under all circumstances....

It is objected to the defenders of American slavery, that they have changed their ground; that from being apologists for it as an inevitable evil, they have become its defenders as a social and political good, morally right, and sanctioned by the Bible and God himself. This charge is unjust.... The present slave States had little or no agency in the first introduction of Africans into this country; this was achieved by the Northern commercial States and by Great Britain. Wherever the climate suited the Negro constitution, slavery was profitable and flourished; where the climate was unsuitable, slavery was unprofitable, and died out.

117 / *"God...established slavery"*

One of the fundamental paradoxes of the South's slave system is that while slavery was a highly commercial, efficient, productive, and profitable institution, slaveholders tended to subscribe to an "anti-industrial" ideology, generally hostile to the forms of "modernization" taking place in the North. Even though slave plantations made extensive use of an extensive division of labor and factorylike discipline, the South was slow to embrace public schools and manufacturing, and many potential sources of investment, particularly in urban trade, went untapped. Like other slave societies, the South failed to develop many cities, whose interactions with the surrounding countryside were the engine of economic growth in the antebellum North. In this selection, a southern theologian defends slavery as a divinely sanctioned, paternalistic institution.

THORNTON STRINGFELLOW, "THE BIBLE ARGUMENT: OR, SLAVERY IN THE LIGHT OF DIVINE REVELATION," *Cotton Is King*, ED. E.N. ELLIOTT, GLC 5115

[Slavery] is branded by one portion of the people, who take their rule of moral rectitude from the Scriptures, as a great sin; nay the greatest of sins that exist in the nation. And they hold the obligation to exterminate it, to be paramount to all others.

If slavery be thus sinful, it behooves all Christians who are involved in the sin, to repent in dust and ashes, and wash their hands of it, without consulting with flesh and blood....

I propose, therefore, to examine the sacred volume briefly, and if I am not greatly mistaken, I shall be able to make it appear that the institution of slavery has received, in the first place,

1st. The sanction of the Almighty in the Patriarchal age.

2d. That it was incorporated into the only National Constitution which ever emanated from God.

3d. That its legality was recognized, and its relative duties regulated, by Jesus Christ in his kingdom; and

4th. That it is full of mercy....

[The abolitionists'] hostility must be transferred from us to God, who established slavery by law in that kingdom over which he condescended to preside; and to Jesus, who recognized it as a relationship established in Israel by his Father, and in the Roman government by men, which he bound his followers to obey and honor.

118 / *"Let us refer to figures and facts"*

An apologist for slavery appeals to statistics to try to refute the argument that slavery is unproductive and unprofitable.

Samuel A. Cartwright, "The Education, Labor, and Wealth of the South," *Cotton Is King*, ed. E.N. Elliott, pp. 879, 891–92 GLC 5115

It has long been a favorite argument of the abolitionists to assert that slave labor is unproductive, that the prevalence of slavery tends to diminish not only the productions of a country, but also the values of the lands. On this ground, appeals are constantly made to the non-slaveholders of the South, to induce them to abolish slavery; assigning as a reason, that their lands would rise in value so as to more than compensate for the loss of the slaves.

That we may be able to ascertain how much truth there is in this assertion, let us refer to figures and facts....

The statistics of the American churches prove that the slaveholding States contain more Christian communicants, in proportion to the population, including black and white, than the non-slaveholding. The report proves that in the cotton and sugar region, the white people who have few or no Negroes, are poor and helpless, but when supplied with seven times their own number of Negroes, they are the richest and most powerful agricultural people on earth. The census will prove that the landed property of those who are thus supplied with from three to seven times their own number of Negroes, if sold at its assessed value, and the proceeds of sales divided equally among all the inhabitants, black and white, each individual would have a larger sum than any Pennsylvanian, New Yorker, or New Englander, would have....

119 / *"Will ye be led away by a cruel and misguided philanthropy, or by designing demagogues?"*

In the concluding remarks of the volume *Cotton Is King*, the volume's editor argues that antislavery represents an attempt by Northerners to divert attention from their own society's mounting problems of inequality, social breakdown, and societal unrest.

E.N. Elliott, ed., *Cotton Is King*, pp. 897–99, GLC 5115

...Many, however, in the North are engaged in the [antislavery] crusade to divert attention from their own plague-spot—Agrarianism. We all recollect the Patroon of Albany

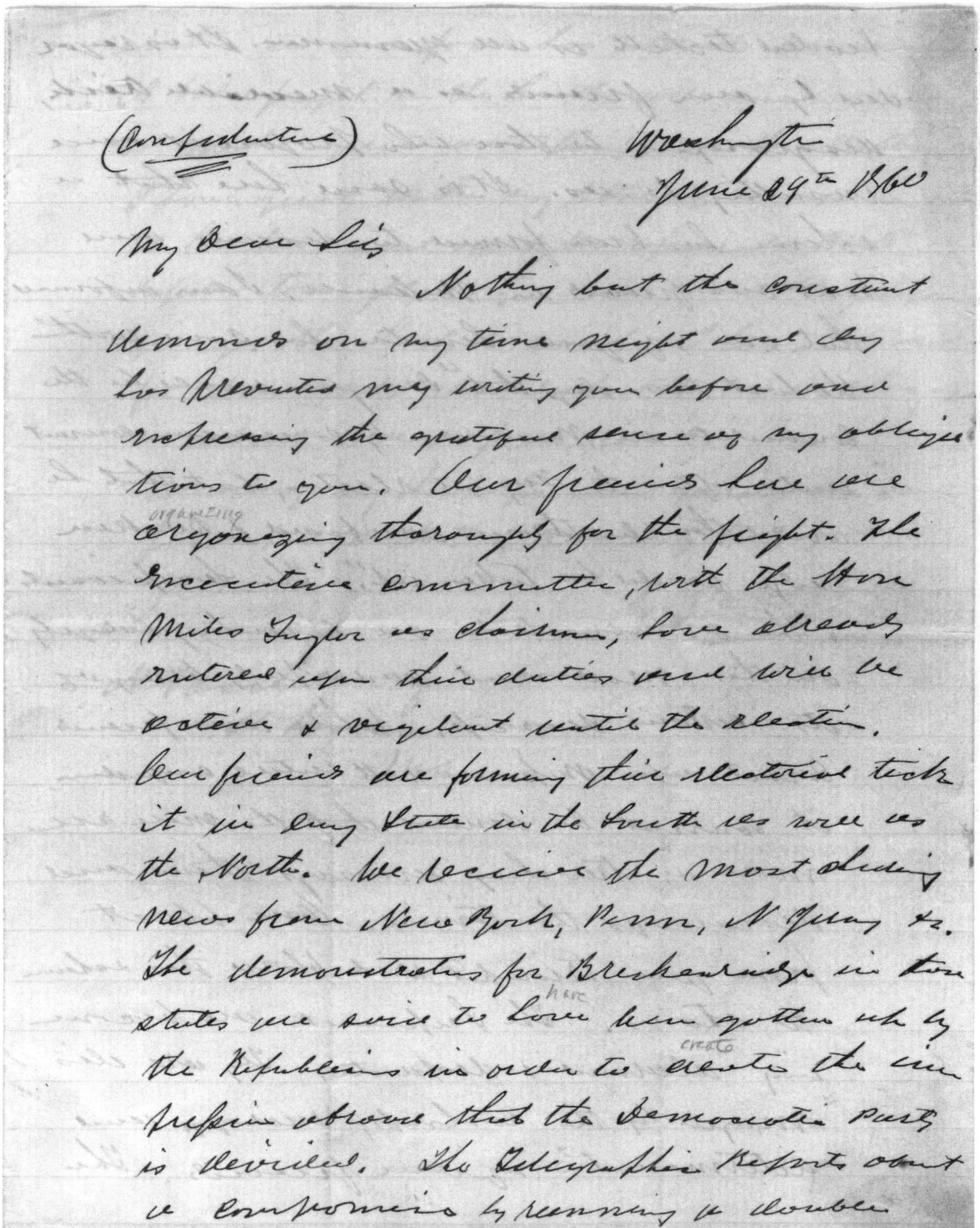
(Confidential)

Washington
June 29th 1860

My Dear Sir,

Nothing but the constant demands on my time night and day has prevented my writing you before and expressing the grateful sense of my obligations to you. Our friends here are organizing thoroughly for the fight. The Executive Committee, with the Hon Miles Taylor as chairman, have already entered upon their duties and will be active & vigilant until the election. Our friends are forming their electoral ticket in every State in the South as well as the North. We receive the most cheering news from New York, Penn, N Jersey &c. The demonstrations for Breckinridge in those states are said to have been gotten up by the Republicans in order to create the impression abroad that the Democratic party is divided. The Telegraphic Reports about a compromise by running a double

Stephen A. Douglas. Autograph letter signed, to N. Prescott, 1860/06/29. The Gilder Lehrman Collection, on deposit at the Pierpont Morgan Library. GLC 4625

and the Van Rensellaer mobs,—the Fourierism and Socialism of the free States, and the ever-active antagonism of labor and capital.... For the time perhaps they have succeeded in hounding on the rabble in full cry after the South, and in diverting attention from themselves. But how will they be in the end.... Will they spare the hoarded millions of the money-prices and nabobs of the North?... Ye capitalists, ye merchant princes, ye master manufacturers, you may excite to frenzy your Jacobin clubs...but remember! the guillotine is suspended over your own necks!!...

Ye people of the North, our brothers by blood, by political associations, by a community of interest; why will ye be led away by a cruel and misguided philanthropy, or by designing demagogues? So long as you confine yourself to making or hearing abolition speeches, or forming among yourselves antislavery societies...you neither injure nor benefit the slaves.... But when you attempt to circulate among them incendiary documents, intended to render them unhappy, and discontented with their lot, it becomes our duty to protect them against your machinations. This is the sole reason why most, if not all the slave States, have forbidden the slaves to be taught to read. But for your interference, most of our slaves would have been able to read the word of God for themselves, instead of being so dependent, as they now are, on that oral instruction, which is now so generally afforded them....

120 / "Our friends...are organizing thoroughly for the fight"

In retrospect, it seems likely that a majority of white Americans, North and South, may well have shared Stephen Douglas's views: his spread-eagle nationalism, his hostility toward Britain, his ardent support for westward expansion, his racism, and his lack of concern over the morality of slavery. But as political opinion grew increasingly polarized, Douglas would lose out.

In April 1860 the Democratic Party assembled in Charleston, South Carolina, to select a presidential nominee. Southern delegates insisted that the party endorse a federal code to guarantee the rights of slaveholders in the territories. When the convention rejected the proposal, delegates from the Deep South walked out. The remaining delegates reassembled six weeks later in Baltimore and selected Stephen Douglas as their candidate. Southern Democrats proceeded to choose John C. Breckinridge as their presidential nominee.

In this confidential letter, Stephen Douglas candidly assesses the political problems he faced during the 1860 campaign.

Stephen A. Douglas, June 29, 1860 (dated Washington), to N. Prescott, GLC 4625

Confidential

Nothing but the constant demands on my time night and day has prevented my writing you before and returning the grateful service of my obligations to you. Our friends here are organizing thoroughly for the fight. The executive committee...have already entered upon their duties and will be...vigilant until the election. Our friends are forming their electoral ticket in every State in the South as well as the North. We receive the most alarming news from New York, Penn, N Jersey etc. The demonstrations for Breckenridge in the states are said to have been gotten up by the Republicans in order to elevate the crisis.... The Telegraphic reports about a compromise by running a double headed ticket is...recognized by our friends as a miserable trick, disgraceful to those who propose it and insulting to us. It is said here that a scheme has been formed to deceive...our friends.... I am informed that one of your Senators has said within the last two days that "Douglas would be the candidate in Missouri by common consent until after the August election, but that he would be thrown overboard & Breckenridge would be taken up." The Secessionists & the administration are counting largely on this movement['s] success.... It cannot be denied that...[this act of] treachery...discourages the timid. One blast from your trumpet will blow this scheme to atoms. The Secessionsts are becoming alarmed & desperate. They are dismayed by the coolness, energy and determination of your friends. The reaction in our favor has already commenced. A bold fight in the South will enable us to make great [gains] at the North.

121 / "The foundations of the Republic tremble under the shock of contending factions"

In May the Constitutional Union Party, which consisted of conservative former Whigs, Know-Nothings, and pro-Union Democrats, nominated John Bell of Tennessee for president. This short-lived party denounced sectionalism and tried to rally support around a platform that supported the Constitution and Union. Meanwhile, the Republican Party nominated Abraham Lincoln on the third ballot.

The 1860 election revealed how divided the country had become. There were actually two separate sectional campaigns: one in the North, pitting Lincoln against Douglas, and one in the South, between Breckinridge and Bell. Only Stephen Douglas mounted a truly national campaign. The Republicans did not campaign in the South, and Lincoln's name did not appear on the ballot in ten states.

Intense anti-Union feelings marked the campaign in the South, where groups such as the Southern Rights Vigilance Club of Savannah, Georgia, threatened secession in the event of Lincoln's election. In the final balloting, Lincoln won only 39.9 percent of the popular vote but received 180 electoral college votes, 57 more than the combined total of his opponents.

Resolutions of The Southern Rights Vigilance Club of Savannah, 1860, GLC 837

In the present excited State of the Country, when the foundations of the Republic tremble under the shock of contending factions, and the mass of the people are distracted and divided by designing demagogues, we The Southern Rights Vigilance Club of Savannah regretting the apathy that prevails among us, and the culpable neglect in failing to prepare for the coming issue, while every breeze from the north brings us tidings of the mustering of the abolition hordes under the names of Wide Awakes, for the avowed purpose of forcing their loathsome Candidate and territorial doctrines upon an unwilling section. We The Southern Rights Vigilance Club of Savannah professing loyalty to the constitution yet preferring first and last our own institutions to every other

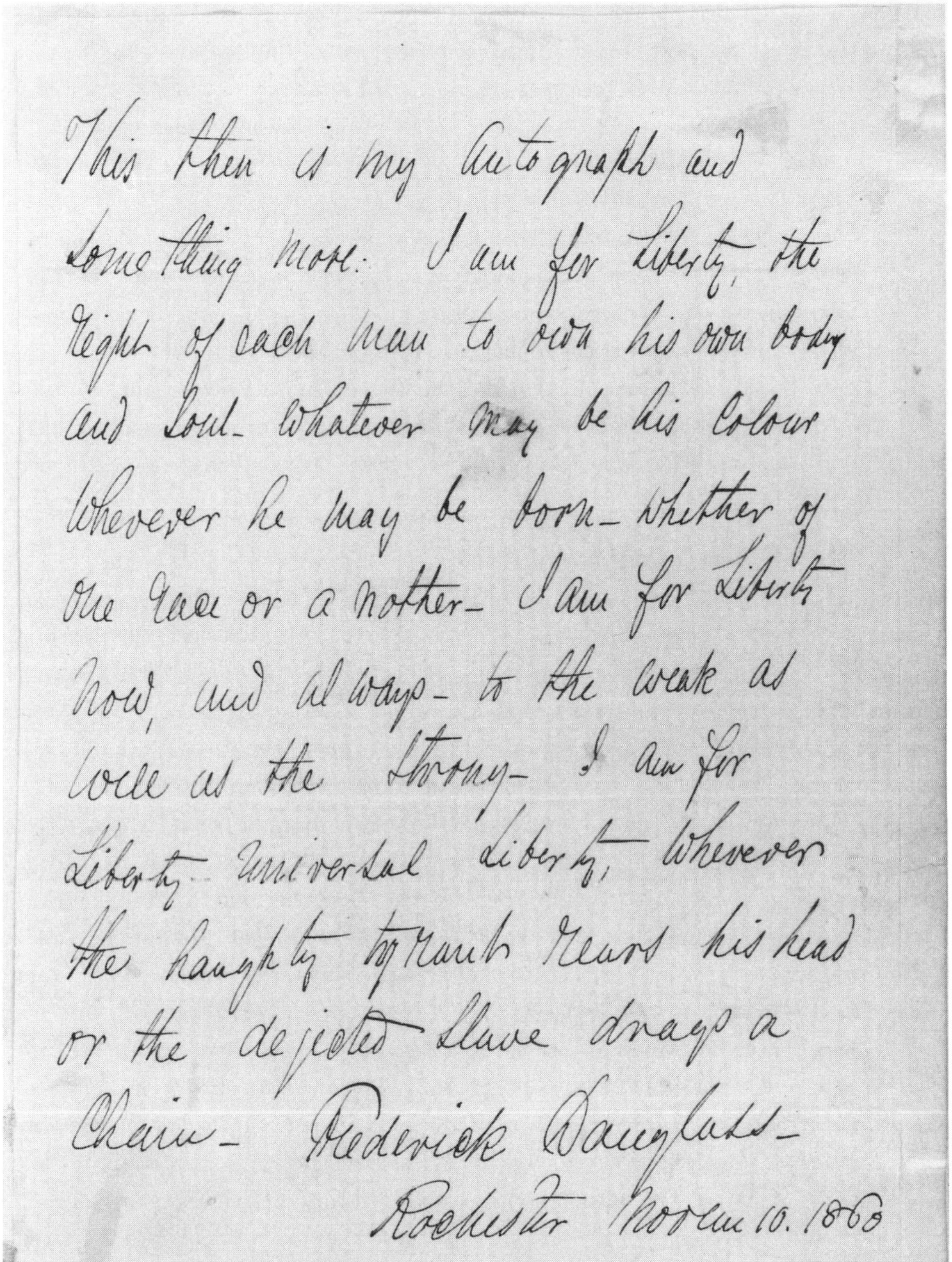
This then is my Autograph and
something more: I am for Liberty, the
right of each man to own his own body
and Soul— Whatever may be his Colour
Wherever he may be born— whether of
one race or another— I am for Liberty
now, and always— to the weak as
well as the Strong— I am for
Liberty— universal liberty, wherever
the haughty tyrant rears his head
or the dejected slave drags a
Chain— Frederick Douglass—
Rochester Novem 10. 1860

Frederick Douglass. Autograph manuscript signed, "I am for liberty, the right of each man to own his own body and soul…", 1860/11/10. The Gilder Lehrman Collection, on deposit at the Pierpont Morgan Library. GLC 4035.04

and loving our own Sunny South with an affection warmer and more devoted than the present so called Union, after waiting in vain for older heads to take steps to vindicate the honor and preserve the social organization of our section, have banded ourselves to-gether for her support. And that all may know the solemn and earnest object of our union.

Be it Resolved

1st That in the event of the election to the Presidency of Abraham Lincoln that we will unite with any organization that will resist and prevent his inauguration.

2nd That we offer our services to any State which shall secede from the union and refuse to submit to a government administered by abolitionists.

3rd That we pledge ourselves to make Savannah too warm a climate for any man who may degrade himself and disgrace our city by accepting office under such an administration.

4th That we pledge ourselves to join any organized body in protecting slave property in the territories.

122 / "I am for...Universal Liberty"

Frederick Douglass (1817–95)—one of America's most brilliant authors, orators, and organizers, and the nineteenth century's most famous black leader—was the first fugitive slave to speak out publicly against slavery. The pioneering feminist Elizabeth Cady Stanton recalled her first glimpse of Douglass on an abolitionist platform: "He stood there like an African prince, majestic in his wrath, as with wit, satire, and indignation he graphically described the bitterness of slavery and the humiliation of subjection."

Douglass (originally named Frederick Bailey) was born in 1818, the son of a Maryland slave woman and an unknown white father. Separated from his mother almost immediately after his birth, he remembered seeing her only four or five times before her death. Beginning at age six, he worked as a slave on plantations and in Baltimore's shipyards; he also learned to read and discovered the existence of reasoned antislavery arguments.

In 1838, after his owner threatened to take away his right to hire out his time, Douglass decided to run away. With papers borrowed from a free black sailor, he boarded a train and rode to freedom. Beginning in 1841, when he first spoke at a convention of the Massachusetts Anti-Slavery Society, Douglass electrified audiences with his first-hand accounts of slavery. Douglass supported many reforms, including temperance and women's rights. He was one of the few men to attend the first women's rights convention, held in Seneca Falls, New York, and he was the only man to vote for a resolution demanding the vote for women.

But his main cause was the struggle against slavery and racial discrimination. In the 1840s and 1850s he also raised funds to help fugitive slaves reach safety in Canada, and during the Civil War he lobbied President Lincoln to organize black regiments and make slave emancipation a war aim. Following the Civil War Douglass was appointed marshal and register of deeds for the District of Columbia and minister to Haiti. He retained the fiery attitudes of his youth into old age. When asked what young African Americans should do, he replied, "Agitate! Agitate! Agitate!" He died in 1895, at age seventy-seven, after attending a women's rights meeting with Susan B. Anthony.

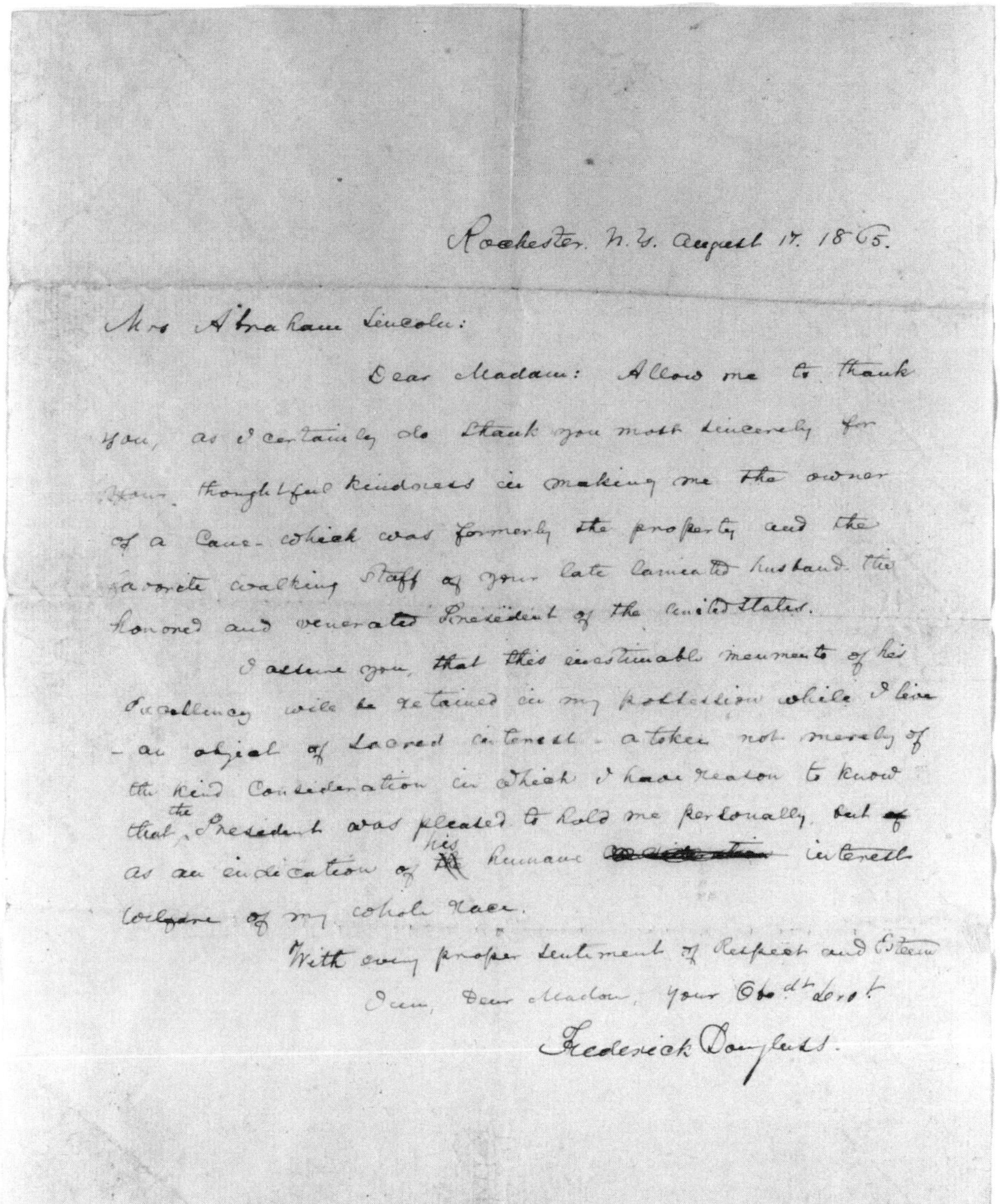

Rochester. N.Y. August 17. 1865.

Mrs Abraham Lincoln:

Dear Madam: Allow me to thank you, as I certainly do thank you most sincerely for your thoughtful kindness in making me the owner of a Cane which was formerly the property and the favorite walking staff of your late lamented husband the honored and venerated President of the United States.

I assure you, that this inestimable memento of his Excellency will be retained in my possession while I live - an object of sacred interest - a token not merely of the kind consideration in which I have reason to know that the President was pleased to hold me personally, but ~~of~~ as an indication of his humane interest welfare of my whole race.

With every proper sentiment of Respect and Esteem
I am, Dear Madam, your Obdt Servt.
Frederick Douglass.

Frederick Douglass. Autograph letter signed, to Mary Lincoln, 1865/08/17. The Gilder Lehrman Collection, on deposit at the Pierpont Morgan Library. GLC 2474

MEN OF COLOR

TO ARMS! TO ARMS!

NOW OR NEVER

This is our golden moment! The Government of the United States calls for every Able-bodied Colored Man to enter the Army for the

Three Years' Service!

And join in Fighting the Battles of Liberty and the Union. A new era is open to us. For generations we have suffered under the horrors of slavery, outrage and wrong; our manhood has been denied, our citizenship blotted out, our souls seared and burned, our spirits cowed and crushed, and the hopes of the future of our race involved in doubt and darkness. But now our relations to the white race are changed. Now, therefore, is our most precious moment. Let us rush to arms!

FAIL NOW, & OUR RACE IS DOOMED

On this the *soil* of our birth. We must now awake, arise, or be forever fallen. If we value liberty, if we wish to be free in this land, if we love our country, if we love our families, our children, our home, we must strike *now* while the country calls: we must rise up in the dignity of our manhood, and show by our own right arms that we are worthy to be freemen. Our enemies have made the country believe that we are craven cowards, without soul, without manhood, without the spirit of soldiers. Shall we die with this stigma resting upon our graves? Shall we leave this inheritance of Shame to our Children? No! a thousand times NO! We WILL Rise! The alternative is upon us. Let us rather die freemen than live to be slaves. What is life without liberty? We say that we have manhood; now is the time to prove it. A nation or a people that cannot fight may be pitied, but cannot be respected. If we would be regarded *men*, if we would forever silence the tongue of Calumny, of Prejudice and Hate, let us Rise Now and Fly to Arms! We have seen what Valor and Heroism our Brothers displayed at Port Hudson and Milliken's Bend, though they are just from the galling, poisoning grasp of Slavery, they have startled the World by the most exalted heroism. If they have proved themselves heroes, cannot WE PROVE OURSELVES MEN?

ARE FREEMEN LESS BRAVE THAN SLAVES

More than a Million White Men have left Comfortable Homes and joined the Armies of the Union to save their Country. Cannot we leave ours, and swell the Hosts of the Union, to save our liberties, vindicate our manhood, and deserve well of our Country. MEN OF COLOR! the Englishman, the Irishman, the Frenchman, the German, the American, have been called to assert their claim to freedom and a manly character, by an appeal to the sword. The day that has seen an enslaved race in arms has, in all history, seen their last trial. We now see that our last opportunity has come. If we are not lower in the scale of humanity than Englishmen, Irishmen, White Americans and other Races, we can show it now. Men of Color, Brothers and Fathers, we appeal to you, by all your concern for yourselves and your liberties, by all your regard for God and humanity, by all your desire for Citizenship and Equality before the law, by all your love for the Country, to stop at no subterfuge, listen to nothing that shall deter you from rallying for the Army. Come Forward, and at once Enroll your Names for the Three Years' Service. Strike now, and you are henceforth and forever Freemen!

E. D. Bassett,	Rev. J. Underdue,	P. J. Armstrong,	Rev. J. C. Gibbs,	Elijah J. Davis,
William D. Forten.	John W. Price,	J. W. Simpson,	Daniel George,	John P. Burr,
Frederick Douglass,	Augustus Dorsey,	Rev. J. B. Trusty,	Robert M. Adger,	Robert Jones,
Wm. Whipper,	Rev. Stephen Smith,	S. Morgan Smith,	Henry M. Cropper,	O. V. Catto,
D. D. Turner,	N. W. Depee,	William E. Gipson,	Rev. J. B. Reeve,	Thos. J. Dorsey,
Jas. McCrummell,	Dr. J. H. Wilson,	Rev. J. Boulden,	Rev. J. A. Williams,	I. D. Cliff,
A. S. Cassey,	J. W. Cassey,	Rev. J. Asher,	Rev. A. L. Stanford,	Jacob C. White,
A. M. Green,	James Needham,	Rev. Elisha Weaver,	Thomas J. Bowers,	Morris Hall,
J. W. Page,	Ebenezer Black,	David B. Bowser,	J. C. White, Jr.,	J. P. Johnson,
L. R. Seymour,	James R. Gordon,	Henry Minton,	Rev. J. P. Campbell,	Franklin Turner,
Rev. William T. Catto,	Samuel Stewart,	Daniel Colley,	Rev. W. J. Alston,	Jesse E. Glasgow.

A Meeting in furtherance of the above named object will be held

____

And will be Addressed by ______________________________

U. S. Steam-Power Book and Job Printing Establishment, Ledger Buildings, Third and Chestnut Streets, Philadelphia.

Frederick Douglass. Broadside, Men of Color: To Arms To Arms! Now or Never… [recruitment broadside], 1863? The Gilder Lehrman Collection, on deposit at the Pierpont Morgan Library. GLC 2752

In this brief note, written in an autograph album, Douglass sums up his philosophy.

FREDERICK DOUGLASS, NOVEMBER 10, 1860, GLC 4025.04

I am for Liberty, the right of each man to own his own body and Soul, whatever may be his colour, wherever he may be born—whether of one race or another—I am for Liberty now, and always—to the weak as well as the Strong—I am for Liberty—Universal Liberty, whenever the haughty tyrant rears his head or the dejected Slave drags a Chain.

123 / *"Sixteen rifle Cannons...Also, One Hundred thousand (100,000) pounds of lead"*

Even before a single state had seceded from the Union, the state of Georgia negotiated a contract with a New York rifleworks company to supply the state with armaments. Paul Jones Semmes (1815–63), who signed this contract, was a Georgia banker and plantation owner who served as a brigadier general in the Confederate Army. He led Georgia troops at the Battle of Gettysburg, where he received a wound from which he died during the retreat to Virginia. Semmes made the contract with Robert P. Parrott, who invented a superior rifled cannon known as a "Parrott Gun."

PAUL JONES SEMMES, DECEMBER 19, 1860, GLC 474

This Contract made and entered into this nineteenth day of December 1860 between Paul J. Semmes, Agent for the State of Georgia...and Robert P. Parrott...That the said Robert P. Parrott hereby covenants and agrees to manufacture furnish and deliver...

(16) Sixteen rifle Cannons of 3.3 in (3 3/10 in) Calibre and of (1000) one thousand pound weight each.... Also (3500) Three thousand five hundred "Dyer" solid shot of ten (10) pounds weight when finished. Also (4000) Four thousand "Dyer" Cannon Shrapnel shot.... Also (500) Five hundred Canister Shot of the ordinary kind.... Also, One Hundred thousand (100,000) pounds of lead....

THE SECESSION CRISIS

124 / *"The People of South Carolina...have solemnly declared that the Union...is dissolved"*

Convinced that a Republican administration would attempt to undermine slavery by appointing antislavery judges, postmasters, military officers, and other officials, a secession convention in South Carolina voted unanimously to secede from the Union on December 20, 1860. The convention issued a declaration in which it attempted to justify its decision. Drawing on arguments developed by John C. Calhoun, the convention held that the states were sovereign entities that could leave the Union as freely as they joined. Among the many indictments of the northern states and people, nothing seems more central than the issue of trust with respect to the capture and return of fugitive slaves.

James L. Petigru (1789–1863), a staunch South Carolina unionist, reportedly responded to the Palmetto State's actions by saying that his state was too small for a country and too large for an insane asylum.

South Carolina Convention (1860)
Declaration of the Immediate Causes which Induce and Justify the Secession of South Carolina from the Federal Union and the Ordinance of Secession, GLC 4483

The People of the State of South Carolina, in Convention assembled, on the 26th day of April, A.D., 1852, declared that the frequent violations of the Constitution of the United States, by the Federal Government, and its encroachments upon the reserved rights of the States, fully justified this State in then withdrawing from the Federal Union; but in deference to the opinions and wishes of the other slaveholding States, she forbore at that time to exercise this right. Since that time, these encroachments have continued to increase, and further forbearance ceases to be a virtue....

In the year 1765, that portion of the British Empire embracing Great Britain, undertook to make laws for the government of that portion composed of the thirteen American Colonies. A struggle for the right of self-government ensued, which resulted, on the 4th July, 1776, in a Declaration by the Colonies, "that they are, and of right ought to be, FREE AND INDEPENDENT STATES...."

They further solemnly declared that whenever any "form of government becomes destructive of the ends for which it was established, it is the right of the people to alter or abolish it, and to institute a new government." Deeming the Government of Great Britain to have become destructive of these ends, they declared that the Colonies "are absolved from all allegiance to the British Crown...."

In pursuance of this Declaration of Independence, each of the thirteen States proceeded to exercise its separate sovereignty; adopted for itself a Constitution, and appointed officers for the administration of government in all its departments—Legislative, Executive, and Judicial. For purposes of defence, they united their arms and their counsels; and, in 1778, they entered into a league known as the Articles of Confederation, whereby they agreed to entrust the administration of their external relations to a common agent, known as the Congress of the United States, expressly declaring, in the first article, "that each State retains its sovereignty, freedom and independence...."

Thus were established the two great principles asserted by the Colonies, namely: the right of a State to govern itself; and the right of a people to abolish a Government when it becomes destructive of the ends for which it is instituted....

In 1787, Deputies were appointed by the States to revise the Articles of Confederation, and...these Deputies recommended, for the adoption of the States...the Constitution of the United States.

The parties to whom this Constitution was submitted, were the several sovereign States; they were to agree or disagree, and when nine of them agreed, the compact was to take effect among those concurring; and the General Government, as the common agent, was then to be invested with their authority....

By this Constitution, certain duties were imposed upon the several States, and the exercise of certain of their powers were restrained, which necessarily implied their continued existence as sovereign States. But, to remove all doubt, an amendment was added, which declared that the powers not delegated to the United States by the Constitution, nor prohibited by it to the States, are reserved to the States, respectively, or to the people....

We hold that the mode of its [the United States's] formation subjects it to a...fundamental principle: the law of compact. We maintain that in every compact between two or more parties, the obligation is mutual; that the failure of one of the contracting parties to perform a material part of the agreement, entirely releases the obligation of the other.... We assert, that fourteen of the States have deliberately refused for years past to fulfill their constitutional obligations....

The Constitution of the United States, in its 4th Article, provides as follows:

"No person held to service or labor in one State, under the laws thereof, escaping into another shall, in consequence of any law or regulation therein, be discharged from such service or labor, but shall be delivered up, on claim of the party to whom such service or labor may be due."

But an increasing hostility on the part of the non-slaveholding States to the Institution of slavery has led to a disregard of their obligations.... [The northern] States...have enacted laws which either nullify the Acts of Congress, or render useless any attempt to execute them.... Thus the constitutional compact has been deliberately broken....

The right of property in slaves was recognized by giving to free persons distinct political rights, by giving them the right to represent, and burthening them with direct taxes for three-fifths of their slaves; by authorizing the importation of slaves for twenty years; and by stipulating for the rendition of fugitives from labor.

Those [nonslaveholding] States have assumed the right of deciding upon the propriety of our domestic institutions; and have denied the rights of property established in fifteen of the States and recognized by the Constitution; they have denounced as sinful the institution of Slavery; they have permitted the open establishment among them of societies, whose avowed object is to disturb the peace [and]...property of the citizens of other States. They have encouraged and assisted thousands of our slaves to leave their homes; and those who remain, have been incited by emissaries, books and pictures to servile insurrection.

For twenty-five years this agitation has been steadily increasing, until it has now secured to its aid the power of the Common Government. Observing the *forms* of the Constitution, a sectional party has found within that article establishing the Executive Department, the means of subverting the Constitution itself. A geographical line has been drawn across the Union, and all the States north of that line have united in the election of a man to the high office of President of the United States whose opinions and purposes are hostile to slavery. He is to be entrusted with the administration of the Common Government, because he has declared that the "Government cannot endure permanently half slave, half free," and that the public mind must rest in the belief that Slavery is in the course of ultimate extinction.

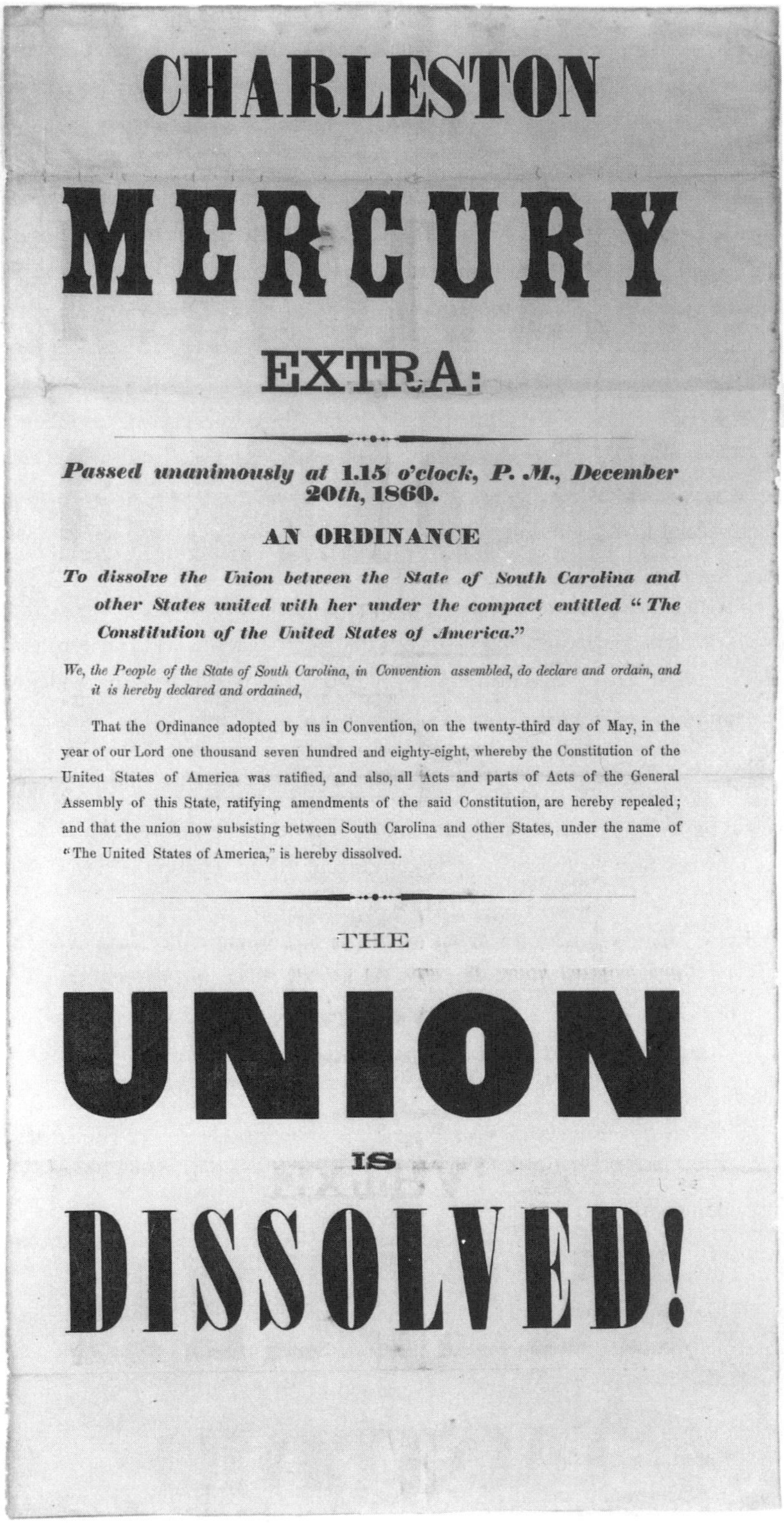

CHARLESTON MERCURY

EXTRA:

Passed unanimously at 1.15 o'clock, P. M., December 20th, 1860.

AN ORDINANCE

To dissolve the Union between the State of South Carolina and other States united with her under the compact entitled "The Constitution of the United States of America."

We, the People of the State of South Carolina, in Convention assembled, do declare and ordain, and it is hereby declared and ordained,

That the Ordinance adopted by us in Convention, on the twenty-third day of May, in the year of our Lord one thousand seven hundred and eighty-eight, whereby the Constitution of the United States of America was ratified, and also, all Acts and parts of Acts of the General Assembly of this State, ratifying amendments of the said Constitution, are hereby repealed; and that the union now subsisting between South Carolina and other States, under the name of "The United States of America," is hereby dissolved.

THE

UNION

IS

DISSOLVED!

Charleston Mercury. Broadside, The Union is dissolved! [Charleston Mercury, Extra Ed.], 1860/12/20. The Gilder Lehrman Collection, on deposit at the Pierpont Morgan Library. GLC 2688

This sectional combination for the subversion of the Constitution, has been aided in some of the States by elevating to citizenship persons, who, by the Supreme Law of the land, are incapable of becoming citizens; and their votes have been used to inaugurate a new policy, hostile to the South, and destructive to its peace and safety.

On the 4th of March next, this party will take possession of the Government. It has announced, that the South shall be excluded from the common Territory; that the Judicial Tribunals shall be made sectional, and that a war must be waged against slavery until it shall cease throughout the United States.

The Guarantees of the Constitution will then no longer exist; the equal rights of the States will be lost. The slaveholding States will no longer have the power of self-government, or self-protection, and the Federal Government will have become their enemy....

125 / *"Every body is rampant in favor of disunion"*

Writing two days after his state decided to leave the Union, a South Carolinian describes the strength of secessionist sentiment in the state.

William P. Gibson, December 22, 1860, to his sister Sarah [Gibson] Humphreys, GLC 4501.092

A happy Christmas to you—may each returning one be, to you, full of heartfelt joys. Pecuniary want keeps us at home, else we should have been at the old homestead several days ago. We are determined never to leave home again without the hope, at least, of making a trip of pleasure. Complaints, troubles and poor folks should be kept at home....

Political excitement was never so high—every body is rampant in favor of disunion. We had an election on this question one day before yesterday [December 20] and it is predicted by the knowing ones that the State will go 30,000 votes majority for the secession ticket. I say hurrah for the biggest party.

126 / *"The unanimity...of the feeling...in opposition to the... Union"*

In just three weeks, between January 9, 1861, and February 1, six states of the Deep South joined South Carolina in leaving the Union: Georgia, Florida, Alabama, Mississippi, Louisiana, and Texas. Unlike South Carolina, where secessionist sentiment was almost universal, there was significant opposition in the other states. Although an average of 80 percent of the delegates at secession conventions favored immediate secession, the elections at which these delegates were chosen were very close, particularly in Georgia, Alabama, and Louisiana. To be sure, many voters who opposed immediate secession were not unconditional Unionists. But the resistance to immediate secession did suggest that some kind of compromise was still possible.

In the Upper South, opposition to secession was even greater. In Virginia, on February 4, opponents of immediate secession received twice as many votes as proponents, while Tennessee voters rejected a call for a secession convention.

A correspondent from Galveston, Texas, describes attitudes toward the Union and secession in the Lone Star State two weeks before a secession convention voted to leave the Union.

New York Herald, January 14, 1861, From: Texas: Our Galveston Correspondent

I do not know that I can find language sufficiently strong to express to you the unanimity and intensity of the feeling in this region in opposition to the perpetuation of the Union under the rule of President Lincoln and a black Republican administration. That there are among us men of a conservative tendency, and hopeful of preservation of the rights and honor of the Southern States in the confederation, is true, and also a class upon whom the present depression of all material interests acts more powerfully than considerations of future political or social stability. But these are few, very few, in number, while the great majority are for secession without compromise on any terms.

As in the rest of the Gulf States that I have visited, the desire for revolution is paramount among the people, and the Union is constantly spoken of as both a danger and a disgrace that is to be averted and avoided. The benefits that it has conferred upon all sections of the country are never referred to, and seem to be entirely forgotten; and the fact that a revulsion of public sentiment may have occurred in the North, equal to that which has taken place in the South since the Presidential election, never seems to be for a moment considered possible. The popular majority which all the free States have exhibited for Lincoln is looked upon as irreversible, and the party slogan that slavery is "an evil and a crime," and must be belted in with a line of socially hostile States, is accepted as the permanent opinion of the Northern people. It is not alone the fear of danger to their social organization that rouses the Southern community to resistance and revolution; the moral obloquy that is conveyed in the sweeping condemnation of an institution which, in a community of mixed races, is considered to be the most wise, and consequently the most productive of high moral results, touches the honor of every Southern man and woman, and leads to that blind resentment which discards all considerations of material interest. The coming administration of Lincoln is looked upon as the embodiment of this moral slur upon Southern society and hence it is believed that submission to it will be an admission of inferiority in the face of the whole world.

This sentiment has swept away all the old party distinctions in the South, and made revolutionists of Breckinridge men and Bell men alike to such a degree that formerly recognized party leaders are now partyless and powerless, and the masses have shown themselves to be far in advance of those to whom they have hitherto been accustomed to look for counsel in public affairs. So ripe is the feeling for revolution here, that it is today attacking the State government, as well as the general government. Governor [Sam] Houston had refused to assemble the State Legislature for the purpose of considering the present political crisis, and had assigned valid reasons of State policy for his course. These were generally admitted to be binding upon him; and yet the people were determined to assemble in convention and take revolutionary action, in which the State government must have acquiesced or be superseded. In consequence of this state of things Governor Houston has changed his course, and issued his proclamation for the assembly of the Legislature....

It is stated in some quarters that the Lone Star men are in favor of exhausting every measure for obtaining guarantees for Southern institutions in the Union before resorting to secession, and it is probable that the coming political conflict in this State will take the shape of a struggle to remain in the confederation with new constitutional guarantees for the South, or a return to the old condition of the independent republic of Texas.

Such a course opens grand visions of achievement and glory to all young minds. It is believed that Arizona will unite with us and give us a Pacific as well as an Atlantic shore. In the present dilapidated condition of Mexico, large accessions from her territory to the new republic are deemed possible. Tamalipas, Nuevo Leon, Coahuila, Chihuahua and Sonora offer a vast field for enterprise and the carrying out of numerous fortunes in their fertile lands and prolific mineral resources, and thousands upon thousands of energetic and ambitious youth would leave the disintegrated States of a disrupted confederacy and seek a new future under the Lone Star of Texas. How long it will be before these anticipations are realized will depend upon the representatives in Congress of the Northern States, if they persist in their hostility to the present necessary social organization of the South, nothing can preserve the present Union. None of the extreme Southern States will remain in the confederacy except upon the admitted equality of Southern to Northern society, and the recognized wisdom of domestic servitude for the inferior race where whites and blacks are living in community.

Herein lies the great doubt of the Southern people. They see the feeling of hostility to African slavery pervading the churches, the Sunday schools, the moral propagandist societies, the school books, and every kind of moral and religious organization in the North, and they believe that the Northern people are so indoctrinated with hatred to an institution which they know theoretically only, through the most exaggerated and highly colored representations of those evils that are to be found in every constituted society, that they despair of justice being rendered to them. Hence the prevailing wish to sever the bonds of political union. The anti-slavery oligarchy, which rules the North through the clergy and the demagogues, are believed to be immutably enthroned there, whether their policy be for weal or woe to the country. It is for the Northern people to disabuse this belief, and only by so doing can the Union and its immense benefits be preserved to us.

New York Herald, January 14, 1861, p. 8.

127 / "The South cannot be conquered"

On February 1, a secession convention in Texas voted to leave the Union. Three weeks later, a popular vote ratified the decision by a three-to-one margin. Texas governor Sam Houston (1793–1863), who owned a dozen slaves, repudiated secession and refused to take an oath of allegiance to the Confederacy. As a result, he was forced from office. Houston predicted: "Our people are going to war to perpetuate slavery, and the first gun fired in the war will be the [death] knell of slavery." His opponents, however, confidently looked forward to the future.

Robert Campbell, February 1, 1861, to James Beale (dated Austin, Texas), GLC 5127.01

I am here attending upon the Convention. Today we adopted an Ordinance of Secession. Our connexion with the U.S. ends on the 2d....

You will recall what I said to you last summer. The Union is defunct—dead, never to be revived. *No concessions now would occasion its reconstruction—The South cannot be conquered.* Peace we prefer but do not dread war. The cost has been counted and we are ready to pay it.

We had a glorious country, great in all respects. Blind infatuation has destroyed it. Had simple equality been evinced, the South would have submitted to every other wrong.

128 / "The temper of the Black Republicans is not to give us our right in the Union, or allow us to go peaceably out of it"

In early February 1861, the states of the Lower South established a new government, the Confederate States of America, in Montgomery, Alabama, and drafted a constitution. Although modeled on the U.S. Constitution, this document specifically referred to slavery, state sovereignty, and God. It explicitly guaranteed slavery in the states and territories, but prohibited the international slave trade. It also limited the president to a single six-year term, gave the president a line-item veto, required a two-thirds vote of Congress to admit new states, and prohibited protective tariffs and government funding of internal improvements.

As president, the Confederates selected former U.S. senator and secretary of war Jefferson Davis (1808–89). The Alabama secessionist William L. Yancey (1814–63) introduced Davis as Confederate President by declaring: "The man and the hour have met. Prosperity, honor, and victory await his administration."

At first glance, Davis seemed much more qualified to be president than Lincoln. Unlike the new Republican president, who had no formal education, Davis was a West Point graduate. And while Lincoln had only two weeks of military experience, as a militia captain, without combat experience in the Black Hawk War, Davis had served as a regimental commander during the Mexican War. In office, however, Davis's rigid, humorless personality; his poor health; his inability to delegate authority; and, above all, his failure to inspire confidence in his people would make him a far less effective chief executive than Lincoln. During the war, a southern critic described Davis as "false and hypocritical...miserable, stupid, one-eyed, dyspeptic, arrogant...cold, haughty, peevish, narrow-minded, pig-headed, [and] malignant."

Following secession, the Confederate states attempted to seize federal property within their boundaries, including forts, custom houses, and arsenals. Several forts, however, remained within Union hands, including Fort Pickens in Pensacola, Florida, and Fort Sumter in the channel leading to the harbor of Charleston, South Carolina.

Jefferson Davis, January 13, 1861, to South Carolina Governor Francis W. Pickens, GLC 4624

I cannot place any confidence in the adherence of the [Lincoln] administration to a fixed line of policy. I take it for granted that the time allowed to the garrison of Fort Sumter

> has been diligently employed by yourselves, so that before you could be driven out of your earthworks, you will be able to capture the fort which commands them. I have not sufficiently learned your policy in relations to the garrison at Fort Sumter, to understand whether the expectation is to compel them to capitulate for want of supplies, or whether it is only to prevent the transmission of reports and the receipt of orders. To shut them up with a view to starve them into submission would create a sympathetic action much greater than any which could be obtained on the present issue. I doubt very much the loyalty of the garrison, and it has occurred to me that if they could receive no reinforcements—and I suppose you sufficiently command the entrance to the harbor to prevent it—and there could be no danger of the freest intercourse between the garrison and the city.... We are probably soon to be involved in that fiercest of human strife, a civil war. The temper of the Black Republicans is not to give us our rights in the Union, or allow us to go peaceably out of it. If we had no other cause, this would be enough to justify secession, at whatever hazard.

129 / "I feel that I have been...an humble instrument in the hands of our Heavenly Father"

Threats of secession were nothing new. Some Southerners had threatened to leave the Union during a congressional debate over slavery in 1790, the Missouri Crisis of 1819 and 1820, the nullification crisis of 1831 and 1832, and the crisis over California statehood in 1850. In each case, the crisis was resolved by compromise. Many expected the same pattern to prevail in 1861.

Four months separated Lincoln's election to the presidency and his inauguration. During this period there were two major compromise efforts. John J. Crittenden (1787–1863) of Kentucky, who held Henry Clay's old Senate seat, proposed a series of constitutional amendments, including one to extend the Missouri Compromise line to the Pacific Ocean, in defiance of the Compromise of 1850 and the Dred Scott decision. The amendment would prohibit slavery north of the line but explicitly protect it south of the line. On January 16, 1861, however, the Senate, which was controlled by Democrats, refused to consider the Crittenden compromise. Every Republican senator opposed the measure, and six Democrats abstained. On March 4 the Senate reconsidered Crittenden's compromise proposal and defeated it by a single vote.

Meanwhile, Virginia had proposed a peace convention to be held in Washington, D.C., February 4, 1861, the very day that the new Confederate government was to be set up in Alabama. Delegates, who represented twenty-one of the thirty-four states, voted narrowly to recommend extending the Missouri Compromise line to the Pacific. The delegates also would have required a four-fifths vote of the Senate to acquire new territory. The Senate rejected the convention's proposals, 28 to 7.

Compromise failed in early 1861 because it would have required the Republican Party to repudiate its guiding principle: no extension of slavery into the western territories. President-elect Lincoln made the point bluntly in a message to a Republican in Congress: "Entertain no proposition for a compromise in regard to the *extension* of slavery. The instant you do, they have us under again; all our labor is lost, and sooner or later must be done over....The tug has to come and better now than later."

With compromise unattainable, attention shifted to the federal installations within the Confederate states, especially to a fort in the channel leading to Charleston Harbor. In November 1860 the U.S. government sent Colonel Robert A. Anderson (1805–71), a pro-slavery Kentuckian and an 1825 West Point graduate, to Charleston to command federal installations there. On December 26, under cover of darkness, he moved his forces (ten officers, seventy-six enlisted men, forty-five women and children, and a number of laborers) from the barely defensible Fort Moultrie to the unfinished Fort Sumter. On January 9, 1861, President James Buchanan made an effort to reinforce the garrison, but the supply ship was fired on and driven off. In this letter, Anderson describes South Carolina's mood.

ROBERT A. ANDERSON, JANUARY 21, 1861, TO ANTHONY THORNTON, GLC 5748

Your affectionate and complimentary letter of the 14 inst. has given me very great pleasure. All give me much more credit for what has been done here, than I deserve. I feel that I have been merely an humble instrument in the hands of our Heavenly Father, and I trust that he will be pleased to dispel the dark and threatening clouds which still hang over our poor country. I fear that as a nation we have taken too much upon ourselves—that we have thought most of self and of worldly vanity and pride than we have of our Maker and that He may now bring us under subjection to his will by severe punishment. Never had a people better reason—if any be needed—than ours to be grateful to God.

These people seem to me to have lost all love for the Union, and to think that S. Carolina is all *the world* to them. The time will come, I think, when their children's children will think kindly of me for having, for a time, at least, saved their ancestors from civil strife. I am heartily tired of my position here, and hope that it will not be a long time before I may be enabled to join my wife and children.

130 / *"The duty of getting possession of the Forts now held within our limits"*

By late February, Fort Sumter had become a key symbol of whether the Confederate states exercised sovereignty over their territory. South Carolina demanded that President Buchanan surrender Fort Sumter in exchange for monetary compensation. To the rebels' surprise, he refused. As the following letter from Jefferson Davis makes clear, any decision about forcing the surrender of the fort by force carried profound consequences. Eight slave states in the Upper South remained in the Union. But their stance would clearly depend on the steps that South Carolina and the federal government took toward Fort Sumter.

JEFFERSON DAVIS, FEBRUARY 22, 1861, TO SOUTH CAROLINA GOVERNOR FRANCIS W. PICKENS, GLC 1958

...A resolution which devolves upon the general government of the Confederate States the duty of getting possession of the Forts now held within our limits by the forces has been adopted and a copy is I am informed to be confidentially sent to you this day.

A letter was shown to me this morning which indicated a purpose on the part of the military to attack Fort Sumter on the 25th of this month—I hope you will be able to prevent the issue of peace or war for the Confederate States from being decided by any other than the authorities constituted to conduct our international relations.

The most ardent and sensitive men should believe that we will not be unmindful or regardless of the rights and honor of South Carolina [to fire the first shots].

The importance of success whenever the attack is made upon a garrison to take one of our forts from the possession of the United States, is too apparent not to be appreciated by even the most heedless, and the technical knowledge necessary to solve the problem of attack and defense which is before you can have only been obtained by much both of military study and experience.

PART EIGHT

Civil War

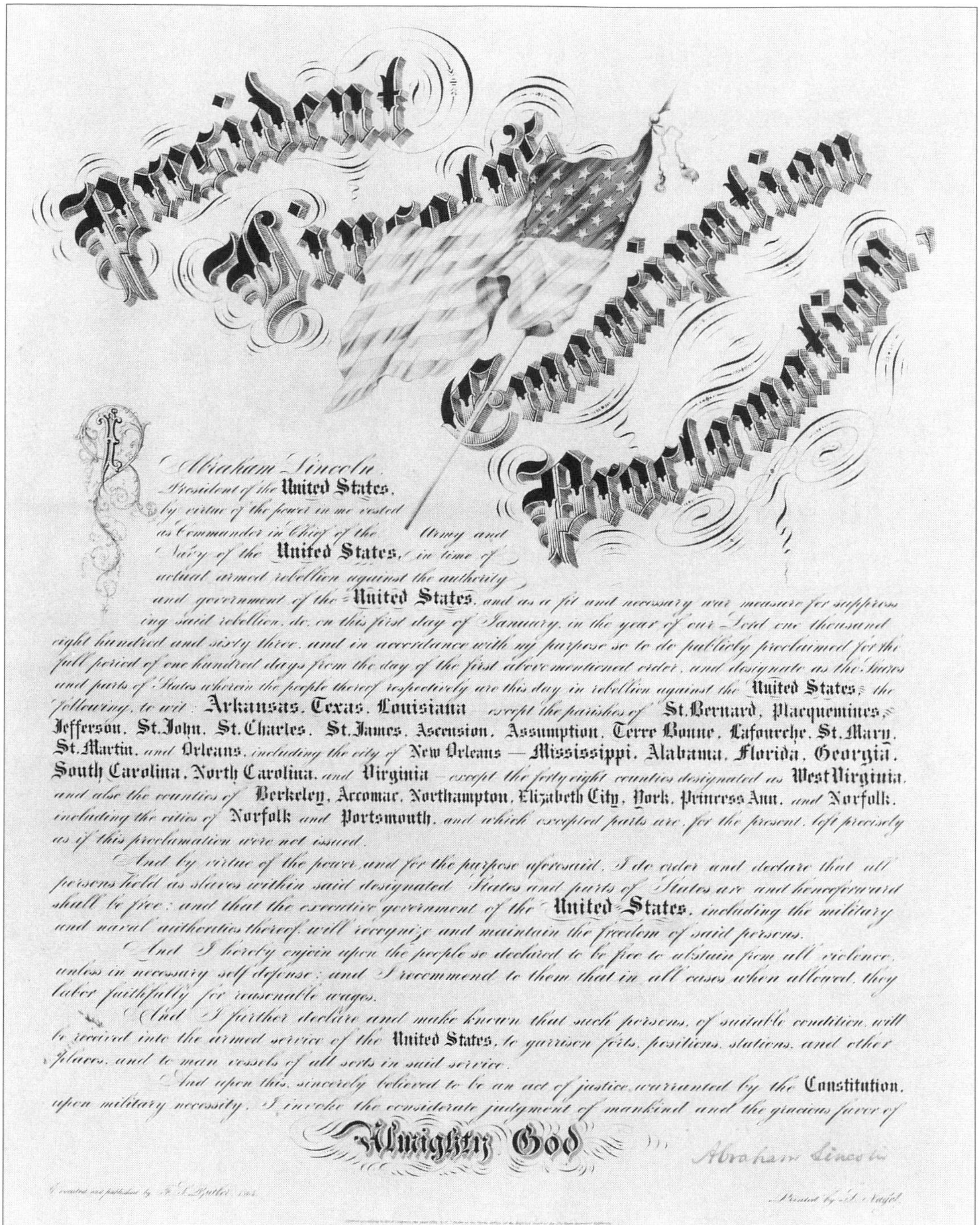

President Lincoln's Emancipation Proclamation.

I, Abraham Lincoln, President of the United States, by virtue of the power in me vested as Commander in Chief of the Army and Navy of the United States, in time of actual armed rebellion against the authority and government of the United States, and as a fit and necessary war measure for suppressing said rebellion, do, on this first day of January, in the year of our Lord one thousand eight hundred and sixty three, and in accordance with my purpose so to do publicly proclaimed for the full period of one hundred days from the day of the first above mentioned order, and designate as the States and parts of States wherein the people thereof respectively are this day in rebellion against the United States, the following, to wit: Arkansas, Texas, Louisiana except the parishes of St. Bernard, Plaquemines, Jefferson, St. John, St. Charles, St. James, Ascension, Assumption, Terre Bonne, Lafourche, St. Mary, St. Martin, and Orleans, including the city of New Orleans — Mississippi, Alabama, Florida, Georgia, South Carolina, North Carolina, and Virginia — except the forty eight counties designated as West Virginia, and also the counties of Berkeley, Accomac, Northampton, Elizabeth City, York, Princess Ann, and Norfolk, including the cities of Norfolk and Portsmouth, and which excepted parts are, for the present, left precisely as if this proclamation were not issued.

And by virtue of the power, and for the purpose aforesaid, I do order and declare that all persons held as slaves within said designated States and parts of States are and henceforward shall be free; and that the executive government of the United States, including the military and naval authorities thereof, will recognize and maintain the freedom of said persons.

And I hereby enjoin upon the people so declared to be free to abstain from all violence, unless in necessary self defense; and I recommend to them that in all cases when allowed, they labor faithfully for reasonable wages.

And I further declare and make known that such persons, of suitable condition, will be received into the armed service of the United States, to garrison forts, positions, stations, and other places, and to man vessels of all sorts in said service.

And upon this, sincerely believed to be an act of justice, warranted by the Constitution, upon military necessity, I invoke the considerate judgment of mankind and the gracious favor of Almighty God.

Abraham Lincoln

Executed and published by [illegible]

Printed by L. Nagel.

Lincoln signed Emancipation Proclamation (California lithograph with flag in background). The Gilder Lehrman Collection, on deposit at the Pierpont Morgan Library. GLC 742

In his inaugural address, Lincoln attempted to be both firm and conciliatory. He declared secession to be wrong; but he also promised that he would "not interfere with the institution of slavery where it exists." He announced that he would use "the power confided to me...to hold, occupy, and possess the property and places belonging to the Government." But he assured Southerners that "there would be no invasion, no using of force against or among the people anywhere."

When he delivered his inaugural address, the new president assumed that there was time for southern pro-Union sentiment, which he greatly overestimated, to reassert itself, making a peaceful resolution to the crisis possible. The next morning, however, he received a letter from Robert Anderson informing him that Fort Sumter's supplies would be exhausted in four to six weeks and that it would take a twenty-thousand-man force to reinforce the fort.

Lincoln received conflicting advice about what to do. Winfield Scott, his commanding general, saw "no alternative to surrender," convinced that it would take eight months to prepare naval and ground forces to relieve Fort Sumter. Secretary of State William H. Seward also favored abandoning the fort to avoid provoking a civil war, but also considered the possibility of inciting a foreign war (probably with France or Spain) as a way to reunite the country. Lincoln's postmaster general, Montgomery Blair, and treasury secretary, Salmon P. Chase, favored dispatching a force of warships and transports to relieve the fort and assert federal authority, since "every hour of acquiescence... strengthens [the rebels'] hands at home and their claims to recognition as an independent people abroad."

In the end, Lincoln decided to try to peacefully resupply the fort with provisions and to inform the Confederate government of his decision beforehand. Unarmed ships with supplies would try to relieve the fort. Only if the South Carolinians used force to stop the mission would warships, positioned outside Charleston Harbor, go into action. In this way, Lincoln hoped to make the Confederacy responsible for starting a war.

1 / *"Terrible News!"*

Upon learning of Lincoln's plan, Jefferson Davis ordered General Pierre G. T. Beauregard (1818–93) to force Fort Sumter's surrender before the supply mission could arrive. At 4:30 A.M. on April 12, Confederate guns began firing on Fort Sumter. Thirty-three hours later, the installation surrendered. Incredibly, there were no fatalities on either side.

Ironically, the only fatalities at Fort Sumter occurred just after the battle ended. During the surrender ceremony, a pile of cartridges ignited, killing one soldier, fatally wounding another, and injuring four.

Reefs Curios Marietta Ohio (1861)

HOME NEWS EXTRA, APR. 13, 11 P.M.

TERRIBLE NEWS!

THE FIGHT RAGES!

FORT SUMTER ON FIRE!

Washington in Danger!

SURRENDER OF FORT SUMTER!

REBEL VICTORY!

The Fleet to Enter the Harbor.

NEW YORK, April 13.

The opinion prevails that an attempt will be made before sunrise to run the light draught vessels of the fleet up to Fort Sumter to reenforce Major Anderson and also supply him with provisions.

The Battle Still Raging.

CHARLESTON, April 13.

The cannonading is going on fiercely from all points, from the vessels outside and all along the coast.

It is reported that Fort Sumter is on fire.

Fort Sumter on Fire!

CHARLESTON, April 13—1 P.M.

The roof of Fort Sumter is in a sheet of blaze. Major Anderson has ceased firing to extinguish it. Two of his magazines have exploded. The shells are flying over and around Fort Sumter in quick succession. The war vessels cannot get in on account of the ebbing tide. They are at anchor. Fort Moultrie appears to be considerably disabled. The Federal flag still waves over Fort Sumter.

Anderson's Shells fly Thick and Fast.

CHARLESTON, April 13—10 A.M.

At intervals of twenty minutes the firing was kept up all night on Fort Sumter. Major Anderson's strongest shells fly thick and fast, and they can be seen in their course from the Charleston City Battery.

SAVANNAH, April 13.

The lights at Tybee and in this harbor have been discontinued for the present.

How Lincoln Received the News.

WASHINGTON, April 13.

Commander Fox, spoken of in the Charleston dispatches, commands the vessel with provisions which was to lead the expedition into Charleston.

The President received the war news calmly.

The Merrimack Getting Ready.

NORFOLK, April 13.

Orders have been received to fit up the frigate Merrimack immediately.

The War News in Boston.

BOSTON, April 13.

The war news from Charleston creates a profound sensation in this city and throughout the State. The general sentiment is that the Federal Government is right and shall be sustained.

The Traitor Tyler at Richmond.

RICHMOND, VA., April 13.

Hon. John Tyler received this morning from Montgomery copies of the official dispatches between Gen. Beauregard and Maj. Anderson and Secretary of War Walker. They were printed and circulated through the country.

Rhode Island Offers Troops.

PROVIDENCE, April 13.

Gov. Sprague has tendered the Government the service of the Marine Armory and 1000 Infantry, and offers to accompany them himself.

Army Officers Removed.

WASHINGTON, April 13.

The President has directed that Capt. W. B. St. John, 3d Infantry, and Lieut. Abner Smead, 1st Artillery, cease to be officers of the army. The regular troops here have been ordered to proceed to the outskirts of the city to watch every avenue thereto, while the Volunteers guard the Armory and public buildings. Videttes are constantly seen riding through the streets. There is comparatively but little excitement here relative to affairs in Charleston.

The Confederate Flag to Wave Over the Frderal Capitol!

MONTGOMERY, April 13.

The President and Secretary of War were serenaded last night. The latter was called out. He said the Confederate flag would soon be waving over Fort Sumter and from the Federal Capitol.

Good News from Texas.

NEW YORK, April 13.

Dispatches from Col. Wade, commander of the Texan forces states that a strong Union feeling is growing.

Gov. Houston predicts the return of the secessionists to their allegiance, they are terrible taxed. Houston has been offered armed support by the Mormons in every part of the State.

Sumter in Distress!

CHARLESTON, April 13, 4 P.M.

The flag on Fort Sumter is at half mast—signal of distress.

Sumter Shows the White Flag!

CAARLESTON, April 13, 6 P.M.

The White Flag was raised, and Fort Sumter surrendered this evening.

Broadside, Home News Extra: Terrible News! The Fight Rages! Forst Sumter on Fire!, 1861/04/13. The Gilder Lehrman Collection, on deposit at the Pierpont Morgan Library. GLC 1545.06

Marietta (Ohio) Home News EXTRA, APRIL 13, 1861, GLC 1545.06

TERRIBLE NEWS!
THE FIGHT RAGES!
FORT SUMTER ON FIRE!
WASHINGTON IN DANGER!
SURRENDER OF FORT SUMTER!
REBEL VICTORY!

The Fleet to Enter the Harbor

The opinion prevails that an attempt will be made before sunrise to run the eight draught vessels of the fleet up to Fort Sumter to reenforce Major Anderson and also supply him with provisions.

The Battle Still Raging

The cannonading is going on fiercely from all points, from the vessels outside and all along the coast.

It is reported that Fort Sumter is on fire.

Fort Sumter on Fire!

The roof of Fort Sumter is in a sheet of blaze. Major Anderson has ceased firing to extinguish it. Two of his magazines have exploded. The shells are flying over and around Fort Sumter in quick succession. The war vessels cannot get in on account of the ebbing tide. They are at anchor. Fort Moultrie appears to be considerably disabled. The Federal flag still waves over Fort Sumter.

Anderson's Shells fly by Thick and Fast

At intervals of twenty minutes the firing was kept up all night on Fort Sumter. Major Anderson's strongest shells fly thick and fast, and they can be seen in their course from the Charleston City Battery.

How Lincoln Received the News

The President received the war news calmly.

Good News from Texas

Dispatches from Col. Wade, commander of the Texan forces states that a strong Union feeling is growing.

Gov. [Sam] Houston predicts the return of the secessionists to their allegiance, they are terrible taxed. Houston has been offered armed support by the Mormons in every part of the State.

Sumter in Distress

The flag on Fort Sumter is at half mast—signal of distress.

> *Sumter Shows the White Flag!*
>
> The White Flag was raised, and Fort Sumter surrendered this evening.

2 / *"Invasion of our soil will be considered as an act of war"*

Lincoln was convinced that the Confederate states had seceded from the Union for the sole purpose of maintaining slavery. Like President Jackson before him, he considered the Union to be permanent, an agreement by the people and not just of the states. Further, he strongly agreed with the sentiments voiced by Daniel Webster (1782–1852) when that Whig senator declared in 1830, "Liberty and Union, now and forever, one and inseparable." Lincoln, too, believed that a strong Union provided the only firm safeguard for American liberties and republican institutions. By attacking Fort Sumter, the Confederacy had directly challeged federal authority. And so the war came.

Lincoln responded to the attack on Fort Sumter by calling on the states to provide seventy-five thousand militia men for 90 days service. Twice that number volunteered. But the eight slave states still in the Union refused to furnish troops, and four—Arkansas, North Carolina, Tennessee, and Virginia—seceded.

One individual who felt especially torn by the decision to support the Union or join the Confederacy was Robert E. Lee (1807–70) of Virginia. Lee was Winfield Scott's choice to serve as field commander of the Union army, but when a state convention voted to secede, he resigned from the U.S. army, announcing to his sister that he could not "raise my hand against my birthplace, my home, my children. Save in defense of my native state, I hope I may never be called on to draw my sword." After joining the Confederate army, he predicted "that the country will have to pass through a terrible ordeal, a necessary expiation perhaps for national sins."

> ROBERT E. LEE, APRIL 24, 1861, TO GENERAL PHILIP ST. GEORGE COCKE, GLC 3874
>
> Establish your Head Quarters as necessary. Establish camps of instruction, and have your troops instructed in the use of their different arms. Make the necessary arrangements for their support. No bacon is to be had in Virginia. Consult with merchants in Alexandria as to the feasibility of obtaining bacon from Ohio, or Kentucky, if this is not practicable, beef & mutton must be your meat ration; the Valley of Virginia will naturally suggest itself to you as the point, from which this part of the ration can be obtained.
>
> Let it be known that you intend to make no attack; but invasion of our soil will be considered as an act of war.
>
> Very few officers of experience have as yet reported, as soon as possible some will be sent to you....

3 / *"The battle [is] opened"*

Many Northerners felt confident of a quick victory. In 1861 the Union states had 22.5 million people compared to just 9 million in the Confederate states (including 3.7 million slaves). Not only did the Union have more manpower, it also had a larger navy, a more developed railroad system, and a stronger manufacturing base. The North had 1.3

million industrial workers, compared to the South's 110,000. Northern factories manufactured nine times as many industrial goods as the South; seventeen times as many cotton and woolen goods; thirty times as many boots and shoes; twenty times as much pig iron; twenty-four times as many railroad locomotives; and thirty-three times as many firearms.

But Confederates also felt confident. For one thing, the Confederacy had only to wage a defensive war and wait for northern morale to erode. In contrast, the Union had to conquer and control the Confederacy's 750,000 square miles of territory. Further, the Confederate army seemed superior to that of the Union. More Southerners had attended West Point or other military academies, had served as army officers, and had experience using firearms and horses. At the beginning of 1861 the U.S. army consisted of only 16,000 men, most of whom served on the frontier fighting Indians. History, too, seemed to be on the South's side. Before the Civil War, most nations that had fought for independence, including, of course, the United States, had won their struggle. A school textbook epitomized southern confidence: "If one Confederate soldier can whip seven Yankees," it asked, "how many soldiers can whip 49 Yanks?"

In this selection, a resident of Marietta, Ohio, reports the mood in his town.

Frederic Pearce, May 13, 1861, to his father (Marietta, Ohio), GLC 66.128

Nothing new here in the way of war items. The people here are wide awake on the subject, and quite a number of companies are drilling, and putting themselves in a state of readiness for anything that may happen. It is not expected, however, that we shall be disturbed, as it is thought eastern Virginia will soon have her hands full without giving much attention to us. It seems now that before long a culmination point will be reached, and the battle opened—It should and doubtless will be the prayer of all Christians that it may be speedily terminated and the rebellion crushed.

4 / "We had an alarm last night"

The Civil War was the deadliest war in American history. Altogether, more than six hundred thousand died in the conflict, more than in World War I and World War II combined. A soldier was thirteen times more likely to die in the Civil War than in the Vietnam War.

One reason why the Civil War was so lethal was the introduction of improved weaponry. Cone-shaped bullets replaced musket balls, and beginning in 1862, smoothbore muskets were replaced with rifles with grooved barrels, which imparted spin on a bullet and allowed a soldier to hit a target a quarter of a mile away. The new weapons had appeared so suddenly that commanders did not immediately realize that they needed to compensate for the increased range and accuracy of rifles.

The Civil War was the first war in which soldiers used repeating rifles (which could fire several shots without reloading), breechloading arms (which were loaded from behind the barrel instead of through the muzzle), and automated weapons such as the Gatling gun. The Civil War also marked the first use by Americans of shrapnel, booby traps, and land mines.

Outdated strategy also contributed to the high number of casualties. Massive frontal assaults and massed formations resulted in large numbers of deaths. In addition, far larger numbers of soldiers were involved in battles than in the past. In the Mexican War, no more than fifteen thousand soldiers opposed each other in a single battle, but some Civil War battles involved as many as one hundred thousand soldiers.

Any hopes for a swift northern victory in the Civil War were dashed at the First Battle of Bull Run (called Manassas by the Confederates). After the surrender of Fort Sumter, two Union armies moved into northern Virginia. One, led by General Irvin McDowell (1818–85), had about thirty-five thousand men; the other, with about eighteen thousand men was led by General Robert Patterson (1792–1881). They were opposed by two Confederate armies, with about thirty-one thousand troops, one led by General Joseph E. Johnston (1807–91), another led by General Pierre G.T. Beauregard (1818–93). Both Union and Confederate armies consisted of poorly trained volunteers.

McDowell hoped to destroy Beauregard's forces while Patterson tied up Johnston's men; in fact, Johnston's troops eluded Union forces and joined Beauregard. At Bull Run in northern Virginia twenty-five miles southwest of Washington, the armies clashed. While residents of Washington ate picnic lunches and looked on, Union troops launched several assaults. When Beauregard counterattacked, Union forces retreated in panic, but Confederate forces failed to take up pursuit.

An Indiana soldier describes life in his camp a day after the First Battle of Bull Run.

James R. Kelly, July 22, 1861, to Mary Kelly, GLC 4197.02

...This is a dreary wet day, it has been raining all day long so hard that we cant do anything but write to our friends.... Something must be terribly wrong in the post office department, there has been but 2 letters recd in our regiment, since we left Indianapolis.... I tell you now there can be no pleasure for any man in the army, & especially while on the march. I don't know what I should do if I should take sick here in these mountains. Most of the time it has been wet & cold, especially at night, a sick man has but little chance for his life here.... The tops of the mountains have been completely enveloped in dense clouds all day—the high ranges of mountains in the distance have the appearance of a volcano in full blast, with the fog curling above the dark clouds below....

We had an alarm last night at 10 o'clock. We all expected a fight, one of the Sentinels got frightened, & fired his gun, & then the alarm paged all around the camp until some guns were fired, all the men was called out, & placed in line of battle, where we stood ready to fire on any one approaching the camp, all in the most perfect silence for three long hours. When we were told the alarm was failed, & ordered to our quarters. It was amusing to see the boys...coming out half dressed, some without their guns, others their shoes and hats....

5 / *"We have an agency...for the abolition of slavery in the...war"*

In July 1861 Congress adopted a resolution by a vote of 117 to 2 in the House and 30 to 5 in the Senate that read: "This war is not waged...for the purpose of overthrowing or interfering with the established institutions of those States, but to maintain the

States unimpaired; and that as soon as these objects are accomplished the war should cease." Fearful of alienating the slave states that remained in the Union—Delaware, Kentucky, Maryland, and Missouri—or of antagonizing Northerners who would support antiwar Democrats if the conflict were transformed into a war to abolish slavery, Lincoln felt that he had to proceed cautiously. Nevertheless, opponents of slavery, such as the abolitionist attorney John Jay (1817–94), the author of this letter and grandson of the Revolutionary War patriot, regarded the war as a providential opportunity to destroy slavery and the slave power.

JOHN JAY, JULY 24, 1861, TO AN UNKNOWN RECIPIENT, GLC 2222

We have an agency at work for the abolition of slavery in the pending war more powerful than all the Conventions we could assemble. Every battle fought will teach our soldiers & the nation at large that slavery is the great cause of the war, that it is slavery which has brutalized & barbarized the South & that slavery must be abolished as our army advances as a military necessity....

I look presently see the entire north...demanding the abolition of slavery not from their Christian regard for the rights of the slave but from motives that partake rather of self-interest—& from a conviction induced only by arguments and by facts that it is slavery alone that has reduced us to our present state.

The continuance of the war, with the unanimous and hearty approval of the whole north...I would not run the risk of weakening it by an active antislavery movement. Let us polish our tones in patience—for I think I have already seen the beginning of the end.

6 / "The men who have struck this blow at our government are playing for a bigger stake than the right to...extend slavery"

In its analysis of the Civil War's causes, the *Times* of London rejected the notion that this was a war about slavery. It argued that the conflict had the same roots as most wars: territorial aggrandizement, political power, and economic supremacy. But few Northerners or Southerners saw the war in such simple terms. To many white southern soldiers, it was a war to preserve their liberty and their way of life, to prevent abolition and its consequences—race war, racial amalgamation, and, according to one militant Southerner's words, "the Africanization of the South." To many northern soldiers, it was a war to preserve the Union, uphold the Constitution, and defeat a ruthless slave power that had threatened to subvert republican ideals of liberty and equality.

In the following letter, a Philadelphian offers his reflections on the war's causes.

DAVID HOPKINS, AUGUST 18, 1861 (DATED PHILADELPHIA), TO HIS BROTHER, GLC 3043

...There are many wrongs to be righted beside the one done to the Negro race. Sailors today in both the Merchants and Navy services of the U.S. are worse used than the slaves in the South. I don't mean by this any apology for the "Sacred Institution"...I believe that slavery is the cause of this war. The men who have struck this blow at our government are playing for a bigger stake than the right to hold or extend slavery. It is intended to be a death blow to our form of Government. Some three years ago...[a southern] Gov[ernor]...said...he was opposed to every thing that had the word *free* prefixed. He meant just what he said—and he and others have played their cards accordingly ever since.

7 / *"I propose to offer you a few* suggestions"

The initial Union strategy involved blockading Confederate ports to cut off cotton exports and prevent the import of manufactured goods; and using ground and naval forces to divide the Confederacy into three distinct theaters. These were the far western theater, west of the Mississippi River; the western theater, between the Mississippi and the Appalachians; and the eastern theater, in Virginia. Ridiculed in the press as the "Anaconda Plan," after the South American snake that crushes its prey to death, this strategy ultimately proved successful. Although about 90 percent of Confederate ships were able to break through the blockade in 1861, this figure was cut to fewer than 15 percent a year later. Although the Union army suffered repeated defeats and stalemates in the East, victories in the western theater undermined the hopes for Confederate independence.

The following letter suggests how active a role President Lincoln played in the formulation of military strategy.

Abraham Lincoln, October 24, 1861, to General David Hunter, GLC 1212

The command of the Department of the West having devolved upon you, I propose to offer you a few *suggestions*. Knowing how hazardous it is to bind down a distant commander in the field to specific lines and operations, as so much always depends upon a knowledge of localities and passing events. It is intended therefore to leave a considerable margin for the exercise of your judgement and discretion.

The main rebel army (Price's) west of the Mississippi is believed to have passed Dade County in full retreat upon North Western Arkansas, leaving Missouri almost freed from the enemy, excepting in the South East of the State. Assuming this basis of fact, it seems desirable as you are not likely to overtake Price, and are in danger of making too long a line from your own base of supplies and reinforcements, that you should give up the pursuit, halt your main army, divide it into two corps of observation, one occupying Sedalia and the other Rolla, the present *termini* of Railroads, then recruit the condition of both corps by reestablishing and improving their discipline and instruction, perfecting their clothing and equipment and providing less uncomfortable quarters. Of course, both Railroads must be guarded and kept open, judiciously employing just so much force as is necessary for this. From these two points Sedalia and Rolla, and especially in judicious cooperation with Lane on the Kansas border, it would be so easy to concentrate and repel any army of the enemy returning on Missouri from the South West, that it is not probable any such attempt to return will be made by the enemy before or during the approaching cold weather. Before Spring the people of Missouri will probably be in no favorable mood to renew for next year the troubles which have so much afflicted and impoverished them during this.

If you adopt this line of policy, and if, as I anticipate, you will see no enemy in great force approaching, you will have a surplus of force, which you can withdraw from these points, and direct to others as may be needed; the Railroads furnishing ready means of reinforcing the main points, if occasion requires. Doubtless local uprising will, for a time, continue to occur: but these can be met by detachments, and local forces of our own, and will, ere long, tire out of themselves.

While, as stated in the beginning of this letter a large discretion must be, and is left with yourself, I feel sure that an indefinite pursuit of Price, or an attempt, by this long and circuitous route, to reach Memphis, will be exhaustive beyond endurance, and will end in the loss of the whole of the force engaged in the attempt.

8 / *"Nathaniel Gordon was indicted and convicted for being engaged in the Slave Trade"*

Early in the war, Lincoln handled the slavery issue cautiously to avoid losing the support of the border states. He did, however, take a major symbolic step when he became the first president to approve of the execution of an illegal slave trader.

Abraham Lincoln, February 4, 1862, GLC 182

Whereas, it appears that at a Term of the Circuit Court...for the Southern District of New York held in the month of November A.D. 1861, Nathaniel Gordon was indicted and convicted for being engaged in the Slave Trade, and was by the said Court sentenced to be put to death by hanging by the neck, on Friday the 7th day of February, A.D. 1862;

And whereas, a large number of respectable citizens have earnestly besought me to commute the said sentence of the said Nathaniel Gordon to a term of imprisonment for life, which application I have felt it to be my duty to refuse;

And whereas, it seemed to me probable that the unsuccessful application made for the commutation of his sentence may have prevented the said Nathaniel Gordon from making the necessary preparation for the awful change which awaits him;

Now, therefore, be it known, that I, Abraham Lincoln, President of the United States of America have granted and do hereby grant unto him, the said Nathaniel Gordon, a respite of the above recited sentence, until Friday the twenty first day of February, A.D. 1862, between the hours of twelve o'clock at noon and three o'clock in the afternoon of the said day when the said sentence shall be executed.

In granting this respite, it becomes my painful duty to admonish the prisoner that, relinquishing all expectation of pardon by Human Authority, he refer himself alone to the mercy of the Common God and Father of all men.

9 / *"I would like the bill to have...three main features"*

In August 1862 Lincoln stated: "If I could save the Union without freeing any slaves I would do it; and if I could save it by freeing all the slaves I would do it; and if I could save it by freeing some and leaving others alone I would also do that." In fact, by that time, immense pressure was building to end slavery, and Lincoln had privately concluded that he could save the Union only by issuing an emancipation proclamation, which he had already drafted.

The pressure came from a handful of field commanders, Republicans in Congress, abolitionists, and slaves themselves. In May 1861 General Benjamin Butler (1818–93), who had been a lawyer and a politician before the war, had declared slaves who escaped to Union lines "contraband of war," not returnable to their masters. In August Major General John C. Frémont, commander of Union forces in Missouri, had issued an order freeing the slaves of Confederate sympathizers in Missouri. Lincoln, incensed by Frémont's assumption of authority and fearful that the measure would "alarm our southern Union friends, and turn them against us," revoked the order, but allowed Union generals discretion in providing refuge to fugitive slaves.

Congress, too, adopted a series of antislavery measures. In August 1861 it passed the Confiscation Act, authorizing the seizure of all property, including slaves, used for Confederate military purposes. Then in the spring and summer of 1862 Congress abolished slavery in the District of Columbia and the territories; prohibited Union officers from returning fugitive slaves; allowed the president to enlist African Americans in the army; and called for the seizure of Confederate property.

The border states' intransigence on the issue of slave emancipation also pushed the president in a more active direction. In the spring of 1862 Lincoln persuaded Congress to pass a resolution offering financial compensation to states that abolished slavery voluntarily. Three times Lincoln met with border state members of Congress to discuss the offer, and even discussed the possibility of emancipation over a thirty-year period. In July, however, the congressmen rejected Lincoln's offer.

This letter, marked "Private," was written six months before his final decision to issue the Emancipation Proclamation.

Abraham Lincoln, March 24, 1862, to Horace Greeley, MA 6027

If I were to suggest anything it would be that as the North are already for the measure, we should urge it *persuasively* and not *menacingly*, upon the South. I am a little uneasy about the abolishment of slavery in this District, not but I would be glad to see it abolished, but as the time and manner of doing it. If some one or more of the border-states would move fast, I should greater prefer it[.]....

I would like the bill to have...three main features—gradual—compensation—and vote of the people.

10 / "A great number...were killed on Sunday"

Under the Anaconda Plan, Union forces in the West were to seize control of the Mississippi River while Union forces in the East tried to capture the new Confederate capital, in Richmond. In the western theater, the Confederates had built two forts, Fort Donelson along the Cumberland River and Fort Henry on the Tennessee River, which controlled the Kentucky and western Tennessee region and blocked the Union's path to the Mississippi.

The Union officer responsible for capturing these forts was Ulysses S. Grant (1822–85), a West Point graduate who had resigned from the army because of a drinking problem and who was working in his father's tanning shop when the war began. In February 1862, gunboats under Grant's command took Fort Henry, and ten days later Grant's men took Fort Donelson, forcing thirteen thousand Confederates to surrender.

Grant and some forty-two thousand men then proceeded south along the Tennessee River. A Confederate force of forty thousand men, under the command of Beauregard and Johnston, tried to surprise Grant before other Union forces could join him at the Battle of Shiloh. In two days of heavy fighting during which there were thirteen thousand Union casualties and more than ten thousand Confederate casualties, Grant successfully pushed back the southern forces. By early June, Union forces controlled the Mississippi River as far south as Memphis, Tennessee.

A firsthand account of the Battle of Shiloh, written by a northern soldier, follows.

EDGAR PEARCE, APRIL 17, 1862, TO HIS BROTHER FREDERIC, GLC 66.075

I received your letter last Sunday morning and will freely admit that I was very much pleased to see that you had really devoted a whole sheet to your unworthy brother away down South in Dixie and in the midst of Secesh [the Confederacy], but although it is a[n] exciting fact, it is here that we are in the midst of Secesh [Confederates] for they lay all around us in the shelf of death, and now only a few rods from [us are]...over 250 dead bodies and *all* secesh, we did not bury Union men & rebels together at all.... A great number of them were killed on Sunday & when I rode on the field on Friday last dead bodies could still be seen lying round in the brush. It was an useful 24 hours work, but thank fortune now all is quiet and we still sit...in our own beds.... But...we know not at what time the hole may open again in all its fury. We are directly in the advance, but now they have moved hosts of our army to the front and we are back of the center, and cannot be surprised as we were before....

He [Gen. Beauregard] will at least make a desperate *resistance*, if he does not make another *attack* himself, he is said to have an army of 120,000 at his command, but he may not hold this number, 5 rebel deserts that came here a day or two ago say there he used all the eloquence he was master of to get his men to make an advance on us again but was unable to get his men to come up to fire. If this is true than it shows that his men are *sensible to the last*, for the probability is great they will get whipped most *outrageously*, if they do try again, for we are the conquerors, and *they* are *whipped* and *disheartened*.... We are flushed with *victory* and they are disheartened by *defeat*, they were too confident on last Sunday evening a week ago, when Beauregard telegraphed home that this was a second *Manassas* [Bull Run], that the Yankees fought with stubbornness, and with the bravery of *despair*, but the *southern* blood was too much for them, and that the Federals were completely whipped, in the next morning, he would take and *kill* the whole of the Federal forces....

[Confederate] General Beauregard is an able General, or he would not have caught us in the way he did before. I can't help *admiring* him as a military man, though I do wish someone had been lucky enough to shoot him. However Sidney A. Johnston [sic], who was the Commander in Chief *was* killed, and I have stood over his body....

I have rode over this field and through the dead...when the stench was so *intolerable* that my company, and old soldiers at that, had to throw their dinners all overboard, and that on horseback too.... I had human bodies for my landmarks from Monday till

> Friday night, and by that time they were so bloated that you could hardly tell what they were, and Union men at that...literally torn all to pieces, heads gone and bodies cut right in two...."

11 / "Shall our mothers, our wives, our daughters and our sisters, be... outraged by the ruffianly soldiers of the North"

The Civil War witnessed a will to destroy and a spirit of intolerance that conflicted with Americans' self-image as a tolerant people committed to compromise. Not only did the conflict see the use of shrapnel and booby traps, it also reportedly saw a few southern women wear necklaces made of Union soldiers' teeth. In a notorious 1862 order, Union general Ulysses S. Grant expelled all Jews from his military department on the grounds that they were speculating in cotton.

While Grant was driving toward the Mississippi from the north, northern naval forces under Captain David G. Farragut (1801–1870) attacked from the south. In April 1862 Farragut steamed past weak Confederate defenses and captured New Orleans. In New Orleans, Union forces met repeated insults from the city's women. Major General Benjamin F. Butler ordered that any woman who behaved disrespectfully should be treated as a prostitute. Reaction in the North was mixed. Southern reaction to "Beast" Butler was predictably harsh.

> *General Order No. 28, New Orleans, May 15, 1862*
> As the officers and soldiers of the United States have been subject to repeated insults from the women (calling themselves ladies) of New Orleans, in return for the most scrupulous non-interference and courtesy on our part, it is ordered that hereafter when any female shall, by word, gesture or movement, insult or show contempt for any officer or soldier of the Untied States, she shall be regarded and held liable to be treated as a woman of the town plying her avocation.
> By command of Major General Butler

General Pierre G.T. Beauregard referred to this order in an attempt to bolster Confederate forces' morale.

> *General Pierre G.T. Beauregard, General Order No. 44, May 19, 1862, GLC 666*
> Men of the South! shall our mothers, our wives, our daughters and our sisters, be thus outraged by the ruffianly soldiers of the North, to whom is given the right to treat, at their pleasure, the ladies of the South as common harlots? Arouse friends, and drive back from our soil, those infamous invaders of our homes and disturbers of our family ties.

12 / "Our country is involved in desolating war"

In the eastern theater, Union General George McClellan's plan was to land northern forces on a peninsula between the York and James Rivers southeast of Richmond and then march on the southern capital. In March 1862 McClelland landed more than one hundred thousand men on the peninsula, only to find his path along the James River blocked by an ironclad Confederate warship, the *Virginia*. Nevertheless by May, McClellan's forces were within six miles of Richmond.

The Confederacy was in desperate straits. The Confederate government had packed up its official records and was prepared to evacuate its capital. It had already lost most of Tennessee, much of the Mississippi Valley, and New Orleans, its largest city and most important port. Between March and June Confederate forces suffered serious military defeats in Arkansas, Kentucky, Louisiana, North Carolina, and Tennessee.

In June, however, Robert E. Lee assumed command of the Confederate Army of Northern Virginia. As a diversionary move to prevent Union forces from concentrating on Richmond, Lee relied on General Thomas J. ("Stonewall") Jackson to launch lightning-like raids from Virginia's Shenandoah Valley. Then, in a series of encounters between June 26 and July 2, 1862, known as the Seven Days' Battles, Lee and Jackson forced McClellan, who mistakenly believed he was hopelessly outnumbered, to withdraw to the James River.

Union forces still hoped to capture Richmond and bring the war to a quick end. But ten days after President Davis offered the following assessment of the conflict, Lee again repulsed a northern advance. At the Second Battle of Bull Run, Union General John Pope found his army almost surrounded and retreated, giving the Confederacy almost total control of Virginia.

Jefferson Davis, August 18, 1862, speech to the Senate and House of Representatives of the Confederate States, GLC 699

It is again our fortune to meet for devising measures necessary to the public welfare whilst our country is involved in desolating war. The sufferings endured by some portions of the people excite the deep solicitude of the government, and the sympathy thus evoked has been heightened by the patriotic devotion with which these sufferings have been borne. The gallantry and good conduct of our troops, always claiming the gratitude of the country, have been further illustrated on hard fought fields, marked by exhibitions of individual prowess which can find but few parallels in ancient or modern history. Our Army has not faltered in any of the various trials to which it has been subjected, and the great body of the people has continued to manifest a zeal and unanimity which not only cheer the battle-stained soldier, but give assurance to the friends of Constitutional liberty of our final triumph in the pending struggle against despotic usurpation.

The vast army which threatened the Capital of the Confederacy has been defeated and driven from the lines of investment, and the enemy, repeatedly foiled in his efforts for its capture, is now seeking to raise new armies on a scale such as modern history does not record, to effect the subjugation of the South so often proclaimed as on the eve of accomplishment.

The perfidy which disregarded rights secured by compact, the madness which trampled on obligations made sacred by every consideration of honor, have been intensified by the malignity engendered by defeat.

These passions have changed the character of hostilities waged by our enemies, who are becoming less regardful of the usages of civilized war and the dictates of humanity. Rapine and wanton destruction of private property, war upon non-combatants, murder of captives, bloody threats to avenge the death of an invading soldiery by slaughter of unarmed citizens, orders of banishment against peaceful farmers engaged in the cultivation of the soil are some of the methods used by our ruthless invaders to enforce the submission of a free people to foreign sway. Confiscation bills of a character so atrocious as to ensure, if executed, the utter ruin of the entire population of these States, are passed by their Congress and approved by their Executive. The moneyed obligations of the Confederate Government are forged by citizens of the United States and publicly advertised for sale in their cities, with a notoriety that sufficiently attests the knowledge of their government; and its complicity in the crime is further evinced by the fact that the soldiers of the invading armies are found supplied with large quantities of these forged notes, as a means of despoiling the Country people by fraud of such portions of their property as armed violence may fail to reach. Two, at the least, of the Generals of the United States are engaged, unchecked by their government, in exciting servile insurrection and in arming and training slaves for warfare against their masters, citizens of the Confederacy. Another has been found, of instincts so brutal as to invite the violence of his soldiery against the women of a captured city [New Orleans]. Yet the rebuke of civilised man has failed to evoke from the authorities of the United States one mark of disapprobation of his acts; nor is there any reason to suppose that the conduct of Benjamin F. Butler has failed to secure from his government the sanction and applause with which it is known to have been greeted by the public meetings and portions of the press of the United States....

The acts passed at your last session intended to secure the public defence by general enrollment [by a military draft], and to render uniform the rules governing troops in the service, have led to some unexpected criticism that is much to be regretted. The efficacy of the law has thus been somewhat impaired; though it is not believed that in any of the States the popular mind has withheld its sanction from either the necessity or propriety of your legislation....

I am happy to inform you that in spite both of blandishments and threats used in profusion by the agents of the Government of the United States, the Indian Nations within the Confederacy have remained firm in their loyalty and steadfast in the observance of their treaty engagements with this government.

Nor has their fidelity been shaken by the fact that, owing to the vacancies in some of the offices of agents and superintendents, delay has occurred in the payments of the annuities and allowances to which they are entitled....

We have never-ceasing cause to be grateful for the favor with which God has protected our infant Confederacy.

13 / *"The Cherokee People...desire... ample Military Protection for life and property"*

In 1861 many Cherokees, Chickasaws, Choctaws, Creeks, and Seminoles decided to join the Confederacy, in part because some of the tribes' members owned slaves. In return, the Confederate states agreed to pay all annuities that the U.S. government had provided and let the tribes send delegates to the Confederate Congress. A Cherokee chief, Stand Watie (1806–71), served as a brigadier general for the Confederacy and did not surrender until a month after the war was over. The author of the following letter, Chief John Ross (1790–1866), joined the Confederacy early in the war, accepted a commission in the Confederate army, and then switched sides when a federal army invaded the trans-Mississippi West.

After the war these nations were severely punished for supporting the Confederacy. The Seminoles were required to sell their reservation at fifteen cents an acre and buy new land from the Creeks at fifty cents an acre. The other tribes were required to give up half their territory in Oklahoma. This land would become reservations for the Arapahoes, Caddos, Cheyenne, Comanches, Iowas, Kaws, Kickapoos, Pawnees, Potawatomies, Sauk and Foxes, and Shawnees. In addition, all these nations had to allow railroads to cut across their land.

In this letter, Ross, the Cherokee leader, assures President Lincoln of the Cherokees' support for the Union cause. A week and a half later, Lincoln responded in a cautious and lawyerly way, mindful of the fact that Ross had initially sided with the Confederacy. "I shall...cause a careful investigation...to be made," Lincoln wrote. "Meanwhile the Cherokee people remaining practically loyal to the federal Union will receive all the protection which can be given them consistently with the duty of the government of the whole country. I sincerely hope the Cherokee country may not again be over-run by the enemy; and I shall do all I consistently can to prevent it."

John Ross, September 16, 1862, to President Abraham Lincoln, GLC 1233.02

I...beg leave, very respectfully, to represent,

1st. That the relations which the Cherokee Nation sustains towards the United States have been defined by Treaties entered into between the Parties from time to time, and extending through a long series of years.

2nd. Those Treaties were Treaties of Friendship and Alliance. The Cherokee Nation as the weaker party placing itself under the Protection of the United States and no other Sovereign whatever, and the United States solemnly promising that Protection.

3rd. That the Cherokee Nation maintained in good faith her relations towards the United States up to a late period and subsequent to the occurrence of the war between the Government and the Southern States of the Union and the withdrawal of all protection whatever by the Government.

4th. That in consequences of...the overwhelming pressure brought to bear upon them the Cherokees were forced for the preservation of their Country and their existence to negotiate a Treaty with the "Confederate States"

5th. That no other alternative was left them surrounded by the Power & influences, that they were, and that they had no opportunity freely to express their views and assume their true position until the advance into their Country of the Indian Expedition during the last summer.

6th. That as soon as the Indian Expedition marched into the Country the great

Mass of the Cherokee People rallied spontaneously around the authorities of the United States and a large majority of their warriors are now engaged in fighting under their flag....

The advance of the Indian Expedition gave the Cherokee People an opportunity to manifest their views by taking [as] far as possible a prompt and decided stand in favor of their relations with the U.S. Govt.

The withdrawal of that Expedition and the reabandonment of that People & Country to the forces of the Confederate States leaves them in a position fraught with distress, danger and ruin! What the Cherokee People now desire is ample Military Protection for life and property; a recognition by the Govt. of the obligations of existing Treaties and a willingness and determination to carry out the policy indicated by your Excellency of enforcing the Laws and extending to those who are loyal all the protection in your power.

14 / "To the question 'Why was not the rebel army bagged...?... you answer 'That is not the game'"

The United States achieved independence in part because foreign countries such as France and Spain entered the war against Britain on the American side. The Confederacy, too, hoped for foreign aid. In a bold bid to win European support, the Confederacy sought to win a major victory on northern soil.

In September 1862 Lee launched a daring offensive into Maryland. No one could be sure exactly what Lee planned to do. But in an incredible stroke of luck, a copy of Lee's battle plan (which had been wrapped around three cigars) fell into the hands of Union General George B. McClellan. After only a brief delay, on September 17, 1862, McClellan's forces attacked Lee at Antietam Creek in Maryland.

The Battle of Antietam (which is sometimes referred to as the Battle of Sharpsburg) produced the bloodiest single day of the Civil War. Lee suffered eleven thousand casualties; McClellan, thirteen thousand. Lee was forced to retreat, allowing the North to declare the battle a Union victory. But Union forces failed to follow up on their surprise success and decisively defeat Lee's army.

Lincoln deeply mistrusted McClellan, an obsessively cautious general and a Democrat who bitterly opposed the Emancipation Proclamation and who called Lincoln the "Gorilla." In the following exchange of letters, Lincoln expresses his anger over the statement of one officer, Major John J. Key, whose brother was a key McClellan adviser, that it was not the objective of the war to crush the Confederate army. Instead, Key implied, the goal was simply to drag the war out until both sides gave up and the Union could be restored with slavery intact. Key was the only officer to be dismissed from service for uttering disloyal sentiments.

ABRAHAM LINCOLN, SEPTEMBER 26, 1862, TO MAJOR JOHN J. KEY, GLC 228

I am informed that in answer to the question "Why was not the rebel army bagged immediately after the battle near Sharpsburg?" propounded to you by Major Levi C. Turner, Judge Advocate &c. you answer "That is not the game." "The object is that neither army shall get much advantage of the other; that both shall be kept in the field till they are exhausted, when we will make a compromise, and save slavery."

I shall be very happy if you will, within twenty four hours from the receipt of this, prove to me by Major Turner, that you did not, either literally, or in substance, make the answer stated.

[Lincoln recounted his interview with Major Key on September 27, 1862:]

At about 11 o'clock AM. Sep. 27. 1862. Major Key & Major Turner appear before me. Major Turner says, "As I remember it, the conversation was, I asked the question why we did not bag them after the battle at Sharpsburg? Major Key's reply was that was not the game, that we should tire the rebels out and ourselves; that was the only way the Union could be preserved, we come together fraternally, and slavery be saved."

On cross-examination Major Turner says he has frequently heard Major Key converse, in regard to the present troubles, and never heard him utter a sentiment unfavorable to the maintenance of the Union. He has never uttered anything which he Maj. T would call disloyalty.

[After the interview, Lincoln wrote:]

In my view it is wholly inadmissable [sic] for any gentleman holding a military commission from the United States to utter such sentiments as Major Key is within proven to have done. Therefore let Major John J. Key, be forthwith dismissed from the Military service of the United States.

[On November 24, 1862, Lincoln wrote directly to Key (GLC 496.045):]

I sincerely sympathize with you in the death of your brave and noble son.

In regard to my dismissal of yourself from the military service, it seems to me you misunderstand me. I did not charge, or intend to charge you with disloyalty. I had been brought to fear that there was a class of officers in the army, not very inconsiderable in numbers, who were playing a game to not beat the enemy when they could, on some peculiar notion as to the proper way of saving the Union; and when you were proved to me, in your own presence to have avowed yourself to be in favor of that "game" and did not attempt to controvert the proof, I dismissed you as an example, and a warning, to that supposed class. I bear you no ill will; and I regret that I could not have the example without wounding you personally. But can I now, in view of the public interest, restore you to the service, by which the army would understand that I indorse, and approve that game myself? If there was any doubt of your having made the avowal, the case would be different. But when it was proved to me, in your presence, you did not deny or attempt to deny it, but confirmed in my mind by attempting to sustain the position by argument.

I am really sorry for the pain this case gives you, but I do not see how, consistently with duty, I can change it.

THE SIGNIFICANCE OF NAMES

During the Civil War, the Union and Confederate armies tended to give battles different names. Thus the battle known to the Union as Bull Run was called Manassas by the Confederacy. Similarly, the Battle of Antietam was known by the Confederacy as the Battle of Sharpsburg. In general, the North tended to name battles and armies after bodies of water (such as the Army of the Potomac or the Army of the Mississippi), while the Confederacy tended to name battles after towns, and armies after land areas (such as the Army of Northern Virginia or the Army of Kentucky). It seems plausible that the Confederacy used such names to convey a sense that its soldiers were defending something of pivotal importance: their homeland.

THE EMANCIPATION PROCLAMATION

15 / *"All persons held as slaves within any State... in rebellion...shall be...free"*

On September 22, 1862, less than a week after the Battle of Antietam, President Lincoln met with his cabinet. As one cabinet member, Samuel P. Chase, recorded in his diary, the president told them that he had "thought a great deal about the relation of this war to Slavery":

> You all remember that, several weeks ago, I read to you an Order I had prepared on this subject, which, since then, my mind has been much occupied with this subject, and I have thought all along that the time for acting on it might very probably come. I think the time has come now. I wish it were a better time. I wish that we were in a better condition. The action of the army against the rebels has not been quite what I should have best liked. But they have been driven out of Maryland, and Pennsylvania is no longer in danger of invasion. When the rebel army was at Frederick, I determined, as soon as it should be driven out of Maryland, to issue a Proclamation of Emancipation such as I thought most likely to be useful. I said nothing to any one; but I made the promise to myself, and (hesitating a little)—to my Maker. The rebel army is now driven out, and I am going to fulfill that promise.

The preliminary emancipation proclamation that President Lincoln issued on September 22 stated that all slaves in designated parts of the South on January 1, 1863, would be freed. The president hoped that slave emancipation would undermine the Confederacy from within. Secretary of the Navy Gideon Welles reported that the president told him that freeing the slaves was "a military necessity, absolutely essential to the preservation of the Union....The slaves [are] undeniably an element of strength to those who [have] their service, and we must decide whether that element should be with us or against us."

Fear of foreign intervention in the war also influenced Lincoln to consider emancipation. The Confederacy had assumed, mistakenly, that demand for cotton from textile mills would lead Britain to break the Union naval blockade. Nevertheless, there was a real danger of European involvement in the war. By redefining the war as a war against slavery, Lincoln hoped to generate support from European liberals.

Abraham Lincoln, September 22, 1862, GLC 1208

That on the first day of January, in the year of our Lord one thousand eight hundred and sixty-three, all persons held as slaves within any State or designated part of a State, the people whereof shall then be in rebellion against the United States, shall be then, and

H.P. Moore. Photograph(s), Civil War and African-American photographs, 1860–1865 ca.. The Gilder Lehrman Collection, on deposit at the Pierpont Morgan Library. GLC 5140.01

thenceforward, and forever, free; and the Executive government of the United States, including the military and naval authority thereof, will recognize and maintain the freedom of such persons, and will do no act or acts to repress such persons, or any of them, in any efforts they may make for their actual freedom.

That the Executive will, on the first day of January aforesaid, by proclamation, designate the States and parts of States, if any, in which the people thereof respectively, shall then be in rebellion against the United States; and the fact that any State, or the people thereof, shall on that day be in good faith represented in the Congress of the United States, by members chosen thereto at elections wherein a majority of the qualified voters of such State shall have participated, shall, in the absence of strong countervailing testimony, be deemed conclusive evidence that such State, and the people thereof, are not in rebellion against the United States.

Now, therefore, I, Abraham Lincoln, President of the United States, by virtue of the power vested in me as commander-in-chief of the army and navy of the United States, in time of actual armed rebellion against the authority and government of the United States, and as a fit and necessary war measure for suppressing said rebellion, do, on this first day of January, in the year of our Lord one thousand eight hundred and sixty-three, and in accordance with my purpose so to do, publicly proclaimed for the full period of one hundred days from the day first above mentioned, order and designate as the States and parts of States wherein the people thereof, respectively, are this day in rebellion against the United States, the following to wit: Arkansas, Texas, Louisiana (except the Parishes of St. Bernard, Plaquemines, Jefferson, St. John, St. Charles, St. James, Ascension, Assumption, Terre Bonne, Lafourche, St. Mary, St. Martin, and Orleans, including the City of New Orleans), Mississippi, Alabama, Florida, Georgia, South Carolina, North Carolina, and Virginia (except the forty-eight country designated as West Virginia, and also the counties of Berkeley, Accomae, Northampton, Elizabeth City, York, Princess Ann, and Norfolk, including the cities of Norfolk and Portsmouth.) and which excepted parts are for the present left precisely as if this proclamation were not issued.

And by virtue of the power and for the purpose aforesaid, I do order and declare that all persons held as slaves within said designated States and parts of States are and henceforward shall be free; and that the Executive government of the United States, including the military and naval authorities thereof, will recognize and maintain the freedom of said persons.

And I hereby enjoin upon the people so declared to be free to abstain from all violence, unless in necessary self-defence; and I recommend to them that, in all cases when allowed, they labor faithfully for reasonable wages.

And I further declare and make known that such persons, of suitable conditions, will be received into the armed service of the United States, to garrison forts, positions, stations, and other places, and to man vessels of all sorts in said service.

And upon this act, sincerely believed to be an act of justice warranted by the Constitution upon military necessity, I invoke the considerate judgment of mankind and the gracious favor of Almighty God.

16 / *"Lincoln's proclamation will produce dissensions and trouble at the North"*

In a letter to his son, Confederate major general Mansfield Lovell (1822–84) predicts that Lincoln's Emancipation Proclamation "will produce dissensions and troubles at the North and...thus indirectly benefit our Cause." Lovell, a West Point graduate who had served in the Mexican War, had unsuccessfully defended New Orleans against a Union fleet in April 1862.

Even before Lincoln issued the Emancipation Proclamation, Postmaster General Montgomery Blair (1813–83), a former Democrat from Maryland, had warned the president that this decision might stimulate antiwar protests among northern Democrats and cost the administration the fall 1862 elections. In fact, Peace Democrats did protest against the proclamation and Lincoln's assumption of powers not specifically granted by the Constitution. Among the "abuses" they denounced were his unilateral decision to call out the militia to suppress the "insurrection," impose a blockade of southern ports, expand the army beyond the limits set by law, spend federal funds without prior congressional authorization, and suspend the writ of habeas corpus (the right of persons under arrest to have their case heard in court). The Lincoln administration imprisoned about thirteen thousand people without trial during the war, and shut Democratic newspapers in New York, Philadelphia, and Chicago for varying amounts of time.

The Democrats failed to gain control of the House of Representatives in the fall 1862 elections, in part because the preliminary Emancipation Proclamation gave a higher moral purpose to the northern cause.

Confederate major general Mansfield Lovell, October 30, 1862, to his son Joseph Lovell, GLC 3790

I received your letter, my dear Jos.... Tell mother she must put you all to school, no matter what it costs and that she must have you escort her to table.... I am glad to hear that you are improving in arithmetic, my Son. You do not take to it easily or naturally and for that reason will have to apply yourself more studiously, than you would to anything that you learned without trouble. The greater the difficulty of any study the greater exertion you must use—

I think Lincoln's proclamation will produce dissensions and trouble at the North, and will thus indirectly benefit our Cause. The Democratic party there is not willing to go headlong into any abolition war. And the elections will show that Lincoln's policy will be condemned. Give my best love to your little brother and sister and write to me as often as you wish. It will help to improve you in writing in expressing your thoughts. Be a good boy and take care of your beautiful mother while I am gone.

17 / *"An incalculable element of strength to the Union cause"*

In July 1862, about two months before President Lincoln issued the preliminary Emancipation Proclamation, Congress adopted a second confiscation act calling for the seizure of the property of slaveholders who were actively engaged in the rebellion. It seems unlikely that this act would have freed any slaves, since the federal government would have to prove that individual slaveholders were traitors. (In fact, one of the largest slaveholders in South Carolina was a Baltimore Unionist). Lincoln felt that Congress lacked the legal authority to emancipate slaves; he believed that only the President acting as commander-in-chief had the authority to abolish slavery.

In recent years, it has sometimes been charged that the Emancipation Proclamation did not free any slaves, since it applied only to areas that were in a state of rebellion, and explicitly exempted the border states, Tennessee, and portions of Louisiana and Virginia. This view is incorrect. The proclamation did officially and immediately free slaves in South Carolina's sea islands, Florida, and some other locations occupied by Union troops. Certainly, the Emancipation Proclamation was only a crucial first step toward complete emancipation, but in effect it transformed the Union forces into an army of liberation.

At the time he issued the preliminary proclamation, Lincoln defended it as a war measure necessary to defeat the Confederacy and preserve the Union. But it seems clear that Lincoln regarded this argument as necessary on tactical grounds. When he issued the final proclamation on January 1, 1863, he described it not only as "a fit and necessary war measure for suppressing said rebellion," but an "act of justice."

In July 1863, Hannah Johnson, the daughter of a fugitive slave, heard an erroneous report that Lincoln was going to reverse the Emancipation Proclamation. She wrote the President: "Don't do it. When you are dead and in Heaven, in a thousand years that action of yours will make the Angels sing your praises...."

In the following selection, a northern publisher speaks out strongly on behalf of the Emancipation Proclamation.

Rufus Blanchard, ca. 1863, GLC 5508.272 (Blanchard's footnote upon his printed broadside of the Emancipation Proclamation)

The Proclamation is an incalculable element of strength to the Union cause. It makes an alliance between the Rebels and Foreign States as impossible as it is for millions of Bondsmen to love Slavery better than Freedom. They loving our Government in proportion as it becomes a free land of promise and shelter from oppression, thus saving thousands of precious lives and millions of treasure from being lost in foreign wars. It perfects the purposes of the Declaration of Independence and impairs no constitutional rights, those whom it would affect having forfeited those rights by proving false to their country, to humanity and religion. No real support to the Union cause will be lost by this Proclamation, while time-serving traitors, who always covertly opposed the war, will be exposed. It will be a powerful incentive to the slave to fight for the Union instead of his rebel master, and when it becomes executed and Freedom reigns throughout the land, the colored man will leave the Northern regions, whither he has fled from slavery, and join his kindred beneath those sunny skies where nature invites him. Labor will be rewarded, justice fulfilled, and the Old Ship of State will again sail majestic o'er the unrippled waters of Liberty and Peace. Confusion and shame rest upon those who fight against a free government, and songs of thankfulness and love glorify its defenders.

18 / *"How is the Proclamation to be enforced?"*

A Northerner reflects on the significance of the Emancipation Proclamation, which went into effect sixteen days before this letter was written.

AMOS LEWIS, JANUARY 16, 1863, TO HIS NEPHEW SETH LEWIS, GLC 3229

The partial Proclamation has gone forth from the White House that the slaves of rebels shall be free while the slaves of union men are to remain in bondage till dooms day unless their masters are willing to sell them to the government for a stipulated price.... But how is the Proclamation to be enforced? Through fields of Hope and carnage, something in death groans, for the rebels will never surrender their long loved institution only at the cannon's mouth and the point of the bayonet. Why did not the Doctor remove the cause before the Patient was worn out by the disease; he knew how but was afraid to administer [the medicine]...for fear...that the border states would be lost to the Union.

19 / *"The administration are generally damned by the soldiers"*

There can be no doubt that some northern soldiers who were willing to fight to preserve the Union were unwilling to fight to abolish slavery. An unidentified soldier in the 12th Vermont Militia expresses his opposition to the Emancipation Proclamation.

A SOLDIER IN THE 12TH VERMONT MILITIA, JANUARY 18, 1863, TO R. W. SOUTHGATE, GLC 2617

We are going on in the same old sorts—plenty to do, plenty to eat, plenty of grumbling and plenty of damning and plenty of preaching—while the Country all together seems to be going to the devil if possible at a faster rate than ever.

Old Abe['s] stock is clear down——Stanton-Halleck-Seward and in fact all the administration are generally damned by the soldiers and their friends wherever they have any....

The Journal of Commerce editorials are more popular with the army than those of any other newspapers—it is a dreadful shame that the administration should have forced this thing or this state of feeling upon us but here it is....

[The soldiers] unanimously want to go home and let the Southern Confederacy, Negroes, our own administration, and all go to the devil together—and save what they can for themselves and of themselves.

Many are sick of fighting if is purely on the Negro question and now that really seems to be made the whole question—or to determine who shall or shall not be the next president and whose friends shall do the big stealing—or what is the same thing, manage the contract business.

Our company has...shot at the rebels...and are now only anxious to be...sent home.

You have probably heard all about Stuart's Cavalry charge upon us—it was not much of an affair as they were taken by surprise and were routed and run before they or we had time to figure much on what it was best to do next. They all did well and were deservingly highly praised by the Gen[eral] and other officers—besides which we nearly froze to death then in the woods waiting for them to come out and the brush did not last far enough to warm us. We have nobody hurt very badly wounded 14 that were left by there on their route...as of no further use.

20 / "We have not been paid anything since I was at home"

The Civil War separated families in unprecedented numbers and freed women to assume many new roles. With the departure of many men into the military, women entered many occupations previously reserved for men only: in factories, shops, and especially, the expanding civil service, where women took jobs as clerks, bookkeepers, and secretaries. A number of women also served as spies (like Rose O'Neal Greenhow (1814–1864), a Confederate spy in Washington) and even as soldiers (like Albert Cashier, whose real name was Jennie Hodgers).

But it was as nurses that women achieved particular prominence. Louisa May Alcott and Clara Barton were among thousands of women, North and South, who carried supplies to soldiers and nursed wounded men on the battlefield and in hospitals. Through organizations like the Christian Commission (formed by the North's YMCAs) and the U.S. Sanitary Commission (one of whose founders was Elizabeth Blackwell, the first American woman to earn a medical degree), women agents distributed medical supplies, organized hospitals, passed out Bibles and religious tracts, and offered comfort to wounded or dying soldiers.

The following soldier's letter, written by a private in the 12th New Jersey Volunteers, suggests some of the strains caused by the wartime separation of spouses.

DAVID V.M. SMITH, OCTOBER 5, 1862, TO HIS WIFE, ELIZABETH, GLC 4189.08

...We have not been paid anything since I was at home and I don't know when we will get paid but as soon as I get it I will send it to you. And if you will try to do as near Right as I think I am trying to do there will be no dispute between us and may God of heaven help us to say & do as near Right as we possibly can and find fault with one another when we know there is no cause when then the less we do of it the better. We have everything a going on here that was ever thought...but I cannot see any pleasure in playing cards and myself therefore I have not had a game of any kind for I made a promise to myself...that I would not do anything of the kind while was I was in the Army and I intend to live up to it. We have had and have now several men and I suppose they would like to be called men one of them has to carry his knap sack filled with stones for one week 2 hours in each day, one has to walk two hours each day with a flour barrel; one head of the barrel is out and the other head has a hole in it just big enough to let the man's head through; one is marched through the camp with a board on his back & 1 on his breast—with the word theif *{sic}* on each by 12 soldiers and a band playing the Rogues march. There is a number of other but I will not mention any more.

21 / "We left...numbering near 3600.... To day we do not number more than 1200"

Almost as many soldiers died during the Civil War as in all other American wars combined. Union combat deaths totaled 111,904; another 197,388 died of disease, 30,192 in prison, and 24,881 as a result of accidents. Another 277,401 Union solders were wounded. Confederate casualties were nearly as high, with approximately 94,000 combat deaths, 140,000 deaths by disease; and 195,000 men wounded.

More than half of all deaths were caused by disease. As a result of poor sanitation, primitive medical practices, and contaminated water supplies, the average regiment lost half its fighting strength from disease during the first year. This letter underscores the war's human cost–as well as the soldiers' willingness to risk their lives for their comrades and country.

George C. Burling, October 25, 1862, to Hon. William A. Menill, GLC 4921

> Excuse the liberty I take in addressing you this letter knowing you to be a Jersey man to the core. I want you to have a thorough knowledge of the 2nd Brigade. We left our camp last April numbering near 3600 men, for duty. To day we do not number more than 1200. Where is the rest? Virginia's soil made sacred with the blood and bodies of a large number of the deficiency. The balance in Hospitals suffering from wounds or sickness. I have no fault to find with this that is what we left home and its comforts for, to sacrifice health and even life, to sustain our glorious flag and Country, and the remainder though few in numbers are brave in spirit, and are ready and willing to stand to the last man, in defense of our Common Country.

22 / "I proposed a national Banking system"

During the war, the Republican-controlled Congress enacted a series of measures that carried long-term consequences for the future. The Homestead Act of 1862 provided public land free to pioneers who agreed to farm the land for five years. The Morrill Act of 1862 helped states establish agricultural and technical colleges. Congress also authorized construction of the nation's first transcontinental railroad.

The Civil War also brought vast changes to the nation's financial system. Before the Civil War, the federal government did not issue paper money. Instead, paper notes were issued by more than fifteen hundred state banks in 1860, which issued more than ten thousand different kinds of currency.

To end this chaotic system and to impose federal regulation on the financial system, Congress enacted two important pieces of legislation. The Legal Tender Act of 1862 authorized the federal government to issue paper money. Because these notes were printed on green paper, they became known as greenbacks. The National Banking Act of 1863 created the nation's first truly national banking system.

In the following letter, Secretary of the Treasury Samuel P. Chase (1808–73), writing to his eventual successor, describes his plan to make banks more trustworthy and stable. As finally adopted by Congress, the National Banking Act of 1863 chartered national banks that met certain requirements, made the notes of national banks legal tender for all public and private debts, and levied a tax of 2 percent on state bank notes, which rate gradually increased over time. By imposing a tax on state bank notes, the federal government forced state banks to join the federal system. By 1865 national banks had 83 percent of all bank assets in the United States. After 1870, interestingly, state banks made a comeback; they avoided the tax on their bank notes by issuing checks.

Samuel P. Chase, January 27, 1863, to William Pitt Fessenden, GLC 1574.01

In my first report (July 1861) I suggested a tax on bank notes as well as other internal taxes: but at that session no internal duties at all were imposed. We all hoped that the increased customs duties & the direct tax might suffice.

In my second report—just before the Suspension—I proposed a national Banking system and a tax on circulation.... It is my considered judgment that had these views been adopted at the last session...there might have been comparatively little financial embarrassment at the time.

But Congress thought otherwise. The system of conversion was adopted and the Banking Association Bill was only ordered...for public information & consideration.

23 / *"We seem to have the whole world against us"*

By early 1863 the Civil War had begun to cause severe hardship on the southern home front. Not only was most of the fighting taking place in the South, but also, as the Union blockade grew more effective and the South's railroad system deteriorated, shortages grew increasingly common. In Richmond, food riots erupted in April 1863. A war department clerk wrote: "I have lost twenty pounds, and my wife and children are emaciated."

The Confederacy also suffered rampant inflation. Fearful of undermining support for the war effort, Confederate leaders refused to raise taxes to support the war. Instead, the Confederacy raised funds by selling bonds and simply printing money without gold or silver to back it. The predictable result was skyrocketing prices. In 1863 a pair of shoes cost $125; a coat, $350. A chicken cost $15; a barrel of flour, $275.

Defeatism and a loss of will began to spread across the Confederacy. Military defeats suggested divine disfavor. Hardships on the home front generated discontent within the ranks. In a letter to North Carolina's governor, Zebulon B. Vance (1830–94), Confederate Major General Daniel H. Hill (1821–89) describes his men's deteriorating morale.

Major General Daniel H. Hill, March 9, 1863, to Zebulon B. Vance, governor of North Carolina, GLC 2701

Colonel Wheeler goes up to the county of Wilkes to arrest numerous deserters. I have directed him to call upon you for orders to the Militia Officers to act in concert with him. I think that there will be no trouble with these disloyal men, when they find both state and Confederate authorities opposed to them. *God help us*! We seem to have the whole world against us, Yankees, Irish, Germans, Danes, Swedes, Poles, Italians, *Tories & Negroes*.

24 / *"They are all moving to Texas with their Negroes"*

As the war dragged on, enthusiasm faded and class tensions flared. In the North, the worst mob violence in American history took place in New York City in July 1863, two weeks after the Battle of Gettysburg. About 120 people were killed, mainly by police and soldiers. Irish Catholic immigrants and their children had been egged on by

Democratic leaders who told them that Republicans wanted to free the slaves to bring them north to replace Irish workers. During four days of rioting, mobs lynched at least a dozen African-American men, destroyed draft offices, and burned and looted black neighborhoods and the homes of leading Republicans and abolitionists.

In the South, the imposition of a military draft in April 1862 produced protests that this was "a rich man's war and a poor man's fight." Although the law made all abled-bodied men of ages eighteen through thirty-five liable for three years' service, the draft law allowed draftees to pay a substitute to serve for him (the North adopted a similar draft law in March 1863). Further aggravating tension was enactment of the "Twenty Negro Law" in October 1862, which exempted one white man from the draft on every plantation with twenty or more slaves.

In the following selection, General William Tecumseh Sherman (1820–91) mentions that some slaveowners were fleeing with their slaves to Texas to avoid wartime disruptions.

General William Tecumseh Sherman, March 30, 1863, to Admiral David D. Porter, GLC 2501

They are all moving to Texas with their Negroes. God grant all may go there and that our Government will open the back door wide and promise to let them stay there in Peace.

25 / "If I could not command a Co[mpany] of white men, I would not command any"

By early 1863, voluntary enlistments in the Union army had fallen so sharply that the federal government instituted an unpopular military draft and decided to enroll black, as well as white, troops. Indeed, it seems likely that it was the availability of large numbers of African-American soldiers that allowed President Lincoln to resist demands for a negotiated peace that might have included the retention of slavery in the United States. Altogether, 186,000 black soldiers served in the Union army and another 29,000 served in the navy, accounting for nearly 10 percent of all Union forces and 68,178 of the Union dead or missing. Twenty-four African Americans received the Congressional Medal of Honor for extraordinary bravery in battle.

Three-fifths of all black troops were former slaves. The active participation of black troops in the fighting made it far less likely that African Americans would remain in slavery after the Civil War.

While some white officers, such as Robert Gould Shaw (1837–63), who commanded the 54th Massachusetts Regiment, were proud to lead black troops in battle, others, as this letter suggests, exhibited a deep resistance.

Joseph M. Maitland, April 22, 1863, to his brother, GLC 3523.10.63

[F]or my part[,] if I could not command a Co[mpany] of white men, I would not command any. I believe in arming and equipping them and making them fight for their freedom, but I would rather be excused from having anything to do with them, there are enough of Abolitionists to do that.

26 / *"I am very sorry to hear that the Rebels are in Pennsylvania"*

After the Battle of Antietam, Lee's forces retreated into Virginia's Shenandoah Valley with almost no interference. Frustrated by McClellan's lack of aggressiveness, Lincoln replaced him with General Ambrose E. Burnside (1824–81). In December 1862 Burnside attacked seventy-three thousand Confederate troops at Fredericksburg, Virginia. Six times Burnside launched frontal assaults on Confederate positions. The Union army suffered nearly thirteen thousand casualties, twice the number suffered by Lee's men, severely damaging northern morale.

After the defeat at Fredericksburg, Lincoln removed Burnside and replaced him with Joseph Hooker (1814–79). In May 1863 Hooker tried to attack Lee's forces from a side or flanking position. In just ten minutes, Confederate forces routed the Union army at the Battle of Chancellorsville. But the Confederate victory came at a high cost. Lee's ablest lieutenant, Stonewall Jackson, was accidently shot by a Confederate sentry and died of a blood clot.

Despite Confederate victories at Fredericksburg and Chancellorsville, the Union showed no signs of giving up. In a bid to shatter northern morale and win European recognition, Lee's army launched a daring invasion of Pennsylvania.

In this letter, a Union soldier mentions Lee's offensive into Pennsylvania and offers insight into his own attitudes toward race.

Samuel Shenk, June 25, 1863, to his wife (dated Norfolk, Va.), GLC 267.232

Dear and Beloved Wife this afternoon I take the Pleasure to answer your kind and welcome letter I received today. I was very glad to learn that you was well at the time of writing I am well at the Present and I hope the Lord may let me have my good health During this Campaign.... I am very sorry to hear that the Rebels are in Pennsylvania But I hope the men will be Patriots enough to turn out and Chase or Drive the traitors from our soil. War news we have not as much as you have at home for all the news we have here come from our native State that is from Pennsylvania you need not get scared yet the Rebs will not get there yet you will stay where you are yet and don't be scared.... I think if our government would take more interest to how they used the Poor Soldiers and less these stinken old worn out Negroes for the Rebs to feed and take that which to give to the Negroes I think this war would a great deal quicker get settled. But they take better care of the Negroes then they do of a Poor white Soldier.

GETTYSBURG

27 / *"Worrying will do no good"*

When his forces drove northward into Pennsylvania, Lee assumed, mistakenly, that Union forces were still in Virginia. When he suddenly realized that Union forces were in close pursuit, he ordered his forces, which were strung out from Maryland to Harrisburg, Pennsylvania, to converge at Gettysburg, Pennsyvania, a central location where a number of roads met. Lee, who did not want to risk a battle until he had gathered all his troops

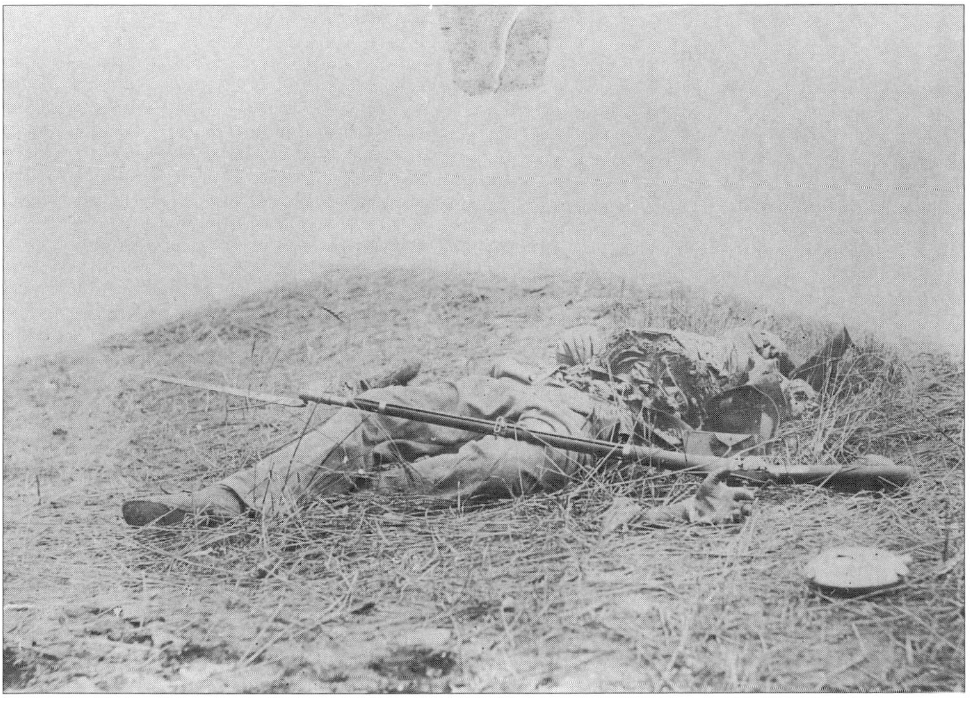

#142 Corpse at Rose Woods (Gettysburg) [From collection: Civil War photograph collection: Brady, Gardner; Lincoln [separate inventory], 1865–1870 ca.. The Gilder Lehrman Collection, on deposit at the Pierpont Morgan Library. GLC 5111

together, ordered his men not to engage the enemy. But on July 1, 1863, a Confederate brigade ran into Union cavalry near Gettysburg, and the largest battle ever fought in the Western Hemisphere broke out before anyone realized what was happening.

On the evening of July 1, most of Lee's army of seventy-five thousand reached Gettysburg. Meanwhile, most of the ninety-thousand-man Union army of General George Meade (1815–72) arrived at Gettysburg that same evening.

On July 2 Lee tried to attack Union positions from the left and right flanks, but northern troops repelled the attack. The next day the Union army, which expected Lee to attack again on the flanks, reinforced its flanks. But Lee launched a frontal attack on the center of the Union lines, which came as a shock and a surprise. However, a frontal assault against a well-fortified defensive position on a hill was very unlikely to succeed. Some fifteen thousand Confederate troops, led by General George E. Pickett (1825–75), marched three-quarters of a mile into withering Union rifle and artillery fire. Although about a hundred Confederate soldiers succeeded in temporarily breaking through the Union defenses, the northern lines held firm. When Lee finally ordered a retreat back into Virginia, it became clear that the Confederacy had suffered a disastrous defeat.

Nearly twenty-five thousand Confederate soldiers were killed, wounded, or missing in action at the Battle of Gettysburg. After Gettysburg, Lee was never able to mount another major offensive.

Writing a day after the battle ended, a Union soldier describes the momentous events of the preceding three days.

Captain Josiah C. Fuller, Company C, 32nd Regiment, Massachusetts Volunteers, July 4, 1863, to his wife, GLC 653.06

My own dear wife. I am "sitting on a rail" but can hardly realize this 4th of July. Am all wet with sweat and don't feel good on that account. Tis so sticky and disagreeable, otherwise I am first rate, and we can hurrah with good grace, for yesterday, we gave the rebs a severe drubbing and have Genl. Hill and from 5 to 10,000 prisoners. Genl. Barksdale (Reb) is dead. This morning everything is quiet and report says the Johnnies have left. The prisoners seemed to be scattered all about and many no doubt have got back. We took the whole of Pickets Division prisoners. Day before yesterday it was terrible fighting.

The rebs tried to turn our left and get possession of a road we came on and thus have a full play on our trains. It was a terrible attack and only hard fighting and stubborn resistance that prevented [defeat]. We were obliged to move Hd Qtrs 2 times that afternoon on account of shell and shot coming among us. The 32nd came along that Thursday afternoon. We saw them as they past and in a half an hour some were going back wounded. Yesterday we moved up to the same ground Hd. Qtrs. were on the day before. We were told that at two o'clock or later the shot and shell would fly in there thick and fast as the rebel line of battle with their batteries was in plain sight opposite and but a half mile distant. But no orders came to move, or be ready to move. I was asleep on the ground and a large part of the company were in the same situation when wizz, bang, burr, chug came the solid shot and shell thicker than I ever knew before. I roused up and took my sword and belt off the stack of arms and told the men to hurry up and while buckling on my belt and sword I turned away to see where the Genl. and his staff were or what they were going to do, and when I had put these on, turned to the company and the most of them had gone and the wagons with them. Our own team had not got out, and I told John to turn them round and put to the rear and right the sooner to get out of range and moved Hamilton's chair out of the way. By this time all had gone and I started to find and get them together again carrying H-['s], chair.

Soon came upon the red wagon (the Genls.) and got 8 or 10 men together. After we had got out of range and in a safe place I ordered them with H to remain there while I went back to where we were to see what in the men's haste had been left behind and if any of the men had been hurt. I went clear back and picked up some things left behind by the men and got safely back. The red wagon had moved and I had some trouble in finding it, and was actually compelled to lay down and rest. I never was before tired as I have been. I did not run a step of the way, but it was terribly hot, and I was lugging a gun and 2 canteens and a haversack and bottle of tamarinds or pickles. I had picked up the last I shall look at by and by, the others belonged to the men. I do not think I was frightened and was not obliged to go back but being a little ashamed of the way the compy. left and not knowing but some of them might be killed or wounded, I thought it best to go see. I certainly did think of home and you all & on your account prayed to be spared. Very near did cannon balls come to me and pieces of shell flew within two feet certain of my head. Some shells burst with a report like a cannon right over head, and as I was coming back the second time, a percussion shell struck the ground a little way ahead and exploded throwing the pieces singing through the air.

The Genl was off to the rear soon as any one and had his horse shot in the rump & had to leave him. H- had a horse and George started with it, but an artillery man took it away from him. H. may get it again. The town of Gettysburg was occupied by our forces this morning and the rebs left so suddenly they could not parole our wounded men they had possession of, and we took many of the Johnnies prisoners. It has been terrible fighting and great loss on both sides. I fear we are too crippled or short of ammunition to follow up the rebs in their retreat. Our Reg't had yesterday forenoon, Col. and Lt. Col. and Major wounded. Capt. Tay, and Dana and Shepherd ditto and other Officers and men ditto. Lt. Barrows...killed and only one or two others that I could find out certainly about.

All the Plymouth men in company E were well. I saw Mr. Eleazer Shaw carrying along the body of Lt. Barrows to bury. I did not understand that the Col. or Lt. Col. were very seriously wounded. Genl. Sickles lost a leg. Genl. Reynolds very recklessly exposed himself (tis said) and is killed. The wounded are every where. I looked into the hospital of two or three different Corps and saw amputation going on and cutting out pieces of shell and musket balls, and though all were suffering and lying around in stable yards, on barn floors, under trees, beside fences and in every place where there was a chance to lay or sit a man. I did not hear so much noise as May used to make in having a tooth out. Just think if you should go up to Uncle John's and see his barn and sheds and outhouse, orchards and yards full of men wounded in every sort of way, and that is as it looks in more than a hundred barns near here. The only difference they would not suffer for water in Plympton and they do not in some places here. There are many lying around yet with their wounds not yet dressed....

Don't worry about me. I am safe and well so far and we will trust to God for the future. Worrying will do no good. Look out for all at home and wait.

28 / "Our wickedness...has brought [us] to what we are"

The four days between July 1 and July 4, 1863, marked a major turning point of the Civil War. Beginning in mid-May, Ulysses S. Grant's troops had begun a siege of Vicksburg, Mississippi. Located on a bluff overlooking the Mississippi, Vicksburg allowed the Confederacy to control river traffic between Memphis and New Orleans. The day after the defeat of Lee's army at Gettysburg, Vicksburg surrendered. Five days later, Union forces captured Port Hudson, Louisiana. These victories gave the North complete control of the Mississippi River and isolated Confederate territory west of the Mississippi from areas east of the river.

After the defeats at Gettysburg and Vicksburg, southern morale began to sag, as the following soldier's letter reveals. Yet despite military defeats, inflation, shortages, desertions, the flight of thousands of slaves, and flagging resolve, the Confederacy continued to fight for another twenty-two months. The following letter, written by a private in the 54th Virginia Volunteers, gives a poignant expression of flagging southern morale.

Christian M. Epperly, August 15, 1863, to his wife, Mary Epperly, GLC 2715.67

My Most Dear Companion

I am happy to say to you that I am well and have another opportunity of answering your kind letter which came to hand last evening which gave me great pleasure to hear from you and to hear that you and the Children was well you don't know how glad I am when I hear you are so favorable blest with health. I hope God will still bless us with such grate blessing while we happen to be apart. and I hope the Time not far distant when we will have the pleasure of meeting in person again. You don't no how glad I would be if I was just there with you. This morning to see the sun rise over the hills in Virginia again for everything seems so sad and desolate here this morning. It seems like the ashes of dear friends and the present conflictions of things has brought deep reflection and sadness upon every heart.... but I hope this is a sign God has provided to bring this time of sorrow to an end and to give us peace in our land again. Though I believe the South first started on a just course but our wickedness and disobedience has brought to what we are: I firmly believe we will be bound to give up to subjugation. I don't think the South will stand much longer and I am sorry to say it, for we will be a ruined people.... But we ought to submit to every thing to have this awful war ended and I pray to God it will end yet....

Dear Mary you wrote in your letter that I should write whether we got plenty to eat or not: we can make out on what we get by buying things at a very high price: we draw a pound of meal a day without being sifted and a pound of bean and 1/3 of a pound of bacon. That is all.... The meal...makes very bad bread. Potatoes cost us six dollars a bushel and beans a dollar a peck only you cant buy many at that price. As to other things they are so high we cant buy at all.

29 / *"I am...in the midst of death in every form and shape"*

Black soldiers participated in the war at great threat to their lives. The Confederate government threatened to summarily execute or sell into slavery any captured black Union soldiers—and did sometimes carry out those threats. Lincoln responded by threatening to retaliate against Confederate prisoners whenever black soldiers were killed or enslaved.

In July 1863 the 54th Massachusetts Infantry, the first black regiment raised in the North, led an assault against Fort Wagner, which guarded Charleston, South Carolina's harbor. Two of Frederick Douglass's sons were members of the regiment. More than 40 percent of the regiment's members were killed or wounded in the unsuccessful attack, including Colonel Robert Gould Shaw, a member of a prominent antislavery family, who was shot dead in the charge.

This soldier's letter reveals the grim realities of the war as Union forces attempted to conquer Charleston.

Abram Bogart, September 9, 1863, to his wife (dated South Carolina), GLC 2970

It is with pleasure that I send a few lines to let you know that I am in the land of the living and in the midst of death in every form and shape, some by fever some by dysentry which goes hard here and some by rebels balls for we have drove the rebels off Amorros Island and have taken Port Wagner. Greg and Sumter they surrendered this week Monday and now the channel is clear to the harbor and city....

Our folks found a horrible sight when they went into the forts they found legs and arms and pools of blood and pieces of flesh all over the forts and by kicking up the sand they would find the dead just out of sight and the smell was too much to bear so they don't occupy the forts.... They say our men are gaining on Charleston every day but slow for it is a hard road to face a fortified enemy to his den but it will be done.... well I don't suppose you care much how the war goes if I only get home safe well that is the way with a good many here if they was out of the way they would give up their claims on government and go home peneless and say good by trouble now I am a good deal of their opinion.... I am out of money entirely for it cost me two months pay on the gun and equipage that was turned in when I went to hospital for I didn't get no receipt of it from the quartermaster....

30 / *"The whites...will not allow their Ind[ian]s to roam in their midst much longer"*

In the midst of the Civil War, a thirty-year conflict began as the federal government sought to concentrate the Plains Indians on reservations. Violence erupted first in Minnesota, where, by 1862, the Santee Sioux were confined to a territory 150 miles long and just 10 miles wide. Denied a yearly payment and agricultural aid promised by treaty, these people rose up in August 1862 and killed more than 350 white settlers at New Ulm. Lincoln appointed John Pope (1822–92), commander of Union forces at the Second Battle of Bull Run, to crush the uprising. Pope promised to deal with the Sioux "as maniacs or wild beasts, and by no means as people with whom treaties or compromises can be made." When the Sioux surrendered in September 1862, 1,808 were taken prisoner and 303 were condemned to death. Defying threats from Minnesota's governor and a senator who warned of the indiscriminate massacre of Indians if all 303 convicted Indians were not executed, Lincoln commuted the sentences of most, but did finally authorize the hanging of 37. This was the largest mass execution in American history, but Lincoln lost many votes in Minnesota as a result of his clemency.

In 1864 fighting spread to Colorado, after the discovery of gold led to an influx of whites. In November 1864 a group of Colorado volunteers, under the command of Colonel John M. Chivington (1821–1894), fell on a group of Cheyenne at Sand Creek, where they had gathered under the governor's protection. "We must kill them big and little," he told his men. "Nits make lice" (nits are the eggs of lice). The militia slaughtered about 150 Cheyenne, mostly women and children.

In this letter, an Ojibway leader describes relations between Indians and missionaries to the clergyman who had helped to persuade Lincoln to commute most of the death sentences in Minnesota.

George Bonga, October 22, 1863, to Rev. Henry B. Whipple, GLC 5121

...The Missionaries & the Gov[ernmen]t has been trying for many years, to educate & civilize the Ind[ian].... I am one of the many, who think it almost impossible to civilize the Ind[ian] as long as he inhabits this thick wooded country without a very large expenditure of money.... I have now been 35 years a pretty close observer of Ind[ian] affairs between the Gov[ernmen]t & Missionaries, & the Ind[ian]s. & I have always noticed, that after the Gov[ernmen]t has fulfilled its treaty stipulations about farming, never anything was done by Ind[ians] after, not even to enlarge his own garden. It could not be expected of Missionaries, to have such large means, so as to show them what benefit they could derive by cultivating the soil and thereby induce them to adopt the habits of the whites.

The Ind[ian] & his father before him have been used to the chase, altho hard work, he is proud of it & thinks to cultivate the soil is only the work of hirelings & squaws & most of the men are ashamed to work in that way. Many a good advice has been given to them, all to no purpose. Starvation will come to him first, before he will cut down trees & dig up roots; when he very well knows it would much better his condition. It would seem, that they can't perceive, that when their game is all killed off, which is disappearing very fast, they will then have to come down to the very lowest depth of degradation, if they are not exterminated, before that time reaches them....

The little I know of the whites leads me to think, that they will not allow their Ind[ian]s to roam in their midst much longer as well as all the Ind[ian]s who live near the white settlements, if the Ind[ian] could be induced to see his own good he would learn that the sooner he was removed from the whites, the better it would be for himself & for his children after him. Having lived the most of my life time with the Ind[ian]s, I easily perceive that the Ind[ian] of today is not the same kind of Ind[ian] that was 40 years ago, altho the same band. In those days we lived and mingled with them, as if we all belonged to one & the same family, our goods often out without lock & key, never fearing anything would go wrong. Far different is it now a days. There is that suspicion on either side, that when we hear of 10 or more Ind[ian]s gathered together, we feel anxious & ask each other, what that can mean, if it is not some bad design & on the Ind[ian] side, they have always some complaint to make. Some imaginary promise that the Gov[ernmen]t has not fulfilled, has led them to that belief, that the whites are combined to try & destroy them. It appears to us all, that there is something smoldering in the breast of the Ind[ian] that it will not take much to set it to a blaze. If that should ever take place, no one can foretell how far the flames will extend....

31 / *"The condition of the Freed Negroes...is daily becoming worse"*

In a letter to President Lincoln, aid workers offer a graphic portrait of the plight of wartime refugees.

James E. Yeatman et al., Western Sanitary Commission, November 6, 1863, to President Lincoln, GLC 1545.11

The undersigned, members of the Western Sanitary Commission, most respectfully represent, that the condition of the Freed Negroes in the Mississippi Valley is daily becoming worse, and [that there are] not less than fifty thousand, chiefly women and children, now within our lines, between Cairo [Illinois] and New Orleans, for whom no adequate provision has been made. The majority of them have no shelter but what they call "brush tents," fit for nothing but to protect them from night dews. They are very poorly clad—

H.P. Moore. Photograph(s), Civil War and African-American photographs, 1860–1865 ca.. The Gilder Lehrman Collection, on deposit at the Pierpont Morgan Library. GLC 5140.01

many of them half naked—and almost destitute of beds and bedding—thousands of them sleeping on the bare ground. The Government supplies them with *rations*, but many unavoidable delays arise in the distribution so that frequent instances of great destitution occur. The army rations (*beef and crackers*) are also a kind of diet they are not used to; they have no facilities of cooking, and are almost ignorant of the use of wheat flour; and even when provisions in abundance are supplied, they are so spoiled in cooking as to be neither eatable nor wholesome. Add to these difficulties, the helplessness and improvidence of those who have always been slaves, together with their forlorn and jaded condition when they reach our lines, and we can easily account for the fact that sickness and death prevail to a fearful extent. No language can describe the suffering, destitution and neglect which prevail in some of their "camps." The sick and dying are left uncared for, in many instances, and the dead unburied. It would seem, now, that one-half are doomed to die in the process of freeing the rest....

We now respectfully ask permission and authority to extend our labors to the suffering freed people of the South-West and South. If you will give us your endorsement in the undertaking before the people, we think we can raise large sums of money, and accomplish great good. Nor would it be only a work of philanthropy, but equally of patriotism, for it would remove an increasing reproach against the Union cause, and by lessening the difficulties of emancipation, would materially aid in crushing the rebellion. At present, hundreds of the blacks would gladly return to slavery, to avoid the hardships of freedom; and if this feeling increases and extends itself among them, all the difficulties of the situation will be increased; while, at the same time, a most effective argument is given to the disloyal against our cause.

32 / *"The recruitment of colored troops has become the settled purpose of the Government"*

During the war, African-American troops also faced a different kind of battle: a battle against discrimination in pay, promotions, and medical care. Despite promises of equal treatment, blacks were relegated to separate regiments commanded by white officers. Black soldiers received less pay than white soldiers, inferior benefits, and poorer food and equipment. While a white private was paid $13 a month plus a $3.50 clothing allowance, blacks received just $10 a month, out of which $3 was deducted for clothing. Furthermore, black soldiers were not provided with the enlistment bonuses commonly given to white soldiers, and, until the end of the war, the federal government refused to commission black officers.

Within the ranks, black troops faced repeated humiliations; most were employed in menial assignments and kept in rear-echelon, fatigue jobs. They were punished by whipping or by being tied by their thumbs; if captured by the Confederates, they faced execution. But despite these trials, African-American soldiers won their battle for equal pay (in 1864), and in 1865 they were allowed to serve as line officers. Drawing upon the education and training they received in the military, many former troops became community leaders during Reconstruction.

One Union captain explained the significance of black military participation on the attitudes of many white soldiers. "A great many [white people]," he wrote, "have the idea that the entire Negro race are vastly their inferiors. A few weeks of calm unprejudiced life here would disabuse them, I think. I have a more elevated opinion of their abilities than I ever had before. I *know* that many of them are vastly the *superiors* of those...who would condemn them to a life of brutal degradation."

In the following selection, General Benjamin F. Butler directs his men to treat black soldiers with respect and declares his opposition to the government's policy of paying African-American soldiers less than white soldiers. This document is extremely revealing and illustrative of the most "liberal" and "best-intentioned" values of the 1860s.

Major General Benjamin F. Butler, General Order No. 46, 18th Army Corps, Department of Virginia and North Carolina, Virginia, December 5, 1863, GLC 698

The recruitment of colored troops has become the settled purpose of the Government. It is therefore the duty of every officer and soldier to aid in carrying out that purpose, by every proper means, irrespective of personal predilection. To do this effectually, the former condition of the blacks; their change of relation; the new rights acquired by them; the new obligations imposed on upon them; the duty of the Government to them; the great stake they have in the war; and the claims their ignorance, and the helplessness of their women and children, make upon each of us, who hold a higher grade in social and political life, must all be carefully considered.

It will also be taken into account that the colored soldiers have none of the machinery of "State aid" for the support of their families while fighting our battles, so liberally provided for the white soldiers, nor the generous bounties given by the State and National Governments in the loyal States—although this last is far more than compensated to the black man by the great boon awarded to him, the result of the war—FREEDOM FOR HIMSELF AND HIS RACE FOREVER!

To deal with these several aspects of this subject, so that as few of the Negroes as possible shall become chargeable either upon the bounty of Government or the charities of the benevolent, and at the same time to do justice to those who shall enlist, to encourage enlistment, and to cause all capable of working to employ themselves for their support, and that of their families—either in arms or other service—and that the rights of Negroes and the Government may both be protected, *it is ordered*:

I.... In this Department, after the 1st day of December, instant, and until otherwise ordered, every able bodied colored man who shall enlist and be mustered into the service of the United States for three years or during the war, shall be paid as bounty, to supply his immediate wants, the sum of ten (10) dollars....

II.... To the family of each colored soldier so enlisted and mustered, so long as he shall remain in the service and behave well, shall be furnished suitable subsistence, under the direction of the Superintendents of Negro Affairs, or their Assistants; and each soldier shall be furnished with a certificate of subsistence for his family, as soon as he is mustered; and any soldier deserting, or whose pay and allowances are forfeited by Court Martial, shall be reported by his Captain to the Superintendent of the District where his family lives, and the subsistence may be stopped—provided that such subsistence shall be continued for at least six months to the family of any colored soldier who shall die in the services by disease, wounds or battle.

III.... Every enlisted colored man shall have the same uniform, clothing, arms, equipments, camp equipage, rations, medical and hospital treatment as are furnished to the United States soldiers of a like arm of the service, unless upon request, some modification thereof shall be granted from these Head Quarters.

IV.... The pay of the colored soldiers shall be ten ($10) per month—three of which may be retained for clothing. But the non-commissioned officers, whether colored or white, shall have the same addition to their pay as other non-commissioned officers. It is, however, hoped and believed by the Commanding General [Butler], that Congress, as an act of justice, will increase the pay of the colored troops to a uniform rate with other troops of the United States. He can see no reason why a colored soldier should be asked to fight upon less pay than any other. The colored man fills an equal space in ranks while he lives, and an equal grave when he falls.

VIII.... Political freedom rightly defined is *liberty to work* and to be protected in the full enjoyment of the fruits of labor; and no one with ability to work should enjoy the fruits of another's labor: *Therefore*, no subsistence will be permitted to any Negro or his family, with whom he lives, who is able to work and does not work. It is, therefore, the duty of the Superintendent of Negro Affairs to furnish employment to all Negroes able to labor, and see that their families are supplied with the necessaries of life. Any Negro who refuses to work when able, and neglects his family, will be arrested and reported to these Head Quarters, to be sent to labor on the fortifications, where he will be made to work. No Negro will be required to labor on the Sabbath, unless upon the most urgent necessity.

IX.... The Commanding General is informed that officers and soldiers in the Department have, by impressment and force, compelled the labor of Negroes, sometimes for private use, and often without any imperative necessity.

Negroes have rights so long as they fulfill their duties: Therefore it is ordered, that no officer or soldier shall impress or force to labor for any private purpose whatever, any Negro; and Negro labor shall not be impressed or forced for any public purpose, unless under orders from these Head Quarters, or because of imperative military necessity, and where the labor of white citizens would be compelled, if present....

X.... The theory upon which Negroes are received into the Union lines, and employed, either as laborers or soldiers, is that every Negro able to work who leaves the rebel lines, diminishes by so much the producing power of the rebellion to supply itself with food and labor necessary to be done outside of military operations to sustain its armies; and the United States thereby gains either a soldier or a producer. Women and children are received, because it would be manifestly iniquitous and unjust to take the husband and father and leave the wife and child to ill-treatment and starvation. Women and children are also received when unaccompanied by the husband and father, because the Negro has the domestic affections in as strong a degree as the white man, and however far South his master may drive him, he will sooner or later return to his family....

XI.... In consideration of the ignorance and helplessness of the Negroes arising from

> the condition in which they have been heretofore held, it becomes necessary that the Government should exercise more and peculiar care and protection over them than over its white citizens, accustomed to self-control and self-support, so that their sustenance may be assured their rights respected, their helplessness protected, and their wrongs redressed; and that there be one system of management of Negro affairs....

33 / *"You are directed to have a transport... sent to the...colony established...at...San Domingo"*

For much of his political career, Lincoln, like his political idol Henry Clay, was an advocate of colonization, based on Lincoln's belief that "the great mass of white people" would refuse to extend equal rights to African Americans. This assumption and prediction, Lincoln believed, "whether well or ill-founded, cannot be safely disregarded." In 1862 the president met with a group of African Americans at the White House (no previous president had dreamed of inviting blacks to the White House), and, in what was perhaps the lowest point of his presidency, seemed to blame blacks for the Civil War and predicted that they would have to emigrate overseas. Lincoln said "your race are suffering, in my judgment, the greatest wrong inflicted on any people...but on this broad continent, not a single man of your race is made the equal of a single man of ours."

Frederick Douglass condemned the president's remarks. "No sincere wish to improve the condition of the oppressed has dictated" his words, Douglass wrote. "It expresses merely the desire to get rid of them, and reminds one of the politeness with which a man might try to bow out of his house some troublesome creditor or the witness of some old guilt."

In that year, 450 African Americans were recruited to settle on the island of Vache, off the coast of present-day Haiti. Smallpox and mismanagement by a white government-appointed manager contributed to the colony's failure. The transport ship dispatched by President Lincoln picked up only 368 survivors.

Abraham Lincoln, February 1, 1864, to Edwin M. Stanton, GLC 3973

> You are directed to have a transport (either a steam or sailing vessel as may be deemed proper by the Quartermaster General) sent to the colored colony established by the United States at the Island of Vache, on the coast of San Domingo to bring back to this country such of the colonists there as desire to return. You will have the transport furnished with suitable supplies for that purpose, and detail an office of the Quartermaster's Department who, under special instructions to be given, shall have charge of the business. The colonists will be brought to Washington, unless otherwise hereafter directed and be employed and provided for at the camps for colored persons around that City. Those only will be brought from the island who desire to return, and their effects will be brought with them.

34 / *"Neither slavery nor involuntary servitude...shall exist"*

The Emancipation Proclamation freed only those slaves in states still at war. As a wartime order, it could subsequently be reversed by presidential degree or congressional legislation. The permanent emancipation of all slaves therefore required a constitutional amendment.

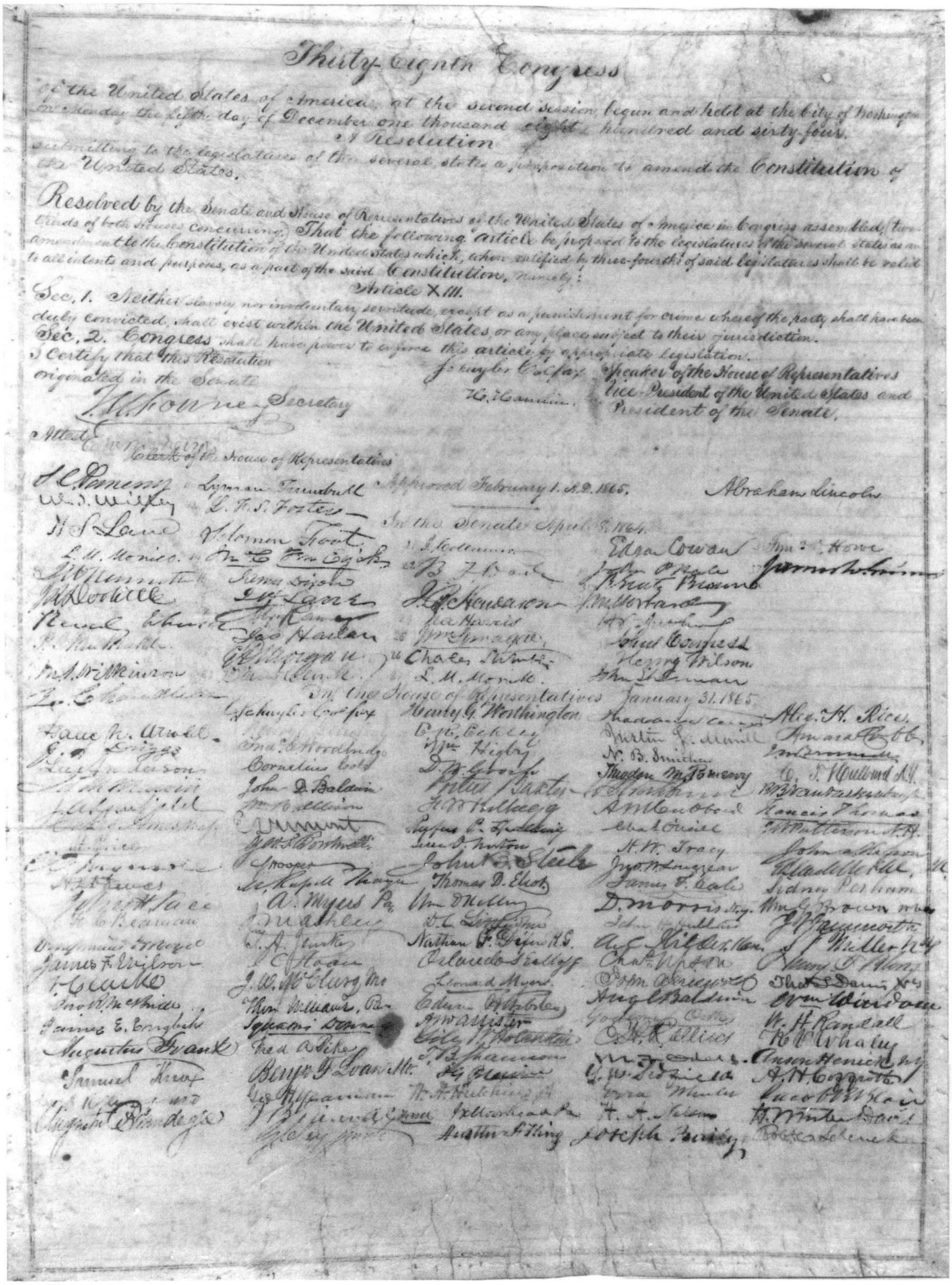
Thirty-Eighth Congress

of the United States of America, at the second session, begun and held at the City of Washington on Monday the fifth day of December one thousand eight hundred and sixty-four.

A Resolution

Submitting to the legislatures of the several states a proposition to amend the Constitution of the United States.

Resolved by the Senate and House of Representatives of the United States of America in Congress assembled, two-thirds of both houses concurring, That the following article be proposed to the legislatures of the several states as an amendment to the Constitution of the United States which, when ratified by three-fourths of said legislatures shall be valid to all intents and purposes, as a part of the said Constitution, namely:

Article XIII.

Sec. 1. Neither slavery nor involuntary servitude, except as a punishment for crime whereof the party shall have been duly convicted, shall exist within the United States, or any place subject to their jurisdiction.

Sec. 2. Congress shall have power to enforce this article by appropriate legislation.

I certify that this Resolution originated in the Senate

Secretary

Schuyler Colfax Speaker of the House of Representatives

H. Hamlin. Vice President of the United States and President of the Senate

Attest

Clerk of the House of Representatives

Approved February 1. A.D. 1865.

Abraham Lincoln

In the Senate April 8. 1864.

In the House of Representatives January 31. 1865.

Abraham Lincoln. Document signed, Thirteenth Amendment resolution ["Congressional" copy on vellum], 1865/02/01. The Gilder Lehrman Collection, on deposit at the Pierpont Morgan Library. GLC 263

In April 1864 the Senate passed the Thirteenth Amendment to abolish slavery in the United States. Opposition from Democratic representatives prevented the amendment from receiving the required two-thirds majority. If McClellan and the Democrats had won the election of 1864, as Lincoln and most Northerners expected in the summer, the amendment would almost certainly have been defeated and slave emancipation repudiated as a war aim. Only after Lincoln was reelected did Congress approve the amendment. Ratification by the states was completed in December 1865.

THIRTEENTH AMENDMENT RESOLUTION, APRIL 8, 1864, GLC 263

Article XIII.

Sec. 1. Neither slavery nor involuntary servitude, except as a punishment for crime, whereof the party shall have been duly convicted, shall exist within the United States, or any place subject to their jurisdiction.

Sec. 2. Congress shall have power to enforce this article by appropriate legislation.

35 / "*Be* prepared *for* the worst"

Initially, Lincoln and his generals anticipated a conventional war in which Union soldiers would respect civilians' property. Convinced that there was residual unionist support in the South, they expected to preserve the South's economic base, including its factories and rail lines. But as the war dragged on, the Civil War became history's first total war, a war in which the Union sought the Confederacy's total defeat and unconditional surrender. To achieve success, Union officers such as Ulysses S. Grant and William Tecumseh Sherman believed that it was necessary to break the South's will to fight. Sherman summed up the idea of total war in blunt terms: "We are not only fighting hostile armies," he declared in 1864, "but a hostile people, and must make old and young, rich and poor, feel the hard hand of war."

A year earlier, a general order was issued that declared that military necessity "allows of all destruction of property" and "appropriation of whatever an enemy's country affords necessary for the subsistence and safety of the Army." This order allowed soldiers to destroy anything that might be of use to the Confederacy.

By the fall of 1864 the Confederacy was beginning to show signs of collapse. It extended the draft ages from seventeen to fifty. By early 1865 the need for manpower was so great that the Confederate Congress authorized arming three hundred thousand slave troops.

LIEUTENANT JOHN MCKINLEY GIBSON, APRIL 12, 1864, TO HIS FATHER, TOBIAS GIBSON, GLC 4501.94

We are both glad to hear that you were all well, and that the Federals had given you no more than the ordinary trouble. I suppose you have the same trials that you had when I was with you. There is no such thing as satisfying a Negro without slavery. They do not know their own wants and unless there is some one to teach them, they are but as little children. I hope they may in some way be made to feel that they are not the *superiors* of the whites....

Have you seen the "Currency Bill" passed by the C[onfederate] S[tates's] Congress at its last session. One hundred dollar notes are taxed firstly with a discount of 83 percent and there is a tax of ten cents on a dollar every month. So that in a short time they will be valueless.... I am sorry I did not bring out with me all the Confederate money I could get. I was afraid something would be done to reduce the redundancy of the currency, which would result in a great depreciation of the old issue. Follow Lee's advice as far as practicable. I do not look upon matters in exactly the same light that he does though you should be *prepared* for *the worst*.

36 / "White children are to...mix in the same cabin with the Negro with the same Yankee Marm for the teacher!"

A supporter of the Confederacy criticizes the Union army of occupation.

TOBIAS GIBSON, APRIL 14, 1864 (DATED OAK FOREST, LOUISIANA), TO HIS DAUGHTER LOULA GIBSON, GLC 4501.95

I know you have reason to conclude that I have almost forgotten you, to judge by the infrequency of my letters to you, but nothing could be more erroneous than such an idea. When you knew how much trouble I had in 1861, that was nothing to my trials and troubles since [Union troops occupied the area]....

American ideas of liberty have totally changed since the Negro war organ [the occupation government] and education for them [the freedmen] is soon to be the order of the Day by Regular Military order. While as far as I know the white children are to grow up in ignorance or mix in the same cabin with the Negro with the same Yankee Marm for the teacher! How much farther this system is to go is broadly hinted at in the newspapers of the North with what real foundation I have as yet no means of judging but with the prevailing tendency to fanaticism at the North I would not be at all surprised if "miscegenation" became the fashion as well as the Sentiment of those people....

We are fixed to our present boundaries by the lever of "military necessity." And we only wish that we may be as well off as we are at the end of the present year. I dread the events of the immediate future filled as it is of potent events for good or evil to all. You no doubt look with painful anxiety to the fate of these last days in the conflict of arms, which cannot be very far off in the future.

37 / "Sad and awful Execution[s] which [have] taken place"

Military desertions were treated harshly. A Confederate soldier describes the fate of men who tried to leave their companies and were recaptured.

CHRISTIAN M. EPPERLY, 54TH VIRGINIA VOLUNTEERS, MAY 8, 1864, TO HIS WIFE MARY EPPERLY, GLC 2715.91

I haven't any news to write to you at this time, only the sad and awful Execution which taken place in our Brigade yesterday which was too cruel for mortal man to behold. There was 14 North Carolinians shot to Death yesterday with musketry. 10 belonging to the 58 North Carolina and 4 to the 60 Regt. Their cries and groans, how sad they did sound. They were tied to stakes by their Captains and then cruelly murdered by the order of a few wicked men and had done nothing...but left the army and went home to see their Families and Friends. [If they had] done anything else I never heard say anything about it.... I have often times seen wicked things done, but this was the cruelest thing ever.... God forbid that I Should witness another such deed committed by men.

38 / *"If the South gains its independence plenty of slaves can be got from Africa"*

Slaves played a critical role in their own liberation. Southern slaves deserted plantations and fled to Union lines. Slaves also staged a few small insurrections during the war as the slave system itself began to unravel. Planters were stunned to see trusted house slaves and field drivers lead field hands in deserting to the Union army. Eventually 150,000 former slaves fought as soldiers in the Union army.

The following letter suggests how the plantation system of labor and discipline was beginning to break down in the face of protracted war.

TOBIAS GIBSON, AUGUST 3, 1864, TO HIS DAUGHTER SARAH GIBSON, GLC 2715

The blacks are getting worse every day & at the end of this year I think they will be *intolerable* in account of bad work and the condition of the crops. I told them they must work Saturday evening but they would not do it, and a dozen of the best men, Wesley at the head, went off to Thibodeux...and last night got back with a paper from Genl. Cameron requiring them to work until the Provost Marshall had investigated the matter.... I have abandoned half the cotton on this place in order to save the remainder but there is a great likelihood that the caterpillar will take what is left.... So in fact our prospect is not bright by any measure.

You will see by the inclosed slip that there is to be another call on our plantations for col[ore]d soldiers. How many will be taken can not be told at present but we shall soon know. The demand for labor will be so great [in] another year that no large plantation can be carried on at the force that will work. I shall try to lease mine out if I could. Fear to do so with safety. After the war if the South gains its independence plenty of slaves can be got from Africa and to let the North take what it likes and make the most of them.

39 / *"All the senators are more anxious to have Mr. Lincoln live than...ever...before"*

The 1864 presidential election was one of the most critical in American history. At stake was whether the war would end in unconditional surrender or a negotiated settlement, which might result in the preservation of slavery as a legal institution. Even though hundreds of thousands of slaves deserted to Union lines during the war, it is not at all inconceivable that slavery could have survived if the president had not been committed to emancipation. During the American Revolution a third of Georgia's slaves had been freed by the British, and tens of thousands of Virginia's slaves had escaped bondage. Nevertheless, slavery survived the revolutionary upheavals in the South and soon began to flourish and expand. Similarly, slavery was temporarily reinstituted by the French in St. Domingue and greatly expanded in Guadeloupe, Martinique, and other colonies despite the Haitian Revolution and the French emancipation decree of 1794.

In August 1864 Lincoln expressed his view in moving words. Observing that more than 130,000 blacks were fighting to preserve the Union, he said that they were motivated by the "strongest motive...the promise of freedom. There have been men who proposed to me to return to slavery the black warriors. I would be damned in time & in eternity for so doing. The world shall know that I will keep my faith to friends and enemies, come what will."

Deeply anxious about the election's outcome, Republicans and prowar Democrats formed the National Union Party, which renominated Lincoln and selected Andrew Johnson (1808–75), a former Democratic senator from Tennessee, for vice president. Johnson replaced Lincoln's first vice president, Hannibal Hamlin (1809–91), a former U.S. senator from Maine. In this letter, a young girl suggests how some ardent Republicans viewed Johnson.

MARY Y. PRENTISS, MARCH 8, 1865, TO HER FRIEND OR SISTER "ABBA," GLC 2319

All the senators are more anxious to have Mr. Lincoln live than they ever were before. People say they wanted Lincoln and Hamlin [Lincoln's first-term vice president], but not Mr. Lincoln and Johnson....

Of course you have heard of the shocking condition that the vice president was in when he took the oath. He was too drunk to preside in the Senate Monday or Tuesday.

40 / *"How shall we End the Rebellion...Coax it, or Crush it?"*

As their presidential nominee, the Democrats chose General George B. McClellan, who opposed the Emancipation Proclamation and who ran on a platform that condemned Lincoln for "four years of failure" and called for a negotiated end to the war.

Some Radical Republicans also opposed Lincoln's reelection. Lincoln had asked Congress to seat representatives from three recently conquered Confederate states—Arkansas, Louisiana, and Tennessee—and also announced that when 10 percent of the voters in the rebel states (excluding high Confederate officials) pledged loyalty to the Union (including government actions concerning slavery), they would be readmitted to the Union. Radicals denounced the "10 Percent Plan" as too lenient. Congress in July 1864 adopted a much more radical measure, the Wade-Davis Act, which required rebel states to abolish slavery, repudiate the Confederate war debt, disfranchise Confederate leaders, and require 50 percent of the citizens to pledge loyalty to the Union. The radicals nominated General John C. Frémont for president, but he withdrew a month before the election.

Lincoln feared that northern battlefield victories might be lost at the polls. During the summer of 1864 he confessed, "it seems exceedingly probable that this administration will not be reelected." There seems little doubt that a McClellan victory would have resulted in an agreement to maintain slavery in the United States.

The capture of Atlanta, a major southern railroad and manufacturing center, in September, electrified northern voters, who gave Lincoln a resounding victory. He received 55 percent of the popular vote to just 21 percent for McClellan.

"The Two Roads to Peace," GLC 701

How shall we End the Rebellion—Shall we Coax it, or Crush it?

Every American citizen wants the Rebellion ended and Peace restored. Two plans have been proposed for doing it: one, by a Convention which met in Baltimore June 7; the other by a Convention which met in Chicago, August 30. Read and compare the two. Here they are:—

The Chicago [Democratic] Platform.

Resolved, That in the future, as in the past, we will adhere with unswerving fidelity to the Union, under the Constitution, as the only solid foundation of our strength, security, and happiness as a people, and as a framework of government equally conducive to the welfare and prosperity of all the States, both Northern and Southern.

Resolved, That this Convention does explicitly declare, as the sense of the American people, that after four years of failure to restore the Union by the experiment of war, during which, under the pretense of military necessity or war power higher than the Constitution, the Constitution itself has been disregarded in every part, and public liberty and private right alike trodden down, and the material prosperity of the country essentially impaired, justice, humanity, liberty, and the public welfare, demand that IMMEDIATE EFFORTS BE MADE FOR A CESSATION OF HOSTILITIES, with a view to the ultimate Convention of all the States, or other peaceable means, to the end that at the earliest practicable moment peace may be restored on the basis of the Federal Union of the States.

Resolved, That the direct interference of the military authority of the United States in the recent elections in Kentucky, Maryland, Missouri, and Delaware, was a shameful violation of the Constitution, and the repetition of such acts in the approaching election will be held as revolutionary, and resisted with all the means and power under our control.

Resolved, That the aim and object of the Democratic party is to preserve the Federal Union and the rights of the States unimpaired; and they hereby declare that they consider the Administrative usurpation of extraordinary and dangerous powers not granted by the Constitution, the subversion of the civil by military law in States not in insurrection, the arbitrary military arrest, imprisonment, trial and sentence of American citizens in States where civil law exists in full force, the suppression of freedom of speech and of the press, the denial of the right of asylum, the open and avowed disregard of State rights, the employment of unusual test-oaths, and the interference with and denial of the right of the people to bear arms, as calculated to prevent a restoration of the Union, and the perpetuation of a government deriving its just powers from the consent of the governed.

Resolved, That the shameful disregard of the Administration to its duty in respect to our fellow-citizens who now and long have been prisoners of war in a suffering condition, deserves the severest reprobation, on the score alike of public interest and common humanity.

Resolved, That the sympathy of the Democratic party is heartily and earnestly extended to the soldiery of our army, who are and have been in the field under the flag of our country; and in the event of our attaining power, they will receive all the care and protections, regard and kindness that the brave soldiers of the Republic have so nobly earned.

The Baltimore [Republican] Platform.

Resolved, That it is the highest duty of every American citizen to maintain against all their enemies, the integrity of the Union, and the paramount authority of the Constitution and laws of the United States; and that, laying aside all differences of political opinions, we pledge ourselves as Union men, animated by a common sentiment, and aiming at a common object, to do everything in our power to aid the Government in quelling, BY FORCE OF ARMS, the rebellion now raging against its authority, and in bringing to the punishment due to their crimes the rebels and traitors arrayed against it.

Resolved, That we approve the determination of the Government of the United States, not to compromise with rebels, nor to offer any terms of peace except such as may be based upon an unconditional surrender of their hostility, and a return to their just allegiance to the Constitution and laws of the United States, and that we call upon the Government to maintain this position and to prosecute the war with the utmost possible vigor to the complete suppression of the rebellion, in full reliance upon the self-sacrifice, the patriotism, the heroic valor, and the undying devotion of the American people to their country and its free institutions.

Resolved, That as slavery was the cause, and now constitutes the strength of this rebellion, and as it must be always and everywhere hostile to the principles of republican government, justice and the national safety demand its utter and complete extirpation from the soil of the Republic, and that while we uphold and maintain the acts and proclamations by which the Government, in its own defense, has aimed a death blow at this gigantic evil, we are in favor, furthermore, of such an amendment to the Constitution, to be made by the people in conformity with its provisions, as shall terminate and forever prohibit the existence of Slavery within the limits or the jurisdiction of the United States.

Resolved, That the thanks of the American people are due to the soldiers and sailors of the army and navy, who have periled their lives in defense of their country, and in vindication of the honor of its flag; that the nation owes to them some permanent recognition of their patriotism and valor, and ample and permanent provision for those of their survivors who have received disabling and honorable wounds in the service of the county; and that the memories of those who have fallen in its defense shall be held in grateful and everlasting remembrance.

Resolved, That we approve and applaud the practical wisdom, the unselfish patriotism, and unswerving fidelity to the Constitution and the principles of American liberty, with which Abraham Lincoln has discharged, under circumstances of unparalleled difficulty, the great duties and responsibilities of the presidential office; that we approve and endorse, as demanded by the emergency and essential to the preservation of the nation, and as within the Constitution, the measures and acts which he has adopted to defend the nation against its open and secret foes; that we approve especially the Proclamation of Emancipation, and the employment as Union soldiers of men heretofore held in slavery and that we have full confidence in his determination to carry these and all other constitutional measures essential to the salvation of the country into full and complete effect....

Resolved, That the Government owes to all men employed in its armies, without regard to distinctions of color, the full protection of the laws of war, and that any violation of these laws or the usages of civilized nations in the time of war by the rebels now in arms, should be made the subject of full and prompt redress.

Resolved, That the foreign immigration, which in the past has added so much to the wealth and the development of resources and increase of power to this nation—the asylum of the oppressed of all nations—should be fostered and encouraged by a liberal and just policy.

Resolved, That we are in favor of the speedy construction of the Railroad to the Pacific....

Resolved, That we approve the position taken by the Government that the people of the United States can never regard with indifference the attempt of any European power to overthrow by force, or to supplant by fraud, the institutions of any republican government on the Western continent; and that they will view with extreme jealousy, as menacing to the peace and independence of their own country, the efforts of any such power to obtain new footholds for monarchical governments, sustained by a foreign military force, in near proximity to the United States [referring to French efforts to take over Mexico].

AMERICANS! Here you have two plans for ending the Rebellion, restoring peace, and preserving the Union. They differ in every essential feature. They agree in scarcely anything. Here are some of their points of contrast:

1. The Chicago platform says not one word in condemnation of the Rebellion or of those who have wrapped the nation in the flames of civil war. The Baltimore platform brands the Rebellion as a gigantic crime, and demands the punishment of the rebels and traitors who have brought it on. With which do you agree?

2. The Chicago Platform proposes that the Rebellion be stopped by IMMEDIATE EFFORTS FOR A CESSATION OF HOSTILITIES on the part of the Government. The Baltimore Platform proposes to "quell it by FORCE of ARMS." The first is Surrender—the last VICTORY! Which do you prefer?

3. The Chicago Platform brands the war in which thousands and tens of thousands of our sons have shed their blood, and millions of treasure have been expended,—in which our Soldiers have won imperishable renown by their gallant devotion to the flag of their country—in which more victories have been achieved than were ever achieved before by any nation—in which the rebels have been stripped of three-fourths of the territory they held at the start—in which one after another of their strong places have been captured, and one after another of their armies have been destroyed, and which is just about to end in a final and glorious triumph of the old Flag and Constitution,—this war the Chicago platform brands as a FAILURE, and demands that it be abandoned and stopped! The Baltimore platform demands that it be "prosecuted with the utmost vigor to the complete suppression of the Rebellion." With which do you agree?

4. The Chicago Platform says not a syllable against the rebellion, but denounces, with intense bitterness and venom, everything the Government has done to put it down. The Baltimore platform applauds and upholds the Government in its efforts to subdue the rebels, and promises continued support in this endeavor. Which is the most patriotic?

5. The Chicago Platform has no thanks or honors, nothing but "sympathy," for the gallant soldiers and sailors who have suffered and died in upholding the honor of the Stars and Stripes, and promises them only "care and protection" in the event of their attaining power. The Baltimore Platform demands for them at the hands of the American people the highest thanks and honors which a grateful nation can bestow. Which is the best and the truest praise?

6. The Chicago Platform denounced our own Government on account of the sufferings of our prisoners in rebel hands; but it has not a word of censure for the rebels themselves, who inflict these sufferings and who persist in continuing the war which has brought them on.

7. The Chicago Platform has not a word to say against slavery, which has caused the war, and which is to be the cornerstone of the new Confederacy the rebellion seeks to establish. The Baltimore Platform brands it as a curse to the country, and calls for its complete extirpation from the soil of the Republic, at the hands of the people, through an amendment of the Constitution. Which is the wisest and best for the country?

Fellow Citizens! These are plain and practical issues: Study them well. These are plain and practical questions: Answer them wisely! This is not a party contest. Political distinctions have nothing to do with it. It is a contest for the life of the Nation! If we surrender to the rebellion, the Union is gone forever. If we fight the rebels a little longer it is safe forever. If we give them to understand in November next, the only Road to Peace lies through the Victory of the National arms, the contest is over! THE ELECTION OF LINCOLN AND JOHNSON IS THE DEATH-KNELL OF THE REBELLION!!

41 / "I think a majority of the soldiers are for Lincoln"

A Union lieutenant in the 1st Connecticut Artillery offers his opinion of McClellan's presidential campaign.

ANDREW KNOX, SEPTEMBER 10, 1864, TO HIS WIFE, GLC 3523.20(16)

...Reinforcements are coming to this army daily so active times will soon be on hand. At present I have nothing to do but eat and sleep and go visiting when I choose, which is not very often. This idleness would be very pleasant to some, but it is far from being agreeable to me. I am living quite respectable now on codfish and mackerel. Potatoes too are plenty at 4 cents a pound. I don't think I would wish anything better if I could have it as well as not. I lived bad enough though during the first three months. But I managed to get along without much complaint. In speaking about Gen. McClellan's election, on the platform of the late convention I do not think he stands any sight whatever. It is decidedly a peace platform. I doubt if he will get many votes from the soldiers if he accepts the nomination under those principles. In fact I hear many soldiers already denouncing him, and but few speak in his favor. Perhaps if he would come out with a strong war acceptance these things may be changed. There is no denying but that he has a host of friends in the army, militarily speaking. But after all I think a majority of the soldiers are for Lincoln. There is few left of the old Army of the Potomac that was in when he commanded it. Consequently it is much less McClellan than it was by a good deal.

42 / "The cry [is]...on to Richmond"

In March 1864 Lincoln gave Ulysses S. Grant command of all Union armies. Vowing to end the war within a year, Grant launched three major offenses. General Philip E. Sheridan's task was to lay waste to farmland in Virginia's Shenandoah Valley, a mission he completed by October. Meanwhile, General William Tecumseh Sherman advanced southeastward from Chattanooga and seized Atlanta, a major southern rail center, while Grant himself pursued Lee's army and sought to capture Richmond, the Confederate capital.

Grant started his offensive with 118,000 men; by early June, half of his men were casualties. But Lee's army had been reduced by a third, to 40,000 men. In a month of fighting in northern and eastern Virginia, Grant lost almost 40,000 men, leading Peace Democrats to call him a "butcher." But Confederate losses were also heavy—and southern troops could not be replaced. At the Battle of the Wilderness, in northern Virginia, Lee's army suffered 11,000 casualties; at Spotsylvania Court House, Lee lost another 10,000 men. After suffering terrible casualties at Cold Harbor—12,000 men killed or wounded—Grant advanced to Petersburg, a rail center south of Richmond, and began a nine-month siege of the city.

At the same time that Grant was pursuing Lee's army, Sherman, with a force of 100,000 men, marched toward Atlanta from Chattanooga, and captured the rail center on September 2, 1864. After leaving Atlanta in flames, Sherman's men marched across Georgia toward Savannah. To break the South's will to fight, Sherman had his men destroy railroad tracks, loot houses, and burn factories. Sherman seized Savannah on December 21, then drove northward, capturing Charleston and Columbia, South Carolina, then heading through North Carolina to Virginia. Sherman summed up the goal of his military maneuvers in grim terms: "We cannot change the hearts of those people, but we can make war so terrible...[and] make them so sick of war that generations would pass away before they would again appeal to it."

A.R. LORD, U.S. SANITARY COMMISSION, APRIL 5, 1865, TO RUGG (DATED RICHMOND), GLC 2034.01

Having a few leisure moments this morning I will use them up by troubling you with a few lines from this portion of Uncle Sam's Domain, which at this time is an object of no small amount of attention. The cry of on to Richmond is now played by the occupation of the late residence of the arch traitor Jeff [Davis] by the Uncle Sam's brave boys in blue. You ought to have been with us when we entered the city [Richmond]. The citizens were out in goodly numbers, and were not at all offended by the sight of Old Glory [Stars & Stripes]. On the contrary they cheered the flag most heartily though it was born in the hands of the darker hued of Uncle Sam's brave defenders. The first troops that put into practical effect the long continued cry of on to Richmond was those portions of the 24 (white) and 25 (Col[ore]d) Corps (Army of the James) that were left on the right of the James when the other portion of the Army of the James moved across the James and joined with the Army of the Potomac in castigating the minions of Lee, which the boys done in fine style. The fighting at the left of Petersburg and vicinity was very severe, and of course our loss was quite large, though much smaller than that of the rebs. It is hardly worth while for me to write you the particulars as you will doubtless have learned them through the columns of the Boston Journal as lines reach you as Carleton is here, there and everywhere where there is ought to be obtained in the line of reliable news. He was in Petersburg this morning and now he is in Richmd. But I have not time to write more this morning. I told you I would write you from Richmond before I returned home—and here is the best that I have time to do. We are all in the A. No. 1 tip topest of spirits while the down-in-the-mouth representatives of Jeff and his ignoble supporters the northern copperheads are on the double quick.

43 / *"The Army...has been compelled to yield to overwhelming numbers and resources"*

By April 1865 Grant's army had cut off Lee's supply lines, forcing Confederate forces to evacuate Petersburg and Richmond. Lee and his men retreated westward, but Grant's troops overtook him about a hundred miles west of Richmond. Recognizing that further resistance would be futile, Lee surrendered at Appomattox Court House, Virginia. The aristocratic Lee wore a full-dress uniform, with a ceremonial sash and sword, while Grant wore a private's coat.

The next day, in a final message to his troops, Robert E. Lee acknowledged that he was "compelled to yield to overwhelming numbers and resources." Three quarters of the Confederate white male population of military age had fought in the war, but by 1865 the North had four times as many troops as the Confederacy. At the time he surrendered, Lee's entire army had shrunk to just 35,000 men, compared to Grant's total of 113,000. Lee's decision to surrender, however, probably helped to prevent large-scale guerrilla warfare.

Robert E. Lee, General Order 9, April 10, 1865 (dated Appomattox, Virginia), GLC 1432

After four years of arduous service marked by unsurpassed courage and fortitude, the Army of North Virginia, has been compelled to yield to overwhelming numbers and resources.

I need not tell the brave survivors of so many hard fought battles who have remained steadfast to the last, that I have consented to this result with no distrust of them; but feeling that valour and devotion could accomplish nothing that would compensate for the loss that would have attended the continuance of the contest, I determined to avoid the useless sacrifice of those whose past services have endeared them to their countrymen.

By the terms of the agreement officers and men can return to their homes and remain there until exchanged.

You will take with you the satisfaction that proceeds from the consciousness of duty faithfully performed, and I earnestly pray that a Merciful God will extend to you his blessing and protection.

With an unceasing admiration of your constancy and devotion to your country and a grateful remembrance of your kind and generous consideration for myself, I bid you all an affectionate farewell.

44 / "'The President is murdered'"

At noon on Good Friday, April 14, 1865, Major General Robert Anderson raised the U.S. flag over Fort Sumter. It was the same flag he had surrendered four years before.

That evening, a few minutes after ten o'clock, John Wilkes Booth (1838–65), a young actor and Confederate sympathizer (who had spied for Richmond and been part of a plot to kidnap Lincoln), entered the presidential box at Ford's Theater in Washington and shot the president in the back of the head. Booth then leaped to the stage, but he caught a spur in a flag draped in front of the box. He fell and broke his leg. As he fled the theater he is said to have cried out: "Sic semper tyrannis" (thus always to tyrants), the motto of the state of Virginia.

Simultaneously, a Booth accomplice, Lewis Paine, brutally attacked Secretary of State William Seward (1801–72) at his home with a knife. Seward survived because Paine's knife was deflected by a metal collar he wore from a severe accident. Seward slowly recovered from his wounds and contined to serve as secretary of state under Lincoln's successor, Andrew Johnson.

Lincoln was carried unconscious to a neighboring house. He was pronounced dead at 7:22 A.M., April 15. A few minutes later, Secretary of War Edwin M. Stanton (1814–69) stepped outside and announced to the assembled crowd, "He belongs to the ages."

J.B. Stonehouse, April 14, 1865, to Johnny (dated Washington), GLC 368.01

Since I have been here this time the most exciting times that this country ever saw have taken place.

Thursday evening Washington was crazy with joy over the surrender of Lee, every one of the Public Buildings was illuminated, and every private house was blazing with candles from top to bottom. the people were wild with excitement. Men women & children were all out of doors.

The next evening a grand performance was advertised to be given at Fords Theatre and it was announced that the President & ladies and Genl Grant and wife were to be present.

Just as I was going to bed a man ran in breathless and pale enquiring which of the Theatres the President was attending—he said he must find him at once as Mr. Seward had been murdered in his bed. We followed him to the door and there met people rushing from the Theatre saying "the President is shot." "The President is murdered." Such a time I never before beheld and never want to again.

At first no one seemed to believe it but it soon became certain that it was all true.

Just as I got to Fords Theatre they were carrying the President to a house across the street. He did not move or speak after he was shot.

You have seen in the papers a full account of it I have no doubt.

I was at Secretary Sewards house several times yesterday. I saw the knife the assassin stabbed Mr. Steward with and the Pistol with which he broke Mr. Frederick Sewards skull. There is blood and hair sticking to it still Neither of the men have as yet been caught.

45 / *"The news...came...like a clap of thunder in a clear sky"*

Following the shooting, Booth fled to Maryland on horseback. A friend then helped him escape to Virginia. On April 26, two weeks after he had shot Lincoln, federal troops tracked Booth down and trapped him in a barn near Port Royal, Virginia. When Booth refused to surrender, his pursuers set the barn on fire. Booth was found dead, apparently of a self-inflicted gunshot wound.

W. Henry Pearce, April 16, 1865, to Lena (Selina), GLC 66.150

The news of course, came to all, like a clap of thunder in a clear sky.... The first thought on hearing that President Lincoln, to whom we had looked as the leader and even the savior of our nation, had been assassinated, was that all was lost and our country ruined. But...we find in Andrew Johnson a man who...is fitted to the instrument in God's hand of carrying out His vengeances...the uppermost feeling in men's minds is "Death to all traitors and sympathizers" there has already been several shot in Cincinnati for rejoicing at the death of the President.... I never saw such a day of gloom before...each felt as if he had lost a relative....

46 / *"It is a very hard blow for this nation to lose our President"*

Lincoln's assassination was part of a larger plot to murder other government officials, including Vice President Andrew Johnson, Secretary of State William H. Seward, and General Ulysses S. Grant. Only Lincoln was killed. Following the assassination, Secretary of War Edwin M. Stanton ordered War Department agents to apprehend the conspirators. Despite wild rumors of involvement by top Confederate officials, the actual conspirators included, apart from Booth, an ex-Confederate soldier, a carriagemaker, and a druggist's clerk. Eight individuals were arrested; a military commission found all of them guilty. Four were hanged. Of the remaining four, one died in prison in 1867 and three others received presidential pardons in 1869.

In the following letter, an unidentified Union soldier reacts to Lincoln's assassination. Like many Northerners, he blamed the Confederate leadership for the president's death. His anger and thirst for vengeance against "traitors," sentiments that were surely widespread, make it all the more remarkable that the North's victory was not followed by a massive and bloody extermination of Confederate leaders and their northern sympathizers.

Union soldier's letter, April 18, 1865, to his parents (dated Burksville Station, Va.), GLB 218

I will now try to quote a few lines to you to inform you that I am enjoying good health at present and I hope that these few lines will find you enjoying the same.... I have learnt since I have been in the service not to let my mind be troubled till trouble comes. Then its time enough.... Father we have heard that President Lincoln has been killed by some traitor in Washington. If that is true I say that we ought to hang every damn rebel in the Southern Confederacy. I go in for killing every one and burn every traitor up north by a stake. I think instead of taken Lee's Army prisoners it would have been better to have hoisted a black flag and butchered every one but now they have paroled them and what are they doing. They are awaiting an opportunity to kill some of our best men. Last Saturday the devilish rebs tried to blow the arsenal at City point but we here caught it because they had done it and some that were paroled and on their way to Richmond tore up the railroad but they were caught and ought to hang and I say they ought to hang every one. I tell you it is a very hard blow for this nation to lose our President at this present time but I still hope it is not true but I fear it is for there are many traitors up North that are first the ones that would kill him. If it had not been for the traitors of the north this war would have ceased long ago but they are trying to destroy this government. They are aiding the South every day. Now, if true, they have killed President Lincoln to aid this rebellion....

47 / "Our country is now in a disturbed condition"

As a result of the Civil War, the South lost a fourth of its white male population of military age, a third of its livestock, half of its farm machinery, and $2.5 billion worth of human property. Factories and railroads had been destroyed, and such cities as Atlanta, Charleston, Columbia, and Richmond had been largely burned to the ground. In South Carolina the value of property plunged from $400 million in 1860, ranking it third in the nation, to just $50 million in 1865. In this letter a former supporter of the Confederacy responds to Lincoln's death, describes conditions in the postwar South, and expresses distrust toward President Andrew Johnson.

Prior to the Civil War, McCaleb, at age 17, had spoken out publicly against secession and in support of the sovereignty of the federal government. After the war broke out, he served as an officer in the Confederate army. In this letter, he expresses his willingness to accept military defeat and the abolition of slavery, as long as the South was allowed to maintain a system of white supremacy. It would be this commitment to white supremacy that would undercut federal efforts to extend the civil rights of African Americans during Reconstruction.

EDWIN H. MCCALEB, JUNE 1, 1865, TO T. P. CHANDLER, GLC 1594

...As mail communication has been partially reopened with the North I avail myself of this my first opportunity to write to you. I have not been with the army since my release from prison. I can never forget the kindness shown me by yourself & family and I shall cherish to the day of my death sentiments of profound gratitude & esteem for your noble generosity & christianlike charity....

Our country is now in a disturbed condition caused by the fiery ordeal through which we just passed & the total absence of both military or civil law in all parts of this state except the few garrisoned towns. Were it not for the national quiet and law abiding disposition of our people we would be subjected to the augur of lawlessness and outrage. All good citizens deeply deplore the assassination of Pres. Lincoln...Mr. L—was a great man and more than that was a good man and the country could ill afford to lose his services at this important crisis.... Mr. Johnson has disregarded the requirements of the Constitution & undertakes to enact military governments over the states that have hitherto only been at war with the Federal Government. And more than this, men are now being tried for their lives before military courts...instead of the civil tribunals of the land.

This is in direct violation of the Constitution as these...were in no way connected with the Army.

This looks very much as that he has assumed arbitrary power & was overstepping his oath of office. I hoped he would convene Congress in Extra Session or take the counsel & advice of the able & learned statesmen of the Country. But even this he has failed to do. All the good men of the land desire to return to their peaceful avocations & be permitted to enjoy the blessings of liberty transmitted by our ancestors who fought side by side through the Revolution & on the plains of Mexico. But this they are not permitted to do & they are told that those who have taken up arms of defense of what they believed to be their rights under the old Federal Compact have no claims but mercy upon the General Government and those who now hold...power.... By this sudden system of Emancipation, this spasmodic transformation of the ignorant Negro from a peaceful laborer who has been accustomed to have all needs...provided...both in sickness & health to a self reliant citizen will paralyze the productive resources of the South. It...can cause a famine in this our fertile land. If we could have a system of gradual emancipation & colonization our people would universally rejoice & be glad to get rid of slavery which has ever been a cancer upon the body politic of our social organization.... We would gladly substitute white for slave labor but we can never regard the Negro our equal either intellectually or socially. The doctrine of "Miscegenation" or as the word which is a Latin compound ("Misco" to mix & "genus" race) signifies an amalgamation of the races, is odious, destructive & contrary to the laws of God & Man. If such a detestable dogma becomes a law we shall soon have a race of mulattoes as fickle & foolish as the Mongrel population of Mexico never content with their present condition but always desiring a change of government & rulers. The government ought to pursue a magnanimous merciful & conciliatory course toward those who have striven to be honorable...& who have acknowledged ourselves fairly beaten. Let the northern people arise in the majesty of their power & stay the uplifted hand of official oppression & hatred.... Let not the pages of American history be stained with a second recital of the reign of terror like the frightful record of the French Revolution in the memorable days of Danton & Robespierre. The only way to avoid these disasters is by a strict compliance with the Constitution & the laws.

I was only 17 years of age when this war commenced & the last speech I made before leaving college for the army was against secession and advocating the sovereignty of the Federal Government and yet I am now among the proscribed because I held a petty office in the army.

TOWARD RECONSTRUCTION

The Civil War was over and the Union had been preserved. But several fundamental questions remained unanswered: What would be the South's place in a reunified country? What systems of labor and race relations would replace slavery? The most important question involved the status of African Americans. The Thirteenth Amendment abolished slavery in December 1865. But whether the end of slavery would bring full legal and political freedom remained to be seen.

Except for Haiti, the American South was the only region in the Western hemisphere in which slavery was overthrown by force of arms. Southern slaveholders were the only slaveholders, except for those in Brazil and a number of French and Hispanic masters, who received no compensation for the loss of their slave property. And the South was the only region, except for Guadeloupe and Martinique, in which former slaves received civil and political rights. Furthermore, the South was the only post-emancipation society in which large number of slaveholders were deprived of the right to hold public office and in which former slaves formed successful political alliances with whites.

Despite these steps, the abolition of slavery did not mean that former slaves had achieved full freedom. Throughout the Western Hemisphere, the abolition of slavery was followed by a period of reconstruction in which race relations were redefined and new systems of labor emerged. In former slave societies throughout the Americas, ex-slaves sought to free themselves from the gang system of labor on plantations and establish small-scale, self-sufficient farms. Planters (even black landowners in Haiti), often with the assistance of government, sought to restore the plantation system. The outcome, in many former slave societies, was the emergence of a caste system of race relations and a system of involuntary labor, such as peonage, apprenticeship, contract labor, and tenant farming.

The story of Reconstruction in the American South echoes a broad concern with labor control. Immediately following the war, all-white southern legislatures passed "black codes" designed to force freed blacks to work on plantations, where they could be put to work in gangs for long contractual periods. These codes denied African Americans the right to purchase or even rent land. Vagrancy laws allowed authorities to arrest blacks "in idleness" and assign them to a chain gang or auction them off to a planter for as long as a year. Other statutes required blacks to have written proof of employment and barred blacks from leaving plantations. The Freedmen's Bureau, ostensibly designed to aid former slaves, helped to enforce laws against vagrancy and loitering and refused to allow ex-slaves to remain on land they had occupied during the war. One black army veteran asked rhetorically: "If you call this Freedom, what did you call Slavery?"

Such efforts to virtually reenslave the freedmen led congressional Republicans to seize control of Reconstruction from President Andrew Johnson, to deny representatives from the former Confederate states their congressional seats, to pass the Civil Rights Act of 1866, and to write the Fourteenth Amendment to the Constitution, extending citizenship rights to African Americans and guaranteeing them equal protection of the laws. In 1870 the country went even farther by ratifying to Fifteenth Amendment, which gave voting rights to black men. The most radical proposals advanced during Reconstruction—to confiscate plantations and redistribute portions to the freedmen—were defeated.

The freedmen, in alliance with carpetbaggers (Northerners who had migrated South during or after the Civil War) and southern white Republicans known as scalawags, temporarily gained power in every Confederate state except Virginia. Altogether, more than six hundred African Americans served as legislators in Reconstruction governments (though blacks comprised a majority only in the lower house of South Carolina's legislature). The Reconstruction governments drew up democratic state constitutions, expanded women's rights, provided debt relief, and established the South's first state-funded schools. During the late 1860s and 1870s, however, internal divisions within the southern Republican Party, white terror, and northern apathy allowed white Democrats who called themselves Redeemers to return to power in the South's state governments. The North's failure to enforce the Fourteenth and Fifteenth Amendments permitted racial segregation and disfranchisement in the South.

During Reconstruction, former slaves, and many white small farmers, became trapped in a new system of economic exploitation known as sharecropping. Lacking capital and land of their own, many former slaves were forced to work for large landowners. Initially, planters, sometimes with the support of the Freedmen's Bureau, tried to restore gang labor under the supervision of white overseers. But the freedmen, who wanted autonomy and independence, refused to sign contracts that required gang labor. Ultimately, sharecropping emerged as a sort of compromise.

Instead of cultivating land in gangs supervised by overseers, landowners divided plantations into 20- to 50-acre plots suitable for farming by a single family. In exchange for land, a cabin, and supplies, sharecroppers agreed to raise a cash crop (usually cotton) and to give half the crop to their landlord. The high interest rates landlords and merchants charged for goods bought on credit transformed sharecropping into a system of economic dependency and poverty. The freedman found that "freedom could make folks proud but it didn't make 'em rich."

Nevertheless, the sharecropping system did allow freedmen a degree of freedom and autonomy greater than that experiences under slavery. As a symbol of their newly won independence, freedmen had teams of mules drag their former slave cabins away from the slave quarters into their own fields. Black wives and daughters sharply reduced their labor in the fields and instead devoted more time to child care and housework. For the first time, black families could divide their time in accordance with their own family priorities.

Chattel slavery had been defeated. The gang system of labor, enforced by the whip, was dead. Incredibly, about 20 percent of African Americans in the South managed to acquire their own land by 1880. Real gains had been won, though full freedom and equality before the law remained unfulfilled promises.

THE NATURE AND HISTORY OF THE GILDER LEHRMAN COLLECTION

by David Brion Davis

In early January 1995 I spent several days immersing myself in the Gilder Lehrman Collection of American history at the Pierpont Morgan Library in New York. I soon discovered that a genuine exploration of the tens of thousands of documents (now exceeding an estimated thirty-five thousand separate items—documents, letters, manuscripts, prints, photographs) would require many months of concentrated effort. Indeed, it almost seemed as if a team of the most renowned American historians, having access to the Library of Congress and all the archives of the major university libraries and historical societies, had selected representative documents to illustrate important themes, events, conflicts, tragedies, and achievements from the colonial era to the end of the Civil War (with some sources stretching back to Columbus and forward to Theodore Roosevelt and Richard Nixon).

No less remarkable, the materials ranged from letters of Washington, Franklin, Jefferson, the two Adamses, Marshall, Jackson, and Lincoln—some of which have never been printed—to the letters and archives of former slaves, unknown soldiers, and eloquent women such as Mercy Otis Warren and Lucy Knox, the wife of Washington's secretary of war. Immense special collections, such as the Livingston-Redmond Family Papers, including documents in English, French, Dutch, and Algonkian, shed light on the manorial system and political intrigues of upstate New York from the early colonial period to the mid-nineteenth century. And the rich meanings conveyed by pen were complemented by a wealth of pictorial imagery that ranges from cartoons, broadsides, and prints to dazzling Civil War photographs. In the forty-odd years I had devoted to historical research, in Britain, France, Brazil, the West Indies, and many American states, I had never encountered such a breathtaking single collection. And I was particularly struck by the vivid way the manuscripts documented the origins and history of the struggle against slavery that finally led to the Civil War. How on earth, I kept wondering, had Richard Gilder and Lewis E. Lehrman acquired and made public such a priceless window on the American past?

People who have never committed themselves to serious collecting find it difficult to understand the collector's mixture of passion and systematic achievement. Lewis Lehrman began collecting a few historical documents when he was an undergraduate history major and then in 1961 a lowly paid Carnegie teaching fellow at Yale. I can testify that in 1962, when Lehrman moved on to Harvard Graduate School as a Woodrow Wilson fellow and earned an M.A. degree in history, rare letters and pamphlets were astonishingly cheap. But with a stipend of $50 a week, Lehrman had no illusions about the realistic goals of an academic collector.

As it turned out, however, Lehrman decided not to pursue an academic career but still found an outlet for his historical interests and training as he moved into business. By the late 1970s and early 1980s the success of his Rite Aid Corporation, of which he was president, encouraged him to begin purchasing some expensive Lincolniana, a tribute to the historical figure he most revered. When in the late 1980s Lehrman became a managing director at Morgan Stanley, he was able to expand the scope of his collecting while concentrating especially on the Revolutionary, antebellum, and Civil War periods, the years that laid the foundations and refoundations of the great republic that was to emerge in the twentieth century. For the professional historian acclimated to public and university archives, it is astounding to learn that vast quantities of invaluable American source material have been and still are scattered about in private hands, in Europe as well as America, available for purchase if one can pay enough. Lehrman himself was amazed at the availability of what might be thought of as priceless documents. The problem was how to find sufficient funds for such investments on an expanding and systematic basis.

In 1990 Lehrman founded his own investment firm and also formed a partnership with Richard Gilder to expand the collection and make the materials available for scholars and teachers and public exhibitions. Gilder, the highly successful head of the investment brokerage firm Gilder, Gagnon, Howe & Co., had joined Lehrman in earlier philanthropic and educational projects before developing an interest in historical collecting. When he decided to make the Gilder Lehrman Collection a major part of his philanthropic spending, it enabled the team to employ a network of agents—in Europe as well as America—and to acquire an almost immediate reputation among dealers in rare books and manuscripts for generous and prompt payments. Even in the late 1980s Lehrman had acquired a reputation for knowing what he wanted and for quickly authenticating documents (in a market awash with fakes and forgeries). In effect, the Gilder Lehrman project became a gigantic magnet. As news of their interests and methods spread among dealers in various geographic regions, the Manhattan magnet pulled in a growing stream of documents for inspection and possible purchase.

Since one of Gilder and Lehrman's central goals was to rescue important manuscripts from private obscurity and make them available for scholarly and educational purposes, they decided in 1992 to put the rapidly expanding collection on deposit at the Pierpont Morgan Library.

Although the immense Gilder Lehrman Collection enables us to give quite thorough coverage to most aspects of American history, we have felt it necessary in the earliest colonial period to include some outside documents to ensure an accurate and coherent view of a given subject. For example, some isolated Gilder Lehrman manuscripts on colonial Virginia and the witchcraft trials in Salem, Massachusetts, take on added meaning when contextualized with outside documents. We have also included a few outside documents concerning women's right in the nineteenth century. Yet in many cases, it should be stressed, Gilder and Lehrman have purchased at least early copies of these outside documents.

Index